PRINTING ESTIMATING

Costing Methods for
Digital and Traditional Graphic Imaging

PRINTING ESTIMATING

Costing Methods for
Digital and Traditional Graphic Imaging

Fourth Edition

Philip Kent Ruggles

California Polytechnic State University

Delmar Publishers

I(T)P An International Thomson Publishing Company

Albany • Bonn • Boston • Cincinnati • Detroit • London • Madrid
Melbourne • Mexico City • New York • Pacific Grove • Paris • San Francisco
Singapore • Tokyo • Toronto • Washington

NOTICE TO THE READER

Cover design by Rachel Baker

Delmar Staff:
Senior Admisistrative Editor: John Anderson
Development Editor: Barbara Riedell
Art & Design Coordinator: Nicole Reamer
Production Manager: Larry Main

COPYRIGHT © 1996
By Philip Kent Ruggles

Printed in the United States of America

For more information, contact:

Delmar Publishers
3 Columbia Circle, Box 15015
Albany, New York 12212-5015

International Thomson Editores
Campos Eliseos 385, Piso 7
Col Polanco
11560 Mexico D F Mexico

International Thomson Publishing Europe
Berkshire House 168-173
High Holborn
London, WC1V 7AA
England

International Thomson Publishing GmbH
Königswinterer Strasse 418
53227 Bonn
Germany

Thomas Nelson Australia
102 Dodds Street
South Melbourne, 3205
Victoria, Australia

International Thomson Publishing Asia
221 Henderson Road
#05-10 Henderson Building
Singapore 0315

Nelson Canada
1120 Birchmont Road
Scarborough, Ontario
Canada, M1K 5G4

International Thomson Publishing—Japan
Hirakawacho Kyowa Building, 3F
2-2-1 Hirakawacho
Chiyoda-ku, Tokyo 102
Japan

10 9 8 7 6 5 4 3   XXX 01 00 99 98 97

Library of Congress Cataloging-in-Publication Data

Ruggles, Philip Kent.
   Printing estimating : costing methods for digital and traditional
graphic imaging / Philip K. Ruggles.
         p.   cm.
   ISBN 0-8273-6439-3
   1. Printing industry--Estimates.   I. Title.
   Z285.R83   1996   96-12480
   686.2'068'1--dc20   CIP

To Joanne and Lauren
for their continuing encouragement,
support, and love

Delmar Publishers' Online Services

To access Delmar on the World Wide Web, point your browser to:

http://www.delmar.com/delmar.html

To access through Gopher:

gopher://gopher.delmar.com

Visit the Delmar Desktop Café™ for an online resource center devoted to graphic communications. Point your browser to:

http://www.desktopcafe.com

(Delmar Online is part of "thomson.com," and Internet site with information on more than 30 publishers of the International Thomson Publishing organization.)

For more information on our products and services:

email: info@delmar.com

Or call 800-347-7707

Contents

Preface

This fourth edition of *Printing Estimating: Costing Methods for Digital and Traditional Graphic Imaging* is literally a new book compared to the third edition published just five years ago. Much has changed in graphic imaging technology in that brief, five-year span of time.

The task of researching and writing this fourth edition, which took fifteen months, has been challenging, given the range and depth of change in the way graphic images are sold, estimated, produced, and distributed.

The objective of this book is to provide readers with procedures for estimating and pricing their graphic products and services, as opposed to completing the process using guesswork. This has proven to be a formidable task, as digital technology has shifted numerous prepress choices from printers to customers—this coupled with the continued constant diversification of both product and process. While the printing industry enjoys an increasing level of computer literacy through skilled employees, and ever-improving software and hardware, at the same time it lacks clearly defined standards and methods used by everyone in the same way. The problem is further complicated by the continuing push toward reduction of cycle times at all levels and the with a wide variation in philosophies and styles for operating many graphic imaging businesses.

This text includes numerous illustrative materials from industry contributors. Listed alphabetically by company, thanks to each of these industry colleagues and their companies or organizations for their contributions to the text:

Lisa Sunok and John Gagliano (ASG Sherman Graphics, Chicago, Illinois)

Gordon Nash (Bay State Press, Framingham, Massachusetts)

Don Parker (Boise, Idaho Chapter, Pacific Printing & Imaging Association)

Jim Birkenseer (Circus Lithographic Prepress, San Francisco, California)

Dave Bascom (Communigraphics Corporation, Denver, Colorado)

Terry Bell (ColorGraphics, San Francisco, California)

Mark Wright (Folder Express, Omaha, Nebraska)

Bob Gans (Gans Ink and Supply Company, Los Angeles, California)

George Ryan, Frank Benevento, and Rich Adams (Graphic Arts Technical Foundation, Pittsburgh, Pennsylvania)

Jeff Heesacker (H & H Printing Company, Salem, Oregon)

Lydia Bos and Nick Orem (Logic Associates, White River Junction, Vermont)

Greg Van Wert and Jackie Pantaliano (National Association of Printers and Lithographers, Teaneck, New Jersey)

Ray Roper and Gail Cotten (Printing Industries of America, Alexandria, Virginia)

Jerome Bannister (Samy's Digital Imaging, Los Angeles, California)

Gregory Dean (Scitex Graphic Arts Users Association, Nashville, Tennessee)

Timm Crull (Watermark Press, San Francisco, California)

Zellerbach Paper (Claude Brown and Lester Barker, San Francisco, California)

Special thanks to Bob Lindgren, Executive Director of Printing Industries of Southern California, for the use of PIA-SC's *1994–95 PIA-SC Bluebook* materials, and to Printing Industry of Northern California's Executive Director, Dan Nelson, for use of materials from their *1995 PINC Buyers Guide*.

Numerous industry colleagues and friends have provided information or inspiration for this text in different ways. Listed alphabetically: Thanks to Larry Aaron (International Publishing Management Association), Tom Crouser (Crouser and Associates), Jim Frey (Printing & Imaging Association of the Mountain States), Don Goldman (G/A Consulting), Hank Hatch (International Prepress Association), Brian Lawler (consultant), Art LeFebvre (Waterless Printing Association), Bob Leveque (R.R. Donnelley & Sons), Lynn Conlan Mrachek (R. R Donnelley & Sons), Jim Olson (Pacific Printing & Imaging Association), Joe Polanco and the late Nolan Moore (Printing Industries of Texas), John Robisch (Xerox), Larry Rolufs (Bureau of Engraving and Printing), Mike Serra (DuPont), Roger Siminoff (Silicon Graphics), Bill Stickney (Printing Industry of Central Ohio), John Walter (R. R. Donnelley & Sons), and Dan Witte (National Association of Quick Printers).

Special thanks to consultant Dick Gorelick (Gorelick & Associates) for his timely observations on a wide range of industry topics. Little of importance escapes Dick's thoughtful analysis and witty insight.

Thanks to my teaching colleagues in the Graphic Communication Department at California Polytechnic State University for their continuing dedication to excellence in teaching and research. Special thanks to Professor Michael Blum for his expertise in all aspects of digital imaging and his patience in sharing this knowledge with students and faculty. Thanks also to Hank Apfelberg, Lee Brown, Harvey Levenson, Steve Mott, Patrick Munroe, and Bob Pinkin for their assistance in various research segments of this book. Thanks as well to industry expert and Rochester Institute of Technology Professor Frank Romano for his timely insights on digital imaging, effectively communicated through his many articles and public presentations on the subject.

My students have also contributed in numerous ways to this book. While many students have had an impact in more ways than they know, special thanks to Andrew Biggers for researching and writing about electronic prepress production standards.

The Delmar team of Barbara Riedell, Developmental Editor, John Anderson, Senior Administrative Editor, and Kathy Fagan, Marketing Manager, deserve thanks. Special appreciation to Barbara Riedell for her patience, flexibility and continuously positive attitude. Thanks as well to reviewers Rich Bundesgaard, Arkansas State University, George Elliott, Texas State Technical College, Olesegun Odesina, Central Connecticut State University, Jesus Rodriguez, Pittsburgh State University, Scott Williams, Georgia Southern University, Jim Barter, Print Northwest, and Lou Berkley, Express Quality Printing for their feedback and insight.

Finally, thanks to my parents, the late Arthur and Janet Ruggles, who first exposed me to the fascinating world of graphic imaging and who influenced my career in countless ways. Thanks also to my wife Joanne and daughter Lauren for their patience and unwavering support over the many months and hundreds of hours this book took to complete.

Philip K. Ruggles
San Luis Obispo, California
January, 1996

Chapter 1

The Scope and Function of Printing Estimating

1.1 Introduction

Cost Estimating Procedure   Price Estimating Procedure

1.2 Emerging Estimating Trends for a Changing Printing Industry

Increasing Use of Computer Estimating Methods

Increasing Use of Price Estimating

Increasing Use of Fast-Pass Estimating

More No-Quote Situations

Declining Emphasis on Estimating in Operating the Business

1.3 The Interrelationship of Estimating to Other Plant Duties

Accounting, Cost Controls, and Finance

Customer Service

Management Decision Making

Order Entry

Pricing

Production Scheduling and Control

Materials Purchase and Buyouts

Sales

1

1.4   What the Estimator Needs to Know

Cost Information
Customers
Data Collection and Computer Management Methods
Material Costs and Buyouts
Mathematics

Operating Personnel and Personnel
    Policies
Printing Production Equipment
Production Methods and Sequences
Quantification Techniques and Derivation of Production Data

1.5   General Procedure for Selling, Estimating, Pricing, and Quoting Printing

Request for Estimate
Estimating the Job

Setting the Job Price
Job Proposal and Quotation

1.6   Standard Production Times and Budgeted Hour Cost Rates

Standard Production Times

Budgeted Hour Cost Rates

1.7   Other Methods Used to Estimate or Price Printing

Tailored Price Lists or Pricing Templates
Pricing Using Standardized Industry
    Systems
Pricing Based on Past Jobs
Pricing Using a Ratio System

Using the Competition's Price
Using a Chargeback System
Pricing by the Customer's Ability
    and Willingness to Pay
Intuitive Pricing

1.8   The Estimator's Work Environment

Office Location and Equipment

Estimating Tools

1.9   Selecting an Estimator or an Estimator Trainee

Preparing a Job Description
Advertising
Hiring from Inside or Outside the
    Plant

Using a Weighted Rating System
Interviewing and Testing

1.10   How to Develop an Estimating Training Program

1.11   Some Rules for the Printing Estimator

1.1   Introduction

Printing estimating is a process used to evaluate the financial impact of potential orders on a printing company. Printing estimating can be segmented into two general procedures: cost estimating and price estimating.

Cost Estimating Procedure

Cost estimating is a method by which a printing order is reviewed to determine the cost impact of the job on the printing company. Cost estimating requires evaluating the job relative to the customer's job specifications and the anticipated production methods the printer will use. Cost estimating requires two sequential steps:

1. developing a production plan to manufacture the product
2. assigning costs using the production plan developed in Step 1

Production Planning. In Step 1, production planning, the estimator first analyzes the product to be manufactured, then carefully breaks the job into component production operations which reflect the steps necessary to manufacture the product.

Once the production plan is developed, the estimator breaks it into two types of production segments: (1) those likely to be completed most economically inside the printing plant and (2) those likely to be produced most economically outside the printing plant. Following this breakdown, the estimator goes to work completing the cost estimate (Step 2).

Assigning Costs. For production operations completed inside the printing plant, the estimator first carefully evaluates each production step, then assigns these steps production times and hourly cost factors known as budgeted hourly rates (BHRs). (For more information on BHRs, see the Budgeted Hour Cost Rates section later in this chapter or Chapter 3.) Next the estimator determines the costs of all materials required for the job. These typically include raw materials such as paper and ink, as well as consumable materials such as film and plates that are not part of the final product.

In addition to assessing the costs of production operations completed inside the plant, the estimator sometimes estimates production segments purchased from outside vendors. The costs of these external production segments, which are known as buyouts or outside purchases, are added to the total costs of the internal production segments. Thus, the formula for cost estimating is:

$$\text{estimated cost to produce the job} = (\text{standard production time} \times \text{BHR})$$
$$+ \text{ material costs} + \text{buyout costs}$$

Establishing the selling price for a printing order is done after cost estimating is completed because the price should recover, at minimum, the estimated cost to produce the job. Pricing is usually done by a printing company executive who understands the nuances and key points of pricing printed products and services.

Cost estimating is completed manually and by computer. Many computer estimating systems are developed using the cost estimating procedure previously described. Although cost estimating requires a thorough set of job specifications and sometimes takes a long time to complete, it is popular because it is accurate and provides detailed cost data on a printing order.

Many large printing manufacturing operations, which have complex production equipment and specialized product lines, separate production planning and cost estimating tasks. These companies employ job planners, also known as production planners, who determine the best production sequences for the work. Once a job planner has completed this task, the planned job sequence is given to an estimator who applies time and cost data. In some plants, the job planner may also follow up work-in-process as feedback to evaluate actual versus estimated production operations.

Like the job planner, the estimator in a large operation may also take on other responsibilities, such as reviewing and verifying production standards, reviewing job costs, and establishing BHRs. For the most part, splitting production planning and cost estimating duties is desirable because it allows for greater specialization in each of the functions, which translates to more accurate estimates.

Price Estimating Procedure

Many printing companies use price estimating procedures in which printing orders are estimated using a price list or some other pricing system. The primary advantages of price estimating are speed and simplicity because price estimating requires little training and minimum job details. With the growth of on-demand printing, rapid technological changes in prepress, and a continuous reduction of lead time for producing printing (from three weeks in the early 1980s to less than one week today), price estimating methods have increased in use. Price estimating is done by printing companies of all sizes, as well as by digital imaging service bureaus, trade shops, on-demand printers, and other graphic products and public-consumption service providers.

The pricing formats and pricing methods companies use vary. Some companies use tailor-made price lists, while others use commercially prepared pricing systems. In addition, various types of computer-assisted pricing (CAP) systems are available. Price estimating and CAP are discussed in detail in Chapter 4.

1.2   Emerging Estimating Trends for a Changing Printing Industry

A number of crucial issues have coalesced that impact the way printing is estimated. The first and most pronounced issue is the emergence of digital imaging technology, which includes desktop publishing, electronic prepress, on-demand printing, and compact disc read-only memory (CD-ROM) production. Although certain portions of photomechanical prepress production remain in wide use, the shift to digital production has been swift and pronounced.

The complexities of these new avenues of digital technology have caused numerous cost estimating problems: There are few established production standards, production methods are varied and unpredictable, and customers and printers lack experience with the technology. Perhaps the first and biggest problem is that desktop publishing has shifted important production choices to the customer or the digital file originator who is frequently unable or unprepared to make them properly.

Second, the emerging theme "customers are 'kings' " is having a panoramic effect on printing and on all American business. This concept has caused many printers to abandon some of their past business practices to meet a wide range of customer demands. The competition between printers has intensified this "need to serve." If Printer A does not meet this need, Printer B will be happy to. The effect on estimating has been pronounced: "It's okay if the customer cannot specify all parts of a job," printers now say. "We'll estimate the job with what we know and hope for the best if we win the order."

The third issue, which is driven by digital technology, is the ever-compressing cycle time necessary to produce a printed product. Consider this: The average lead time for producing a printing order in the early 1980s was approximately twenty days or about three weeks. The lead time in the mid-1990s was five days or fewer. As cycle times have shortened, customers have grown accustomed to faster responses in other areas, such as estimating and sales.

The fourth issue is that investments in digital technology are substantial and require a company to be productive or lose money. The focus on productivity, in conjunction with reduced cycle times, forces many printers to compromise estimates when jobs are presented for bids. This is a vicious cycle: High investment requires substantial production, which can only be maintained when prices and costs are lowered to encourage volume. Thus, estimating is forced into a backseat while technology and production drive the operation of the printing company.

Other problems are also evident. These include difficulty in obtaining estimating job specifications from customers; the lack of technically skilled and knowledgeable sales, customer service, and estimating staff; and continuing technological advances in digital production that make accurate estimating difficult to accomplish because processes and methods change frequently.

These paradigm shifts have caused printers to reevaluate the role of estimating on their business environment, which has led, in turn, to the following estimating trends.

Increasing Use of Computer Estimating Methods

There is clear acceptance and increased use of computer-assisted or computer-generated estimating and the related use of computer management systems for operating graphic arts companies of all kinds and sizes. Because this subject is important, it is covered in detail in Chapter 2.

Increasing Use of Price Estimating

In many segments of the printing industry there is an increased use of price estimating methods in which quotations are based on price lists or price-driven matrices. Both manual and computerized pricing models, which can be tailored to meet the pricing requirements of most printing companies, have emerged. Although price estimating is not new to the printing industry, the advantages of speed and simplicity have energized its use. As mentioned earlier, Chapter 4 covers price estimating in detail.

Increasing Use of Fast-Pass Estimating

Driven primarily by the printer's interest in meeting the customer's time-compressed requirements, "fast-pass" or "ballpark" estimating has increased in use. In this estimating procedure the printer generates a cost or price estimate based on the customer's subjective job specifications and the printer's best guess of what the job will require. This system is common when the customer has a clear need for the printed product yet is unsure of the quality or type of artwork or is unable to identify other job specifications.

The fast-pass estimate can be presented as a written quotation or stated orally as a verbal quote. When it is used, it is wise for the printer to issue a disclaimer to ensure that the quote is not fixed. Once the customer accepts the printer's fast-pass estimate, the job enters production and work proceeds. Throughout the production process the customer is free to modify the job and the printer is free to charge for the modifications. Although fast-pass estimating provides both the customer and the printer with production flexibility, both parties must communicate clearly to achieve a quality final product. The fast-pass system is frequently an early sign of an emerging strategic alliance between a customer and a printer because it necessitates that both parties work in a cooperative, proactive manner.

More No-Quote Situations

With increasing frequency, printers and customers are agreeing to produce printing orders without estimates or quotations. This typically occurs when any one or a combination of the following three factors is present:

1. The job is very time compressed (the job, from artwork to final product, must be produced in an extremely short time period).
2. The job is expected to be complex and production is unpredictable.
3. An environment of trust and cooperation has been established between the printer and customer.

When a job is completed without an estimate or a quote, typically the printing order is produced using a time-and-materials chargeback system which is discussed later in this chapter. For data accuracy, printers working in this no-quote environment frequently use real-time data collection systems to track time and materials consumption of jobs (see Chapter 2). Once a job is completed, the customer is invoiced for the job based on the time and material records, plus an additional amount of profit for the printer.

Declining Emphasis on Estimating in Operating the Business

Some printing companies today consider estimating printing, and particularly cost estimating, to be less important than meeting customer needs and the associated time constraints necessary to do business. Although estimating remains a critical and key element for many printing companies, other printers have downgraded estimating from essential to important or, in some plants, from important to "nice to know." This is a trend where caution must be applied.

One sign of this trend is the shift of estimating duties from estimating staff to customer service representatives (CSRs), sales representatives, and other staff. Sometimes, when companies reorganize (and downsize), estimating and customer service departments converge. When this happens, the job tasks of the two positions marry: Estimators complete customer service job duties and CSRs pick up estimating tasks. Because in-depth training is typically not included in such a reorganization, and because estimating requires specific and detailed knowledge gained through experience and training, a company may be forced to revise or modify its complex cost estimating methods to obtain less complex ones. Frequently, price list estimating emerges as a result.

Another sign of the decline of estimating value is the shift of the bulk of the estimator's daily job tasks from estimating to invoicing and billing, data collection review, production management, and other types of nonestimating duties.

Few printing companies are operated in precisely the same way relative to the way jobs are specified, estimated, priced, quoted, and produced. However, it should be clear that any trend that has the probability of compromising the financial good health of a printing company must be carefully evaluated. Thus, it is unwise for a printing company to implement any type of estimating process, or to neglect to estimate jobs, without assurances that the financial risk to the company is minimal.

1.3   The Interrelationship of Estimating to Other Plant Duties

The estimator's assigned duties may vary depending upon the size of the printing plant, the specialization of product and process, the size and quality of the estimating staff, the type of estimating procedures the company uses, the speed by which estimates are completed, and the computer system available to aid the estimating staff. Company management typically determines the estimator's job mix according to the realities of daily business operation. Many printing companies complete estimates by computer as opposed to manual estimating procedures using a calculator, paper, and pencil.

Although small printing plants and quick printers may have no formal estimators, they usually have individuals assigned to handle a range of estimating duties that includes customer pricing, material purchasing, buyout arranging, and price list analyzing. Large commercial printing plants and high-volume printers typically use full-time cost estimators to handle estimating plus other duties. Some very large printing firms use estimating specialists who concentrate on particular products or process segments. Usually, each individual's task becomes more specialized as the estimating staff grows. If various estimating and pricing systems are intermixed, the job duties of the estimator vary accordingly. The following alphabetized sections briefly summarize the areas in a printing company in which a printing estimator may have input or responsibility.

Accounting, Cost Controls, and Finance

Because of the mathematical interrelationship of estimating and the variety of plant production and operating functions, estimators may be asked to assist in the company's accounting, cost control, and finance areas. There is an array of accounting duties necessary to operate any plant and, as a general rule, an accountant is engaged to handle these duties. However, the cost estimators' knowledge and background in cost accounting is beneficial, perhaps even necessary, to develop accurately the costing systems used in the company. In some plants, financial matters such as cash flow, banking practices, equipment leasing, capital borrowing, and similar decision-making concerns may be part of the estimator's duties. Because estimators may deal extensively with costing methods that reflect on certain types of financial statements, such as profit and loss evaluation, their general knowledge in this area may be of assistance to top management.

Customer Service

Progressive printers, particularly large printers and those practicing Total Quality Management (TQM), are using CSRs as a vital link between customer and company. Although CSRs may have varied duties from company to company, they generally serve as liaisons with customers, sales representatives, estimators, and production staff. Individuals serving in CSR positions also work to coordinate production segments of customers' jobs, address customers' problems and complaints, and support other areas by conducting press checks and directing customer contact during job production.

The CSRs in some companies complete estimates as part of their job duties. This requires the CSRs to be familiar with the company's production sequences, job specification completion methods, computer estimating systems, and proposal and quotation procedures. In fact, printers who require their CSRs to estimate generally ask their sales representatives to work closely with the customers in sales capacities only, because once the job is well established and the customers are "sold," the sales representatives can transfer the customers to the CSRs. This exchange of duties allows the sales representatives to maintain a larger group of clients and to pursue new ones while ensuring the important company connection is maintained via the CSRs.

Management Decision Making

In most printing plants, the estimator's position is a staff or an advisory job instead of a line position, which is production related. As advisors, estimators may sometimes be asked to take part in certain decision-making efforts at the management level. Like the estimator's finance decisions, these management decisions, such as production data and costing information, usually relate to the mathematics of the business operation. For example, if top management is considering the purchase of a new press, they may ask the estimator to compare output of the potential new press with the output of existing equipment.

It is generally recognized that the estimator's position is ideal training ground for a future management position in a printing company. Many printing plants, especially medium-size plants and larger, begin new employees in their estimating departments. In these departments the new employees are put in touch immediately with a wide array of plant data and begin to familiarize themselves with many important segments of printing manufacturing. All of the information the employees gather is extremely helpful should they desire to become top management candidates.

Order Entry

Order entry is the process of launching a customer's job into the plant production system and converting the customer's estimate to actual work-in-process. Some estimators are responsible for completing the order entry process as part of their estimating duties. When an integrated computer management system is in place, order entry typically requires the conversion of a cost estimate to a work-in-process order and the generation of a job ticket that details the customer's order in terms of necessary materials, outside purchases, and production operations inside the plant. Detailed information on computerized order entry is provided in Chapter 2.

Pricing

Pricing a printing job is the process of adding profit dollars to the cost of a job after all production costs have been included in the cost. Pricing methods vary extensively in the printing industry. Many factors help determine the final price of a job.

Selling price is the basic unit of price estimating. Although the cost estimator's job is to determine all costs in a given job based on a detailed production plan, top management should be responsible for determining the price of the job because the cost of producing a customer's job is only one critical issue that must be considered. In sum, pricing printing orders is complex and requires extensive knowledge and consideration of risk issues, which are duties best left to top management. Further information on pricing methods and philosophies is presented in Chapter 4.

Production Scheduling and Control

In small printing companies and quick printing firms, it is common for the estimator or the person assigned estimating duties to schedule work into production in a way that achieves the immediate results the customer desires. As a company grows or volume increases, increased job scheduling usually necessitates that a production control system and a more complex production and delivery interface are developed. A growing number of printing companies are using computer-aided scheduling (CAS) as discussed in Chapter 2.

Estimators commonly perform certain duties that are related to scheduling jobs into the plant production system or that are part of the production control process. With skilled labor at a premium, these assignments appear to be reasonable extensions of the estimators' duties because the estimators are concerned with such information when estimating. As products and processes diversify in large commercial printing firms and high-volume plants, estimators are sometimes more specialized. In these circumstances, the estimators may be indirectly responsible for production control or may schedule certain jobs, but they are usually busy enough with estimating duties alone.

To ensure a smooth flow of jobs through the plant, many large printing operations use production coordinators or customer service coordinators who work with sales representatives, estimators, production control staff, and customers. These coordinators focus primarily on minimizing job errors, maximizing plant production, and servicing customer needs fully.

Materials Purchase and Buyouts

Because estimators are required to determine the cost of materials necessary to complete printing orders, many plants require that estimators also handle purchasing duties.

In quick printing companies and small commercial printers, the plant manager typically completes purchasing duties and may also do some estimating. As company volume increases, however, estimators sometimes take over purchasing duties because they already must calculate material costs and coordinate buyouts to complete their estimates. For these reasons, estimators must remain current with respect to the various discounts and bargains offered by suppliers.

In some companies estimators may be the only plant staff continually dealing with suppliers. Large printing companies, which usually benefit from combined purchasing power in many supply categories, may have purchasing agents or purchasing departments. When this is the case, it is necessary to coordinate the efforts of the purchasing staff with the efforts of the company's estimators, who determine material costs. This cooperative effort keeps company inventories at reasonable levels.

Sales

The relationship between estimating and sales is clear-cut—the sales representative meets with the customer, determines the job specifications of the customer's order, then requests that the estimator prepare the estimate. Sales and estimating are different yet vital aspects of a printing business, and the two should be compatible.

The most important duty the sales representative performs for the estimator is obtaining exact and complete job specifications from the customer. Without accurate specifications, estimating is like trying to put a puzzle together with some of the pieces missing. Estimators can aid the sales representatives in turn by completing estimates quickly so the sales representatives can provide quotations to customers just as quickly. Experienced estimators and sales representatives understand the coordination necessary for their relationship to work smoothly.

Given the interactive relationship between sales and estimating, some printing managers believe that the duties of estimators and sales representatives should be integrated. Two approaches are common: (1) requiring the sales representatives to do their own estimating or (2) requiring estimators to handle sales duties.

In some plants, estimators sell reorder jobs and walk-in business. At other plants, sales representatives carry estimating information so they can estimate in the field. The specific mixture of estimating and sales duties is best determined by each company. Considerable problems may arise if job duties are not clearly defined or if management appears to support sales over estimating or estimating over sales.

Printing brokers represent one way for printers to increase sales volume without adding sales personnel or increasing sales costs. A printing broker is a sales representative who works independent of any printing company. After printing brokers sell printing jobs, they locate printers to complete them. When the jobs are finished, the brokers deliver them and bill the customers. The printers then bill the brokers from whom the orders were placed.

Printing brokers' success is driven by their skills at providing superior customer service and competing successfully against conventional printing sales representatives. The printing brokerage business has grown in the past ten years and has particularly affected small commercial printers and quick printers. Estimators in these printing companies now commonly work with brokers and generally accept working with them as working with their own sales representatives.

1.4   What the Estimator Needs to Know

Successful printing estimators are knowledgeable in many areas. A brief discussion of each of these areas (listed alphabetically) follows. Discussions of these areas are found in other parts of this book. ·

Cost Information

One of the estimator's primary duties is to understand the range of costs that affects printing production. It is critical that estimators understand how BHRs are derived and how these cost rates impact the company and the customer. They should understand how fixed and variable components contribute to the costing system, how to determine chargeable and nonchargeable production, and where to modify costs without impacting the company or the customer adversely. This area is further detailed in Chapter 3.

Customers

The estimator's contact with customers and print buyers varies from very little to extensive; some estimators work with customers frequently. The estimator usually initiates the contact by calling the customer or communicating with the customer by fax. Frequently the estimator requests information for a pending estimate or for confirmation of a job specification that is unclear, incorrect, or requires modification. The primary reason for direct contact is to speed the estimating/pricing process.

Some estimators are very good at dealing with customers and buyers. These estimators prefer to take job specifications directly from the customers or buyers instead of having to take the job specifications from sales representatives. Other estimators, however, prefer not to deal with customers unless absolutely necessary and insist that the sales representatives provide them with full job specifications before they complete their estimates. If a printing company has a customer service department, the estimator's direct customer contact is usually minimized because the estimator obtains any required information through the CSR. Further information relative to customers and print buyers is provided in Chapter 5.

Data Collection and Computer Management Methods

Due to the growing use of data collection systems and computer estimating methods in printing, estimators should understand how to work with their companies' computer management systems. Although estimators should not be required to become computer programmers or computer technologists, they should be computer literate to levels that they can work competently with their companies' computer management information systems (MISs). Chapter 2 provides extensive detail in the area of computer systems for printing company operation.

Material Costs and Buyouts

Material costs are the out-of-pocket costs of materials needed to complete a customer's order. They typically include paper, ink, film, plates, and other job supplies. As mentioned earlier in the chapter, buyouts are products or services purchased from outside sources for a specific job. Material costs are covered in this text as they relate to the specific material required for that area of the estimate.

In the printing industry, outside suppliers are usually categorized as service bureaus, electronic prepress trade houses, trade binders, or an array of other vendors that provide specialized products. For example, if electronic prepress production is completed outside the plant, it is ordered from the appropriate service bureau or electronic trade house and is considered a buyout in the estimate. With increased specialization in the printing and publishing industry, buyouts from more than one outside vendor in a printing job are common.

The estimator should understand how to calculate material costs and what inventory impact these materials have on the company's cash position. The estimator should also know how to purchase outside services as well as how to estimate the costs of these services so they can be included in the estimate without slowing the quoting process.

Mathematics

Estimators must be comfortable with mathematics. They should have a good understanding of addition, subtraction, multiplication, and division. Estimators should also understand basic algebra and should have a practical, working knowledge of electronic calculators and other similar devices. They should develop a commonsense relationship with number values to minimize decimal errors and other typical mistakes. As estimators become more experienced, they should work to develop an ability to mentally compare all or part of an estimate-in-process with previous estimates of similar type to see if the two estimates are in line. Use of mathematics is needed in all chapters of this text where estimating production time and cost is completed.

Operating Personnel and Personnel Policies

Estimators do not need to be human resource experts, but they should have a good knowledge of company personnel policies because these policies affect costs and production. These policies include coffee breaks, vacation and holiday procedures, overtime factors, multiple shifts, and appropriate union contract parameters when applicable. In addition, estimators should personally get to know plant operating personnel as appropriate. Furthermore, estimators should remember that production data are derived from a mix of employees, machines, and materials. Many of these policy areas and their impact on company costs are discussed in Chapter 3.

Printing Production Equipment

Estimators should understand all equipment parameters-output speeds, adjustments made during setup and operation, sizes and types of products produced, and maintenance information, to name a few. If possible, estimators should have practical experience with all major plant equipment. In this text, equipment parameters are provided as they relate to the specific area discussed.

Production Methods and Sequences

In the modern printing plant, there are numerous options, methods, and procedures for producing quality printed products. These include photomechanical and digital methods, lithographic and waterless press production, and finishing and bindery production. Estimators should have a thorough, working knowledge of all such available procedures. They should remain abreast of new technology that could change production operations. They should, if possible, have hands-on production experience before estimating. Finally, estimators should be aware of plant production bottlenecks. In this text, production methods are clarified as the production area is discussed.

Quantification Techniques and Derivation of Production Data

Estimators should thoroughly understand the standard production data used for estimating and how these data are derived. As a general rule, such information comes from data collection methods which are linked to historical production data. This information may also come in published form or in the form of new equipment performance projections. Once estimators know how such production data are derived, they must understand completely the data's application and practical use when preparing estimates. Chapter 2 covers data collection. Chapter 3 details quantification of BHRs and production standards, and numerous other chapters provide specific information relative to quantification methods, including time and cost benchmarks for estimating printing and digital imaging.

1.5   General Procedure for Selling, Estimating, Pricing, and Quoting Printing

The following section describes the general procedure for selling, estimating, pricing, and quoting printed work. It is discussed in detail in Chapter 5.

Request for Estimate

The estimating process typically begins with the printing sales representative, who contacts customers to determine their printing needs. When consulting with the customer, the sales representative completes a job specification form which details factors necessary to completely describe the customer's desired product. It helps if the customer can provide a sample of the work. Next, the sales representative returns to the plant and transfers this information from the job specification form to a request for estimate form. The purpose of transferring this information is to allow the sales representative to carefully review and clarify the job specifications the customer has provided. The request for estimate form is then forwarded to the estimator. Many plants combine the job specification and the request for estimate forms to prevent the sales representatives from having to repeat information and to allow them more time to make sales contacts.

If the company provides the sales representative with a price list or another on-the-spot method of job pricing, the sales representative may price and quote a job immediately in the customer's place of business. This bypasses the remaining steps in the request for estimate process. Even when a job is sold by the sales representative from a price list, some printers have their in-house estimating staff double-check the sales representative's pricing to be certain it has been properly completed and that the job fits the price list used.

Estimating the Job

Once the estimator receives the request for estimate form, he thoroughly evaluates the requested product, then determines the production plan that dictates the manufacturing segments necessary to produce the product. If cost estimating is used, the estimator may complete the estimating process either manually (using a paper estimate form, pencil or pen, and a calculator) or by computer. Sometimes cost estimating templates are developed to speed the process.

Although manual estimating is common, many printing companies use computer estimating systems because they provide accuracy, speed, and flexibility. If the estimator price estimates a job that has not been estimated on the spot, she evaluates the job and applies the appropriate pricing information. Customer quotations are then generated from this information.

Whether cost estimating or price estimating is used, and whether the estimate is completed manually or by computer, the estimator should evaluate the job and develop a probable production plan. If cost estimating is used, the estimator first assigns production times and appropriate BHR values, then adds material costs and costs of outside purchases. When the cost values are summed, they represent the manufacturing cost for the job. Factors such as the required number of copies (quantity) and the desired quality level are critical because they have a major bearing on production time and cost. The chosen production plan is also important because there are usually numerous options, each with a different cost value. If time permits after estimating is complete, the estimate should be double-checked for errors that might have occurred during the estimating procedure.

Setting the Job Price

If the job is price estimated, the quotation can be generated and delivered to the customer. If the job has been cost estimated and has been verified as accurate, the quotation is forwarded to top management to determine the price the customer will pay (the job's selling price). As mentioned earlier, pricing is the process of adding an established dollar amount to the cost of a job to provide the company with a profit. The person who does the pricing is typically a top manager or a company executive-a sales manager, a vice president of sales, or perhaps the company president.

Sometimes management will ask an estimator to price a job based on a standard or fixed profit markup percentage. The estimator does so, then calculates the total cost to manufacture the product and adds the specified amount for profit. Many computer estimating systems are programmed to automatically provide the profit markup over cost, which is typically known as default pricing.

Job Proposal and Quotation

After the selling price is assigned and confirmed, a proposal is generated either manually or by computer. The proposal may be mailed conventionally to the customer, delivered to the customer by the sales representative or company messenger, transmitted to the customer by fax or fax/modem, or picked up by the customer.

The proposal, which is a tentative offer made to a customer for producing printing goods and related services, details all job requirements, specifications, and selling prices for these goods and services. The customer may accept, reject, or modify the proposal. Once the customer and management have agreed on all aspects of the job, including selling price, a quotation is issued to the customer. When the customer accepts the quotation in writing, it becomes a binding, legal agreement between the printing company and that customer at the specified selling price, quantity, and quality of product. Some plants combine the proposal and quotation functions and generate one "proposal/quotation" document.

It is not unusual for commercial printing operations—that is, companies doing general printing of all types including advertising and promotion—to depart from the procedures described here depending upon their sizes, types of customer, product lines, and general business philosophies.

1.6 Standard Production Times and Budgeted Hour Cost Rates

As illustrated earlier, accurate cost estimates are a product of standard production times and BHRs, to which material costs and buyout costs are added. It is important to understand standard production times and BHRs.

Standard Production Times

Every printing company, whether it is a quick printer, a commercial printer, or a high-volume printer, needs a certain amount of equipment to produce some portion of the final product. Some of this equipment may require sophisticated electronic systems and may operate at high speeds; other equipment may require more manual effort and may therefore operate more slowly.

In addition to needing equipment, printing companies need skilled employees to operate the equipment. The employees' abilities and production outputs can vary tremendously depending on their training and experience.

Standard production times are average outputs per unit of time for each production operation performed in a plant. Such standards may be expressed as hours per 1,000 impressions, sheets per hour, or any similar output as a function of time. Machinery operating without employee interference tends to be consistent, but most production machinery operates with worker interference. This means that any production that requires employee-machine interaction exhibits differing levels of output. This variation is largely the result of employee training, knowledge, and ability. No standard is precise, so average production outputs must be used. Averages allow a given set of standards to reasonably predict approximate times needed for given production operations under normal operating conditions. Any major change in employee or equipment methods or procedures requires the standards to be revised to reflect such changes.

Consider the operation of a small vertical process camera. A skilled camera operator can expose and process one 10 inch x 12 inch film negative of line work at a rate of one film image each 6 minutes. The standard production time for this example may be restated in decimal hours as 0.10 hour (6 minutes/60 minutes per hour = 0.10 hour). In 0.10 hour, the camera operator must place the copy in the camera copyboard, adjust for enlargement or reduction, calculate and set exposure, position the film in the vacuum of the camera, expose the film, and automatically process the sheet of film. Should this work sequence change, however, the standard production time must be reevaluated.

Budgeted Hour Cost Rates

Every printing plant can be segregated into production or cost centers, which are areas where productive work is completed continuously. A list of cost centers in which a typical printing company regularly incurs production costs might include an electronic prepress platform, a process camera, a printing press, and a folding machine.

Some of the costs in a cost center remain constant regardless of output; these costs are termed "fixed costs" and include items such as insurance, taxes, and rent. Other costs, such as the cost of labor, are known as "variable costs" and are generated only when production occurs in the cost center. The tool for summing these costs and then dividing them into hourly increments is the BHR. Other job costs, such as material costs and outside purchases, are not included in the BHR. These costs must be calculated and charged to the customer separately.

Consider the process camera example discussed in the Standard Production Times section. Assume that the camera operator must produce 10 camera negatives, each 10 inches x 12 inches, for a customer. At the standard production rate of 0.10 hour per negative, it will take the camera operator 1 hour to complete work on all 10 images (10 images x 0.10 hour = 1.0 hour). If the BHR for the small vertical process camera has been determined to be $40.00 per hour, then the customer would owe $40.00 for using the camera, the camera operator, and all associated facilities ($40.00 x 1 hour). Add to this an estimated material cost of $8.00 for film and processing chemistry and the customer owes an estimated $48.00 for camera work and film materials. To complete this order, costs for additional manufacturing steps such as film assembly, platemaking, presswork, and bindery must follow. Each of these costs would also be evaluated at the applicable production standards and multiplied by the BHR for the production center in which the work was completed. These costs would be summed and added to the material costs. The total cost of the job would include the internal manufacturing expense for each segment of the customer's order.

1.7   Other Methods Used to Estimate or Price Printing

In addition to, or in place of, the cost estimating procedure detailed previously, the following eight procedures can be used to estimate or price printing. One major difference between these techniques and cost estimating is that each of these eight techniques is based on the selling price of a job. Estimating using selling price—or price estimating a job—is defined as calculating the total dollar amount the customer pays when the job is completed. As mentioned earlier, selling price is the sum of all manufacturing, material, and overhead costs, plus profit.

There are two important differences between price estimating and cost estimating in printing. First, profit markup has been included in the figure used for price estimating, so there is no need to add an additional amount for profit. Second, price estimating does not normally require a specific breakdown of production segments that details how the job will be produced. Together these two differences provide price estimating with a significant advantage over cost estimating: Price estimating is a much faster estimating procedure. In general, price estimating allows an estimator to complete more estimates per day, and it allows the company to quote on more printing orders.

The disadvantages of price estimating offset its advantage, however. The built-in profit margin makes modifying profit on a particular job difficult for management. In addition, no production times are assigned during price estimating, so when and if the job begins production, it is not easy to schedule it into plant workflow. Chapter 4 provides detailed information on price estimating methods, including how to establish a price list system for estimating standard products.

Figure 1.1 compares the general characteristics of cost estimating and eight common price estimating methods with respect to accuracy, speed of system use, system complexity, ease of modification, computer adaptability, training time, and shop performance data. The following discusses each method.

Tailored Price Lists or Pricing Templates

All types of printers—quick printers, commercial printers, high-volume printers, electronic service bureaus, and specialty printers—commonly estimate from price lists or pricing templates if the product line of the price list item is standardized. For example, many printers offer standard sizes and colors of paper, standard colors of ink, defined quantities, and routine production which make price lists convenient, reliable, and fast.

Depending on the printer's assessment of the competition and other factors, price lists may be printed and distributed to customers. When this is done, customers can use the price lists to determine the price of the work they are contemplating before they contact the printer. When price lists are published and made available to customers, they should be dated with the month and year of effective use, and they should include the statement, "Prices may change without notice." These two factors protect the printer from problems regarding price changes and out-of-date lists.

For accuracy, price lists should be developed using cost estimating techniques. Tailoring price to a particular printing company is very important because it is likely that the costs of production, labor, and materials may vary and recovering the full cost of a job plus a profit is desired. Price lists should also be revised using cost estimating techniques, especially if equipment is new or production changes have been made. A price update revision may be done as a percentage markup based on current prices. However, this percentage markup should be determined accurately to reflect real changes in material, labor, and other costs.

There is no question that estimating from a tailored price list is fast and convenient for customer and company alike. These advantages are significant, but price list estimating does not provide any information about production times, which is a disadvantage for most large, complex, or specialized jobs. Price lists are very accurate for work that is locked into the established product lines of a company that uses standard production techniques, but they should not be used for jobs that deviate from standard production routines. Should a customer

	System accuracy	Speed of use	Complexity of basic system	Ease of modification	Computer adaptability	Time to learn/ training time	Provides shop performance data
Cost estimating	excellent	manual: slow computer: faster	fairly high	good	excellent	may be extensive	yes (when job costing is included)
Tailored price lists or pricing templates	excellent (when based on cost estimating)	moderate to fast	varies with system	varies with system	good	moderate to low	not extensive data
Standardized Industry pricing systems	good to fair	moderate to fast	fairly low	done by vendor	fair	moderate to low	not extensive data
Past work basis	good	good	varies with system	good	good (but based on system design)	moderate to low	not extensive data
Ratio system	good to fair (depends on index used)	moderate to fast	moderate	good	varies with system	varies with system	not extensive data
Using the competition's price	depends on production and pricing similarities	varies with system	varies with system	cannot modify	varies with system	varies with system	not extensive data
Chargeback	good	no estimating completed	low	varies with system	varies with system	varies with system	yes
Customer's ability and willingness to pay	poor	moderate to fast	low	easily modified	none	hard to determine	no
Intuitive method	poor	fast	low	poor	none	hard to determine	no

Figure 1.1 Chart comparing various methods for cost estimating and price estimating printed goods

desire a product not specifically covered in the price list, the product should be cost estimated for accuracy.

It is common for large printing companies that offer standardized products, such as labels or business forms, to develop price list books that cover literally all of the products they produce. These books, which are usually referenced as "confidential prices," are carried by all sales representatives, who have been trained to use them. When a customer desires a price for a certain quantity and type of label listed in the price book, the sales representative can find and quote the customer a firm price on the spot. This quick price estimating is a distinct advantage in selling standardized products. Of course, this type of price list estimating, which is completed in the customer's office and in the customer's presence, can be embarrassing if the sales representative makes an error or misquotes a price.

Price lists are extremely valuable pricing tools when they are developed accurately, updated frequently, and are used for the product lines for which they were designed. Because specialization is a key profitability ingredient in the printing industry, price estimating jobs from tailored price lists has become increasingly popular. This trend toward tailored price lists is driving the recent development of computerized pricing systems for such microcomputer applications as portable laptops and notebook computers.

Pricing Using Standardized Industry Systems

Three standardized printing industry pricing systems are enjoying wide use, primarily by quick printers and small commercial printers. In alphabetical order the three are *Bill Friday's Counter Price Book*, *The Crouser Guide to Estimating Printing*, and *Franklin Estimating Systems*. All three are available in both computerized and printed formats nationwide and all three vendors provide telephone customer service to support their pricing products. The address and telephone number of each are in the computer vendor listing in the appendix of this book. In addition, each of the three systems provides procedures to adjust or modify prices based on job quality and customer issues, thereby providing flexibility. Following is a brief description of each.

Bill Friday's Counter Price Book. *Bill Friday's Counter Price Book* can be found on the sales counters of quick printers and small commercial printing firms throughout the nation. This system, which is offered through Prudential Publishing Company, is available to lease. It is updated each time small press printing costs go up 3 percent. The primary purpose of this book is to provide quick, consistent pricing for customers who order the fast-turnaround products that are largely available through quick printing enterprises. A computer version of this book is also available.

Counter Price Book prices are based on jobs produced on normal quick printing equipment, such as an Itek-type camera/platemaker and an A.B. Dick press. The prices in the *Counter Price Book* represent Prudential Publishing's best judgment of fair selling prices. No specific amount of profit is indicated or guaranteed; the efficiency of the printer's operation affects the cost of production and determines the amount of profit that is obtained or the amount of loss that is absorbed.

The Crouser Guide to Estimating Printing. *The Crouser Guide to Estimating Printing*, also known as *The Crouser Guide*, is primarily aimed at small format press printers. It is based on the cost of direct materials and uses a base BHR and standard estimating times. It includes tables for using a second color head on small format presses, and it allows the user to note the press time for scheduling purposes.

The Crouser Guide is actually broken into three pricing guides: low cost (35th percentile or 35 percent of printers are at this cost or lower), medium cost (50th percentile), and high cost (70th percentile).

Crouser and Associates, who developed this product, also offer the Crouser Quick Estimator. This point-of-purchase computer program allows printers to quickly estimate jobs using their own BHRs, paper stocks, press setup times, press running times, markups, spoilage factors, capacity utilization percents, production cost markups, and total cost markups. The Quick Estimator then prints the estimate, work order, and invoice.

Finally, Crouser's Book Program offers a tailored pricing system, which is similar to *The Crouser Guide* but is built specifically for the costs of an individual company, and the Crouser Quick Job Tracker. The latter system, when used with the Quick Estimator, provides computerized job tracking through various production stages and prints reports by production center or customer.

Franklin Estimating Systems. *The Franklin Catalog*, the "granddaddy" of standardized print pricing systems, was first published in paper format in 1917. Sometimes called *The Porte Book* after the Porte Publishing Company that first produced it, *The Franklin Catalog* provides a price estimating system for literally all kinds of commercial printing jobs. Franklin estimates are based on selling price dollars, which may be directly quoted from the catalog or adjusted to meet competitive needs.

Franklin also offers five pricing books, computer estimating software, and real-time data collection. The pricing books are the *Franklin Offset Pricing Book, Franklin Small Press Pricing Book, Franklin Letterpress Pricing Book, Franklin Quick Print Pricing Book,* and *Franklin Desktop Publishing Pricing Book*. As their titles suggest, each book covers a specific graphic arts production area. *The Franklin Offset Pricing Book*, which is directed at general commercial printing shops, is the most popular. The two most recent Franklin additions are the *Franklin Quick Print Pricing Book* and the *Franklin Desktop Publishing Pricing Book*.

The Franklin Estimator is a computer estimating software package that is available for both IBM-compatible and Macintosh computer platforms. Although they differ slightly in use, both packages allow the estimator to either use the Franklin pricing rates or to develop an estimate separate from the Franklin rates. Both packages also provide customer files that hold up to 2,000 customer names that can be sorted in various ways, and both provide various types of printed reports, including customer quotes, detailed estimates, job tickets, and price lists.

The three standard (catalog) pricing systems, like their tailored price list companions, are fast and convenient. When pricing data are properly and consistently applied to them, catalog pricing systems provide a uniform pricing base from which to sell printing. However, catalog pricing systems have generally recognized drawbacks. First, the systems usually have no production plans, which means that production times for scheduling the work in the plant are unavailable. Second, they typically offer limited ability to modify their systems for production variations within plants or from one plant to the next.

A third drawback is that the prices used in standard catalogs are the same for all parts of the United States. Printing managers recognize that geographic location has a direct bearing on their costs and eventually on the prices they charge for their products. Because standard catalog prices do not vary geographically, plants or users must adjust prices relative to their geographic regions. Methods to make these adjustments vary, which in turn may compromise the consistency of the prices.

Pricing Based on Past Jobs

A common technique for estimating in the printing industry, especially when a wide mix of products is produced in the same plant, is price estimating based on past work. In general, the past work-based process is fast and accurate. The technique also sometimes shifts the company's marketing direction toward specialized products that may be most profitable for the company in the long term.

To use this system, management establishes and maintains a file of past jobs that were profitably produced and for which production had been streamlined. From this file, sales representatives develop a sample portfolio for contacts with customers. Frequently, a client selects a product from the sample, then requests a different color, a slightly different page size, or some other change than can be easily completed. Back at the plant, the estimator pulls the standing estimate for the job, reviews it, makes necessary changes to reflect the modifications the customer requested, and finally prepares a proposal. The sales representative then returns to the customer with the proposal which states exact prices for various quantity levels of the desired product.

In some cases, this procedure can be modified. The estimator may maintain a card file or a database system of past job quotations. The sales representative, who knows about past jobs done by the company, sells work without a sample portfolio and brings the work to the plant to be estimated. At this point, the estimator refers to the database for a similar job done perhaps three months ago, and uses that price as a reference against which to set the price for the job under consideration. It is best if the database or card filing system is indexed and cross-referenced because it saves the estimator time.

It is important to note that cost estimating should be used to periodically verify the costs of the products in the past work system. Increased costs may change prices. Also, as new products are added to the portfolio, cost estimating should be used to establish their initial prices.

Pricing Using a Ratio System

This technique involves establishing a dollar ratio of paper or some other job component to the selling price of the job. The most common ratio item is the cost of paper because it is a part of most printing orders and can normally be estimated quickly and accurately.

To use the ratio system with paper as the indexed item, the estimator estimates the cost of paper for an order, then multiplies the paper cost by a specific ratio. The product represents the selling price for the printing order as a function of paper cost.

This technique is not intended to reflect specific, actual costs incurred during the manufacture of a product, but it is accepted because it is easy to execute and, in the view of some plant owners, it is accurate enough. The key to the accuracy of this technique is first carefully identifying the component item common to the products produced by the company. The next step is developing a ratio that most accurately provides for full job-cost recovery and profit. To ensure a continuing high profitability, the ratio should be based on past profitable jobs done by the company. It is important that all jobs estimated using the ratio system have similar manufacturing components as well as the same level of product quality. When either of these conditions is not met, either a different ratio should be used or the job should be estimated some other way.

Using the Competition's Price

Using the prices competing printers charge as a basis for estimating is fairly common practice in the printing industry. Such information is available from many sources—published price lists, customers who check around for the best prices on their jobs, supply salespeople, former employees, or "table talk" at a local association meeting. Once the information is obtained, it may be used to adjust or establish a price for a job under consideration.

Two major problems exist when pricing by competition, however. First, it is difficult to verify if the prices are accurate for the described product at the quantity and quality levels requested unless the competitor's prices are taken from a published list. Second, there may be few similarities between the companies comparing prices. Each company may have an entirely different type of equipment, production technique, and personnel. There may also be widely different accounting, costing, and estimating procedures. Therefore, the use of the competition's prices is driven less by manufacturing and investment considerations and more by free-market and commodity-based methods.

The advantages of pricing by competition are that it is simple and direct once the competitor's information has been obtained. It is possible to undercut the competition's price and to subsequently increase personal volume of work by winning jobs that normally would go elsewhere. Of course, although production volume may increase, costs to cover that production may not be recovered because the costs were reduced simply to beat the competition and win the jobs. The net effect over time is struggling survival or dissolution of the company through bankruptcy.

Consider this situation: If each printing plant in the community priced work by comparing with the competition, a price-cutting cycle could easily begin. Plants that refused to cut prices would lose business to the firms that were offering the best deals. The plants that cut prices would do a tremendous volume of work, perhaps much of it at cost or below. Price cutting is a vicious cycle that can hurt the entire printing community.

It is safe to say that most estimators and sales representatives attempt to meet or beat the competition's price on jobs they consider important. In fact, it is reasonable to assume that some printing plants price their work as much as possible on competitors' bids and may even make money if the competitors know their costs and pricing structures well. Consistently making a profit when pricing by competition, however, is more a product of luck than of skill.

Using a Chargeback System

Although a chargeback system is not an estimating or a pricing method per se, its use for printing companies and other graphic arts firms that adopt "no estimate" policies is growing. The chargeback system is also used extensively for operating the in-plant (or captive) printing departments commonly found in large hospitals, school systems, and corporations.

Simply put, the chargeback procedure is a "time-and-materials" method in which the actual time and material costs are tracked during production and summed when the job is completed. Thus, the chargeback system is not actually an estimating method but is more of an ex post facto review of actual costs that is followed by the addition of a certain number of profit dollars. When this method is used by in-plant printing operations that do captive work for larger parent corporations, profits may or may not be added. When the chargeback system is used in the commercial printing segment, profit is typically added to the total actual costs to arrive at a final selling price for the customer.

One advantage of the chargeback method is that the customer pays for the actual time worked and the actual materials consumed for a job, which eliminates any differences between the estimated and actual costs of the job. Because a customer is invoiced based on actual time and materials, chargeback procedures eliminate or reduce the estimator's involvement because prices are based on actual and not estimated times. Using chargeback with other quoting methods saves the estimator time because chargeback jobs do not require estimating.

One disadvantage of chargeback in the commercial printing segment is that because no estimate is prepared, no proposal or quotation is offered. As a result, a customer may be surprised at the final price of a job and may even consider it excessive. Without a proposal or a quotation stating specific dollar amounts, the question of whether a contractual agreement exists between the printer and the customer may arise.

As just mentioned, commercial printers who use the chargeback system do so as part of their "no estimate" policies. Frequently these customers have established accounts and wish to expedite production on their jobs, especially on their repeat printing orders or their routine jobs. In such cases, a climate of trust exists between printer and customer.

In-plant printing operations, such as printing facilities within insurance companies, typically find the chargeback system desirable because the customers—the departments within the parent company—use the procedure as a budget control process. For example, when printing is done for a department, the cost is tracked during production and then charged against that department's budget or operating fund. The printing department's income is then generated by the volume of chargeback work done for the various departments it supports within the parent organization.

Pricing by the Customer's Ability and Willingness to Pay

This pricing procedure is subjective and is typically driven by the printing company's history with the customer. This history may include the customer's payment patterns and the printer's observed customer successes in his own markets and business activities.

The sales representatives or company management evaluate customers with respect to their willingness and ability to pay for jobs. When possible, an index such as a credit rating can be used as a base for arbitrarily establishing selling price. Once prices are communicated to customers, the customers may accept, reject, or attempt to negotiate the figures downward. Because the customers, not the costs incurred in producing the product, are the focal point of the pricing system, it is not unusual for the quoted prices to be higher than if normal estimating procedures were used.

Printing companies that price in this manner may not want to take the time to estimate the jobs, or they may have no defined procedures by which estimates can be accurately completed. Pricing exclusively by the customer's ability or willingness to pay for the work appeals largely to the entrepreneurial printer and may border on guesswork, depending on how the "willingness to pay" and "ability to pay" factors are determined. However, there is merit to the concept. Printers can subjectively price on what the "market will bear" and can therefore earn substantial profits if their observations and feelings about customers are correct.

Intuitive Pricing

Some printing managers believe that cost estimating jobs, or developing tailored price estimating systems, is a waste of time. They base their reasoning on the facts that cost estimating requires standard times and budgeted costs, both of which are averages and are thus imprecise; that many mistakes occur during the estimating process; and that too many changes occur during production to simply be determined during estimating. So, instead of estimating, these managers use intuition to determine a price for each job. In some cases, they review the production requirements of the job and include those requirements in their guesses. In other cases, they quote a price based on a quantity or a type of product with no other input at all.

Guessing at a price for a printed product is an inaccurate pricing procedure. Nonetheless, it is a technique practiced today by those who believe that intuition is better than averaging when pricing printing or by companies faced with excessively large numbers of estimates to complete in a limited amount of time.

1.8   The Estimator's Work Environment

The following addresses the work environment of the typical commercial printing estimator. Quick printers and commercial printers doing fast-turn-around work usually complete the pricing process at the counter manually with an electronic calculator, by countertop computer system or point-of-purchase computer, or at the cash register when the order is tallied. In instances where the quick-print customer requests a competitive price before placing an order, the counter employee may complete such pricing and give it to the owner/operator or store manager for approval. When such orders are complex or are for fairly high quantities, the customer may consider price differences between quick printing production and commercial "metal lithographic plate" production.

Office Location and Equipment

The physical location of the printing estimator's office is important because the office services sales representatives, CSRs, management, and customers. It must be easily accessible, but not in the center of traffic or major plant activity. It should also be quiet, so location immediately adjacent production is undesirable. When possible, outside windows should be used to provide natural lighting. Artificial white lighting of normal intensity is also needed, and is preferably color balanced to compare true color values of printed products. A heating/air conditioning system should provide a comfortable working environment.

The office should be large enough for conferences with sales representatives, customers, other estimators, and management. A large table with chairs should be available and distinctly separate from the estimator's work area. Some plants provide estimators with conference areas as part of their offices; other plants locate the estimator's office adjacent a conference room shared by other estimators and company staff. Because estimators lay out and inspect artwork and printed press sheets in their offices, there must be ample space to spread out large sheets.

Each office should be furnished with a large desk and an additional large table for greater working space. A comfortable, ergonomically designed computer work area should be adjacent the estimator's desk. Ample filing space in closed cabinets for job tickets and other documents should be easily accessible. A bookcase should be available for reference materials. Some estimators prefer manual card filing systems to record and quickly review and compare jobs. However, a good microcomputer database and a spreadsheet program can replace a manual system. One or more telephones should be accessible to visitors as well as to the estimator. A fax telecommunication unit or a fax/modem computer connection is also desirable, although these can be contained in a room close to the estimator's office and shared with other estimators and company staff.

The estimator's office should be a pleasant environment in which to work. If financially possible, the office should be carpeted. Carpeting soundproofs a room, provides insulation, and adds decorative flavor. Stylized furniture and framed artwork are additional options.

Estimating Tools

The estimator needs certain tools to assist in accurate estimating. Normal office supplies such as pencils, pens, erasers, and graph paper are needed, and convenient access to a copying machine is required. A microcomputer with appropriate spreadsheet, database, and related application software, and a connected printer, are necessities. A typewriter for typing proposals and quotations is common.

In addition to a microcomputer and a printer, each estimator should have access to two types of calculators: a printing calculator and a pocket calculator. The printing calculator provides a paper record for all input figures and operations so the figures can be rechecked at a future time. Printing calculators are desk models that operate on normal electrical current. The handheld portable pocket calculator, which may be solar or battery powered, is used for calculations that require no future record. A model with built-in memory that allows storage of intermediate figures during calculations is preferred.

Other tools are also needed for estimating. A magnifying glass or loop, which aids in inspecting samples and press sheets; a paper thickness gauge; a proportion scale, which aids in fitting artwork; rulers and tape measures, which help measure accurately; and gauges, which determine screen rulings and angles of screens, are all standard tools for estimating. In addition, reference books containing production standards, costing information, and process considerations are very helpful. Providing the estimator with an efficient, pleasing office and the proper tools and resources necessary for executing estimates is very important if accurate estimates are desired.

1.9   Selecting an Estimator or an Estimator Trainee

Turnover of estimating staff can be high, so establishing a process for selecting individuals who have the backgrounds to become estimators is important. In addition, establishing a process for training estimators is helpful so that the company is prepared when estimators leave or move to other areas of the company.

Estimators commonly request transfers within the company to enhance their experience and breadth of knowledge. Although they may move to any area, they tend to focus on three specific areas: production management, customer service, and sales. It is important that company management graciously approve such transfers so that the estimators can continue to grow personally and professionally. Because transfer requests from estimators are common, management should have a process to select and train new estimating staff.

Preparing a Job Description

The initial step in selecting a printing estimator or a printing estimator trainee is developing a job description that specifically states the duties of the position in the organization. For example, an estimator's duties in a small printing plant, which may have one estimator for fifteen production and management personnel, may include office management and over-the-counter sales. In a larger plant, estimators may have far narrower breadth of duties. They may be required to concentrate their estimating skills in production planning or in certain product lines or processes. Regardless of the breadth and scope of the estimator's job, it is important to determine accurately the range of duties the estimator will complete. Hiring is then a matter of fitting each applicant into as many categories of the job description as possible.

It is sometimes desirable to develop an expanded job description that breaks down all duties the estimator will perform. The more detailed and specific the expanded job description is, the easier it is to determine who should be hired.

Advertising

Once the job description is complete, it should be used in advertising and in external communication with potential job applicants. Depending upon available funds and the importance top management assigns this hiring, advertising may be done either in a limited geographic region or nationally. A local newspaper may be one advertising source, but it may not provide the best coverage, especially when attempting to reach applicants who completely meet the job description. In order to reach experienced applicants, advertising is often done in national trade journals as well as in numerous regional graphic arts publications. A general rule is the more applicants the better the selection, and the better the selection, the lower the training costs once an individual is hired.

Hiring from Inside or Outside the Plant

A traditionally good source for estimating trainees are current employees working in the plant in production or operating management capacities. A department head, a management trainee, and a knowledgeable production employee are possible candidates.

The major advantage of hiring from within is that management and other employees know the individual under consideration. The individual's general job performance, attitude, personality, and printing background have been observed daily. One of the most significant disadvantages of hiring from within relates to the impact of the decision not to hire the employee. If employees are not accepted for estimating positions, they may be discouraged and disappointed and may ultimately become unhappy and unproductive.

When there are no internal applicants, or when a wider selection of applicants is desired, outside recruiting is used. External sources include college or university graphic communication or printing management programs, classified newspaper advertisements, word of mouth, or referrals via local industry trade associations. The most common recruiting media are classified advertisements in newspapers and trade magazines.

Hiring an individual who is unknown to company management requires carefully assessing the applicant's background, printing knowledge, personality, and potential for success. Job history is also very important. In most cases, applicants under final consideration should be invited to the plant, which incurs travel and related costs. Testing the final applicants may also be desired, which is an additional expense.

Using a Weighted Rating System

Interviewing and hiring the right person for an estimating position is an art. To aid in this endeavor, the weighted rating system in Figure 1.2 is provided. The criteria in the left column cover the major areas for estimating: knowledge of printing, mathematical ability, technical printing competence, personality factors, logic ability, computer knowledge and literacy, and educational background. Note that each has been weighted according to its relative importance in estimating. Of course, should an expanded job description indicate that other factors are more important, or that the weight of one factor outweighs the others, the chart should be modified. Top management should make these decisions before interviewing and testing candidates.

When using the weighted system, which is an attempt to objectively categorize and define subjective values, the interviewer must attempt to accurately determine the competence levels of each candidate. Point values for each category must be fairly assigned and then totaled for final assessment. At the bottom left of the chart is a total point evaluation, which is intended to aid management in assessing their choices.

Interviewing and Testing

It is vital that the interviewer rate every candidate consistently and accurately. Resources to do so are not limited to personal interviews; they may include discussions with former teachers and employers and educational transcripts which contain general aptitude test results. All inputs should be as unbiased as possible. Should the interviewer be unable to rate the candidate confidently in three or more categories (of these, two should be among the last four categories listed in Figure 1.2), further information from additional sources may be necessary.

The subject of testing deserves discussion. Although few tests are designed specifically for selecting an estimator, there are tests available for purchase in most of the category areas. The Graphic Arts Technical Foundation (Pittsburgh, Pennsylvania) and the Educational Testing Service (Princeton, New Jersey) are two sources for such tests. Of course, most employment services and professional psychologists provide testing in their respective disciplines. If tests are

	Weight factor	Excellent (8)	Good (6)	Fair (4)	Poor (2)	Total (factor x pts.)
Knowledge of printing. Includes the applicant's understanding of process, products, and workflow for printing manufacturing.	3.0					
Mathematical ability. Assess the applicant's knowledge, understanding, and use of mathematics. May be related to high school or college test scores.	2.5					
Technical printing competence. Assess the applicant's awareness and understanding of the technical factors involved in the production of printed materials; includes knowledge of materials used, costs, and job components.	2.5					
Personality factors. Assess the applicant's basic personality profile-maturity, ability to work independently, frustration level in solving problems, general character, disposition, and so on.	2.0					
Logic ability. Assess the applicant's ability to think and speak logically; effective and clear reasoning capability; may relate to mathematical ability closely.	2.0					
Computer knowledge and literacy. Assess the appliant's understanding of computer applications and the functions and operations of a computer system; includes the individual's ability to quickly learn and master computer estimating and related software programs; includes the individual's knowledge of spreadsheet software.	1.0					
Educational background. Assess the applicant's ability to deal effectively with theoretical and practical problems; school grades may be a good indicator of future success.	0.5					

Total point evaluation

Excellent	95-108 points
Applicant has good potential	68-94 points
Questionable potential	41-67 points
Best not to hire	Under 40 points

Rating total _____

Figure 1.2   Sample of weighted rating system for evaluating printing estimator candidates

administered by the interviewer, they should be reviewed and evaluated before they are used with applicants. Sometimes the best way to do this review is to have the interviewer or a top management candidate take the test. It must be noted that test results, for obvious reasons, cannot provide a total basis from which to make any hiring decision. They reflect only what the test covers and may have built-in biases.

If the weighted rating procedure in Figure 1.2 is used, remember that the weight factor can be modified to better reflect the type of individual to be hired, the job description, and other contingencies. Total point evaluation may also be reassessed if desired.

1.10   How to Develop an Estimating Training Program

One of the most difficult problems with printing estimating is the continual turnover of estimating staff. This is expected for a number of reasons. First, estimating serves as an ideal entry-level area for management training, as well as a good place for CSRs or future sales representatives to "learn the ropes" of a printing company. Although estimators' in-service time varies, sooner or later they tend to transfer to other plant areas where they can capitalize on their estimating knowledge. Second, estimating requires continually applying numbers, much as an accountant constantly works with figures. This makes the job stressful and less desirable in the long run for some types of people. Third, estimating requires constant attention to numerous job details, which also makes it somewhat stressful over the long term. Fourth, the estimators' salaries do not always reflect the responsibility, knowledge, and stress required for the job. This sometimes leads estimators to move into customer service, sales, or management positions where financial compensation is more aligned with the work performed.

Figure 1.3 is a flowchart with step-by-step points for training a printing estimator. Although it is general, it outlines how such training should be completed. The following explains the steps in further detail.

Step 1

Once it has been determined that an estimator trainee is needed, people with the proper aptitude and interest level should be interviewed and carefully selected. In many cases, choosing someone from inside the plant—a person with known skills, personality, and work record—proves less problematic in the long term than choosing an outside candidate.

Step 2

Basic estimating theory is best taught away from the plant by skilled industry professionals. Seminars, workshops, and short courses are forms of this basic

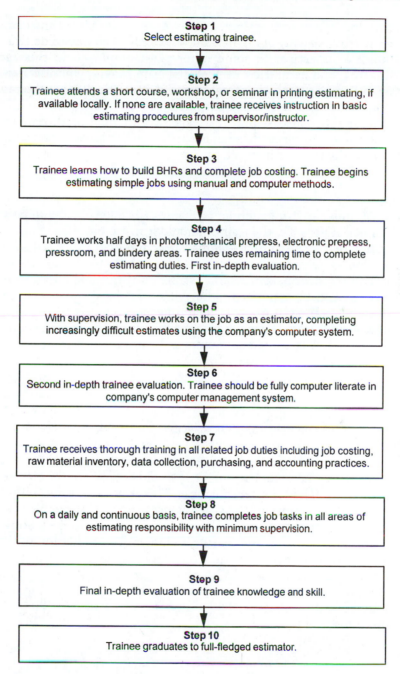

Figure 1.3 Flowchart for training an estimator

instruction. Many Printing Industries of America (PIA) offices offer basic courses in estimating, usually at night or on weekends. If courses are not available, the estimating supervisor or some other plant employee who is familiar with estimating and is skilled at training can provide instruction. Using the company's computer estimating system as a teaching tool is acceptable, but the system tends to overlook important basic estimating concepts. Estimating training is most successful if it uses slower manual methods so concepts are clearer. However, once these concepts are understood, computer estimating should be the focus of instruction.

Step 3

Trainees must learn the rudiments of how to develop plant production standards and BHRs. If possible, the trainee should learn to build and tailor BHRs to the printing firm using a computer spreadsheet. If the company has a functional data collection system, the trainee should learn how to complete the job costing process of comparing actual and estimated times and costs. In addition, the trainee should be exposed to the range of jobs done in the company, the production methods used, and scheduling production, perhaps by working for a short time in the production management area of the company. Trainees should understand how to complete manual and computer estimates.

Step 4

At this point it is suggested that trainees divide the workday into halves. They should spend the mornings of at least one week in conventional prepress, electronic prepress, and pressroom areas and the afternoons completing estimates. Although all production areas are critical, if one area were to be selected as "most important" for the trainee it would be a mix of the electronic prepress and conventional film assembly areas. This is because these areas tend to have many author's alterations (AAs) and house errors (HEs), and they also tend to be a mix of many production details that cannot be overlooked. Sometime during this step the trainee should receive an in-depth introduction to the company's computer management system. This can be done away from the plant at the computer vendor's office or in house by a person skilled in teaching all parts of the computer system. Once this training is completed, computer estimating should be routinely used. The trainees should receive their first in-depth evaluations in this step.

Step 5

After the trainees complete the four-week "back shop" working commitment with a one-week minimum of half-day training in conventional prepress, electronic prepress, pressroom, and bindery areas, they should begin full-time estimating duties. This should require full use of the company's computer estimating system and other modules of the computer system, such as raw material inventory and job costing, as needed. The time spent in this step should be from two to four weeks, or longer based on the training leader's informal evaluation. This step should encourage the trainee to follow a positive work routine so that estimates are processed quickly and accurately. There should also be a focus on estimating details. Supervisor observation should provide evidence that the trainee enjoys the task of estimating.

Step 6

The trainee's progress should be evaluated in depth for the second time in this step. The speed with which the training progresses depends on many factors, including the trainee's interest and ability in learning the procedures, applicable printing experience, knowledge of production planning, desire to be an estimator, knowledge of the company's computer estimating system, and focus on completing the training. If trainees lose their interest or motivation to estimate, the training leader should determine the reasons. Training should not continue unless the company and trainee mutually agree the effort is fruitful and worthwhile for both parties.

Step 7

If the trainees receive positive second evaluations, they should be provided with in-depth training in related job duties using the company's computer management system as the primary tool. This includes thorough training in the company's pricing policies, order entry, data collecting, job costing, raw material inventory control, purchasing, and applicable accounting practices. This training provides the trainees with a broad knowledge base. The computer vendor can provide partial training in theory-based areas; on-the-job training should focus on the practical application of these areas.

Step 8

Once training has been provided and completed in all aspects of the company's computer management system, the trainees should focus primarily on completing a range of on-the-job tasks that include job costing, purchasing, order entry, and direct customer contact. The trainee should be fully knowledgeable and capable in these tasks, and they should require minimum supervision while completing them.

Step 9

A third in-depth evaluation should be given in this step. The training leader or supervisor and the trainee should honestly assess the trainee's areas of strength and weakness, and training should be provided in any area where the skills are deemed inadequate. Training should continue until the trainee and the training leader agree that the trainee is fully knowledgeable and capable of performing all estimating and related estimating duties for the company.

Step 10

In this step, the trainee completes training and graduates to master estimator. A pay raise or salary increase is one way to congratulate the full-fledged estimator and to help ensure the newly trained estimator's interest remains with the company. To celebrate this event and other promotions in the company, a company-sponsored luncheon or dinner might be appropriate. A framed certificate also might be given to the trained estimator.

Some additional training points:

1. The estimating training program should be focused and follow a clear plan. The program should detail major points and provide a time breakdown for the training to be completed.
2. Texts like this one are important resources for training an estimator. Also available is The Printing Estimating Workbook by Philip K. Ruggles (P.O. Box 46, San Luis Obispo, CA 93406, 805/543-5968 or fax 805/543-9579). The Printing Estimating Workbook is collateral to this text and contains more than 200 practical estimating problems that cover estimating paper, ink, and all related production operations. Together these two books provide an excellent training program for the estimating trainee.
3. Training should be a continuous process that is supported by the company at the company's expense and on the company's time. If estimators have to work "double-duty" during training, they should receive overtime compensation and other benefits.
4. It is possible to write a legal training agreement that ties the trainee and the company together for a specified period of time when training concludes. As long as the agreement is not overboard in terms of its requirements, and is entered into clearly and openly by the trainee, it should be generally acceptable. A lawyer will likely need to aid in drafting and reviewing such a document.
5. If the company is close to a junior college, university, or other academic facility that has a printing or graphic communication curriculum, a faculty member may provide special resources for estimating training. Also consider any type of estimating training program offered through an associa-

tion such as the National Association of Printers and Lithographers (NAPL), PIA, or any of PIA's regional offices. Such programs are usually packed with information and have great educational value.

6. Most vendors of computer management systems, including vendors of computer estimating software, provide training for entry-level trainees either at their corporate locations or at companies. Typically a training fee is required and the training is condensed into a few intense days. The training vendors provide should receive serious consideration because it provides hands-on application of the company's software and may be faster and more convenient than learning the computer estimating process through trial and error.

1.11   Some Rules for the Printing Estimator

There are areas of difficulty that the printing estimator frequently encounters. The following guidelines are suggestions to help resolve some of these issues.

1. Before estimating any job, find out who will supply the artwork, whether the artwork will be mechanical or electronic, and what general quality level the artwork will be. When artwork is clarified and defined, fewer problems and surprises arise when the job enters production. Remember: "As goes art, so goes the job."
2. Before estimating, determine the customer's needs exactly through complete job specifications.
3. Use up-to-date production standards, BHRs, material costs, and outside purchase costs.
4. Always include a reasonable profit for the job.
5. Double-check estimates for math and logic errors before the proposal/quotation is issued.
6. Establish and use a good filing system and keep track of all estimates completed. Keep paper and electronic copies of all quotations/proposals, estimating worksheets, and other items.
7. Make minimum assumptions when estimating by requiring complete job specifications from the sales representative or the CSR.
8. Plan production carefully and estimate every job using the most likely production sequence, not the ideal sequence. Be realistic.
9. Do not make arbitrary exceptions to established plant rules and policies.
10. When estimating, work slowly and carefully. Try not to estimate in the customer's presence.
11. Foster a teamwork environment between sales representatives, estimators, and CSRs. No team member should exert pressure on another.
12. Delivery dates should be carefully established and always kept.

13. If buyouts from trade suppliers are part of the estimate, try to get firm estimates from the suppliers or establish a process by which these buyouts can be estimated in house.

14. Use a profit markup system that relates the price of the job to market factors for that particular customer, job type, value added, and other important pricing factors. It is best not to use a markup percentage that applies to all customers.

Chapter 2

Computers for Production and Management in the Printing Industry

2.1 Introduction

2.2 The Electronic Printing Company

2.3 Computer Applications in a Printing Company

Mainframes, Minicomputers, and Microcomputers

Information Processing and Printing Production Applications

Typesetting and Word Processing

Electronic Prepress Systems and Desktop Publishing

Data Collection and Database Applications

Number Crunching and Spreadsheets

Telecommunication, Electronic Transmission, Fax Systems, and the Internet

Electronic Press Controls, Waterless Printing, On-Demand Publishing, and Digital Presses

2.4 Computer Management Systems for Printers
Outside Service Suppliers   In-House Systems

2.5 Modular Building Blocks for Computerizing a Printing Company
Module Descriptions   Accounting Group (Modules 10
Production Group (Modules 1   through 17)
   through 9)

2.6 Key Points on Computer Management Systems for Printing and Publishing

2.7 Information versus User-Friendliness

2.8 List of Vendors of Computer Management Systems for Printing and Publishing (Appendix C)

2.1   Introduction

Computers have been used in the printing industry since the mid-1960s. It is generally acknowledged that the first computer applications in printing were heralded with the introduction of the Compugraphic phototypesetting system, followed with a variety of faster electronic typesetting systems by the mid-1970s. Computer systems for management purposes, which were developed primarily to complete printing estimating duties, were introduced to printers in the late 1960s.

During these early years, computer methods for management generally took a backseat to the development and use of computer systems for production applications. In the early 1980s computerized printing management systems, including integrated systems for completing estimating, order entry, inventory, accounting, and a range of other duties, began to emerge in mass.

Today computers and electronic systems utilizing microprocessors are in wide use in the printing industry and handle an increasingly expanding range of manufacturing and management tasks. Technological advancements in both hardware and software have provided continuous improvement that will continue unabated into the twenty-first century.

During the late 1980s and to the mid-1990s, the following changes occurred to facilitate computer integration throughout the printing industry:

1. Hardware platforms continued to be significantly improved through electronic advancements and enhanced processing power. Hardware was downsized in both space and cost, making powerful computer systems easily affordable to even the smallest printing company.

2. A wide and growing variety of powerful software programs covering a range of management and production areas became available. These included desktop publishing (DTP) and electronic prepress software and estimating, inventory control, scheduling, and BHR programs. Many of the programs could be used interactively. Cost was low and user-friendliness was continually enhanced.

3. Automated data collection methods in which electronic production units were directly connected to computer management systems emerged. As such direct machine interconnectedness continues to emerge, printing company management will be able to monitor work-in-process at all times. This will allow for such capabilities as instantaneous rescheduling of plant production, targeted delivery information, real-time activity and materials reporting, and important management controls for inventory, order entry, accounting, and so forth.

4. Printing industry computer vendors who developed and marketed management information systems generally stabilized. Many of these vendors

were national and offered to professionally support their installed systems. In addition, these systems continued to improve in functionality and ease of use while costs remained easily affordable for even the smallest printing company.

5. Inexpensive, interchangeable mass storage devices, including SyQuest removable media and similar other removable media, emerged. The transportable electronic media were inexpensive, troublefree, and easy to use. CD-ROM technology and Photo CD had become well established and represented important technological steps in digital transportation and electronic image conversion methods.

6. Electronic prepress production systems forever changed the way jobs enter production. Customers enthusiastically embraced these electronic methods and printers were forced to provide supporting electronic prepress services. These systems caused significant shifts in manufacturing methods for printers and structurally changed the customer-printer relationship at its very core.

7. Technological advances in computer systems used for graphic imaging, including Xerox DocuTech, Heidelberg-DI, IRIS, Xiekon, and Indigo digital imaging systems, continued to emerge throughout the printing industry. The type of production these systems facilitated moved the industry to a just-in-time (JIT) delivery environment and changed the paradigm of how printing is manufactured and delivered. The development of an array of different electronic and computer-based systems for conventional printing manufacturing in prepress, press, and finishing continued unabated. Lead times for printing were reduced from many days to a few days, and increasingly from a few days to one day or a few hours.

8. The electronic interconnectedness between customers and printers through interactive computer network systems became a reality. Communication via facsimile or fax, modem exchange, ISDN (Integrated Digital Services Network), and direct digital telecommunication were common methods to translate information and images. The Internet and the World Wide Web also served as an electronic communication medium for printers and customers. Its potentially significant impact on digital image transfer included serving as a medium for marketing and selling graphic images.

Clearly the electronic and computer changes were extensive to both the manufacturing and management segments of the printing industry. This chapter focuses on MISs available to printers. An overview of electronic and computer devices for printing production is also covered briefly in this chapter. The seventeen modules necessary to fully computerize a printing company are presented in depth, and a list of computer vendors serving the printing industry is provided.

2.2 The Electronic Printing Company

It is clear that the printing industry is in transition in all segments of the graphic arts, moving from conventional, manual methods and ink-on-paper products to electronic methods and electronic products. The transition is well underway and the result will ultimately be the "electronic printing company."

Today's graphic arts enterprise can be described as a business that uses an increasing number of electronic platforms and electronic devices to manufacture ink-on-paper products. Conventional production methods are still frequently used, however, particularly in press and finishing areas. At the same time, new equipment is increasingly driven by electronic methods.

Increasingly, printing companies link this electronic equipment with electronic computer management systems. When jobs enter production, the orders are converted from computer-assisted estimates to electronic job tickets. The customers provide electronic artwork and production is monitored by electronic data collection and direct machine interface (DMI) tools. Management benefits from numerous electronic decision-making tools. Electronic production equipment of all kinds and at all production stages controls quality, speed, and output of final products.

As a result, printing employees have become less craft oriented but increasingly computer literate. The move is now toward employing highly skilled technologists. Hierarchical management methods, less often the norm, are being replaced with various forms of TQM. Employee empowerment, continuous improvement, statistical process control (SPC), and outstanding customer service are increasingly understood and accepted concepts.

There is no question that, in various forms, the previous description fits a growing number of printing companies. In addition, one more major graphic arts component is likely to go electronic: the products. Certain ink-on-paper products are in transition to various forms of magnetic media. Computer-based information systems are "printed" on CD-ROM to replace encyclopedias printed on paper. Electronically interactive products such as maps, reference manuals, and catalogs have been reconfigured and "printed" in electronic form, not on paper. Although paper products in some forms will remain viable for many years because they are portable, easy to use, flexible, and inexpensive, electronic products will most likely become the new paradigm as their public acceptance increases and their cost diminishes.

The electronic printing company will be integrated in all areas: Its digital products will be produced using electronic methods and operated with computer management systems. In the short term a fairly broad range of ink-on-paper products will remain the primary products of some printing companies. The long term, however, is likely to show printing companies producing a growing number of electronic products using digital methods.

There is no force on the horizon to challenge the electronic revolution inside the graphic arts, or among the customers, as the shift from ink-on-paper to electronic products occurs in some markets. An increasing number of graphic arts companies are becoming purveyors of both ink-on-paper and electronic products using electronic equipment and computer management systems. These businesses represent the electronic printing companies of the present. As this transition continues, it appears likely that someday not too far in the future the all-electronic printing company will produce electronic graphic products on electronic equipment managed with a fully integrated computer MIS.

2.3   Computer Applications in a Printing Company

The following discussion covers the production and management uses of computers in a typical printing company.

Mainframes, Minicomputers, and Microcomputers

Computers have been generally categorized by decreasing size into three basic hardware platforms: mainframes, minicomputers, and microcomputers. Today, because of hardware improvements, distinctions between these categories are much less defined. Although mainframes and minicomputers still exist, they have been downsized to fit into very small areas and have thus begun to appear like larger versions of the microcomputer.

Information Processing and Printing Production Applications

It is important to distinguish between computer systems for management that are used largely for processing information of various kinds and computer systems that are developed to aid in manufacturing printed goods. Although these two general groups of computer systems have fairly clear distinctions, there is growing overlap or blurring in some cases. For example, some types of computer systems serve dual roles whereby they can be used to complete both management and printing production functions. In addition, because electronic systems can be tied together, interconnectedness between computer management and electronic production systems is common.

The type of computer platform relative to the application in a printing company varies. In general, printers use Macintosh platforms for graphic imaging and electronic prepress, while personal computers (PCs) with Microsoft Windows and UNIX-based networked systems are commonly used for business management applications, including MISs. Some small printers use one computer platform to complete both production and management duties, but the cost of microcomputer platforms is low enough that even small printers have two or more computers.

The quick printer and the small commercial printer have seen the rapid evolution of a number of computer systems. This evolution has been led by the Macintosh as well as by computerized peripheral attachments including laser printers, black-and-white copiers, and color copiers with electronic controls. For the quick printer or the small commercial printer, the Macintosh represents a computer platform that is economically feasible and versatile enough to handle both graphics and information processing. In fact, piggybacking information processing and graphic production duties on a Macintosh is common for this industry segment.

For example, during normal working hours one Macintosh running DTP software such as PageMaker or QuarkXPress can be used to generate original artwork. In the evening and during "off" hours, the same Macintosh can be used to complete various business and management duties, including invoicing, inventory control, and estimating. Other uses of Macintoshes, IBMs, and IBM compatibles are discussed with the prepress areas in Chapter 8.

Large printers and high-volume printers purchase and use numerous computers for both manufacturing and management applications. These larger firms have hundreds of customers, dozens of jobs-in-process at any given time, and literally thousands of pieces of information to track and monitor. Without computers to aid in and expedite the information flow, details would be forgotten, too many mistakes would be made, and a plethora of unhappy customers would arise.

Typesetting and Word Processing

Typesetting, an important graphic design component and a vital art form for graphic communication, has largely been replaced with word processing software that is linked to PostScript output devices. Some experts lament that this trend has lowered the quality of typeset materials to what appears to be a secondary role in the graphic imaging process, while others argue that a "good enough" philosophy relative to type quality is perfectly acceptable.

Regardless of these issues and differences of opinion, it is clear that word processing software and related DTP software have, for all intents and purposes, replaced typesetting as production operations in the printing industry. These operations, when done by printers, are typically completed on inexpensive microcomputer platforms, such as Macintoshes or Disk Operating System-based (DOS-based) or Microsoft Windows 95®-based computers, that use a range of popular word processing programs like Microsoft Word or WordPerfect. Because customers can save money when they complete the input/typesetting process, they commonly provide printers with disks containing their manuscripts in digital form.

Service bureaus also provide printers with type matter. Many of today's service bureaus are former typesetting companies that have become film output providers who work between customers and printers. As PostScript output software and imagesetting equipment have been enhanced, and as Adobe and other type software vendors have refined and expanded the typeface selection to literally thousands of choices, type quality has generally improved over the first versions available in the mid-1980s.

There remain certain kinds of front-end typesetting systems with specific application to certain types of customers, such as magazines and newspapers. However, dedicated word processors or general-purpose, front-end typesetting systems are not commonly found in typical printing companies today.

Electronic Prepress Systems and Desktop Publishing

Of the areas affected by electronics and computer systems, it is clear that prepress, which includes design/art production, typesetting, photography, film assembly, proofing, and platemaking, has been the most drastically changed. In sum, prepress includes those areas of printing production necessary before any ink-on-paper printing is completed.

Prepress History. The revolution in electronic prepress began with the introduction of the Macintosh 128K computer in January 1984. The introduction of Aldus PageMaker software, Adobe PostScript output language, and the Apple LaserWriter followed in 1985. These advances combined to allow the integration of type and graphic images at one time. The final product was a fully composed, imaged page.

Thus the process of imagesetting was born, and the printing industry for the first time was changed from outside industry boundaries by computers and software. No longer did printers control all parts of the manufacturing process—from artwork to finished product—as they had since Johanes Gutenberg, who is considered the "father of printing," developed movable type around A.D. 1450.

Prepress Today. Today, prepress done without computerization or electronic aid is labor intensive, but many printers continue to complete all or parts of their jobs in this manner because they lack computer equipment and/or the ability to use it effectively. Thus, mechanical artwork and table stripping are still found in many printing companies, but this type of work is craft oriented and tends to be fairly slow because it is paced to the operator's manual skills.

Electronic prepress, the emerging de facto standard for graphic arts prepress, is also labor intensive. However, because the same electronic platforms and software are available to customers and clients of the printing company, there has been a significant shift in prepress production from the printer's plant to the customer's office. Thus, the customer and not the printer bears the initial labor in a job by supplying electronic art. For many printers it is increasingly common for customers to supply fully imaged electronic artwork, including typesetting, thereby bypassing prepress production traditionally done by the printer.

This shift to customer-supplied electronic artwork via computer imaging systems represents a major structural change in the printing industry. Survival requires that printers maintain competence in all conventional prepress methods, which have attendant high labor costs and generally slow production output, while providing an array of complex electronic prepress services, which have different, labor-intensive problems. This pressure has affected printers of all levels and sizes, although some printers have been less affected than others.

Today, computer systems to complete both management and production in printing are pervasive. This chapter focuses on computer management systems while Chapter 8 addresses various production and estimating issues for DTP and electronic prepress.

Data Collection and Database Applications

Data collection in a printing plant has evolved into a fast, convenient, and fairly inexpensive process. Sometimes known as "shop floor data collection (SFDC)" or "real-time data collection," this process uses electronic units to track work-in-process. An installed electronic factory data collection (EFDC) system consists of user-friendly terminals or computers located at strategic production points throughout the plant. These terminals are connected to one large computer to which all information is sent and stored. Employees doing production work log all activities performed, the materials used, production notes, and other vital production data into the data collection terminals. The employees are also required to "log on" and "log off" to begin and end the workday respectively and when they take lunch and work breaks. Ultimately the employees' workdays can be reviewed relative to the jobs on which they worked, the times they spent in various activities on a job-by-job basis, the times that are chargeable to customers and those that are nonchargeable, material usage, and so on. The EFDC system is ideal for immediate job cost review, which is discussed in depth later in this chapter.

Databases (D-bases) for microcomputers are marvelous tools for processing vast amounts of data quickly and accurately and for building and maintaining complex numerical files. Database software is typically integrated into a computer management system purchased from a printing industry computer vendor, but it can be a stand-alone system to control inventory or to track work-in-process. For example, a stand-alone database for inventory control may require inputting stock-on-hand weekly to update the inventory quantities and stocks available.

Database software may be relational, where data in one field can be associated with data in another, or nonrelational, where data are generally not intended to interface. Instead of installing an expensive factory data collection (FDC) system, a printing company could build its own microcomputer database to analyze production or inventory information quickly and accurately.

Number Crunching and Spreadsheets

As they do with data collection and data processing, computers also speed "number crunching" duties (e.g., numerical analysis) in the printing plant. Because they are mathematically error free, computers are valuable tools for a diverse series of important numerical analysis chores.

One of the most significant number-crunching duties is estimating, which is discussed throughout this text relative to the software applications available. Many printing industry computer vendors develop their own proprietary software for completing cost estimating by computer. This includes developing BHRs, completing detailed cost estimates of customers' jobs, assessing material costs and buyouts, and adding company profits. Price estimating using a computer-driven price matrix or price list is also available.

One option for completing price estimating and cost estimating by computer is to use electronic spreadsheet programs which are typically developed in house by estimators or other staff and are tailored to meet a company's specific needs. A spreadsheet is a row-and-column arrangement of numerical data. These data can be related by establishing formulas upon which cell information is generated. Cell data can be based on formulas or on an identified piece of data. A cell is where a row and a column intersect. Column and row locations are referenced using letters and numbers respectively.

Initially, to develop a spreadsheet, a general-purpose spreadsheet program is purchased for, and loaded into, a microcomputer. Spreadsheet programs such as VisiCalc®, SuperCalc®, MultiPlan®, Microsoft Excel®, and Lotus 1-2-3® are available for purchase at most computer stores and run on an array of microcomputers. The microcomputer with spreadsheet software then becomes a stand-alone estimating system for the company.

To create a spreadsheet, the estimator develops a series of blocks of information or cells via the computer monitor. Each cell is cross-referenced by a number for its row and a letter for its column so that "A-1" is the first cell to accept data. For example, the cells of the first row might be built to contain titles of desired data, such as "Press Number" (A-1), "Average Imp./Hr." (A-2), "Quantity Needed/Job" (A-3), "BHR $/Hr." (A-4), and "Total Press $/Job" (A-5). The cells of the second row directly below the first row would then receive standard estimating data such as "6,000 Shts./Hr." (B-2) to represent "Average Imp./Hr." in Cell A-2 or "25,000 pss" (B-3) to represent "Quantity Needed/Job" in Cell A-3, which would vary from job to job. Chapter 3 provides detailed discussion of spreadsheet development.

Thus the spreadsheet forms a model by which "what if" questions can be asked and answered. For example, changing the "Quantity Needed/Job" in Cell

B-3 from 25,000 pss to 35,000 pss changes the "Total Press $/Job" figure in Cell B-5. The spreadsheet system allows for very fast calculations that are done automatically when the variable data are changed. The spreadsheet can ultimately be developed to estimate all segments of a normal printing job using both a reasonably responsive, simple matrix of fixed plant production standards and hourly costs and variable data that pose "what if" questions. Because each company develops its spreadsheet data based on its individual information, the system can be tailored for the company.

Some of the other number-crunching duties that can be quickly and accurately done by computer—and done easily on spreadsheet programs—include BHR development, "what if" comparisons of all kinds, machine loading, payroll services, accounting, purchasing, sales forecasting, production, cash flow management, and budget preparation.

Telecommunication, Electronic Transmission, Fax Systems, and the Internet

Telecommunication. The oldest and least expensive telecommunication unit is the modulator-demodulator or modem, an electronic interface between computers using a normal telephone line. A modem changes the sending computer's digital code into transmittable electronic signals that are picked up by the receiving computer and converted back to digital code. The speed, or baud rate, at which modems transmit these electronic signals is commonly 9,600 baud to 28,800 baud. Because digitized graphic images such as color separations tend to generate large file sizes, and because modems transmit at slow rates compared to other forms of data transmission, modems are less frequently a source for the expeditious movement of large files or digital images.

Electronic Transmission. For transmitting large data groups such as color separations, fully digitized pages, or DTP materials, either direct electronic transmission or shipment of transportable magnetic media is common. Electronic transmissions using Switched 56, ISDN, and direct digital "T" lines are increasingly popular.

Transmission of electronic pages, which is popular among publication printers, provides high-speed digital interconnectedness for remote proofing and immediate image revision. Another popular method for transporting large digital files is to first format the files to a SyQuest cartridge or to another type of removable cartridge. These cartridges, which are available in various megabyte sizes, are then shipped by Federal Express, United Parcel Service (UPS), or other overnight carrier.

Fax Systems. Facsimile or fax machines provide a fast, convenient method for transmitting information between two remote sites and are extensions of modems. Essentially a fax is a tabletop electronic input/output (I/O) unit which translates graphic images or text on paper to digital signals and sends these signals over normal telephone lines to an accepting fax. Fax units can either send or receive, usually operating between 4,800 baud and 9,600 baud transmission rates. Typically fax machines output to paper, but image quality is generally not good. Thus, the fax machine is used for transmitting information and not graphic images intended for reproduction.

Use of the fax/modem, where a modem is used to either send or receive digital signals between two computers, is also popular and reduces paper usage. Because the image quality of paper-output fax units is poor, the most common use of fax machines is to telecommunicate information, including estimates, job specification information, job details, and invoices, between customers and printers.

The Internet and World Wide Web. Today the Internet (and World Wide Web) represents the largest interactive network ever developed. These electronic exchanges provide worldwide interconnectedness of electronic systems whereby any user who has a computer system with telecommunication capability, a connection path, and an Internet address can log on and travel through the extensive byways the Internet has available. At this writing there are thousands of bulletin boards and other types of information-sharing cubbyholes, as well as direct communication with any other user on the network. It is, in sum, the world's largest electronic communication system. It allows for information queries and on-line information exchange between individuals and/or groups and serves as a source for research of all kinds, as an advertising medium, and, for some, just a place to "roam around looking at the scenery." Because the Internet and "the Web" are worldwide, fast, convenient, available to anyone with a computer and a modem, and very inexpensive, they represent a telecommunication network of potentially great power to printers.

Electronic Press Controls, Waterless Printing, On-Demand Publishing, and Digital Presses

Conventional lithographic sheetfed and web printing processes continue to be significantly improved by computerization and electronic systems, which aid and assist in controlling the quality and speed of the printed product. In addition to these changes in conventional printing methods, the emergence of waterless printing, on-demand publishing systems, and PostScript output devices as electronic printing presses have emerged.

Electronic Press Controls. Electronic and computer changes in conventional lithographic press production can be divided into two broad categories: (1) makeready and press preparatory improvements and (2) process controls during printing. Together these improvements have had significant effect on the structure of the pressroom, the quality and cost of the final product, and the speed with which the product is delivered.

When completing a makeready for a job, the time from the beginning of the makeready period to the point when the first sheet is approved for customer acceptance has always been a key productivity issue for printing managers. The longer a makeready takes, the higher the fixed costs to produce the first salable sheet and the more costly the product to both the customer and the printer. Technological changes to reduce makeready times—and thus, costs—include plate scanning devices which electronically read image densities for ink adjustments prior to start-up, accurate plate registration controls, image movement via electronic consoles, and various feeding and delivery controls allowing both simplified makeready and higher running speeds.

During the printing process, newer sheetfed and web presses are operated from an electronic console that provides the operator with instantaneous control over literally every aspect of the image being printed on the sheet. In addition, computer devices read ink densities and automatically adjust ink controls to provide precise, preset values that are consistent through the pressrun. These changes have improved the quality and speed of production while reducing the number of skilled employees required in the pressroom to operate the equipment.

The Heidelberg Direct Image (DI) and the Heidelberg Quickmaster (QM) presses are linked with Presstek laser imaging for making plates, thus bypasssing traditional film and stripping methods. They have emerged as important electronic imaging systems for lithographic plates. Essentially the Presstek plate imaging process, which is driven by a Macintosh or another electronic platform, provides for the laser imaging of lithographic plates directly on press from fully prepared electronic artwork. This imaging process is fast and the final ink-on-paper printed product can be delivered within thirty minutes of initiation of the process.

Waterless Printing. Waterless printing, which is printing without any type of dampening solution, represents an emerging technology that is likely to become significant as it is improved and reduced in cost. The major advantages of printing without using a fountain solution are that it enhances color fidelity and color brightness while removing the necessity of chemical controls and alcohol use. At the same time, waterless inks undergo temperature increases during printing, so presses must be retrofitted with ink chiller rollers or air cooling methods to keep the ink at the proper temperature for graphic reproduction. These systems are computer driven to maintain precise temperature accuracy.

Waterless printing of computer-generated halftones has been evaluated experimentally with methods commonly known as "stochastic halftoning" or "stochastic screening," and the results appear most favorable. Research and legal issues have yet to be overcome when waterless printing and stochastic screening are used in combination, but it is likely that the two will grow in use in certain parts of the graphic arts industry. The Heidelberg-DI and Quickmaster presses print exclusively using waterless methods.

On-Demand Publishing. On-demand graphic reproduction, which is also known as print on demand (POD), uses digital methods to mass-produce graphic products on an as-needed basis. Essentially POD systems are used to produce a printed product from a digital file immediately, without waiting. This means customers can order and receive printed goods within minutes of placing their orders, and that they no longer are forced into maintaining large inventories of printed products because their products can be printed on demand. As POD systems are perfected, they will revolutionize both the manufacturing and business methods for any printer using them. This subject is discussed in detail in Chapter 10.

In terms of black-and-white printing, the leader in the development and implementation of POD technology is Xerox DocuTech, which has its roots in electrostatic imaging methods. Other companies providing digital press equipment for black-and-white on-demand publishing are Eastman Kodak's Lionheart and Siemans PageStream. Digital color POD systems include Indigo's E-1000, Xiekon's DCP-1, Agfa ChromaPress, and others.

The most popular on-demand black-and-white system is the Xerox DocuTech, where images are designed and prepared using a computer platform and conventional DTP software. When the imaged file is fully prepared, it is transferred by electronic network to the DocuTech system where printing is done immediately using electrostatic methods. To produce the common products books and booklets, the entire file is prepared, sent to the DocuTech, and the product is produced on demand for the number of copies needed at that time.

Because the DocuTech system is fast and on demand, there is no need to print and inventory any product. This allows the DocuTech customer to implement a JIT inventory system by ordering the quantity needed, when it is needed. It also allows the customer to change or revise products between orders, so continuously updating and revising a book or booklet is easily completed. However, DocuTech output is currently limited to single-sided or duplexed (double-sided) products printed in black.

Full-color digital presses are an explosive POD technology. Two digital printing systems with "engine" or printing unit configurations are taking the lead at this time: the Indigo E-1000 press and the Xiekon (Agfa's ChromaPress uses a Xiekon engine). The Indigo E-1000 prints flat sheets while the Xiekon utilizes web technology. Although each differs in PostScript imaging and engine configuration, each produces a final flat-sheet product that is duplexed in full color and is printed from a computer platform using common DTP software. Because all digital presses are imaged directly from computer files, they bypass labor-intensive prepress operations, thereby saving both time and money. As a result, there is no film, no plates, no labor costs for stripping, and so on. Although there currently is a high cost for either full-color press configuration, it is likely that their costs will drop significantly as the equipment is perfected and details are resolved.

2.4   Computer Management Systems for Printers

Computer systems serving the printing and allied industries can be classified into two general groups: systems with services provided by outside service suppliers, including service bureaus and time-sharing companies, and systems purchased by printers to be used in-house. The latter group is generally broken down into turnkey, microcomputer, and customized system segments.

Outside Service Suppliers

As just discussed, outside service supplies are divided into two general groups: service bureaus and time-sharing companies. Today neither enjoys significant use in the printing industry for many reasons. Certainly the fact that computer hardware and software have become affordable to even the smallest company is a major factor, as is the increased level of computer literacy throughout the United States. Also contributing are the facts that computer systems have been demystified and the level of user-friendliness has been heightened.

As mentioned in Chapter 1, service bureaus are organizations that offer complete data processing using the computer hardware and software in their offices. The printer provides whatever source materials are needed, such as time cards for payroll. The service bureau would process these time cards and provide the printer with payroll checks and all financial information related to payroll transactions.

Service bureau functions are typically not tailored to a printer's precise needs, but they can be made available by the bureau if desired. Service bureaus usually charge monthly, and the printer pays a flat fee for all processing completed during the last transaction period.

With time-sharing, printing companies rent time on large mainframe computers that hold their programs. Printers typically communicate with the computers at time-sharing facilities through terminals in their printing plants. Employees enter information in the terminals which is translated via a modem and telephone line to the mainframe computers. The information is then processed by the mainframes and returned to the printing companies via modem either as a display on the computer monitor or in printed form. Sometimes report documents can be printed at the time-sharing facility and mailed to the printer.

In-House Systems

The following summarizes the four approaches available for selecting an in-house computer management or an MIS system. The final choice is determined by a wide and varied group of needs, including the size of the company, the present and future computer needs, employee needs, and dollars available to spend on the system.

Approach One: Microcomputer and Application Software. Using this approach requires the printing company to first purchase a stand-alone microcomputer, then to separately purchase an application software package ("canned software") from a printing industry computer vendor. This "micro and software" (M&SW) system package generally appeals to quick printers, small commercial printers, and large printers who are purchasing a first-time computer system for management purposes or who wish to utilize an existing microcomputer now dedicated to typesetting or some other internal production function.

The microcomputer world is generally divided into two major hardware and operating system camps: the IBM and IBM-compatible systems and the Macintosh system. The IBMs and the IBM compatibles typically run the popular Microsoft DOS (MS-DOS or, more commonly, DOS) or Operating System 2 (OS/2). The use of Microsoft Windows® and Windows 95 are also popular on IBMs, and many printing industry computer vendors have converted their DOS software to function in a Windows® environment.

The Macintosh runs with a system specific to it, which is known as a System File. The System File is coupled with a Finder that locates and opens files for use. The Macintosh System File, which contains the operating program, may also contain utility programs, desk accessories, font data, and a message file.

Vendors who develop application software for M&SW systems must write programs in a language that is compatible with the microcomputer's operating system. Because programming for IBMs and IBM compatibles has largely focused on DOS, and because IBM and IBM-compatible equipment was heavily purchased in the 1980s, most printing software vendors originally developed programs for the DOS environment and, to a lesser degree, OS/2 or UNIX. In addition, the reduction in cost for IBM machines that contain the faster 386, 486, and Pentium microprocessors has boosted sales of this group of computers.

At the same time, as the Macintosh computer became faster through microprocessor improvements, and as its hard disk capacity became more readily available and reduced in price, a few vendors began offering Macintosh estimating programs to the industry. However, the development of Microsoft Windows® software shifted DOS into a significantly more user-friendly environment, further keeping IBM-compatible computers more popular systems for M&SW.

As the Macintosh became the system of choice for printers of DTP and electronic prepress, an increasing number of printing industry management computer vendors began to offer production and estimating software for the Macintosh. In almost all cases the targeted markets for these programs were the quick printer and the small commercial printer.

There are two changes that may affect the M&SW choice between DOS and Macintosh. The first change is that the Power Personal Computer, or PowerPC, provides the hardware capability for cross-platform interchangeability between two distinctly different systems. This means that choosing DOS or Macintosh may not be important in the future. The second change is the explosion of electronic prepress use throughout the printing industry and the emerging interest in tracking production time through data collection. Because the Macintosh is the system of choice for DTP and electronic prepress, and because data collection then requires the direct interconnection of Macintosh platforms, this second change could lead to an increased focus on the Macintosh for management purposes.

Major advantages of M&SW systems include:

1. Most M&SW systems are much less expensive than other systems.
2. Installation time is usually very short, allowing almost immediate use of the system.
3. The microcomputer can be used to complete other tasks, such as word processing and DTP functions, when not being used for management functions.
4. Documentation from national software-only vendors is generally good.
5. If the change to a more sophisticated system is done before too much time and effort is invested to make the M&SW system fit growing demands, the financial and time commitments with the M&SW system are minimized.
6. System expandability through networking is simply accomplished, allowing the system to grow with the user.

Some of the major disadvantages of M&SW systems are:

1. Some of the application software, which has built-in inflexibility, is limited in part by the memory capacity of the microcomputer and in part by the effort of the developer to write a generic program for many possible purchasers-users.
2. It is possible that some of the vendors providing software may go out of business, leaving the printer with a system that will not be upgraded or supported over time.
3. EFDC is more difficult to implement because the M&SW system capacity is generally limited.

4. Documentation may be limited or not complete, and the vendor may not have an established process by which software support is easily provided.

5 . System files are difficult to integrate due to the size capacities of random-access memory (RAM) and the fact that production and accounting software may run with different background software.

6. Expanding the system as a business grows likely points out the major system limitations and the printer's desire to upgrade to a better system. Because there is typically little interchangeability between vendor products, changing to a new vendor's system can be complex.

Approach Two: The Turnkey System. The second approach, which is typically taken by medium-size to very large printing firms, is to purchase and implement a turnkey system. Here a single vendor provides all hardware and a fully integrated software package and thus a full MIS. This system can handle all production and accounting duties from order entry and estimating to inventory control, accounting, and financial statements.

Turnkey systems are designed, programmed, produced, and sold as complete packages of hardware and software. The purchaser "turns the key" to begin operating the system. Most turnkey vendors purchase hardware from major manufacturers and assemble the computer systems from various selected components. Programming is completed by individuals knowledgeable in both computer programming for the configured hardware and in printing. The vendors sell the complete packages under their companies' names and are called original equipment manufacturers (OEMs).

Figure 2.1 provides a view of a typical, modular, turnkey approach to computerizing a graphic arts company with a full MIS. There are two distinct layers for the system-production and accounting. Installing a typical MIS turnkey system, as indicated in Figure 2.1, begins with estimating and job planning/engineering (Module 1), followed by BHR development (Module 2) and pricing/quotation control (Module 3). These modules are likely to take from thirty days to ninety days to install, but it is possible to install them more quickly or slowly, depending on many factors.

Once Modules 1 through 3 are operational, order entry (Module 4), data collection (Module 5), and job costing (Module 6) should be implemented. Once these are operational, raw material inventory (Module 7) and purchase order control (Module 8) should go on line. Sometime after these modules are fully operational, job/machine loading and plant scheduling (Module 9) are installed. Using the modular approach, system implementation can be focused on, and operator training restricted to, one function at a time.

Frequently the accounting group modules (Modules 10 through 17) are installed at the same time the production modules are implemented. This speeds the implementation process. Also, because some accounting modules are linked to production modules, the integration of data between modules can be im-

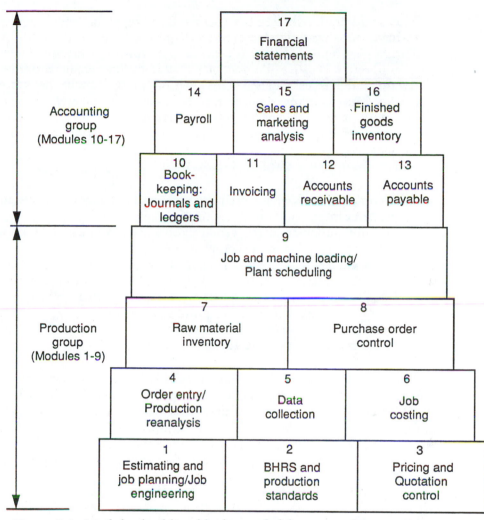

Figure 2.1 Modular building blocks needed for a complete computer management system in a graphic arts company

mediately utilized. For example, in a typical turnkey system, a customer's name and address are necessary to initiate an estimate. After the customer's name and address have been entered for the first time, they can be automatically linked to appear on future estimates, job proposals, all job tickets, and invoices during the billing cycle. Thus, an advantage of the turnkey system is the linking and integration between modules of interactive data. For additional information on modular building blocks, see the Modular Building Blocks for Computerizing a Printing Company section later in this chapter.

Turnkey systems represent the easiest way for a typical printing company to computerize because the vendor has already chosen both hardware and software and has established a foundation upon which the system will function. Most turnkey vendors who have been in the industry for five or more years have established a pool of users and a history of system installation and attempt to upgrade systems and installation procedures on a continual basis.

Major advantages of turnkey systems include:

1. A complete package is purchased and available for immediate use in, or modular integration into, the printing plant.
2. Documentation from the vendor is usually available from the time the system is installed in the company.
3. The vendor likely provides support through a hot line which allows for fairly immediate resolution of glitches and programming problems.
4. Usually the system has been fairly well debugged through field testing (e.g., beta site testing) with selected printing companies.
5. System integration provides a fairly complete MIS.
6. EFDC is usually a simple add-on.

It is important to note that many established printing industry turnkey vendors encourage, work with, and/or support user groups that usually meet from one to four times per year to discuss shared experiences, problems, and solutions. As the number of users of any turnkey system increases, the users' collective ability to have a specific, system-wide problem addressed is usually quite good. This could also be considered an advantage in selecting a turnkey system.

Some of the disadvantages of turnkey systems include:

1. Turnkey systems can be moderately to extremely expensive.
2. Once a turnkey system is on line, it is very difficult to shift to another computer system or to a different turnkey vendor.
3. Any packaged program may require compromise or may be incompatible with the specific needs of the user.
4. Software support costs can be expensive, but they are essential to be certain the system is always functional.
5. Software for the system may include more than what is desired by the user, but it may be impossible for the vendor to unbundle the undesired modules or parts. This means that the undesired modules must be purchased with the system even though they will not be used.
6. The user almost entirely depends on the vendor for support.

Approach Three: Open Architecture Software on Company-Owned Hardware. The third approach to selecting a computer management or an MIS system is to purchase an "open architecture" application software package that runs on the printer's network environment and uses the printer's PCs. This software is typically available from turnkey vendors and is patterned to follow the vendor's turnkey modules, which are modified for network use.

The open architecture approach allows the printer to adapt software to whatever network needs are desired and facilitates tailoring the software to the company's production and accounting requirements. This approach evolved because it removes turnkey vendors from providing hardware maintenance and support and because it appeals to any printing company that has invested heavily in the PC environment. Sometimes the vendor provides source code of the software program, thereby allowing the program to be restructured to the printer's exact desires. Vendor support is typically good, but this approach can be costly depending on the amount of tailoring and reprogramming desired and on the additional hardware that may be necessary.

Advantages of the open architecture approach are:

1. Computer hardware owned by the printing company can be used and networked in any manner that is workable. Also, used computer equipment can be purchased at lower cost.
2. The open architecture system can be carefully tailored to the company's production and accounting needs.
3. Usually there is vendor support available, and the level of support is flexible and controlled by the printer.
4. Any system modifications are completely controlled and executed in the manner the printer desires.
5. The purchase of source code and the license to modify the original software gives the printer considerable flexibility in all aspects of tailoring the system to meet specific company needs.
6. The printer is able to obtain software support from nonvendor sources and has the ability to hire in-house employees to work on the system.

Some of the disadvantages of the open architecture approach are:

1. When printers tailor the systems to meet their needs, there is no documentation for the unique systems unless the printers take the time to develop it in house.
2. Some printers philosophically desire the freedom to develop their own software, but they simply do not execute this when given the opportunity.
3. Purchasing an open architecture system forces the printer into developing an in-depth knowledge about this area, which is frequently beyond the level needed or desired.

4. Without vendor support and direction, the printer can go overboard in tailoring the system to meet company needs.
5. The printing company alone can make changes to the system, so knowing how and what to change is sometimes difficult to identify.
6. Frequently the open architecture system requires outside consultants to assist in system revisions, which can be costly.

Approach Four: Customized or Homegrown Systems. A customized computer system that operates any size or type of printing company provides the most tailored, precise result but at generally great time and cost because the process of developing the system is borne completely by the printing firm. It is not unusual for a printing company to become frustrated with canned software or a turnkey package that it finds does not address its production, estimating, inventory, or other needs. This is particularly true of small printing operations and quick printers. Vendors largely ignore these small firms or afford them little interest because both their sales costs and their support costs are high. Why would vendors sell and support many small shop installations when they can sell one system, which is easier to install and to support, to one large firm for the same income?

This text addresses the two extremes of customized systems with the understanding that there are intermediate customizing solutions between them. On the one end, which addresses the needs of the first-time or "low-end user" or the small firm, a microcomputer and generic spreadsheet software are all that are required. On the other end, which addresses the needs of the large printer or the "high-end user," customized programs, hardware, and support are purchased through a company or a person professionally selling such services.

For the small printer or the quick printer, a customized estimating, inventory, or production control system can be accurately built using a microcomputer and a spreadsheet package such as Lotus 1-2-3®, MultiPlan®, Excel®, or VisiCalc®. It is critical that the people building the spreadsheets understand the interrelationships of each cell and are familiar with the processes they are attempting to computerize. For example, building a spreadsheet program to reflect specific BHRs for a company should be attempted only once the person doing this work understands, in detail, how BHRs are manually calculated. Essential spreadsheet information is presented in the Number Crunching and Spreadsheets section earlier in this chapter.

Advantages of spreadsheets as number-crunching tools are:

1. The cost of the spreadsheet software is low.
2. The system can be tailored to meet the specific needs of the person or the company for whom or for which the spreadsheet is intended.

3. When it is not running the spreadsheet program, the microcomputer can be used to complete other tasks such as scanning and DTP functions.
4. The commercial spreadsheet programs are usually thoroughly debugged, have clearly written documentation, and are easy to use.
5 . Development time can be very short, allowing almost immediate use of the spreadsheet.
6. Modifications can be quickly and effectively completed without the aid or the expense of any outside sources.

Some disadvantages of spreadsheets are:

1. It is not difficult to leave out or forget a specific item or element, and catching such an error may be difficult if the only person building the spreadsheet is also the primary one using it daily. By like token, spreadsheets do not provide any outsider's input with respect to what is being completed. Professional software vendors check and recheck the software they sell.
2. There is a dollars versus time component consideration. The printer is faced with balancing the time required to build a spreadsheet program versus purchasing a canned program that may do almost all of the functions desired of the spreadsheet.
3. Data and calculations built into one spreadsheet are not easily interconnected with another spreadsheet. This means that although two separate spreadsheet programs, such as estimating and BHRs, may be interconnected, such links are complex to build and can be problematic.
4. Spreadsheet cells require that data be quantifiable or be able to be "boiled down" to clear mathematical facts. This is sometimes hard to do within the cell framework.
5. Although spreadsheets handle number-crunching duties easily, they are only one component of the information processing system needed to run a printing firm. Expanding a business also may force a company to consider a different solution to handling estimating or other duties.
6. The people building the spreadsheets—the people who know the spreadsheets best—might move to other jobs and take their skills at modifying programs with them. Also, it is likely that the author of the spreadsheet provided no written procedures or documentation clarifying the spreadsheet, making it difficult to revise the spreadsheet at a future time.

While spreadsheets represent the small company's method of tailoring a computer package to its printing company, the large printer's spreadsheets are faced with different requirements. Large printers and high-volume printers, due to the intensely competitive cost/price/volume relationships they encounter and the hundreds of customers and minute details of each job they have in production, need computer systems that track everything occurring in the plant as well the details of each customer's job. This amounts to literally thousands of detailed pieces of information daily, with minimum errors allowed.

The solution for the large printer or the high-volume printer may be to employ a person or a company specifically to develop a full MIS system that is tailored to its needs. Vendors providing customizing services work closely with printers to determine both present and future computer needs, then select hardware and write (or develop) software specific to the printer's requirements. Custom vendors usually also coordinate the installation of their systems and train employees in the systems' use. These vendors may also provide extended service contracts to maintain the systems.

Advantages of a fully customized MIS system include:

1. The system is tailored to fit the printer's needs exactly.
2. The system can be fully integrated, incorporating full production and accounting functions with minimum difficulty.
3. The printer can have complete say as to the way the system is developed and worked on daily.
4. Expanding the system is easily accomplished because a professional software developer always includes expansion plans in the system design.
5. The system can be easily changed or modified because no part of the system is proprietary.
6. The printer can exercise more control over both hardware and software maintenance procedures.

Some disadvantages of a fully customized MIS system include:

1. The cost of initially developing and implementing the system is high.
2. Training times and costs are higher and must be fully paid by the user-printer, as opposed to turnkey system training costs, which are factored into the cost of a typical system and are thus recovered by the collective number of system users.
3. Software modification is not ongoing but is completed only when the printer wishes it to be done. Its full cost is borne by the printer.
4. Because the system is tailored to the user-printer, there is typically little documentation written to support the system.
5. System development and implementation can be long-term processes, taking more than one year to complete.
6. The user-printer is required to support the system once it is fully operational using company employees. Some custom vendors provide software service support after the system has gone on line, but this can be expensive.

As mentioned earlier, between the low-end, number-crunching spreadsheets for the small printer and the fully customized, information-processing MIS packages for the large printer, there are intermediate solutions for customizing computer systems for printing companies. There are also a variety of programming languages (e.g., BASIC, COBOL, C, RPG, DBMS, UNIX) for this purpose. In addition, it is possible for time-sharing vendors to have specific programs written in languages and operating systems that fit their equipment, much as custom programs could be written by printing industry vendors for specific printing firms.

Shareware has also become a way to find a program that is largely oriented to a specific printer's needs. Shareware is computer software that is developed and initially shared at no cost with potential buyers, with the understanding that the potential buyer will pay for the software if it serves a useful purpose. Some printers, frustrated with canned package inadequacies, have built their own estimating, inventory, and other packages, usually for IBM or IBM-compatible microcomputers running with DOS operating systems and Windows®. These software authors feel other printers should have the opportunity to use their packages, which are customized for their companies' operations, and therefore make their software available through shareware groups such as Printer's Shareware (see the listing in Appendix C of this chapter for more information).

2.5 Modular Building Blocks for Computerizing a Printing Company

The best, most effective MIS for a printing or publishing company is built using a modular approach. As discussed in the Approach Two: The Turnkey System section earlier in this chapter, Figure 2.1 provides a graphic display of the seventeen key modular components divided into two groups: production and accounting.

When operating properly, modules are electronically connected to one another. This provides smooth, seamless integration whereby modules are automatically linked to share data with other modules. For example, cost estimating typically requires the interactive use of BHRs and production standards, so this module (Module 2) should be linked to the cost estimating program (Module 1). The data collection module (Module 5) should be linked to raw material inventory (Module 7) because part of the data collection process is tracking and monitoring available inventory levels. Another example would be to link estimating (Module 1) to order entry (Module 4) so that an estimate could be quickly converted to a live job. In this example, order entry (Module 4) would then be linked to data collection (Module 5) so that the customer's job details could be tracked during production. Many other examples of system integration could be provided in this discussion, but the key point is that links between modules represent improved operating efficiency and a faster, more user-friendly computer environment.

The ease of use of each module and of the system as a whole are important for day-to-day operation. Working characteristics have improved greatly in the past five or so years, driven by customer feedback, faster hardware, and increased competition between vendors for customers. The approach taken by most vendors has been to simplify the options available to the user as much as possible while keeping the details in the background as supporting data that can be used if needed.

For example, estimating tends to be complex because it requires user choices that have significant bearing on job cost and company profitability. Many of today's computer-assisted estimating (CAE) packages streamline the estimator's choices by simplifying the foreground operations performed by the operator while completing the estimating details automatically as background information via the computer software. This means that while estimating by computer requires limited input by the estimator, the final estimate is filled with detail that is generated by the computer software and is based on the estimator's foreground input.

Other current system considerations of note: Icon- or window-based systems tend to be easier to use and are therefore popular. Systems that do not require complicated keyboard operations or are macro-driven are desired. Faster system response time through higher operating speeds is a key issue and has been cited by many users as an important buying consideration. Systems that are interconnected to portable laptop or notebook computers are of interest to computer-literate sales representatives (a small but increasing number given the time-compressed requirements of quoting jobs) because these systems function on electronic job specifications, allowing faster estimates/proposals.

As TQM and ISO 9000 have become functioning parts of the printing and publishing industry, interest in application software that provides an SPC interface has grown. This SPC software allows for ease in setting up statistical analyses of problems, defects, and variances so these problems and defects can be evaluated for correction. For printing and publishing companies interested in continuous process improvement, SPC software is a potential and desired requirement. Both TQM and ISO 9000 are discussed in Chapter 13.

Module Descriptions

As mentioned previously, Figure 2.1 shows that there are two groups of modules—the production group containing modules 1 through 9 and the accounting group containing modules 10 through 17.

Although the purchase and implementation of the modules within the production and accounting groups of a fully integrated, modular MIS system should be completed in numerical sequence, this is not a fixed rule. To implement a module or a system means to install the software on workable, functioning computer hardware known as a platform and to then follow the installation with employee training and use of the software on a daily basis. Thus, computerizing printing production should begin with the purchase and implementation of Modules 1, 2, and 3. After this is done, Modules 4, 5, and 6 should be installed, then Modules 7 and 8. Finally, Module 9 should be purchased and implemented.

There is no established amount of time necessary for fully implementing any module or group of modules. It might take one week for Company A to implement Modules 1, 2, and 3, for example, but it might take four months for Company B to fully install the same three modules. Further information on implementation procedures and methods is covered in Chapters 3 and 5.

The accounting group modules can be implemented either with or separate from the production modules at any time. Thus, it is possible to implement the accounting modules weeks or months before the production modules, or to implement production Modules 1, 2, and 3 with the appropriate staff while the accounting modules are installed at the same time.

Linking accounting to production is typically desirable, but it cannot be completed unless all modules to be linked are fully installed and operational. For example, accounts receivable (Module 12) might be linked to pricing/quotation control (Module 3) and order entry/production reanalysis (Module 4), while invoicing (Module 11) might be linked to job costing (Module 6). Deciding which modules are linked and providing this integrated format is largely decided by the printing company with assistance from the computer vendor providing the software.

There are two sources of computer accounting software for printing and publishing companies: (1) the computer vendors listed in Appendix C of this chapter who serve the printing industry and (2) national vendors of generic computer accounting software which is not specific to printing. Some printing industry vendors offer prospective printing companies/purchasers a choice: either the accounting package they have developed as part of their own system software or an interface with the more popular generic accounting software programs. Thus, if printers are currently using better-known generic accounting packages on their PCs and they wish to computerize the production sides of their businesses, they contact vendors who provide automatic interfaces with the companies' current accounting software. This saves time and money and is an option worth investigating.

Production Group Modules (Modules 1 through 9)

This group of modules covers the production data needed to fully computerize a printing company. If any module is missing, full computerization is not achievable.

Production Modules 1, 2, and 3. These modules are usually the first three to be installed because they represent the core data the remaining production modules draw upon. They are usually installed at the same time and are linked together because of similar data needs.

Module 1 Estimating and Job Planning/Engineering. As discussed in Chapter 1, there are two types of estimating methods: cost estimating and price estimating. Cost estimating requires the customer to provide sufficient job specifications so that the estimator can first develop a production plan of the job, then analyze the specific time and material costs the job will require. Cost estimating uses total job cost as a baseline for final pricing. Price estimating uses sales dollars to estimate and quote the order. Of the two methods, cost estimating is more accurate and detailed; price estimating is faster and less complex.

Both cost estimating and price estimating are completed using computer systems. Computer-assisted price (CAP) estimating is divided into two general categories: (1) look-up pricing schedules from which quotes are either manually completed or computer generated and (2) pricing templates where jobs are "built" from a series of price component matrices that are based on job details. Chapter 4 provides information on price estimating and CAP methods.

Because of the detail and accuracy that can be obtained, cost estimating procedures using CAE and computer-generated estimating (CGE) systems remain popular, even though price estimating methods are faster and less complex. For this reason, the following discussion centers on estimating and job engineering using CAE and CGE systems.

Cost estimating is an important decision-making tool for printing company management. It allows company management to (1) evaluate how the job will fit into the normal production routine offered by the company, (2) assess what bottlenecks the job might present, (3) provide the customer with viable alternatives that could save money or better serve the client's needs, and (4) provide a core dollar cost of production that should be included in setting the price of the job.

It is important to note that the term "estimate" is commonly used by print buyers and customers—and by many printing industry professionals—to mean a "price proposal" or a "price quotation." This term should be clarified. An "estimate" in printing is a document that details the anticipated production flow, materials, and outside vendor purchases that comprise the production cost of a job. Estimates do not typically include profit markup. Thus, an estimate is the anticipated dollar amount to produce the job in the plant, based on analysis of the job specifications provided by the customer.

The terms "proposal" or "quotation"—or "price proposal" or "price quotation"—represent the selling price of the job to the customer, which includes a profit markup for the company. It should be clear that the selling price for a printing job, which is offered to the customer through a proposal or a quotation, should factor in all relevant production and material costs (which come from the estimate), as well as a desired profit for the company. Thus, estimating precedes pricing—an "estimate" is not a "price proposal" but an internal evaluation of the job from production planning and cost perspectives.

The objective of cost estimating is to break down a given set of job specifications into individualized job components from which production and cost data are derived. These data represent the company's initial "window" on the job; data from the estimate are commonly used as a basis for detailed production analysis, cost evaluation, production scheduling, value added analysis, and profitability considerations. In sum, estimating data are the printing company's first—and usually most detailed—analysis of a potential printing order. Estimating provides the company with the primary set of data for production and job costs.

The cost estimating process begins by taking a customer's proposed job specifications, planning the anticipated production sequence, then breaking these production operations into specific time components. Once these production times are identified, they are multiplied by an all-inclusive BHR (Module 2). Then all materials and outside purchases are added. The following cost estimating formula represents the approach taken for computerizing the estimating process:

$$\text{selling price} = [(\text{production time x BHR}) + \text{material costs} + \text{outside purchases}] + \text{profit}$$

Accurate cost estimating requires that each job be carefully planned. However, identifying these specific job components can be a laborious process. Cost estimating is completed before the job enters production and must be based on accurate job specifications from the customer. These specifications are typically provided to the estimator through a company sales representative. Most experienced estimators acknowledge that it is not unusual for these job "specs" to be inaccurate or unclear, causing the desired estimating accuracy to be compromised, sometimes excessively. For this reason, profitable printing companies diligently and assertively work to pin down customers on job details, then carefully engineer jobs to take the most expeditious, cost-saving production path.

Estimates completed by computer can be classified into two formats: detail estimates and summary (or general) estimates. Detail estimates provide the greatest detail of job analysis. Each job component and all materials are included. Detail estimates break each job into its most discrete production components by specifically identifying each production step, such as "0.8 hours in typesetting input," "1.2 hours in graphic image manipulation," and "1.4 hours in PostScript output to film." Detail estimates take more time to complete, but they provide far more accurate sets of production data for scheduling the job and for completing the job costing process. Both types of estimates are discussed later in this chapter.

Summary estimates provide a breakdown of each job by plant area or cost center. They provide production data for these areas in a general sense, such as "3.4 hours in electronic prepress," "1.8 hours in platemaking," or "7.6 hours in sheetfed press." When estimating software provides detail estimating capability, summary estimates are totals of the detail components by cost center and for the entire job. Summary estimates allow for an overall view of the job by cost center and are helpful when analyzing the job for pricing and production planning.

The CAE systems provide valuable assistance in completing the estimating process because they offer a way to manage, evaluate, and control numerous job details; provide cost analysis benefits; and complete related mathematics quickly and accurately. A fully functional CAE system, when operated by a knowledgeable person, can complete a detailed estimate in a matter of minutes, thus reducing estimating turnaround and enhancing the company's potential to sell more work. One way to speed the cost estimating process is to use estimating templates, which are preformatted lists of job components. Further information is provided on template estimating in Chapters 5 and 8.

As noted earlier, there are two general options for computer cost estimating of printing production: CAE and CGE. The essential difference between them is that CGE is automated, whereby the computer is preplanned to make certain production choices. An estimate is then "generated" using a computer-driven, preprogrammed job planning process. On the other hand, CAE requires the estimator to make many key production choices in the process of completing an estimate.

On a comparison basis, CGE systems tend to be faster than CAE systems. However, because of the automated production decision making, the choices selected by the computer are sometimes not in the best interests of the company or the customer. Thus, CGE systems tend to be less accurate when compared to CAE systems, which require a step-by-step review of each production step during estimating. The adage that "faster estimating systems tend to compromise accuracy of the estimate" remains true when comparing CGE to CAE.

Even in light of the accuracy issue, CGE systems remain an important option or choice when investigating computer estimating systems for the following reasons:

1. Many CGE systems provide the option of manually overriding what the computer has chosen. For example, a faster press would be automatically selected by the computer, but the estimator could override this and select a slower press for the job. Although these choices take time to evaluate and complete, they also significantly improve the accuracy of the estimate. Thus, CGE systems with the override option, when monitored by knowledgeable estimators or production people, provide the best of both worlds: they offer the advantage of increased estimate throughput while providing the accuracy found in CAE systems.

2. When printing production is standardized to the point that there is little variation from job to job, CGE systems offer a potentially desirable

solution. As printers become more specialized in niche markets, CGE systems have the potential to offer a streamlined estimating/quoting solution.

3. Given customer-driven requirements for reducing estimate/proposal turn-around time, and the fact that CGE systems can be accurate if properly used, CGE systems may serve the estimating needs of some kinds of printing companies.

The decision as to what type of computer estimating package to purchase is critical because estimating provides the single key source of production data, as well as sets a dollar cost baseline for pricing the job. The advantages and disadvantages for both CAE and CGE may affect the way other modules interface, which should be factored into the decision regarding the estimating module.

Module 2   BHRs and Production Standards. (Note: Both BHRs and production standards are complex subjects that are overviewed here and covered in depth in Chapter 3 of this text.)

Budgeted Hour Cost Rates. The objective of determining a BHR, which utilizes cost accounting procedures, is to arrive at an hourly dollar value that, when charged to customers over a projected yearly number of hours, will pay back the printing company for all equipment-based fixed and variable costs. As noted in the cost estimating formula presented earlier in this chapter, job-specific materials and outside purchases are separately calculated and added to the customer's job cost.

Figure 2.2 is an example of a BHR developed for a 2-color Komori lithographic press. Key figures show a TOTAL ANNUAL CENTER COST (between Lines 26 and 28, right-hand column) of $147,896. If this press can be used to produce work chargeable to customers for 1,510.40 annual hours (see Line 31: BHR cost 80%), then the BHR is $147,896 ÷ 1,510.40 or $97.92 per hour.

Four points must be made about BHRs. First, each printing company needs to tailor its BHRs to fit its own costs and production requirements. Therefore, using published industry BHRs tends to reduce accuracy. Second, because BHRs are used as part of the cost estimating process, their accuracy has a direct effect on the accuracy of the estimates completed with them. Accurate estimating is possible only with accurate BHRs. Third, both over-time and multiple shifts change printing company costs significantly, so separate BHRs or modification procedures should be used in such instances. Fourth, many printing industry computer vendors offer their versions of BHRs generally following the logic and accounting procedures similar to what are shown in Figure 2.2.

BUDGETED HOUR COST RATE Center title: Komori 2/c litho press	Calculation method or basis	Total company	General factory overhead	Selling and admin. overhead	Annual center cost (one shift)
Investment cost		$2,600,000	$24,000	$72,000	$219,000
Number of employees in center		24	2	6	1
Square feet of working area		4,600	350	600	320
Total motor horsepower					5.9
Arc lamp wattage					0
Wage scale 1			$9.00		$18.00
Wage scale 2			$7.50		$0.00
Wage scale 3					$0.00
Paid days off: Sum vacation days and holidays					24
Weekly hours paid		40	40	40	40
Annual hours paid			2,080	2,080	2,080
FIXED COSTS (ANNUAL)					
1 Fixed overhead (sq. ft.)	$3.00		$1,050	$1,800	$960
2 Insurance (Per $1,000 value)	$3.00		$72	$216	$657
3 Property taxes (Per $100 value)	$1.25		$300	$900	$2,738
4 Depreciation 1 (33% value)	33%				
5 Depreciation 2 (10% straight or other method)	10%		$2,400	$7,200	$21,900
6 Cost of new software (estimate for year)	estimate cost				$0
7 Center R & D activities (estimate for year)	estimate cost				$500
8 Training & retraining costs (estimate for year)	estimate cost			$4,000	$2,500
9 TOTAL FIXED COSTS			$3,822	$14,116	$29,255
VARIABLE COSTS (ANNUAL)					
10 Direct labor cost, No. 1	scale*annual hrs.		$18,720	$320,000	$37,440
11 Direct labor cost, No. 2	scale*annual hrs.		$15,600		
12 Direct labor cost, No. 3	scale*annual hrs.				
13 Total cost: Direct labor			$34,320	$320,000	$37,440
14 Cost of indirect labor (20% direct labor)	20%		$6,864	$64,000	$7,488
15 Total cost: Direct and indirect labor			$41,184	$384,000	$44,928
16 Employee taxes and benefits (direct plus indirect)	30%		$12,355	$115,200	$13,478
17 Overhead lighting cost (kWh)	$0.10		$218	$374	$200
18 Electrical power cost (kWh)	$0.10				$915
19 Arc cost (kWh)	$0.10				$0
20 Department supplies (8% total labor)	8%		$3,295	$30,720	$3,594
21 Repairs (2% value)	2%		$480	$1,440	$4,380
22 TOTAL VARIABLE COSTS			$57,532	$531,734	$67,496
23 Total fixed and variable costs			$61,354	$545,850	$96,750
24 Proration: General factory overhead	% investment				$5,168
TOTAL FACTORY COST					$101,918
26 Proration: Administration and selling overhead	% investment				$45,977
TOTAL ANNUAL CENTER COST					$147,896
	Chargeable hrs.				
28 Manufacturing cost 80%	1,510.40				$67.48
29 Manufacturing cost 70%	1,321.60				$77.12
30 Manufacturing cost 60%	1,132.80				$89.97
31 BHR cost 80%	1,510.40				$97.92
32 BHR cost 70%	1,321.60				$111.91
33 BHR cost 60%	1,132.80				$130.56

Figure 2.2 BHR for a two-color Komori lithographic press

Production Standards. A production standard is an hourly value representing the average time anticipated for completing a defined task during printing production. Production standards, when used in plural form, are then a group of times representing all of the component operations for all production areas of printing. The production standards for a printing company are a listing of all component operations and the times required to complete each operation. Traditionally, average time values are used because they provide mid-range hourly figures, but median hourly rates are also sometimes used.

Production standards are used with BHRs to determine the cost of production. For example, assume the 2-color Komori press in Figure 2.2 with a BHR of $97.92 (80 percent utilization) has an established production standard of 0.40 hours for makeready (both printing units). Assume also that a 2-color job requires 1 makeready on this press. To calculate the makeready cost, multiply the production standard of 0.40 by 1 makeready (0.40 x 1 = 0.40 hour of makeready), then multiply the result by the BHR of $97.92 (0.40 x $97.92 = $39.17) to determine the production cost for makeready.

Printing industry computer vendors typically do not provide production standards when setting up computer systems. They instead request that the printing companies provide their own, which means that developing these standards is a company requirement. For companies that purchase, install, and use data collection, and then complete job costing as part of the production management process, these data become available over time. However, data collection and job costing are not required to establish (or maintain) production standards. Thus, in printing companies setting up their first computer management systems, which typically is done when setting up estimating software, the first set of production standards may be "best guess" or generic standards taken from a published source or borrowed from another printer.

Of particular difficulty is establishing production standards for electronic prepress, because the technology has been changing quickly and the production operations are hard to define. Printing industry experts believe that as electronic prepress production stabilizes in both technology and customer-based issues (i.e., what the customer will provide and how the electronic art will interface with the printing company's production cycle), this problem will lessen in complexity.

Module 3 Pricing/Quotation Control. One of the most important functions of a computer management system is to provide clear, accurate proposals or quotations to customers. The terms "quotation" and "proposal" are used interchangeably in this discussion. Each can be defined as the written dollar amount the printing company charges the customer to complete a printing order. As noted earlier, the term "estimate" is not the same as a proposal or a quotation, even though it is frequently used by customers, printing sales representatives, and printing company management to mean the same thing.

Although they are used interchangeably, proposals and quotations are not the same. In the printing industry, a proposal is a tentative offer to produce a product at a certain dollar amount, and it may be modified by negotiation between the printer and the customer. This negotiating is usually done when customers are unclear about specific parts of the jobs they are seeking. In contrast, a quotation is a firm, fixed dollar offer from printer to customer, and it is usually the result of proposal negotiation. Many printers do not distinguish between these two terms, so they are frequently interchanged. For simplicity, they are interchanged in this book.

In general, a proposal should contain:

1. the customer's name, address, and other relevant information
2. the printing company's name, address, and other relevant information
3. the date from which the proposal validity begins and the proposal duration
4. a summary of the customer's job that provides all specifics that have significant bearing on the final product and all costs that will be incurred in producing the product
5. prices for the job, broken down by quantity, as well as prices for additional quantities
6. any additional costs that are possible, such as proofs, shipping, and AAs
7. reference to applicable legal terms and conditions or to the Printing Trade Customs (normally printed on the back of the proposal or quotation)
8. a signature by an appropriate printing company authority as commitment to the proposal
9. a signature and date line for the client to accept the document

Computer management systems typically offer a range of proposal/quotation formats. Most systems allow the proposal or quotation to be graphically individualized to the printer's wishes; most also provide that the proposal can be output on the printing company's stationery. With the laser output devices currently available, the professional appearance of a proposal or a quotation is not difficult to achieve.

Some vendors provide a fax/modem telecommunication connection so the proposal or quotation can be sent directly from the computer system without generating paper copy. However, it is prudent for a paper copy to be produced and mailed to the customer as well. A file copy should be maintained for printing company records.

A key aspect of the proposal/quotation relates to the evaluation and establishment of a selling price for the job under consideration, which is normally broken down by quantity to be delivered. Setting this price is a critical step in the business cycle because this price is directly related to company profitability, which in turn is related to the long-term survival of the company. Experts dealing with pricing printed products and services agree that pricing is a delicate matter driven by many factors, issues, and requirements. The law of elasticity of demand affects printing: High prices tend to reduce the volume of work coming into the printing plant, and low prices tend to increase the volume of work. Thus, low prices mean the printer may have more jobs in his plant at any given time, even though these jobs make little, if any, profit for the company.

Many computer systems provide a link between the cost estimating module (Module 1) and the pricing/quotation control module (Module 3). This relationship makes sense because the cost of a job typically represents a critical factor in setting the job's price. However, there are many other related and important questions to be addressed: How much profit markup should a company add to the cost? Should materials such as paper be marked up separately? Should certain production areas be marked up for greater profit than others? Should the company add profit based on the job cost or on the job value added (the amount of dollars after pass-through material and outside purchases have been deducted)? Which person—the estimator, sales representative, sales manager, CSR, controller, company president—should be responsible to complete the profit markup process?

Pricing factors and issues are covered in Chapter 4. At this point it must be noted that the general areas of pricing and how the computer system handles pricing linked to estimating are important areas to consider when reviewing this module.

An important computerized estimating/pricing/quoting issue relates to the way the computer system completes the profit markup process prior to generating a quotation. Although systems vary, some allow for the establishment of a "default" pricing percentage in which all jobs—unless they are excluded—are automatically marked up by the computer based on a company-determined profit percentage. (A common industry markup is 35 percent over estimated cost, which means a job that costs $100 would sell for $135).

The problem with using default pricing as a continuous pricing method is that it:

1. sets a de facto pricing standard below what some customers might be willing to pay;
2. streamlines the pricing process instead of requiring the careful review of each job;
3. lulls the printing company into a "good enough" pricing philosophy; and
4. reduces potential profits to the company because it does not take into account many important intangible issues that affect price.

Default pricing, if carefully evaluated in light of the previous issues, may be of benefit to some users because it streamlines the generation of quotes.

High-profit printers know that pricing printing products and services is best done by marking up each job based on an evaluation of the specific customer needs and related customer-driven issues. These printers know that using a standard markup system—a pricing system that offers no flexibility or variability in setting price on a job-by-job basis—is not desirable. Thus, when picking a computer management system, the process of quotation control through individual, customized pricing should be an important component.

As discussed earlier in the chapter, some computer management systems provide a "price list" or "job pricing" module in addition to, or in place of, a pricing system driven by cost estimating. The objective of any "direct pricing system," which uses manual price lists (on paper) or computer-generated prices, is to speed the quoting process, which in turn means the company can quote more orders. Computerized direct pricing systems may be configured as stand-alone pricing modules, or they may be built around a CGE package which combines the speeds of CGE and direct pricing methods.

Regardless of whether the system is stand-alone or part of a CGE package, the advantage is producing fast quotes. The disadvantage is that many production details are glossed over or neglected, which tends to reduce profitability. Also, as will be noted later in the discussion of plant scheduling (Module 9), selling work on the basis of price alone—with no production time evaluation—does not lend itself to implementing a CAS process.

Production Modules 4, 5, and 6. These modules, which are installed following Modules 1, 2, and 3, represent the second phase of installation. Typically Modules 4, 5, and 6 are installed as soon as the first three modules are being used in a satisfactory manner.

Module 4 Order Entry/Production Reanalysis. The objective of order entry is to initiate the job into production. Order entry is completed after the customer has committed the job to be produced, usually by accepting the proposal or quotation.

Ideally the original production plan and the resultant estimate require little revision as the job is converted to an actual order. However, prudent printing companies, whether they are computerized or not, typically begin the order entry process with a reevaluation or review of the original estimate. Sometimes this review suggests a modified or different job plan or a reengineering of the production sequence to enhance one or more aspects of production. These suggestions might include production changes to reduce job turnaround time, a different production approach to save the printing company money, or a production enhancement to improve quality.

Most computer systems link the estimating module (Module 1) to the order entry/production reanalysis module (Module 4). Thus, once the order is placed by the customer, the original estimate is reviewed and reanalyzed. Changes are made if desired. When completed, the estimate is automatically converted to a functional job ticket or job jacket, which is traditionally an envelope or a folder in which job materials are placed. Such job materials include mechanical artwork, color swatches, samples of past jobs or samples to be matched, notes on the job, and other information relevant to production.

As computer management systems have become more sophisticated, the electronic job ticket has gained interest. Here the conventional job ticket system is replaced by computer terminals strategically located throughout the plant. Any terminal on the network provides instantaneous production and job details. In practical terms an envelope or a job jacket containing important physical job materials sometimes leads the job, but the job data are only available electronically.

Advantages of the electronic job ticket system include the ability to reconfigure or reengineer the job at any time, the ability to view the current status of the job, and the ability to determine cost or profitability of the job at any point in the production cycle.

Computerized order entry is an important module because mistakes in translating the estimated job details to the job ticket format are minimized. Job complexities, which took time to determine at the estimating stage, are automatically transferred to the order entry file. The estimate-to-order entry transfer retains the anticipated production sequence from the estimate and establishes a format for EFDC. Also at the order entry stage, raw material inventory is checked against the estimate materials for the job, and an inventory commitment or purchasing request is then completed. In sum, the entire order entry process, which is based substantially on the original estimate, is streamlined so initiating the job into production is a simplified task.

Module 5 Data Collection. Data collection, also known as factory data collection (FDC) or shop floor data collection (SFDC), can be defined as capturing discrete production information reflecting the employees, production activities, and materials on a real-time basis as the printing job is manufactured. As computer management systems have grown in sophistication, and as they have provided electronic methods to capture and evaluate data, FDC has grown in popularity. For the cost-conscious printing company, data collection has become an important tool in computer managing the company.

There are three primary objectives of a data collection system in printing:

1. to gather data on production time by tracking the discrete activities completed by employees as they work on specific parts of a job;
2. to track materials consumed during production; and
3. to monitor all company production activities in the form of nonchargeable HEs and chargeable AAs, for which the customer pays.

To set up an FDC system, the first step is to divide the printing company into production or cost centers where chargeable work is performed. Once this is done, each cost center is then subdivided into discrete and specific production operations or production activities that are performed in the center, as well as specific material items that are used in the center and employees who work in the center. When this description process is complete, the company will have developed a list of hundreds of discrete items, sometimes called "operating codes," each of which contributes to the cost of operating the company. This framework then is ready to accept data as it is generated during the production of a given job.

The best data collection systems provide "real-time" input, which implies that the information is captured at approximately the moment it occurs. If a data collection system is not real time, the accuracy is lessened because the data are captured after the fact and could be compromised in some way.

There are three methods for data collection:

1. manual factory data gathering using employee handwritten methods
2. electronic factory data capturing using terminals requiring employee data input
3. automated electronic factory data capturing using devices that are directly connected to equipment and require little employee input

Each is described in the following.

Method 1: Manual Data Collection. Manual data input requires that company employees complete the data gathering process primarily by handwritten methods, sometimes assisted with a time clock for "punching in" and "punching out" as activities are completed. Most companies using this tedious data collection technique develop standard forms that are completed by employees as they do their normal daily production work. After the data are collected, they are manually cross-referenced by employee, cost center, production activity, materials used, and whether the item is chargeable or nonchargeable. Manual data collection is not used extensively because both entering and evaluating the data are done manually, making the process labor intensive. Also, manual techniques make cross-checking categories a complex and laborious task.

Method 2: Electronic Factory Data Collection. As mentioned earlier in the chapter, EFDC is a process by which employees enter job-related data into electronic terminals that are strategically located throughout the plant and are networked to a central computer.

There are three types of EFDC systems: keypad input, bar code input, and computer terminal workstations. The keypad input system, first introduced to the printing industry in 1984 by Covalent Systems, Inc., consists of one or more programmable keypad collection terminals which are hardwired to a network, which in turn inputs data into a hard disk storage medium. Each keypad unit is programmed for the specific production operation codes, material codes, employee codes, and any other relevant production codes of an operating center. Because prepress operations differ from press or finishing operations—and even prepress operation codes differ between conventional prepress and electronic methods—the keypad terminals must be able to be individually tailored when the system is first installed in the company.

When the keypad input system is in use, production employees begin their day by logging on—"starting shift"—into their keypad terminals. Then, throughout the day, they enter their production activities as they complete them, their materials as they consume them, and so on. At the end of the day the employees log off—they "end shift." The captured data have been sent to the hard disk of the central computer for storage and can be viewed, sorted, and printed as needed by production management staff at any time. Because the employees begin and end their workday by logging on and logging off respectively, there is a data collection link to payroll.

The second type of EFDC, bar code input, has emerged with the acceptance of bar code inventory and the retail pricing systems that have come out in the past twenty years. It works like this: Each employee, production activity, or material item has its own individual bar code combination. It is common for employees to have badges that contain their bar codes. Each center has all of its production operations, with applicable bar codes, listed on a sheet of paper near an input source, which is typically a handheld scanning wand.

To "begin a shift," an employee first passes the scanning wand over the bar code that indicates the "begin shift" function. She then passes the scanning wand over the bar code on her employee badge to input herself as starting to work. To input a production operation, she passes the scanning wand over the production bar code that represents the activity.

The bar code input system is fast, simple, and easy to use, and is generally less expensive when compared to keypad input. However, bar code data collection requires the purchase of at least one bar code printer to generate master bar codes.

The third type of EFDC is to use computer terminal workstations that are strategically positioned throughout the plant. Keyboard input or touch-screen versions are both available. To use this system, the employee first enters the code describing a job, activity, or material. This code is then transmitted to the computer storage device. Although these computer terminals can be expensive, they allow the company to use the electronic job tickets previously discussed in the Module 4 Order Entry section of this chapter. The terminals can also be used to access the computer system from any location, which enhances the possibility of using them for other activities, such as reporting production problems or transmitting electronic messages.

Method 3: Fully Automated Data Collection. The third type of data collection method is represented by an emerging group of systems which electronically link production equipment and data collection devices so that all data collection is fully automated and completed without operator intervention. This has become known as Fully Automated Data Collection, or FADC. One of the first companies in this important area was Logic Associates of White river Junction, Vermont, who named this type of data collection method "Direct Machine Interface" and trademarked the name and its abbreviation (Direct Market Interface™ or DMI™). Both "FADC" and "DMI" are now commonly used throughout the industry to identify generically this emerging type of data collection process.

The advantage of FADC is that tracking is done automatically as production occurs, causing minimum production disruption. Current FADC systems remain generally limited to production areas that produce highly mechanized output, such as sheetfed and web presses and some postpress operations. Various printing industry computer vendors are working to expand fully automated data collection to track electronic prepress production, which has proven difficult to do for various reasons. Once FADC is perfected for electronic prepress, it is likely to emerge as the de facto data collection standard, replacing EFDC.

Some experts believe that the printing plant of the future—the electronic printing company discussed in Chapter 1—will be managed through a group of networked, interactive computer terminals that will complete all data collection automatically, view electronic job tickets, complete electronic scheduling, and monitor real-time work-in-process. These terminals would tie together electronic printing systems such as DocuTech and CD-ROM, as well as a range of electronic prepress and digital output devices now emerging as the next generation of imagesetting equipment.

Following are some final data collection comments. Because data collection systems must be electronic to work interactively with a computer management system, manual data collection is not an option for interactive systems. The data collection module is one of the most interactive of all modules because it involves employees, production operations, materials, and chargeable and non-chargeable time. For that reason, any printing company that desires to install and implement a full-blown computer management system must plan for the additional expense and time a data collection system requires. It is, however, a worthwhile investment over the long term.

A word of caution is necessary here. The EFDC system should always be considered a production management tool and not a management feedback system to evaluate employee performance. Management should not use the data collection system to evaluate employee productivity or to track and blame employees for job errors or excessive material use. If this happens, employees will sabotage the process and considerable money and effort will be wasted.

Module 6   Job Costing. The objective of job costing is to compare estimated production times and costs to actual production times and costs. Job costing requires a functional data collection system for gathering actual production times and a detailed cost estimating module that establishes times and costs during the estimating process. Each of these topics is covered earlier in this chapter.

Job costing can be done either manually or using a computerized job costing system. Manual job costing is completed with manual data collection, manual estimating, and manual comparison of times and costs. Computerized job costing requires the use of EFDC, a computerized estimate, and computerized job costing software. Computerized job costing, which is the focus of the following discussion, is preferred because it is fast and convenient compared to the very slow manual methods.

The job costing process begins when the potential order is cost estimated. In cost estimating the job is broken into specific operational tasks to which times and costs are assigned. After cost estimating, the job is priced and the proposal is sent to the customer. The customer accepts the job proposal and the job moves from estimating to order entry where it is reviewed and production changes are made. Then the job "goes live" and becomes work-in-process. As production is completed, production data are collected electronically. When the job is finished, there exists a full, detailed data collection record covering all production.

At this point an important job costing question must be asked: Should the job costing review be completed prior to invoicing the job, or should it be completed later and not be related to the invoicing process? In the first case, where job costing is completed immediately after the job is finished but before the invoice is generated, the invoice may include all chargeable costs and materials—that is, all approved and chargeable AAs. It may also include accrued job costs that were not author approved nor on the original estimate. It should be clear that when job costing is completed prior to invoicing, it must be done expeditiously—within one day of job completion is suggested—to avoid increasing the accounts receivable collection period and slowing customer payment. This means that there must be a continuous focus on completing job costing daily, which may require extra staff.

In the second instance, where job costing is completed separately from the invoicing process, the job costing is completed primarily for feedback and internal evaluation of specific areas where job cost was too high or too low, as well as for specific production feedback on estimating standards, production errors, and excessive material usage. When job costing is not linked to the invoicing cycle, less time is required to complete reviews and fewer staff are required. However, this option does not allow the company to include additional chargeable costs to the customer's job, which tends to diminish profits because the company and not the customer bears those costs.

There are three desired benefits of the job costing process. To achieve these benefits, the job to be costed should have an existing, detailed computer estimate and a complete EFDC file that was generated as the job was produced.

Benefit No. 1. Job costing flags production variations in time and cost, which allows management to investigate reasons for these variations and to take corrective action in future jobs. The key to this review is a computer-generated variance report that lists cost centers and production activity by code, then shows columns containing estimated production times next to actual production times. The structure of the report allows for quick evaluation of variances between the estimated values and the actual values and provides a tool to quantify gains and losses.

Benefit No. 2. Job costing allows management to quickly assess and clarify any alterations completed during production and to determine whether these alterations should be invoiced to the customer as reasonable charges. There are three types of job changes typically found in printing production:

1. House errors (HEs) are internal production mistakes not normally charged to the customer.
2. Author's alterations (AAs) are traditionally charged to the customer as long as the customer approved the alterations before they were made.
3. Nonchargeable alterations (NAAs) are job changes that have been made but will not be charged to the customer.

Because the variance report compares estimated production to actual job activity, any unplanned production may be quickly noted and categorized as one of these three types of job changes, and appropriate invoicing action may be taken.

Benefit No. 3. Job costing represents an important feedback mechanism for revising production standards used for estimating and for analyzing chargeable hour usage. Carefully studying job cost variance reports and comparing report findings between jobs provide excellent feedback for changing estimating production standards. In general this process requires the person completing the review to look for patterns where estimates are continually too high or too low compared to actual production. When such patterns are noted over a period of time and with a series of similar jobs, it is wise to modify estimating standards so that future estimates more closely align with actual production.

During this review process it is also common for the reviewer to evaluate equipment utilization, which links to BHRs and is correlated with the level of use applied during estimating. In Lines 31 to 33 of Figure 2.2, the levels of use are 80 percent, 70 percent, and 60 percent respectively. If a pattern showing greater or less utilization is noted, it is prudent to raise or lower the estimating BHR rate to fit that revised utilization pattern. Using Figure 2.2 as an example, if estimating is completed using an 80 percent BHR of $97.92, and job costing shows that the actual use of the press is 70 percent or $111.91, it would be prudent to shift to the 70 percent BHR for all future estimates. If the 80 percent BHR would continue to be used, the company would, in effect, lose $13.99 per hour sold on this press.

Production Modules 7 and 8. These modules are important because they monitor raw material inventory levels and the purchase of new materials to sustain the company's current work-in-process and future jobs.

Module 7 Raw Material Inventory. Because printing manufacturing is a materials-intensive business, monitoring and tracking available inventory is an essential function which is greatly assisted by computerization. One objective of a good inventory control system is to provide sufficient material at all times so the company is not placed in a position whereby an inventory item is thought to be available but is not. Because the company's inventory can require a substantial cash commitment for purchasing the products as well as a physical commitment to storing these products, another objective is to keep certain inventory items at levels that do not require excessive cash or storage space. Historically some cases of raw material inventory, such as when inventory levels are excessive or when expensive inventory items are used infrequently, have been dilemmas for printers. Too much inventory ties up valuable cash dollars and is like "putting cash on the shelf" for a printing company.

Computerized raw material inventory systems, such as daily inventory-on-hand, committed work-in-process inventory, and minimum inventory, tend to be elaborate because they are designed to handle inventory at different points in time. Application software to track raw material inventory varies relative to the way data are set up as well as to the way the system functions. As a result, the following descriptive information is general in nature.

For a fully computerized management system, the raw material inventory module (Module 7) should be linked with the order entry module (Module 4) to establish the future commitment of raw materials and to the data collection module (Module 5) to monitor daily inventory transactions. In general, the inventory segment of the order entry process works this way: As each order is entered into production based on the estimated quantities of raw materials from the estimating module (Module 1), a raw material "transaction commitment" is made and is linked to an anticipated date when the raw material is needed.

The date in the transaction commitment for the use of the raw material is important because inventory levels constantly change—when the job requires raw material there may be none available, or there may be too much. Thus, the computer inventory program monitors all raw material transaction commitments by job number, by established minimum quantity levels of raw materials, and by date. As a result, if a negative inventory balance is indicated for the date a job requires raw materials, an "order flag" is generated to note that the required raw material will not be available when needed. In such a case, the order flag is linked to the purchase order control module (Module 8, the next production module to be discussed), which establishes a purchasing record that will be acted upon if the negative raw material inventory balance is confirmed upon management review.

Following the inventory order entry commitment, production on the job begins. If the company has a functioning real-time data collection system, actual materials consumed for the job are entered by employees. This information is then transferred to the computer inventory control file where it is checked against the transaction commitment for the job, the transaction commitments for other jobs-in-process, and the current real-time inventory level. The result is a daily inventory-on-hand quantity, which might indicate that a reasonable level of inventory remains, or that the inventory on hand is too high or too low. If it is too low, a purchasing decision would be initiated.

Sometimes the estimated raw material quantity committed for the job from the order entry and the actual quantity of the raw material are very different. A common reason for this is that too much raw material (e.g., paper) was spoiled during production. This situation, which requires immediate action, occurs more frequently when company policy is to keep minimum inventory levels or when a JIT inventory system is in place.

Once the problem is resolved so that the job can be delivered, a review should be completed to determine the reasons for the excessive spoilage or other problem. This review could be used to initiate corrective action to modify spoilage data schedules for estimating and to resolve future production problems. Unpredictable raw material inventory levels are undesirable and should occur infrequently. A functional computer inventory control system is a great help in keeping inventory in check. When unplanned inventory gaps occur more frequently than necessary, SPC could be used to focus on, analyze, and correct the problem.

Some MIS systems link raw material inventory to the computer estimating system. This link is reasonable as long as it is used primarily for checking general availability of raw materials and not for making raw material commitments. A commitment to allocate raw materials at the estimating stage is unwise because the job has not yet been ordered by the customer.

Module 8 Purchase Order Control. This module is linked to the order entry module (Module 4), the raw material inventory module (Module 7), and the accounts payable module (Module 13). It may also be linked to the estimating module (Module 1).

The objectives of purchase order (PO) control are to initiate the purchase of raw materials and outside purchases for work-in-process and to interface with accounts payable so that purchases are handled in a timely manner. The connection between order entry and purchase order control from the raw material inventory perspective is described in the previous section and is not covered again here. Another equally important order entry objective is to determine what goods and services are necessary to order from outside vendors. These goods and services are commonly called buyouts, outside purchases, or trade purchases.

Buyouts are usually based on what has been estimated for the job and should be clearly noted as the estimate is transferred to the order entry module (Module 4). In cases where the buyout has been noted, the process of specifying and ordering the product is generally not difficult. However, when a buyout is not clearly indicated, has been overlooked during estimating, was not originally specified as part of the job, or when the customer changes his mind and has decided to let the printer provide the outside purchase, the process of specifying and ordering the product may be complicated. Resolution here requires a CSR or an assigned employee to first evaluate the needed buyout, which is usually done through direct customer contact, and to determine the appropriate vendor(s). The employee then prepares a purchase order and obtains the product. This process is not exceptionally difficult but it can be time consuming.

The relationship of purchase order control to accounts payable (Module 13) is primarily informational. Accounts payable should be informed once a raw material item or an outside purchase order has been initiated. Later, when the ordered material or buyout has been received and invoiced for payment, it becomes an active account payable and should be paid as determined by company management. Cross-checking the purchase order to the vendor's invoice, which should include reviewing specific purchases for such characteristics as quantity and quality, should be completed prior to paying the invoice.

Module 9 Job/Machine Loading and Plant Scheduling. Computerized job/machine loading and plant scheduling represent the final module in the production group and draw upon data that are provided directly or indirectly from each of the other eight modules in the production group.

Job loading, sometimes called machine loading, is a process by which a group of jobs to be produced are queued for a specific piece of equipment—a printing press, a folder, an electronic prepress platform—to achieve the most efficient production. Because computerized job loading evaluates a stand-alone production area and not a group of interactive processes that are locked into a necessary sequence, it is not a complex process. Times for determining the load sequence are available via a computer link with the order entry module (Module 4) and typically originate from the job estimating module (Module 1).

In contrast, plant scheduling, when done either manually or by computer, is a complex and difficult process. The objective of any good plant scheduling system, termed a CAS system here, is to arrange all current work-in-process into the most efficient production sequence whereby all job requirements, critical production factors, targeted delivery dates, and quality levels are met. A functioning computer scheduling software package is the ultimate in detail management.

For example, consider the following typical printing plant scheduling problem: Assume there are twelve jobs-in-process. Three are in various electronic prepress stages, one is being tablestripped, three are in various platemaking stages, three are on three different presses, and two are in bindery—one is on the folder and the other is being collated. Delivery dates vary from one day to four days. Two of the twelve jobs require outside bindery work. Tomorrow it is anticipated that there will be five new jobs beginning production—three with three-day turnarounds and two with six-day turnarounds. Of these five new jobs, three will have customer-supplied electronic artwork, one will have fully mechanical art, and one will have a mix of electronic and mechanical art. Of the seventeen total jobs, "excellent" quality is anticipated for fourteen; "good enough" is anticipated for the remainder. Even with this fairly simple sketch, which omits many details, it is clear that scheduling these seventeen jobs would be a challenging data management problem.

Now that the overall objective of a fully functional CAS package is clear, the specific goals are to ensure:

1. the customer's jobs are always delivered on time;
2. production employees work at maximum efficiency;
3. cost centers achieve maximum productivity;
4. costs are minimized throughout the production process; and
5. product quality is achieved on continuous and consistent bases.

Although these five goals are the cornerstones of a great scheduling system, assuring that the customers' jobs are delivered on time and at the quality expected is paramount because the environment in printing is intensely competitive. Doing this ensures repeat customers, sustains increased volume, provides a higher price ceiling, and, most importantly, provides a lever to enhance company profitability.

Scheduling to the customer's stated delivery date—the job due date—is essential. All CAS packages should be able to schedule from "due date backward to today," from "today to due date," from "a given production point to due date," or from "due date backward to a given production point." A "what if" analysis using these target date parameters is an option as well. This type of flexibility, which focuses on meeting the customer's delivery date requirement while considering all other work-in-process, makes CAS an important and essential management tool.

The CAS offers a workable solution to this complex data management problem as long as estimating (Module 1), BHRs and production standards

(Module 2), order entry (Module 4), data collection (Module 5), and raw material inventory (Module 7) are integrated parts of the system. The following discusses some of the issues, dilemmas, and problems faced when using a CAS package that relates to these modules.

CAS Can Schedule Only Jobs for Which a Computer Estimate Exists. The CAS system can schedule only those orders (work-in-process) for which production time records exist in the computer. This means that all jobs to be scheduled must reside in the computer database with time allocations. The computer cannot schedule jobs that have not been entered in the computer with production time records.

As noted when discussing estimating and order entry earlier, such time records are initially generated through the development of a job estimate using the system estimating module (Module 1). The more detailed the estimate, the more accurate the estimate. However, typically more time is needed for such accuracy.

The estimated production time and cost records serve as a baseline for pricing the job. Later, once the customer has accepted the quoted price and has ordered the job, this estimating information is transferred to order entry (Module 4) and the job becomes work-in-process.

This system works well as long as all jobs are estimated by computer. However, building full cost estimates on all jobs is sometimes not completed. This may be due to a rush situation or a job for which a customer simply cannot identify all specifications. Sometimes estimating is only completed on key items such as paper or prepress. Also, many jobs are quoted and sold on price alone (e.g., by price list or other pricing method). Some estimators do not like the way computer estimating software functions; some refuse to become computer literate and continue estimating all of their jobs manually using their own methods.

To provide estimating data for scheduling when jobs have not been estimated, one of two paths is commonly followed. The first path is to complete a detailed computer estimate at the order entry stage after the job has been priced and sold but before it begins production. Because this estimating occurs after the job has been priced and sold, costs that were not anticipated may come to light, or it may become apparent that the production plan does not provide the final price on which the job was sold.

The second path is to intuitively determine or "guesstimate" production times and to input these approximations into the computer. This gives the CAS system approximate times with which to schedule production.

CGE Systems Do Not Provide Scheduling Data. Previously there was a discussion of CGE systems that are automated to speed the estimating process. However, typical CGE systems do not break out production times and therefore do not provide the time data needed to complete scheduling. If a CGE system is being considered and CAS is desired, it is wise to investigate this issue.

Price Estimating Methods Do Not Provide Scheduling Data. Also discussed previously, price quoting systems, which are systems using price lists or other price-driven methods, are popular throughout the printing industry. They are fast, convenient, easily modified, and generally uncomplicated. However, when any type of price quoting system—from a price sheet printed on paper to a computer-driven pricing module—is used, no cost estimate is generated to support the price and therefore no times are available for scheduling. Thus, even though price quoting systems are a common method of quoting printing, they complicate CAS methods.

Customer Unknowns Complicate Scheduling at All Levels. Sometimes as the order entry process starts the job, customers still do not know certain production requirements of their jobs. These unknowns affect plant scheduling. For example, prepress production is a common problem because a customer's electronic artwork may only be partially complete or problematic, or it may mix electronic and mechanical formats. Press and finishing decisions on jobs are also not always known, which effectively negate any attempts at accurately scheduling a customer's job.

CAS Requires Accurate Real-Time Data Collection. It is not possible to have a CAS system without a fully functional, real-time EFDC or FADC system. The latter is an essential feedback loop because scheduling production requires both estimated times and work-in-process links. The EFDC system should also have a fully functional link to raw materials inventory so that material availability is ensured at all times.

There Are Numerous Unexpected Scheduling Unknowns. Many scheduling factors cannot be anticipated or are so pervasive that they simply cause scheduling havoc. These include customers who do not meet their deadlines and obligations when their jobs begin, many small mistakes or one or two big mistakes that are made during production, equipment that does not work properly or cannot achieve the desired result, employees who are too slow or unable to produce the needed results, trade purchases that arrive late or are improperly done, customer-supplied materials that are incorrect and need to be redone, delivery dates that are too compressed for the quality and/or quantities of the products, unexpected problems that arise with raw materials, equipment that breaks down, and union or other employee problems that occur. An effective CAS program provides organization and control of all work-in-process by eliminating bottlenecks and the unpredictable.

CAS is the most complex and difficult to execute segment of a printing company's MIS. Over time, as the industry moves toward the "electronic printing company," integrated scheduling will become a reality. In the meantime, given the many complications indicated here, the ultimate wish of many printing company managers regarding computerized scheduling—"to hit a key to find out today's production schedule"—remains unfulfilled.

Accounting Group Modules (Modules 10 through 17)

These modules tend to follow traditional accounting practices, although some printing industry computer vendors have added their own enhancements. The discussion that follows summarizes these modules as they apply to graphic arts companies.

Module 10 Bookkeeping: Journals and Ledgers. This module provides the framework of data on which the company's accounting system interfaces. A journal is a record of an original transaction made by the company. It is supported by sales slips and other documents. Journals commonly cover a range of categories, including sales transactions, purchasing, shipping, payroll, bank transactions, and travel and entertainment records. Journals require daily recording of data covering all transactions made by the company.

A ledger, sometimes called a general ledger, is a file that is divided into homogenous categories where accounting data from journals are posted on a timely basis. A journal category is also commonly a ledger category, so the ledger represents a summary of the journals in one file. The general ledger is an important document because it is a single-source summary covering all transactions for the business.

Bookkeeping is the process by which journals and ledgers are maintained. The journal and ledger module interfaces with all other accounting modules (Modules 11 through 17), so it must be reliable. Because computer-assisted bookkeeping is today a fairly defined process, some printing industry computer vendors rely on generic PC-based accounting packages such as Peachtree Software or Great Plains Software to provide journal, ledger, and related accounting documents.

It should be noted that some of the other modules in the accounting group are components of this module (Module 10). They have been broken out of Module 10 because they require separate discussion or have been traditionally problematic for printers.

Module 11 Invoicing. One of the most important issues with respect to invoicing is for management to focus on getting an error-free invoice in the customer's hands as quickly as possible after the job has been produced and is ready for delivery. Invoicing begins the cash turnaround cycle, so any delay means a delay in revenue. Even though the printing job is not physically in the hands of the customer—it may be in transit or yet to be shipped—quickly completing the invoicing process is essential. With the advent of good computer systems, fax transmission, fax/modems, and overnight mail, putting an error-free invoice quickly in the hands of the customer is not a problem.

If data collection (Module 5) were used to collect shop floor data on the job, management must decide whether job costing (Module 6) will be completed prior to generating the invoice and therefore whether the customer will be charged for all job-related production not included on the original estimate. These chargeable areas may include customer-approved AAs, alterations made to the job that were not approved at the time but should be chargeable, or other customer-ordered work on the job that was not included in the original estimate. In general, customers do not mind paying additional costs for work performed on their jobs as long as there are clear reasons for the charges and the charges are not excessive.

Because job costing is a detailed process, it tends to slow the invoicing cycle. No more than two days should lapse between job completion and invoicing. Same-day invoicing is preferred.

Some printing companies do not complete job costing because they have found it slows their invoicing processes too much. These companies complete job costing some time after their invoices are sent to their customers. This is unwise if real-time data collection systems are operational because job costing could be easily completed if staff were organized to immediately do it. Why invest money in EFDC equipment and have employees take the time to enter the data during production if only part of the benefits are achieved? Also, in this era of incomplete electronic artwork, the likelihood is high that some electronically prepared printing jobs will have additional alterations and costs that should be invoiced to the customer. If these costs are not billed to the customer, and if they must be paid, then they will ultimately come out of the company's profit on the job.

It is important to note that studies have shown that when an invoice has an error of any kind, the customer tends to request a corrected invoice, which slows payment. This applies to the situation in which an AA that has not been approved or may have been queried is charged to the customer. Also, invoices that are confusing or unclear slow payment until clarification is provided by the company.

Module 12 Accounts Receivable. This module is used to monitor all customer accounts that have been billed and are currently due. An array of receivable reports should be available, including aged receivables and receivable lists sorted by invoice date, customer, order number, and sales representative. Accounts receivable should be linked to invoicing (Module 11), sales and marketing analysis (Module 15), finished goods inventory (Module 16), and financial statements (Module 17).

It is important that accounting staff closely monitor the accounts receivable collection period (ARCP), which is defined as the time in days from the mailing or faxing of the invoice to the customer to the date the payment of the amount due is received. Linked to monitoring the ARCP via the invoicing module (Module 11) is the aged receivable list, by which receivables are tracked for length of time overdue. Timely invoices are mailed or faxed when receivables change to the next aging category.

Studies have shown that when a printing company charges an interest penalty (i.e., 1.5 percent on the outstanding balance each 30 days) or offers a discount for early payment (i.e., 2 percent net 10 days), it has little effect in speeding payment. An exception to this is when the discount is 5 percent or greater.

Module 13 Accounts Payable. This module is linked to purchase order control (Module 8), where outside purchases are contractually made, and order entry (Module 4), which initiates the purchase order request. The accounts payable module provides reports for monitoring payments due on raw materials, outside purchases, and other payable materials and services contracted by the company. In some systems this module is linked to the actual check writing process.

Past payment practices and vendor relationships drive a typical printing company's accounts payable practices. For example, some vendors require immediate or speedy payment for a raw material or trade service, while other vendors extend credit without hesitation. If a printing company is consistently late in meeting payment to a vendor or a supplier, the vendor may require cash on delivery (COD) or immediate payment before the raw material is provided. This may burden the company's cash reserves, which in turn tends to cause financial stress and should be avoided. Cash cycles, cash turnaround, and the flow of dollars through the company are important issues and in some systems are monitored from this module.

Module 14 Payroll. The monitoring and generating of payroll documents is a straightforward module that receives continuous use. As a result, it tends to be error free and functional. If the company has a data collection system in place, and if the system requires production employees to log on and off the system in completing their normal daily work cycles, this logging on and off is linked to the payroll module. Thus, detailed tracking of all employees for payroll purposes is fully computerized so time cards or other manual methods are not needed.

Module 15 Sales and Marketing Analysis. This module has increased in importance as world-class customer service and niche markets have received increased focus throughout the graphic arts industry. Although sales and marketing analysis is not a functioning part of accounting process, it has been placed in the accounting group due to its active connections with invoicing (Module 11), accounts receivable (Module 12), finished goods inventory (Module 16), and financial statements (Module 17). It also draws on production modules for pricing/quotation control (Module 3), order entry (Module 4), and estimating (Module 1). Regardless of its placement in Figure 2.1, the sales and marketing module should be available to facilitate the development of new markets, analyze the needs of current customers, and provide data on a range of important areas such as accounts receivable collection and pricing.

A variety of sales and marketing reports are most helpful in monitoring this critical area of any printing company. The MIS systems that provide this module with information may focus on building and maintaining databases on current and past customers, as well as on potential future clients. These databases should provide for a wide range of information, such as client location, type of business performed, client markets, company officers, potential sales volume in the customer's market, growth profiles, current and past printers, accounts receivable payment records, ratios of proposals submitted to jobs won, and so on. These databases should also be open ended so they include any information that has a bearing on the client or the company as a current or future customer.

As part of the database, it may prove beneficial to evaluate current clients relative to their prevailing working relationships with the printing company and, if appropriate, the anticipated future direction of the printing company. These are subjective issues and, to the extent possible, should remain within the circles of company management. Some of these issues might include ranking the customer's ease of workability with the printing company, the quality of customer-supplied job materials relative to payment for chargeable AAs (particularly related to electronic artwork), the customer payment practices and receivable collection time, the customer's attitude with respect to the printing company, and the stability of the customer's business relative to potential printing volume over the long term.

Many printers want their computer systems to provide them with the abilities to generate mailing lists of customers and to print functional mailing labels. These printers also want their computer systems to provide for culling and sorting these customer lists so they can target a certain type of customer by specific product or service.

Module 16 Finished Goods Inventory. The objective of the finished goods inventory module is to monitor all finished goods until they are in the hands of the customer. Typical components of this module include preparing shipping/delivery documents, arranging for shipping/delivery services, monitoring arrival of finished goods at the customer's desired location, and tracking in-house storage inventory.

This module is generally not complex but requires daily maintenance. It should be linked to invoicing (Module 11), accounts receivable (Module 12), and raw material inventory (Module 7) if the same facilities are used to store both raw materials and finished goods.

Module 17 Financial Statements. This is a critical module. Some top managers believe it is the most important module. It requires links to most other modules so that the data that build the financial statements are accurate and reliable. Computer accounting software has taken the drudgery out of preparing the financial statements and, when it is linked with production modules, streamlines and simplifies the entire financial statement preparation process. Following are some brief observations on the subject.

Financial statements are the link between accounting and finance. The two most important financial statements are the income statement, also called the profit and loss statement or the P & L statement, and the balance sheet. The income statement, which reports revenue and expenses for a specific period of time, reflects the results of operations during that period. The balance sheet shows the financial position of the company on a specific date and is generally regarded as a snapshot view of "the house the printer lives in."

The function of the accountant is to gather and prepare financial statements. The function of the company's finance person—the company president in a small business—is to analyze those statements and determine, with other company objectives, in which direction the company should go. Financial statements indicate the health of the company and are of great interest to the owners of the firm (e.g., the stockholders), as well as to banks, lenders, investors, and tax agencies.

To be effective, financial statements must be prepared and reviewed at least monthly; annual financial statements are too broad and their data are generally too old for any response to be effective. If desired, computer-assisted accounting systems, which are capable of generating income statements and balance sheets more frequently than monthly, can be used to provide management with a timely look at income and expenses as well as the general health of the company.

Sadly, business failure in printing, particularly in small printing companies, has been linked to top management who are unable to understand their own financial statements and are therefore unable to take timely and appropriate action. This is changing as computer-aided accounting systems and MIS systems emerge with graphical ("gooey") interfaces, which allow complicated data and analyses to be presented in picture form such as pie charts. Nevertheless, understanding the content of an income statement—revenue, cost of goods sold, gross margin (profit), operating expenses, net income, and retained earnings—remains important. Also important is understanding the content of the balance sheet, which is a critical financial statement that provides a snapshot of the company's assets, liabilities, and owner's equity at a given point in time.

When completing financial analysis, ratio measurements are of great assistance. These ratios are developed from financial statements in combination with computer-assisted accounting data and are indicators of company liquidity, financial leverage, activity, and profitability. Ratios are commonly compared over time to show trends and patterns within companies, as well as between companies when industry-wide ratio data are available.

Most managers select and monitor certain ratios as their personal choices for noting the company's financial health and direction. Because cash flow continues to be a major problem with small businesses, including graphic arts companies, ratios evaluating receivable collection periods and average daily credit sales are important. Ratios for return on sales (ROS), return on investment (ROI), inventory turnover, debt-to-equity, and current ratio and quick ratio also receive frequent use.

2.6   Key Points on Computer Management Systems for Printing and Publishing

Following are some key points regarding the evaluation and selection of a computer management system or an MIS for a graphic arts company.

First, there is no perfect or ideal system that "thinks just like people do" or that can meet a person's every wish and desire. The evaluation of any computer management system is subject to a person's years of experience and knowledge, which will not be the same as the experience and knowledge of that person's coworkers. Although a specific computer estimating module may appear to work exactly as expected, its order entry may not fit the company's needs. Similarly, although the job costing system may be liked, the report format for indicating variances in job cost may seem confusing. The strengths and weaknesses of any system under review are not always apparent. An MIS may seem the ideal solution on first review, but it may not be quite so perfect when used day to day and month to month.

Second, current systems are not always as bad as they seem. Sometimes the printing company is not using the system fully or has not implemented recent software upgrades. Change in the printing industry is pervasive—electronic prepress is a perfect example of this. Vendors of today's systems frequently enhance their software to reflect the current production environment. Before doing all of the work necessary to switch to a completely new MIS, which can be time consuming and expensive, be certain that the current system is clearly unable to meet the present and future needs of the company.

Third, the process of selecting, buying, and implementing a computer management system requires a different perspective than is traditionally used for purchasing and implementing production equipment such as a press or a folder. The following reasons can be noted for this:

1. Computer management systems require a basic level of computer knowledge that must be interfaced with a wide range of knowledge of how the

business operates in many areas, from estimating and purchasing to accounts receivable, invoicing, and machine loading.

2. The chosen system will have far-reaching, dynamic effects on most company employees, not just a few.

3. Printing company management traditionally has used a subjective decision-making system for purchasing production equipment. However, the purchase of a computer system, which ties together many discrete functions but does not provide a salable product per se, does not fit into a single production environment and cannot be easily evaluated. The concept that "we'll make the computer system work," or "we'll figure that out after the system is installed and operating," can be disruptive.

4. The old adage "software before hardware" remains as true today as it was in the past. High on the list of reasons for this is that intense competition among hardware manufacturers has significantly reduced hardware costs for almost all varieties of equipment. Clearly, such cost reductions make hardware choices easier because the paybacks are faster and the immediate effects on cash flow are reduced. In addition to significantly reducing hardware costs, this competition has improved the speed, system capability, and capacity of technical hardware. Finally, there is a steady convergence to a single platform system. Hardware is becoming so similar that there may be no need to make a distinct hardware choice in a few years. The PowerPC is a recent example of this convergence.

5. The more removed and distant top management is from the review, selection, and implementation of an MIS, the less successful the system will be in the long term. Although this book suggests a team approach to selecting and implementing a computer management system, it is clear that top management's active participation throughout the process is essential for success. In addition, top management's involvement must be continuous, direct, and clear to employees over the long term, or full system use may be jeopardized.

6. The company's chosen computer management system must streamline tasks, reduce the complexities of the work done by company employees, provide customer benefits that are pronounced and clear, and provide company management with a functional tool to operate the business more profitably. The system must also improve employee productivity by reducing errors and simplifying employees' work activities while providing a tool to meet the time-compression realities of customers. If a system does not provide these employee and customer benefits, it should either be replaced by a new system or reinstalled with upgraded software and hardware. Finally, the system should improve the ability of company management to profitably operate the company at all levels—operating management for production, mid-level management for accounting, and

top-level management for financial reports, operating statements, and global financial issues.

7. If a printing company wants to successfully move into the twenty-first century and beyond, it has no choice except to computerize its management functions. This is true despite the obvious complexities of what computer system to choose, the system's potentially high cost in both dollars and time, the disruption of employees due to training and implementation issues, and the frustrations the computer system causes as it is installed and debugged.

2.7   Information versus User-Friendliness

The reasons to computerize are clear and pronounced, but there is no greater frustration than working with a computer system that does not return significant benefits for the time, effort, and money invested. For this reason it makes sense that one of the major reasons a printing company computerizes is to provide organization and rhyme and reason to its thousands of pieces of information. Computerization allows the company to be more organized and logical, thereby providing a structure for better decision making at all company levels. This means that a computer management system is primarily an information tool.

However, all of the information in the world is no good if it is not presented in a friendly, convenient, manageable, and understandable manner. Computer use is greatest when there is a balance between the information presented and how that information is displayed.

The function of a computer terminal or monitor is to display information electronically. How each screen shows data in terms of the data's general presentation, user-friendliness, image size, and logical organization is an important factor for everyday use and is critical to receiving the desired feedback. Printers, who sometimes sidestep the information on the screen, frequently purchase (or do not purchase) systems based on their first views of certain screen displays. Some vendors, who believe, "You never get a second chance to make a first impression," work diligently to make their screen displays aesthetically pleasing. They may go overboard, however, and limit the information that is displayed or present information that is "nice to know" but not essential. In sum, there should be a balance between the attractiveness of the screen display and the information that is presented so that the daily use of the system is not compromised.

Reports that are printed from the computer system and their information, or their lack thereof, deserve equal scrutiny. Reports or printouts should be evaluated with respect to the quality and quantity of information they provide. Some systems provide a "report generation" function, which allows the user to tailor her printouts from a list of available data. This feature is desired because predesigned management reports tend to represent the information the computer vendor decided was important, and not what the user considers important.

Above all, reports printed to paper represent management's primary source of information for evaluating the company. These printouts must be orderly. The more they can be tailored to the specific desires and needs of company management, the better. There is little reason to computerize a graphic arts company unless it is kept in mind that one of the key objectives of a computer system is to obtain and use accurate information to ultimately ease decision making and improve profits.

2.8 List of Vendors of Computer Management Systems (Appendix C)

Appendix C is an alphabetical list of eighty-two vendors who provide a range of computer management products and services for the printing and allied industries. Each vendor's name, address, telephone number, fax number, and contact person were correct at the time of publication. For reference, the vendor's target market and general type of computer management product are also indicated.

The vendor's target market is the type or size of graphic arts firm the vendor is seeking. It is indicated by one of the following four categories:

Target Market 1   Small and quick printers (sales under $2 million annually)
Target Market 2   Medium printers (sales between $2 million and $10 million annually)
Target Market 3   Large printers (sales over $10 million annually)
Target Market 4   Specialty graphic arts firms (includes screen printers, service bureaus, trade shops, business forms printers, and label printers)

In terms of products, most of the vendors offer either software (SW) application programs (or group of software modules) or turnkey (TK) systems, which include hardware and software. Some vendors provide software modules that stand alone, such as estimating or BHRs, while other software vendors offer a group of modules that, when purchased and installed, builds to make a full MIS system. It should be clear that each vendor offers a unique solution—a different approach—to each module. Thus, there is little compatibility of software between vendors and little potential of interchangeability between application programs as a result.

For specific information on any vendor, contact the vendor directly.

Chapter 3

Developing a Cost Estimating System

Establishing Production Components, Production Time Standards, and BHRs

3.1 Introduction

3.2 Defining Production Centers, Production Components, and Operation Codes

3.3 Defining and Using Production Time Standards
How Production Standards Are Used
Categories of Production Standards
Standardizing, Specializing, and Automating Printing Production

3.4 Five Important "Rules of the Road" for Establishing and Using Production Standards and BHRs
Rule 1: Divide Production Areas into Specific Centers
Rule 2: Tailor All Data to the Company's Production Conditions
Rule 3: Review and Revise Standards and Costs at Least One Time per Year
Rule 4: Keep All Data Written and Secure
Rule 5: Share Information with Employees on a "Need to Know" Basis

99

3.5 Methods for Establishing Production Standards

Method 1: Standards Based on Historical Plant Data through Job Costing

Method 2: Standards Based on Intuition

Method 3: Standards Based on Published Information

Method 4: Standards Borrowed from the Competition

Method 5: Standards Based on Equipment Manufacturers' Data

Method 6: Standards Based on Plant Engineering Evaluation

3.6 Keeping Production Standards Current

3.7 Developing BHRs

General Rules for BHR Use

General Steps in BHR Development

Step-by-Step BHR Development for a Komori 1-Color Press

Line-by-Line Analysis of Figure 3.4

Some Further Comments and Pointers on Developing and Using BHRs

3.8 Overtime Considerations and Cost Savings for Additional Shifts

3.9 Effects of Automation on BHRs and Chargeable Hours

3.10 Cost Markup

Estimating Methods

Material Markups

3.11 Establishing Prorated Costing

System Overview and Description

Database Needed to Establish Prorated Costing

Appendix: All-Inclusive BHRs

3.1   Introduction

This chapter provides detailed information on the development of two critical aspects of cost estimating: standard production data and BHRs. As indicated in Chapter 1, these two bodies of data work together to provide estimated production costs and production times for a customer's job. Estimated production costs are used by management when pricing the job; estimated production times are used when scheduling each production step to be completed on the job.

As noted in Chapter 2, it is possible for any company to use generic spreadsheet software (e.g., Lotus 1,2,3® or Microsoft Excel®) on a microcomputer to collect, massage, and evaluate these two sets of data. Many printing industry computer vendors provide services in data collection and BHR development which can be tailored to meet the specific needs of a printing company.

As was also mentioned previously, production standards are the basic time units required for production operations. For example, the production standard for line exposures on a process camera might be 0.10 hour (6 minutes) and 0.15 hour (9 minutes) for halftone production. If a job requires 12 line exposures and 4 halftones, the estimated time for production is 1.8 hours [(12 x 0.10 hour) + (4 x 0.15 hour) = 1.8].

The BHRs are an accounting procedure by which all costs are first identified for each production center of the plant, such as an electronic prepress platform, a process camera, or a printing press, then are broken down into hourly amounts that are used to estimate a customer's job. For example, if a process camera has a BHR of $50.00 per hour, then (1.8 hours of estimated production time) x ($50.00 per hour) = $90.00, which is the estimated production cost of the job. Material costs, in this example the costs of the film and the developer, must be added to the estimated production cost to arrive at an estimated cost for process camera production for this job.

Estimators should have a thorough knowledge of BHR development and of the production standards specific to their plants. Without these two groups of data, accurate cost estimating is impossible. Also, as noted in Chapter 2, most CAE systems require establishing these two cores of data for system initialization.

3.2   Defining Production Centers, Production Components, and Operation Codes

A production center or a cost center is a working area in a printing plant where production activities are completed on a printing job. A cost center might be a printing press, a cutter or a folder in the bindery, an electronic prepress platform, or a light table. In printing production, most cost centers have employees who operate the equipment. As a job moves through a printing plant, numerous cost centers are used. Each adds incrementally to the final product's completion and cost. Standard production times and BHRs are used to charge customers based on the amount of time the job resides in each production center.

Within each production center the company must identify and define all production components, which are specific operations or activities performed in the center. In any given production center there may be a few or dozens or hundreds of production components; the number varies relative to the range of operations and job activities that can be completed in the center. For example, a single-color press may have three makeready production components identified as simple, average, and difficult levels. An electronic prepress production center may have a range of scanner input production components that are based on resolution of desired output, size of original, and type of scanner.

Once the company develops the production components of a production center, the components are assigned numbers and become known as operating or operation codes. The system of production centers and operation codes is important for three reasons. First, it provides a framework by which a data collection system can be established and used. Chapter 2 covers this subject in detail. Second, the system allows every production operation to be quantified based on time units so that estimating and scheduling activities can be performed. Third, identifying centers is essential to building BHRs used for estimating internal production costs of a customer's job.

3.3   Defining and Using Production Time Standards

Accurate cost estimating mandates that production standards, which are identified by operating codes for each cost center, are developed and used. As just discussed, a production standard is an hourly unit value that represents the average output of a particular operating area producing under specified conditions. Output can be measured as a quantity unit of material, such as sheets of paper, number of signatures, pounds of paper, or sheets of film. The hourly value then becomes a function of the number of units produced. The terms "production standards" and "standard production data" are used interchangeably. For example, the output of a printing press may be measured in the number of press sheets produced per hour, the number of press sheets per shift, or any other output per unit of time. Both output and time relationships vary with respect to the type of product produced and the relative speed and operating conditions of the equipment and personnel.

How Production Standards Are Used

Two common and interrelated methods of applying standards of production are used in the printing industry: one measures output per unit of time and one measures a value of time per output quantity. An example of the first production standard, which measures output per unit of time, is 6,000 sheets printed per hour for a lithographic sheetfed press. That is, in one sixty-minute time period on the press, 6,000 sheets of paper are printed. The second production standard, which measures time per output quantity, relates production on a decimal hour base. The last example of 6,000 sheets printed per hour may be converted to 0.1667 hour per 1,000 sheets or 0.1667 hour per M sheets. Calculation of this production standard is as follows:

1,000 sheets ÷ number of sheets/hour = number of hours/M sheets

Then substitute:

1,000 sheets ÷ 6,000 sheets/hour = 0.1667 hour/M sheets

If 0.1667 is used as the production standard, multiplying the number of sheets (in thousands) by the hours/M sheets (which is the production standard) yields the estimated production time. Thus, if 4,000 sheets were to be printed on this lithographic press at the production standard of 0.1667 hour/M sheets, the following calculation would apply:

4,000 sheets x 0.1667 hour/M sheets = 0.6668 hour

This answer translates to 40 minutes (0.6668 hour x 60 minutes/hour).

If the production standard is known as a value of time per output quantity, in this case 0.1667 hour/M sheets, the following formula can be used to convert it to a measure of output per unit of time:

1,000 ÷ number of hours/M sheets = number of sheets/hour

Then substitute:

1,000 ÷ 0.1667 hour/M sheets = 6,000 sheets/hour

It is important to remember that standard production data are averages of production and are based on all of the operating conditions for a specific piece of equipment or work area. Averages are necessary because equipment differs (much equipment sold in the printing industry contains optional devices that cause differences in output), because the skill levels of the various plant production employees differ, and because the criteria affecting the work produced on the equipment differ. Far too many small and unaccountable differences exist, even on a day-to-day basis with production employees, to allow such figures to be anything other than averages.

Categories of Production Standards

Five categories of production standards generally apply to any printing company: procedural, machine, manual, integrated, and performance. These standards are discussed in the following paragraphs.

Procedural Standards. Sometimes referred to as "technical standards," these standards state specifically the recognized technique or procedure for a given job, as well as the expected outcome. They are not time standards but serve as a framework for developing accurate time assignments. For example, the procedural standard for the proper exposure and development of a lithographic plate would include a step-by-step analysis of job components. The procedural standard for opaquing a line negative would include all component operations needed to complete the job successfully. Procedural standards define the job duties and expected outcomes as thoroughly as possible.

Machine Standards. These time standards are established specifically for automated production operations in which the significant portion of output is completed by machine operation and not manually. Examples of equipment that apply for machine standard rates are stand-alone units such as film processors and phototypesetting equipment of some kinds.

Manual Standards. These time standards are developed specifically for operations done entirely by hand with no aid from automated equipment. Many bindery operations, pasteup, and stripping are examples of operations to which manual standards would be applied.

Integrated Standards. Because printing manufacturing is essentially a combination of manual and automated operations, these standards apply more frequently than either the machine or manual types. These time standards are developed after procedural standards have been delineated. Integrated standards are by far the most difficult type of standard to develop accurately and require continual monitoring and reassessing on the part of production management.

Performance Standards. These are written standards that define and clarify each employee's tasks and represent a set of criteria against which employees are measured for work performance. In sum, performance standards describe the specific job duties and operating methods for each company employee. Although they are not time standards per se, they may include quantitative production information as one method of setting performance goals. From a human resource standpoint, it is generally agreed that an employee's job performance is a subjective matter covering a range of employee performance factors, not just factors for which quantified standards exist. Thus, it is important to use quantitative performance standards as one part of an employee's evaluation but not the only part.

Standardizing, Specializing, and Automating Printing Production

Due to the repetitive nature of manufacturing activity, success in printing production requires standardizing processes, which are generally undertaken to reduce costs. For many printers, such standardization lends itself naturally to the development of specialized products, which can then be manufactured more quickly and with higher quality as the process is automated. Thus, process standardization, product specialization, and automation are linked and interconnected for many printers.

Standardization of Process. Establishing thorough procedural standards for product and process provides for more efficient production. Such efficiency reduces the cost of manufacturing the product and eventually gives management a flexibility of price not enjoyed by competing printers who do not standardize. In sum, the more efficient the manufacturing operation, the more manufacturing costs can be reduced and the greater the competitive advantage for the company.

Process standardization relates to the equipment and to the employees who complete production operations. In recent years, the printing industry has been fortunate to have suppliers and equipment manufacturers who have researched, developed, and marketed hundreds of new products and equipment, most of them standardized for improved efficiency. Thus, when a printing company decides to purchase a rapid-access automatic film processor, it in effect standardizes film sizes, types of rapid-access films to be used, exposure times, and operational procedures. When a job is in production, the processor not only speeds film processing in the photographic area, it also requires that standard procedures be used for handling and exposing all film images. Such standardization has made photographic workflow simple and efficient, and the resultant film images are of excellent quality. Many other examples of standardized manufacturing processes, with accompanying standardized materials, can be found in the modem printing plant.

Product Standardization. Product standardization is the development of a group of products that have significant common elements yet unique characteristics. Some product standardization is due to equipment factors, and some is due to the increasing marketing interests of printing management with respect to product specialization. In terms of equipment, for example, web presses, which have fixed cutoffs, mandate that products remain within common size formats. Otherwise, extreme costs from high paper waste may result. Some bindery equipment is also manufactured only for specific product sizes.

Market Specialization in Printing Production. Both process and product standardization as discussed previously tend to be inextricably connected to market specialization in a growing number of successful printing companies. The growth of specialized product marketing, in which a certain type of product with perhaps slight variation is manufactured for a range of customers, has emerged as a key for success in the 1990s. In general, the more a product line is specialized, the greater the likelihood that standardizing production is possible, which provides a desired cost efficiency for the company.

Although standardization and specialization are connected in successful printing companies, they are also independent of each other. It is possible to specialize in a particular product or process and utilize little standardization, or to standardize greatly while attempting to meet every customer's total printing needs.

Automation of Printing Production. In the past ten years there has been an increasing use of production automation throughout the printing manufacturing process. In general, the use of automated systems tends to be a fairly significant capital investment cost up front, but its intent is to reduce labor costs in the long term. Common areas that have automation include materials handling in web and sheetfed production, film processing, electronic prepress production, and numerous binding and finishing operations. The cost of automated systems are built into the BHR, so the payback is spread out over the amount of time charged to customers.

One of the key reasons to automate is to ensure a specified level of product quality while increasing production throughput. Thus, automated equipment may modify production times significantly. This is an important reason to review production methods and production times yearly or more frequently.

3.4   Five Important "Rules of the Road" for Establishing and Using Production Standards and BHRs

The following rules are important to keep in mind regarding the development and use of production standards and BHRs.

Rule 1: Divide Production Areas into Specific Centers

When establishing BHRs and production times, the company should be divided into working production areas or production centers. As mentioned earlier, these centers typically consist of employees who operate equipment, but it is possible to have a center that is fully automated, such as a film processor, or completely manual. Centers are frequently defined by the square footage they occupy, which normally includes aisle space and adjacent storage area necessary for center operation. Using square footage as a basis for developing centers for BHRs assumes that the floor plan and workflow are efficient.

Rule 2: Tailor All Data to the Company's Production Conditions

All developed data for each production center should be tailored to the company's production methods, personnel, equipment, and operating procedures. This means that all quantified information—costs, times for production, equipment use, and so on—should be developed and tailored to company production. Although using the competition's standards or Blue Book Standards provides for comparison with other companies, it does not provide an accurate reflection of the specific costs incurred by the plant for which the standards were built.

Rule 3: *Review and Revise Standards and Costs at Least One Time per Year*

Given no significant changes in production methods or costs, reviewing production time standards and BHRs should be completed one time per year at minimum. The review should be thorough and detailed. In cases where major production or cost changes occur—equipment peripherals are added to existing equipment, software becomes faster, employee costs change, the plant layout is revised—the review should be completed when such changes occur. Of course, when completely new equipment is added to the current production capacity, initial standards and costs should be immediately established, even if the quantified data do not precisely represent production times or costs. If computerized job costing or time tracking systems are used to track production times and costs, reviewing and revising data can be done easily and frequently, perhaps every three months.

Rule 4: *Keep All Data Written and Secure*

All data should be written on paper and kept with a "master file," perhaps a notebook of written standards and BHRs, in a secure location. Working copies should be made for estimators, planners, schedulers, and others who typically use this information on a frequent basis. Because the information tends to be sensitive, copies should be assigned only to responsible employees who need them, and the copies should not be taken from the company nor photocopied for use by others inside or outside the company. Some companies claim that their tailor-made, company-specific production standards and BHRs are trade secrets. This is an attempt to stress the importance of keeping this information within the company.

Rule 5: *Share Information with Employees on a "Need to Know" Basis*

In general, production standards and BHRs are not secret, but they are sensitive company information that should not be available to all employees. Thus, this information should be controlled to those who need it to complete their daily jobs. Of course, production employees may wish to learn about company costs or the production times used for scheduling their work or costing their jobs. Sharing this information with them is acceptable—they have a "need to know" as a matter of personal interest—as long as it is clear to them that the information is sensitive and should not be discussed outside of the company. In such cases, the information should be verbally presented and explained; copies should not be made for distribution. The primary intent in sharing this information is to demonstrate trust in company employees.

3.5   Methods for Establishing Production Standards

There are six methods in the printing industry for establishing production standards. The comparison chart in Figure 3.1 shows the relative merits of each. The methods should be used in combination with one another when time and cost permit to ensure accuracy of data.

In some printing plants, establishing production standards is completed by an individual in estimating or production management. In other companies a group or a committee establishes the standards. For the most part, the people who are involved in the process are middle management staff with experience in the production aspects of the business. Such people have the best judgment regarding procedural and time standards.

Method 1: Standards Based on Historical Plant Data through Job Costing

The collection and review of historical plant data—the most popular of the six methods—utilizes job costing procedures. Job costing is a comparison of actual versus estimated times and costs and is done after the job is completed. Thus, for a job to be job costed, it requires that the job have: (1) a completed cost estimate and (2) a functional data collection system for gathering real-time data during production for all work done on the job.

The three primary purposes for completing job costing are to:

1. evaluate overall job and cost center profit or loss by comparing actual to estimated times and costs;
2. update existing production standards for greater estimating accuracy; and
3. track and charge for billable costs (e.g., AAs) approved by the customer during production so the customer can be invoiced for these charges. As discussed in Chapter 2, AAs are customer-approved work done on the job which are chargeable to the customer.

Job costing is completed before invoicing when a company wants to include AAs as part of the invoice. In such a case, job costing must be completed quickly and accurately enough to capture all AAs. If the primary reason for job costing is to update production standards or to study the job for profit or loss, the job costing process is less time compressed and can be done after the job is delivered. However, given the cost and time necessary to gather the data, and because AAs, particularly in prepress, may be significant, many companies that job cost do so before invoicing.

	Accuracy	Relative cost	Time needed	Outside experts or consultants	Impact on employees and production
1	Standards based on historical plant data through job costing	excellent (over time)	high (over time)	considerable	optional	may be extensive
2	Standards based on intuition	poor to terrible	low	modest to little	none	little
3	Standards based on published information	fair to good	low to moderate	little	none	little
4	Standards borrowed from the competition	varies (depends on production similarity)	low	modest	none	little
5	Standards based on equipment manufacturers' data	initially poor	low	little	yes	little
6	Standards based on plant engineering evaluation	excellent	expensive	considerable	sometimes	may be extensive

Figure 3.1 Comparison chart of six methods used for establishing production standards in printing

A general, step-by-step plan for establishing production standards using job costing follows:

1. Accurately collect data during production. Chapter 2 covers data collection methods and procedures in detail.
2. Analyze the collected data via variance report methods. This provides a comparison of actual versus estimated times and costs.
3. Based on the study of variances, overtime, and numerous jobs, adjust production standards to more accurately reflect true production output.

As suggested by Step 3, the job costing process requires continuing effort and attention. It is possible to review estimating times and costs using a manually generated variance report or computerized reports like the one shown in Figure 3.2. Computerized job costing is fast and convenient and provides important feedback.

Method 2: Standards Based on Intuition

Using intuition is a common procedure for establishing production standards in the printing industry, but this is not to say that the technique provides accuracy. Although the opposite is sometimes the case, this method is low in cost, very easy to complete, and has little impact on employees. Sometimes estimators and production planners use intuitive standards for a particularly complex manufacturing procedure or for a new piece of equipment when no other standards have been developed. Small printing plants also develop standards by intuition.

The major problem with basing production standards on intuition is that human nature gives each person an outlook that may not be realistic. People tend to assess quantifiable data in different ways and with different standards. The individual's personality has a significant bearing on the standards he establishes. Although it may be possible for a production manager to watch an employee carefully during a normal working situation and then establish standards based on such observations, the standards are not necessarily accurate or consistent.

Using the intuitive method as a cross-check or judgment check of other procedures is acceptable, especially if a standard appears grossly out of line. The observer should be thoroughly familiar with the procedural standards required for the job and should attempt to overlook personal feeling and bias while watching the individual performing the task. The working conditions should be as normal as possible. It is unwise to attempt to judge and assign a time value for a production sequence at the beginning or end of any shift or close to a break period. It is best to let employees know that they are being evaluated but that such results will have no impact on their jobs.

```
Watermark Press Ltd.
Job No: 33188                        Desc: ^Multiprotocal Inter:(Part.#:A1
Cust.:                               PO#:                 FOB:(2) Cust.
Slsmn:                               Due:  02/10/95  Shipped: 02/10/95
Planner:                             Date Booked: 02/02/95
Est. Sale:$2861    Quoted: Yes       Product:   65 6 color Half Size
Quantity: 3000     %Overs: 0.00      Estimate#:5100051 Mod#: 1 R#: 1 QT:1
Price/M: 953.57    RC:New Job         Target Sales$:2861   Value+ $:2358
Open/Closed Status:CLOSED            Includes open & closed transactions
Today 13:40 09/11/95                 Data updated thru: 09/10/95, #940442
-------------------------------------LABOR -------------------------------
Operation            Employee      Date  Units   Avg %Std  Hours   Cost
File Review          Ron Sunseri   02/02    3   6Min  92    0.3     26
Processing 2400 Text Ron Sunseri   02/02                    0.0      3
Processing 2400 Text Ron Sunseri   02/02                    0.2     16
Processing 2400 Text Stephen Balschi 02/08                  0.0      2
General Editing      Stephen Balschi 02/08                  0.2     20
Sub Total **Elec PrePress**                         92     0.8     65

Selectset 2400 Text  Select Set 5000 02/02    1  3Min 133   0.1      4
Selectset 2400 Text  Select Set 5000 02/08    1  3Min 133   0.1      4
Sub Total **Imagesetting**                         133     0.1      9

Press Sheet Rule Up  David Peltz   02/09    1  12Min  83    0.2     16
Press Sheet Rule Up  David Peltz   02/09    1   5Min 200    0.1      6
STRIP                David Peltz   02/02                    1.5    118
STRIP                Neil Woldman  02/08                    0.7     54
Sub Total **STRIPPING**                            117     2.4    194

BLUELINE             Ann Reichert  02/02   18   3Min 150    0.8     47

MAKE PLATES          Lisa Bell     02/07   12   3Min 200    0.6     35
MAKE PLATES          Lisa Bell     02/08    5   4Min 150    0.4     20
MAKE PLATES          Lisa Bell     02/08    9   5Min 120    0.7     39
Sub Total **PLATEMAKING**                          156     1.7     93

6/25 Feeder          Jerail Jackson 02/09                   0.5     0*

Makeready-Heid 6/25  Larry Minetti 02/09    6  24Min  71    2.4    569
Makeready-Heid 6/25  Anthony Clem  02/09    2  14Min 121    0.5    115
Makeready-Heid 6/25  Larry Minetti 02/09    1  18Min  94    0.3     72
Run 6/C - Heid 6/25  Anthony Clem  02/09 2600  7429   93    0.3     84
Run 6/C - Heid 6/25  Larry Minetti 02/09 2700  2288   29    1.2    283
Washup - Heid 6/25   Anthony Clem  02/09    2   9Min 139    0.3     72
DRYING TIME          Larry Minetti 02/09                    0.9    228
Sub Total ** Heid 6/25 **                           73     5.9   1423

MR Cutting           Eric Armstrong 02/10                   0.1      7
Cutting Post Press   Eric Armstrong 02/10                   0.1      8
Helper Cutting       Rudy Montoya  02/10                    0.1      7
Sub Total **Cutting**                                      0.3     22

Set Up Folder        Rudy Montoya  02/10                    0.4     28
Fold - LTR or 4pg    Ayewin Maung  02/10 5250 10294   86    0.5     34
Folder Helper        Ayewin Maung  02/10                    0.2     16
```

Figure 3.2 Sample computerized job cost report. (Reproduced with permission of Watermark Press, San Francisco, and Logic Associates, White River Junction, VT.)

Method 3: Standards Based on Published Information

Using standards based on published information is a valuable and an inexpensive way to obtain data. Published sources require little investigative time, no outside consultants (unless desired), and offer no impact on production or employees in the normal working situation. The single biggest problem with published standards is that they may not reflect the exact procedures used in a specific company, which makes extreme accuracy almost impossible. Regardless, published standards are a good cross-checking source for standards verification.

There are four major sources for published information. The first sources are national associations serving the printing industry, including PIA, NAPL, and the National Association of Quick Printers (NAQP). The PIA's published sources include Production Profit Targets and Production Benchmarks. Out-of-date publications from PIA, which are still found in some printing plants, are PIA-Production PAR and PIA Sim-PAR. Some of NAPL's published materials, which provide production standards, include *Increase Your Profits with Production Standards, Controlling Sheetfed Waste and Spoilage, Controlling Web Press Waste and Spoilage, An Overview of Waste and Spoilage in the Bindery*, and *Simple Scheduling Methods*. NAQP offers publications that relate exclusively to quick and small commercial printing production, including annual studies on copier and small press productivity.

The second sources for published standards are books and textbooks serving industry and education. The major advantages of these books are that they are inexpensive and fairly easy to obtain. Their primary disadvantage is that they sometimes address older technology and may not effectively cover current machines and newer technological processes.

The third sources of published information, ones that offer various amounts of standard production data plus articles on estimating and related topics, are trade magazines serving the graphic arts. Major monthly periodicals serving the broad-based commercial industry include *Graphic Arts Monthly, American Printer*, and *Printing Impressions*. Two magazines, *Quick Printing Magazine* and *Instant & Small Commercial Printer*, serve the quick printer with excellent articles, including many that address price list development and estimating and marketing issues. *High Volume Printing* directs its editorial and advertising efforts to the needs of the larger web and sheetfed printers. *In-Plant Reproductions Magazine* serves printing facilities within corporations.

The fourth and final sources are published catalogs and regional studies that contain both production standards and cost rates. The catalog in widest circulation is *The Franklin Catalog* (Porte Publishing Company, Salt Lake City, Utah), which is described in Chapter 1. Franklin is a system for pricing printing that contains various production standards as well. A number of PIA regional offices produce standards for their own geographic membership, equipment, and staffing considerations. Printing Industries Association of Southern California (PIA-SC) publishes the *Blue Book of Production Standards and Costs for the Printing Industry*, a reference source which is updated annually and is very popular among estimators and production planners in the southwestern United States. Other PIA regional offices, including Printing Industry of Ohio (PIO), Printing Industries Association of Texas, Printing Industries of Northern California (PINC), and Pacific Printing and Imaging Association (PPI), provide similar information for their memberships.

Published information on printing estimating, including production standards, must be scrutinized because the type of publication and its anticipated user have a great deal to do with the accuracy and reliability of the information. However, even though their accuracy may vary, published data are very modest in cost and, for the most part, require little time to obtain. Also, published sources are excellent sources to use when cross-checking against existing production standards and other estimating data.

Method 4: Standards Borrowed from the Competition

The problems noted in Chapter 1 that exist when pricing by competition are very much the same as those encountered when borrowing production data from the competition. Inaccurate data are possible because equipment and production techniques may not be the same. Also, gathering and verifying data are sometimes awkward. Although the cost of obtaining such information is low, and although there is little impact on plant production employees, the time needed to gather the data can fluctuate depending on the range and kind of competitive sources used.

In regions where large numbers of printing establishments exist, exchanging information between competitors is not uncommon. Typically the information is shared as employees move from one printing company to another—they take their previous employers' standards to their new companies. With quick printers and small commercial printers, equipment may vary somewhat but typically the time and hour rates are very similar. In larger commercial plants, which have many different avenues of production and different equipment, production data and hour rates are less similar and therefore exchange of data is less likely. Of course, when competitive pressures in a market niche are intense, the sharing of production standards and methods that is done between competing firms is much more closely scrutinized by printing management.

Opinion varies significantly with respect to how much production data should be shared among printers. Certainly one of the functions of the trade associations—PIA, NAPL, NAQP, and others—is to encourage the exchange of such information to better the industry. The International Association of Printing House Craftsmen (IAPHC), a social club for printing personnel from all phases of the industry with affiliate branches across the country, openly promotes such "sharing of knowledge."

Method 5: Standards Based on Equipment Manufacturers' Data

Equipment manufacturers are a source for production information when the purchase of a new piece of equipment is being considered. Small equipment items require a modest amount of standard data. The sellers of large printing equipment, however, usually offer potential purchasers extensive production standards to compare with the standards of competitive equipment. Sometimes equipment manufacturers are willing to develop comparison studies between existing equipment in the plant and the equipment under consideration for purchase. Usually these studies are done by sales representatives, sales teams, or, in cases of very large purchases, groups of staff consultants working for equipment manufacturers. Because the equipment manufacturers undertake these studies, the cost to the printing company is low.

The data generated and used by manufacturers are usually accurate and provide a good base from which to begin estimating once the equipment is operational. Of course, there may be a tendency on the part of the manufacturers to present the standard data under optimum or exaggerated conditions. For this reason, standard data generated by equipment manufacturers should be reevaluated following the break-in period of the equipment. Also, manufacturers will not include in their analyses of standard production data those less determinable conditions affecting the equipment, such as changes in markets, varying degrees of product quality, and differing training and skill levels of personnel operating the equipment. These factors may have tremendous bearing on production standards, and the manufacturer of a piece of equipment cannot possibly include such assessments.

Method 6: Standards Based on Plant Engineering Evaluation

This method for determining production standards, which is precise, is commonly used to initially establish production standards when a new piece of equipment is installed for use or when a company redesigns its manufacturing floor plan. Large printing companies use time and motion study methods to focus on maximizing production output. These large companies are more likely to be capable of affording the time and effort necessary to complete the process.

Time and motion study is implemented using a three-stage process which begins with redesigning production workflow, followed by motion study analysis, and then production time analysis. Engineers who are usually trained in mechanical engineering direct the study process. They must be knowledgeable of each piece of printing equipment to be used and of the nuances of printing manufacturing methods, as well as the development of time and motion study methods. The process can be complex.

The first step begins with a careful assessment of past and anticipated production output for existing and new equipment to be used. It is followed with the development of a new manufacturing floor plan. Although usually the main objective of redesigning the floor plan is to increase production output, many other issues, including human factors for employees who will work in the redesigned area, are involved. Once the new production floor plan is checked thoroughly, equipment is moved physically into this new production layout. Because moving highly technical and sensitive equipment such as presses is complex and incurs costs, there is a considerable study and evaluation period prior to actually moving equipment when many options are considered. Because production is completely shut down during the move, which is costly, the time for physical movement is normally as compressed as possible.

Once the manufacturing floor plan is operable, motion study methods are employed in the second step. Motion study is a procedure by which a particular job or job sequence is broken down into its component elements and is analyzed in terms of movements. Motion study uses charts, graphs, and photography to break all operations into their detailed operational components. Human tasks are also carefully evaluated. A major objective of this step is to simplify the employee's job task so she can produce more product in less time and with less physical activity. All methods to produce the same product are investigated, with emphasis on efficiency improvement. Such operations analysis is particularly useful in manufacturing areas that require considerable handwork and the establishment of manual standards, such as the binding and finishing areas of a printing plant. This analysis is also used for establishing integrated standards. The overall intention is to streamline procedures and techniques to make them more efficient.

Once the best, most efficient movement method has been developed and tested, time study may be used to establish standard production times. Standard times are developed for each hand or body movement, for an entire sequence of movements, or for an entire production operation. This task requires the services of a knowledgeable time study engineer as well as those of a methods engineer. The latter services are typically found in a professional mechanical engineer. If a specialized small printing facility considers motion and time analysis, it should also consider hiring a consulting engineer to complete the job. Rarely does the printing manager have the tools, skills, or time necessary to effectively perform this task. Because the cost of the study can be high, the expected cost savings over time should be considered in relation to the cost of the engineer or consultant. Sometimes this cost-effective determination is difficult to make, however.

Motion and time study may not be popular with plant employees. Generally, employees oppose detailed study of their work situations using micromotion analysis, flowcharts, and videotapes. Thus, plant employees should be informed well in advance of any such study. Perhaps incentives could also be provided for their cooperation. If employees are not notified, a work stoppage or slowdown might result. When the announcement is made, it should be pointed out that no individual will be singled out for study. The methods/time engineer, with the aid of management and employees, selects and studies a sample of a size that is sufficient to develop reliable standard data for the company.

Motion and time study is one of the most exacting methods by which plant production standards can be established. It is also expensive, time consuming, and may have undesirable effects on the company labor force.

3.6 Keeping Production Standards Current

It is common for changes in production techniques, equipment, and personnel to occur as time passes. These changes require modification of standard production data. Continuously using job costing and data collection methods provides the necessary updating of these standards.

The following alterations represent the usual range of changes that necessitate revising standards:

- adding new equipment or laborsaving devices to existing equipment to increase output in the plant
- adopting new materials that expedite production or modify the quality of the product
- making any physical change or modifying a product
- undergoing greater specialization
- changing the flow of production because of any revision of the physical plant (e.g., implementing a new layout in the existing or new building, selling a specific process to another printer, making changes that modify production lines and procedures)
- changing the mix of materials on the buyout list, thereby reducing output of products in the plant
- increasing experience levels of shop personnel through additional or improved on-the-job training

Every few years it is desirable to fully review the entire plant's production center setup and its related production components and operation codes. In addition, at this time it is prudent to review production workflow to be certain that the most efficient production methods and sequences are being used.

3.7   **Developing BHRs**

Developing and using BHRs, sometimes termed machine hour rates (MHRs) or all-inclusive hour rates (AIHRs), is a common procedure in the commercial printing industry and in high-volume printers; it is growing in acceptance among smaller commercial printers and quick printers. The intent of the procedure is to accurately recover all costs incurred in the production, sales, and administration of the printed product. The procedure includes many cost areas for which the customer must pay: equipment, rent and heat, labor, and support labor, among others. The cost of materials and outside purchases are not recovered by the BHR process, but are determined and added separately during estimating.

The BHRs, when used for cost recovery, must be accurately determined so the customer is not overcharged or undercharged for cost items. If the customer is charged too much, prices will be too high and will threaten to reduce volume in the plant, which might lead to layoffs and other negative actions. If the customer is charged too little, prices will be too low and perhaps no profit will be made. Thus, using BHRs is a "fine-line" procedure of cost determination. In sum, BHRs must, as accurately as possible, reflect the costs the company incurs and the customer pays without inflating or minimizing either cost.

As detailed in Chapter 1, the usual cost estimating procedure includes breaking the job into operational components and then assigning standard production times to each operation. The cost estimating formula is:

estimated cost to produce the job = (standard production time x BHR) + material costs + buyout costs

Because each manufacturing segment of the production plan requires different equipment and different employee skills, separate cost rates must be developed to reflect these differences. If the estimated time is accurate and the BHR provides for all operational costs incurred in the production area, then the product of the two figures (estimated time x BHR) represents the manufacturing cost of the product. Along with the costs of paper, ink, film, and plates, which are substantial, the costs of materials whose use can be noted and quantified in the manufacture of a particular product are added to the manufacturing cost. Other materials that are more difficult to identify with any one job, such as solvents, industrial towels, and lithographic blankets, are included in the BHR recovery system. For a halftone in a process camera center, the following formula would apply:

total cost for halftone = (estimated time to expose and process one halftone x BHR) + (film and chemistry costs)

The initial establishment of a BHR system should be completed by someone familiar and experienced with variations of the procedure—a company accountant, a production management staff member or estimator, a team of plant personnel who are each knowledgeable in a certain area, or outside consultants. Various industry associations have extensive experience with BHRs and have personnel knowledgeable in the installation of such procedures.

General Rules for BHR Use

There are some general rules for using BHRs. First, it is most important that each plant develop and use its own individual cost figures when starting its BHR procedure. This is because costs can vary extensively due to many factors that act on production, such as company finances, purchasing methods for equipment, and depreciation. For example, assume that Plant A and Plant B have the same model of lithographic press. Plant A has purchased its press outright with inherited capital (no interest charges), has located it in a building with low rent (but in a bad area of town, which increases fire and sprinkler insurance costs), and pays an operator $18.50 per hour (no fringe benefits) to run it. Plant B, on the other hand, is financing its press over five years, has located it in a building with high rent (but excellent fire protection), and pays an operator $12.25 per hour (with paid health insurance). Clearly each company has different cost values for the same press, so the calculated BHR for each is different. The point is that accurate BHRs are possible only when they are tailored to fit the company. Costs simply vary too much to be applied generally.

Many electronic MISs for printing contain ready-to-run software that quickly and accurately calculates BHRs once the printer provides the necessary basic cost information. When this software is used, it is possible for the printer to update BHRs frequently—perhaps monthly—and to adjust them for variations in chargeable hours, wages, and so on. Computerized systems save time for company staff who would normally develop such BHRs manually. They also allow for quick and easy storage of BHRs, but it is suggested that they also be written down or printed out for backup protection.

General Steps in BHR Development

Because electronic spreadsheet programs are simple, available, and accurate, they are commonly used to complete BHRs. Any commercially developed spreadsheet format, such as Microsoft Excel® or Lotus 1-2-3®, works for this purpose. The following discusses the development of BHRs by spreadsheet and assumes the reader has a general knowledge of spreadsheet methods. Chapter 2 provides an overview of number crunching and spreadsheet methods for reference.

When building spreadsheet BHRs from scratch, the process begins by carefully building a master spreadsheet format similar to the one in Figure 3.3. Next, one company center is chosen and specifications are developed to represent that center. In the next step, the BHR is manually calculated, line by line, and is followed with the electronic development of the spreadsheet, which is carefully checked against the manually calculated BHR. Once the BHR is built and checked for accuracy, it can be copied and used to develop all other company BHRs. Figures 3.3 through 3.8 were completed using spreadsheet software and appear as they do on the computer screen.

Step-by-Step BHR Development for a Komori 1-Color Press

As just noted, Figure 3.3 is a blank BHR sheet in spreadsheet format. In spreadsheets, letters are used for columns and numbers are used for rows. They intersect to identify a specific location—or cell—on the spreadsheet. In Figure 3.3, Column A details the fifty-four lines necessary to complete the BHR process. Cell A1 has a blank line where the production center title could be written. (See the following Center Identification (Column A) section). Cell A8 is the eighth row of the A column and shows "Wage scale 1."

Spreadsheet cells may be alphanumeric like the ones in Figure 3.3 or they may contain only text or only numbers. The number formats may be percentages, dollar figures, or any other number values, including decimals. Cells can be related mathematically using addition, subtraction, multiplication, division, or combinations of these functions. These functions allow the spreadsheet to be an extremely powerful mathematical tool. As long as a spreadsheet formula is properly written, mathematical computations are extremely fast and error free.

Figure 3.4 is a completed BHR form for a 1-color, 20 inch x 26 inch Komori S26 lithographic press. Figure 3.5 is the identical spreadsheet reconfigured to show the formulas and calculations necessary to achieve the figures in Figure 3.4. The text that follows describes how Figure 3.4 is developed and references both Figure 3.4 and Figure 3.5. Figure 3.4 is the primary focus of discussion; references to Figure 3.5 are cited as needed. All dollar amounts, percentages, and other numerical data are for example only and are not intended to represent any printing company. To ease their use, the spreadsheets in this book contain grid lines and row/column alphanumeric references. However, one or both of these reference aids can be easily removed.

Center Identification (Column A). As discussed earlier, Cell A1 of this column identifies that the BHR to be generated is for a production center titled "Komori S26, 20x26, 1/C press." As mentioned earlier, a production center is a defined area of production for some portion of the printed product. The production center must be properly identified, defined, and titled. It may contain one piece of equipment operated by one employee, one piece of equipment operated by a complement of employees, or one employee working without a piece of equipment.

	A	B	C	D	E	F
1	**BUDGETED HOUR COST RATE** Center title: _____	Calculation method or basis	Total company	General factory overhead	Selling and adminstrative overhead	Annual center cost (one shift)
2	CENTER SPECIFICATIONS					
3	Investment cost/equipment value					
4	Number of employees in center					
5	Square feet of working area					
6	Total motor horsepower					
7	Wattage requirements					
8	Wage scale 1					
9	Wage scale 2					
10	Wage scale 3					
11	Paid days off: Sum vacation days and holidays					
12	Weekly hours paid					
13	Annual hours paid					
14	FIXED COSTS (ANNUAL)					
15	Fixed overhead (sq. ft.)					
16	Insurance (Per $1,000 investment cost)					
17	Property taxes (Per $100 investment cost)					
18	Depreciation 1 (33% investment)					
19	Depreciation 2 (10% straight or other method)					
20	Cost of new software (estimate for year)					
21	Center R & D activities (estimate for year)					
22	Training and retraining costs (estimate for year)					
23	TOTAL FIXED COSTS					
24	VARIABLE COSTS (ANNUAL)					
25	Direct labor cost, No. 1					
26	Direct labor cost, No. 2					
27	Direct labor cost, No. 3					
28	Total cost: Direct labor					
29	Cost of indirect labor (20% direct labor)					
30	Total direct and indirect labor cost					
31	Employee taxes and benefits (direct plus indirect)					
32	Overhead lighting cost (kWh)					
33	Electrical power cost (kWh)					
34	Wattage cost (kWh)					
35	Department supplies (8% total labor)					
36	Repairs (2% investment cost)					
37	TOTAL VARIABLE COSTS					
38						
39	Total fixed and variable costs					
40						
41	Prorate: General factory overhead					
42						
43	TOTAL FACTORY COST					
44						
45	Prorate: Administration and selling overhead					
46						
47	TOTAL ANNUAL CENTER COST					
48		Chargeable hours				
49	Manufacturing cost @ 80%					
50	Manufacturing cost @ 70%					
51	Manufacturing cost @ 60%					
52	BHR cost @ 80%					
53	BHR cost @ 70%					
54	BHR cost @ 60%					

Figure 3.3 Blank BHR form

	A	B	C	D	E	F
1	BUDGETED HOUR COST RATE Center title: Komori S26, 20x26, 1/C press	Calculation method or basis	Total company	General factory overhead	Selling and adminstrative overhead	Annual center cost (one shift)
2	CENTER SPECIFICATIONS					
3	Investment cost/equipment value		$2,600,000	$24,000	$72,000	$125,000
4	Number of employees in center		24	2	6	1
5	Square feet of working area		4,600	350	600	150
6	Total motor horsepower					6.2
7	Wattage requirements					0
8	Wage scale 1			$9.00		$18.50
9	Wage scale 2			$7.50		$0.00
10	Wage scale 3					$0.00
11	Paid days off: Sum vacation days and holidays					20
12	Weekly hours paid		40	40	40	40
13	Annual hours paid			2,080	2,080	2,080
14	FIXED COSTS (ANNUAL)					
15	Fixed overhead (sq. ft.)	$3.00		$1,050	$1,800	$450
16	Insurance (Per $1,000 investment cost)	$3.00		$72	$216	$375
17	Property taxes (Per $100 investment cost)	$1.25		$300	$900	$1,563
18	Depreciation 1 (33% investment)	33%				
19	Depreciation 2 (10% straight or other method)	10%		$2,400	$7,200	$12,500
20	Cost of new software (estimate for year)	estimate cost				$500
21	Center R & D activities (estimate for year)	estimate cost				$2,500
22	Training & retraining costs (estimate for year)	estimate cost			$4,000	$2,000
23	TOTAL FIXED COSTS			$3,822	$14,116	$19,888
24	VARIABLE COSTS (ANNUAL)					
25	Direct labor cost, No. 1	scale*annual hrs		$18,720	$320,000	$38,480
26	Direct labor cost, No. 2	scale*annual hrs		$15,600		$0
27	Direct labor cost, No. 3	scale*annual hrs				$0
28	Total cost: Direct labor			$34,320	$320,000	$38,480
29	Cost of indirect labor (20% direct labor)	20%		$6,864	$64,000	$7,696
30	Total direct and indirect labor cost			$41,184	$384,000	$46,176
31	Employee taxes and benefits (direct plus indirect)	30%		$12,355	$115,200	$13,853
32	Overhead lighting cost (kWh)	$0.10		$218	$374	$94
33	Electrical power cost (kWh)	$0.10				$962
34	Wattage cost (kWh)	$0.10				$0
35	Department supplies (8% total labor)	8%		$3,295	$30,720	$3,694
36	Repairs (2% investment cost)	2%		$480	$1,440	$2,500
37	TOTAL VARIABLE COSTS			$57,532	$531,734	$67,279
38						
39	Total fixed and variable costs			$61,354	$545,850	$87,166
40						
41	Prorate: General factory overhead	% investment				$2,950
42						
43	TOTAL FACTORY COST					$90,116
44						
45	Prorate: Administration and selling overhead	% investment				$26,243
46						
47	TOTAL ANNUAL CENTER COST					$116,359
48		Chargeable hours				
49	Manufacturing cost @ 80%	1,536.00				$58.67
50	Manufacturing cost @ 70%	1,344.00				$67.05
51	Manufacturing cost @ 60%	1,152.00				$78.23
52	BHR cost @ 80%	1,536.00				$75.75
53	BHR cost @ 70%	1,344.00				$86.58
54	BHR cost @ 60%	1,152.00				$101.01

Figure 3.4 BHR form for one-color Komori S26 lithographic press

As a printing job moves through a company, numerous production centers perform work on that job and time is tracked for production. The cost of each production center is calculated by multiplying the time needed for the production center by the BHR for that center. The total cost of the job is the sum of all final values for the customer's job.

Calculation Method or Basis (Column B). This column lists the dollar values or percentages necessary for calculating the noted item. The figures used in this

	A	B	C	D	E	F
1	BUDGETED HOUR COST RATE	Calculation method or basis	Total company	General factory overhead	Selling and admin. overhead	Annual center cost
2	CENTER SPECIFICATIONS					
3	Investment cost/equipment value		2600000	24000	72000	125000
4	Number of employees in center		24	2	6	1
5	Square feet of working area		4600	350	600	150
6	Total motor horsepower					6.2
7	Wattage requirements					0
8	Wage scale 1			9		18.5
9	Wage scale 2			7.5		0
10	Wage scale 3					0
11	Paid days off: Sum vacation days and holidays					20
12	Weekly hours paid		40	40	40	40
13	Annual hours paid			=D12*52	=E12*52	=F12*52
14	FIXED COSTS (ANNUAL)					
15	Fixed overhead (sq. ft.)	3		=D5*B15	=E5*B15	=F5*$B$15
16	Insurance (Per $1,000 investment cost)	3		=D3/1000*B16	=E3/1000*B16	=F3*$B$16/1000
17	Property taxes (Per $100 investment cost)	1.25		=D3/100*B17	=E3/100*B17	=F3*$B$17/100
18	Depreciation 1 (33% investment)	0.33				=F3*$B$18
19	Depreciation 2 (10% straight or other method)	0.1		=D3*B19	=E3*B19	=F3*$B$19
20	Cost of new software (estimate for year)	estimate cost				500
21	Center R & D activities (estimate for year)	estimate cost				2500
22	Training & retraining costs (estimate for year)	estimate cost			4000	2000
23	TOTAL FIXED COSTS			=SUM(D15:D22)	=SUM(E15:E22)	=SUM(F15:F22)
24	VARIABLE COSTS (ANNUAL)					
25	Direct labor cost, No. 1	scale*annual hrs		=D8*D13	320000	=F8*F13
26	Direct labor cost, No. 2	scale*annual hrs		=D9*D13		=F9*F13
27	Direct labor cost, No. 3	scale*annual hrs				=F10*F13
28	Total cost: Direct labor			=SUM(D25:D27)	=E25+E26+E27	=F25+F26+F27
29	Cost of indirect labor (20% direct labor)	0.2		=D28*B29	=E28*B29	=F28*$B$29
30	Total direct and indirect labor cost			=D28+D29	=E28+E29	=F28+F29
31	Employee taxes and benefits (direct plus indirect)	0.3		=D30*B31	=E30*B31	=F30*$B$31
32	Overhead lighting cost (kWh)	0.1		=(D5*D13*3*B32)/1000	=E5*E13*3*B32/1000	=(F5*F13*3*$B$32)/1000
33	Electrical power cost (kWh)	0.1				=(F6*F13*0.746)*$B$33
34	Wattage cost (kWh)	0.1				=(F7*F13*$B$34/1000)*0.5
35	Department supplies (8% total labor)	0.08		=D30*B35	=E30*B35	=F30*$B$35
36	Repairs (2% investment cost)	0.02		=D3*B36	=E3*B36	=F3*$B$36
37	TOTAL VARIABLE COSTS			=SUM(D30:D36)	=SUM(E30:E36)	=SUM(F30:F36)
38						
39	Total fixed and variable costs			=D23+D37	=E23+E37	=F23+F37
40						
41	Prorate: General factory overhead	% investment				=F3/$C$3*$D$39
42						
43	TOTAL FACTORY COST					=SUM(F39+F41)
44						
45	Prorate: Administration and selling overhead	% investment				=F3/$C$3*E39
46						
47	TOTAL ANNUAL CENTER COST					=SUM(F43+F45)
48		Chargeable hours				
49	Manufacturing cost @ 80%	=(F13-(F12/5)*F11)*0.8				=F43/$B$49
50	Manufacturing cost @ 70%	=(F13-(F12/5)*F11)*0.7				=F43/$B$50
51	Manufacturing cost @ 60%	=(F13-(F12/5)*F11)*0.6				=F43/$B$51
52	BHR cost @ 80%	=(F13-(F12/5)*F11)*0.8				=F47/$B$52
53	BHR cost @ 70%	=(F13-(F12/5)*F11)*0.7				=F47/$B$53
54	BHR cost @ 60%	=(F13-(F12/5)*F11)*0.6				=F47/$B$54

Figure 3.5 Spreadsheet formulas showing Figure 3.4 BHR development

column must be tailored to actual company costs and therefore change from company to company. Spreadsheet calculations draw on these figures, each of which appears in its own cell. For example, Figure 3.4 shows Cell A15 to be "Fixed overhead (sq. ft.)," which identifies the cost area, and Cell B15 to be $3.00, which notes the cost basis upon which calculations are made. Any stand-alone number in the B column is mathematically applied using spreadsheet formulas.

All numerical figures appearing in the Calculation method or basis column (Column B) should be carefully determined from the company's accounting records. Spreadsheets cannot mathematically relate words, so when words and not numbers appear in this column, they merely indicate the necessary method or procedure to be used. Details of how the calculations are completed are provided in the line-by-line analysis that follows.

Total Company (Column C). This column identifies total company investment cost as well as other essential information, such as total number of employees. Cell C3 of Figure 3.4 shows a total company investment of $2,600,000, Cell C4 shows there are 24 employees in the production center, and Cell C5 shows production covers a 4,600 square foot area in the company. As mentioned earlier, this is a fictitious company, for example only.

General Factory Overhead (Column D). This column represents all shared or common areas used by company employees, thus the term "general factory." For this example general factory areas include the employee lunchroom or cafeteria, bathrooms, immediate storage areas that are not part of a specific production center, vehicle and driver costs for a company messenger or delivery service, and janitorial services for these areas. A proration method is used to divide and distribute general factory overhead so that each production center in the company pays a portion of this expense. As is noted in Cell F41, the general factory overhead to be paid by this Komori press center is $2,950. The specific calculation process is covered when Line 41 is addressed later in this chapter.

Selling and Administrative Overhead (Column E). This column covers the cost of sales representatives and administrative support of the product, including sales representative and executive salaries, company-paid autos, and related sales and administrative expenses. Anticipated sales commission draws are included for all sales representatives and executives, but sales commissions are not included. Cell E25 shows a direct labor cost of $320,000, which supports the six company sales and management employees in Cell E4.

The Komori press must pay a portion of the cost burden of these sales and administrative employees. This portion, which Cell F45 shows is $26,243, is prorated based on a developed percentage of investment method. The proration method is explained in detail when Line 45 is addressed later in this chapter.

Annual Center Cost (One Shift) (Column F). This column contains only numeric figures, which are either provided as specifications or as mathematically calculated dollars. As the column title suggests, the cost data are based on one shift's use of the press. Round dollar figures are used to simplify the mathematics.

Shaded areas of the column represent center specifications that change for each center. These areas include Cells F3 through F13 and Cells F20 through F22. (In Column B, Cells B18 and B19 are also shaded.) Nonshaded areas in Column F require either a specific numeric entry or a formula that calculates the dollar amount in the cell.

When the spreadsheet is fully built and error free, only the shaded areas require data changes. The spreadsheet program automatically completes the calculations. A spreadsheet can thus be an extremely useful tool to evaluate "what if" cost situations for a company, which is sometimes necessary when considering a new piece of equipment, a fringe benefit increase, a change in working time for employees, and so on.

Line-by-Line Analysis of Figure 3.4

The following provides detailed information for each line of Figure 3.4; references to Figure 3.5 are provided as needed. The general working procedure is line by line from top to bottom of the spreadsheet. As just discussed, all shaded areas represent data that change with each cost center. Again, Figure 3.5 shows the formulas used to achieve the final answers in Figure 3.4.

Center Specifications (Lines 3 through 13). The specifications of the production center establish the parameters of the center and provide a basis on which to establish the BHR. The specifications, which appear shaded in Cells F3 through F13, should be carefully determined and tailored to the company's actual operating conditions. Specifications must be determined individually for each production center in the plant.

Investment Cost/Equipment Value (Line 3). This line should include all installation costs and the cost of any peripherals. In general, three types of dollar figures could be used here, each representing a different view of how the company wishes to recover its costs:

1. Full investment cost regardless of the age of the equipment ensures the dollar figure remains the same every year.
2. Depreciated cost, which diminishes as the equipment is used or becomes older, effectively reduces the dollar figure by the depreciated amount each year.

3. Replacement cost value is a consideration as the time for replacing the equipment approaches.

Arguments can be advanced for each of these three approaches and it is management's task to decide which approach to use. Full investment cost, if it is used unchanged each time the BHR is calculated, inflates the actual value of the equipment because older, depreciated equipment is worth less. Using a full investment cost basis thus also inflates the BHR because it recovers dollars that have been written off. In sum, when full investment cost is used, the BHR is inflated, which makes the company less competitive. Using full investment cost can be significant in centers that require high capitalization costs. Cell F3 on Line 3 of Figure 3.4 shows the investment cost basis for this Komori press is $125,000.

In contrast to using a full investment cost basis, using a depreciated cost basis lowers the investment amount to a level that realistically reflects the company's investment. However, it does not take into account the expensive replacement of equipment that will be necessary at some point.

Number of Employees in Center (Line 4). This line indicates the number of employees who work in the center. There may be a fraction of a person when multiple pieces of equipment are operated simultaneously by one employee, or there may be more than one person if a crew is necessary to operate the center. Cell F4 on Line 4 in Figure 3.4 shows that this press requires one operator.

Square Feet of Working Area (Line 5). This is the actual measured floor space the press occupies, including the storage and aisle space necessary for daily operation of the press. Cell F5 on Line 5 in Figure 3.4 shows that this press occupies 150 square feet.

It should be noted that a common assumption among printing company owners is that their printing plants utilize efficient production flows and that the floor space taken up by each piece of equipment approaches what would be ideal. Unfortunately, this assumption is frequently incorrect. When a new piece of equipment is bought, it is common practice to first casually and arbitrarily decide how much floor space it requires, then to install the piece of equipment and never rethink this decision. It is wise for plant owners to periodically review their production flows and equipment square footage allocations to ensure efficient production and maximum use of expensive floor space.

Total Motor Horsepower (Line 6). Total motor horsepower (hp) is determined from equipment data or from specification plates that are attached to the motor on the press or another piece of equipment. If more than one motor is used in the production center, or if some motors operate at different rates or times than others, a weighting factor should be used to determine hp demand.

Cell F6 on Line 6 of Figure 3.4 shows that a 6.2 hp motor is needed. This figure is used to calculate the cost of electrical power cost on Line 33.

Wattage Requirements (Line 7). The figure on this line is the input wattage requirement of the high-intensity light sources that are used to expose photographic materials. These sources include cameras, contact frames, and plate-making equipment, but they do not include the overhead or general area lighting equipment which is covered under Fixed overhead (sq. ft.) on Line 15.

In Figure 3.4, Cell F7 on Line 7 shows 0 wattage requirements. However, should any piece of equipment be fitted with a peripheral electric device, the wattage amount would be indicated here. For example, if this press were retrofitted with an electric ink drying unit, a wattage amount would be indicated. Line 7 wattage is used to calculate Line 34 wattage cost in kilowatt-hours (kWhs).

Wage Scales 1, 2, and 3 (Lines 8 through 10). These lines identify the hourly rates of pay for each person with direct working responsibility in the production center. These wage scales do not include fringe benefits, which are calculated separately in Cell F31 on Line 31 of Figure 3.4 as a percentage of the gross annual labor cost. More than one wage scale is provided for centers that require crew components. Cell F8 on Line 8 shows one employee earning $18.50 per hour. There are no other employees in the center, so Cells F9 and F10 on Lines 9 and 10 respectively are $0.

Paid Days Off: Sum Vacation Days and Holidays (Line 11). This line represents the total amount of days of company-paid time off the employee(s) in the production center receive. This time includes paid vacation, holidays, sick leave, and jury duty if provided by the company. If more than one employee works in the center, an average for all center employees is used. Cell F11 on Line 11 of Figure 3.4 shows the one employee in this example receives 20 paid days off, which could be broken down into any mix of days off with pay that totals 20, such as 10 paid holidays and 10 vacation days.

Weekly Hours Paid (Line 12). This line carries the number of hours per week the employee is paid for working in the production center. Cell F12 on Line 12 of Figure 3.4 shows the one employee working in this center works a 40-hour week. No overtime is included in this BHR calculation, nor is any additional shift use of the center. Both overtime and multiple shifts affect center cost and BHR rates, which are discussed later in this chapter.

Annual Hours Paid (Line 13). The figure on this line is calculated by multiplying the number in Cell F12 by 52 weeks per year. It represents the maximum amount of hours the employee is paid for the year, including vacation and holiday hours because these hours are paid by the company. Cell F13 on Line 13 of Figure 3.4 shows this number is 2,080 (40 hours per week x 52 weeks per year).

Four points are important to mention regarding cell formulas and calculations. First, when a formula is built in a spreadsheet, an equals sign (=) is used to begin the cell formula and is a standard notation that a mathematical equation follows. The equation being built may draw on the other cells in the spreadsheet, which are referenced by letters and numbers such as F15 and B15, or a number can be entered into the cell by the operator.

Second, when a dollar sign ($) appears before a cell column and row, such as $B$15, the cell reference is fixed to that cell and no others. This is important when spreadsheet cells are copied and moved because cells that do not contain dollar signs shift references to their new locations. Thus, any cell letter or number that is preceded by a dollar sign never changes its line or column cell position and keeps its reference position absolute.

Third, the multiplication operation in spreadsheet cells is initiated by an asterisk (*), division by a slanted line (/), addition by a plus sign (+), and subtraction by a minus sign (-). These symbols are typically found on the numeric keypad portion of a computer keyboard.

Fourth, preestablished rounding rules for spreadsheets use the following protocol: Any number that is 50 or greater, such as 50¢, is rounded up to the next number (or dollar), and any number that is 49 or less is rounded down to the current number (or dollar). For example, if a dollar amount were calculated to be $456.55 and the spreadsheet cell was set to round to whole dollars, the spreadsheet would round this amount to $457.00. Given this, when spreadsheet cells are defaulted to calculate dollars in whole dollar amounts, it is possible that numbers may be rounded higher or lower than the actual amount when calculated to the penny. This is normal rounding protocol and has marginal effect on the final outcome of the spreadsheet answers.

Fixed Costs (Annual) (Lines 15 through 23). Fixed costs are defined as costs that remain constant over a period of time—they do not change when production changes in the production center. For example, the cost of insurance for the Komori press in Figure 3.4, which is paid as part of the company's annual fire and sprinkler insurance premium and which may also include business interruption insurance, is a fixed annual dollar amount and is not affected by the volume of production completed in the center over the premium period.

Fixed Overhead (Sq. Ft.) (Line 15). Fixed overhead provides for the recovery of all fixed costs necessary to maintain the environment in the production center. Included are rent, heating and air conditioning, and general utility costs such as water, sewer, and natural gas. Any electrical power costs used to maintain the general center environment should be included as well. However, power requirements for specific equipment operation are considered a variable cost and are recovered on Lines 32 through 34.

As the specifications in Figure 3.4 indicate (shaded Cells F3 through F13), the

Komori press requires 150 square feet of plant area (Cell F5) and the production center environment is maintained around the clock. Using a cost per square foot of $3.00 (Cell B15), the total annual cost for fixed overhead for this press is $3.00 x 150 sq. ft. = $450 (Cell F15).

The $3.00 per square foot basis (Cell B15) is normally derived by summing the company's annual environment and rent costs for all production areas, then dividing the resulting figure by the total number of square feet of production space. Sales, administrative, and shared areas should be excluded from this analysis because their costs are recovered using General factory overhead (Column D) and Selling and administrative overhead (Column E).

As has been mentioned earlier, Figure 3.5 is presented in this text to facilitate the development of spreadsheets. Cell F15 on Line 15 of Figure 3.5 shows the formula for calculating the $450 annual center cost in Cell F15 on Line 15 of Figure 3.4: =F5*$B$15. Cell F5 of Figure 3.5 shows 150 square feet and Cell B15 shows $3.00.

Insurance (Per $1,000 Investment Cost) (Line 16). This line covers the cost of premiums for fire and sprinkler insurance and for business interruption insurance if it is provided by the company. Cell B16 on Line 16 of Figure 3.4 shows a premium cost of $3.00 for each $1,000 of production center investment. To calculate the figure in Cell F16 of Figure 3.4, use the corresponding formula in Cell F16 on Line 16 of Figure 3.5: =F3*$B$16/1000, which is (Cell F3) x [(Cell B16) ÷ 1,000] or $125,000 x [($3.00) ÷ $1,000] or $125,000 x 0.003 = $375.

Property Taxes (Per $100 Investment Cost) (Line 17). This line provides for the recovery of the cost of property taxes to be paid on the production center investment. When used, the formula should reflect the method or procedure used for property tax payments in the area or region where the company is located. Cell B17 on Line 17 of Figure 3.4 shows a tax base of $1.25 per each $100 of investment cost. To calculate the figure in Cell F17 of Figure 3.4, use the corresponding formula in Cell F17 of Figure 3.5: =F3*$B$17/100, which is (Cell F3) x [(Cell B17) ÷ 100] or $125,000 x [($1.25) ÷ $100] or $125,000 x 0.0125 = $1,562.50. The final amount is rounded up to $1,563 using spreadsheet rounding protocol.

Depreciation 1 (33% Investment) and Depreciation 2 (10% Straight or Other Method) (Lines 18 and 19). Depreciation is the method by which owners are compensated for the wear and tear of their equipment or software over time. In other words, the depreciation process is the way the owner of the equipment is compensated for his investment risk. The cost basis for depreciation may be the equipment's new, depreciated, or replacement cost. If equipment is leased by the company, the annual cost of the lease is used as the depreciated amount, and it is entered in Cell F18 or F19. In sum, whether the cost basis is in depreciated dollars (from ownership) or in out-of-pocket dollars paid for leasing, the amount used represents a dollar amount to be paid back to the owners or lessors.

Two depreciation percentage rates are used here: 33 percent (Line 18) and 10 percent (Line 19). The 33 percent depreciation rate applies to any equipment that is largely electronic, such as the computer hardware and software used in electronic prepress. The working life of such equipment and software is generally anticipated to be three years, so each year there is a depreciation of one-third of the computer hardware and software investment. The 10 percent depreciation provides a write-off over a ten-year period and applies to equipment that is largely mechanical, not electronic. Because the press in this example is lithographic or mechanical, the 10 percent depreciation value applies as shown in Figure 3.4.

Cost of New Software (Estimate for Year) (Line 20). This line represents the estimated annual cost of all anticipated purchase of software that will be directly used in the production center. The $500 dollar amount shown in Cell F20 on Line 20 of Figure 3.4 is an estimate based on what is anticipated to be spent on software in the next year. Because this cell is shaded on the spreadsheet, this amount is likely to change from center to center.

Center R&D Activities (Estimate for Year) (Line 21). Some companies actively engage in research and development (R&D) in order to improve the products and services they offer. Line 21 provides for the company to recover costs for such research, and Cell F21 on Line 21 of Figure 3.4 shows an estimated $2,500 is anticipated to be spent. The figure in this cell is usually an estimated amount.

Training & Retraining Costs (Estimate for Year) (Line 22). Training and retraining are important to maintain a high skill level for the production center employee(s) and their costs must be included as part of the BHR cost. Cell F22 on Line 22 of Figure 3.4 shows an estimated $2,000 in training is provided to the one employee operating the center in this example.

Total Fixed Costs (Line 23). This line is the sum of all fixed costs—Line 15 through Line 22 and Cell F15 through Cell F22—which totals $19,888 as shown in Cell F23 on Line 23 of Figure 3.4. As noted in Cell F23 on Line 23 of Figure 3.5, the formula for summing is =SUM(F15:F22), which means that a range of cells from Cell F15 to Cell F22 is added. Because summing can also be accomplished by using a positive sign (+) in the formula, Cell F23 of Figure 3.5 could have also been written: =F15+F16+F17+F18+F19+F20+F21+F22. Any combination of cells can be added, not necessarily just those that are consecutive.

Variable Costs (Annual) (Lines 25 through 37). Variable costs are costs that change (e.g., increase or decrease) with changes in production output. The major variable costs incurred in printing manufacturing are the cost of labor and associated labor support costs such as fringe benefits.

Direct Labor Costs (Nos. 1, 2, and 3) (Lines 25 through 27). The cost of labor is calculated by multiplying the wage scale by the number of annual straight time hours the employee is paid. Lines 8, 9, and 10 are linked directly to Lines 25, 26, and 27, and the labor cost calculations are completed in Cells F25, F26, and F27 respectively of Figure 3.4. For example, Cell F25 on Line 25 of Figure 3.4 shows that the direct labor cost of the one press operator in this example is $38,480.

Total Cost: Direct Labor (Line 28). This line is the sum of all direct labor costs on Lines 25, 26, and 27.

Cost of Indirect Labor (20% Direct Labor) (Line 29). Indirect labor covers employees working in the plant who have partial or intermittent responsibilities to the production center. These people include working forepeople, supervisors, and miscellaneous employees who provide hands-on management or support to work done in the center. In this example, indirect labor costs are 20 percent of direct labor, which translates to roughly one full employee for every five cost centers the company has. Cell F29 on Line 29 of Figure 3.4 shows an indirect labor cost of $7,696.

The best procedure to determine the percentage of indirect labor is to first identify all support labor personnel who perform a portion of their job tasks in the center, then to sum all labor costs for these individuals and divide the total by the sum of all direct labor costs for all of the centers in which these individuals work. It should be noted that any employee who performs a job that benefits the company as a whole and not just a specific center or group of centers is considered a general factory employee and is cost recovered as General factory overhead in Column D and not as indirect labor.

Total Direct and Indirect Labor Cost (Line 30). This is the sum of all direct and indirect labor costs on Lines 28 and 29 (Cells F28 and F29). Cell F30 on Line 30 of Figure 3.4 shows a total cost of $46,176.

Employee Taxes & Benefits (Direct & Indirect) (Line 31). This line covers all fringe benefits, including health care, retirement, social security taxes, worker's compensation, unemployment compensation, and related employee support costs. For Figure 3.4 the calculation method in Cell B31 on Line 31 indicates that the cost is 30 percent of direct and indirect labor, which is 0.30 x $46,176 = $13,853 (rounded up).

Because fringe benefits are complex and tend to carry a high cost burden, computation accuracy could be increased here by building a list of fringe benefits separately at another location on the spreadsheet and breaking it down by individual category of fringe benefit and by the amount paid annually for the employee(s). The total of this separate cell would then be referenced to Cell F31, in which the total cost of the fringe benefits would appear. This process tailors the employee's fringe benefit costs to the center instead of generalizing them.

Overhead Lighting, Electrical Power, and Wattage Costs (In kWhs) (Lines 32 through 34). Light and power costs are most accurately apportioned to each production cost center by summing annual lighting and electrical power costs, then allocating these costs back to each working area on a square footage or usage basis. This can be difficult, however, because a typical printing company receives one monthly electric bill and breaking out the specific electric costs can be complex. For this reason another popular procedure—the one used in this book—is to mathematically calculate the cost of electrical power using standard, proven formulas. This provides approximate lighting and power cost determinations and sufficient accuracy to substitute for the more difficult apportioning method.

The cost of electric power used in the examples in Figure 3.4 is $0.10 per kWh, but the rate varies throughout the country contingent upon geographical location, demand usage for the printing company, electric company charges, and other factors. Although electrical power is the most common energy source for a printing plant, natural gas is also sometimes used. The BHR in Figure 3.4 has no line to recover for the natural gas cost of a specific center. However, this line should be included for companies that have natural gas requirements beyond normal plant heating and air conditioning (Line 15). As with electrical power costs, natural gas costs should be prorated from monthly bills according to approximate usage requirements for the centers that consume the product.

Example 3.1—Overhead Lighting Cost (kWh) (Line 32). As was discussed earlier, there is a total of 150 square feet for the Komori press in this example (Cell F5 of Figure 3.4) and the lighting level is 3 watts (W) per square foot. Electrical power cost is $0.10 per kWh (Cell B33).

To determine the cost annually to light this production center operating one shift at 40 hours per week, three variables must be known:

1. the number of annual hours worked
2. the lighting coverage in watts per square foot
3. the cost per kWh for power

The steps in this example are represented by the following formula, which can be used for lighting cost problems in general:

lighting cost = [(number of annual hours worked x wattage per square foot) ÷ (1,000 W/kilowatt)] x cost per kWh x number of square feet in center

The figure 1,000 W/kilowatt (kW) is a constant. To determine the lighting costs in this example, take the following steps:

Step 1. Determine the number of kilowatts per square foot:

3 W/sq. ft. ÷ 1,000 W/kW = 0.003 kW/sq. ft.

Step 2. Determine the number of annual operating hours:

40 hr./wk. x 52 wk./yr. = 2,080 hr./yr.

Step 3. Determine the number of annual kWh per square foot:

0.003 kW/sq. ft. x 2,080 hr./yr. = 6.24 kWh/sq. ft./yr.

Step 4. Find the annual lighting cost per square foot:

6.24 kWh/sq. ft./yr. x $0.10/kWh = $0.624/sq. ft./yr.

Step 5. Find the lighting cost per year for the press center:

$0.624/sq. ft./yr. x 150 sq. ft. = $93.60/yr.

(This figure is rounded up to $94 in Cell F32 of Figure 3.4.)

Example 3.2-Electrical Power Cost (kWh) (Line 33). To determine the annual cost of electrical power for the 6.2-hp motor used to power the Komori press in Figure 3.4, three variables must be known:

1. the number of annual hours worked in the center
2. the total of all motor hp in the center
3. the cost per kWh for electricity

The steps in this example are represented by the following formula, which can be used for cost of power problems in general:

power cost = total hp of motors x number of annual hours
worked x 0.746 kW/hp x cost per kWh

The figure 0.746 kW/hp is a constant. To determine electrical power costs in this example, take the following steps:

Step 1. Determine the number of annual operating hours:

40 hr./wk. x 52 wk./yr. = 2,080 hr./yr.

Step 2. Determine the number of annual horsepower hours (hp-hr.):

2,080 hr./yr. x 6.2 hp = 12,896 hp-hr./yr.

Step 3. Determine the number of annual kWh using 0.746 kW/hp as a constant:

0.746 kW/hp x 12,896 hp-hr./yr. = 9,620 kWh/yr.

Step 4. Find the annual cost of electrical power to run the motor:

9,620 kWh/yr. x $0.10/kWh = $962.00/yr.

Example 3.3-Wattage Cost (kWh) (Line 34). In this example determine the cost annually to operate a 3,000-W platemaker center (3,000-W arc lamp) operating one shift at 40 hours per week. The platemaking unit operates 50 percent of the time with the arc lamp in use. Power cost is $0.10 per kWh. Four variables must be known to make cost of arc lamp calculations:

1. the number of hours worked per week
2. the arc lamp input wattage for the platemaker or camera
3. the cost per kWh for power
4. the usage adjustment factor

The steps in this example are represented by the following formula, which can be used for arc lamp cost problems in general:

arc lamp cost = (number of rated input watts of source ÷ 1,000 W/kW) x number of annual hours worked x cost per kWh

The figure 1,000 W/kW is a constant. To determine the wattage costs in this example, take the following steps:

Step 1. Determine the number of kW:

3,000 W ÷ 1,000 W/kW = 3 kW

Step 2. Determine the number of annual operating hours:

40 hr./wk. x 52 wk./yr. = 2,080 hr./yr.

Step 3. Determine the number of annual kWh:

2,080 hr./yr. x 3 kW = 6,240 kWh/yr.

Step 4. Make usage adjustments using 50 percent use:

6,240 kWh/yr. x 0.50 = 3,120 kWh/yr.

Step 5. Find the arc lamp cost per year for the platemaker center:

3,120 kWh/yr. x $0.10/kWh = $312.00/yr.

Department Supplies (8% Labor) (Line 35). This line is a catchall category for material costs that are incidental to the center and are not direct material costs of a customer's job. These include items such as paper, ink, plates, and film. Typically these items are not easily identifiable or quantifiable to the production center but are necessary to produce work.

Examples of department supplies for the Komori press in this example are ink-cleaning solvents for washup, lithographic blankets, cotton wipes, shop towels, and plate cleaner. Other production centers have different direct supplies. Equipment repair items are not included here, nor are materials that are directly charged to the customer, such as lithographic plates, unless the company decides to do so. For example, management might decide to cost ink as a department supply instead of estimating ink cost and quality for a specified type of job or kind of work.

The best way to determine departmental costs is to develop a list of all incidental items for the center, determine the annual costs of these items, and sum these costs. This figure is then entered in Cell F35. Because this process necessitates a detailed bookkeeping effort, many companies establish a percentage and relate this percentage to another accurately defined cost. Figure 3.4 uses 8 percent of total labor cost to calculate the cost of department supplies (Line 35), but both the percentage and the item to which it is referenced—in this case total labor cost—are used for example only and could change.

Repairs (2% Investment Cost) (Line 36). The cost of repairing mechanical equipment can be approached in different ways. The age and condition of the equipment, its usage level, and preventative maintenance procedures all play a part in the cost of equipment repair. One method for establishing repair costs is to adopt an upwardly sliding scale that is based on use and increases 1/2 percent per year (e.g., 1 percent for equipment that is one year old, 1 1/2 percent for equipment that is two years old, 2 percent for equipment that is three years old).

A second method is to use an average percentage that is based on the investment cost and does not vary. Other methods include using the previous year's repair cost to determine repair costs for the current year or to simply estimate the anticipated repair costs for the next year and to enter that figure in Cell F36. Because Figure 3.4 uses a 2 percent of equipment investment method (Line 36), the repair cost in this example is 2 percent of $125,000 (Cell F3) or $2,500.

Total Variable Costs (Line 37). This is the sum of all variable costs on Lines 30 through 36 (Cells F30 through F36). The amount in Cell F37 on Line 37 of Figure 3.4 is $67,279.

Total Fixed and Variable Costs (Line 39). This line is the sum of the fixed and variable costs totaled on Lines 23 and 37 (Cells F23 and F27). In Cell F39 on Line 39 of Figure 3.4 the total is $87,166.

Careful observation shows that there is a $1 difference when adding Cells F23 and F37. This relates to the rounding protocol of spreadsheets. Line 23 calculates at $19,887.50 (to the penny) and Line 37 calculates at $67,278.52 (to the penny). These figures have each been rounded up to the next higher dollar amount in their respective spreadsheet cells because they are each over 50 cents. However, when these figures are added in Cell F39, they total $87,166.02 (to the penny). Because spreadsheets round up to the next dollar at 50 cents or more, and stay at the same dollar amount at 49 cents or less, and because the exact amount here is below 49 cents, the sum is rounded to $87,167, or $1 less than they total when added manually. If precise accuracy to the penny is required, the spreadsheet cells must be defaulted to show answers in pennies, and rounding is not a problem. In developing BHRs, this rounding protocol is not a problem.

Proration: General Factory Overhead (Line 41). Prorated costing is the process of distributing dollars using a ratio comparison formula, which proportionately spreads the cost of the shared area among all production centers using the area. Various indexes, such as floor space or direct labor cost, can be used.

In Figure 3.4, the proration basis is the annual investment cost of the center (Cell F3) divided by the total company investment (Cell C3) ($125,000 ÷ $2,600,000), which is then multiplied by the general factory cost of $61,354 (Cell D39) to yield a rounded prorated cost of $2,950 (Cell F41). This dollar figure represents the amount the Komori press center contributes annually for its share of the general factory expense. When all other centers contribute proportionally to the general factory overhead, the sum of their prorated dollars totals $61,354.

Total Factory Cost (Line 43). This line is the sum of total fixed costs (Line 23) and total variable costs (Line 37) plus general factory overhead (Cell 41). Cell F43 on Line 43 of Figure 3.4 shows a total factory cost of $90,116.

Proration: Administration and Selling Overhead (Line 45). The same proration formula and method used for general factory overhead on Line 41 is used for prorating administration and selling overhead on Line 45. The formula is: center investment (Cell F3) divided by company investment (Cell C3) ($125,000 ÷ $2,600,000), which is then multiplied by the total fixed and variable cost of $545,850 (Cell E39) to yield a rounded product of $26,243 (Cell F45). This amount is collected by applying this BHR costing method to the Komori press, which contributes $26,243 (Cell F45) to the total amount needed for administration and selling cost burdens.

Total Annual Center Cost (Line 47). This line is the sum of the annual dollars the center requires to produce work (total factory cost in Cell F43 and administration and selling overhead in Cell F45), which in this example is $116,359 (Cell F47). It is important to note that this figure is "pure cost" because only cost dollars have been used and no profit has been included at any point in the BHR calculations. In sum, this Komori press must generate $116,359 in income over the year to pay its portion of costs incurred by the company.

Chargeable Hours (Cells B49 through B54). Chargeable hours represent the number of hours the company anticipates will be sold yearly in this center (e.g., the estimated number of hours that can be charged to customers' jobs for which the customers will pay). It is difficult to precisely and accurately project what this figure will be for the next year, so many companies typically use the past year as a guide. Example 3.3 that follows shows the calculation process to determine the chargeable hours anticipated for the Komori press in this example annually. Figure 3.5 shows the formulas that drive the Figure 3.4 chargeable hour amounts.

Example 3.4. Remember that the single employee in Figure 3.4 works 40 hours per week. This person receives 20 paid days off. Production management wants to evaluate her amount of actual working time or utilization at 80 percent, 70 percent, and 60 percent levels. To determine how many chargeable hours will this employee work annually, take the following steps:

Step 1. Find the total annual hours:

40 hr./wk. x 52 wk./yr. = 2,080 hr./yr.

Step 2. Determine annual time-off hours:

20 days off/yr. x 8 hr./day = 160 hr./yr.

Step 3. Find the maximum annual chargeable hours:

2,080 hr./yr. - 160 hr./yr. = 1,920 hr./yr.

Step 4. Determine the actual annual chargeable hours at the three desired percentages:

80%:1,920 hr./yr. x 0.80 = 1,536 hr./yr.
70%1,920 hr./yr. x 0.70 = 1,344 hr./yr.
60%:1,920 hr./yr. x 0.60 = 1,152 hr./yr.

Manufacturing Costs at 80%, 70%, and 60% (Lines 49 through 51). These costs are calculated by dividing the total factory cost of $90,116 (Cell F43) by the chargeable hours at a specific percentage of utilization (Cells B49 through B51). Using the 80 percent chargeable hours in Cell B49 of Figure 3.4, the calculation is $90,116 ÷ 1,536 hours = $58.67 (rounded). When chargeable hours are reduced to 70 percent (Cell B50), manufacturing cost rises to $67.05; when they are further reduced to 60 percent (Cell B51), manufacturing cost increases to $78.23 (rounded).

Manufacturing cost represents the internal cost to make the product and does not include any costs for administering or selling the product. It can also be used to determine rework costs of correcting job errors in the center and as a measurement tool for value added.

BHR Costs at 80%, 70%, and 60% (Lines 52 through 54). The BHRs recover for all costs incurred in the manufacture of the product, including administration and selling overhead (Line 45). In Cell F43 of Figure 3.4, the total factory cost is $90,116. When the prorated amount of $26,243 for administrative and selling overhead (Cell F45) is added to the total factory cost, the total annual center cost (Line 47) becomes $116,359. If this cost is then divided by the number of chargeable hours at the determined percentage of use, the product is the BHR cost per chargeable hour. Thus, Figure 3.4 shows that one hour of time on this Komori press at an 80 percent utilization level ($116,359 in Cell F47 divided by 1,536 hrs. in Cell B49) costs the customer $75.75 (rounded in Cell F52). When the percentage is reduced to 70 percent (Cell B50), the BHR cost rises to $86.58; when it is reduced to 60 percent (Cell B51), the BHR cost increases to $101.01 (rounded).

As discussed previously, BHR cost figures are necessary when estimating jobs using the cost estimating process described in Chapters 1 and 4. The BHRs are also used for determining the cost of AAs or any other chargeable work to be completed as a part of the customer's order.

Deciding which BHR utilization level to use is important in estimating, and in general the following rule is used: When estimating a job, honestly evaluate and apply the level of utilization that best represents the company's production situation when the job is anticipated to enter the production center being estimated. For example, if the estimator chooses to apply the 80 percent BHR level, the cost result will be lower than with the 70 percent or 60 percent level and will tend to reduce the price of the job to the customer. However, the 80 percent level may not accurately reflect the true cost the job will entail, which will result in the company losing income. Conversely, if the estimator chooses the 60 percent BHR cost level, the price to the customer will be greater than the actual cost might be, which makes the company less competitive when quoting the job and risks winning the order.

Figures 3.6 and 3.7 are two completed BHR sheets. Figure 3.6 is for a production center titled "electronic design production" (Cell A1); Figure 3.7 is for a Polar 92EM cutting machine.

Figure 3.8 demonstrates the BHR process in Figures 3.4 and 3.5 for multiple centers in a printing company. It provides for six centers (Columns F through K) and is intended to show how the BHR process would be extended to cover an entire printing plant. Keep in mind that all figures appearing in this chapter are provided for example only and are not intended to reflect costs or hour rates for any particular printing company.

The appendix to this chapter provides all-inclusive BHRs representative of the Southern California geographic region. These rates are based on prevailing

	A	B	C	D	E	F
1	**BUDGETED HOUR COST RATE** **Center title:** **Electronic design production**	Calculation method or basis	Total company	General factory overhead	Selling and administrative overhead	Annual center cost (one shift)
2	CENTER SPECIFICATIONS					
3	Investment cost/equipment value		$2,600,000	$24,000	$72,000	$15,000
4	Number of employees in center		24	2	6	1
5	Square feet of working area		4,600	350	600	120
6	Total motor horsepower					0.1
7	Wattage requirements					2,000
8	Wage scale 1			$9.00		$15.00
9	Wage scale 2			$7.50		$0.00
10	Wage scale 3					$0.00
11	Paid days off: Sum vacation days and holidays					20
12	Weekly hours paid		40	40	40	40
13	Annual hours paid			2,080	2,080	2,080
14	FIXED COSTS (ANNUAL)					
15	Fixed overhead (sq. ft.)	$3.00		$1,050	$1,800	$360
16	Insurance (Per $1,000 investment cost)	$3.00		$72	$216	$45
17	Property taxes (Per $100 investment cost)	$1.25		$300	$900	$188
18	Depreciation 1 (33% investment)	33%				$4,950
19	Depreciation 2 (10% straight or other method)	10%		$2,400	$7,200	
20	Cost of new software (estimate for year)	estimate cost				$2,000
21	Center R & D activities (estimate for year)	estimate cost				$1,000
22	Training & retraining costs (estimate for year)	estimate cost			$4,000	$1,200
23	TOTAL FIXED COSTS			$3,822	$14,116	$9,743
24	VARIABLE COSTS (ANNUAL)					
25	Direct labor cost, No. 1	scale*annual hrs		$18,720	$320,000	$31,200
26	Direct labor cost, No. 2	scale*annual hrs		$15,600		$0
27	Direct labor cost, No. 3	scale*annual hrs				$0
28	Total cost: Direct labor			$34,320	$320,000	$31,200
29	Cost of indirect labor (20% direct labor)	20%		$6,864	$64,000	$6,240
30	Total direct and indirect labor cost			$41,184	$384,000	$37,440
31	Employee taxes and benefits (direct plus indirect)	30%		$12,355	$115,200	$11,232
32	Overhead lighting cost (kWh)	$0.10		$218	$374	$75
33	Electrical power cost (kWh)	$0.10				$16
34	Wattage cost (kWh)	$0.10				$208
35	Department supplies (8% total labor)	8%		$3,295	$30,720	$2,995
36	Repairs (2% investment cost)	2%		$480	$1,440	$300
37	TOTAL VARIABLE COSTS			$57,532	$531,734	$52,266
38						
39	Total fixed and variable costs			$61,354	$545,850	$62,008
40						
41	Prorate: General factory overhead	% investment				$354
42						
43	TOTAL FACTORY COST					$62,362
44						
45	Prorate: Administration and selling overhead	% investment				$3,149
46						
47	TOTAL ANNUAL CENTER COST					$65,511
48		Chargeable hours				
49	Manufacturing cost @ 80%	1,536.00				$40.60
50	Manufacturing cost @ 70%	1,344.00				$46.40
51	Manufacturing cost @ 60%	1,152.00				$54.13
52	BHR cost @ 80%	1,536.00				$42.65
53	BHR cost @ 70%	1,344.00				$48.74
54	BHR cost @ 60%	1,152.00				$56.87

Figure 3.6 BHR form for a prepress electronic design production center

	A	B	C	D	E	F
1	**BUDGETED HOUR COST RATE** **Center title:** **Polar 92EM cutting machine**	Calculation method or basis	Total company	General factory overhead	Selling and adminstrative overhead	Annual center cost (one shift)
2	CENTER SPECIFICATIONS					
3	Investment cost/equipment value		$2,600,000	$24,000	$72,000	$56,850
4	Number of employees in center		24	2	6	1
5	Square feet of working area		4,600	350	600	145
6	Total motor horsepower					4.2
7	Wattage requirements					0
8	Wage scale 1			$9.00		$16.25
9	Wage scale 2			$7.50		$0.00
10	Wage scale 3					$0.00
11	Paid days off: Sum vacation days and holidays					20
12	Weekly hours paid		40	40	40	40
13	Annual hours paid			2,080	2,080	2,080
14	FIXED COSTS (ANNUAL)					
15	Fixed overhead (sq. ft.)	$3.00		$1,050	$1,800	$435
16	Insurance (Per $1,000 investment cost)	$3.00		$72	$216	$171
17	Property taxes (Per $100 investment cost)	$1.25		$300	$900	$711
18	Depreciation 1 (33% investment)	33%				
19	Depreciation 2 (10% straight or other method)	10%		$2,400	$7,200	$5,685
20	Cost of new software (estimate for year)	estimate cost				$500
21	Center R & D activities (estimate for year)	estimate cost				$2,500
22	Training & retraining costs (estimate for year)	estimate cost			$4,000	$2,000
23	TOTAL FIXED COSTS			$3,822	$14,116	$12,001
24	VARIABLE COSTS (ANNUAL)					
25	Direct labor cost, No. 1	scale*annual hrs		$18,720	$320,000	$33,800
26	Direct labor cost, No. 2	scale*annual hrs		$15,600		$0
27	Direct labor cost, No. 3	scale*annual hrs				$0
28	Total cost: Direct labor			$34,320	$320,000	$33,800
29	Cost of indirect labor (20% direct labor)	20%		$6,864	$64,000	$6,760
30	Total direct and indirect labor cost			$41,184	$384,000	$40,560
31	Employee taxes and benefits (direct plus indirect)	30%		$12,355	$115,200	$12,168
32	Overhead lighting cost (kWh)	$0.10		$218	$374	$90
33	Electrical power cost (kWh)	$0.10				$652
34	Wattage cost (kWh)	$0.10				$0
35	Department supplies (8% total labor)	8%		$3,295	$30,720	$3,245
36	Repairs (2% investment cost)	2%		$480	$1,440	$1,137
37	TOTAL VARIABLE COSTS			$57,532	$531,734	$57,852
38						
39	Total fixed and variable costs			$61,354	$545,850	$69,853
40						
41	Prorate: General factory overhead	% investment				$1,342
42						
43	TOTAL FACTORY COST					$71,195
44						
45	Prorate: Administration and selling overhead	% investment				$11,935
46						
47	TOTAL ANNUAL CENTER COST					$83,130
48		Chargeable hours				
49	Manufacturing cost @ 80%	1,536.00				$46.35
50	Manufacturing cost @ 70%	1,344.00				$52.97
51	Manufacturing cost @ 60%	1,152.00				$61.80
52	BHR cost @ 80%	1,536.00				$54.12
53	BHR cost @ 70%	1,344.00				$61.85
54	BHR cost @ 60%	1,152.00				$72.16

Figure 3.7 BHR form for a Polar 92EM cutting machine

#	BUDGETED HOUR COST RATE / Center title: / Six plant production centers	Calculation method or basis	Total company	General factory overhead	Selling and adminstrative overhead	Electronic design production	Electronic scanning production	PostScript output devices	Komori 1/C press, 20x26	Komori 4/C press, 20x28	Polar 92EM cutting machine
1											
2	CENTER SPECIFICATIONS										
3	Investment cost/equipment value		$2,600,000	$24,000	$72,000	$15,000	$95,000	$125,000	$125,000	$986,500	$56,850
4	Number of employees in center		24	2	6	1	1	1	1	2	1
5	Square feet of working area		4,600	350	600	120	60	100	150	300	145
6	Total motor horsepower					0.1	0.2	0.2	6.2	8.9	4.2
7	Wattage requirements					2,000	4,000	4,000	0	0	0
8	Wage Scale 1			$9.00		$15.00	$17.00	$16.50	$18.50	$19.25	$16.25
9	Wage Scale 2			$7.50		$0.00	$0.00	$0.00	$0.00	$15.50	$0.00
10	Wage scale 3					$0.00	$0.00	$0.00	$0.00	$0.00	$0.00
11	Paid days off: Sum vacation days and holidays					20	20	20	20	20	20
12	Weekly hours paid			40	40	40	40	40	40	40	40
13	Annual hours paid			2,080	2,080	2,080	2,080	2,080	2,080	2,080	2,080
14	FIXED COSTS (ANNUAL)										
15	Fixed overhead (sq. ft.)	$3.00		$1,050	$1,800	$360	$180	$300	$450	$900	$435
16	Insurance (Per $1,000 investment cost)	$3.00		$72	$216	$45	$285	$375	$375	$2,960	$171
17	Property taxes (Per $100 investment cost)	$1.25		$300	$900	$188	$1,188	$1,563	$1,563	$12,331	$711
18	Depreciation 1 (33% investment)	33%				$4,950	$31,350	$41,250			
19	Depreciation 2 (10% straight or other method)	10%		$2,400	$7,200				$12,500	$98,650	$5,685
20	Cost of new software (estimate for year)	estimate cost				$2,000	$1,000	$500	$500	$500	$500
21	Center R & D activities (estimate for year)	estimate cost				$1,000	$1,500	$1,000	$2,500	$500	$2,500
22	Training & retraining costs (estimate for year)	estimate cost			$4,000	$1,200	$1,500	$1,000	$2,000	$500	$2,000
23	TOTAL FIXED COSTS			$3,822	$14,116	$9,743	$37,003	$45,988	$19,888	$116,341	$12,001
24	VARIABLE COSTS (ANNUAL)										
25	Direct labor cost, No. 1	scale*annual hrs		$18,720	$320,000	$31,200	$35,360	$34,320	$38,480	$40,040	$33,800
26	Direct labor cost, No. 2	scale*annual hrs		$15,600						$32,240	
27	Direct labor cost, No. 3	scale*annual hrs									
28	Total cost: Direct labor			$34,320	$320,000	$31,200	$35,360	$34,320	$38,480	$72,280	$33,800
29	Cost of indirect labor (20% direct labor)	20%		$6,864	$64,000	$6,240	$7,072	$6,864	$7,696	$14,456	$6,760
30	Total direct and indirect labor cost			$41,184	$384,000	$37,440	$42,432	$41,184	$46,176	$86,736	$40,560
31	Employee taxes and benefits (direct plus indirect)	30%		$12,355	$115,200	$11,232	$12,730	$12,355	$13,853	$26,021	$12,168
32	Overhead lighting cost (kWh)	$0.10		$218	$374	$75	$37	$62	$94	$187	$90
33	Electrical power cost (kWh)	$0.10				$16	$31	$31			
34	Wattage cost (kWh)					$208	$416	$416	$962	$1,381	$652
35	Department supplies (8% total labor)	8%		$3,295	$30,720	$2,995	$3,395	$3,295	$3,694	$6,939	$3,245
36	Repairs (2% investment cost)	2%		$480	$1,440	$300	$1,900	$2,500	$2,500	$19,730	$1,137
37	TOTAL VARIABLE COSTS			$57,532	$531,734	$52,266	$60,941	$59,843	$67,279	$140,994	$57,852
38											
39	Total fixed and variable costs			$61,354	$545,850	$62,008	$97,943	$105,831	$87,166	$257,335	$69,853
40											
41	Prorate: general factory overhead	% investment				$354	$2,242	$2,950	$2,950	$23,279	$1,342
42											
43	TOTAL FACTORY COST					$62,362	$100,185	$108,781	$90,116	$280,614	$71,195
44											
45	Prorate: administration and selling overhead	% investment				$3,149	$19,945	$26,243	$26,243	$207,108	$11,935
46											
47	TOTAL ANNUAL CENTER COST					$65,511	$120,129	$135,023	$116,359	$487,722	$83,130
48		Chargeable hours									
49	Manufacturing cost @ 80%	1,536.00				$40.60	$65.22	$70.82	$58.67	$182.69	$46.35
50	Manufacturing cost @ 70%	1,344.00				$46.40	$74.54	$80.94	$67.05	$208.79	$52.97
51	Manufacturing cost @ 60%	1,152.00				$54.13	$86.97	$94.43	$78.23	$243.59	$61.80
52	BHR cost @ 80%	1,536.00				$42.65	$78.21	$87.91	$75.75	$317.53	$54.12
53	BHR cost @ 70%	1,344.00				$48.74	$89.38	$100.46	$86.58	$362.89	$61.85
54	BHR cost @ 60%	1,152.00				$56.87	$104.28	$117.21	$101.01	$423.37	$72.16

Figure 3.8 BHR form for six production centers in a typical printing company

1994-95 wages for the greater Southern California area using a 40-hour work week. They have been reproduced with permission from the Printing Industries Association, Inc., of Southern California from its 1994-95 *Blue Book of Production Standards and Costs*. Copies of the complete book, which is revised annually, may be obtained by contacting the Management Services Department, PIA-SC, 5800 South Eastern Avenue, Los Angeles, CA 90040.

Some Further Comments and Pointers on Developing and Using BHRs

The following are important points regarding the development and use of BHRs using spreadsheets as working tools.

Spreadsheet Literacy Is a Must. As noted earlier, the BHR process is very much expedited when the person building the BHRs has a working knowledge of spreadsheet development on a microcomputer platform. Again, Figure 3.5 shows the formulas that represent this process and support Figure 3.4. As noted in Chapter 2, spreadsheets are also frequently used as estimating tools, in addition to being used in numerous calculation and "what if" analysis methods in printing companies of all sizes.

BHRs Are Not Selling Prices. The BHRs represent a composite of all costs to produce work in a particular location in the plant, which has defined personnel and equipment and a specific rate of production. It is important to note that BHRs are not selling prices because they do not include any profit markup. When properly calculated, BHRs are first multiplied by the number of estimated hours anticipated for a job. When material and buyout costs are added, management has the baseline cost of the job with no profit. Typically the profit markup on a printing order includes this base dollar cost so that the company recovers all costs.

Enter Annual Costs When Developing BHRs. Annual center costs as listed in Column F of Figure 3.4 are sometimes difficult to accurately determine using a calculation process or a formula. In fact, in some cases it may be easier to determine the cost in some other manner and to then enter the cost in the column. For example, if the cost of department supplies (Line 35) can be accurately summed from last year's purchase orders, there is no reason to calculate this cost using a formula because this summed figure could be more easily entered in the spreadsheet cell.

As Chargeable Hours Go Down, Costs Go Up. A critical concept of BHR costing is that as the number of chargeable hours decreases, the cost per hour increases and, conversely, as the number of chargeable hours goes up, the BHR cost per hour goes down. It is therefore clear that if Printing Company A utilizes its Komori press less often than Printing Company B uses its Komori press, then

Printing Company A must apply a higher BHR rate and is less competitive than Printing Company B.

This discrepancy can be overcome if Printing Company A's customers are less concerned about Company A's competitive costs than they are about its outstanding service, fast job turnaround, or high product quality. Nevertheless, it is clear that production costs lower when there is a focus on increased productivity, which is achieved when any cost center has more chargeable time usage. This develops into a cycle: High center utilization reduces BHR costs, which allows the company to be more competitive, which in turn allows the company to win more orders and effectively keep chargeable hours high and BHR costs low.

Production Efficiency Affects BHRs. Any time a job requires significant production time—and when the work on the job will be continuous—production efficiencies can reduce the BHR. Reducing costs via production efficiencies keeps the printing company in a stronger competitive position. This concept is logical, but the problem is how much to reduce costs and yet maintain an accurate cost basis.

No studies have been done on this subject, but a general rule of thumb can be applied: When a minimum of three hours of continuous production is anticipated, reduce the BHR by 5 percent per hour after the first full hour of normal BHR activity. For example, if a job were in production on the Komori press for three consecutive hours and there was a BHR of $50.00, the total cost would be: $50.00 (first hour), $47.50 (second hour), $45.14 (third hour) = $142.63 for three hours instead of $50.00 x 3 hours = $150.00. Passing savings to the customer by lowering job price is important if the company wishes to remain competitive.

Use Incremental Costing Methods for Reduced, Limited Production. The length of production time for some jobs, particularly jobs in electronic prepress, may be just a few minutes and not hours. Some prepress suppliers, who are also known as film output providers, establish dollar minimums for these types of job, such as one-half hour or one-half of the hourly BHR cost. This recovers reasonable costs for jobs that take perhaps fifteen minutes.

It is clear, however, that for electronic prepress production that is broken or discontinuous—when each job requires a very small amount of time—costs for processing the job is typically higher. Thus, as BHRs can be adjusted downward when production is likely to be continuous and long, BHRs can also be raised when job production is very short. This is also a rule-of-thumb adjustment: Increase the BHR cost by 10 percent for jobs requiring short, incremental production.

For example, adding 10 percent to a normal BHR of $50.00 for an electronic prepress center used for a series of short, broken jobs increases the BHR to $55.00. If one unit is a 6-minute increment, the cost per units is $5.50 because there are ten 6-minute increments in one hour ($55.00 ÷ 10 increments). Thus, a 30-minute job requires 5 units (30 minutes ÷ 6 minutes), which when multiplied by the cost per unit costs $27.50 (5 x $5.50). Keep in mind that this percentage increase is a rule of thumb. Also remember that as costs increase, prices typically increase accordingly, which makes the film output provider less competitive yet compensates the company for losing productivity when jobs have very short production times.

3.8   Overtime Considerations and Cost Savings for Additional Shifts

One of the critical production management decisions that must be made from time to time relates to whether or not to start a second or third shift. Typically, the cost centers that are the most labor and capital intensive are the ones that require this decision. One guideline that is sometimes used is that when overtime consistently approaches 40 percent of the straight time hours worked, a complete new shift should be considered. For example, if an employee running a single-color press consistently works three hours over each eight-hour day, which is a 37.5 percent increase in center usage, a complete additional shift should be seriously considered.

There are advantages to running second and/or third shifts. Essentially, additional shifts save money for the company by reducing overtime and spreading fixed costs for the center over a larger time block, which reduces center costs. With added shifts, the company can significantly increase its volume of work without additional equipment purchases.

However, there are also some other important considerations prior to initiating an additional shift. First, the company should plan to increase the volume of its plant through increased sales efforts or other methods. Second, additional shifts—second shifts and especially third or "graveyard" shifts—typically present both employee and supervisory staffing problems. Because many employees do not wish to be moved to a late afternoon/evening work time, or because they do not wish to work at night (even though they earn a shift differential pay increase from 5 percent to 20 percent over straight time pay), it may be hard to find competent personnel to work during the second or third shift. Third, employees working overtime make one and one-half or double their straight pay scale. This additional pay situation essentially ends with the addition of a new shift, which makes employees who earned overtime pay disgruntled at losing the extra income. Finally, additional shifts represent increased equipment wear. For example, a press that normally might last ten years on a one-shift basis would probably last only three years on a three-shift operation.

In terms of the major advantage of additional shifts—cost savings to the plant—some general rules can be made. Because the center's fixed costs are spread over a larger working time and do not increase with increases in production, a significant savings in hour cost results. For example, a second shift may save from 10 percent to 20 percent in BHR over the first shift and the third shift may save from 5 percent to 15 percent in BHR over the second shift. Thus, for a center working on all shifts at 75 percent production and with a first shift BHR of $50.00, the second shift BHR would reduce the BHR to $42.50 per hour (a 15 percent savings over the first shift), and a third shift would reduce the BHR to $39.10 per hour (an 8 percent savings over the second shift). It is important to note that the savings percentages may vary with respect to the type of equipment, operating factors, labor rates, and fringe benefits paid to employees, among some of the more important conditions.

3.9   Effects of Automation on BHRs and Chargeable Hours

As previously discussed, BHRs are used with standard production times to determine estimated selling costs. One particularly important aspect to study here relates to the effects of automation on BHRs, especially when comparing new, automated equipment to older, less automated units. To make this comparison, refer back to Figure 3.4, which is a BHR form for a Komori 1-color press. Note the two "bottom line" components in Figure 3.4: the total annual center cost of $116,359 (Cell F47) and the chargeable hours at 70 percent utilization, which is 1,344 hours annually (Cell B50). The BHR for this press is then $116,359 divided by 1,344 annual hours, which equals a rate of $86.58 (Cell F53). Now assume that this Komori press is retrofitted with electronic controls which enable it to be 25 percent more productive. Consider the following examples.

Example 3.5. After the BHR sheet is redone line by line, the additional electronic gear is found to increase the total annual center cost by $10,000 from $116,359 (Cell F47) to $126,360, with no reduction in labor costs. Chargeable hours are reduced by 25 percent because there has been no increase in volume in the center, which makes the chargeable hours (at 70 percent utilization in Cell B50) 1,008 hours (1,344 - [0.25 x 1,344] = 1,008). To determine the BHR for the retrofitted Komori press, do the following calculation:

$126,360 total annual center cost ÷ 1,008 hr. = $125.36/hr.

Example 3.6. Total annual center cost remains at $126,360, with no reduction in labor costs. Chargeable hours are increased by 25 percent through increased sales efforts, which puts them back at 1,344 hours (70 percent utilization in Cell B50). To determine the BHR for the Komori press, do the following calculation.

$126,360 total annual center cost ÷ 1,344 hr. = $94.02 hr.

Example 3.7. Because of a nonunion environment and added electronic gear, only $10,000 can be saved in labor costs, which reduces the total annual center cost to $106,360 ($116,359 in Cell F47). However, with no increase in volume in the center, chargeable hours are 25 percent less, or 1,008 hours (1,344 - [0.25 x 1,344] = 1,008). To determine the BHR for the Komori press, do the following calculation:

$106,360 total annual center cost ÷ 1,008 hr. = $105.52 hr.

Example 3.8. The total annual center cost remains at $106,360 because of the $10,000 savings in labor costs. With a 25 percent increase in volume through increased sales, the chargeable hours increase back to 1,344 (at 70 percent utilization in Cell B50). To determine the BHR for the Komori press, do the following calculation:

$106,360 total annual cost center ÷ 1,344 hr. = $79.14 hr.

Even with arbitrary figures, the preceding examples demonstrate that the impact of automation on hourly costs can be significant. Both top management and the estimating staff have a responsibility to work out such annual cost and productivity values, which should include increasing sales volume to keep the automated equipment busy so that BHRs are current and reasonable for the company.

3.10 Cost Markup

In a nationwide study by NAPL based on a 1994 NAPL/American Printer "Let's Get the FACTS" survey (NAPL Special Report S146), estimating methods, material markup percentages, and information on areas where printers charge for additional services were investigated. This was a follow-up study from NAPL's initial study published in 1985.

Cost markup is an additional dollar amount included in the overall cost of a job or in any material or outside purchase as part of the job. A markup is usually a percentage figure that is added to the calculated cost base of the material or outside purchase. For example, if the cost of paper for a given job is $100 and the company applies a 30 percent markup, the selling price of the paper is $130.

The theory behind cost markups on materials and outside purchases is to recover for any real costs incurred in addition to the actual cost. Markups are not intended as "hidden" profits for the company, but are dollar amounts to compensate the printer for the real costs incurred in making the material or outside service available as part of the customer's job. In the case of materials such as paper, ink, film, and plates, the cost markup percentage should recover for the printer's true costs of purchasing and inventorying the materials. This would include recovering for the cost of physically storing the material as well as the cost for using company dollars as an ROI. In the case of outside services, the markup percentage should recover for direct staff costs required to ensure that the service is properly completed, including transportation, handling, and other essential charges.

Establishing this cost markup percentage should be based on accurately gathering factual cost data for each material item or outside purchase, which are then translated to a percentage that is applied during estimating. Some printers find it difficult to accurately determine cost markup percentage given the complexity of assessing the true costs of material storage or ROI dollars. Even so, the printer should strive to carefully establish the markup percentage so that it reflects only real costs. If this is improperly done and the percentage is too high, the printer risks inflating the overall job cost and losing the order; if the percentage is too low, the printer has effectively given the customer a cost discount on the job and has neglected to add dollars that the customer should have paid for the material or outside purchase.

Estimating Methods

As noted in Figure 3.9, 65 percent of printers responding to the study indicate that they estimate jobs using time and materials with all-inclusive hourly cost rates (BHRs), which is considered the traditional method for cost estimating discussed throughout this text. Other estimating methods, with respondent percentages in parentheses, are: time and materials at manufacturing cost rates (15 percent), price lists (10 percent), time and materials at out-of-pocket hourly cost rates (5 percent), and other methods (5 percent), which include *The Franklin Catalog* and other types of standardized pricing systems as discussed in Chapter 1.

Material Markups

It is common for printers to mark up the cost of materials used to produce printing orders. The 1994 survey provides information for the average markups on film, ink, plates, paper, and outside services/labor. The report details how

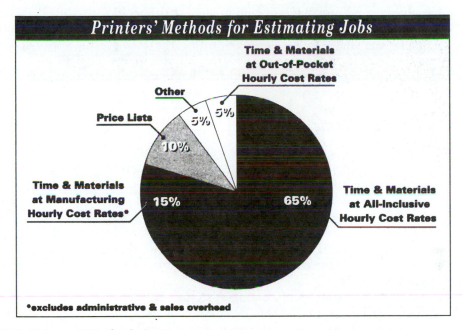

Figure 3.9 Printers' Methods for Estimating Jobs. Reproduced from NAPL's *Special Report* S146 titled "The Art of Determining Cost Markup," September 1995. For information contact NAPL at 201/342-0700.

the markups vary by company size and geographic location. For a copy of "The 'Art' of Determining Cost Markup" (S146), contact NAPL Customer Service at 1-800-642-6275, extension 1315.

3.11 Establishing Prorated Costing

Prorated costing may have particular appeal to small commercial printers and quick printers who do not wish to establish full BHRs but who may wish to cost recover for general areas of their plants. For example, a small commercial printer or quick printer may have a small stripping department which is used somewhat infrequently or which has "roaming" employees who complete many other plant duties, including stripping, platemaking, press operating, and bindery. Because prorated costing is more of a "global" costing system for a printing firm, it more easily accommodates these varied types of production situations.

It is also important to point out that prorated costing allows for separate development of fixed and variable costs, which is also on a more global basis. This provides the small printer or quick printer with a view of the total fixed or variable cost picture that is unencumbered with specific, intricate details of cost as derived by the BHR process. This is not to say that the BHR system does not work for the small printer or quick printer. Prorated costing simply provides a less specific costing system. Its accuracy approximates the BHR process if time is taken to be certain the data used and the process followed are correct.

System Overview and Description

Different types of allocation or prorated units may be used depending upon available information. The most popular allocation base is square footage as physically measured in the plant. Sometimes the number of employees or the amount of capital investment in a working center may be the allocation base. It must be noted that the criteria for selecting the prorated base should be such that the base for the units is common to all centers and reasonably reflects plant production capacities in each center. For example, Example 3.9 that follows uses square footage as the allocation base and assumes the plant is utilizing its floor space efficiently.

As with most types of costing systems, different approaches and philosophies can be taken. For this discussion of prorated costing, there are two different methods. The first, called the all-inclusive center (AIC) method, allows the administrative areas of the plant to represent a cost center, just as if administration were a production-oriented portion of the plant. The administrative center then has a calculated cost base. It is not desirable to use the AIC method for estimating purposes because printing production is normally not completed in administrative areas. Of course, the AIC method provides a specific hourly cost value that may be helpful for comparing the cost of administrative centers over time or with the costs of other segments of the plant.

The second method, called the production center (PC) method, subtracts the administrative units from the total number of units. Thus, fixed and variable costs are then prorated over only those centers specifically dedicated to production. The PC method is preferred by the estimator because it more accurately reflects the true costs that must be paid for each order moving through the plant. Administrative variable costs are prorated over production centers.

Database Needed to Establish Prorated Costing

The five groups of information that follow are needed to complete prorated costing.

1. *Employee demographics.* This information includes (1) the number of hours worked per week per employee, (2) the average number of days of

vacation per employee, and (3) the average number of paid holidays per employee per year.

2. *Plant square footage by working area or center.* Aisle and storage space should be included only as they apply. If an area is not dedicated to production, it should be classified as a "special area" or an administrative area.

3. *Utilization time.* This information includes the percentage of time (which is based on the annual total of chargeable hours) each center utilizes space or equipment.

4. *Annual fixed costs.* These costs include fixed overhead (e.g., rent, heat, and general utilities), insurance on equipment, applicable property taxes, and depreciation.

5. *Total annual variable (labor) cost.* This information should include the cost of all labor in the plant whether salaried or waged. All fringe benefits should be included as a dollar amount, as should support labor costs such as social security, retirement, unemployment compensation, and medical insurance. In the administrative category, costs should include administrative and selling expenses paid by the company, as well as sales representatives' commissions, which are paid annually.

The more accurate the collected data, the more precise the results. Keep in mind that such information gathering may be the most difficult task in establishing costs precisely. In many cases, collecting the proper array of information and formatting it in a manner that is sympathetic to the system is more difficult than mastering the mechanics of the system itself.

Example 3.9. For this example assume the following information has been gathered:

Employee demographics: All employees work 35 hours per week, take an average of 15 days paid vacation per year, and receive an average of 10 paid holidays annually.

Square footage and utilization time, by center:

Center	No. of units (sq. ft)*	Utilized time (percent)
Administration	25 (250)	100
Camera	15 (150)	70
Stripping and platemaking	5 (50)	65
Pressroom	30 (300)	80
Total	75 units	

*Any equivalent ratio system, such as the number of employees or capital investment in dollars, may be used.

Annual fixed costs: $41,600

Total annual variable (labor) cost, by center (number of employees indicated in parentheses):
Administration (6): $88,600
Camera (2): $31,500
Stripping and platemaking (4): $14,200
Pressroom (4): $58,500
Total labor cost: $192,800

To determine the prorated cost per hour for each center using the AIC method, see Figure 3.10.

If costs and hours hold as determined on an annual basis and customers are charged the indicated dollar values, cost recovery should be effective. Of course, many tangential variables enter to change this status, which implies that any such system must be monitored to maintain consistency and accuracy. The AIC method generates a cost for the administrative areas of the plant. The PC method, which is presented next, does not.

In the PC method, variable and fixed costs are prorated over only those centers that are actually dedicated to production. In addition, the variable costs of administration are prorated over the other production centers. The total number of units does not include administration. The problem data from Example 3.9 are used so comparisons can be made with Example 3.10 that follows. The total of annual production hours and chargeable hours used in the AIC method applies to the PC method with no changes except that administrative hours are not used in Example 3.10.

Example 3.10. To use the data in Example 3.9 to determine the prorated cost per hour for each center according to the PC method, see Figure 3.11.

When comparing method results, note that the high utilization of administration, as well as the averaging of administrative costs over working production centers, causes differences between solutions. Remember that as chargeable hours increase, hourly costs decrease. This fact has stimulated printing management to automate production techniques. Such automation reduces the long-term cost of labor, which has been rising considerably.

Production Standards and Budgeted Hour Cost Rates in the Printing Industry

Determining Annual Production Hours and Chargeable Hours

35 hr/wk × 52 wk/yr:		1820 hr
subtract vacations and holidays		
(25 da × 7 hr/da):		− 175 hr
annual max production hr:		1645 hr

Center	Maximum Production Hours		Utilization		Number of Chargeable Hours
Administration	1645 hr	×	100%	=	1645 hr
Camera	1645	×	70	=	1152
Stripping and Platemaking	1645	×	65	=	1070
Pressroom	1645	×	80	=	1316

Fixed Cost Proration (AIC Method)

annual fixed cost ÷ total units = annual fixed cost/unit:
$41,600 ÷ 75 units = $554.67/unit/yr

Center	Units		Cost/Unit		Annual Cost/Center		Number of Chargeable Hours		Fixed Cost/Center/Hour
Administration	25	×	$554.67	=	$13,867	÷	1645 hr	=	$ 8.43
Camera	15	×	554.67	=	8,320	÷	1152	=	7.22
Stripping and Platemaking	5	×	554.67	=	2,773	÷	1070	=	2.59
Pressroom	30	×	554.67	=	16,640	÷	1316	=	12.64
	75				$41,600				$30.88

Variable Cost Proration (AIC Method)

Center	Annual Wage and/or Salary		Number of Chargeable Hours		Variable Cost/Center/Hour
Administration	$ 88,600	÷	1645	=	$ 53.86
Camera	31,500	÷	1152	=	27.34
Stripping and Platemaking	14,200	÷	1070	=	13.27
Pressroom	58,500	÷	1316	=	44.45
	$192,800				$138.92

Totals Summation

Center	Fixed Cost/Center/Hour		Variable Cost/Center/Hour		Total Cost/Center/Hour
Administration	$ 8.43	+	$ 53.86	=	$ 62.29
Camera	7.22	+	27.34	=	34.56
Stripping and Platemaking	2.59	+	13.27	=	15.86
Pressroom	12.64	+	44.45	=	57.09
Figure 3.11	$30.88	+	$138.92	=	$169.80

Figure 3.10 AIC method solution for Example 3.9

Fixed Cost Proration (PC Method)

annual fixed cost ÷ total production units* = annual fixed cost/unit

$41,600 ÷ 50 units = $832.00/unit/yr

Center	Units		Cost/Unit		Annual Cost/Center		Number of Chargeable Hours		Fixed Cost/Center/Hour
Camera	15	×	$832.00	=	$12,480	÷	1152 hr	=	$10.83
Stripping and Platemaking	5	×	832.00	=	4,160	÷	1070	=	3.89
Pressroom	30	×	832.00	=	24,960	÷	1316	=	18.97
	50				$41,600				$33.69

Variable Cost Proration (PC Method)

administrative variable cost ÷ total production units = annual variable cost/unit

$88,600 ÷ 50 units = $1772.00/unit/yr

Center	Units		Administrative Cost/Unit		Administrative Cost/Center		Center Annual Wage		Annual Labor Cost		Chargeable Hour		Variable Cost/Center/Hour
Camera	15	×	$1772	=	$26,580	+	31,500	=	58,080	÷	1152 hr	=	$ 50.42
Stripping and Platemaking	5	×	1772	=	8,860	+	14,200	=	23,060	÷	1070	=	21.55
Pressroom	30	×	1772	=	53,160	+	58,500	=	111,660	÷	1316	=	84.85
	50				$88,600		104,200		192,800				$156.82

Totals Summation

Center	Fixed Cost/Center/Hour		Variable Cost/Center/Hour		Total Cost/Center/Hour
Camera	$10.83	+	$ 50.42	=	$ 61.25
Stripping and Platemaking	3.89	+	21.55	=	25.44
Pressroom	18.97	+	84.85	=	103.82
	$33.69		$156.82		$190.51

*75 total units minus 25 units for administration

Figure 3.11 PC method solution for Example 3.10

Appendix to Chapter 3

All-Inclusive BHRs

Figure 3A.1 Composition including DTP, color publishing systems, work-stations, and output devices

Figure 3A.2 Lithographic preparatory including process cameras, film processors, vacuum frame platemakers, automatic plate processors, and stripping

Figure 3A.3 Scanners

Figure 3A.4 Duplicators and small presses

Figure 3A.5 Offset presses, one- and two-color

Figure 3A.6 Offset presses, four-, five-, and six-color

Figure 3A.7 Offset presses, seven- and eight-color

Figure 3A.8 Letterpress and flexographic press

Figure 3A.9 Bindery cutters

Figure 3A.10 Bindery folders

Figure 3A.11 Perfect binders, collators, and bindery systems

Figure 3A.12 Other bindery equipment

The figures in this appendix were reproduced with permission of Printing Industries Association, Inc., of Southern California from its *1994-1995 Blue Book of Production Standards and Costs for the Printing Industry*. Note that all rates are based on prevailing wages in Southern California and a standard 40-hour work week.

ALL-INCLUSIVE HOURLY COST RATES
BASED ON PREVAILING WAGES IN SOUTHERN CALIFORNIA
AND A STANDARD 40 HOUR WORK WEEK

NAME OF COST CENTER	SIZE	APPROXIMATE INVESTMENT IN EQUIPMENT	CREW	COST PER HOUR AT PRODUCTIVITY OF 60%	70%	80%
COMPOSITION						
Proofreading	N/A	1412.40	1	46.38	39.75	34.80
Hand Composition	N/A	16831.10	1	54.93	47.08	41.22
Photo-Typositor	N/A	8738.69	1	50.68	43.44	38.03
Pasteup and Copy Prep	N/A	1412.40	1	48.38	41.46	36.30
IBM Electric Composer	N/A	13182.40	1	52.52	45.01	39.41
DESKTOP PUBLISHING						
Entry Level System Quadra 605, 600 DPI Laser Prtr Color Monitor, Scanner	N/A	5940.00	1	62.79	53.82	47.12
Basic Production System Quadra 605, Thermal Laser, Color Monitor, Scanner	N/A	19690.00	1	72.19	61.87	54.17
Imagesetting & Film Process. Quad 650, RIP, Clr Monitor, Processor, Laser Imagesetter	N/A	39468.00	1	84.98	72.83	63.76
Imagesetting System with Processor & Color Proofing Quad 650, RIP, Color Monitor Processor, Laser Imagesetter	N/A	57915.00	1	87.79	75.24	65.87
High Production System Quad 950, Color Monitor, CD-ROM, Drum Scanner, Laser Color Copier	N/A	117700.00	1	123.70	106.01	92.81
COLOR PUBLISHING SYSTEMS						
Designer/Creative Scanner, Platform, Laser Prtr, Imagesetter, Software, Training	N/A	67430.00	1	91.68	78.57	68.79
Mid-Level Production Scanner, Platform, Network, Laser Prtr, Imagesetter, Software, Training, Disk Storage	N/A	249150.00	1	177.82	152.40	133.42
Professional Pre-Press Color Scanner, Network, Platform, Laser Prtr, Color Prtr, Color Proofer, Imagesetter, Software, Disk Storage, Train & Support	N/A	702350.00	1	315.77	270.63	236.94
WORKSTATIONS						
VariColor 2960 Layout Mac IIvx, SM Color Monitor, Internal CD-ROM, Software	N/A	6928.90	1	60.43	51.79	45.34
PC Photoshop Processor 486, SM Color Monitor, Software, 32MB RAM	N/A	13194.50	1	64.04	54.89	48.05
MAC Photoshop SM Multimode Monitor, Software	N/A	17594.50	1	66.87	57.31	50.18
VariColor 2992B Processor, Software, 1GB Hard Disk, Supports up to 7SCSI Devices	N/A	19644.90	1	68.10	58.36	51.10

Figure 3A.1 Budgeted hour cost rates: Composition including desktop publishing, color publishing systems, workstations, and output devices

ALL-INCLUSIVE HOURLY COST RATES

BASED ON PREVAILING WAGES IN SOUTHERN CALIFORNIA AND A STANDARD 40 HOUR WORK WEEK

NAME OF COST CENTER	SIZE	APPROXIMATE INVESTMENT IN EQUIPMENT	CREW	COST PER HOUR AT PRODUCTIVITY OF		
				60%	70%	80%
OUTPUT DEVICES						
Low Level Imagesetter Film Processor, 2 PG Format,	N/A	43725.00		18.74	16.06	14.06
Mid-Range Imagesetter Film Processor, 2 PG Format,	N/A	84150.00		35.45	30.38	26.60
High Resolution Imagesetter Film Processor, 2 PG Format, Process Color, 3000DPI+	N/A	125950.00		52.72	45.18	39.56
High Resolution Imagesetter Film Processor, 4 PG Format, Process Color, 3000DPI+	N/A	185845.00		77.38	66.32	58.06
High Resolution Imagesetter Film Processor, 8 PG Format, Process Color, 3000DPI+	N/A	280500.00		116.44	99.79	87.37

Figure 3A.1 *(continued)*

LITHOGRAPHIC PREPARATORY

CAMERAS

				60%	70%	80%
Horizontal	14 X 18	5085.00	1	49.54	42.46	37.17
Horizontal	14 x 18	6780.00	1	50.08	42.92	37.58
Vertical	14 x 18	3955.00	1	46.45	39.81	34.85
Vertical	14 x 18	7910.00	1	47.72	40.89	35.80
Vertical	16 x 20	4746.00	1	46.79	40.10	35.11
Vertical	16 x 20	8362.00	1	47.94	41.09	35.97
Vertical	16 x 20	10848.00	1	48.74	41.77	36.57
Horizontal	20 x 24	12995.00	1	66.42	56.93	49.84
Vertical	20 x 24	16498.00	1	64.82	55.55	48.64
Horizontal	20 x 24	21018.00	1	68.99	59.13	51.77
Vertical	20 x 24	24408.00	1	67.35	57.72	50.53
Horizontal	20 x 24	36883.20	1	74.07	63.48	55.57
Vertical	20 x 24	37290.00	1	71.47	61.25	53.63
Horizontal	32 x 32	33109.00	1	75.37	64.60	56.55
Horizontal	32 x 32	39595.20	1	77.45	66.37	58.11
Horizontal	32 x 32	50646.60	1	80.98	69.40	60.76
Lowbed	30 x 40	42985.20	1	79.76	68.35	59.84
Overhead	30 x 40	50172.00	1	81.15	69.55	60.89
Overhead	30 x 40	58308.00	1	83.75	71.78	62.84
Horizontal	40 x 40	40680.00	1	86.28	73.95	64.74
Overhead	40 x 40	56952.00	1	91.49	78.41	68.65
Overhead	40 x 40	72094.00	1	96.33	82.56	72.28

FILM PROCESSORS

				60%	70%	80%
	20"	7458.00	1	46.41	39.78	34.83
	20"	11808.50	1	47.81	40.97	35.87
	20"	14916.00	1	48.80	41.82	36.62
	26"	13921.60	1	49.19	42.16	36.91
	26"	19888.00	1	51.10	43.79	38.34
	26"	23617.00	1	52.29	44.81	39.24
	26"	27843.20	1	53.64	45.97	40.25
	26"	34306.80	1	55.71	47.75	41.80
	26"	37290.00	1	56.67	48.56	42.52
	32"	16159.00	1	57.87	49.60	43.42
	32"	21131.00	1	59.46	50.96	44.62
	32"	34804.00	1	63.84	54.71	47.90
	32"	42013.40	1	66.15	56.69	49.63
	48"	27346.00	1	62.43	53.51	46.84
	48"	33561.00	1	64.42	55.21	48.34
	48"	39278.80	1	66.25	56.78	49.71
	48"	47606.90	1	68.91	59.06	51.71

Figure 3A.2 Budgeted hour cost rates: Lithographic preparatory including process cameras, film processors, vacuum frame platemakers, automatic plate processors, stripping

ALL-INCLUSIVE HOURLY COST RATES
BASED ON PREVAILING WAGES IN SOUTHERN CALIFORNIA AND A STANDARD 40 HOUR WORK WEEK

NAME OF COST CENTER	SIZE	APPROXIMATE INVESTMENT IN EQUIPMENT	CREW	COST PER HOUR AT PRODUCTIVITY OF 60%	70%	80%
VACUUM FRAME PLATEMAKERS						
	17 x 22	2237.40	1	45.80	39.25	34.36
	17 x 22	3107.50	1	46.08	39.49	34.57
	23 x 27	4599.10	1	48.07	41.20	36.07
	23 x 27	7085.10	1	48.87	41.88	36.67
	24 x 28	4350.50	1	48.08	41.20	36.07
	24 x 28	7085.10	1	48.95	41.95	36.73
	28 x 32	4226.20	1	55.30	47.39	41.49
	28 x 32	6960.80	1	56.17	48.14	42.15
	30 x 40	6893.00	1	56.82	48.70	42.63
	30 x 40	10735.00	1	58.05	49.75	43.56
	30 x 40	12430.00	1	58.59	50.22	43.96
	30 x 40	14916.00	1	59.39	50.90	44.56
	35 x 45	6893.00	1	57.53	49.30	43.17
	35 x 45	9153.00	1	58.25	49.92	43.71
	35 x 45	11187.00	1	58.90	50.48	44.20
	35 x 45	14125.00	1	59.84	51.29	44.90
	40 x 50	12091.00	1	65.16	55.84	48.89
	40 x 50	15820.00	1	66.35	56.86	49.78
	40 x 60	14803.00	1	67.32	57.70	50.51
	40 x 60	18645.00	1	68.55	58.75	51.44
	48 x 60	14351.00	1	67.18	57.57	50.41
	48 x 60	22261.00	1	69.71	59.74	52.31
AUTOMATIC PLATE PROCESSORS						
	24″	8079.50	1	58.23	49.90	43.69
	24″	12656.00	1	59.69	51.16	44.79
	24″	14916.00	1	60.41	51.78	45.33
	24″	18984.00	1	61.72	52.89	46.31
	32″	10814.10	1	59.71	51.18	44.81
	32″	16385.00	1	61.50	52.70	46.14
	32″	18419.00	1	62.15	53.26	46.63
	32″	20792.00	1	62.91	53.91	47.20
	40″	11413.00	1	60.79	52.10	45.61
	40″	18984.00	1	63.21	54.18	47.43
	40″	21752.50	1	64.10	54.94	48.10
	48″	15288.90	1	67.68	58.01	50.78
	48″	22374.00	1	69.95	59.95	52.48
	48″	28837.60	1	72.02	61.72	54.04
	48″	34804.00	1	73.93	63.36	55.47
	48″	64636.00	1	84.13	72.10	63.12
	60″	25357.20	1	72.13	61.82	54.12
	60″	31323.60	1	74.04	63.46	55.56
	60″	35030.00	1	75.23	64.47	56.45
	60″	67009.00	1	85.87	73.59	64.43
STRIPPING						
Small Presses(Black & White)		900.00	1	46.81	40.12	35.12
Mechanical Color		1100.00	1	58.00	49.71	43.52
Large Presses, Process Color		1750.00	1	80.94	69.37	60.73

Figure 3A.2 *(continued)*

ALL-INCLUSIVE HOURLY COST RATES
BASED ON PREVAILING WAGES IN SOUTHERN CALIFORNIA
AND A STANDARD 40 HOUR WORK WEEK

NAME OF COST CENTER	SIZE	APPROXIMATE INVESTMENT IN EQUIPMENT	RATED SHEETS PER HOUR	CREW	COST PER HOUR AT PRODUCTIVITY OF		
					60%	70%	80%

SCANNERS

DRUM PMT SCANNERS

NAME OF COST CENTER	SIZE	INVESTMENT	RATED SHEETS	CREW	60%	70%	80%
ScanMate Magic	8 x 10"	14300.00		1	62.23	53.33	46.69
ScanMate	8.5 x 11"	19800.00		1	64.97	55.68	48.75
ScanMate Plus	8.5 x 11"	26400.00		1	67.80	58.10	50.87
ScanMate 5000	8.8 x 11.9"	49500.00		1	76.17	65.28	57.15
Magnascan Plus	20 x 25"	108900.00		1	119.58	102.48	89.72
D/C 636EQ	20 x 25"	164450.00		1	138.06	118.32	103.59
D/C 636MQ	20 x 25"	197450.00		1	148.62	127.37	111.51
D/C 656EA	20 x 25"	230450.00		1	160.60	137.64	120.50
ChromaGraph S3500	17.72 x 20.08"	115500.00		1	122.40	104.90	91.84
ChromaGraph S3700	17.72 x 20.08"	139700.00		1	131.56	112.75	98.71
ChromoGraph S3800	25.6 x 20.08"	160600.00		1	139.87	119.87	104.95

Figure 3A.3 Budgeted hour cost rates: Scanners

DUPLICATORS & SMALL PRESSES

NAME OF COST CENTER	SIZE	INVESTMENT	RATED SHEETS	CREW	60%	70%	80%
Multi, 1250, chute del.	10 x 15	14690.00	9000.00	1	52.01	44.57	39.02
Multi, 1250, chain del.	10 x 15	18080.00	9000.00	1	52.85	45.29	39.65
Hamada 500CDA	11 x 15	16950.00	9000.00	1	52.55	45.04	39.43
Multi, 1650, chute del.	12 x 16	15820.00	11000.00	1	52.57	45.05	39.44
Multi, 1650, chain del.	12 x 16	18984.00	10000.00	1	53.37	45.74	40.05
Heidelberg TOM	11 x 15	38060.00	10000.00	1	58.17	49.85	43.64
Heidelberg TOK	11 x 15	39160.00	10000.00	1	58.44	50.08	43.85
AB Dick 8820	11 x 17	15678.75	10000.00	1	52.51	45.01	39.40
AB Dick 1-8855S, 2/c	11 x 17	22569.49	10000.00	1	54.69	46.87	41.03
Ryobi 2800 CD	11 x 17	19097.00	9000.00	1	53.39	45.75	40.06
Hamada 600 CD	11 x 17	17628.00	9000.00	1	53.00	45.42	39.77
Ryobi 3200 CD	12 x 17	23730.00	9000.00	1	54.69	46.87	41.03
Embassy Super Maxim	12 x 18	26555.00	10000.00	1	61.02	52.29	45.78
AB Dick 9810	13 x 17	20057.50	10000.00	1	59.41	50.91	44.57
AB Dick 9810, 2/c	13 x 17	27120.00	10000.00	1	61.42	52.64	46.09
Multi 1960, chute del.	18 x 15	20453.00	8500.00	1	60.06	51.47	45.06
Multi 1960, chain del.	18 x 15	24860.00	8500.00	1	61.19	52.44	45.91
Multi 3650 Auto, chute del.	12 x 16	23504.00	10000.00	1	55.04	47.17	41.30
Multi 3650 Auto, chain del.	12 x 16	28024.00	10000.00	1	56.16	48.13	42.14
Multi 1650, 2/c, chain del.	12 x 16	22600.00	10000.00	1	60.62	51.95	45.48
Multi 1962, 2/c, chain del.	18 x 15	33561.00	8500.00	1	63.37	54.31	47.55
Multi 3875 Auto	12 x 18	62715.00	9000.00	1	71.12	60.95	53.36
Hamada 700 CD	18 x 14	21357.00	9000.00	1	60.83	52.13	45.64
Ryobi 500N	14 x 18	28024.00	8000.00	1	62.50	53.56	46.90
Ryobi 500N-NP	14 x 18	41132.00	8000.00	1	66.00	56.56	49.52
Davidson 702PJ	14 x 17	38024.50	8000.00	1	65.00	55.71	48.77
Ryobi 3200PFA, 2/c	12 x 17	50850.00	9000.00	1	67.85	58.15	50.91
Ryobi 3302M	12 x 17	61020.00	9000.00	1	70.70	60.59	53.05
Hamada 800 CDX	14 x 20	31527.00	9000.00	1	63.64	54.54	47.75
Multi Eagle	15 x 20	58760.00	10000.00	1	70.47	60.40	52.88
Davidson 901, chain del.	15 x 20	25190.00	9000.00	1	62.07	53.20	46.57
A.B. Dick 9890	17 x 22	31182.35	10000.00	1	68.69	58.87	51.54
A.B. Dick 9890, 2/c	17 x 22	41233.70	10000.00	1	71.20	61.02	53.42

Figure 3A.4 Budgeted hour cost rates: Duplicators & small presses

ALL-INCLUSIVE HOURLY COST RATES
BASED ON PREVAILING WAGES IN SOUTHERN CALIFORNIA
AND A STANDARD 40 HOUR WORK WEEK

NAME OF COST CENTER	SIZE	APPROXIMATE INVESTMENT IN EQUIPMENT	RATED SHEETS PER HOUR	CREW	COST PER HOUR AT PRODUCTIVITY OF 60%	70%	80%

OFFSET PRESSES

ONE COLOR PRESSES

NAME OF COST CENTER	SIZE	INVESTMENT	RATED SHEETS	CREW	60%	70%	80%
Heidelberg GTO52	14 x 20	71775.00	8000.00	1	73.53	63.02	55.17
Heidelberg MO	19 x 25	145640.00	12000.00	1	97.74	83.77	73.34
Komori S26	20 x 26	123585.00	11000.00	1	93.86	80.44	70.42
MAN Roland 201	20 x 29	162800.00	12000.00	1	104.59	89.64	78.48
Heidelberg SORM	20 x 29	153450.00	12000.00	1	101.98	87.40	76.52
Heidelberg SORS	28 x 40	228800.00	12000.00	1	133.01	113.99	99.80

TWO COLOR PRESSES

NAME OF COST CENTER	SIZE	INVESTMENT	RATED SHEETS	CREW	60%	70%	80%
Heidelberg GTOZP *	14 x 20	171930.00	8000.00	1	109.79	94.09	82.38
Heidelberg MOZP *	19 x 25	301730.00	12000.00	1	146.65	125.68	110.03
Komori S226	20 x 26	229515.00	11000.00	1	129.24	110.76	96.97
Komori S226P *	20 x 26	277145.00	11000.00	1	141.67	121.41	106.30
Komori Lithrone 226-II	20 x 26	358985.00	13000.00	1	162.05	138.88	121.59
Akiyama BT228	20 x 28	390500.00	13000.00	1	169.93	145.63	127.50
Komori Lithrone 228-II	20 x 28	429605.00	13000.00	1	183.61	157.36	137.77
MAN Roland 202	20 x 29	262900.00	12000.00	1	141.80	121.53	106.40
Heidelberg SORMZ	20 x 29	259930.00	12000.00	1	140.94	120.79	105.75
MAN Roland MP104*	28 x 40	638000.00	13000.00	1	242.45	207.79	181.92
MAN Roland 702	28 x 40	880000.00	15000.00	1	302.18	258.98	226.73
Heidelberg SORSZ	28 x 40	359700.00	12000.00	1	172.22	147.60	129.22
Komori Lithrone 240P *	28 x 40	582615.00	11000.00	1	229.21	196.44	171.99
Komori Lithrone 240-III	28 x 40	659120.00	13000.00	1	248.34	212.83	186.34
Akiyama 240	28 x 40	617100.00	13000.00	1	237.19	203.28	177.97
Komori Lithrone 244-III	32 x 44	853325.00	13000.00	1	305.31	261.66	229.08
Komori Lithrone 250-III	38 x 50	1474000.00	13000.00	1	462.08	396.02	346.71
MAN Roland 800 55	39 x 55	1073600.00	10000.00	1	366.91	314.46	275.31
MAN Roland 800 55C	39 x 55	1501500.00	10000.00	1	473.71	405.99	355.44
MAN Roland 800 63	47 x 63	1256200.00	10000.00	1	418.17	358.39	313.77
MAN Roland 800 63C	47 x 63	1685200.00	10000.00	1	525.28	450.18	394.13

* denotes Perfector
C denotes Coater

				CREW	60%	70%	80%
Feeder				1	42.80	36.69	32.12
Second Pressman				1	60.75	52.06	45.58
Floor Help				1	32.07	27.49	24.07

Figure 3A.5 Budgeted hour cost rates: Offset presses, 1- and 2-color

ALL-INCLUSIVE HOURLY COST RATES
BASED ON PREVAILING WAGES IN SOUTHERN CALIFORNIA AND A STANDARD 40 HOUR WORK WEEK

NAME OF COST CENTER	SIZE	APPROXIMATE INVESTMENT IN EQUIPMENT	RATED SHEETS PER HOUR	CREW	COST PER HOUR AT PRODUCTIVITY OF		
					60%	70%	80%

OFFSET PRESSES

HOURLY RATES FOR PRESSES FOUR COLOR AND LARGER, WILL BE LISTED BY EQUIPMENT CONFIGURATION, SIZE AND INVESTMENT RATHER THAN BY A SPECIFIC MANUFACTURER.

FOUR COLOR PRESSES

NAME OF COST CENTER	SIZE	INVESTMENT	RATED SHEETS	CREW	60%	70%	80%
Basic Model	14 x 20	333520.00	8000.00	1	158.52	135.85	118.94
Perfector	14 x 20	366410.00	8000.00	1	167.47	143.52	125.65
Console	14 x 20	464915.00	10000.00	1	191.70	164.30	143.84
Console, Hi Pile Feed	19 x 25	728200.00	12000.00	1	265.13	227.23	198.94
Console, Hi Pile, Perfector	19 x 25	765270.00	12000.00	1	274.32	235.10	205.83
Console	20 x 26	700315.00	13000.00	1	260.93	223.62	195.78
Console, Coater	20 x 26	870391.50	13000.00	1	303.55	260.15	227.76
Console	20 x 28	591800.00	13000.00	1	235.08	201.47	176.39
Console, Coater	20 x 28	979852.50	13000.00	1	331.42	284.04	248.67
Console	20 x 28	986480.00	13000.00	1	333.82	286.10	250.48
Console	20 x 28	794475.00	13000.00	1	288.85	247.56	216.74
Console	20 x 29	825000.00	12000.00	1	297.18	254.69	222.98
Console, Coater	20 x 29	938300.00	12000.00	1	325.25	278.75	244.05
Console	28 x 40	1205600.00	13000.00	1	397.16	340.38	298.00
Console, Perfector	28 x 40	1158300.00	13000.00	1	386.10	330.90	289.70
Console, Coater, Perfector	28 x 40	1426700.00	13000.00	1	454.77	389.76	341.23
Console	28 x 40	1246300.00	13000.00	1	408.30	349.92	306.36
Console, Coater	28 x 40	1743500.00	15000.00	1	532.87	456.69	399.83
Console, Coater	28 x 40	1467400.00	13000.00	1	464.40	398.01	348.46
Console	28 x 40	1122000.00	13000.00	1	377.98	323.95	283.61
Console, Coater	28 x 40	1353000.00	13000.00	1	436.00	373.67	327.15
Console	32 x 44	1595000.00	13000.00	1	502.12	430.33	376.76
Console, Coater	32 x 44	1980000.00	13000.00	1	597.95	512.46	448.66
Console	38 x 50	2772000.00	13000.00	1	796.90	682.97	597.94
Console, Coater	38 x 50	3223000.00	13000.00	1	914.12	783.43	685.89
Console	39 x 50	1917300.00	10000.00	1	590.53	506.10	443.09
Console	39 x 55	2008600.00	10000.00	1	620.48	531.77	465.56
Console, Coater	39 x 55	2436500.00	10000.00	1	728.18	624.08	546.38
Console	47 x 63	2169200.00	10000.00	1	664.69	569.67	498.74
Console, Coater	47 x 63	2597100.00	10000.00	1	771.77	661.43	579.08

Console has remote inking, dampening and registration controls.

Feeder				1	43.66	37.42	32.76
Second Pressman				1	66.90	57.33	50.19
Floor Help				1	33.41	28.63	25.07

Figure 3A.6 Budgeted hour cost rates: Offset presses, 4-, 5-, and 6-color

ALL-INCLUSIVE HOURLY COST RATES
BASED ON PREVAILING WAGES IN SOUTHERN CALIFORNIA
AND A STANDARD 40 HOUR WORK WEEK

NAME OF COST CENTER	SIZE	APPROXIMATE INVESTMENT IN EQUIPMENT	RATED SHEETS PER HOUR	CREW	COST PER HOUR AT PRODUCTIVITY OF		
					60%	70%	80%

OFFSET PRESSES

HOURLY RATES FOR PRESSES FOUR COLOR AND LARGER, WILL BE LISTED
BY EQUIPMENT CONFIGURATION, SIZE AND INVESTMENT RATHER THAN BY A
SPECIFIC MANUFACTURER.

FIVE COLOR PRESSES

NAME OF COST CENTER	SIZE	INVESTMENT	SHEETS/HR	CREW	60%	70%	80%
Basic Model	14 x 20	410080.00	8000.00	1	192.66	165.12	144.56
Console	14 x 20	464915.00	10000.00	1	206.36	176.86	154.84
Console, High Pile Feed	19 x 25	859210.00	12000.00	1	309.27	265.06	232.06
Console, High Pile, Perfector	19 x 25	969540.00	12000.00	1	338.03	289.70	253.64
Console	20 x 26	818015.00	13000.00	1	301.13	258.08	225.94
Console, Coater	20 x 26	999823.00	13000.00	1	347.68	297.97	260.87
Console	20 x 28	912175.00	13000.00	1	329.78	282.63	247.45
Console, Coater	20 x 28	1097552.50	13000.00	1	375.72	322.01	281.92
Console	20 x 28	718300.00	13000.00	1	280.69	240.56	210.61
Console, Coater	20 x 28	998800.00	12000.00	1	350.84	300.68	263.25
Console	20 x 29	886600.00	12000.00	1	322.40	276.31	241.91
Console	28 x 40	1195700.00	13000.00	1	407.61	349.33	305.84
Console	28 x 40	1482800.00	13000.00	1	480.64	411.93	360.64
Console, Coater	28 x 40	1744600.00	13000.00	1	546.79	468.62	410.27
Console	28 x 40	1507000.00	13000.00	1	484.18	414.96	363.30
Console, Coater	28 x 40	1584000.00	13000.00	1	506.00	433.66	379.67
Console	28 x 40	1353000.00	13000.00	1	447.41	383.45	335.71
Console	32 x 44	1826000.00	13000.00	1	570.47	488.91	428.04
Console, Coater	32 x 44	2200000.00	13000.00	1	664.83	569.78	498.84
Console	38 x 50	3003000.00	13000.00	1	867.38	743.38	650.82
Console, Coater	38 x 50	3454000.00	13000.00	1	981.90	841.52	736.75
Console	39 x 50	2524500.00	10000.00	1	751.38	643.96	563.78
Console, Coater	39 x 50	2953500.00	10000.00	1	858.74	735.97	644.34
Console	39 x 55	2526700.00	10000.00	1	754.06	646.26	565.79
Console, Coater	39 x 55	2954600.00	10000.00	1	861.15	738.03	646.15
Console	47 x 63	2798400.00	10000.00	1	827.88	709.52	621.18
Console, Coater	47 x 63	3226300.00	10000.00	1	936.05	802.23	702.35

Console has remote inking, dampening and registration controls.

				CREW	60%	70%	80%
Feeder				1	43.66	37.42	32.76
Second Pressman				1	66.90	57.33	50.19
Floor Help				1	33.41	28.63	25.07

Figure 3A.6 *(continued)*

ALL-INCLUSIVE HOURLY COST RATES

BASED ON PREVAILING WAGES IN SOUTHERN CALIFORNIA AND A STANDARD 40 HOUR WORK WEEK

NAME OF COST CENTER	SIZE	APPROXIMATE INVESTMENT IN EQUIPMENT	RATED SHEETS PER HOUR	CREW	COST PER HOUR AT PRODUCTIVITY OF		
					60%	70%	80%

OFFSET PRESSES

HOURLY RATES FOR PRESSES FOUR COLOR AND LARGER, WILL BE LISTED BY EQUIPMENT CONFIGURATION, SIZE AND INVESTMENT RATHER THAN BY A SPECIFIC MANUFACTURER.

SIX COLOR PRESSES

NAME OF COST CENTER	SIZE	INVESTMENT	RATED SHEETS	CREW	60%	70%	80%
Console	14 x 20	670890.00	10000.00	1	267.83	229.54	200.96
Console	20 x 26	935715.00	13000.00	1	340.58	291.89	255.54
Console, Coater	20 x 26	1070481.50	13000.00	1	375.70	321.99	281.90
Console	20 x 28	797500.00	13000.00	1	311.72	267.16	233.90
Console	20 x 28	1210000.00	13000.00	1	413.95	354.77	310.60
Console, Coater	20 x 28	1474000.00	13000.00	1	477.69	409.40	358.43
Console	20 x 29	980100.00	12000.00	1	354.44	303.76	265.94
Console, Coater	20 x 29	1092300.00	12000.00	1	383.91	329.03	288.06
Console, Perfector	28 x 40	1607100.00	13000.00	1	520.93	446.45	390.87
Console, Coater, Perfector	28 x 40	1871100.00	13000.00	1	588.44	504.31	441.52
Console	28 x 40	1661000.00	13000.00	1	536.75	460.01	402.74
Console, Coater	28 x 40	1923900.00	13000.00	1	603.16	516.93	452.57
Console	28 x 40	1767700.00	13000.00	1	560.40	480.28	420.49
Console, Coater	28 x 40	1983300.00	13000.00	1	616.17	528.08	462.33
Console	28 x 40	1316700.00	13000.00	1	449.12	384.91	336.99
Console, Coater	28 x 40	1772100.00	13000.00	1	564.98	484.20	423.92
Console	28 x 40	2031700.00	15000.00	1	628.30	538.47	471.43
Console, Coater	28 x 40	2293500.00	15000.00	1	696.17	596.64	522.36
Console	32 x 44	1936000.00	13000.00	1	611.36	523.95	458.72
Console, Coater	32 x 44	2332000.00	13000.00	1	715.49	613.20	536.86
Console	38 x 50	3234000.00	13000.00	1	941.26	806.70	706.26
Console, Coater	38 x 50	3685000.00	13000.00	1	1056.03	905.05	792.37
Console	39 x 50	2835800.00	10000.00	1	851.31	729.60	638.77
Console, Coater	39 x 50	3264800.00	10000.00	1	959.30	822.16	719.80
Console	39 x 55	2919400.00	10000.00	1	872.03	747.36	654.31
Console, Coater	39 x 55	3346200.00	10000.00	1	980.39	840.22	735.61
Console	47 x 63	3078900.00	10000.00	1	926.44	793.99	695.14
Console, Coater	47 x 63	3516700.00	10000.00	1	1038.79	890.28	779.43

Console has remote inking, dampening and registration controls.

Feeder				1	48.14	41.25	36.12
Second Pressman				1	66.90	57.33	50.19
Floor Help				1	33.41	28.63	25.07

Figure 3A.6 (continued)

ALL-INCLUSIVE HOURLY COST RATES

BASED ON PREVAILING WAGES IN SOUTHERN CALIFORNIA AND A STANDARD 40 HOUR WORK WEEK

NAME OF COST CENTER	SIZE	APPROXIMATE INVESTMENT IN EQUIPMENT	RATED SHEETS PER HOUR	CREW	COST PER HOUR AT PRODUCTIVITY OF 60%	70%	80%
OFFSET PRESSES							

HOURLY RATES FOR PRESSES FOUR COLOR AND LARGER, WILL BE LISTED BY EQUIPMENT CONFIGURATION, SIZE AND INVESTMENT RATHER THAN BY A SPECIFIC MANUFACTURER.

SEVEN COLOR PRESSES

NAME OF COST CENTER	SIZE	APPROXIMATE INVESTMENT	RATED SHEETS PER HOUR	CREW	60%	70%	80%
Console	28 x 40	1986600.00	13000.00	1	627.26	537.58	470.65
Console, Coater	28 x 40	2249500.00	13000.00	1	694.99	595.63	521.47
Console	28 x 40	2029500.00	13000.00	1	638.05	546.83	478.75
Console, Coater	28 x 40	2245100.00	13000.00	1	696.53	596.95	522.63
Console, Perfector	28 x 40	1835900.00	13000.00	1	590.98	506.49	443.43
Console, Coater, Perfector	28 x 40	2099900.00	13000.00	1	659.24	564.99	494.65
Console	28 x 40	1765500.00	13000.00	1	573.37	491.40	430.22
Console, Coater	28 x 40	2002000.00	13000.00	1	633.65	543.06	475.45
Console, Coater	28 x 40	2531100.00	15000.00	1	766.10	656.57	574.83
Console	28 x 40	2268200.00	15000.00	1	698.36	598.52	524.00

Console has remote inking, dampening and registration controls.

Feeder				1	**48.85**	**41.87**	**36.66**
Second Pressman				1	**73.73**	**63.19**	**55.32**
Floor Help				1	**34.64**	**29.69**	**25.99**

EIGHT COLOR PRESSES

NAME OF COST CENTER	SIZE	APPROXIMATE INVESTMENT	RATED SHEETS PER HOUR	CREW	60%	70%	80%
Console	28 x 40	2290200.00	13000.00	1	715.61	613.30	536.94
Console, Coater	28 x 40	2505800.00	13000.00	1	772.85	662.36	579.89
Console, Perfector	28 x 40	2064700.00	13000.00	1	658.57	564.42	494.15
Console, Coater, Perfector	28 x 40	2328700.00	13000.00	1	726.99	623.06	545.48
Console, Coater	28 x 40	2244000.00	13000.00	1	706.00	605.07	529.73
Console	28 x 40	2002000.00	13000.00	1	643.03	551.10	482.49
Console, Coater	28 x 40	2871000.00	15000.00	1	862.30	739.02	647.01
Console	28 x 40	2609200.00	15000.00	1	794.42	680.85	596.08

Console has remote inking, dampening and registration controls.

Feeder				1	**48.85**	**41.87**	**36.66**
Second Pressman				1	**73.73**	**63.19**	**55.32**
Floor Help				1	**34.64**	**29.69**	**25.99**

Figure 3A.7 Budgeted hour cost rates: Offset presses, 7- and 8-color

ALL-INCLUSIVE HOURLY COST RATES
BASED ON PREVAILING WAGES IN SOUTHERN CALIFORNIA
AND A STANDARD 40 HOUR WORK WEEK

NAME OF COST CENTER	SIZE	APPROXIMATE INVESTMENT IN EQUIPMENT	RATED SHEETS PER HOUR	CREW	COST PER HOUR AT PRODUCTIVITY OF 60%	70%	80%

LETTERPRESS PRESSES

HOURLY RATES FOR PRESSES FOUR COLOR AND LARGER, WILL BE LISTED BY EQUIPMENT CONFIGURATION, SIZE AND INVESTMENT RATHER THAN BY A SPECIFIC MANUFACTURER.

LETTERPRESS

NAME OF COST CENTER	SIZE	APPROXIMATE INVESTMENT IN EQUIPMENT	RATED SHEETS PER HOUR	CREW	60%	70%	80%
Heidelberg, Stamp & Emboss.	10 x 15	29622.95	5500.00	1	62.33	53.42	46.77
Heidelberg, Stamp & Emboss.	13 x 18	42802.14	4000.00	1	66.07	56.63	49.58
Kluge, Stamp & Emboss.	14 x 22	38207.56	4000.00	1	65.14	55.83	48.88
Platen, Hand-fed*	8 x 12	1815.00	1800.00	1	50.03	42.88	37.54
Platen, Hand-fed*	10 x 15	1864.50	1800.00	1	50.04	42.89	37.55
Platen, Hand-fed*	12 x 18	2090.50	1800.00	1	55.05	47.18	41.31
Heidelberg Platen	10 x 15	26419.40	5500.00	1	61.20	52.45	45.92
Kluge Automatic	11 x 17	15113.75	4500.00	1	58.84	50.42	44.15
Heidelberg	13 x 18	41109.40	5500.00	1	65.40	56.05	49.07
Kluge Automatic	13 x 19	18136.50	5000.00	1	57.81	49.55	43.38
Heidelberg*	15 x 20	10615.00	5000.00	1	56.49	48.41	42.38
Cylinder Press*	14 x 20	11770.00	5000.00	1	58.48	50.12	43.88

*Reconditioned Equipment

Floor Help				1	**37.68**	**32.29**	**28.27**

FLEXOGRAPHIC PRESS

Mark Andy 830	3 Color, 7"	33000.00		1	68.55	58.75	51.43
Mark Andy 2200	6 Color, 10"	165000.00		1	106.06	90.90	79.58
Webtron 750	6 Color, 7.5"	157646.50		1	102.47	87.82	76.89
Mark Andy 830	3 Color, 7"	335621.00		1	149.33	127.98	112.05
Mark Andy 830	3 Color, 7"	193561.50		1	113.96	97.67	85.51

Figure 3A.8 Budgeted hour cost rates: Letterpress & flexographic press

ALL-INCLUSIVE HOURLY COST RATES
BASED ON PREVAILING WAGES IN SOUTHERN CALIFORNIA
AND A STANDARD 40 HOUR WORK WEEK

NAME OF COST CENTER	SIZE	APPROXIMATE INVESTMENT IN EQUIPMENT	CREW	COST PER HOUR AT PRODUCTIVITY OF		
				60%	70%	80%

BINDERY

CUTTERS

NAME OF COST CENTER	SIZE		CREW	60%	70%	80%
Challenge 20, w/o/s	20"	7260.00	1	46.71	40.03	35.05
Polar 58 EM	22.625"	18348.00	1	49.89	42.76	37.43
Challenge Diamond 26, w/o/s	26.5"	13200.00	1	48.88	41.89	36.68
Challenge Champion, w/o/s	30.5"	14850.00	1	49.29	42.24	36.98
Challenge MPX	30.5"	18700.00	1	50.24	43.06	37.70
Challenge CRT	30.5"	22000.00	1	51.06	43.76	38.31
Polar 76 EM	30"	32956.00	1	53.78	46.09	40.35
Brausse PE 78	30.75"	33825.00	1	53.99	46.27	40.51
Polar 92 EM	36.25"	54131.00	1	71.83	61.56	53.90
Polar 92 Monitor	36.25"	59774.00	1	73.23	62.76	54.95
Brausse PE 92	36"	39600.00	1	68.23	58.48	51.20
Challenge 420 CRT	42"	52800.00	1	71.84	61.57	53.90
Itoh 115 FC	45.25"	76945.00	1	78.31	67.12	58.76
Brausse PE 115	45"	49500.00	1	71.51	61.29	53.66
Polar 115 EM	45.25"	76219.00	1	78.13	66.96	58.63
Polar 115 Monitor	45.25"	82258.00	1	79.63	68.25	59.75
Polar 137 Monitor	54"	93236.00	1	83.04	71.17	62.30
Brausse PE 137	54"	59400.00	1	74.65	63.98	56.01
Itoh 137 FC	54"	87945.00	1	81.73	70.04	61.32
Polar 155 Monitor	61"	105666.00	1	87.30	74.82	65.50
Itoh 160 FC	63"	104445.00	1	87.40	74.91	65.58

Figure 3A.9 Budgeted hour cost rates: Bindery cutters

FOLDERS

NAME OF COST CENTER	SIZE		CREW	60%	70%	80%
Baum Econofold	14 x 20	2420.00	1	37.92	32.50	28.45
Baum 714 XE	14 x 20	5934.50	1	38.79	33.25	29.11
O & M F14	14 x 20	13475.00	1	40.74	34.91	30.56
Stahl B-14 4-4	14 x 20	37158.00	1	46.60	39.94	34.97
Shoei SPT 49 4-4	19 x 26	33000.00	1	60.51	51.86	45.41
Stahl B-20 4-4	20 x 30	35970.00	1	61.50	52.71	46.14
Baum 2020 Model 3-3	21 x 33	23094.50	1	58.31	49.97	43.75
Baum 2020 Model 3-3-3	21 x 33	32994.50	1	61.76	52.93	46.34
Shoei SPT 59 4-4	23 x 35	48345.00	1	65.06	55.76	48.82
Stahl B-23 4-4-4	23 x 35	57750.00	1	67.64	57.97	50.75
Shoei SPT 59 4-4-4	23 x 35	60445.00	1	68.06	58.33	51.07
MBO B123 4-4 Pile	23 x 36	34100.00	1	61.78	52.95	46.35
Baum LD 23 4-4	23 x 38	17600.00	1	57.69	49.44	43.29
Baum LD 23 4-4-4	23 x 38	26400.00	1	59.93	51.36	44.97
MBO B23 4-4-4 Cont.	23 x 50	43450.00	1	64.53	55.31	48.42
Shoei SPT 66 4-4	26 x 40	62645.00	1	69.27	59.37	51.98
Shoei SPT 66 4-4-4	26 x 40	74745.00	1	72.27	61.94	54.23
Baum LD 26	26 x 40	60500.00	1	69.02	59.15	51.79
Stahl B-26 4-4-4	26 x 45	76263.00	1	73.17	62.71	54.90
MBO B26 4-4-4 Cont.	26 x 50	58850.00	1	68.35	58.58	51.28
Stahl B-30 4-4-4	30 x 45	81972.00	1	75.11	64.37	56.35
MBO B30 4-4-4 Cont.	30 x 50	63250.00	1	71.67	61.42	53.77
Stahl B-37 4-4-4	37 x 52	115302.00	1	84.73	72.62	63.58
MBO T102	40 x 59	118855.00	1	86.40	74.05	64.83
Stahl B-44 4-4-4	44 x 60	121495.00	1	86.81	74.40	65.13
MBO T112	44 x 65	125532.00	1	88.14	75.54	66.13
Stahl B-56 4-4-4	56 x 63	327800.00	1	142.27	121.93	106.75

Figure 3A.10 Budgeted hour cost rates: Bindery folders

ALL-INCLUSIVE HOURLY COST RATES

BASED ON PREVAILING WAGES IN SOUTHERN CALIFORNIA AND A STANDARD 40 HOUR WORK WEEK

NAME OF COST CENTER	SIZE	APPROXIMATE INVESTMENT IN EQUIPMENT	CREW	COST PER HOUR AT PRODUCTIVITY OF 60%	70%	80%

BINDERY

PERFECT BINDERS

NAME OF COST CENTER	SIZE	APPROXIMATE INVESTMENT IN EQUIPMENT	CREW	60%	70%	80%
M-M Panda	8 Station	127690.00	1	107.37	92.02	80.56
M-M Panda	12 Station	145770.00	1	114.00	97.71	85.54
M-M Panda	14 Station	154810.00	1	118.68	101.71	89.05
M-M Pony		45200.00	1	61.65	52.84	46.26
Rosback 880 Binder		18645.00	1	53.64	45.97	40.25
Bourg 361		11675.16	1	53.34	45.72	40.02
Bourg 361 "S"		14712.60	1	54.10	46.36	40.59
Bourg BB3000		27025.08	1	57.15	48.98	42.88
MK III Auto Minabinda		23730.00	1	54.83	46.99	41.14
SB 200	3 Clamp	63280.00	1	66.33	56.85	49.77
SB 2500	10 Clamp	68930.00	1	67.94	58.23	50.98
SB 240	15 Clmp & Coll.	254250.00	1	143.12	122.66	107.39

COLLATORS

NAME OF COST CENTER	SIZE	APPROXIMATE INVESTMENT IN EQUIPMENT	CREW	60%	70%	80%
Watkiss 222	22 Bin	14690.00	1	44.69	38.30	33.53
Watkiss 243	43 Bin	20340.00	1	46.11	39.52	34.60
Bourg Modulen	5 Station	53479.51	1	54.59	46.79	40.96
Bourg AE 10 "S"	10 Bin	14449.31	1	45.02	38.59	33.78
Bourg AE 16 "S"	16 Bin	22553.67	1	47.03	40.31	35.29
Bourg AE 22 "S"	22 Bin	28865.85	1	48.60	41.65	36.46
Bourg BC 15	W Stitcher	13330.61	1	45.33	38.85	34.01
Bourg BC 20	W Stitcher	16287.82	1	46.06	39.48	34.56
Bourg AE 46 "S"	46 Bin	66866.62	1	58.95	50.52	44.23
106C	9 Station	53675.00	1	55.56	47.61	41.69

BINDERY SYSTEMS

NAME OF COST CENTER	SIZE	APPROXIMATE INVESTMENT IN EQUIPMENT	CREW	60%	70%	80%
MB 250 Multibinder	9 Station	76840.00	1	78.25	67.06	58.71
MB 320	15 St.Cl./Gth SB	101700.00	1	85.69	73.44	64.30
SP 455 Sdl Stch/Trim	6 Station	96050.00	1	84.29	72.24	63.24
SP 562 Sdl Stch/Trim	6 Station	192100.00	1	112.79	96.67	84.63
SP 650 Sdl Stch/Trim	6 Station	248600.00	1	126.79	108.67	95.14
Rosback 203 Bind Sys	6 Station	56500.00	1	65.81	56.41	49.38
MM Minuteman Sdl Stchr	6 Pocket	92660.00	1	85.11	72.94	63.86
MM Fox Sdl Stchr	6 Pocket	157070.00	1	101.32	86.83	76.02
MM 385 Sdl Stchr	6 Pocket	229390.00	1	118.99	101.98	89.28
MM Fox Sdl Stchr	4 Pocket	100570.00	1	77.11	66.08	57.85
Bourg AE 10 "S"	10 Bin, 40 Pg	39388.41	1	61.57	52.77	46.20
Bourg AE 16 "S"	16 Bin, 64 Pg	47465.65	1	63.58	54.49	47.70
Bourg AE 22 "S"	22 Bin, 88 Pg	53522.45	1	65.08	55.77	48.83
Bourg Modulen	5 Station	83583.84	1	80.63	69.10	60.50
Bourg Modulen	9 Station	110956.96	1	89.48	76.69	67.14
Bourg Modulen	17 Station	165347.25	1	105.49	90.41	79.15
Bourg Modulen	21 Station	192657.09	1	115.86	99.29	86.93
ST-90	4 Pocket	117920.00	1	91.21	78.17	68.44
ST-90	6 Pocket	142120.00	1	99.74	85.48	74.83
ST-90	8 Pocket	164120.00	1	108.78	93.23	81.62

Figure 3A.11 Budgeted hour cost rates: Perfect binders, collators, bindery systems

ALL-INCLUSIVE HOURLY COST RATES
BASED ON PREVAILING WAGES IN SOUTHERN CALIFORNIA
AND A STANDARD 40 HOUR WORK WEEK

NAME OF COST CENTER	SIZE	APPROXIMATE INVESTMENT IN EQUIPMENT	CREW	COST PER HOUR AT PRODUCTIVITY OF		
				60%	70%	80%
BINDERY						
OTHER EQUIPMENT						
Challenge JF Drill	Single Head	1576.35	1	35.67	30.57	26.76
Challenge EH-3A Drill	3-Head	5650.00	1	37.05	31.76	27.80
Challenge MS-10A Drill	5-Head	12430.00	1	39.32	33.69	29.50
Baum NDS-MT Drill	3-Head	8794.50	1	38.06	32.62	28.56
Baum ND10 Drill	5-Head	13475.00	1	39.47	33.83	29.62
DL Super Duty A-3 Drill	3-Head	20845.00	1	41.13	35.25	30.86
DL Classic Horizontal	DBL Station	39050.00	1	45.93	39.37	34.47
DL Classic Slanted	DBL Feed	50490.00	1	48.77	41.80	36.59
Rosback Trueline Perforator	20″	4520.00	1	40.94	35.09	30.72
Rosback Trueline Perforator	26″	5650.00	1	41.28	35.38	30.98
Rosback 240 Perforator	30″	20679.00	1	45.63	39.11	34.24
Rosback 201 Auto Stitcher		10170.00	1	50.63	43.39	37.99
Interlake Model A Stitcher		2825.00	1	48.38	41.46	36.30
Interlake 53A Stitcher		5424.00	1	49.02	42.01	36.78
Interlake P Stitcher		6215.00	1	49.22	42.18	36.93
Moll Pocket Folder	Glue & Fold	40700.00	1	51.25	43.93	38.46
Moll Pocket Folder	Glue & Fold	66000.00	1	65.75	56.35	49.34
Rollem Auto-4	18″	14839.00	1	5.54	4.75	4.16
Rollem TR System	36″/Sgl Head	47289.00	1	14.00	12.00	10.51
Rollem TR System	36″/Dbl Head	59389.00		17.29	14.82	12.97
Rollem Champion 990	36″,Score/Perf	7689.00		3.57	3.06	2.68
Rolle, Slipstream	Slitter/Collator	429000.00		115.88	99.31	86.95
Small Machines		11000.00	1	39.28	33.66	29.47
Hand Bindery		1100.00	1	32.18	27.58	24.14
Bindery helper			1	29.89	25.62	22.43

Figure 3A.12 Budgeted hour cost rates: Other bindery equipment

Chapter 4

Price Estimating in the Printing Industry

4.6 Key Factors When Establishing Prices

4.7 Setting Up a Tailored Price List

4.8 Important Pricing Concepts and Issues

Who Should Establish Prices?
Customer-Differentiated Pricing
Baseline Price Estimating
Price Cutting

Pricing for the Best and Worst Customers
Pricing for Long-Term Contract Commitment

4.9 Computer-Assisted Price Estimating

Price List Estimating Using a Spreadsheet

Price Matrix Estimating Using Computer Templates

4.10 Some Difficult Pricing Areas for Printers

Filler Work
Repeat Work
Trade Work from Other Printers
Rush Work
Charity Work

Work for New or First-Time Customers
Work for Friends and Family
Rerun Work Due to Customer Error
Contract Work

4.11 Price Discrimination

4.1   Introduction

Price estimating, the process in which printing is estimated using the selling price for an identified graphic product, is practiced extensively and with increasing frequency in the printing industry. Speed coupled with simplicity are the primary advantages of price estimating. The process allows for fast quotes, which give the printing company the ability to bid on more work and thus increase production volume.

The emergence of DTP has provided an environment in which many customers and print buyers have shifted their buying patterns. Today's print buyer purchases printing in smaller quantities and more frequently. This means there are more quotations per customer. Buyers also capitalize on the intense competition between printers for their work. This competition allows customers to "shop around," which increases the number of estimates printers are asked to complete. Because customer service is a factor in obtaining and keeping customers, fast quotations have become an important way for customers to choose and stay with a printing company.

From a printer's standpoint, understanding how price affects the company's revenue and profit picture is vital. Although costs are important to know and monitor, clearly price is the primary generator of revenue for a printing company. Price is frequently adjusted relative to the customers and markets the company serves, the company's competitive position, and the volume of work in the company.

This chapter addresses price estimating methods and procedures for a printing company. It includes discussions of pricing philosophies for printed products, the relationship between cost estimating and price estimating, complications when using price estimating, how a price estimating system is developed, computerized pricing systems, pricing templates, and some thorny pricing issues for a typical printing company.

4.2   Proactive Pricing: Key Pricing Points and Pricing Rules for Printing Companies

The prices a printing company charges for the products and services it provides are the single most important factor in the economic survival of the company. These prices determine whether the company retains or loses customers, which in turn keeps company volume high or low. Prudent pricing recovers all costs and requires basing prices on a knowledge of all costs of production. Most importantly, prices—not costs—drive whether the company wins or loses jobs, which in turn drives the revenue of the company.

The principle of elasticity of demand, an economic condition affecting many printers who engage in pure "head-to-head" competition, states, "As prices go up, volume (e.g., jobs won by the company) goes down, and as prices go down, volume increases." To put it another way, if a printer's prices are too high, customers send their jobs to other printers, which results in the high-priced printer earning no revenue, recovering no fixed costs, and losing any profit opportunity. Conversely, if a printer's prices are low, jobs tend to be plentiful, but costs may not be fully recovered, which may diminish company profits to the point that income is reduced to below costs and the company is placed in financial jeopardy.

Key Pricing Points

To resolve this dilemma, successful printers take a proactive view of pricing. They recognize pricing as a key element for success because it drives both volume and revenue, which in turn drive growth and profits. The following are critical points in this proactive pricing strategy, which yields improved profits.

Key Point 1. Profit (or income) in printing is driven by the prices charged for the goods and services delivered to customers. Costs are important, but prices are more important and represent the key to controlling volume and generating revenue.

Key Point 2. For a printing company to control its prices, management must identify customers and markets willing to pay those prices. Thus, strategic evaluation of markets and customers is inextricably linked to an effective pricing system.

Key Point 3. Customer perception of the company and the products it produces is critical to the pricing discipline practiced by the company. Perceived high value establishes a higher price potential. Successful pricing requires that customers consistently perceive a high level of added value in the goods and services the company provides, even though it is possible that competing companies sometimes provide greater added value at lower prices.

Key Point 4. An important pricing factor as a whole are the various services the company provides to customers, not necessarily the finished product alone.

Key Point 5. Achieving efficient production by keeping costs low, maintaining consistent and high product quality, and minimizing rework improves the likelihood of increased profitability, but it does not ensure it.

Key Point 6. As a printing company increasingly utilizes digital technology, employees must be trained and empowered to make decisions that affect product and process, which in turn affect costs and prices. Thus, as employee skills improve and as employees take active parts in decisions regarding their work environment and production responsibilities, prices are affected.

Key Point 7. Profits are a reflection of the positive aspects of any company's customers, employees, suppliers, and leadership. Profits are not achievable when the mix of these four components is negative.

Pricing Rules Based on a Proactive Pricing Philosophy

Given the previous key pricing points, the development and use of any price-based system or method for a printing company should include the following pricing rules. These rules apply when pricing printing orders on a job-by-job basis using the cost estimate as a baseline or when establishing a price list or price template system.

Pricing Rule No. 1. The selling price for the good or service provided by the printing company is *the* revenue generator for the company. No job should be sold and produced by the printing company without adding a reasonable amount of profit dollars to the cost dollars required to produce the job. Taken individually or collectively, controlling costs, increasing volume, or niche marketing, without focusing on prices, tends to have little effect on profits.

Pricing Rule No. 2. Using a fixed price markup system covering all customers and products does not maximize profits and should be avoided. Top management should establish a method to price each job based on flexible criteria that address specific customer needs. This is because customers vary in what they are willing to pay for the goods and services provided by the printing company, and because profit dollars can easily be lost using any type of pricing system that lumps or categorizes customers into a fixed profit markup environment.

Pricing Rule No. 3. If a printing company desires high profits, its prices are likely to be higher compared to competing printing companies. In order to maintain volume at these higher prices, the company must proactively justify its higher prices by actions—not promises—that demonstrate exceptional customer service, consistently high quality, timely delivery, attention to job details, clear and friendly communication with customers, attention to customer feedback and customer complaints, and an environment of continuous and positive interaction. Without such a proactive response, the company with higher prices cannot maintain a solid customer base at a stable volume level in the long term.

Pricing Rule No. 4. If the price of a job has been carefully and fairly determined, cutting that price to get the order should not be done unless all cost and profit consequences are evaluated carefully. Cutting prices may be justified in some cases, but it should be the exception, not the rule.

Pricing Rule No. 5. Unless extraordinary or unique circumstances exist, the selling price of a job should always exceed the sum of all costs to produce the job. Cost is driven by internal production processes, materials, and buyouts, while price is driven by numerous market, buyer, and customer service factors. Given these facts, cost should represent the baseline or "floor" dollar amount at which prices begin. It is therefore unwise and imprudent to quote any job without considering all costs related to that job. The quote should be higher than the estimated manufacturing cost of the job unless extraordinary reasons exist.

Pricing Rule No. 6. The president's job in a commercial printing company should be concentrated in four principal areas:

1. reviewing and setting prices
2. determining the marketing strategy and how it is implemented
3. addressing personnel matters such as finding, training, and keeping employees
4. dealing with the financial aspects of the company

Pricing Rule No. 7. Establishing a fair price for a printed product is complicated and impacted by many factors, both tangible and intangible. Thus, there is no easy way or simple formula to price goods and services in any segment of the highly competitive printing industry.

The previous seven key pricing points and seven pricing rules, which effectively establish the pricing philosophy practiced by profitable printing companies, are discussed as appropriate throughout this chapter and other parts of this book.

4.3   Price Estimating Methods

Price list estimating and price matrix estimating are the two general approaches for price estimating graphic products and services.

Price List Estimating

Price list estimating is the generation of a price estimate or quotation from a list of prices which has been tailored to meet the printing company's products. Price list estimating requires that the customer's desired product fits the parameters upon which the price list was based. Normally the "fit" of the customer's product to the price list is determined by the sales representative and the customer as they discuss the job.

Price list estimating is usually a two-step process. The first step involves using a basic price table to locate the proper base price for the job without special operations or services. The second step involves covering additional charges for special operations or extra services that enhance the product beyond its basic value.

Figures 4.1, 4.2, and 4.3 are examples of price lists used for estimating. Each demonstrates, with some variation, the "base price plus additions" method just described. Even though each of the price lists has a different format, the simplicity and ease of use of each is also apparent.

Price Matrix Estimating

Estimating using a price matrix format is more complicated than price list estimating and somewhat resembles cost estimating methods except that all-inclusive prices—not costs—are used. Figure 4.4 illustrates this format.

When setting up a price matrix estimating system, the printing company is first divided into production centers. Each center is then broken into production components (e.g., production operations) that are completed in the center. Following this, codes are assigned to the components and all-inclusive selling prices are developed for each unit of production component used. The term "all-inclusive selling price" means that the price includes all costs plus profit markup. A unit may be measured in time needed (e.g., hours or portions of hours) or products (e.g., finished proof or final film).

To use the price matrix estimating system, the estimator or sales representative evaluates the customer's job, determines the number of units needed, multiplies that number by the selling price, then multiplies that number by a penalty factor intended to adjust for expected problems or job complications (a penalty factor of 100 percent means there is no penalty charge). The result is a final selling price by production component. As noted in Figure 4.4, Operation/component code 600 (second row, second column) requires 1 unit at $30 with no penalty, which yields a final selling price of $30. When the calculations in this example are completed for each anticipated production code using matrix pricing, the total price for this DTP job is estimated to be $864 (lower right-hand corner).

The matrix pricing system integrates well with cost estimating because it follows the cost estimating process of dividing the company into production activities and component codes. Thus, once the value of a unit is defined by matrix pricing, using cost estimating methods to generate all-inclusive selling prices is not difficult. When the units are established as functions of time, or can be related to time, it is possible to interface the price matrix system with the company's scheduling package.

4.4 Price Estimating Compared to Cost Estimating

Compared to cost estimating, price estimating from a price list or a price matrix is a streamlined process. Price estimating begins with company management

QUALITY OFFSET PRINTING

FREE PICKUP in the Salem area
363-5491

FREE DELIVERY
FAX 503-375-9646

FRIENDLY FACES
1-800-484-9622-9397

Quantity	5 1/2 x 8 1/2		8 1/2 x 11		8 1/2 x 14		11 x 17	
	1-side	2-side	1-side	2-side	1-side	2-side	1-side	2-side
250	$17.70	$21.75	$18.50	$21.50	$24.15	$34.45	$38.00	$51.50
500	19.50	23.25	21.50	26.45	26.10	36.10	42.10	58.60
1000	22.50	33.25	26.45	45.30	35.40	47.65	78.50	136.50
2000	40.40	45.80	45.30	73.60	55.10	83.50	108.50	175.10
2500	49.50	61.30	55.90	85.20	69.50	102.75	111.90	184.50
5000	86.75	94.95	109.50	178.50	131.50	195.50	251.30	322.30
Add'l M's	18.20	21.50	22.10	33.10	28.75	38.75	28.50	41.10

(Above pricing is for 20# white bond.)

Camera ready means that your copy is ready to be photographed. What you see on your original copy is what you will see on the finished work. To reproduce good quality halftones (pictures) we need originals or screened prints. CAMERA CHARGE: to convert glossy photos or shaded illustrations into halftones add $7.00 each for size up to 4 x 5. Print area is not to exceed : 11x17 not to exceed 10x16; 8 1/2 x14 not to exceed 8 x 13; 8 1/2 x 11 no to exceed 8 x 10. If needed we can reduce copy to above sizes for 5.00 each side of sheet. IF NO SPECIAL INSTRUCTION OR PAYMENT IS RECEIVED WE WILL PRINT COPY AS IS. COLOR PAPER: 20# CANARY, BLUE, PINK, GREEN, IVORY, GOLD (INDICATE 2ND CHOICE). 8 1/2 x 11 $5.00/1000 (MIN. CHARGE $5.00). 8 1/2 x14 $5.50/1000 (MIN $5.50). 11x17 $9.00/1000 (MIN. $9.00).

Other services
Collating:$10.00 per 1000 (flat sheets) min. $10.00
Color ink: $17.50 per job
Cutting: $3.00 per cut 1000; $1.00 set up
Drilling:standard 3 hole, $7.10 per 1000 sheets
Folding:
8 1/2 x 11 fold in half 1¢ per fold ($5.00 min.) Over 5M get quote
8 1/2 x11 tri-fold 1.5¢ per fold ($7.00 min.) Over 5M get quote
11 x 17 in half 1.75 ¢ per fold ($9.00 min.) Over 5 M get quote
Numbering: $33.50 per 1000 sheets (state starting number)
Padding in 50's: $6.50 per 1000 (min. $6.50)
Padding in 100's $5.50 per 1000 (min. $5.50)
Perforating/Scoring: $17.50 setup, plus $9.00/1000 sheets
Stapling: 4¢ per staple
Business Cards: 500 $15.00; 1000 $23.50; 2000 $44.99 (Base price)

Envelopes

	1000 size #10
White regular	$32.50; add'l 1000 $27.50
White window	$39.95; add'l 1000 $32.50
	1000 size #6 3/4
White regular	$30.00; add'l 1000 $24.50
White Window	$36.00; add'l 1000 $22.50

NCR Forms			
8 1/2 x 11	500	1000	5000
2 part	$44.98	$76.24	$337.42
3 part	63.96	115.75	515.69
4 part	84.26	157.99	606.19
5 1/2 x 8 1/2	500	1000	5000
2 part	$31.85	$47.00	$213.33
3 part	42.90	69.51	286.83
4 part	55.97	91.68	422.94

Figure 4.1 Sample price list. (Reproduced with permission of H&H Printing Co., Salem, Oregon.)

Booklet Prices

NO. OF PAGES	5 1/2 x 8 1/2 PAGE SIZE					8 1/2 x 11 PAGE SIZE				
	250	500	1000	2500	Add'l 1000s	250	500	1000	2500	Add'l 1000s
8	$94.00	$114.00	$134.00	$218.50	$59.00	$148.00	$160.03	$227.55	$505.66	$140.85
12	105.00	133.00	169.00	328.00	81.00	196.30	224.50	333.20	731.22	174.50
16	135.00	153.00	199.00	352.00	99.00	256.87	284.40	452.00	920.90	331.76
20	165.00	199.00	249.00	445.25	132.00	327.85	410.81	654.38	1061.21	395.10
24	186.00	217.00	306.00	667.00	174.00	372.64	508.64	680.74	1433.45	469.48
28	206.00	262.00	361.00	757.00	196.00	547.06	585.45	772.84	1596.18	562.55
32	227.00	278.00	405.00	825.00	207.00	517.21	653.26	865.41	1820.99	633.16
36	272.00	302.00	438.00	971.00	273.00	542.03	676.36	895.33	2014.46	709.54

For booklets over 36 pages, please write, call, or fax for a quote.

PRICES INCLUDE: Printing in black ink on 60# white offset from your camera-ready copy, collating, 2 staple, folding, trimming and free delivery within the Continental USA. (Please give a street address as we ship UPS only.)
SUBMIT ORIGINALS taped together in proper page sequence ready for camera (if unsure, call for a free booklet planner). Your copy must have sufficient gripper margin (3/8" white margin on all four edges of the sheet). Unless you advise us otherwise, we will reduce your copy slightly in order to have this required margin.

BOOKLET SPECIFICATIONS

5 1/2 x 8 1/2 booklets are printed on 8 1/2 x 11 sheets. They are folded in half and saddle stitched. 4 pages are printed on each 8 1/2 x 11 sheet (2 pages on each side of the sheet). Example: a 28-page booklet is printed on 7 8 1/2 x 11 sheets.

8 1/2 x 11 booklets are printed on 11 x 17 sheets. They are folded in half and saddle stitched. 4 pages are printed on each 11 x 17 sheet (2 pages on each side). Example: a 32-page booklet is printed on 8 11 x 17 sheets.

COVER OPTIONS: 67# Vellum Bristol - reasonably priced.
5 1/2 x 8 1/2 booklet, add $35.00 per 1000
8 1/2 x 11 booklet, add $45.00 per 1000
Please give a 2nd and 3rd choice of colors.
Many other covers available—call, write, or fax for quote.

Color Paper for inside pages
(60# offset):
Your choice of color available: green, gold, canary, blue, ivory, and pink. Each sheet equals 4 pages. (Prices are additional to standard price above.)
5 1/2 x 8 1/2 booklet $7.50/1000 sheets
8 1/2 x 11 booklet $11.50/1000 sheets

PAGE SETUPS
(Dummy Booklet)
If you supply individual pages, we will "dummy" them for printing at $1.00 per page. A 36-page dummy booklet will cost $36.00. There is no dummy charge if we are printing from a printed book or you lay out your own booklet.

SPECIAL BOOKLETS/BOOKS: Side-stitched (booklets); Perfect Bound (books) - ask for quote.

Most jobs completed within 7 to 10 working days.

FREE DELIVERY
H&H Printing Co.
P.O. Box 7603 • Salem, Oregon 97303
503-363-5491 • 1-800-484-9622-9397
FAX: 503-375-9646

Figure 4.1 *(continued)*

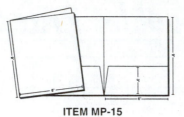

ITEM MP-15
6 x 9 Folder

- Slightly larger than a half sheet of paper, this folder fits inside a portfolio notebook.
- Due to pocket dimensions, only the E-1 business card slit is available. Illustration on page 16.

ITEM MW-99

4 x 9¼ Four-Pocket Folder

- The optimal ticket folder for the travel industry. Offering four pockets that are glued at the outside edges and open at the spine.
- No business card slit is available on this product.

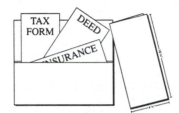

ITEM MW-34
4½ x 10¼ Document Folder

- This wallet-style folder has many uses. Its wide pouch is glued at both ends and is ideal for storing 8½ x 11" folded documents.

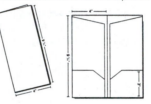

PRICE LIST FOR ITEMS: MW-34, MW-99, MP-15

Production time: 7 working days   Ground Freight included for the 48 contiguous United States

BASE FOLDER PRICE (prices reflect cost per folder)									
	250	500	1,000	1,500	2,000	3,000	5,000	7,500	10,000
One Color	$ .870	$ .608	$ .446	$.399	$.354	$.330	$.309	$.299	$.293
Two Color	1.271	.805	.544	.462	.399	.360	.327	.311	.302
4 Color Process	3.894	2.144	1.242	.944	.762	.622	. .512	.456	.428
Foil Stamped 16 sq. in.	.995	.680	.493	.431	.382	.353	.328	.316	.309
Embossed 8 sq. in.	1.250	.785	.525	.439	.379	.340	.307	.291	.282
ADD TO ABOVE PRICES FOR PROCESS DESIRED									
Additional Ink Color	$.404	$.217	$.137	$.110	$.094	$.067	$.050	$.045	$.043
Heavy Ink Coverage	.187	.104	.063	.049	.042	.035	.029	.027	.025
UV Coating	.127	.120	.117	.117	.117	.117	.117	.117	.117
Laminate One Side	.148	.140	.137	.137	.137	.137	.137	.137	.137
ADD TO ABOVE PRICES FOR SPECIAL PAPERS									
Group 2 Papers	$.070	$.063	$.058	$.055	$.052	$.051	$.050	$.049	$.049
Group 3 Papers	.095	.085	.078	.074	.070	.069	.068	.067	.066
Group 4 Papers	.147	.132	.122	.115	.109	.106	.105	.104	.102
Group 5 Papers	.177	.159	.146	.138	.131	.128	.126	.124	.123

PAPERS

Group 1 — 12 pt. Carolina C1S, Champion 80 lb. Linen
Group 2 — 12 pt. Carolina C2S, Benefit 80 lb. Recycled, Cordwain 90 lb. Leatherette, Concept 80 lb. Fibered, Kromekote 12 pt. C1S
Group 3 — 16 pt. Carolina C1S, Concept 80 lb. Deep Colors Fibered, Champion 80 lb. Linen Medium Colors, RSVP 80 lb. Felt, Cambric 80 lb. Linen
Group 4 — Champion 80 lb. Linen Deep Colors, Currency Cover 10 pt. Smooth, RSVP 80 lb. Felt Deep Colors
Group 5 — Kromekote 12 pt. C2S, Cambric 80 lb. Deep Colors

FOLDER EXPRESS — 1-800-322-1064

Figure 4.2 Sample price list. (Reproduced with permission of Folder Express, Omaha, Nebraska.)

Samy's Digital Imaging

Rental Stations Now Available!

RENTAL WORK

Quadra 950 with 40MB of RAM, 17" monitor, 44/88/200 MB SyQuest, 6 x 9 Wacom Tablet. CoolScan 35mm slide scanner and flatbed scanner available for an additional charge. — $16.00/hour

FUJIX PICTRO

This is the finest print available in digital imaging!

Seeing is believing these 24-bit Photographic quality, continuous-tone silver-halide digital color prints.

8¾" x 12" print size
2759 x 3800 pixels
8.54" x 11.77" max. image area

Resolution	Image size in inches	Image size in pixels	RGB Price	PostScript
400 dpi	6.90" x 9.50"	2759 x 3800	$15.00	$21.00
320 dpi	8.58" x 11.77"	2745 x 3767	$15.00	$21.00
267 dpi	8.57" x 11.76"	2288 x 3139	$15.00	$21.00
200 dpi	8.58" x 11.77"	1716 x 2354	$15.00	$21.00
133 dpi	8.560" x 11.80"	1144 x 1569	$15.00	$21.00

8 HOUR TURNAROUND. (Images must be sized to the above pixel specifications. Image centered on paper.)

KODAK XL

203 ppi, 2048 x 2048 pixels
Maximum image area
24-bit Continuous tone
color or b&w dye-sublimation prints

	8½" x 11"	11" x 11"
	1536 x 2048 pixels	2048 x 2048 pixels
	7.56" x 10.08"	10.08" x 10.08"
Prints	$12.50	$15.00
Transparencies	$15.00	$17.50

8 HOUR TURNAROUND. (Images must be sized to the above pixel specifications.)

3M RAINBOW

24-bit continuous tone dye-sublimation prints
300dpi CMYK 11"x17" image area — $34.95 each — $20.00 each addl. print (same image)

CD ROM

NEW! **Multiple Session** Convert costly SyQuest back-up disks to CD-ROM. You can transfer $1000 of Syquest storage onto a $135 CD-ROM.

Media cost $25, Transfer fee of 20¢ per mb – CD-ROM Media has a capacity of 640MB (Formats: ISO 9660, Apple HFS or Multiple Session)

LEAF 45 SCAN

Color or B&W scans
negative or transparency
(Image size shown in pixels)

Format	Max. image size	Price
35mm	2900 x 4350	$20.00 each
35mm	5000 x 7500	$50.00 each
120mm	4800 x 4800	$30.00 each
4 x 5	4800 x 6000	$40.00 each

DRUM SCAN

The highest resolution scans available from 35mm to 8"x10" negative, transparency, or reflective art originals.

Size (K) is the number of pixels on the long dimension, in 1000 pixel increments.

Size	48 hour (turnaround)	24 hour (turnaround)	Approximate Size (RGB file) Square	Rectangle
1-4K	$40.00	$60.00	48.0mb	38.4mb
5K	$50.00	$75.00	75.0mb	38.4mb
6K	$60.00	$90.00	108.0mb	86.4mb
7K	$70.00	$105.00	147.0mb	117.6mb

35MM FILM

From our new Management Graphics Sapphire Film Recorder.
Minimum order is 10 images. Scans not included.
Images should be in TIFF format, 4096 x 2728 pixels or less and in landscape mode.

10-29 images	$4.95 ea.
30+ images	$3.95 ea.

PHOTO CD

3½" x 4½" max. image size.
(Final image centered on 4 x 5 film, sizes shown in pixels.)

Highest resolution, finest quality 4x5 digital color transparency or negative, or b&w negative

Original Size	Res. 40 - $75	Res. 48 - $95	Res. 60 - $95
4 x 5	3556 x 4572	4267 x 5486	5334 x 6858
2¼	3556 x 3556	4267 x 4267	5334 x 5334
35mm	3556 x 4572	4267 x 5486	5334 x 6858
6 x 7	3556 x 4148	4267 x 4978	5334 x 6223

48 HOUR TURNAROUND. (Images must be sized to the above pixel specifications.)

213 **857-9915** • FAX **857-9916** • DATA **857-9917** ▲ 200 S. LA BREA AVENUE, LOS ANGELES, CA 90036

Figure 4.3 Sample price list. (Reproduced with permission of Samy's Digital Imaging, Los Angeles, CA.)

Customer name: Forrest Smith Enterprises   Date: September 25, 1995

Address: 275 Andover Road, Escondido, CA

Telephone: 216/555-1515   Estimator/Sales Rep: Bobby M.

Production component, operation, or activity	Operation/ component code	All-incl. selling price (per unit)	No. units required	Calculated selling price (sell. price x units)	Addl. % markup (penalty)	Final selling price
Design plan/roughs	600	$30	1	$30	100%	$30
DT-image planning	601	$10				
Job routing plan	602	$10	1	$10	100%	$10
File setup for job	610	$10				
Typesetting-straight text	620	$28	3	$84	125%	$105
Typesetting-complex text	621	$32	2	$64	125%	$80
Typesetting-technical text	622	$34				
Typesetting-foreign text	623	$35				
Typesetting-ASCII text	624	$20				
Scanning-position	630	$15	2	$30	100%	$30
Scanning-OPI/APR	631	$20				
Scanning-high res	632	$48	2	$96	100%	$96
Scanning-B&W	633	$27				
Scanning-other	634					
DT-drawing	640	$14				
DT-painting	641	$18	3	$54	100%	$54
DT-illustration	642	$18	2	$36	150%	$54
DT-other graphics	643	$20				
Image modification 1	650	$30	2	$60	125%	$75
Image modification 2	651	$30	3	$90	100%	$90
Image modification 3	652	$30				
Image modification 4	653	$30				
Proofing-thermal	660	$10				
Proofing-color dye	661	$15	6	$90	100%	$90
Proofing-ink jet	662	$15				
Proofing-other	663	$20				
RIP-imagesetter (paper)	670	$5				
RIP-imagesetter (film)	671	$20	6	$120	100%	$120
RIP-to Scitex	672	$15				
Customer support	680	$10	1	$10	100%	$10
System archiving	690	$10	2	$20	100%	$20
				Total selling price for job		**$864**

Figure 4.4 Estimate price matrix estimating worksheet for estimating DTP and electronic prepress

establishing the products. It requires the person completing the task—the estimator, CSR, or sales representative—to identify the graphic product through written or verbal job specifications, a job sample of a similar product, or perhaps simply a general verbal description from the customer.

Once the product is identified, the printing company representative estimates a price for the job using the company price list or pricing matrix and communicates this price to the customer either verbally or in writing. Sometimes discussion or negotiation of the price to meet the customer's budget requirements is included in this process. Because price estimating is completed in sales dollars, it is simple and fast to execute. The dollar value is intended to include all costs incurred by the printing company for the job, plus profit.

It is important to note that the terms "estimate," "proposal," and "quotation" are used interchangeably by printers and customers to generally indicate a dollar amount paid by the customer to the printer for delivering a specified printed product. In practice, each of these terms is slightly different in meaning. An estimate is a printing company's internal dollar evaluation of a job under consideration, which typically does not go to the customer. A proposal, also known as a price proposal, is a printing company's tentative offer to produce a specific graphic product for a specified dollar amount. It is intended to be negotiated or modified between customer and printer. Once a price proposal is modified by the printer and accepted by the customer, it becomes a quotation, which is a legal and binding contract. Thus, when customers want a price on a printing order, they may ask for an "estimate" when what they really want is a tentative price proposal or a firm quotation. Which one is chosen depends on the complexity and negotiability of the job. As printers and customers work together, these three terms are clarified between them.

Pricing estimating, as noted in Figure 4.5, can vary from tailored price list or price matrix methods, which have good to excellent accuracy, to an intuitive pricing method, which has poor accuracy. Other price estimating methods include pricing on the basis of past job prices, pricing using the competition's price, pricing using standard industry pricing systems, customer-based pricing, and ratio-based pricing. Each of these methods was discussed in Chapter 1.

Cost estimating, as previously discussed, can provide a high degree of cost accuracy when properly used. However, cost estimating tends to be complex, time consuming, and labor intensive. Cost estimating can be completed manually using pencil, paper, and an electronic calculator or by computer using appropriate estimating software. Regardless of whether the estimate is done manually or by computer, accurate cost estimates require the development of a full set of job specifications which detail job requirements. After this point the job is planned, whereby it is broken into discrete

	Speed of use	System accuracy	Complexity of basic system	Ease of modification	Computer adaptability	Time to learn/ training time	Provides shop performance data
Tailored price list or price matrix	fast	good to excellent	varies with system	varies with system	excellent	low	not extensively
Pricing on the basis of past jobs	moderate to fast	good	varies with system	good	good (but based on system design)	low	not extensively
Using the competition's price	moderate to fast	depends on similarities	varies with system	can't easily modify	varies with system	varies with system	not extensively
Standardized industry pricing systems	moderate to fast	good to fair	fairly low	done by vendor	fair	moderate to low	not extensively
Pricing on customer's ability and willingness to pay	moderate to fast	depends on customer	low	easily modified	no	hard to determine	no
Pricing based on a ratio system	moderate to fast	good to fair (depends on index)	moderate	good	varies with system	varies with system	not extensively
Intuitive pricing	fast	poor	low	low	none	hard to determine	no
Cost estimating	manual: slow computer: faster	excellent	fairly high	good	excellent	may be extensive	yes (when job costing included)
Chargeback	moderate to fast	good	low	varies with system	varies with system	varies with system	yes

Figure 4.5 Chart comparing various methods for estimating printing

job components representing the production activities and materials needed. These job components are then translated into production times and BHRs are applied. Material costs and outside purchases are estimated and added to yield a manufacturing cost of the graphic product. Pricing—adding profit for the company to the manufacturing cost—follows the costing process and results in the final proposal or quotation.

When comparing cost estimating to price estimating, cost estimating is generally preferred as long as the steps of the process can be completed quickly and accurately. Although price estimating is more streamlined, cost estimating is preferred because it provides a thorough breakdown of production times and costs, as well as important scheduling data and inventory information. It also simplifies order entry, job tracking, and job costing during production.

However, achieving a high level of cost estimating accuracy on a consistent basis presents numerous issues to a printing company. The following describes some of the key areas where cost estimating tends to be problematic.

The accuracy of cost estimating is achieved only when the job specifications accurately describe the graphic product to be produced. This level of accuracy is hard to achieve on a consistent basis.

Determining accurate job specifications remains the single biggest stumbling block for achieving accurate cost estimates. The following lists some of the reasons for this:

1. When customers want estimates, they are unable to provide job details because their jobs are not yet fully envisioned or graphically designed. If job details cannot be identified, developing an accurate cost estimate is impossible.
2. Printing sales representatives are unable to lead or assist the customers in the process of accurately identifying their job specifications. When this occurs, it is usually because the sales representatives do not have sufficient knowledge of printing technology or experience in evaluating printing orders relative to important job details.
3. Printing company management has not established a firm policy that requires printing sales representatives to provide complete job specifications for estimating. This lack of discipline effectively gives sales representatives permission to request estimates with incomplete job information. This, in turn, places the estimator in a position of having to determine specifications directly from the customer or to assume what the customer wants. Frequently the resolution of this problem requires management to insist that sales representatives receive training in printing technology. This coerced training tends to be unpopular with some sales representatives, who find ways to avoid or bypass it, and the problem remains.
4. In instances when a job is accurately specified, the artwork for the job, which is frequently supplied by the customer, may be poorly prepared or completed differently than the customer indicated in the original job specifications. This problem is common when inexperienced artists prepare the art and when electronic artwork is not preflighted (checked carefully) as it enters production. When this happens and time permits, it is prudent to revise the estimate to reflect artwork alterations. Typically this means the revised job quotation will be at a higher price, which frustrates the cooperative effort between customer and printer.

Even when a complete set of job specifications can be obtained, the process of cost estimating may take too long to complete.

Using manual estimating methods, it is possible that a single cost estimate for a complex job could take an experienced estimator an hour or more to complete. Although there is no fixed rule, computer methods typically reduce the time for estimate completion by 50 percent or more. When pro forma or template cost estimating is used, which is the process of basing current estimates on previous similar ones, a cost estimate can be completed in a few minutes. Template estimating is described in Chapter 2 and in Chapter 5 in detail.

Cost estimating tends to be complicated.

Cost estimating requires a thorough knowledge of printing production, consumable materials, BHRs, plant production standards, and experienced people who know how to build estimates. The cost estimating process also requires detailed use of mathematics and faultless logic, sometimes under a time-compressed situation. As a whole the cost estimating process is complicated, especially in light of increasingly complex printing orders and the changing technology of printing production.

The complexity of cost estimating makes the process error prone.

The accuracy of cost estimating is a result of the details used to build the estimate. With such a high level of detail, it is easy for an estimator to skip job details inadvertently or to simply make a mistake on a job detail that could be costly to the company. Manual cost estimating tends to be prone to errors in both logic and mathematics—a 25 percent error rate is considered industry standard for manual cost estimating. Although computer estimating is much more accurate, mistakes also occur with greater frequency than desired.

Cost estimating requires participation by some of the company's most experienced employees, who sometimes prefer to spend their time doing other job tasks.

Accurate cost estimates require knowledgeable sales representatives to provide job specifications, estimators to complete estimates, pricing personnel to set final job prices and quotations, and frequently CSRs to assist where needed. Cost estimating requires these skilled people to take valuable time away from the other important duties they must do, ones they enjoy more than estimating.

Sometimes employees seek shortcuts during their parts of the cost estimating sequence, which compromises the accuracy of the process. It is also possible that too many estimates are requested and that some of the skilled staff do not have sufficient time or interest in meeting their estimating obligations. Thus, the estimating process is bottlenecked to the point that some employees are forced to compensate for others, or customers take their printing work elsewhere because the estimates simply take too long to complete.

In addition, cost estimating is a continuous and complex effort—there are always estimates to complete, revise, reevaluate, review, or replan. As employees gain experience in estimating, there is a tendency for some to "burn out" or lose interest in the process. Also, most company employees involved in the cost estimating process have a range of other job duties. The problem is that once employees are familiar with the complexity and constant discipline required by estimating, they sometimes focus their efforts on the other parts of their jobs they enjoy more. Solving this problem is difficult. For example, replacing an experienced cost estimator with a fresh employee becomes an organizational problem, not to mention the fact that finding new estimating staff with proper training and background is difficult.

In some printing companies, producing accurate cost estimates is "nice to know," but it may be of little practical use in the overall business operation profile of the company.

It is not unusual for some printing companies to be managed and to operate in casual manners and to focus primarily on "getting the jobs out" with less emphasis on estimating, job planning, and operating on a firm cost basis. Sometimes these companies purchase complete computer management systems and take the time to work out functioning computer estimating processes. Even so, company management recognizes that detailed cost estimating is "nice to know" yet not essential for much of the printing work they do. Therefore, they bypass the cost estimating process frequently instead of quoting work on a range of price-driven methods.

Cost estimating simply is not worth the effort for some customer's jobs.

This statement is a common response when comparing price estimating to cost estimating. Given the complexity, time, and hard-to-obtain job specifications necessary for cost estimating, many printing companies conclude that cost estimating simply is not worth the time and effort for most jobs. Sometimes jobs are printed and delivered in less time than it takes to do their cost estimates. Simply stated, the primary benefit of cost estimating is accuracy, but the accuracy of cost estimating is not very important when compared to winning orders from customers. Therefore, why spend valuable time and effort cost estimating? Driving the quotation process with quick, easily referenced prices is clean, simple, fast, and meets the time-compressed needs of a customer-sensitive printing company.

Given that the estimate-to-order conversion ratio tends to be low in some printing companies, spending major time completing cost estimating does not make sense.

Experienced printers know that winning printing orders is a "hit-or-miss" proposition—it is impossible to predict the number of printing orders that will lead to jobs based on the number of estimates provided. These printers conclude that taking extensive time and effort to produce accurate cost estimates can easily become wasted time because the quoted jobs that actually turn into work-in-process (the printers' "hit rates") may be too few to justify the effort. In sum, why waste time on complex cost estimating when a fast price quoting system will do?

Because printing is market driven and is sometimes purchased as a commodity, the customer's price and not the printer's cost is the primary reason a printing company wins the order.

In the competitive printing industry, buyers decide which company receives the printing order by focusing on quoted price, among other key factors. Because the price of printing is market driven and is largely based on competitive issues, a detailed cost estimate is good information for the printer to have but it does not really affect whether the printer gets a printing order or not.

Given the previous discussion of cost estimating issues and problems, it is easy to understand why price estimating is popular and widely used in all parts of the industry. Because price estimating provides fast quotes, it meets the increasingly time-compressed demands of customers. Fast quotes are possible because price estimating is simple enough to be done by any experienced employee, such as the sales representative while talking with a customer at the customer's place of business. Increasingly, laptop computers instead of printed paper pricing methods are being used to build price quotes. Computers ensure accuracy in mathematics and, when linked to portable printers, can output quotes for customers on the spot. Because the quote from a laptop is immediate, it allows the sales representative and the customer to discuss budget constraints and to compare competitive prices if the customer has obtained bids from other printers on the job.

4.5 Areas of Caution When Estimating with Price Lists

Estimating from a price list is found in many parts of the printing industry. Key reasons are simplicity, convenience, and speed. As just discussed, price list estimating is easy to learn and can be done by a sales representative at the customer's place of business, which allows for quick competitive comparisons and on-the-spot quotations. Price list estimating is convenient because it can be computer assisted using a laptop or portable computer. Because quoting is fast in price list estimating, customers tend to make quicker commitments of their orders to the printing company, which increases volume and leads to company growth and potentially greater dollar profits.

The advantages of price list estimating make it appear superior to cost estimating. However, there are important drawbacks and cautions of price estimating. In fact, some of these difficulties are compelling enough to make price estimating far less desirable than cost estimating, even in light of its significant advantages of speed and simplicity. Consider the following areas where price list estimating tends to be problematic.

Oversimplification

First, price list estimating frequently simplifies the cost components and production methods of a printing job too much. Thus, complex jobs are simplified to the extent that the price estimate does not represent the work needed to produce the job. When this occurs, and when the printing company is unable or unwilling to charge for this misalignment of cost and price, company profits are reduced. This is a frequent problem for commercial printers who use price estimating for complicated jobs.

False Sense of Accuracy

Second, price list estimating is so easy and simple that management believes the system is more accurate than it might actually be. In instances where company profits are low, factors other than poor pricing are sometimes cited as reasons; when profits are high, "good" pricing is felt to be the primary reason. The net result is that management operates the company with a false sense of security. In some cases companies with histories of low profitability continue to insist that the reason is not a poor pricing structure, but factors such as production bottlenecks, high labor rates, or excessive material costs. Although these factors may reduce profits, price clearly has a greater leverage on profits than any other factor.

Sacrificing Accuracy and Appropriateness for Simplicity and Speed

Third, once price list estimating is implemented in a printing company, it is hard for company management to force estimators and CSRs to do laborious, time-consuming cost estimates, even though cost estimating is more accurate and more appropriate for certain types of work. In addition, sometimes when cost estimating procedures are abandoned as price estimating takes over, companies lose the ability to cost estimate accurately. These firms become captive to price estimating for its speed and simplicity, forgetting that the development of the pricing system should be rooted in cost estimating procedures.

Flawed Blanket Pricing

Fourth, sometimes a price list is stretched to fit products and services it was not designed to cover. This is usually done when new products and services become available or when a certain product is produced differently because of new equipment. This "blanket pricing" method is inaccurate and may lose the company money when used for jobs outside the parameters within which the prices were developed.

When profits are low, a frequent management reaction is to adjust prices upward and to continue allowing the flawed blanket pricing system to be used. In cases where profits are high, management tends to look proudly at the prices used as the primary source of these profits. However, this strategy ignores the fact that profits might be even greater if the company uses a mix of price estimating for work that fits the price list and cost estimating for work outside the price list parameters.

Inflexible or Outdated Prices

Fifth, frequently the prices used for price estimating, such as the prices in a price list covering a certain standard product, become fixed and inflexible over time, which makes the prices difficult to upgrade as costs incrementally rise. It is common for printing companies to use outdated price lists on the basis that they have been successful in the past, even though company management intuitively suspects that the prices are outdated and reduce profits.

One frequent response to this problem is to simply adjust the old prices by adding a certain percentage or dollar amount to the current prices. These adjustments, however, may not represent the cost impacts that are reducing profits.

Complexity in Price Setting

A sixth caution is that setting the prices for price list estimating is as complex as pricing a job that has been cost estimated. This is because similar market forces and costs drive either pricing decision. As is noted in the next section of this chapter, numerous factors—some tangible and some intangible—have a bearing on establishing the price for printing work.

Failure to Maximize Profit

Seventh, because price list estimating is simple and product-based, it does not meet a cardinal rule of business operation: Maximize profit for *each* job and *each* customer. Instead, price list estimating typically works as follows:

Prices are initially developed around a particular type of product. This approach tends to neglect the type of customer, product differentiation, and important market factors, however. When these prices are used, certain customers are willing to pay more than the estimated prices, but the pricing "mentality" of management allows these customers to pay what everyone else pays, which is less. This is lost profit.

When this problem is recognized, there are two ways it is typically resolved. Both require a separate pricing review step once the job is price estimated. The first way to solve the problem is to build a price list estimating system that recovers all costs with minimum profit markup. Every job is then reviewed and marked up a second time, this time using customer and market factors. The second way to solve the problem is to price estimate the job, then adjust the prices higher or lower based on customer, market, and other factors affecting the job being estimated. In either case, the price is specifically tailored by the printer to meet company profit needs as well as the customer's business conditions.

Although this additional pricing step takes time and may slow the quotation process, it ensures that each job is evaluated with respect to maximum profitability to the company and considers the customer's willingness and ability to pay.

System Misuse or Deception

Eighth, the price list estimating system can be knowingly misused or "stretched" to win a job or beat the competition. For example, a customer may want to order a printed product that is similar to products covered by a price list, so the sales representative or estimator intuitively adjusts the price to reflect this product. Once the price is set, the printing company remains committed to this price because of competitive factors, even though the sales representative or estimator knows that the price is not appropriate for the kind or type of product.

Although it is not unusual for the customer or sales representative to describe a product in a way that makes it fit into the price format of a company product, the final product may require additional prepress or other work that was knowingly not specified. Sometimes management, which does not know about the deception, charges for AAs to make up the difference in manufacturing cost. The customer often objects to paying for these alterations because they were not mentioned at the quotation stage, which creates an awkward situation between the printer and the customer.

Losing Sight of Job Details

Ninth, although price list estimating methods are sometimes simplified to the point that critical job details that affect price are glossed over or not pinned down during estimating, the printing company may quote on the job anyway because of competitive pressure. Then, as the job is being produced, these unidentified but costly details become evident, and the printer must choose either to charge the customer for them or not. If the printer chooses to charge for them, an uncomfortable relationship and hard feelings between the customer and the printer are likely, which may ultimately lead to losing the customer who views the printer as scattered and disorganized. If the printer chooses not to charge for the details, job profits are compromised.

Lack of Production Times

Tenth, price list estimating does not provide the company with production times for job costing and scheduling. As was noted in Chapter 2, plant scheduling cannot be executed unless each job has been broken down into specific operational times by cost center. These times are easily developed when cost estimating is used. However, price estimating typically ignores production times, using dollar amounts to estimate the job instead.

Two methods are available to resolve the problem of scheduling jobs that have been price estimated. The first solution is to review the price estimated job and develop production times for scheduling and job costing during order entry. This requires breaking the job into operational components, which cannot be done unless job details are clarified. Because this procedure is required for cost estimating, it was ignored initially but now must be done.

The second solution is for the printer to develop or purchase a computerized price estimating system that is built with a foreground matrix or list of prices for quoting jobs and is supported by a background matrix or list of production times that is linked to the foreground prices. In use, each price in the matrix is supported by a defined production process and production times. Thus, if a price of $100 were selected from the price matrix, it would reference one or more estimated production times that would be needed to produce the job at the $100 price.

4.6   Key Factors When Establishing Prices

It is important to note here that many printers operate in an intensely competitive environment, which causes them to be reactive and not proactive to the pricing realities of their competition. Because the printing environment is purely competitive, targeting customers by identifying, serving, and directing efforts to specific markets is a vital issue for any printing company. This is discussed appropriately in this chapter and also in Chapter 13.

The price printers charge for printed goods is a function of many factors. Clarifying these factors and then establishing a pricing policy or system based on an understanding of these factors is important. Figure 4.6 summarizes these eighteen pricing factors. The following discusses each of them.

Market Demand for the Product

Market demand for printing products may be either elastic or inelastic. Elastic demand means that as price increases, the volume sold decreases, and that as price decreases, the volume sold usually increases. Inelastic demand signifies

1. Market demand for the product
2. Manufacturing costs
3. Product mix
4. Competition
5. Quality of product
6. Services provided to the customer
7. Quantity of work to be printed
8. Volume of work in the plant
9. Customer's willingness and ability to pay for the job
10. Potential future business from the customer
11. Value added
12. Profit desired by top management
13. Location of the printing company to the customer
14. The customer or print buyer's general attitude
15. The technical difficulty of the job in terms of the printer meeting the service or quality requirements desired by the customer
16. The ego satisfaction gained by printer desiring the customer or customer wanting exclusive printer services
17. Printer's exclusive production capability
18. Customer's resale value of the printed product

Figure 4.6 Factors that influence prices for graphic products and services

that price is not necessarily related to volume: Prices may rise or fall and there may be no direct reduction or increase in volume.

The printing industry characteristically has an elastic demand structure. However, when a printing establishment specializes in a particular product line or in an item that is not easily obtained from other printers, the market becomes inelastic. Typically, the more inelastic the market, the greater the printer's control of prices.

This determination is, in effect, a major conclusion of the 1966 *McKinsey Report to PIA*. This study, which was commissioned by PIA and completed by the management consulting firm McKinsey & Company in 1966, is considered to be a cornerstone investigation of marketing, pricing, and profitability for the commercial printing industry. In general, the report states that profit variation between printing companies is not always related to cost, volume, or price—even though each of these factors plays a part in the profit picture—but to market demand, services provided by the printer, and factors of competition experienced by companies vying for work in those markets. The study stresses that printing managers should consider marketing as well as production manufacturing for enhanced profitability because the industry is heavily market driven. Thirty years after the *McKinsey Report* was released, its findings are still considered relevant to commercial printers because there has been little change in the competitive factors at work in the industry.

In terms of products, the *McKinsey Report* finds that the demand for tailor-made printed products is diversified, but that no printer can reasonably expect to provide all products and services for all customers, even though many seem to try. In terms of procedures used for manufacturing printed products, *McKinsey* reports that there is extreme diversity in process: Some equipment is automated and high speed, while other equipment is slow and requires the individual operator's attention. In fact, the study observes that printing companies are beginning to branch out with the addition of nonimaging processes. Conventional printing techniques of ink-on-paper still were used during printing, but extra equipment, such as special wrapping equipment, was being installed to provide additional services to entice the customers' business.

The McKinsey Report concludes that market diversity and process variation both contribute to the significant and intense competition in the printing industry. Thus, if printers practice specialization of product or process (or both), the intense competition between them for the same types of work would lessen. If a printing company could enter a specialized market and control it, it could then control prices in that market. If such prices were under control, profits would be greater because price exerts tremendous leverage on profitability. Specialization is a way out of the intense, price-cutting free-for-all that many printing managers dislike.

According to *McKinsey*, specializing provides printers with entrance into markets wherein prices can be controlled. If these controlled prices are raised, there is limited volume loss. The report notes that when prices were increased 3 percent in an elastic market, volume decreased by 10 percent, yielding a profit loss of 50 percent (Figure 4.7). Therefore, for the printer in an elastic market who makes 5 percent profit, an attempt to increase prices by even a small amount could be disastrous.

In the same study, *McKinsey* notes that price has tremendous leverage over profit. In fact, it has three times more leverage than other variables, assuming the market is inelastic.

Figure 4.8 from the same report shows that if material costs were reduced 10 percent in an inelastic market, profits increased 66 percent. If labor costs were reduced 10 percent, profits increased 56 percent. If volume was increased 10 percent, profits increased 33 percent. However, if price was increased 10 percent, profits increased 180 percent. These findings are significant because they clearly demonstrate the interrelationship of cost, volume, and price in an inelastic market.

Further information on product and process specialization and market niche development for printing is provided in Chapter 13.

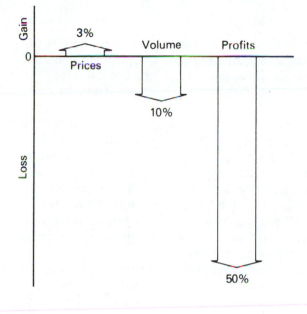

Figure 4.7 A price increase with a resultant volume loss for the commercial printer in an elastic market. (Reproduced from the "McKinsey Report to PIA," with permission from Printing Industries of America, Inc.)

Figure 4.8 The leverage of price over profit for the commercial printer in an inelastic market. (Reproduced from the "McKinsey Report to PIA," with permission from Printing Industries of America, Inc.)

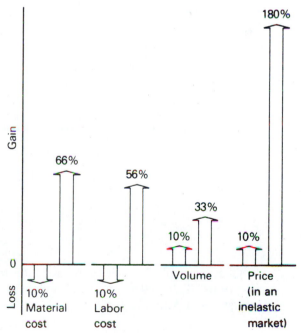

Manufacturing Costs

The dollar amount necessary to manufacture a defined printed product is the total of labor costs, material costs, and equipment costs. Typically the manufacturing cost represents the baseline dollar cost to produce the job inside the plant, without sales and administrative costs and without profit for the company.

There is no established relationship between total manufacturing cost and the selling price of the order from one company to another. For example, one plant may decide to double the total manufacturing cost figure to calculate the selling price of an order, while another may add a very small amount to the total manufacturing cost for final selling price determination. Thus, there is no defined procedure or formula for this cost-price relationship; it is determined on an individual plant basis. In fact, if printing companies in a geographic region attempt to establish prices together at a fixed level, which reduces the competitive relationship, unlawful price collusion may be charged.

In light of the previous information, it should be noted that cost control by itself fails to account for the difference between high- and low-profit printers. Figure 4.9 from the *McKinsey Report* shows that for low-profit printers to achieve equality with high-profit printers in sales—a difference of 8 percent in

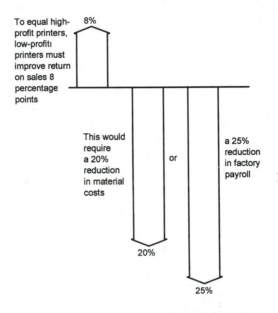

Figure 4.9 Cost control alone fails to account for the difference between low- and high-profit groups. (Adapted from the "McKinsey Report to PIA," with permission of Printing Industries of America, Inc.)

this example—they would need to reduce material costs by 20 percent or factory payroll by 25 percent. Clearly, achieving such profitability through cost control mechanisms is impossible.

Product Mix

With changing technology and manufacturing processes, there have been modifications in the product mixes available through specific printers. Product mix follows the elastic-inelastic market relationship to pricing as discussed previously. However, product mix has another variable.

Even in a narrowed, specialized product array, each product may contribute differently to the overall profit of the firm. Because of this fact, it is wise for management to investigate and determine the profitability for each of the products and services the company offers. Once these determinations are done, and they are neither precise nor simple in many cases, the products that provide the greatest profitability should be emphasized through sales efforts. The less profitable products, depending upon their ease of production and levels of profitability, among other factors, may continue to be produced, they may be dropped, or they may be purchased from outside printers.

Competition

Many printers price their products and services based on what the competition is charging. This method is an inaccurate way to price for two reasons. First, it is sometimes difficult to verify the prices charged by the competition. Second, and more important, there is generally little similarity between competing companies—they vary in type and size of equipment, labor skills, rates of pay, management and sales salaries, production methods, electronic prepress skills, and so on. Typically even minor aspects of two apparently similar companies are likely to be different. Given this, if Printer A bases its pricing structure on the published prices of Printer B, the comparison is not "apples to apples" because the cost dynamics of each company are different.

Using the competition's prices as guideposts is commonly and frequently done between printers. However, printers who enjoy great financial success have learned to watch the competition—and monitor the competition's prices—but not to become overly concerned with competitive issues or competitive pricing.

Quality of Product

The quality of the printed product is established between the customer via the sales representative and the printer and frequently has a direct bearing on price and the customer's willingness to order that product. Typically, higher quality products justify higher selling prices. Generally speaking, defining product quality is a matter of defining specific product points as excellent, good, or poor quality.

When digital technology is used to produce the printing, the level of product quality is driven primarily by electronic equipment and software choices, employee skill, and time to complete production. The price of the job increases commensurate to quality as better equipment, correct software, and highly skilled operators are used for the job. Also, higher quality products frequently require more production time, while lower quality products need less production time.

Services Provided to the Customer

The *McKinsey Report to PIA* indicates that providing services to the customer is key to being a high-profit printer. As demonstrated in Figure 4.10, the preponderance of company presidents in this study who viewed their businesses' orientation as service were high-profit printers, while most of the company presidents who viewed their businesses' orientation as manufacturing were low-profit printers.

Generally the services provided to the customer can be categorized into the four following areas, each of which provides significant profit potential:

1. Preprinting services are services provided by the sales force and affiliated plant personnel in design and other preliminary work on the order. The number and types of preprinting services are extensive in light of electronic prepress and related digital imaging methods.
2. Printing and graphic services are provided during the manufacture of the product.
3. Postprinting services are provided by the company in a range of peripheral areas such storing finished goods, distributing the finished product, mailing and transporting the product, and interfacing with other media such

23 high-profit printers

27 presidents who viewed printing as a service business

21 low-profit printers

23 presidents who viewed printing as a manufacturing business

Figure 4.10 Relationship of service or manufacturing orientation to profit. (Reproduced from the "McKinsey Report to PIA," field interviews, with permission from Printing Industries of America, Inc.)

as CD-ROM or digital areas. This is perhaps the most untouched service area of the four, particularly in fulfillment and distribution services.

4. Customer support services deal with a range of customer-driven needs, including effective communication and handling complaints and problems.

Quality of service and timely product delivery are important factors. When services are not rendered with excellence or in a timely manner, customers feel shortchanged and tend to project their views of poor service performance in one area of the company onto other areas. Thus, poor communication with the customer on job alterations causes the customer to wonder whether the printed product will be flawed.

Quantity of Work to Be Printed

The production of the printed product—that is, the actual manufacture of the product—requires a high fixed cost at the outset, before the first piece is printed. After the order is put into production, costs for preparatory work begin to mount. Mechanical and electronic artwork, electronic prepress, photographic work, film assembly, proofing, corrections, and platemaking must be completed prior to producing the first copy. Then, when the job goes on the press and the initial copy is printed, that single copy bears the total preparatory cost burden, plus the variable cost for labor and materials (in this case, one sheet of paper and the press operator's labor cost.)

When the second press sheet is produced, the fixed preparatory cost is cut in half, but the labor and material cost—that is, the variable cost—increases by another sheet of paper and the associated time for labor. As the number of copies continues to increase, the fixed cost per copy decreases because it is spread over the larger quantity of sheets but the variable costs increase in proportion to the quantity produced.

The net effect is that the total cost to manufacture a printed product is not in direct proportion to the volume produced. For example, assume 1,000 single-color letterheads cost $100 to manufacture. If this order is increased to 2,000 letterheads, the cost does not double to $200, but maybe only to $175. Even though the quantity doubled, the total cost did not double because fixed costs were spread over a larger quantity. Of course, material costs for paper and labor increase in direct proportion to the quantity produced. Thus, certain costs are quantity dependent while others are dependent on time, employees, quality, or other factors.

To study this concept, especially in capital-intensive production areas such as printing presses where equipment costs are high and press size sheets are changeable, management utilizes the break-even or changeover point concept.

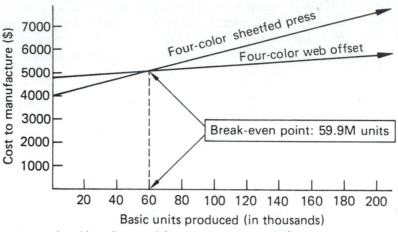

Figure 4.11 Example of break-even/changeover point analysis

The concept of changeover analysis is explained in detail in Chapter 10, where the selection of printing presses is also discussed.

Figure 4.11 demonstrates graphically the changeover point method. Break-even or changeover analysis is a common procedure for comparing profitability between different pieces of equipment. In Figure 4.11 a four-color sheetfed press and a four-color web offset press are compared. The sheetfed press offers dollar savings up to about 60,000 units of production (the break-even point). After that, the web press provides greater savings in costs and thus greater profitability. Actual chart development is based on accurate preparatory (setup) cost calculation and the establishment of a uniform basic unit of product.

With printed products, as quantity increases the total price to the customer increases, but the manufacturing cost per unit decreases. Given this concept, changeover analysis assists in maintaining a good quantity versus cost profile. Further discussion of this subject is also provided in Chapter 10.

Volume of Work in the Plant

Selling price and the amount of work-in-process in a printing company are related. When a printer maintains high prices, customers tend to purchase less and the number of jobs sold is low. However, when the same printer drops his prices, a greater volume of jobs is sold and the number of work-in-process increases.

It is important for printing company management to understand this capacity issue relative to lowering or raising selling price because price changes may result in significant volume shifts in the company. For example, when plant capacity is underutilized, management may adjust normal prices downward, thus encouraging customers to buy. Conversely, when plant capacity is over-utilized, management may opt to increase prices above normal to discourage new orders, thus encouraging customers to take their business elsewhere.

One factor in either pricing scenario is the time delay before the pricing strategy is executed. For example, jobs for which the selling price is dropped may not enter production for days or weeks after their proposals are accepted. When these orders finally do begin production, the company may be running at capacity. These additional orders may cause overtime or multiple shifts to be instituted. In contrast, typically when selling price is increased in an attempt to discourage volume, the effect is generally felt quickly and an immediate volume drop is noticed.

Again, the key point for printing management here is to monitor the price-capacity-time situation. Plant capacity and delivery dates are important and must be factored into the pricing equation at all times.

Customer's Willingness and Ability to Pay for the Job

Based on informal discussions with printers across the country during the 1980s and 1990s, pricing printing by "what the market will bear," which is gauged by the customer's ability and willingness to pay for printing, is fairly common. This is particularly true among small commercial printers and quick printers where the entrepreneurial philosophy of business operation is used. The entrepreneurial printer does not attempt to maximize profit, only to get the job and produce it at a financial gain. Thus, this type of "what the market will bear" pricing procedure fits well in the small printer's philosophy.

How much the customer is willing to pay is, in many cases, difficult to determine without some input from the customer herself. Negotiating price may represent the most common method to determine this aspect. Furthermore, whether the customer has the ability to pay a particular dollar amount for a job can only be determined as the printer and customer work together over time. Thus, whether a customer has the "willingness and ability to pay for the job" is best evaluated with repeat customers, who commonly represent more than half of the client base of the typical small printer or quick printer.

It is fair to say that if a printer believes the customer has both the willingness and the ability to pay for a particular product or job, he might decide to charge the highest possible price he can achieve. If he does so, he must tailor the good or service, which is in this case the printed product, to the customer's needs because various state and federal laws may preclude the printer from charging different prices for exactly the same good or service.

Potential Future Business from the Customer

Similar to "what the market will bear" pricing, adjusting the price based on new or anticipated future printing orders is fairly common. Usually the customer informs the printer that she has a growing business and if the printer will keep the price lower on the current work, her future printing will go to the printer. Again, this pricing process is more common with small printers and quick printers.

The disadvantages of pricing by this method are obvious. First, the printer may be doing the current work at cost or even a loss simply to encourage future business. By the time future work is available, if it ever is, the printer may be out of business. Second, promises are typically not a basis for legal contracts. Therefore the customer's statements are only promises, not facts. Finally, there is no reason for the printer to believe the customer will ever return to place future orders.

It is true that encouraging business through astute pricing is one way to grow the business. This can be done through sales promotions or other special pricing systems that are offered on an infrequent basis. Another way to address the "future business" issue is to enter into a long-term contract with the customer, which locks a specific type of product or quantity of work into a signed agreement.

Value Added

Value added (VA) is an important concept because it forces the company to evaluate areas that contribute to profit separate from those areas that have little effect on the bottom line. By definition, VA is the amount of dollars a product increases in worth due to the various manufacturing and service components that improved it. Sometimes VA is defined quantitatively as the total dollar value of the product (in sales dollars) minus material costs and other directly chargeable costs, commonly known as buyouts or outside purchases. It is stated as the following simple formula:

$$VA = \text{sales dollars} - [\text{material costs} + \text{buyouts}]$$

VA has become a defined measure of profit performance similar to ROS and ROI. It is an important point of view for printing management in that the profit is achieved from sales of products manufactured by their own companies. Sometimes VA is called "inside sales" because it represents sales dollars generated inside the plant, as opposed to sales dollars used for materials and other outside-the-plant requirements. The VA concepts are the same for printing industry service bureaus, trade shops, graphic design firms, and industry suppliers.

It is clear that printers should attempt to maximize their VA by working to reduce material costs, chargeable costs, and buyout charges. This is usually done by doing more production work on a job inside the plant, as opposed to sending it to a trade supplier. For example, Printer A sells a job for $100, $23 of which can be directly traced to paper, $8 for film and plates, and $7 for buyouts, which totals $38. The VA for this job is then $100 − $38, or $62. Printer B sells the same job for $100, $20 of which can be traced directly to paper, $6 for film and plates, and $4 for buyouts, which totals $30. Printer B's VA for this job is then $100–$30, or $70. Thus, Printer B has $8 more than Printer A ($70–$62) to contribute to overhead costs, other costs, and profit. Given the previous VA description, Printer B is more profitable than Printer A.

With the VA concept, it is possible to have lower total sales dollars but greater profit than the competition. For example, Company A has total monthly sales of $175,000, which produces $90,000 in VA. Company B has monthly sales of $150,000 and a VA of $100,000. Even though the total monthly sales of Company A is $25,000 higher than Company B, Company B has $10,000 more than Company A to cover overhead and for profit. Company B appears more profitable than Company A, which should reevaluate its material and buyout cost relationships. Company A might then decide to buy paper and other materials in larger quantities to take advantage of quantity discounts, or perhaps it will begin to do more work directly on some jobs as opposed to sending the work to trade houses as outside purchases.

Keep in mind that the VA figure is improved any time printers do work inside the plant with their own equipment and personnel instead of sending it outside of their facilities. The VA banks on increasing internal production and reducing buyouts when quality or technical factors are not problems.

Some printers use VA to compensate sales representatives—the greater the VA, the greater the sales representative's earned commission, and the lower the VA, the lower the commission. Because it is reasonably easy to determine the cost of paper, other chargeable materials, and buyout costs, which is an advantage of the VA concept, the procedure of determining VA allows the sales representatives to ascertain fairly quickly how much commission they will earn. For this reason, it is easy for sales representatives to direct their efforts at jobs that have high VAs, which means the jobs provide improved profit to the company as well.

Profit Desired by Top Management

Profit provides incentive for the owners of any business. It is the reward for risks taken with invested capital. It allows for the growth of the business and for investment in new technology. Profit provides a general sense of security in the company which is shared by employees and management alike. Continual profits mean continued stability in the operation of any printing business.

In raw figures, profit data may be categorized into gross and net figures. Gross profit is the amount of dollars made by the business before the subtraction of administration and sales expenses, salaries, and taxes. It reflects manufacturing costs for the product but not the cost of sales commissions nor the costs necessary for the administration of the product. Gross profit as a percentage of sales dollars, which varies widely in the printing industry, typically ranges between 10 percent and 40 percent. The PIA Ratio Studies, which provide extensive financial measurement information for a printing company based on industry-wide data, indicate an average gross profit as a percentage of sales to be 23.75 percent in 1995.

Net profit, which is also known as income, is the amount of dollars remaining after all costs, including sales and administrative overhead, have been deducted. Net profit is the dollar amount on which taxes to both state and federal governments are paid and is sometimes referred to as "net profit (before taxes or b.t.)" or "income (b.t.)." While net profit can vary widely, the net profit (b.t.) in the printing industry typically falls between 2 percent and 6 percent of annual sales. Based on 1995 PIA Ratio Studies data, the average income (b.t.) was 3.30 percent of sales dollars for all firms included in the study. The Ratio Studies also provide extensive data for high-profit printers, who are defined as printers whose profits are above the upper quartile point based on profits as a measure of VA dollars.

Three measures of profitability are frequently applied to the printing industry: (1) income as a percentage of sales dollars; (2) income measured against investment dollars, which is known as ROI; and (3) income as a percentage of VA, which was previously discussed.

Income as a percentage of sales dollars, also termed return on sales or ROS, is popular because it is a simple concept to understand and has traditionally been used. In the *1995 PIA Ratio Studies* of 839 respondent companies, the average net profit (before taxes) was 3.30 percent of sales. This statistic means that for every dollar the average printing company sold in products, it kept 3.30 cents (before taxes). Thus, if an average printing company had a total annual sales volume of $1,000,000 and averaged 3.30 percent ROS, it would have before-tax profits of $33,300. In general, this would be considered a fairly low return for the risk and work involved. It is important to emphasize that taxes, which vary from state to state and company to company, have to be paid on this profit amount and could total as much as one-half of the ROS dollar amount. The remainder would then either be distributed to the owners or shareholders of the business or reinvested in the business.

Although the percentage of sales method is simple and easy to execute mathematically, it does not allow for a crucial element in the printing industry—the cost of investment. Because a printing company is so capital intensive—that is, because it requires a considerable amount of money to establish and operate—the ROI concept of measuring profits has grown in popularity.

The ROI is not quite as simple a measure of profitability as the percentage of sales concept. However, it is considered a more accurate measure because it relates net income (profit earned b.t.) to the assets (investment) required to produce that income. Thus:

$$\text{ROI} = \text{net income} \div \text{gross assets or net assets}$$

There are two asset measures by which to calculate ROI: gross asset and net asset. Essentially, the difference between the two relates to the depreciation, or the loss in dollar value from use, of the piece of equipment under consideration. Gross asset ROI makes no adjustment for depreciation and treats each piece of machinery as if it were a new investment, regardless of its year(s) of use. Net asset ROI subtracts depreciation loss. Consider the following examples for a small sheetfed press.

The gross asset ROI method uses the following formula:

$$\text{gross asset ROI} = \text{net income} \div \text{gross assets}$$

In this method, the investment cost remains the same from year to year, but profits diminish due to reduced equipment efficiency and increased wear. Thus, ROI is reduced from 12.5 percent to 5 percent over the eight-year period of use as shown by the following data:

Age of press	Income (profit)	Investment cost	ROI percent
1 year	$1,000	$8,000	12.5
3 years	$ 800	$8,000	10.0
8 years	$ 400	$8,000	5.0

The net asset method uses the following formula:

$$\text{net asset ROI} = \text{net income} \div (\text{gross assets} - \text{depreciation})$$

Thus, with the net asset method, depreciation reduces the investment, but income falls in the typical manner as indicated in the following:

Age of press	Income (profit)	Investment cost	ROI percent
1 year	$1,000	$8,000	12.5
3 years	$ 800	$6,000	13.3
8 years	$ 400	$2,000	20.0

For this example, the investment return on the press in the eighth year is better than any previous year, including when the press was new.

It should be noted that there are different methods to calculate depreciation. The choice of method is made by the owner(s) of the equipment when it is new. Given this, the depreciated dollars may be the same amount over the time period used, which is called "straight line" depreciation, or they may be skewed to be greater for the first few years with declining amounts for the remainder of the depreciation period, which is called "sum of the years digits" depreciation.

It is also important to note that because depreciation is a legitimate business expense, the United States Internal Revenue Service (IRS) has established guidelines for depreciation tax deductions that affect the taxes paid by the company. It is prudent for printers to make any depreciation decisions carefully with the assistance of a professional accountant.

On the one hand, it must be noted that there are numerous depreciation methods, which make comparisons of net asset ROI data inaccurate. On the other hand, because depreciation is not included in gross asset ROI, comparing data using this ROI method is more common.

Publications to Aid in Profit Calculation. The PIA Ratio Studies series mentioned earlier in this section is a valuable financial management tool which exhibits data relative to ROS, ROI, and VA. The studies provide factual, yearly data and financial information related to costs, prices, and profits for the printing industry. The ratio studies are produced annually and provide complete comparative data through their fourteen volumes which are broken out by ROS, ROI, and VA and cross-referenced with company size and types of products and processes used by the responding printers. The ratio studies, which have been produced for more than seventy years, provide long-term financial guidelines for the printing and allied industries.

Another valuable publication to the printing industry is NAPL's *Printing Business Report* (PBR). Figure 4.12 comes from the PBR for the second quarter of 1995 and provides two illustrations to show the type of data presented. Figure C of Figure 4.12 compares printing sales, costs, and profitability for 1993, 1994, and 1995 and shows increasing sales, increasing costs, and generally unchanged profits. Figure D shows the printers' confidence in business conditions.

NAPL's PBR provides up-to-date, insightful financial information on a quarterly basis, which serves as valuable guidepost information from which timely business decisions can be made.

Although various measures of profit have been discussed, the addition of profit during pricing is a decision that normally rests with top management, such as the company president or vice president of sales. Profit markup is best done on a job-by-job, customer-by-customer basis using the estimated total cost as a baseline. The person making such a decision must consider the array of pricing components described in this section and listed in Figure 4.6.

Location of the Printing Company to the Customer

It is said in real estate that the three most important criteria for buying a house or a piece of property are "location, location, and location." It is not unusual for printers, particularly small and quick printers, to experience much the same reaction from their customers—that being physically close to customers is important. This makes communication simple and direct and expedites fast job alterations, press checks, and immediate delivery when the job is done.

With jobs that are larger in quantity, utilize sophisticated digital imaging, are certain types of product specialties, and are purchased by professional print buyers, the physical location of the printing company is of less concern. This is due to the growth of specialized product manufacturing, fast communication

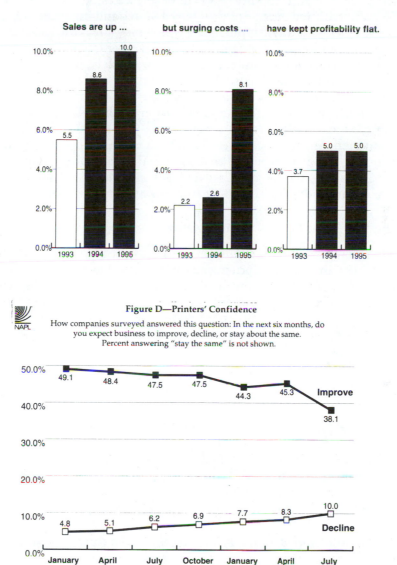

Figure 4.12 Illustrations on Printing Sales, Costs, and Profitability and Printers' Confidence. Reproduced from the National Association of Printers and Lithographers Printing Business Report, Volume 4, No. 3, 2nd Quarter, 1995. For information contact NAPL at (201) 342-0700.

methods, and a wide choice of excellent delivery methods. For example, it is not unusual for a large job to be printed in one region of the country and delivered to the customer in another region or in selected sites, or for a certain product to be manufactured outside of the United States and imported. There also may be tax savings where a job is produced, which may affect the location of production.

An important, emerging change for printers is a shift from the traditional "print and distribute" process described previously, which can incur significant shipping and handling costs when the printer and customer are distant from each other, to the use of the "distribute and print" (D&P) concept. D&P is completed using the telecommunication of digital graphic files to different remote locations where customers reside. The printing is then done by similar equipment at each site. Xerox DocuTech is among the first systems using this concept, and it is expected that as digital interconnectedness expands, other D&P systems will be used. Advantages include significant reduction in print cycle time and reduced product shipping and customer delivery costs.

The Customer's or Print Buyer's General Attitude

This factor can be best expressed as an "ease of working" relationship and may represent an important pricing factor in that some printers do not wish to work for customers who are continually dissatisfied with their jobs; who continually complain about service, price, or quality; or who are simply difficult to get along with. Charging such "difficult" clients premium prices for printing goods and services compensates the printer for difficult, awkward, or pressured working situations.

The Technical Difficulty of the Job in Terms of the Printer Meeting the Service or Quality Requirements Desired by the Customer

As digital production has increased, some types of jobs have become technically more difficult to produce. The printer who has invested in equipment and personnel capable of this high level of technical skill may be able to charge a premium for the work. Also, digital technology has expanded production options, which means customers sometimes choose printers according to their technical skill. This work may also have a price premium to the printer.

The Ego Satisfaction Gained by the Printer Desiring the Customer Wanting Exclusive Printer Services

Assume that Printer A desires to be the printer for Customer 1 and therefore reduces his price to become Customer 1's printer. The printer's ego drive has affected price in this case. The converse might also occur: Customer 2 decides that Printer B is the best printer in the city/state/nation and is therefore willing to pay any price Printer B charges. In this case the customer's ego has caused her acceptance of any price the printer wishes to charge. Both ego-driven conditions are common and can play major roles in the pricing equation.

Printer's Exclusive Production Capability

Specialization is clearly a price lever. If a printer is the only manufacturer or source for a particular product or service, there is no doubt that a definite price advantage exists for that printer. For any printer to have such a unique position is unusual, but it is sometimes evident in remote geographic areas where capital investment is prohibitive or when patents or other legal barriers provide such exclusivity. In general, if these situations do not prevail, the intensely competitive environment of printing results in very few printers having exclusive production capabilities.

Customer's Resale Value of the Printed Product

Some printers factor the value the customer gains into the product they produce for that customer. This is usually a subjective determination because most printing is done for mass distribution and the cost per printed unit is not an issue. Instances where the customer's resale value might be important are for very specific printed goods of limited run, such as serigraphs and artwork, special short-run books, posters, or certain types of packaging products.

4.7   Setting Up a Tailored Price List

Establishing a tailored price list seems, at first glance, to be a simple matter. Perhaps this is because using a price list is simple and convenient. However, such simplicity masks the complexity necessary to achieve the level of accuracy where the price list recovers all costs and provides a good ROI to the owners of the company. The price list used to quote a printing job must recover all fixed and variable costs, as well as consumed material costs and outside purchases. A single price must also include the components of volume, VA, ROS, ROI, customer issues, and other items as noted previously in this chapter and in Figure 4.6. Setting up the prices to be used for a price list estimating system can be deceptively complicated.

Most printing companies, from small quick printers to larger specialized sheetfed printers and web printers, operate in an environment of pure competition, which means typically that many firms with similar products and services compete. One result of these similarities between companies is intense competition, which allows for the establishment of artificially low price ceilings for the goods and services the printers provide. Another outgrowth of this intense competition is elasticity of demand, which means that as prices for printing goods and services go up, volume sold by the printing company is reduced, and that as prices go down, volume sold typically increases. Both of these issues have a bearing on prices.

The following lists the most common methods for developing the pricing structure for printing goods and services. Each method is self-explanatory.

Method 1   Basing prices on the competition's prices.
Method 2   Tailoring prices using the company's cost estimates of products as a baseline; prices always exceed costs.
Method 3   Basing prices on an analysis of profitable jobs done in the past.
Method 4   Basing prices on intuition or educated guessing.
Method 5   Basing prices on a combination of the four previous methods.

The result of any of these methods is a price list that describes the products or services the printer offers. When developing such a price list, one of the first management decisions to be made is whether the company wishes to tailor its prices to its costs using cost estimating or some other defined costing procedure. If the company does not wish to use a defined costing procedure, then typically management allows the prices to be determined in a more arbitrary, that is less defined, manner. Another early issue is management's view of the competition. Prices are sometimes developed with "beat the competition" as the most important criterion, but such an approach neglects internal baseline costs in producing the product.

The discussion that follows, when accompanied by Figure 4.13, provides a framework for how to develop and tailor a price list to represent a printing company's products and services. The procedure assumes that company management has decided to establish prices using baseline cost estimates, which ensures established prices recover internal manufacturing costs.

Step 1—Identify the Products and Services to Be Covered by the Price List

A price list should be developed to cover a specific, clearly identified group of products and services provided or performed by the printing company. There should be no ambiguity relative to what products and services are covered. Thus, management must decide and segment either (1) those products that have a certain amount of support services built into their prices and the parameters of these support services or (2) those products that are supported by stand-alone, a la carte services which add to the products' prices and are selected by the customer in addition to the basic product.

It is unlikely that a single price list covers all of the products and services a typical printing company offers. Usually the list targets a specialized product or defined group of products and related services that the company finds profitable, easy to do, and within all of its production capabilities. The products and services chosen should avoid loss leaders, which are products or services that

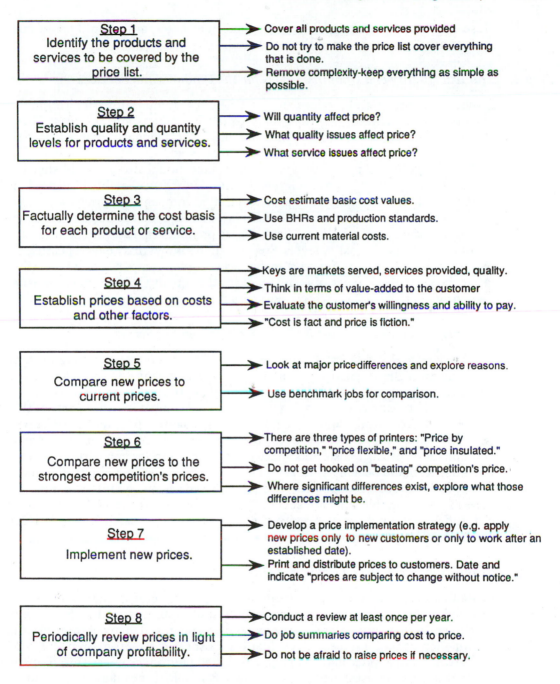

Step 1 Identify the products and services to be covered by the price list.	→ Cover all products and services provided → Do not try to make the price list cover everything that is done. → Remove complexity-keep everything as simple as possible.
Step 2 Establish quality and quantity levels for products and services.	→ Will quantity affect price? → What quality issues affect price? → What service issues affect price?
Step 3 Factually determine the cost basis for each product or service.	→ Cost estimate basic cost values. → Use BHRs and production standards. → Use current material costs.
Step 4 Establish prices based on costs and other factors.	→ Keys are markets served, services provided, quality. → Think in terms of value-added to the customer → Evaluate the customer's willingness and ability to pay. → "Cost is fact and price is fiction."
Step 5 Compare new prices to current prices.	→ Look at major price differences and explore reasons. → Use benchmark jobs for comparison.
Step 6 Compare new prices to the strongest competition's prices.	→ There are three types of printers: "Price by competition," "price flexible," and "price insulated." → Do not get hooked on "beating" competition's price. → Where significant differences exist, explore what those differences might be.
Step 7 Implement new prices.	→ Develop a price implementation strategy (e.g. apply new prices only to new customers or only to work after an established date). → Print and distribute prices to customers. Date and indicate "prices are subject to change without notice."
Step 8 Periodically review prices in light of company profitability.	→ Conduct a review at least once per year. → Do job summaries comparing cost to price. → Do not be afraid to raise prices if necessary.

Figure 4.13 Developing a tailored price list for a graphic arts company

lose the printing company money on consistent bases, and should target customer needs that are frequently in demand.

Step 2—Establish Quality and Quantity Levels for the Products and Services

Once the products and services are identified, it is important to determine the quantity and quality levels that apply to these products and services. These levels should target those quantities that are most frequently ordered, as well as allow for quantity ranges that might be requested.

It may be difficult to do, but quality of product should also be established because it is frequently an issue relative to price. Sometimes establishing product quality is done with samples of products that accompany the price list; sometimes narrative is used to define the quality level. Frequently prices are developed using quality as a primary ingredient, where products are categorized into "excellent" and "good" quality levels. Step 3, which follows, may have a bearing on Step 2 in that quantity and quality are both cost-driven components. It is possible that the anticipated range of quantity or level of quality may be too expensive when evaluated in Step 3, which requires a reassessment of Step 2.

Step 3—Factually Determine the Cost Basis for Each Product or Service

Although prices can be established on the basis of many items, one important ingredient is the internal cost for the printing company to manufacture the product. For this reason, it is prudent to evaluate the products and services on the price list using cost estimating procedures. As noted in other parts of this book, cost estimating requires accurate BHRs, quantitative production times, current material costs, current outside purchase costs, and profit assessment as components. Because costs and prices per unit diminish as quantities rise, cost estimates should be done at target quantities over the expected range of quantities to be offered. Product quality should be fixed because quality and quantity are different variables that affect cost. The precise cost estimating method used should be written down and retained so that it can be repeated for future price increase calculations.

Step 4—Establish Prices Based on Costs and Other Factors

Establishing actual prices is critical because prices factor in many issues and variables. As noted earlier in this chapter and as summarized in Figure 4.6, eighteen components enter into the price assessment, and many of these pricing components require subjective evaluation. Cost estimates from Step 3 provide a starting point or price floor. This step, Step 4, should be completed by company management, not estimating or sales staff. It is sometimes done by executive meeting, where prices are openly discussed and finalized based on consensus. To speed the process, sometimes a company executive sets the prices, then asks other executives to provide their individual review and feedback. Sometimes prices are established by the company owner with no consultation from other employees. Whatever method is used, setting prices is a mix of quantitative and subjective components, which makes this step difficult.

One important issue relative to establishing prices is what the customer is willing to pay for the products and services he purchases. If prices set at Step 4 are too low, volume increases but profit is less than desired; if prices are too high, volume drops, but profits are higher on this reduced volume. To some, establishing prices at Step 4 is a process of identifying high and low dollar amounts, then setting the final price somewhere between these high and low points. Regardless of the approach, management should be mindful of the links between volume, price, and profitability: Prices drive volume, and these prices are directly linked to the level of profits made by the company.

Step 5—Compare New Prices to Current Prices

Once prices are tentatively set, company management should compare the current prices to the new prices under consideration. Sometimes this task is integrated as part of Step 4. The purpose of this comparison is clear: If the new prices are substantially different than the current prices—if they are either too high or too low—the reasons deserve investigation.

If the new prices are lower than the current ones but volume using the old (higher) prices is stable and at a desired level, then intangible factors of the market and not price alone may be driving the business. This situation could be caused by numerous factors which should be explored. Typically the result of this "new prices lower than current prices" scenario is that the company is enjoying prosperity. However, if this is not the case, then there is a real discrepancy between the true costs the business incurs and the estimated costs the business expects. Again, this is a serious problem which should be investigated and corrected as appropriate.

If the new prices are higher than the current ones, which is a more likely scenario than them being lower, a key issue is how much volume will be lost if these higher prices are implemented. As indicated earlier in this chapter, two findings from the *McKinsey Report to PIA* relate to the price-volume-market situation: (1) When prices are increased 10 percent and the market is inelastic (there is no volume loss from the price rise), profits increase 180 percent, and (2) When prices are increased 3 percent and the market is elastic (customers can go elsewhere for the same products and services), there is a subsequent 10 percent loss of volume and a resulting 50 percent loss of profits. Thus, whether the market is inelastic or elastic—that is, whether customers stay or leave when prices are increased—is a critical issue to maintaining viable company volume and turning a profit in the business.

Step 6—Compare New Prices to the Strongest Competition's Prices

This step is important in that it requires comparison of the competition's prices to the suggested new prices. When significant differences are apparent here, evaluation should be done to determine the reasons for them. Because the printing industry is driven by intense competition and artificially low price ceilings set by many printers vying for the same types of printing work, opinion varies widely as to how to address competitive issues and differences in competitive pricing. There are three general, philosophical groups of printers related to price competition:

Group 1: "Price-by-Competition Printers." These printers base the prices for all of the products and services they provide completely on their competition's prices. They operate on the theory that all they have to do is meet or beat the competition and put all other pricing factors aside.

Group 2: "Price-Flexible Printers." These printers base their prices on their competition's prices in areas where they experience strong competition, feel they can dominate, or have a history of reasonable profits. These printers maintain separate pricing methods for other customers (they may use more than one type of pricing) in which they largely ignore the competition's price.

Group 3: "Price-Insulated Printers." These printers ignore the competition's prices and sell their products and services to clients who are willing to pay the prices the printers determine to be fair and reasonable.

There are clear advantages and disadvantages with each group. In general, the greatest profits are enjoyed by Group 3, the "price-insulated printers" who ignore the competition's prices. However, this is true only when these printers operate their businesses in careful, cost-focused, and customer-driven environments. This is not to say that either of the other two groups do not make money, because they do. However, Groups 1 and 2 tend to generate profits in less predictable patterns, perhaps earning profits on the basis of very high volume or from a few customers who are willing to pay more.

Although matching the competition's prices allows Group 1 and 2 printers to maintain volume that might have gone to a Group 3 printer, it is generally acknowledged that the intense competition causes their prices to be lower, and thus their profits are compressed. Group 1 and 2 printers also tend to enjoy higher volumes but lower ROIs, ROSs, and VAs. In general, the most successful printing companies watch the competition and understand the competition's price estimating methods and pricing philosophies but do not become overly engrossed in these subjects. To ensure good volume, successful Group 3 printing companies downplay price and focus on providing world-class service, differentiating their products and services, continuously improving the delivery of their products and services, and fostering TQM environments.

Step 7—Implement New Prices

Implementing a new price estimating system may be done with public fanfare or silently, depending on the approach company management wishes to take. If the prices are organized into a price list format, and management decides that customers should have this information, the price list should be published and distributed to customers. If this is done, the published list should be dated as to when prices are effective and state that "Prices are subject to change without notice."

Various other information, such as cost modifiers, technical tips, normal job turnaround, messenger service, and discounts provided, can also be included in published price lists. The more specific a price list becomes and the more detail that is provided, the more informed the customer is about contractual points that affect the stated price. Published price lists should be graphically pleasing and easy to understand and use. Figures 4.14 and 4.15 are sample price lists which exhibit some of the previous points.

Sometimes a new price estimating system is developed and implemented inside the printing company, and the customers have no knowledge that prices have changed. Typically these are known as "confidential" prices. Over time it is not unusual for these internal, confidential prices to become known to other printing companies, so it is possible that competing printers also have this knowledge.

Step 8—Periodically Review Prices in Light of Company Profitability

Every price estimating system requires periodic review because changing costs, new technology, employee productivity, and other factors have a bearing on price. Although opinion varies, in general prices should be reviewed at least one time per year relative to cost accuracy and profitability to the company.

Signs of mispriced products or services vary. The most common indicator is a significant gain or loss of business volume. Typically a loss of volume, which results because the company's prices are higher than its competing companies, can be noted fairly quickly. Gains in volume, however, which result because the company's prices are lower than its competing companies, tend to be less pronounced. Other common indicators of mispricing are the customer's statements or comments, including increased customer requests to "justify" the company's prices. There is also feedback from company employees who note prices are too high or low based on their intuitive knowledge of the business.

A key feedback tool is the company's P&L statement, which preferably should be available monthly or at least quarterly. If a company does not have a quarterly P&L from which to evaluate the business, the accounting and management practices of the company should be immediately reviewed because these P&L statements provide critical indicators of overall business operation. For exam-

PRICES

FREE DELIVERY ANYWHERE! for most jobs

CAMERA

Film
Line Neg.
Contact Positive

4x10	8.25
10x12	15.00
12x18	20.25
20x24	36.00
24x36	58.00

Stat
Price Includes Neg.

4x10	10.50
10x12	18.75
12x18	25.50
20x24	45.00
24x36	72.50

Halftone

4x10	15.00
10x12	27.25
12x18	42.50
20x24	96.75
24x36	188.25

Print
Velox From Your Film

4x10	7.75
10x12	11.00
12x18	17.00
20x24	31.50
24x36	45.00

SCANNER

Color Separation
Transparency or
Reflective Art to Disk

25 MB	65.00
35 MB	75.00
45 MB	85.00
55 MB	95.00
>55 MB	Call

Black & White
Transparency or
Reflective Art to Disk

10 MB	25.00
15 MB	30.00
20 MB	35.00
25 MB	40.00
>25 MB	Call

POSTSCRIPT® OUTPUT

Film
2540dpi Resolution

12x12	16.50
12x15	18.50
12x18	20.25
12x24	24.25
12x30	28.50
13x22	30.25
18x19	34.50
14x30	52.25
18x30	64.50
22x30	76.00

Paper
2540dpi Resolution

12x12	13.75
12x15	15.25
12x18	16.75
12x24	20.00
12x30	23.50
13x22	38.00*
18x19	43.00*
14x30	64.25*
18x30	79.00*
22x30	93.25*

*Includes Film Neg.

DIGITAL PROOFING

3M Rainbow
PostScript Dye Sub.

11x17	45.00

TRADITIONAL PROOFING

Blueline

4x10	3.50
6x10	4.00
8x10	4.50
10x12	5.25
11x14	5.75
12x19	7.25
19x25	10.25
25x38	12.75
30x40	14.50

3M MatchPrint
Price per Color

7x11	15.75
11x14	21.00
12x19	28.75
19x25	47.25
25x38	67.25

3M Color Key
Price per Color

7x11	13.50
11x14	17.75
12x19	24.50
19x25	40.25
25x30	51.75
25x38	57.25

IMPORTANT PRICING INFORMATION
$25.00 MINIMUM PURCHASE. There will be an additional charge for RUSH work.
Prices are for finished size. NO EXTRA CHARGE for enlargement or reduction.
FILTER, FINE LINE, DROP-OUT and other SPECIAL REQUIREMENTS add at least 25% to listed prices.
(Prices effective: April 1, 1994. Prices subject to change without notice.)

C I R C U S
LITHOGRAPHIC PREPRESS

575 Howard Street
San Francisco 94105

TEL 777-0575

FAX 777-4223

MODEM 777-4636

"ADOBE" FONTS
BUSINESS PARTNER
DISCOUNT PRICES

HOURS

MONDAY THRU FRIDAY
8:00 am–4:30 pm

CLOSED FOR LUNCH
12:00–12:30

Figure 4.14 Sample price list. (Reproduced with permission of Circus Lithographic Prepress, San Francisco, California.)

desktop pricing

Bay State Press
2 Watson Place
Framingham, MA
(508) 877 0116

Merge	Color or B&W 3 min. each plus 15 min. set-up photo x 3 + 15/60 = merge	$175.00 hr.
Varnish Merge	Same as merge except 1 min. each plus 15 min. set-up Varnish x 1 + 15/60 = varnish merge	$175.00 hr.
Postscript	4 min. per film (to stripping) A. x 4/60 Postscript	$75.00 hr.
Rip	8 min. per film (to stripping) A. x 8/60 = rip	$75.00 hr.
PressWise	30 min. per unique printing form	$175.00 hr.
Inspect	Review film prior to moving to stripping 2-5 min. per film based on complexity A. x (2-5)/60 = inspect	$75.00 hr.
Technical	Simple 5-10 min. per page Moderate 5-15 min. per page Complex 15-30 min. per page (Multiple multi-color graphics) B. x (5-30)/60 = technical	$175.00 hr.

A. = Pieces of film stripping is to receive

B. = Number of pages

1. PageMaker - no traps, okay to merge, PageMaker - traps of 4 color screens are okay to merge. Allow time in technical to check.

2. QuarkXpress - merges and traps easily, allow time in technical to check traps.

3. Film size 11¼" x 32" (approx.)

cost per piece of film†

	1693 DPI-No Gradations		2540 DPI- Gradations	
	Letter*	**Tabloid***	**Letter***	**Tabloid***
1-10	24.00	34.00	29.00	40.00
11-25	20.00	27.50	25.00	35.00
26-50	18.00	25.00	23.00	31.50
51-100	16.50	23.00	20.00	27.50
Over 100	Quote	Quote	Quote	Quote

† Film or RC Paper

PC files add 45%.

* Page size is based on the page geometry created in the file.

Additional: PressWise - $175.00 per hour
Technical - $175.00 per hour
Text & Image Merging - $175.00 per hour
Auto Trapping - Additional 50% to above chart (technical may also be needed)

Storage: Jobs are stored for 1 week after job is delivered.
Removable hard disk cartridges are available:
    44 mb Syquest - $129.99   90 mb Bernoulli - $139.97
    88 mb Syquest - $149.99   150 mb Bernoulli - $199.97

All prices are subject to change without notice.

BSP Form 7 11/94 #19297 © GJN

Figure 4.15 Sample price list. (Reproduced with permission of Bay State Press, Framingham, Massachusetts.)

ple, price is a key factor driving income earned, which is directly related to profitability. Because the P&L provides price feedback, it is a critical indicator of the overall level of company profit earned. It should be noted that the P&L does not provide profit and cost feedback on a job-by-job basis. It only indicates that a profit was made, it does not clarify which customers and markets were most profitable. This is because prices established for some types of work may not even recover costs, while other types of production (e.g., production for certain customers or market niches) may be extremely profitable and offset the losses.

The analysis of profits on a job-by-job basis takes time, but this effort can be very worthwhile. Typically the job costing process, in which individual jobs are reviewed for all cost and profitability components, is used. When job costing, care must be taken to accurately correlate actual production costs to estimated costs, which can be obscured behind the pricing format used. Because hundreds of jobs are likely to have been done using a given pricing system, the selection of jobs to be reviewed is frequently done on an nth number basis, where each seventh, eighth, or other job is evaluated. Another way is to specifically select jobs that represent the typical or average job.

4.8   Important Pricing Concepts and Issues

The following are some key points for pricing printed work or developing a pricing system or price matrix for graphic products.

Who Should Establish Prices?

The individual who establishes prices in a printing company should be the person who stands to gain or lose the most by the pricing choices made. Traditionally this is the company owner, although it may also be the company president or another executive. Frequently prices are set by a sales manager or a vice president of sales. Because sales managers tend to have daily involvement in company activity, quotations tend to be turned around fairly quickly by them. Also, sales managers tend to know the company's customers, which allows them the unique opportunity to factor in customer issues that may affect price. Some company presidents elect to be less involved in pricing because they do not wish to maintain a close, continuous role in operating the business. Sometimes, too, presidents are uncomfortable or feel unfamiliar with the range of pricing issues, so they delegate this critical activity to someone else.

From a practical perspective, it makes no difference who establishes the prices as long as company profits are maximized and the pricing process is completed in a timely manner. In general it is best if prices are not set by estimators, billing personnel, production supervisors, or customer service personnel because these individuals actively participate in various aspects of the customer's order and do not typically have the range of knowledge needed for the task. It should be clear, however, that this same group of individuals should be free to participate in the process by providing input relative to establishing the price of the job if asked to do so or by providing information that would directly affect the final price.

Customer-Differentiated Pricing

Bob Lindgren, executive director of PIA-SC, advances the following procedure for customer pricing. He calls it the "power of systematic customer differentiation." It works like this: Take the customers and divide them into three groups. Group 1 customers recognize the company's unique ability to deliver their time-sensitive, high-quality products and are the types of customer the company wishes to have. Group 2 customers are average customers who know the company's products and services well but routinely consider other printers for their work. Group 3 customers are "price shoppers" who get numerous bids on every job and typically buy at the lowest prices; they are negotiators on price who frequently push for cutting reasonable prices even lower.

Consider the following scenario of the normal quoting process:

Group 1 customer quotation	$1,000	Job sells
Group 2 customer quotation	$1,000	Job sells
Group 3 customer quotation	$1,000	Job does not sell (price too high)
Revenue gained	$2,000	

Now consider a pricing strategy done by customer group:

Group 1 customer quotation	$1,100	Job sells
Group 2 customer quotation	$1,000	Job sells
Group 3 customer quotation	$ 900	Job sells
Revenue gained	$3,000	

The key point here is that defining customers by group and establishing a pricing strategy relative to these customers is an important concept that should be considered as a company explores various vertical markets, where customers share common elements, and business expansion. Clearly the revenue gained from pricing by customer group in the second example is greater than the revenue gained from pricing by normal quoting procedure in the first example because the prices in the second example are adjusted to meet the customers' realities.

One assumption made in these examples is that the printer wishes to do business with Group 2 and Group 3 customers, who could well be a mixture of problematic clients. However, sometimes these Group 2 and Group 3 customers advance to Group 1 level and become business partners to the printer instead of price-cutting adversaries. One might also question the fact that the best customer group (Group 1) pays the most while the average customer (Group 2) and the price-cutting customer (Group 3) pay less. This does not appear to provide the best customer with the greatest financial incentive. However, given that the Group 1 customer should be given the absolute best and fastest service the printer can provide, this price differential is justified.

Baseline Price Estimating

Another approach taken to build a price estimating system is to first establish a minimum, baseline price—perhaps the full cost of the job plus 10 percent—then to adjust that base price for each job as needed to compensate for important customer and competitive issues.

An advantage of using this type of pricing strategy is that it gives flexibility yet recovers a base amount that has been determined to be essential. For example, if the company has maximized production to the point that no more production time is available at current prices, baseline price estimating allows for adjusting prices for new work upward. These higher prices tend to discourage additional volume or, when customers choose to purchase at the higher price, ensure that any work done at these higher prices provides a far higher profit. Conversely, if additional production volume is needed, the baseline price estimating process allows for careful, conscientious price reductions that encourage customers to use the price-reduced services.

One disadvantage of this pricing strategy is that baseline price estimating may slow the quoting process because jobs require pricing review by a company insider. It also requires constant staff support because the pricing system is not automated.

Price Cutting

Price cutting is a difficult problem for printers. Essentially price cutting is the lowering of an accurately determined selling price to a point where job profitability is compromised. Typically price cutting occurs when a customer presents the printer with a competitive but lower price quotation on a job the printer would like to have. A key problem is that any time a customer is successful in negotiating a reduced price, for whatever reason, it establishes a pattern. On the one hand, the printer should be committed to developing her prices based on internal costs plus reasonable profits, while on the other hand the competition is always intense but not always driven to make profits as much as gain a larger customer base.

Varying options to counter price cutting can be suggested, none of which provides an ideal solution to the problem. The first option is for company management to adopt a fixed policy whereby no price cutting is allowed, regardless of customer or reason. A key to the success of this option is how customers are informed of this policy: The printer can deliver a hard-core message ("we never cut price") or subtly meet the customer's suggestion of lowering price with silence. A second option is for the company to include a strategic additional markup in its pricing system so that a certain amount of price cutting can be accommodated without negatively effecting profit. A third option is for the company to focus on certain vertical markets and on customers who buy less often on price and more often on service and quality issues. A fourth option is to discuss price cuts only when there is a change in the products or services provided by the printer (e.g., smaller format size, fewer colors, customer supplies final film). A fifth option is for the printing company to streamline production methods or efficiencies, thereby cutting costs to a point that price reduction is possible. A sixth option is for the company to tell all customers at the quotation stage that "our prices are higher, but our service is world class," which suggests that price cuts are not likely.

Pricing for the Best and Worst Customers

Every printing company has good and bad customers, and price is one way that the good customers can be rewarded and the bad customers can be penalized. For the really terrific customers who meet every deadline, provide fully output-ready and properly specified files, pay their invoices in full without complaint, and in general are great to work with, a periodic price reduction, which is perhaps based on volume or a "special reason," might be a realistic consideration. Such a reduction encourages the customers' business and continues a partnership arrangement. Consider the benefits of such a partnership agreement: The customers' production is smooth, their cooperative efforts are great, and having them as customers is enjoyable.

Pricing is also an effective tool to discourage the work of problematic customers: If the price is raised high enough, problem customers go elsewhere. However, it is possible that these problematic, troublesome customers may also have the most creative and experimental jobs or jobs that move the company into an improved quality mode. There are two key questions to be answered in deciding whether a difficult customer should be retained: (1) Does the customer pay his invoices on time, without hassle or argument? and (2) Are the problems the customer presents so overwhelming that absolutely no company employee wants to see him come in the door or work on his jobs? If problem customers pay on time and can be successfully managed, then pricing might be moderately increased to keep their work while earning more profit. However, if they are continually problematic and do not pay on time, substantial price increases would be in order to compensate for their business.

Pricing for Long-Term Contract Commitment

One of the ways to encourage continuous volume in printing is to enter into long-term contractual commitments with selected customers. These commitments, once they are established, initiate partnerships that encourage cooperation between customer and printer. Both customer and printer understand that the long-term arrangement is beneficial and work to encourage its success. Such a commitment provides for a highly cooperative environment between employees of both parties, a far smoother production situation, and a positive working relationship across the board.

The use of long-term contract commitments should be limited to select customers and to the type of work the company finds is most profitable and most expeditiously produced. In other words, the contract should be focused on printing work within the specialty categories and on the products the company does routinely and well. Because the selection of long-term customers is a commitment similar to marriage, before the contract is engaged it is important to evaluate the customer's attitudes, working relationship, and business philosophies for similarities with the same factors in the company.

4.9   Computer-Assisted Price Estimating

As discussed in Chapter 1, computer-assisted pricing (CAP) is a process by which a printing company's prices are formatted to computer software for quick and easy use. Because CAP combines the speed of price estimating and the speed and accuracy of computers, and because laptop and portable notebook computers are becoming more affordable, CAP is growing in popularity.

Price List Estimating Using a Spreadsheet

Most price lists can be formatted to a spreadsheet, which is then linked to a quotation. The user selects base prices and adds extra costs, after which the spreadsheet computes tax and provides the final price in quotation format. Developing this spreadsheet and the linked quotation requires a good knowledge of spreadsheet programming. Following are four suggestions in this area:

1. For price list estimating in the field, the system consists of a laptop computer and a portable printer. For estimating in the office, hardware consists of a computer and a printer or fax/modem. The sales representative in the field or the staff doing the quoting via telephone should be

thoroughly trained in how the system works before using it with customers.

2. The spreadsheet format should provide minimum complexity on the part of the user. It should also allow for "what if" scenarios as jobs are discussed with customers.
3. Flexibility of use is important. Multiple quantities and product variations should be allowed, including the addition of extra costs that may not be on the price list.
4. The spreadsheet should be developed so that it allows for price updates without complete revision of the spreadsheet format.

Some printing industry computer vendors offer commercial versions of price list estimating systems that utilize spreadsheets. Chapter 2 provides information on these systems and on vendors serving the printing industry.

Price Matrix Estimating Using Computer Templates

The price matrix estimating system is best completed using a computer system because it is more complex than price list estimating. The matrix process requires the printing company to develop cost centers, production components, activity codes, and, finally, all-inclusive selling prices for conventional prepress, press, finishing, and any other production it offers for sale. Figure 4.4 is an example of a price matrix estimating format for DTP.

Once all matrices are developed, the company develops a set of price matrix templates to represent the most typical or specialized products it produces. A template is a breakdown of the usual or expected job components a particular product requires. Thus, if a printing company specializes in producing eight-page newsletters with two colors on two sides of a page, the newsletters' template would contain only the production activities and prices need to produce them. Thus, templates streamline the pricing process by providing only specific operations.

Chapter 5 and Chapter 8 discuss template cost estimating procedures in detail, which resemble template price estimating procedures. Also, some printing industry computer vendors offer CAP estimating software.

4.10 Some Difficult Pricing Areas for Printers

The management staff of any printing establishment are faced with the task of pricing company products effectively. The following discussion outlines some of the more difficult problems frequently faced by printers pricing certain types of work. It is wise for the printing company management to discuss and develop a strategy or philosophy to deal with any of the following situations.

Filler Work

Filler work is printing that is used to keep the company busy during normal slowdown periods. Filler work is accepted by the printer to provide company stability by recovering manufacturing costs and reducing employee layoffs. However, the policy for filler work requires thought because, even though costs are recovered, little effort is sometimes made to obtain a profit. At the same time, equipment is being used (and worn out) for no financial gain.

Small printers and quick printers, whose volumes tend to fluctuate somewhat on a day-to-day basis, do not typically experience the problems large commercial and high-volume printers do in dealing with filler work. This is because smaller printers tend to experience less pronounced volume shifts and are usually better able to react to these volume variations because fewer employees are involved.

Many printing companies that aggressively seek filler work cut prices to obtain it. Other printers attempt to schedule production in such a manner that average output is consistent and filler work is unneeded. Still others track customer needs closely and arrange for "last like period" printing to fill these slower periods. For an example of the latter, if a customer ordered a particular job six months ago, the printing sales representative might recontact the customer when the company is experiencing a slack period to sell that customer a repeat run of the job, with or without changes.

Repeat Work

Many printers, particularly commercial and high-volume types, experience repeat orders for printing with no changes, such as reruns of existing jobs. The question in such cases, where all preparatory work has been completed already (perhaps all that needs to be done is to make new plates), is should the printer pass her prepress savings to the customer? On the one hand, if the printer does pass along her savings, the customer will expect this savings on all other repeat work and may try to reduce job changes in the future to enjoy this discount. On the other hand, if the printer does not share such savings with the customer, the printer's profit on the job will appear larger because the dollars paid by the customer for prepress manufacturing on the rerun job would not have actually been spent for this item.

Trade Work from Other Printers

While buyout work is purchased from an outside printing company or a trade house, a buy-in is an order placed in the plant by another printing establishment. The frequency of buy-ins is related to the certain process and product specialty areas the printer makes available to the industry, such as perfect binding, special folding capabilities, or certain specialized copying or prepress operations.

There appears to be an increasing amount of trade work between printers as market specialization accelerates. Service bureaus, which are former typesetters, provide extensive prepress services for printers. Trade binderies provide specialized binding and finishing services for printers who do not wish to buy or maintain expensive equipment in this production area. Printing services are also being affected. On-demand printing using Xerox DocuTech, Indigo, and Xeikon systems provide component parts of jobs that are produced on time-compressed bases.

Normally price reductions for companies providing specialized products and services are reciprocated between printing companies and their suppliers. When the manufacturing operation is truly streamlined, considerable cost savings are possible, and the savings may then be passed to the purchasing company.

Rush Work

Rush work is unexpected or unplanned work customers request on a fast-turnaround, time-compressed basis. This type of work is a market specialty for some printers, but it may represent major difficulties for many types of customers and products. There is no question that the typical lead time, which is the time needed to manufacture the printed product inside the printing company, was compressed during the 1980s, regardless of the type of printing operation. Prior to 1980 industry-wide lead times averaged twenty or more working days for many jobs. By the mid-1980s, lead times had been reduced to an average of ten days; by the mid-1990s lead time had been compressed to five working days for a growing number of products. Certainly lead times vary widely relative to industry segment, type of job, and customer need.

For any printer who is not geared to work overtime or who is not working on a two- or three-shift basis, compressing lead times represents a difficult problem. Providing customers with speedy delivery—a very important customer service requirement—necessitates that the printer do everything in his power to produce the customer's work as desired. If he does not, customers will find another printer who will.

There is no question that all customers need rush printing completed from time to time or even frequently, and there is also no question that market factors and competitive issues require the printer to respond accordingly. However, rush work can be costly and may require overtime for employees, special supplies or processes to expedite production, increased paper waste, and other increased costs. Because these are valid, job-related costs, they should be borne by the customer.

In many cases, customers and print buyers are willing to pay extra for rush work, but how much varies in proportion to how badly the printing is needed and to the buyer's budget constraints. Rush charges may range from the printer's additional costs only to two or three times the original price, which is charged by some printers to discourage customers from habitually requesting fast-turnaround jobs. When rush work is requested by the customer, the printer should provide the customer with a dollar estimate of the additional rush costs. Once a job is committed as rush work, the printer is responsible to meet the compressed delivery date.

Just as rush work has become an issue between the customer and the printer, it has also become an important issue between the trade supplier and the printer. This is particularly true of prepress trade houses and service bureaus supplying the printer with various prepress job components, such as final film, as well as bindery trade shops who finish the job after printing. Because off-site manufacturing is part of the rush order, and because the work is time compressed to the trade supplier too, pricing issues between printers and trade suppliers are a problem.

Two final points need to be made about rush work. First, there is no question that the printer of the 1990s must provide excellent customer service to remain in business and profitable, which means that fast-turnaround work remains a fact of business and that some customers will likely request rush work on a frequent basis. Second, because fast-turnaround work is a market niche, it is likely there will be an increasing number of printers—quick, commercial, and high-volume—who will encourage this type of work. Thus, rush work remains a competitive dimension in an industry already intensely competitive in many other ways.

Charity Work

It is safe to state that most printing companies have been approached by a church, foundation, school, or other nonprofit service organization requesting a free job or a job at a substantially reduced price. Both the advantage and disadvantage of accepting charity work relate to the company's reputation. If the work is done at a reduced price or for free, the company benefits from a good reputation within the community. As this good reputation develops, however, additional organizations may request the same benefits from the printer. Saying no may then be difficult. Some printing plants take charity work at a time-and-materials rate and make no profit; others do small charity jobs for free but do not accept large jobs. Still others accept charity work, run it using normal production practices, price it as regular work, then donate it to the charitable organization and write off its full cost as a donation (provided there are no legal entanglements). Whatever procedure is used, management must establish a policy regarding how to handle work for charities.

Work for New or First-Time Customers

Pricing work for new customers presents a particularly thorny problem to management, especially in printing companies wishing to keep their equipment busy or to impress the new clients with the dependability and service they can provide. There is a tendency for new customers to indicate that they will place more work in the future if they are given a price break on the first job. Although some printers reduce prices initially to get new customers, this practice can be dangerous. After the first order, can prices be raised without question? How much compromising on price will be necessary in the future if the printer begins by cutting prices? Will the customer expect this practice all of the time?

As stated earlier, it is probably best not to put much stock in the customer's promises. It is also good to remember that well over fifty percent of the volume of some commercial printers comes from repeat customers. Thus, if price cutting is done initially, it may become more of a pattern than the printer would like because its long-term effects can be costly.

Work for Friends and Family

Friends and family seem to request discounts, or even free printing, more than the general public. The advantage of reducing prices for a friend or family member, perhaps to costs for time and materials, is that the printer's personal relationship with that person is maintained in a normal manner. The disadvantage is that if the price is reduced, the friend or family member may expect similar treatment in the future and may have a more significant printing request at that time.

Various philosophies exist with respect to dealing with this matter. Some printers use the time-and-materials method; some ask for a favor of equal value in return. Others do the printing as a regular job but with the understanding that the friend or family member will provide something of like value through a barter. Finally, although some printers refuse to do printing for family or friends, they may aid the person in obtaining printing from a reliable source. Whatever policy is used, it should result in fair treatment for both parties in the relationship.

Rerun Work Due to Customer Error

Assume that the customer has approved a press sheet and that the job is printed, finished, and delivered. Later that day the customer notices a major error in the work due to her oversight. The customer insists that job must be reprinted immediately (perhaps because it is time dated) and desires a discounted second run even though she is clearly apologetic.

Scenarios to resolve this problem vary. Some printing companies would rerun the job at a reduced price, perhaps by deducting the cost of prepress. Others would rerun the job using a discounted original price, while still others would rerun the job at a time-and-materials rate. Important issues such as the quality of the job and the quantity of other printing done for this customer may be factors in making this rerun pricing decision.

If the job is rerun at a reduced price, one disadvantage is that errors may occur with future jobs and the customer may expect a reduced price again. One rule of thumb is that the printing company should not rerun the order without first receiving full payment for the first job. Then, if further misunderstandings arise, the company at least has received full payment for the first job and will not pay twice for materials. Certainly, avoiding this situation is desirable.

The best solution is to work diligently to reduce customer errors by thoroughly checking all possible elements of the job during production and double-checking important facts with the customer prior to printing.

Contract Work

Most printing plants bid on contract printing at one time or another. In fact, a growing number of printers encourage contract work to ensure a continuing, predictable printing volume. Sometimes printers become involved in contract work to fill production scheduling gaps. In other instances, that job might appeal to the printer or the printer might have a specialty in that area, in which cases bidding on the contract may be the only procedure by which the printer will be awarded the work.

Perhaps the most important consideration in contract work is for whom the work will be done. State and federal government bids are usually accepted on the lowest dollar amount, but this is not always the case. Criteria for the selection of other types of contract work vary with regard to the type of company, product use, and so on. Some printing companies cut prices on contract work simply to stay busy; others refuse to bid on contract work because it normally requires exacting specifications that cannot be accurately cost estimated and priced.

4.11 Price Discrimination

The intention of the Robinson-Patman Act of 1936, which is actually an amendment to the Clayton Act of 1914, is to eliminate price discrimination. The act essentially prevents the seller of a product, good, or service from offering the same kind of goods, "goods of like grade and quality," to two or more buyers at different prices.

Proving discrimination under Robinson-Patman is not a simple procedure. Because the act is federal law, interstate commerce must be involved in legal proceedings. The buyer must prove that "an unjustified special price, discount, or special service was provided to the customer," while the identical price, discount, or special price was not provided to the complainant.

For the most part, purchasing agents, the people who purchase printing consistently for larger companies, understand that Robinson-Patman is complicated and difficult to interpret. Robinson-Patman is enforced by the Federal Trade Commission through initial use of cease-and-desist orders from a court of law. If price discrimination is proven in court, the offender pays treble damages. Most states have their own laws concerning price discrimination for interstate commerce, but these laws vary in application and intent.

Robinson-Patman and various state laws affect the establishment of prices for printed products. However, because the products are generally tailor made, it is difficult under most circumstances for the buyer to prove that price discrimination exists. Of course, if discounts are used or services are charged at different levels and if interstate commerce applies to the product, Robinson-Patman may be enforced. Should any questions arise concerning the Robinson-Patman Act or state law with respect to price discrimination, contact an attorney.

Chapter 5

Print Order Processing

Sale through Invoice

5.1 Introduction

5.2 Reducing Cycle Time in Print Order Processing

5.3 Selling the Printing Order
Sales Representatives, Customers, and Print Buyers
Printing Brokers and Print Consultants

Walk-In Clients

5.4 Customer Service Representatives

5.5 Job Specifications and Requests for Estimate
Defining Terms: Estimates, Proposals, and Quotations
Procedures for Obtaining Job Specifications

Problems in Obtaining Accurate Job Specifications

5.6   Estimating the Order Based on the Job Specifications

Price Estimate or Cost Estimate the
  Job?
Production Planning Based on the
  Job Specifications
Completing the Cost Estimate
Manual Cost Estimates
Estimating Worksheets

Computer Estimating
Developing a Template or Pro Forma
  Estimating System
Reprint Orders versus New Jobs and
  Their Effects on the Printing Com-
  pany

5.7   Teamwork between Sales, Estimating, and Customer Service

5.8   Estimating Errors, Double-Checking the Estimate, and Checking the Customer's Credit

Categories of Estimating Errors
Double-Checking Cost Estimates

Checking the Customer's Credit

5.9   Price Setting by Top Management

5.10   The Price Proposal, the Price Quotation, and the Contractual Relationship

The Price Proposal

The Price Quotation

5.11   The Order Entry Process

5.12   Production and Delivery of the Job

Problematic Artwork
Production Tracking
Production Scheduling

General Production Rules
Additional Points Regarding Production

5.13   Completing the Job Cost Summary

5.14   Invoicing and Cash Flow

Cash Flow Sequence
Accounts Receivable Collection Period

Effective Cash Flow

5.1   Introduction

The purpose of this chapter is to provide an accurate description of the typical procedures for processing orders for printed products. This chapter covers a number of important areas of printing company operation, including job quotations, price estimating versus cost estimating, template estimating, use of the Graphic Communications Business Practices (also known as the Printing Trade Customs), and invoicing and collection methods.

The procedures in this chapter are followed by printers of all kinds and sizes. However, it should be noted that the printing industry is quite diversified in the products it produces and in the processes it uses to manufacture these products. The use of digital prepress production is now common, on-demand production is increasing, and JIT order fulfillment is growing in popularity. For example, many customers are now providing electronic artwork in disk form, replacing mechanical artwork. Job cycle time has been compressed from weeks to days and, in a growing number of print markets, to hours. Due to various technological production advances, the quality of the printed product remains the same as, or better than, it was ten years ago, but some customers are willing to accept "good enough" quality under certain conditions.

The importance of this chapter cannot be too greatly emphasized because many of the areas discussed are critical to printing company profitability and, in the long term, the survival of the printing company.

5.2   Reducing Cycle Time in Print Order Processing

While the cycle time for printing production was being dramatically reduced since the mid-1980s, the same time compression phenomena was occurring in print order processing. Customers now want quicker estimates, faster customer service response, more timely invoices, and the feeling that the printing company is able to meet their faster graphic needs without error and with quality in both product and service. Many customers perceive that a lack of speed and accuracy in the way a printing business is operated (e.g., slow and unclear estimates) represent a related lack of speed and quality in the printing work the company produces.

Employees who typically complete order processing duties in a printing company include sales representatives and support sales staff, CSRs, estimators, billing and job costing personnel, and company managers or executives assigned to complete pricing and other duties. Small companies, which have limited staff, combine these duties in different ways based on the skills of their employees. For example, a sales representative in a small printing company might also handle billing and provide customer service while the company president might do part-time sales and some estimating.

Compressing time while maintaining quality remains a thorny problem. The following list suggests ways that printing companies can generally address the time-compressed demands that affect their order processing. This list covers general areas for reducing cycle time because meeting time-compressed demands is frequently the manner in which details of a particular operation are handled.

1. Company management should carefully select, buy, and use an integrated computer management system for completing all order processing, estimating, job costing, and invoicing procedures. Choices include computer-generated or CAE systems and CAP systems. These systems are discussed in Chapter 2 and Chapter 4.

2. Management may wish to consider developing a price estimating system for certain standardized products that the company produces on a frequent basis. This would mean the company would abandon more complex cost estimating procedures for certain standardized products and allow the sales representative the quote jobs more quickly. As noted in Chapter 4, the advantages price estimating has over cost estimating include speed, convenience, and simplicity. It should be clear, however, that moving away from cost estimating can be risky because accuracy, production planning, and job scheduling may be compromised. Price estimating is not desirable on jobs that are complex or tailored to customer needs.

3. Every employee involved in order processing should be fully trained in the order entry methods and procedures so they can complete their portions of the print order processing cycle quickly and accurately.

4. Management should encourage the use of order processing teams and the team members should be cross-trained to facilitate meeting immediate customer needs. For example, CSRs should be able to estimate if needed and estimators should be able to handle sales representative duties.

5. There should be a focus on, and a dedication to, achieving minimum errors in all areas of order processing. Errors and error correction activities represent an important area of lost time in order processing and in printing manufacturing overall. The identification and implementation of methods that ensure zero defects can result in substantial time savings.

6. Management should study and implement TQM at a level on which they are comfortable. For printing companies that are hierarchically managed, particularly family-owned printing companies, TQM can be a significant shift in the way the business operates, in which case it may not be possible or desirable to implement. Extensive documentation and reference materials are available relative to TQM in printing.

7. Finally, management should provide support and assistance—not just lip service—to all employees assigned to order processing activities. Because order processing involves estimating, production planning, order entry,

and plant scheduling, management's support of these activities can save thousands of dollars annually.

5.3   Selling the Printing Order

Figure 5.1 shows the steps for selling, estimating, proposing, quoting, printing, and invoicing a typical printing order. The "front-end" portion of order processing is represented by the selling, estimating, proposing, and quoting activities and includes order entry procedures that launch the job into production. The "back-end" portion covers order processing methods during printing and delivery, including the completion of the job cost summary, invoicing, and billing. Figure 5.1 is presented to reflect the typical order processing procedures in a printing company because deviations to the process are common.

The order processing procedure begins when the customer and sales representative meet to discuss a potential printing job. Methods and procedures for selling printing vary widely. Some printing company management provide little marketing direction to their sales representatives relative to customer selection and products to be sold, while some companies offer their sales representatives substantial marketing assistance and related sales support. In terms of profitability, the more a printing company is able to separate the marketing environment from the sales effort, that is, the more the printing company applies marketing as the strategy component and uses sales to execute that strategy, the greater the success the company enjoys. Chapter 13 provides details with respect to marketing as it relates to printing sales.

Sales Representatives, Customers, and Print Buyers

For many printing companies, the sales representatives are the companies' only contact with the customers or print buyers. These salespeople are a key link in the functioning of any printing establishment because they bring in work from outside the plant and serve as the companies' public personas. Ideally, sales representatives are thoroughly trained in the elements and processes of printing, especially paper, electronic, and conventional prepress technology; color and quality issues; and finishing processes. In other words, the sales representative should understand the technology of printing manufacturing and be able to articulately explain the products and services the company offers.

In the intensely competitive environment of commercial printing, sales representatives must be familiar with the elements of good selling, including how to effectively open and close the sales process, how to identify the real buying decision makers of potential clients and then how to secure appointments with them, how to provide fast responses to customer inquiries, how to deal with questions about their companies' service/prices/quality, and how to

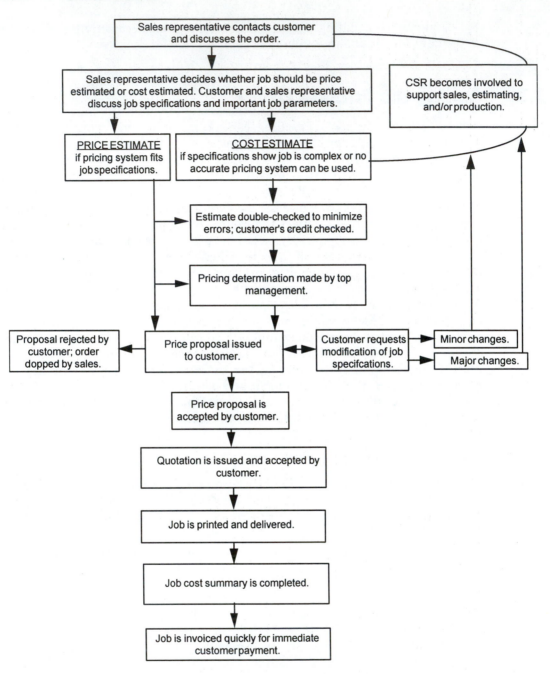

Figure 5.1 Flowchart for selling, estimating, proposing, quoting, printing, and invoicing a typical printing order

maintain high and consistent levels of quality in servicing accounts. Most successful printing sales representatives have unique and engaging personalities, a thorough knowledge of printing production, and a focus on addressing customer needs quickly and professionally. Successful printing sales representatives are not "order takers," but rather are skilled "consultants" who deal openly and fully with all issues related to the customers' and print buyers' printing needs. Because the printing sales representative provides the customer's or buyer's first, and sometimes only, view of the printing company, he should be keenly aware that his public image speaks for the firm. While the sales representative sells printing to the customer, he also sells the company.

The CSRs play quasi-sales roles in most printing companies that use them. Their position is between the sales representative, who is outside the company, and the production of the customer's job, which is inside the company. The CSRs are discussed later in this chapter in greater detail.

As intense competition has forced many printers into becoming more market oriented and more aware of the marketing environment in which they provide products and services, the difference between a customer and a print buyer has become more distinct, but the lines are still somewhat unclear. A customer is generally profiled as a person who represents her company, purchases printing on a fairly infrequent basis, and has limited experience and knowledge of the printing process. In contrast, a professional print buyer is constantly involved in placing orders and evaluating printing as it is produced.

As most sales representatives quickly learn, the typical customer requires a different sales approach and different sales support than does the professional print buyer. For example, the print buyer frequently has a thorough knowledge of how electronic artwork affects production time and cost, while the customer has less knowledge in this area and thus requires greater sales and CSR support. The typical print buyer, in contrast to the typical customer, is an experienced professional: The typical print buyer knows printing manufacturing methods thoroughly, understands the variables of the printing processes, knows finishing techniques, and has a good knowledge of estimating, pricing, and scheduling print production. Print buyers are commonly employed by corporate clients who purchase large quantities of printing. Many print buyers buy printing and related graphic products as full-time jobs or as the primary function of their duties. The products these print buyers purchase total a very large dollar amount of printing purchased in the United States. It is not unusual for print buyers to be former printing sales representatives, estimators, or CSRs.

Printing sales representatives develop their own unique selling procedures based on their personalities, which is one key to achieving success. An important factor related to the sales representative's initiative and drive for success is the method of financial compensation he receives for his efforts. Although sales compensation methods vary (draw on commission, straight commission, and a commission based on a percentage of profit or a percentage of VA are common), most systems allow printing sales representatives to make significant income. It is not uncommon for sales representatives to outearn most other company employees, including estimators and CSRs who assist and support the sales process. When the disparity between the income earned by sales representatives and the income earned by estimators and CSRs is great, teamwork and other cooperative activities tend to suffer. This problem can be difficult to resolve, particularly in a TQM environment where the sales process is a team effort.

In theory, commission compensation methods for the sales representative are intended to encourage the sales representative to be proactive in increasing sales efforts—the more that is sold by the sales representative, the greater the money that is earned by the sales representative. Sometimes this is not the case, however, and the sales representative is actually a well-paid order taker. Frequently the sales compensation method is designed to encourage sales representatives to sell certain types of products or to selected vertical markets (e.g., customers and print buyers) where profits are greater.

Regardless of the type of compensation method, the sales representative should be the most articulate and effective company individual dealing with customer needs and desires. When selling, she should suggest to the customer other services the printing company can provide, such as the design of a new company logo, the development of a house publication, or related communication solutions. Despite which types of printing orders are sold or which markets are served by the sales representative, the sales representative, estimator, and CSR should work together to serve the customer's best interests. They should be committed to providing the client with the best product for the money spent, and that product should be delivered on time and with minimum client hassle.

Sometimes the sales representative provides support to customers even when the printed product is not made by the printing company for whom the sales representative works. For example, if a graphic product cannot be produced by the printing company the salesperson represents, he may arrange for it to be printed by another company, or he may suggest another printer of the product for the customer to pursue. Customers appreciate this type of sales support and tend to continue their relationships with the printing company because of the proactive stance taken by the sales representative.

Printing Brokers and Print Consultants

A printing broker is an independent agent who sells printing goods and services to customers and print buyers, then arranges for printing manufacturing through any printer willing to complete the job. Printing brokers are independent in that they order printing from many different printing companies; they do not sell for one printing company. The income a broker earns comes from the difference between what the customer pays the broker (who bills the customer for the printing) and what the printing company charges the broker for the printing. The greater the difference, the greater the income the broker earns. To a printing company, the advantage of accepting jobs from a broker is that the broker provides the company with increased volume of production without any sales commission or other sales costs.

In the past ten years the number of print brokers has increased, thus increasing the competition in certain market niches. Brokers sometimes sell "head to head" with printing company sales representatives. Frequently the broker has a distinct advantage in that she can select any cooperating printing firm to do her manufacturing, while the printing sales representative is locked into the printing company he represents and has little latitude to consider options that may provide more competitive situations. It is not unusual for a printing broker to be a former sales representative for a printing company who has chosen to work independently.

The most successful printing brokers offer their clients a full range of products and exceptional support services. The broker's success is driven by providing first-rate customer service as well as timely delivery of quality printed products. Customer services provided by the broker might include arranging for electronic or mechanical art through a service bureau, engaging professional photographers for a client, providing design and other creative activities, handling press checks and quality control issues, or ensuring full-service product fulfillment of all parts of a client's graphic needs.

The broker is paid by charging a fee for her services, which is added to all other costs of producing the job. This tends to make broker-ordered printing more expensive than printing done through a printing company which has dedicated sales representatives. The broker invoices the client and, upon receiving payment from the client, pays the printer. Usually the customer never deals directly with the printer. Because world-class service is key, clients who work with successful printing brokers find the process of designing and obtaining printed goods is simple and has minimum hassles, even though its cost may be higher.

Depending on the printing company's experience with brokers, the brokers seem to fit into the extremes of being either very well liked or very well disliked. Printing manufacturers who have found brokers who provide additional volume without detracting from current customers, who are easy to work with, and who pay the printing bills in full and in a timely manner, are the printing manufacturers who accept and may even encourage work from brokers. However, when a broker practices a "hit-and-run" procedure whereby she uses the printing manufacturer to produce brokered printing on a marginally profitable basis for a period of time, then places no orders with that printer, relations between the two parties can become strained. Also, brokers who provide slow payment for printing while taking current brokered work to other printers can cause angry feelings with printers.

Print consultants also play an active role in the printing industry. Instead of providing independent sales and service to a wide and varied customer base as brokers do, the print consultant is retained by a customer or print buyer to ensure consistent quality, to coordinate printing projects at key stages, to manage details of a complex printing order, or to provide fulfillment services. Print consultants are an extension of the busy professional print buyer in that they take over and manage important printing jobs. The print consultants tend to provide services that are focused on very large or very important jobs, on printing work that requires complex manufacturing, or on work that is of critical quality. They also monitor complicated distribution methods of final printed products. Print consultants typically are employed on a per job or retainer basis and work with print buyers who buy large quantities of printing for large corporations.

Walk-In Clients

While large commercial printers and high-volume printers use sales representatives and brokers to provide most, if not all, of their orders, walk-in customers are common to small commercial printers and quick printers. Generally "walk-ins" are geographically close to the printing company; need "on-demand" printing, which is mostly short-run and fast-turnaround work; pay cash for the completed printing; and expect a high level of customer service to be rendered immediately. Walk-in customers are sometimes not familiar with the printing and copying processes and therefore their artwork may be poorly prepared. Some printers assist customers in correcting this artwork as well as provide supplies for customer use to aid the customers in artwork repair before copying or printing. In contrast, experienced walk-in customers may have fully prepared electronic art in floppy disk form or a mix of electronic and mechanical artwork that is properly prepared and immediately ready for graphic reproduction.

Many quick printers and some small commercial printers gear a sizable portion of their businesses toward inside sales activities where walk-in customers provide orders over the counter. For this reason many of these printing firms do not have full-time sales representatives, although they are increasingly moving in the direction of what is called "outside" or "outbound" sales through the use of part-time sales personnel. When a company focuses on inside sales, it must foster a very customer-oriented and pleasant counter environment. This means that employees who handle customer jobs over the counter should be thoroughly trained in a range of customer issues, including handling discount and other pricing issues, customer complaints, and print quality issues.

5.4   Customer Service Representatives

Customer service representatives (CSRs) are important to many commercial printers and high-volume printers primarily due to an increasing need for customer sensitivity and customer focus. The CSRs are considered a vital link between various internal company staff and printing company customers. Printing firms that have adopted TQM concepts consider the role of the CSR to be a key focal point for addressing numerous customer-driven issues.

Generally speaking, the primary job objective of the CSR is to serve as a liaison between the customer and the printing company. Although the CSRs' specific job duties vary from company to company, they work with the sales representatives, estimators, and production staff to ensure the customers' jobs are produced correctly and on schedule. Prior to the mid-1980s, CSRs were commonly known as production coordinators and their focus was largely on internal production and not directly on customer-related matters. It is generally agreed that the primary duties of a printing company CSR are to:

1. coordinate details of work-in-process as a liaison between printing company and customer
2. coordinate activities between estimators, sales representatives, production management, and other internal company staff
3. facilitate timely delivery of each customer's job and maintain an established and expected level of quality
4. provide backup support for sales, estimating, and production management on an as-needed basis
5. continually represent the company positively with customers

As mentioned earlier in the chapter, the job duties of the CSR tend to vary from company to company. For example, some printing firms ask their CSRs to complete estimating in addition to coordinating production tasks. In fact, some printing companies have disbanded their estimating staff because their CSRs have assumed these duties. Other firms have estimating staff but use the CSRs as the primary contacts between the customers and estimators instead of having the estimators contact the customers directly. Some companies ask their sales representatives to hand the customers to CSRs as soon as their quotations or proposals are accepted, which makes the CSRs the key and primary customer contacts very early in the process. This frees the sales representatives to actively pursue new clients. In still other companies, CSRs continue to handle mostly production coordinating duties, with varying amounts of direct customer contact.

Some printing firms compensate their CSRs on a straight-salary basis but ask them to participate in a fairly significant amount of sales service, including direct support of the sales representatives. Driven by the motivation and dynamic nature of the sales representative, these same firms pay their sales representatives on commission, VA, or profit basis. Thus, the CSR sometimes does a large portion of what might be considered "sales," but is paid on a straight-salary basis only. This salary injustice tends to cause problems between the CSR and the sales representative (and the estimator as well). It also tends to lead CSRs from customer service duties to positions as sales representatives quickly, and therefore from straight salaries to compensation packages dictated by their own drives and motivation. The CSR has functioned largely as a sales representative anyway. Some CSRs also move from their customer service roles into full-time estimating, which in many printing companies is also compensated on a straight-salary basis of roughly the same amount of pay.

The CSR function is essential for the survival of commercial printing firms and high-volume printers who handle complex, tailor-made printing orders on a frequent basis. They are the counterparts to the educated, friendly counterpeople working for the quick printer or small commercial printer. With an inherent overcapacity in the industry, increasingly complex printing jobs, thousands of printing firms competing for the same type of work, increasing foreign competition, globalization of printing production, the growing use of digital communication, and artificially low ceilings on prices, there is no question that enhanced customer sensitivity and greatly improved customer satisfaction play key roles in printers keeping customers. The CSR ensures that customer happiness and customer satisfaction are continually monitored and maintained at high levels.

5.5   Job Specifications and Requests for Estimate

In printing, job specifications are the key parameters that define a printing order. Job "specs" should be developed for every job the company produces, but their accuracy is critical when printing orders require complex manufacturing operations or when the job is beyond an expected and defined range of production. As printing orders have increased in color, prepress operations have shifted from mechanical to electronic methods, and printers have recognized the need for quickly meeting customer wishes with high-quality products and services, gathering accurate job specifications has taken on increased importance.

Defining Terms: Estimates, Proposals, and Quotations

It should be noted that the terms "estimate," "proposal," and "quotation" are used interchangeably throughout this book, as they tend to be used in real life. Thus, when a customer requests an "estimate" he is really asking for a proposal or a quotation on a printing order. In theory, each of the three terms is different:

- An estimate is generated and used by the printing company as an internal dollar measurement of the cost required to produce a specified printed product. A cost estimate is normally not shared with the customer.
- A proposal is a tentative offer from the printing company to the customer to produce a specific printed product for a specific dollar amount. A proposal

is subject to negotiation and change based on customer and printer compromises.

- A quotation is an offer from the printer to the customer to produce a printed product for the dollar amount specified as the selling price. It is final and binding to both printer and customer when accepted by the customer.

Procedures for Obtaining Job Specifications

During the job specification discussion with the customer (Figure 5.1), the sales representative normally completes a job specification form (JSF), also known as a request for estimate (RFE) form or a request for quotation (RFQ) form. The primary purpose of this form is to provide essential information that describes the job. From this information the job can be planned and economically evaluated. One of the primary duties of the sales representative is to gather all essential job specification information during this customer meeting so that estimating can be completed without interruption to secure a missing item. Thus, the JSF or the RFE or RFQ form should be tailored to allow for quick and thorough data collection. A sample JSF is shown in Figure 5.2, and an RFQ form is provided in Figure 5.3.

Typically the JSF is in interview format, so it should be arranged in a logical and orderly manner. The information requested should be clearly defined and targeted to relevant job details only; unnecessary information clutters the process. Although each company develops its own JSF and RFQ forms, it usually includes at least the following information:

- the customer's name, address, and telephone number;
- the sales representative's name;
- a general description of the job;
- quantity levels;
- flat sheet and folded dimensions (with possible alternate sizes);
- bleeds and margin information;
- the number of colors;
- complete details regarding all artwork (who will supply it and whether the work will be camera ready);
- complete paper specifications;
- binding, finishing, and other postpress requirements;
- the type of packaging to be used; and
- the type of delivery method.

The graphic presentation of the JSF varies considerably among printing companies and is usually modified to represent the types of products produced by a particular printing company. If a computer system will be used to estimate the job, the JSF should be designed to dovetail smoothly with this process. Some fully integrated computer systems provide for the job specifications to be

Estimate Description

Estimate Due Date: _____

Customer Name/#: _____

Salesperson Name/#: _____

Job Description: _____

Quantity: | | | | | Additional: _____   New Job: Exact Reprint: Reprint w/ Changes:

Special Instructions:

_____

_____

_____

Imposition/Ink

	# of Pages	Page Size	Black	%	PMS	%	Process	%	Varnish	%	Bleeds(T,B,R,L)
Text											
Cover											
Other											

Paper

	Description	Weight	Additional Stock
Text			
Cover			
Other			

Figure 5.2 An estimate description form or JSF. (Reproduced with permission of Watermark Press, San Francisco, California.)

Camera

	Line	size	Reverses	size	Screens	size	Traps & Fits	size
Text								
Cover								
Other								

Supplied Film

	Line	Size	Screened	Size	Color Breaks Inc.	Additional Work Req.
					Y N	
					Y N	

Separations

	4 x 5	5 x 7	8 x 10	11 x 14	16 x 20	Other
Halftones						
Duotones						
4/C Process						

Grade: Best off scanner ☐   Color Match TX ☐   Product Match ☐

Type of Proof: Matchprint ☐   Fuji ☐   Cromalin ☐   Colorkey ☐

Proofs

	Blueline	Colorkey	Contact Prints	Press Check	Other
Text					
Cover					
Other					

Bindery

	trim(size)	fold(type)	Die Cut / Emboss	Binding	Other
Text			Reg		
Cover			Reg		
Other			Reg		

Packing

	Shrink in	Bulk	Skid	Other

Figure 5.2 *(continued)*

CAE REQUEST FOR QUOTATION

ColorGraphics

Customer: _____ Estimate No.: _____

Address: _____ Date: _____

_____ Salesperson: _____

City, State, Zip: _____ Estimate Needed: _____

Telephone: (_____) _____ Fax: (_____) _____ Previous Estimate No.: _____

Contact_____ Previous Job No.: _____

TITLE: _____

DESCRIPTION: _____

BOOKLET   BLEED

☐ UPRIGHT   **PAGES:** _____ Self Cover   Yes ☐ No ☐

☐ ALBUM   **PAGES:** _____ Plus Cover   Yes ☐ No ☐

TRIM Page Size _____ X _____

FOLDER   BLEED

Flat Size _____ X _____   Yes ☐ No ☐

Folded Size _____ X _____

PAPER STOCK:	WT.	Type/Color
Cover (VER 1)		
Cover (VER 2)		
Text (VER 1)		
Text (VER 2)		

PAPER STOCK:	WT.	Type/Color
VER 1		
VER 2		
VER 3		
VER 4		

PREPRESS

CUSTOMER FURNISHES: 1. Camera Ready Art Work   2. Composed Negs.   3. Plate Ready Film   4. Electronic Disk   5. Prepress Only

Describe Artwork Color/Stripping

Tint Areas: _____   Trap Areas? ☐ Yes ☐ No   Crossover? ☐ Yes ☐ No

Colors per Tint: _____   How Many Pages: _____   How Many Pages: _____

Reverses: _____   Number of Furnished Seps: _____

FINAL SIZE	5 x 7	8 x 10	10 x 12	12 x 18	16 x 20	20 x 24	24 x 30	30 x 40	TOTAL	Screen
Transparencies										☐ 133
Reflectives/Flexible										
Camera Halftones										☐ 150
Scanned Halftones										
Camera Duotones										☐ 175
Scanned Duotones										
Scanned Tritone										☐ 200
Outlines										
Outline/Hold Shadow										

ELECTRONIC OUTPUT

Program Used: _____

Are pages setup in: ☐ Single Pages ☐ Readers Spreads ☐ Printers Spreads

Trapping Required: ☐ Yes ☐ No

Electronic Edits: ☐ Yes ☐ No

Vignette Creation/Repl. ☐ Yes ☐ No

Request Hi-Res Scans   ☐ Yes ☐ No   Qty. _____

Request Low-Res Scans   ☐ Yes ☐ No   Qty. _____

Drop-in Scans on table   ☐ Yes ☐ No   Qty. _____

Drop-in Halftones   ☐ Yes ☐ No   Qty. _____

PREPRESS PROOFS (in position)

☐ Bluelines _____ Sets

☐ Press Match

☐ Color Keys

☐ B&W Laser / Digital Color (circle)

COLOR SEPARATIONS

Number of Proofs:

☐ 1 Proof & Corrections

☐ 2 Proofs & Corrections

☐ 3 Proofs & Corrections

Additional Instructions:

_____

_____

_____

_____

Figure 5.3 A request for quotation form for computer estimating orders. (Reproduced with permission of ColorGraphics, San Francisco, California.)

PRESSWORK AND INK COLORS

COVER		Customer OK ☐ Yes ☐ No		Cock Sheet ☐ Yes ☐ No	
	Front	%	Back	%	
Process Colors					
PMS Colors					
Varnish					
Metallic					
Total Colors					
Plate/Version Chgs.					

TEXT		Customer OK ☐ Yes ☐ No		Cock Sheet ☐ Yes ☐ No	
	Front	%	Back	%	
Process Colors					
PMS Colors					
Varnish					
Metallic					
Total Colors					
Plate/Version Chgs.					

TEXT		Customer OK ☐ Yes ☐ No		Cock Sheet ☐ Yes ☐ No	
	Front	%	Back	%	
Process Colors					
PMS Colors					
Varnish					
Metallic					
Total Colors					
Plate/Version Chgs.					

TEXT		Customer OK ☐ Yes ☐ No		Cock Sheet ☐ Yes ☐ No	
	Front	%	Back	%	
Process Colors					
PMS Colors					
Varnish					
Metallic					
Total Colors					
Plate/Version Chgs.					

INSERT		Customer OK ☐ Yes ☐ No		Cock Sheet ☐ Yes ☐ No	
	Front	%	Back	%	
Process Colors					
PMS Colors					
Varnish					
Metallic					
Total Colors					
Plate/Version Chgs.					

FLYSHEET		Customer OK ☐ Yes ☐ No		Cock Sheet ☐ Yes ☐ No	
	Front	%	Back	%	
Process Colors					
PMS Colors					
Varnish					
Metallic					
Total Colors					
Plate/Version Chgs.					

SPECIAL PRESS INSTRUCTIONS (i.e., INDICIA HONE-OFF, PLATE CHGS., WEB GLUE, SCORE, PERF., WEB PREFOLD, ETC.):

FIN. SIZE _____ X _____

BINDERY   ☐ OTHER INST.: _____

UPRIGHT/ALBUM

BINDING
Bind Side: _____ Type of Bind: 1. Saddle 2. Perfect 3. Wire O 4. Side Stitch 5. Spiral 6. Loose Leaf 7. Case/Hard Bound 8. Lay Flat

FOLDING
Folded Size _____ X _____ Type of Fold: 1. Accordion 2. Letterfold 3. Roll 4. Parallel 5. Double Gate 6. Right Angle

FINISHING

☐ DRILL _____"   ☐ PRESS/SCORE   ☐ PRESS/PERFORATE   ☐ UV COTE 1-SIDE   ☐ UV COTE 2-SIDES   ☐ EMBOSS   DIE SIZE _____ X _____

☐ PAD   ☐ DIECUT   ☐ GLUE   ☐ ROUND CORNER ☐ COLLATE   ☐ FOIL STAMPING/COLOR OF FOIL _____

☐ DIE SCORING   ☐ DIE PERFORATE ☐ CONVERT TO ENV. _____ X _____

OTHER FINISHING: _____

PACKAGE/WRAP AND CARTON

☐ SHRINK WRAP IN _____   ☐ PAPER BAND IN_____   ☐ CARTON IN_____

☐ KRAFT WRAP IN _____   ☐ RUBBER BAND IN _____   ☐ SKID PACK

☐ STRING TIE IN _____   ☐ MAILING_____

SHIPPING INSTRUCTIONS   SHIP VIA: ☐ Our Truck
               FOB Los Angeles   FOB San Francisco

QUANTITIES

Figure 5.3 (continued)

completed on a laptop or portable computer by the sales representative. The specifications are then downloaded into the central computer system for estimating. This saves time and minimizes input errors because the specifications go directly from the customer to the estimator via the laptop. Building the job specifications using a computer format saves estimating, quoting, and order entry time.

The person gathering the job specifications (usually the sales representative although the CSR and the estimator also handle this activity) is responsible for ensuring the thoroughness and accuracy of the information. It is critical that the job specifications provide the estimator with accurate and complete details of the job under consideration. If time permits during the process of gathering the job specifications, the sales representative may wish to talk with a CSR, an estimator, or a job planner regarding production details, buyouts, artwork, or other issues.

Skipping, neglecting, or forgetting any job specification can be a source of aggravation to the estimator, particularly when it is an established pattern of behavior for a specific person. This may cause friction between the sales representatives, CSRs, and estimating staff, which is most undesirable. For this reason, company management should discourage any employee from submitting incomplete or inaccurate job specifications for estimating, and they should have a clear procedure as to who handles the follow-up contact for obtaining any unknown information.

Some customers provide their own written job specifications, which are commonly formatted as POs or request for purchase (RFP) forms. However, these documents are sometimes not thorough or detailed enough in terms of the specifications they provide. Some clients, specifically professional print buyers or others who are thoroughly familiar with the process, telephone the plant with specifications for an RFE. In this case the person taking the job specifications should carefully record the information. It is also possible that customers request estimates via fax or fax/modem, letter, or personal appearance. Regardless of the method used by the customer, it is wise to provide the customer with a copy of the complete job specifications and/or the written job proposal which includes the specifications. These documents serve as written clarification and provide the client with complete job information with which to compare estimates from other printers.

When the sales representative handles a standardized product line, the job specifications are related only to the variables offered for that standard product, such as different colors of ink, changes in format size, or changes in type. If a sample portfolio of standard products is available from which the customer can select, the selling effort, especially the difficulties of providing complete job specifications, is simplified. Standardization of product and the accompanying reduction of complex job specifications expedite the sales effort and reduce mistakes and misunderstandings throughout production. Usually this type of standardization provides for the development of a price estimating system, which can be completed either by the sales representative during the customer meeting or by the customer if the price list is published and available. Price estimating is discussed in detail in Chapter 4.

Problems in Obtaining Accurate Job Specifications

Obtaining accurate job specifications for estimating printing has a problematic history, which is compounded today by the four following interrelated issues.

Problem 1: Customer Indecisiveness in Defining Job Parameters. Too frequently a customer or a print buyer contacts a sales representative to order a printed product not really knowing what she wants. What happens is the customer acknowledges the need to develop a graphic product to meet an identified group of objectives, and she has a good idea as to when the graphic product is needed, but she does not know or cannot describe the specifics of her product enough to set defined job parameters. In general, this is an attempt by the customer to ask for help. Frequently the customer wants the sales representative to have a "cookbook solution" or a simple resolution for her graphic needs. Skilled sales representatives understand this indecisiveness and provide the customer with professional assistance, the result of which is a set of job specifications for estimating the order. However, many times job specifications are developed that do not represent the job.

Problem 2: Increasingly Electronic and Customer-Supplied Artwork Is Improperly Prepared. The artwork for any printing job, which is increasingly customer supplied and prepared using electronic methods, establishes important job parameters in prepress, press, and finishing. The old printing adage, "As goes artwork, so goes the printing job," remains a statement of fact today.

Numerous problems exist with customer-supplied art, which translate to potential problems with the specifications of the job. First, too frequently customers want estimates before any artwork is prepared, so the printer makes certain artwork assumptions only to find the assumptions are incorrect. Second, the estimate is requested when the artwork is being produced, but for various reasons the final art does not meet anticipated output requirements. Third, the artwork is fully prepared but time compression or other reasons do not allow the printer to complete a full artwork evaluation before estimating the job. Fourth, the customer has engaged an artwork provider who is incapable of properly completing the artwork for the job or is producing the art on electronic systems that are incompatible with the printing company's systems.

Problem 3: Poor Early Decisions Are Made under Time Pressure. Customers and printers both work under their own time-compressed situations. This pressure of time frequently forces both parties into defining important job specifications too early or making critical job assumptions that appear to be initially minor or inconsequential, but that actually have a costly bearing when the job enters production.

Frequently the situation begins when the customer asks the sales representative for a "ballpark" estimate. To accommodate this request, the sales representative and customer together make unrealistic or too positive assumptions about the job. The ballpark estimate is prepared based on these less-than-accurate specifications. The customer accepts this estimate and the job enters production. As the job is produced, costs begin to increase. By now, however, the customer considers the ballpark estimate a serious job quotation, and misunderstandings result between the customer and the printer.

As noted in Chapter 1, the use of ballpark estimating is a trend that can be an acceptable estimating process only when it is clear to both the customer and the printer that the estimated price and the described job are tentative and subject to change as production is completed.

Problem 4: Sales Representatives Do Not Know Important Printing Technology or Are Incapable of Writing Accurate Job Specifications. An important duty of a printing sales representative is to guide the customer through the maze of job specifications so that the customer's job is accurately detailed for production planning and estimating. Unfortunately, this has become a problem area for an increasing number of printing sales representatives. First, too many sales representatives lack a good working knowledge of computers in general, electronic artwork, integrated electronic printing technology, and modern print manufacturing methods. These same sales representatives often do not participate in company-sponsored training in these important areas. Second, too many printing sales representatives are incapable or unwilling to take the time or make the effort to gather accurate job specifications from the customers. They would rather submit job specifications that are "about right," knowing that the specifications are not correct. Third, too many sales representatives have loose or cavalier attitudes toward job specifications. They feel "an estimate is just an estimate" and that the details will become clear as the job is produced. Fourth and finally, some sales representatives are motivated primarily by the dollar commissions they earn and do not have professional attitudes toward job specification accuracy.

Successful printers resolve these problems using a mix of the following six key components. First, management of the printing company purchases an integrated computer management system and requires basic computer literacy for sales representatives. Second, management insists that all sales representatives use those segments of the company's computer management system that relate to sales activities, including the estimating, order entry, and scheduling segments. Third, management requires all sales representatives to learn appropriate printing technology, including electronic artwork and digital production.

As a result, sales representatives become computer literate and gain key knowledge in electronic imaging as it relates to prepress, press, and finishing operations. Fourth, company management segments their products and customers into defined groups, then develops methods to streamline the process of quickly and accurately gathering job specifications from these target groups. This may lead to the development of a price estimating process for some types of work, while other jobs continue to be cost estimated. Fifth, management establishes customer-sales training programs in electronic prepress and related printing production methods, including methods to preflight electronic artwork so that jobs begin production with minimum rework. Finally, management takes a team approach to selling activities of the company so that sales representatives, CSRs, and estimators are team members and are cross-trained to assist each other as needed.

Even with these efforts to resolve problems relative to job specifications, gathering accurate job data is one area that continues to be troublesome for printers and customers. Lacking a complete set of job specifications places a printer in a difficult position. On the one hand the printer desires to provide the customer with an estimate for his printing order, while on the other hand the lack of specifications compromises the accuracy of the printer's estimate. Complicating this problem is the intense competition from other printers who have no problem quoting on the job without such detail.

Experienced sales representatives quickly learn that a key job specification is the customer's budget or the targeted amount of money the customer wishes to spend on the job. Knowing this figure allows the job to be planned and estimated to meet this important financial condition. Some sales representatives believe that because they work with the customers to keep the jobs within the targeted budgets, they are able to close more printing orders. Sometimes, however, customers are unwilling to indicate targeted budgets for their jobs, perhaps because they honestly do not know what the budgets are or because they believe the printer more honestly estimates the jobs without this information. Regardless of the customer's reason, it is wise for the sales representative to determine a budget figure for the customer's order as part of the job specification process.

Another important job specification is the amount of time in which the printer has to provide the customer with an estimate for the job. While some estimates are time compressed and require extremely fast turnarounds if the printing company has any chance of winning the jobs, other estimates can be done in a more relaxed atmosphere, over longer periods of time. In general, more estimating time provides greater opportunity for printing company staff to evaluate the job plan and cost-saving alternatives, which may lead to dollar savings for the customer. Typically a general sense of when the estimate is needed becomes evident as the customer talks about the job, but no job should be submitted for an estimate without some specific, written due date for estimate completion.

5.6 Estimating the Order Based on the Job Specifications

As noted earlier in the chapter, the estimating process begins when the printing sales representative meets or talks with the customer to determine job specifications. This meeting frequently takes the form of an "interview" with the customer about the particulars of her printing order. The process should be done in a relaxed atmosphere and at a location convenient to the customer. Once the job specifications are identified, the estimating process can begin.

Price Estimate or Cost Estimate the Job?

Based on the job specifications and other factors, a decision must be made as to whether the job should be price estimated or cost estimated. Price estimating, which is discussed in depth in Chapter 4, is convenient and fast but sometimes glosses over job details that may be important. In contrast, while cost estimating tends to be slow and labor intensive, it provides for a thorough analysis of job particulars.

Management should establish and use a clear-cut process to quickly determine whether to price estimate or cost estimate each printing order. Doing this requires the establishment of a "who, what, and when" decision sequence. The "who" component relates to the type of customer and to the importance of the customer to the company's overall marketing strategy. The "what" component relates to whether the job fits into the company's current pricing system. The "when" component is comprised of five decision factors, which default to the use of cost estimating. The five "when" decision factors are:

1. when the job complexity exceeds standard production methods of the company
2. when the job difficulty exceeds normal or routine levels
3. when the job is tailor made and is unlike any other job
4. when the impact of the job on the company's production system or volume capacity is great
5. when the company's potential profitability or financial risk is great

Given the previous information, the decision of price estimating or cost estimating is not difficult to make, but it may be difficult to accept. Sometimes a job clearly fits a price list or a price matrix the company uses, in which case the job should be price estimated. Sometimes a job clearly fits into one or more of the five "when" decision factors in the decision matrix noted above, indicating that cost estimating is the best way to proceed. However, given the intense competition for printing orders and other business factors determined by the sales representative or company management, sometimes printers bend the rules and price estimate jobs that clearly should be cost estimated. When this is done in an intelligent manner, it is not a major problem. However, when it is done with many jobs and over a long time span, the company is placed in a risky situation relative to its long-term financial health. This may jeopardize the survival of the business.

Using price estimating over cost estimating, or vice versa, varies among printers. For example, some printers use price estimating for all jobs and all customers, while other printers use price estimating for certain types of jobs and cost estimating for other types of printing work. When price estimating is the chosen estimating method, and this choice should be carefully made so as to not compromise either the customer or the printer, it may be desirable for the sales representative to estimate the job at the customer's place of business. This provides for quick quotes and may provide the sales representative with increased sales volume. Chapter 4 contains a detailed comparison of price estimating and cost estimating methods and should be reviewed regarding the risks, advantages, and disadvantages of each method.

The discussion that follows assumes that the printing job is of sufficient complexity to require the use of cost estimating methods. The steps of the cost estimating process begin with production planning, then applying cost estimating time and cost standards, and finally adding profit to generate the company's selling price of the job. The selling price is communicated to the customer through a proposal or a quotation, while the cost estimate is an internal document that is not shared with the customer.

Production Planning Based on the Job Specifications

Production planning, or job planning, is the evaluation of manufacturing methods to ensure that the customer's printing order is produced to meet his requirements. For planning to be thorough, it should be done carefully and it should be based on the set of accurate and complete job specifications the customer has provided. The typical procedure for planning production in printing manufacturing includes:

1. assessing the job relative to the route the job is anticipated to take
2. breaking the job into discreet operational components that represent the anticipated route the job will take
3. analyzing and reviewing overall alternative methods of production that might be faster, less costly, or advantageous to the printer and the customer
4. preparing internal plant planning materials such as dummies and rough sketches

In some printing companies, production planning is completed by job or production planners, while estimating is done separately by estimating staff. In other companies production planning and estimating are done by the same people. Generally separation of planning and estimating duties is done when manufacturing complexity is extensive. In many commercial printing companies, estimators complete both planning and estimating and assume these two functions are inseparable.

Frequently a production plan appears simple on the surface only to have hidden areas of difficulty. Given the flexible options for printing production, many printing jobs have numerous choices in prepress, press, and finishing production. It is up to the production planner or estimator to determine the most time- and cost-efficient route for manufacturing the job. The most successful job planners, or the estimators who most successfully do planning as parts of their jobs, learn by experience. This includes understanding the relationship between production planning choices and the profitability of the job for the company. Less experienced planners or estimators, or trainees, should be carefully educated with respect to the many production variables and contingencies possible, always keeping job and company profitability in mind.

Completing the Cost Estimate

Cost estimating is completed after the production plan has been established (e.g., after the job has been broken into its detailed, discrete production components). Cost estimating requires information in the three following areas:

1. time assessments for all operational components identified in the production plan, based on established company production standards
2. application of accurate BHRs, by production center, to determine manufacturing costs
3. addition of all material costs and outside purchases to be charged to the customer as part of the customer's order

The formula for cost estimating is:

$$\text{estimated cost to product the job} = [\text{standard production time x BHR}] + \text{material costs} + \text{outside purchases}$$

A cost estimate is built using a line-by-line analysis of each individual production step, following the anticipated production sequence. Some jobs require many production steps and their cost estimating may be complex and time consuming, while other jobs require a limited number of production steps and their estimating is completed in a few minutes.

Because each manufacturing segment of the production plan frequently requires different equipment and employee skills, separate BHRs must be developed to reflect these differences. In addition, each manufacturing step has a standard production time. Chapter 3 describes both of these components. Assuming that both the BHR and the standard production time for each segment are accurate, when the estimated production time is multiplied by the BHR, the result represents the manufacturing cost to complete that segment of the product. Direct material costs, such as the costs for paper, ink, film, and plates, are then estimated and added to the manufacturing cost. Costs for materials that are more difficult to identify, such as the costs for solvents, industrial towels, and lithographic blankets, are included in the BHR recovery system.

For example, in a process camera production center with a BHR of $50.00 and a standard production time of 0.10 hour per halftone, the total cost for exposing and processing 10 halftones is:

[(estimated time to expose and process 10 halftones) x BHR]
+ film and chemistry costs

First, the estimated time to expose and process 10 halftones is:

[0.10 hr. standard production time x10 halftones] = 1.00 hr. production

Plugging this figure into the original formula yields:

[(1.00 hr. production) x $50.00 BHR] + $12.00 estimated film and chemistry
costs = $62.00 total cost for exposing and processing 10 halftones

Manual Cost Estimates

Cost estimating can be done either manually, by computer, or by a mix of the two. Sometimes estimators complete manual calculations as they prepare estimate worksheets for computer estimating, although a fully computerized estimating system should minimize manual calculations.

Manual cost estimating uses the same general procedure as CAE. The process is completed by the estimator who works on an estimating worksheet with a pencil and a calculator. She carefully breaks the job into various component operations based on an expected production plan, determines the length of time each operation will take, then applies a BHR to determine the cost of each production operation. Material costs for each operation or outside purchase are also estimated. The time and cost for each operation, plus material costs and buyouts, are then added together to represent the total production time and cost.

Manual estimating is labor intensive and requires careful attention by the estimator. It tends to be slow and is prone to errors in mathematics and logic. However, it is frequently used when a job is unique to the company or does not fit the company's typical production pattern.

Estimating Worksheets

Figures 5.4 and 5.5 are sample cost estimating worksheets used to prepare jobs for computer estimating. Manual estimating worksheets are similar but leave more space for calculations, quantity levels, and written details. Estimating worksheets typically contain the following information:

- the customer's name and company organization;
- the names of the sales representative and estimator;
- the date of the estimate;
- the assigned estimate number;
- the quantities desired;
- prepress, press, and postpress job details;
- material and outside purchase details;
- packing, shipping, and delivery details; and
- the date of delivery.

The development of estimating worksheets is usually tailored to each company and is integrated to parallel the company's computer estimating system software. Sometimes the estimating worksheet is integrated with the JSF or RFQ, as is the case with Figure 5.5. Better cost estimating worksheets, as illustrated in Figures 5.4 and 5.5, provide sufficient detail in all areas of the estimate. This attention to detail is critical to ensure accurate estimates.

Computer Estimating

Computer estimating is discussed in detail in Chapter 2. Selecting the appropriate software requires that the estimator determine which type of estimating procedure she desires: CAE or CGE. Figure 5.6 is one page of a sample computer estimate.

The advantages computer estimating has over manual estimating are superior estimating accuracy, detailed time and cost analysis (by cost center) for each production step, the ability to schedule production from the estimated times, and the ability to analyze any part of the estimate in an effort to save money for the customer. Disadvantages include the facts that achieving such estimating accuracy and detail requires accurate job specifications, which can be difficult to obtain; that CAE requires a skilled, computer-proficient estimator to work directly on the computer; and that inflexible software may not meet the range of needs of the company.

If the choice is to use CGE software, the process is simplified and streamlined. The CGE system requires that a company employee, not necessarily an estimator, input predetermined job specification data into the computer, typically by answering a series of questions about the job. Once all data are input, the computer software automatically plans the job, determines costs, and provides a proposal or quotation, as well as an estimate breakdown of the chosen production plan. Advantages of CGE software are speed, simplicity, and the fact that any employee who can understand the job specifications, such as a CSR or a sales representative, can do an estimate.

Cost estimates done by computer also require less time than those completed manually. When computer estimating is done using template or pro forma methods, estimating times can be significantly reduced. Also, as estimators gain experience in completing estimates by computer, estimating time can be substantially cut.

However, one disadvantage is that computer estimating can be troublesome and slow when the job specification details are not formatted or linked directly with the estimating software. Other disadvantages include the fact that the accuracy of the estimate may be compromised because the production plan chosen by the computer may not reflect the actual plan that will be used, as well as the fact that estimate modification can be done by changing the job specifications only, which limits the "what if" questions that could result in cost savings for the customer.

An important part of the estimator's job is investigating alternatives that lower production time and cost for the customer. Such savings are then passed to the customer, keeping the company competitive and providing a valuable customer service. When computer estimating is used, the initial estimate using the customer's job specifications provides a base from which product and process alternatives can be quickly developed using "what if" situations. These alternatives can then be quickly tested against the initial estimate. Although investigating alternative methods and processes takes valuable estimating time, experienced print buyers consider it an important service and a reason to continue buying from the printers offering the service.

The final cost estimate, whether produced by computer or manually, should be kept on file with the job specification information supplied by the customer. Use of an estimating tracking system that is cross-indexed by estimate number, job number, date of order, and customer name, can be of considerable assistance to the printer. If the estimate were completed manually, or if manual calculations were made as the job was planned even though it was produced by computer, these calculations should be kept in the file with the final cost estimate. The estimator should build a file for each customer and cross-reference it by type of job for future use. Copies of all estimates should be printed out and saved in paper form. There should be ample filing cabinet space provided in the estimator's office for this purpose.

Printing industry computer vendors who provide estimating software have each developed their own estimating formats that are generally built to fit into their computer screen displays and to match the other screen forms they provide with their software. Most vendors provide the ability to tailor their estimating

TITLE _____

QUANTITIES _____

File Code _____

CM _____ %

% Overs Accepted _____

☐ New Job
☐ New Customer
☐ Revise of Estimate # _____

☐ Exact Reprint of Job# _____
☐ Reprint w/changes

TEXT FORMS   No. of Pages   ☐ Selfcover Book   ☐ Plus Cover Book

Flat size	Folded size	Bleed			
X	X	Yes No	----- Dylux	----- Color Key	----- Fuji

Type of Stock _____

Ink Colors

				%	S V	O V
Total Colors	____ Side 1			%	S V	O V
Including VN	____ Side 2			%	S V	O V

COVER   No. of Pages

Flat size	Folded size	Bleed			
X	X	Yes No	----- Dylux	----- Color Key	----- Fuji

Type of Stock _____

Ink Colors

				%	S V	O V
Total Colors	____ Side 1			%	S V	O V
Including VN	____ Side 2			%	S V	O V

PREPRESS

	# in Text	# in Cover
____ Halftones*		
____ Duotones*		
____ Seps		
____ Silhouettes		
____ Screens		
____ Reverses		
____ Traps		
____ Crossovers		
____ Tritones		
Special Items		
____ Line Art		
____ Illustrations		
____ Graphs		
____ Charts		
____ Maps		
____ Logos		

*Halftones and Duotones Are Assumed Reflective. If Not Please Specify.

ELECTRONIC PREPRESS
☐ IBM   ☐ MAC
☐ Disk**Program _____
Any multicolored imported graphics?
  ☐ Yes   ☐ No
☐ High resolution scans in file.
☐ No process screens to ouput.
If yes, what **program & how many?
**Program _____
**Program _____
☐ Mechanicals
  All line ☐ Yes ☐ No
☐ One piece negs supplied
  by customer
☐ Flats supplied by customer
☐ BSP pick up film
  Job # _____
☐ BSP pick up flats
  Job # _____
Resolution: ☐ 1693 ☐ 2540
Imposition: ☐ Yes ☐ No
Merge Images: ☐ Yes ☐ No
How Many? _____

SEPARATIONS (Includes Loose Fuji)

	QTY	Finished Size
☐ Trans. _____		x
☐ Reflective _____		x
☐ Other _____	_____	x
QTY Finished Size		
_____ 4 x 5	_____	x
_____ 5 x 7	_____	x
_____ 8 x 10	_____	x
_____ 10 x 12	_____	x

FINISHING   ☐ No Fold   ☐ Collate
☐ Trim to Size ☐ Fold _____   ☐ Pad In ____
☐ Saddlewire   ☐ Barrel   ☐ Gatefold
☐ Perfect Bind ☐ Z fold   ☐ Open
☐ __ Hole Drill ☐ In Half   ☐ Closed

☐ Roto   ☐ Litho   ☐ Letterpress
☐ Score   ☐ Text   ☐ Cover ☐ Other___
☐ Perforate ☐ Text   ☐ Cover ☐ Other___
☐ Rt. Angle
☐ UV Coat 1/s 2/s   ☐ Cover ☐ Text
☐ Film Laminate 1/s 2/s   _____ Mil
☐ Other _____

☐ Pocket   Pockets # _____
Size of pockets _____ BCS ☐ Yes ☐ No
☐ Glue   ☐ No glue
Die supplied by ☐ BSP ☐ Customer
☐ Number from_____to_____
☐ Emboss ☐ Die cut ☐ Foil stamp
Explain in full _____

NOTES _____
_____
_____
_____

ESTIMATE NUMBER   **PRICING**

A		
_____		/EA
		/M
		Total
B		/EA
_____		/M
		Total
C		/EA
_____		/M
		Total

PACKAGING ☐ Other _____
☐ Shrinkwrap in _____   ☐ Pack In Cartons
☐ Elastic band in _____ ☐ Skid Flat Press
☐ Belly Band in_____   Sheets

SPECIAL PACKAGING INSTRUCTIONS
☐ Skid ☐ Hold • ☐ FOB:_____
*FOB: Assumed our Dock Framingham Unless Specified.
How did you hear about Bay State Press? _____

Attn:: City:: Address Customer

Phone: State Customer Number

Fax # Date completed Date in Date

Account Executive Estimator Delivery Date Art Ready Job #

CSR Estimate # Production Art Design Estimate Print Estimate

☐ ☐ ☐

Figure 5.4 Cost estimating worksheet for CAE. (Reproduced with permission of Bay State Press, Framingham, Massachusetts.)

OTHER No. of Pages _____

Flat size	Folded size	Bleed				
X	X	Yes No	----- Dylux	----- Color Key		----- Fuji

Type of Stock _____
Ink Colors

Total Colors ____Side 1	%	S V	O V
Including VN ____Side 2	%	S V	O V

OTHER No. of Pages _____

Flat size	Folded size	Bleed				
X	X	Yes No	----- Dylux	----- Color Key		----- Fuji

Type of Stock _____
Ink Colors

Total Colors ____Side 1	%	S V	O V
Including VN ____Side 2	%	S V	O V

OTHER No. of Pages _____

Flat size	Folded size	Bleed				
X	X	Yes No	----- Dylux	----- Color Key		----- Fuji

Type of Stock _____
Ink Colors

Total Colors ____Side 1	%	S V	O V
Including VN ____Side 2	%	S V	O V

REQUEST FOR DESIGN

Estimate No._____ Estimate Due Date: _____

Project Name: _____

Scope of this Project: (expected client meetings, degree of involvement, etc.)

_____
_____
_____
_____
_____
_____
_____
_____
_____

☐ Client Meeting

_____

PROPOSED SCHEDULE

Initial meeting _____
1st Comps presented _____
Rev'd Comps presented _____
Photo shoot scheduled _____
Manuscript received _____
Photos received _____
1st page proof presented _____
Revisions received _____
Color goes out for separation _____
2nd page proof presented _____
Changes received_____
Prep for output _____
Output _____
Job proceeds to camera _____
Blueprint to client _____
Changes received_____
Stripping changes made/plates _____
Job on press _____
Job in bindery _____
Special Finishing_____
Finished job ships_____

DESIGN

☐ All new design   ☐ Matching previous format/style
☐ Straight production only/no design involved

Expected complexity of Design:
Easy 2 3 4 5 6 7 8 9 Complex

PRESENTATION

☐ Rough sketches   ☐ Comps   ☐ Color comps
☐ Multiple comp presentations will be necessary 1 2 3
☐ Rainbow Color Proof (Purchased Externally)

PRODUCTION ART & TYPE

Type to be received as:

☐ Clean scannable manuscript   ☐ IBM formatted
☐ Mac formatted   ☐ Keystroking needed
☐ ASCII file only

LOGO DEVELOPMENT

☐ New design
☐ Update, refine existing logo

Figure 5.4 *(continued)*

DESIGN ESTIMATE WORKSHEET

	HOURS REQ'D.		ESTIMATED COST	
Client Meetings: (Internal, external, teleconferences)				
Concept/Design:				
Comp/Presentation:				
Project Organization: (Meetings with AEs, internal production advise, outside vendors, etc.)				
Type: (Translating disks, assigning styles, etc.) To be received as: ☐ Clean scannable manuscript ☐ IBM disk (ASCII) ☐ Mac formatted ☐ Keystroking needed ☐ IBM formatted (NOTE: Unexpected tabular matter, graphs, and special formatting will be requoted upon receipt)				
MAC Layout: (Page makeup, flowing text, positioning photos, etc.)				
Proofreading:				
Photo Handling: (Scanning photos, sizing and cropping photos for prepress. Photoshop manipulation, proofing matchprints, etc.)				
MAC Stripping: (Color breaking, traps, special effects, etc.)				
Art Direction: (Photographer/Illustrator/Outside Designer supervision)				
Press Proofing:				
Service Bureau:				
Other outside services: (Materials, services, etc.)				
Logo Development:				

DO NOT WRITE BELOW

LOW   HIGH

Figure 5.4 *(continued)*

LAYOUT SHEET   **PRINTS AS A**

SW, WORK & TURN, TUMBLE
FORM #_____ OF_____   ONE SIDE, PERFECTING FORM, ANGLE
HOW MANY OUT_____ COLOR BARS_____

FRONT

NUMBER OF COLORS
FRONT: _____   BACK: _____
FINISHED PRODUCT WILL BE: _____

SHEET SIZE: _____   BLEEDS: YES ☐   NO ☐
FLAT SIZE: _____

ADDITIONAL INFORMATION _____
_____
_____
_____

LAYOUT SHEET   **PRINTS AS A**

SW, WORK & TURN, TUMBLE
FORM #_____ OF_____   ONE SIDE, PERFECTING FORM, ANGLE
HOW MANY OUT_____ COLOR BARS_____

FRONT

NUMBER OF COLORS
FRONT: _____   BACK: _____
FINISHED PRODUCT WILL BE: _____

SHEET SIZE: _____   BLEEDS: YES ☐   NO ☐
FLAT SIZE: _____

ADDITIONAL INFORMATION _____
_____
_____
_____

SALES NOTES
_____
_____
_____
_____
_____
_____
_____

OUTSIDE SERVICES

Service Quoted	Size	Qty	Vendor 1	Vendor 2	Vendor 3

Revised BSP Form #4 02/95   #19216
© GJN 6/94

Figure 5.4 *(continued)*

☐ **PREPRESS BUYOUTS**

Artwork: _____ $ _____

Artwork: _____ $ _____

	COLOR/STRIPPING	COLOR/STRIPPING	COLOR/STRIPPING	COLOR/STRIPPING
	VENDOR:	VENDOR:	VENDOR:	VENDOR:
	DESCRIPTION:	DESCRIPTION:	DESCRIPTION:	DESCRIPTION:
	USED Y N $	USED Y N $	USED Y N $	USED Y N $

SCANNED SEPS.
(SEE FRONT SIDE)

IMAGING SYSTEM
(SEE FRONT FOR DESCRIPTION)

☐ **HALF, DUO, TRITONES**
(SEE FRONT SIDE)

LINE 11 × 14	LINE 16 × 20	LINE 22 × 28	LINE 30 × 40		
SCREENS 11 × 14	SCREENS 16 × 20	SCREENS 22 × 28	SCREENS 30 × 40	BLUELINE 16 × 20	BLUELINE 22 × 28	BLUELINE 30 × 40
DUPES 11 × 14	DUPES 16 × 20	DUPES 22 × 28	DUPES 30 × 40	COLOR KEY 16 × 20	COLOR KEY 22 × 28	COLOR KEY 30 × 40
CONTACTS 11 × 14	CONTACTS 16 × 20	CONTACTS 22 × 28	CONTACTS 30 × 40	2C CROM 16 × 20	2C CROM 22 × 28	2C CROM 30 × 40
COMPOSING 11 × 14	COMPOSING 16 × 20	COMPOSING 22 × 28	COMPOSING 30 × 40	4C CROM 16 × 20	4C CROM 22 × 28	4C CROM 30 × 40
				6C CROM 16 × 20	6C CROM 22 × 28	6C CROM 30 × 40

FURNISHED FILM | NEGS | FURNISHED SEPS | PU SEPS

PLATE LAYOUTS COMMON FORMS: FW _____ HW _____ SF40 _____

LOW QUANTITY

LAYOUT 1
SF-40 HW FW
OF FORMS _____ PLATE CH. _____
CUST. OK HOURS _____
DRY TIME _____
SW IS W & TR W & TM
1 UP SIZE _____ × _____ OUT _____ M
CONTENTS _____ STOCK _____
LOW Q _____ CWT M C $ _____ /HR
HIGH Q _____ CWT M C $ _____ /HR
XTRA MR _____ PRE FOLD _____ TRIM _____ GLUE _____ PERF
SF RUNS _____ 1ST _____ 2ND
1ST _____ 2ND
CUT Y N COCKED SHEET Y N SLIP SHEET Y N

CF _____ CB _____
TOTAL _____

HIGH QUANTITY

LAYOUT 2
SF-40 HW FW
OF FORMS _____ PLATE CH. _____
CUST. OK HOURS _____
DRY TIME _____
SW IS W & TR W & TM
1 UP SIZE _____ × _____ OUT _____ M
CONTENTS _____ STOCK _____
LOW Q _____ CWT M C $ _____ /HR
HIGH Q _____ CWT M C $ _____ /HR
XTRA MR _____ PRE FOLD _____ TRIM _____ GLUE _____ PERF
SF RUNS _____ 1ST _____ 2ND
1ST _____ 2ND
CUT Y N COCKED SHEET Y N SLIP SHEET Y N

CF _____ CB _____
TOTAL _____

LAYOUT 3
SF-40 HW FW
OF FORMS _____ PLATE CH. _____
CUST. OK HOURS _____
DRY TIME _____
SW IS W & TR W & TM
1 UP SIZE _____ × _____ OUT _____ M
CONTENTS _____ STOCK _____
LOW Q _____ CWT M C $ _____ /HR
HIGH Q _____ CWT M C $ _____ /HR
XTRA MR _____ PRE FOLD _____ TRIM _____ GLUE _____ PERF
SF RUNS _____ 1ST _____ 2ND
1ST _____ 2ND
CUT Y N COCKED SHEET Y N SLIP SHEET Y N

CF _____ CB _____
TOTAL _____

Figure 5.5 Cost estimating worksheet for CAE. (Reproduced with permission of ColorGraphics, San Francisco, California.)

LAYOUT 4

SF-40   HW   CF _____ CB _____
OF FORMS. _____ PLATE CH. _____ TOTAL. _____
CUST. OK HOURS. _____
DRY TIME
SW   IS   W & TR   W & TM
1 UP SIZE _____ x _____ OUT _____ M
CONTENTS _____ STOCK _____
LOW Q _____ CWT M C $ _____ /HR
HIGH Q _____ CWT M C $ _____ /HR
XTRA MR _____ PRE FOLD _____ TRIM. _____ GLUE. _____ PERF _____
SF RUNS. _____ 1ST _____ 2ND. _____
1ST _____ 2ND.
CUT Y N   COCKED SHEET Y N   SLIP SHEET Y N

LAYOUT 5

SF-40   HW   FW   CF _____ CB _____
OF FORMS. _____ PLATE CH. _____ TOTAL. _____
CUST. OK HOURS. _____
DRY TIME
SW   IS   W & TR   W & TM
1 UP SIZE _____ x _____ OUT _____ M
CONTENTS _____ STOCK _____
LOW Q _____ CWT M C $ _____ /HR
HIGH Q _____ CWT M C $ _____ /HR
XTRA MR _____ PRE FOLD _____ TRIM. _____ GLUE. _____ PERF _____
SF RUNS. _____ 1ST _____ 2ND.
1ST _____ 2ND.
CUT Y N   COCKED SHEET Y N   SLIP SHEET Y N

LAYOUT 6

SF-40   HW   FW   CF _____ CB _____
OF FORMS. _____ PLATE CH. _____ TOTAL _____
CUST. OK HOURS. _____
DRY TIME
SW   IS   W & TR   W & TM
1 UP SIZE _____ x _____ OUT _____ M
CONTENTS _____ STOCK _____
LOW Q _____ CWT M C $ _____ /HR
HIGH Q _____ CWT M C $ _____ /HR
XTRA MR _____ PRE FOLD _____ TRIM. _____ GLUE. _____ PERF _____
SF RUNS. _____ 1ST _____ 2ND.
1ST _____ 2ND.
CUT Y N   COCKED SHEET Y N   SLIP SHEET Y N

☐ **FINISHING BUYOUTS**

VENDOR:
OPERATION:
QUOTE #.
USED Y N   SHIP. _____
LOW Q: _____ $ _____
HIGH Q: _____ $ _____

VENDOR INFO.
NAME: _____ DATE. _____
PRICE: _____

☐ **FOLDING**

FOLDS:
FAIT _____ x _____
FOLDED _____ x _____
LOW Q: _____ $ _____
HIGH Q: _____ $ _____

POCKETS:
SIZE _____ x _____
STITCH SIDE

☐ **STITCH**

COVER FEED Y N
LOW Q
SPEED
HIGH Q
SPEED

VENDOR INFO.
NAME: _____ DATE. _____
DELIVERY DATE: _____
PRICE: _____

☐ **DRILL MISC.**

OF HOLES:
FLAT SHEETS _____ BOOKS _____
LOW Q IN. _____ /HR
HIGH Q IN. _____ /HR
COST RATE _____ /HR

A = SHRINK WRAP
B = RUBBER BAND
C = STRING TIE
D = PAPER BAND
E = SLIP SHEET
F = KRAFT WRAP

☐ **PACKAGE**

PCS   PCS./PKG. $/PKG.
LOW Q
HIGH Q

VENDOR INFO.
NAME: _____ DATE. _____
DELIVERY DATE: _____
PRICE: _____

☐ **CARTON**

LBS. PCS
PCS.   PCS./PKG. $/PKG.
LOW Q
HIGH Q

VENDOR INFO.
NAME: _____ DATE. _____
DELIVERY DATE: _____
PRICE: _____

☐ **SHIPPING**

IA
SF
OC

LOW QUANTITY   HIGH QUANTITY

Figure 5.5 (*continued*)

```
DETAILS: 4 pages as 1/4 pages run 2 up W/T, 4 out of press sheet
         Trim size 8.5 x 11

STOCK: 100# Lustro Gloss Cover      MCC# 1000
Stock type: sub 100.00  Mwt 366  coated cover
Price   $373.20/M shts
SPOILAGE: 31.2%
INK side 1: 1 PMS, 4 Process, 1 Varnish
INK side 2: 1 PMS, 4 Process, 1 Varnish

================================================================
LABOR
Description            hours      cost$      sell$       Notes

Complex RIP P  Setup:   1.00      65.00      81.25 :
Complex RIP Pages  :    4.80     576.00     720.00 : 24 1 up
Tiff Images    Setup:   0.25      16.25      20.31 :
Tiff Images        :    0.50      60.00      75.00 : 10 1 up
EPS Charts, I  Setup:   0.50      32.50      40.63 :
EPS Charts, Illustra:   1.60     192.00     240.00 : 8 1 up
Scanning           :    1.35     202.50     253.13 : 3 transparent scans
Set up flats       :    1.47      73.50      91.88 : 8 flatspcs
Strip Complex RIP Pa:   2.00     100.00     125.00 : 24 pcs
Blueline proof     :    2.00     120.00     150.00 : 1 two sd Bluel 0 stp
NAPS proof         :    1.50      90.00     112.50 : 1 NAPS  6 clr 0 stps
                                                   ─────────────────────

=
Est. # 95:06:0175  B.sect # 1                      Page 2

40" Plates         :    2.50     150.00     187.50 : 6 one sd 40" p 1 SR
                     ───────── ─────────── ───────────
Prepress sub-total :   19.47    1677.75    2097.20 :
                     ========= =========== ===========

Bobst & Kluge  - Bobst    16396 impressions
           Setup:       0.17      17.00      19.55 : 1st form only
        Makeready:      1.50     150.00     172.50 : 1 MR/form, 2 passes
              Run:      6.56     656.00     754.40 : 2500i/hr
                     ───────── ─────────── ───────────
Bobst & Klug sub-ttl:   8.23     823.00     946.45 :
                     ========= =========== ===========
Sheetfed Offset - 102S 6/C    16396 impressions
           Setup:       0.42     105.00     120.75 : 1st form only
        Makeready:      2.00     500.00     575.00 : 6 MR/form, 2 passes
      Waiting time:     1.00     250.00     287.50 :
      Drying time:      1.29     322.50     370.88 :
              Run:      2.91     727.50     836.63 : 5639i/hr
           Washup:      0.20      50.00      57.50 : 1 wu per form
                     ───────── ─────────── ───────────
Sheetfed Off sub-ttl:   7.82    1955.00    2248.26 :
                     ========= =========== ===========

Pre-Press Cut/Trim
        Makeready:      0.17      10.20      11.73 : 1 cut(s)
              Run:      0.80      48.00      55.20 : 16 lifts 5Inch ea
Trim Flat Sheets
        Makeready:      0.42      25.20      28.98 : 6 cut(s)
              Run:      1.47      88.20     101.43 : 13 lifts 5Inch ea
                     ───────── ─────────── ───────────
Sub-total          :    2.86     171.60     197.34 :
                     ========= =========== ===========

                     ───────── ─────────── ───────────
Labor total        :   38.38    4627.35    5489.25 :
                     ========= =========== ===========
```

Figure 5.6 One page of a detailed computer estimating report. (Reproduced with permission of Communigraphics, Denver, Colorado, with assistance from Logic Associates, White River Junction, Vermont.)

forms to meet the specific needs of a printing company. Because estimating provides a critical set of production time and cost data, most printing companies sooner or later develop estimating forms that are tailored to meet their particular types of work and production sequencing. For manual estimating, most printing companies develop their own estimating forms to meet their specific needs, and use trial and error to revise the forms until they fit the companies' precise requirements.

One issue that invariably arises is the question of whether employees should have access to the times that have been estimated for their production operations. Opinions vary among managers on this point. However, as computer management systems and EFDC have become more common, as electronic job tickets have been making data available to shop floor employees, and as employee empowerment has pushed decision making down to the shop floor, there appears to be less focus on this issue.

It is essential that the sales representative, the CSR, and the estimator all have clear understandings of their responsibilities to the others. Obtaining job specifications must be carefully and meticulously done, regardless of who does them. An important rule is that the estimator, who receives complete job specifications, owes the others a quick turnaround of the estimate. Because not all jobs are time compressed, there is no fixed turnaround time. However, a one-day or quicker turnaround should be easily achievable when requested. Computer estimating, when coupled with fax and fax/modem telecommunication, is an enhancement to achieve this fast turnaround. The use of cross-trained teams for selling, estimating, and order entry activities is another way to speed the process.

The person supervising the estimating staff, or the cross-trained team of sales representatives, estimators, and CSRs, should be familiar with all of the activities performed by each staff group and preferably has work experience in each area. Frequently the company's vice president of sales or the sales manager is the supervisor in charge. Because estimating is an important part of the sales activity of a company, working directly under a sales-related supervisor seems natural. Advantages of this setup include a cooperative environment and quick mediation between team members should problems arise. Some printing companies position the estimating staff under production management or financial management supervision, which appears to work well too.

Developing a Template or Pro Forma Estimating System

The development and use of a template estimating system is a practical way to compress estimating time while maintaining a high level of accuracy. The template estimating concept is simple: Because some jobs have very similar job specifications, the estimator develops a master form or an estimating template covering these specifications. For use on a specific job, the master template is first copied and titled to reference the job, then the estimator carefully modifies the template to meet the exact job specifications. When jobs are very similar, template estimating can cut estimating time to a few minutes. Jobs that are less similar require the estimator to add the missing components, which takes more time.

Figure 5.7 is a simplified graphic presentation showing the three steps required to establish a template estimating system. Step 1 requires the development of production components for each production operation completed when producing the job. This is done by breaking the company into cost centers where work is performed, then developing a list of all activities performed in each production center. These activities are then evaluated and standard production times are assigned to them. Thus, a production component could be defined as a specific job activity performed by an employee within a specific production time. Printing companies providing full-service graphic imaging capability utilizing prepress, press, and finishing operations have numerous cost centers and hundreds of production components. Many computer management systems require the development of these components when the computer system is first installed because these components drive the cost estimating process. Chapter 2 covers key points relative to the computerization of production activities, while Chapter 3 covers the establishment of hourly production standards.

Step 2 in building a template cost estimating system requires that company staff carefully group jobs with respect to similarity of production. This frequently is done by classifying the types of products the printer produces in common categories of production. Generally the resulting list represents the specialized products the printer provides because specialized products typically require similar manufacturing methods. In Figure 5.7, there six different types of products that are segmented by two criteria: number of colors printed and type of paper. It is important to note that the criteria used for classifying and listing jobs should be carefully developed to keep production similarity the key component because the greater the production similarity the less time that is needed to modify a template during estimating. Artwork, for example, might be an important production variable. Artwork for one group of jobs might be fully electronic and customer supplied, while artwork for another type of job might be pasteup or mechanical art done by the printer.

Step 3 is the development of a group of master templates based on the criteria established in Step 2. As noted in Figure 5.7, there are six products and six templates, each with a different range of production components. These master templates are developed individually whereby each template contains only those production components required for producing that specific type of job. Sometimes a master template for a certain type of job is developed, in which cases submaster templates covering variations in production are developed. It is possible that the master and submaster estimating templates could number in the hundreds, all segmented by production variables.

No precise number of templates and subtemplates is considered the best.

Step 1: Develop the components for every operation in the plant.

Step 2: Classify jobs by similar production operation and component use.

Step 3: Develop templates based on job similarity and product type.

STEP 1

Prepress Components 1-10	Press Components 11-16	Finishing Components 17-20
Conventional production		
Camera	Press 1	Cutting
Stripping and contacting		
Proofing	Press 2	Folding
Platemaking		
	Press 3	Hand bindery
Electronic production		
Customer-supplied disk	Press 4	Stitching
Printer-supplied disk		

- List every possible component for every part of plant (there may be hundreds).
- Begin with "best guess" production times and refine through experience and job costing.

	STEP 2		**STEP 3**	
Product/ size	No. colors	Type paper	Estimating templates	Components
19x25 posters	4/0	80# offset	Template 1	1, 2, 3, 4, 6, 11, 16, 17
16-pg. signatures	1/1	60# offset	Template 2	2, 3, 4, 6, 8, 9, 10, 17, 19
16-pg. signatures	2/2	60-70# offset	Template 3	3, 4, 5, 6, 9, 10, 12, 16, 20
16-pg. signatures	4/4	60-70# offset	Template 4	3, 4, 5, 8, 12, 15, 16, 19, 20
Wine labels	2/C + foil emboss.	label stock	Template 5	2, 3, 4, 6, 9, 10, 17, 18, 19
Wine labels	3/C+foil +varnish	label stock	Template 6	2, 3, 4, 6, 8, 9, 10, 17, 20

Figure 5.7 Illustration of how a template estimating system is developed

However, there should be a balance between the time saved during estimating when one or two components can be quickly added to an existing template and the time required to develop a stand-alone subtemplate for each slight variation of production.

When the system is properly set up, template estimating is streamlined and fast. In Figure 5.7, if an estimate for printing a 19 inch x 25 inch poster job with 4 colors on one side of 80-pound offset book were desired, the estimator, working on a computer, would begin the template estimating process by selecting and copying Template 1 (a master template), then personalizing it by customer name, date, or perhaps estimate number. The choice of Template 1 would be made based on the estimator's experience and knowledge of the proposed job and the templates available. As indicated in Figure 5.7, Template 1 has prepress components 1, 2, 3, 4, and 6; press components 11 and 16; and finishing component 17. It therefore has all of the necessary production times for each of these eight components.

The estimator next moves through the template beginning with Component 1, providing information or modifying the template to fit the precise job specifications of this order. If the estimator discovers that this order requires an additional component that does not appear in the template, it can be added quickly. Correspondingly, if a particular component on the template is not needed, it is simply deleted. These decisions are made carefully but quickly by the estimator. When the template is done, it represents a complete cost estimate upon which the job can be priced and quoted to the customer. When using computerized template estimating, mathematical computations are done instantaneously, which allows the estimator to immediately evaluate production time and cost values.

Like cost estimating, template estimating can be done using either manual or computer methods. Manual template estimating saves time over cost estimating, but it remains labor intensive because of the mathematics that must be completed. Template estimating using a computer system speeds the process substantially by doing the calculations automatically as components are modified, added, or deleted.

Many printing industry computer vendors offer template or pro forma estimating following largely the same concepts described previously.

Reprint Orders versus New Jobs and Their Effects on the Printing Company

Reprint jobs, sometimes called repeat orders, are defined as print orders that have been previously produced by the printer and have been reordered for a second or an additional printing. Reprint work is divided into two general categories: (1) "straight" reprint work, which requires no image changes, and (2) "minimum change" reprint work, which requires minor or incidental image or other changes that can be quickly made. Reprint jobs are distinguished from other types of jobs that come into the plant in that their prepress imaging is, for all intents and purposes, complete and they only require presswork and finishing to provide the customer with a complete order.

When a customer requests a straight reprint order, there is no rework necessary and the manufacturing costs of the job are lower than in the initial run because prepress manufacturing has been fully completed. When a customer requests a minimum change reprint, the estimator must determine the quantity of rework necessary, then add its cost to the existing press and finishing costs. In either reprint situation, because all or most of the prepress work has been completed for the reprint and is paid for by the customer on the first printing, there is a reduced manufacturing cost. Given this, many printing companies provide a reprint discount on the billed price of the first printing. Although discount rates and discounting methods vary, generally a range of between 5 percent and 30 percent off of the initial selling price of the first job is common. This discount passes the reprint cost savings the printer enjoys to the customer.

Even in light of such discounts, in recent years there has been a decline in the frequency of reprint orders. In conjunction, there has also been a trend by customers to order fewer copies (e.g., lower quantities) when they place orders. Thus, customers are ordering fewer initial copies of new jobs and are exercising one of two options when they need to reorder: (1) they order a straight or minimum change reprint at a reduced price, or (2) they order a completely redesigned new product, which is the same as a new job. For example, a few years ago a typical print buyer would order 10,000 copies, which he would estimate to last one year. Today that same buyer orders 2,500 copies of the product-one-quarter of the previous amount—then either orders a reprint or a completely redesigned new job when the quantity is depleted.

The reasons for customer shifts to fewer reprints and reduced-quantity orders are varied. Among them is the customer's belief that graphic image changes are necessary and are a visible sign of the constant improvements in the customer's product or service. Linked to this reduced life cycle of each graphic product is the parallel emergence of DTP, which provides customers with powerful graphic imaging tools that allow each job to be redesigned so that it provides new graphic impact. Other technological advances in printing production, such as on-demand publishing and digital presses, have contributed as well to these trends. Customers and print buyers have also become more adept at estimating their own quantity requirements by targeting their markets more accurately and ordering only what they absolutely need. In so doing they effectively keep their options open for reprinting the job or designing the product as a new job. Also among reasons for the shifts to fewer reprints and reduced quantities are the ever-present intense competition between printers for the customer's business, the recognition of customer service as a key marketing tool for printers, and the eye-opening reality that printers must provide customers with quality printing in an environment that has greatly reduced time available compared to the time available a few years ago.

For the printer, these shifts in how customers order printing have significantly affected company operation. First, the company now experiences a greater number of smaller jobs-in-process at any given time, which increases the quantity of job details and particulars the printer must handle and thus exposes the printer to the potential of increased production problems. Second, the individual dollar values of these smaller jobs are lower, which means the company requires a greater number of small jobs to equal one bigger job in terms of sales volume and revenue earned. Third, these smaller jobs burden the printer's labor-intensive sales, order entry, and estimating efforts because customers increasingly expect significantly reduced cycle times in these areas. Fourth, this greater number of smaller jobs requires company executives to manage the business differently than in the past, with increased trust in employees and support for employee education, training, and teamwork throughout the company and especially in the order processing area.

5.7 Teamwork between Sales, Estimating, and Customer Service

Based on the preceding discussion, maintaining a positive relationship with customers is ensured only when sales representatives, estimators, and CSRs work as a unified group. Teamwork is a key to keeping customers happy as cycle times are reduced and technology constantly shifts. Achieving a team effort requires a commitment from each team member to work toward a unified group of objectives and the dedication of all team members to support each other's actions. Cross-training, cooperative effort, responsibility to each other, and trust are all important parts of the team atmosphere.

As previously discussed, the sales representative's primary focuses are to locate customers who wish to purchase targeted graphic products, to provide the customer with proposals/quotations in a timely manner, to secure the customer's order, and to provide follow-up customer contact as the job is produced and/or delivered. The estimator's primary duties are to take the sales representative's job specifications and use them to plan and estimate the job, including analysis of possible production and cost variations so that the job can be produced efficiently and competitively.

The CSR is a critical bridge between the company and the customer, handling an array of job details to ensure that the job is completed correctly, on time, and at a specified level of quality. In a team environment, each person's duties are handled as they best fit the situation, so CSR duties might sometimes be completed by a sales representative, or estimator duties might sometimes be completed by the CSR.

A problem that frequently emerges in many printing companies, and which makes teamwork hard to achieve, is that management allows, and even encourages, unnecessary differences between sales representatives, estimators, and CSRs to exist. Although the reasons for such unnecessary differences vary, they generally revolve around the three following issues:

1. There is disparity between the dollar incomes sales representatives enjoy, which include more perks and benefits, and the dollar incomes estimators and CSRs earn.
2. Management allows a "most favored status" situation to exist in which sales representatives are taught that they can demand and receive greater respect than CSRs and CSRs are taught that they can demand and receive greater respect than estimators.
3. There is the general belief that estimators and CSRs exist primarily to support the sales effort, not to enhance or improve it.

Overcoming these problems requires management to deal with each of the issues carefully and directly. A solution for one company may not work for another, but it is up to management to accept responsibility and take action to resolve these differences. Only when such problems are met head on and resolved can teamwork between these three job areas be achieved. When this is done, the process of selling, estimating, and providing world-class customer service is far more easily achieved, and the company enjoys significant benefits in terms of happy customers and an energized group of company employees. It is an important step to ensure printing company success in these times of unsure customer loyalty and intense competition.

5.8 Estimating Errors, Double-Checking the Estimate, and Checking the Customer's Credit

Cost estimating is a complex procedure that can lead to errors. Consider this situation: The estimator must develop a detailed plan of production with perhaps dozens of manufacturing steps and then add buyouts and material costs. Then she must accurately assign time and cost values to determine total cost to manufacture the product. In addition, she must estimate in an increasingly time-compressed environment because many customers view quick estimating turnaround as an indicator of how the company performs in all other areas.

When computer estimating is used to estimate the entire job, mathematical errors are eliminated. However, logic errors, inaccurate assumptions based on poor job specifications, and inaccurate communication frequently lead to mistakes. The most important consideration with respect to errors is the relative cost impact on the printing company. If an error causes a significant cost loss to the company, profit dollars must be used to make that loss up. However, if the error causes too high a price for the product, the customer will probably not order the job and the company will lose a potential sale. In essence, a printing company cannot afford to price work at a loss in profits, nor can it afford to overprice work and lose volume in the plant.

Categories of Estimating Errors

Estimating mistakes generally fall into five categories: mathematical, logic, assumption, policy, and written and verbal communication. These categories are discussed in the sections that follow.

Mathematical Errors. Because many estimators use manual estimating methods for specific or select jobs or to complete various intermediate steps of the estimate when computer estimating, math errors remain a problem even though computer estimating is common. When estimates are completed manually using pencil, paper, and electronic calculator, errors in math are too frequent. However, when computer estimating is used for estimating the entire job and the estimator performs no separate math calculations, math errors are eliminated. This is an important advantage of computer estimating.

Logic Errors. Cost estimating requires the identification of each production operation that occurs while a job is being manufactured. Because cost estimating is a detailed process which is usually done quickly and sometimes with interruptions, it is possible that an estimator may either leave out or include certain production activities, thus causing the final estimate to be either too high or too low. While logic errors are inadvertent, they tend to be difficult to discover and may have a significant bearing on the cost of the job, which typically affects job price. In circumstances where estimating templates or pro forma estimating systems are used, there tend to be fewer errors in logic because the errors are eliminated as the template is perfected.

Assumption Errors. Assumption errors usually occur when the estimator is forced into making an assumption due to incomplete job specifications from the sales representative or the CSR. Clearly the fewer the assumptions the estimator must make during estimating, the more accurate the estimate. Correspondingly, the less information and the fewer specifications available during estimating, the less precise the estimate.

Assumption errors may be divided into two categories: job specification assumptions and production planning assumptions. In the case of job specification assumptions, major errors usually result from:

- not knowing what the customer will supply
- not understanding exactly what the customer wants produced
- assuming the use of certain materials that have not been clearly specified

The most common production planning assumption errors are:

- assuming that the first production plan is the best and most economical when other plans should be developed and compared
- assuming certain capacity and production levels apply when they may be different when the order begins production or may not generally represent the plant
- assuming and using a delivery date that is unrealistic or unachievable

There are many other assumption errors that can occur during production planning, but those listed are some of the most common and must be carefully watched.

Policy Errors. Established company policies allow the estimator to work under known conditions and procedures, which reduces misunderstandings. There should be clear guidelines covering job specifications parameters, how estimates are completed, and how proposals and quotes are processed. The company should develop guidelines on policy areas such as buyouts, material purchasing, modification of production standards, development and interpretation of BHRs, relations between production planning and estimating, and so on. It is the job of company management to establish and oversee these key policy areas so that estimators can work quickly and accurately.

Errors in Written and Verbal Communication. These errors occur because of poor or misunderstood communication between the customer and the printing company representative (e.g., the sales representative, CSR, or estimator). To minimize such problems, all parties should communicate on the same level—that is, on the same knowledge and language plane. Every attempt should be made to put important items between the customer and the company in writing. Product samples and sample graphic images should be provided whenever possible to clarify what is desired. Verbal agreements and casual "okays" on job-related items should be avoided or completed in accordance to standing company policy. The more efficient and direct the communication, the fewer the misunderstandings and problems that arise.

Everyone makes mistakes. Doing so is a part of the human condition. No matter how much effort is made to eliminate mistakes, they occur anyway. A focus on reducing errors in job specifications, estimating, and order entry reduces misunderstandings between customer and printing company staff, as well as costly rework when jobs are done incorrectly. Tolerance for errors is necessary, but actively working to reduce them is essential.

Double-Checking Cost Estimates

The best way reduce estimating errors is to review estimates at the two following levels:

1. *At the estimator level.* At this level a second person, perhaps another estimator or a CSR who also does estimating, double-checks the estimate after it has been initially completed but prior to when the job is priced. In some large printing firms, one person, such as the estimating supervisor, completes the double-checking process. Also, some printing companies establish guidelines for checking estimates, which may include checking estimates only for jobs that are above a set dollar value, checking estimates for jobs that are unique or new to the company, and/or checking estimates for a specific category of jobs that has a history of being particularly troublesome in production or not financially rewarding.

2. *At the job costing level.* Job costing, which is a review of actual to estimated times and costs, is essential for providing feedback with respect to estimating errors. Some printing companies job cost every job they produce, while other companies review only certain jobs, such as those above a specified dollar level or those that were troublesome during production. Because job costing is ex post facto, the printer is not normally empowered to charge the customer for estimating and production errors. Thus, job costing is a feedback process so that future estimates can be completed more accurately. The job costing process is discussed again later in this chapter, and has been discussed in both Chapters 2 and 3.

Double-checking estimates is a most effective procedure to eliminate estimating errors. As mentioned earlier, usually such reviews are completed by the estimating supervisor in a large plant (at the estimator level) or by exchanging estimates between estimators. Given the need for fast estimating turnaround, many printing companies establish guidelines whereby estimates are double-checked only when the production plans are complex or when costs for the proposed jobs appear significant. Some companies double-check only those estimates that are not time compressed. Other printing companies double-check estimates on a random or an nth number basis. Given the press for time to complete all of the other activities in order processing, few printing companies double-check all estimates. Certainly, the greater the number of estimates that are double-checked, and the more thorough the checking procedure, the more accurate the estimates that are produced.

Checking the Customer's Credit

At some point during the estimating stage it is prudent to check the customer's credit. This is particularly important when the job is large, when extensive costs appear likely, or when the printer feels that the customer might be irresponsible or slow in paying for the job.

It is generally agreed that the customer's credit should be checked prior to extending a proposal or quotation to the customer. However, this is not always possible in an environment of quick estimating turnaround. In such cases, a statement such as "Prices quoted above are conditional upon company approval of customer's credit" on the proposal or quotation clarifies the company's credit checking process.

Opinion varies among printers as to whose credit should be checked. Some printers check credit for all new customers and depend on the payment history of established customers to indicate credit and payment problems. Other printers check the credit of all customers on a periodic basis, regardless of their credit histories with the companies. Still others rarely, if ever, check credit, or they check credit randomly or only when a job is large and represents a significant impact on the company relative to production and cash needs.

There are essentially three ways to check a potential customer's credit. The first way is for the printer to have the customer complete a credit application which requests relevant creditors and credit references. The application can then be checked with routine telephone calls at little cost to the printer. The format of the credit application varies, but each form should require the signature of a responsible party in case there are questions.

The second procedure for credit checking is for the printer to contact a credit association, which is a commercial firm used by many companies to investigate credit. When the printer frequently does credit checks, he may wish to become a member of the credit association to reduce the overall costs of the process. In instances when the printer uses a credit association intermittently, there are typically initial access charges plus additional other costs.

The third procedure for checking credit is to utilize the credit referral service offered through most PIA regional offices. Although this service is available only to PIA members, it is typically efficient, inexpensive, and accurate.

Credit checks help the company avoid bad debts and slow payment on receivables, which adversely affect the company's cash position and cash flow in general. Later in this chapter effective cash flow is discussed, along with the split invoice technique by which a customer pays a certain amount on a job before production begins—as a deposit—and the remainder after the job is delivered.

5.9   Price Setting by Top Management

Setting the price on a printed product is among the most important functions of company management because the prices charged have a direct bearing on revenue earned and company profitability. As detailed in Chapter 4, numerous factors go into establishing the price of a printed product. Management must understand that to effectively control price in printing requires that markets are targeted and controlled. Specialized product and process applications were mentioned earlier in this regard. Other elements of pricing include estimated manufacturing cost, product mix of the printer, the competition's price, the quality of the product, the services provided to the customer, the volume of work, VA, and the desired profit. Also, a key estimating and pricing issue is the customer's budget for the job, which should be obtained as a job specification so that the printing company can try to meet this target.

As just mentioned, setting price is a top management responsibility. However, in some printing companies, pricing is left up to the estimator or CSR. Also, some printers allow their sales representatives to price jobs as part of the sales process on the basis that it increases sales volume. Experience shows that when the sales representative is given pricing responsibility, she should be limited to specific situations and circumstances or provided with a set of pricing guidelines.

When computer estimating is used to determine manufacturing cost, the quoting process is streamlined because management provides the estimator with profit markup information. This markup is usually a percentage based on the total manufacturing cost of the job. Although markup percentages vary, the most frequent "markup over cost" used by commercial printers is 35 percent. Thus a job with a $100 total cost would be priced at $135.

However, experienced printers know that using a single fixed markup percentage—such as 35 percent over cost—for all jobs does not address the company's true profit potential because each customer may be willing and able to pay more (or less). Thus, when using a percentage "markup over cost" system with computer estimating, it is wise for management to provide the estimator with strategically established target percentages for different customer segments. These percentages should factor in a number of key pricing elements which are discussed in detail in Chapter 4.

As also discussed in Chapter 4, the Robinson-Patman Act, which is federal law, and state laws in most states require that pricing patterns be consistent for like goods and services provided to the customer or within major product groups. Of course, the customer needs the graphic product and the printing company has the skills, personnel, and equipment to provide it. There is no process by which pricing can be simplified in the printing industry because it is solely a company-by-company, top management decision.

As noted earlier in this chapter, prior to the printer making a final commitment to print an order, the customer's credit should be verified as good. Management should consider carefully the aspect of customer credit—that is, the customer's ability to pay for the work—prior to extending a proposal to the client. The more substantial the dollar amount of the job, the more thorough the credit check must be.

5.10 The Price Proposal, the Price Quotation, and the Contractual Relationship

As indicated earlier in this chapter, the terms "estimate," "proposal," and "quotation" are used interchangeably throughout this book, as they tend to be used in real life. Thus, when a customer requests an "estimate," he is really asking for a proposal or a quotation on a printing order. In theory, each of the three terms is different. An estimate is generated and used by the printing company as an internal dollar measurement of the costs required to produce a specified printed product. A cost estimate is normally not available to, nor shared with, the customer. A proposal is a tentative offer from the printing company to the customer to produce a specific printed product. A proposal is subject to negotiation and change. A quotation is a firm offer from the printer to the customer to produce a printed product for a specified dollar amount. It is final and binding to both printer and customer when accepted by the customer.

The Price Proposal

The proposal is a typewritten or computer-generated document that specifies prices for a printing order. It may be sent to the customer by mail, fax, or fax/modem, or it may be delivered by the sales representative or company messenger. A complete proposal describes the work to be done, specifies quality and quantity levels, and provides tentative selling prices to the customer.

Because the proposal suggests tentative prices, the customer may take one of three actions in response to it. First, the customer may accept the proposed price, in which case the proposal becomes a quotation, which is a legal agreement between the printer and customer. Some printers issue a separate quotation upon acceptance of the proposal.

The second option available to the customer, rejection of the proposal, typically occurs because the customer finds the price too high for her budget or because she decides she does not want the job for other reasons. Sometimes the customer makes arrangements with another printing company because it took the first printer too long to complete the estimate-proposal process. Regardless of the reason, when the customer rejects the proposal, the sales representative drops the order and informs the printing company of the customer's decision.

In this case, all of the work done by the printing company to obtain the order was done in vain.

The third action, and perhaps the most frequent, is for the customer to modify the job in one way or another, typically in an effort to reduce the price. When extensive modifications are indicated, it is best for the sales representative to develop a new set of job specifications and submit the job for reestimating. If the modifications are minor, such as a different brand or color of paper stock or minor graphic changes, only those segments of the estimate that are affected need to be recalculated. A second proposal is then issued with the modified price. Minor revisions are normally completed by the estimator revising the original estimate. Major revisions, however, require a complete new estimate.

Price Negotiation. Sometimes the printer must negotiate the price with the customer before the customer agrees to accept the proposal. Price negotiation is handled differently from company to company. Sometimes management sets a minimum lowest acceptable price and allows the sales representative to negotiate directly with the customer to no less than this set lowest price. In other cases, management sets a minimum lowest acceptable price and the sales representative is free to negotiate price with the customer even lower than management's minimum, but the difference comes from the sales representative's commission. In still other cases, management allows the sales representative to negotiate price, but keeps final pricing authority in the hands of a company executive, such as the sales manager, who must approve the negotiated price. Other negotiation methods are also used, usually with established procedures set by company management.

The Price Quotation

Once the price proposal has been agreed upon by the customer and the printer, it has the impact of a legal agreement between the two parties and thus takes the status of a price quotation. However, when the proposal has been through a complex negotiation sequence, the printer may opt to issue a separate confirming price quotation so that job particulars can be clarified in writing. This price quotation, when accepted by the customer, also becomes a legal and binding agreement between the two parties.

Given the legal ramifications of the contract, it is important that the price quotation specify exactly the job to be produced with firm price, quantity, and quality levels indicated. In many cases, it contains additional specifications, such as the date the job is to be completed, shipping and delivery considerations, the type of wrapping for the final packages, the special conditions of the final product, and so on. Figures 5.8 and 5.9 are two sample quotations.

Frequently a copy of the quotation is faxed to the customer and the original copy is sent by mail. Messenger service is also frequently used. The customer

```
┌─────────────┐
│ W A T E R   │
│ M A R K ✒   │
│ P R E S S   │
└─────────────┘
```

Quotation

Client: Mary Agresta   **Estimate Number:**94:1:11

                                Lewis & Partners
                                433 California Street
                                San Francisco, CA

Client's Job Number

Description   Sales Sheet Reprints: 20,00 each of FS-1238,2058

Quantity: 40000

Size: Flat: 8.5x11   Finished: 8.5 x 11   Pages: 2 each

Paper: 100# Productolith Gloss Book

Ink: 4/C process + varnish both sides

Artwork: Film supplied fronts, type changes to backs from disk.

Separations: none

Halftones & Duotones: none

Proofs: Blueline, Color Proof for backs, Press Check

Finishing: Trim

Packaging: Carton pack

Delivery: F.O.B. Watermark

Other:

Costs: 40000
                     $4814

Presented by: Timm Crull   **Accepted by:** _____

Date: 1/20/95   **Date:**

Note: Due to current industry conditions, paper pricing and availability are subject to change without notice.

Figure 5.8 A sample quotation. (Reproduced with permission of Watermark Press, San Francisco, California.)

February 1, 1995   Quote # 6088

Active Systems, Inc.
34 Coolidge Circle
Northboro, MA 01532
Attn: Gordon Jay Nash

Dear Gordon;

We are pleased to quote on the following project(s):

Job Title:	PRODUCT LINE BROCHURE
Qty:	5M
# of pages:	8 Page Self Cover
Size:	17" x 11" Folds to 8 1/2" x 11", No Bleed
Stock:	80# Multiart Silk Text
Ink:	6/6 (process + pms + SGV) vs. 5/5 (process + pms)
Art:	Quark Disk Supplied - (Varnish in File)
Prep:	(3) Min. Seps - square ups, (1) 5" x 7" Sep. - square up
Proof:	Dylux, Fuji Color Proof
Bindery:	Fold, Stitch & Trim
Packaging:	Shrinkwrap in 75's
Shipping:	FOB Our Dock, Framingham
Price:	6/6 = $4623.00 vs. 5/5 = $3979.00

Thank you for the opportunity to submit this printing cost estimate. We pledge to make the best use possible of your Time and our new Technology to develop mutual Trust.

Sincerely,

Kristen Gleason

*All print orders are considered NOT LESS THAN. BSP will bill for over runs up to 5% of the print order.
*Net price does not include sales tax or shipping charges.
All quotes F.O.B. our dock in Framingham, MA 01701 unless specifically stated otherwise.
Baystate Press conforms to Standard Printing Trade Customs, a copy will be sent to you upon request.

2 Watson Place Building 5C Framingham, MA 01701   508 877-0116 FAX: 508 877-7930

Figure 5.9 A sample quotation. (Reproduced with permission of Bay State Press, Framingham, Massachusetts.)

typically notifies the printer of his acceptance using the same delivery method and services. Good business practice dictates that no quotation is modified unless both parties agree to the changes. There should be no verbal agreements regarding any aspect of the quotation made between the customer and any company employee. Such verbal agreements can be misconstrued and easily lead to misunderstandings at some future time.

The Graphic Communications Business Practices. Because the quotation is a legal and binding contract, prudent printers include with it a copy of the Graphic Communications Business Practices (GCBP), also known as the 1994 Printing Trade Customs (Figure 5.10). The current GCBP, which were revised extensively from the 1985 Printing Trade Customs, were researched and drafted by the Graphic Arts Technical Foundation (GATF), NAPL, and PIA through surveys and feedback from hundreds of printers. They were written to reflect the common business practices of the printing industry by defining the working parameters between customer and printer. It should be noted that the GCBP are rooted in language from the Uniform Commercial Code, which defines a trade custom as

> any practice or method of dealing having such regularity of observation in a place, vocation, or trade as to justify an expectation that it will be observed with respect to the transaction in action. The distance and scope of such a usage are to be proved as facts. If it is established that such usage is embodied in a written trade code or similar writing, the interpretation of the writing is for the court.

The 1985 Printing Trade Customs were commonly printed on the back of the proposal or quotation, and thus were incorporated as part of the proposal or quotation. However, the newer 1994 Business Practices, which were revised to include numerous production changes in electronic prepress and DTP, are too long to reasonably fit on one page. Given this, printers who wish to include the GCBP as part of their quotations send the procedures by mail or messenger separate from the quotations as part of the confirming details of their jobs. Another approach is for the printer to have the customer or buyer sign a copy of the GCBP to cover a series of jobs or a specified length of time, such as one year. Having a signed copy of the GCBP on file is important when quotations are completed by telecommunication.

The GCBP require that specific terms and conditions of sale be identified. These terms and conditions should be applied uniformly to all customers. Using the GCBP is optional, however. Some printers elect to use the GCBP while other printers opt to work with no accepted business practices in place. The use of any trade custom is an independent, individual business decision.

Some companies may wish to develop their own terms and conditions of sale whereby they establish and tailor their own contractual provisions to meet their

Printing Trade Customs – 1994 Revision

What are Trade Customs? *In the technical language of the Uniform Commercial Code, a trade custom is defined as: "any practice or method of dealing having such regularity of observation in a place, vocation or trade as to justify an expectation that it will be observed with respect to the transaction in question. The distance and scope of such a usage are to be proved as facts. It is established that such usage is embodied in a written trade code or similar writing, the interpretation of the writing is for the court."* ◆ *Trade customs must still be spelled out in specific terms and conditions governing the agreement between the vendor and the customer.*

1. QUOTATION. A quotation not accepted within 30 days may be changed.

2. ORDERS. Acceptance of orders is subject to credit approval and contingencies such as fire, water, strikes, theft, vandalism, acts of God, and other causes beyond the provider's control. Cancelled orders require compensation for incurred costs and related obligations. **3. EXPERIMENTAL WORK.** Experimental or preliminary work performed at customer's request will be charged to the customer at the provider's current rates. This work cannot be used without the provider's written consent. **4. CREATIVE WORK.** Sketches, copy, dummies, and all other creative work developed or furnished by the provider are the provider's exclusive property. The provider must give written approval for all use of this work and for any derivation of ideas from it. **5. ACCURACY OF SPECIFICATIONS.** Quotations are based on the accuracy of the specifications provided. The provider can re-quote a job at time of submission if copy, film, tapes, disks, or other input materials don't conform to the information on which the original quotation was based. **6. PREPARATORY MATERIALS.** Artwork, type, plates, negatives, positives, tapes, disks, and all other items supplied by the provider remain the provider's exclusive property. **7. ELECTRONIC MANUSCRIPT or IMAGE.** It is the customer's responsibility to maintain a copy of the original file. The provider is not responsible for accidental damage to media supplied by the customer or for the accuracy of furnished input or final output. Until digital input can be evaluated by the provider, no claims or promises are made about the provider's ability to work with jobs submitted in digital format, and no liability is assumed for problems that may arise. Any additional translating, editing, or programming needed to utilize customer-supplied files will be charged at prevailing rates. **8. ALTERATIONS/CORRECTIONS.** Customer alterations include all work performed in addition to the original specifications. All such work will be charged at the provider's current rates. **9. PREPRESS PROOFS.** The provider will submit prepress proofs along with original copy for the customer's review and approval. Corrections will be returned to the provider on a master set marked "O.K.," "O.K. with corrections," or "Revised proof required" and signed by the customer. Until the master set is received, no additional work will be performed. The provider will not be responsible for undetected production errors if: ◆ proofs are not required by the customer; ◆ the work is printed per the customer's O.K.; ◆ requests for changes are communicated orally. **10. PRESS PROOFS.** Press proofs will not be furnished unless they have been required in writing in the providers quotation. A press sheet can be submitted for the customer's approval as long as the customer is present at the press during makeready. Any press time lost or alterations/corrections made because of the customer's delay or change of mind will be charged at the provider's current rates.

11. COLOR PROOFING. Because of differences in equipment, paper, inks, and other conditions between color proofing and production pressroom operations, a reasonable variation in color between color proofs and the completed job is to be expected. When variations of this kind occur, it will be considered acceptable performance. **12. OVER-RUNS or UNDER-RUNS.** Over-runs or under-runs will not exceed 10 percent of the quantity ordered. The provider will bill for actual quantity delivered within this tolerance. If the customer requires a guaranteed quantity, the percentage of tolerance must be stated at the time of quotation. **13. CUSTOMER'S PROPERTY.** The provider will only maintain fire and extended coverage on property belonging to the customer while the property is in the provider's possession. The provider's liability for this property will not exceed the amount recoverable from the insurance. Additional insurance coverage may be obtained if it is requested in writing, and if the premium is paid to the provider. **14. DELIVERY.** Unless otherwise specified, the price quoted is for a single shipment, without storage, F.O.B. provider's platform. Proposals are based on continuous and uninterrupted delivery of the complete order. If the specifications state otherwise, the provider will charge accordingly at current rates. Charges for delivery of materials and supplies from the customer to the provider, or from the customer's supplier to the provider, are not included in quotations unless specified. Title for finished work passes to the customer upon delivery to the carrier at shipping point; or upon mailing of invoices for the finished work or its segments, whichever occurs first. **15. PRODUCTION SCHEDULES.** Production schedules will be established and followed by both the customer and the provider. In the event that production schedules are not adhered to by the customer, delivery dates will be subject to renegotiation. There will be no liability or penalty for delays due to state of war, riot, civil disorder, fire, strikes, accidents, action of government or civil authority, acts of God, or other causes beyond the control of the provider. In such cases, schedules will be extended by an amount of time equal to delay incurred. **16. CUSTOMER-FURNISHED MATERIALS.** Materials furnished by customers or their suppliers are verified by delivery tickets. The provider bears no responsibility for discrepancies between delivery tickets and actual counts. Customer-supplied paper must be delivered according to specifications furnished by the provider. These specifications will include correct

weight, thickness, pick resistance, and other technical requirements. Artwork, film color separations, special dies, tapes, disks, or other materials furnished by the customer must be usable by the provider without alteration or repair. Items not meeting this requirement will be repaired by the customer, or by the provider at the providers current rates. **17. OUTSIDE PURCHASES.** Unless otherwise agreed in writing, all outside purchases as requested or authorized by the customer, are chargeable. **18. TERMS/CLAIMS/LIENS.** Payment is net cash 30 calendar days from date of invoice. Claims for defects, damages or shortages must be made by the customer in writing no later than 10 calendar days after delivery. If no such claim is made, the provider and the customer will understand that the job has been accepted. By accepting the job, the customer acknowledges that the providers performance has fully satisfied all terms, conditions, and specifications. The provider's liability will be limited to the quoted selling price of defective goods, without additional liability for special or consequential damages. As security for payment of any sum due under the terms of an agreement, the provider has the right to hold and place a lien on all customer property in the provider's possession. This right applies even if credit has been extended, notes have been accepted, trade acceptances have been made, or payment has been guaranteed. If payment is not made, the customer is liable for all collection costs incurred. **19. LIABILITY.** **1. Disclaimer of Express Warranties:** Provider warrants that the work is as described in the purchase order. The customer understands that all sketches, copy, dummies, and preparatory work shown to the customer are intended only to illustrate the general type and quality of the work. They are not intended to represent the actual work performed. **2. Disclaimer of Implied Warranties:** The provider warrants only that the work will conform to the description contained in the purchase order. The provider's maximum liability, whether by negligence, contract, or otherwise, will not exceed the return of the amount invoiced for the work in dispute. Under no circumstances will the provider be liable for specific, individual, or consequential damages. **20. INDEMNIFICATION.** The customer agrees to protect the provider from economic loss and any other harmful consequences that could arise in connection with the work. This means that the customer will hold the provider harmless and save, indemnify, and otherwise defend him/her against claims, demands, actions, and proceedings on any and all grounds. This will apply regardless of responsibility for negligence. **1. Copyrights.** The customer also warrants that the subject matter to be printed is not copyrighted by a third party. The customer also recognizes that because subject matter does not have to bear a copyright notice in order to be protected by copyright law, absence of such notice does not necessarily assure a right to reproduce. The customer further warrants that no copyright notice has been removed from any material used in preparing the subject matter for reproduction. To support these warranties, the customer agrees to indemnify and hold the provider harmless for all liability, damages, and attorney fees that may be incurred in any legal action connected with copyright infringement involving the work produced or provided. **2. Personal or economic rights.** The customer also warrants that the work does not contain anything that is libelous or scandalous, or anything that threatens anyone's right to privacy or other personal or economic rights. The customer will, at the customer's sole expense, promptly and thoroughly defend the provider in all legal actions on these grounds as long as the provider: ◆ promptly notifies the customer of the legal action; ◆ gives the customer reasonable time to undertake and conduct a defense. The provider reserves the right to use his or her sole discretion in refusing to print anything he or she deems illegal, libelous, scandalous, improper or infringing upon copyright law. **21. STORAGE.** The provider will retain intermediate materials until the related end product has been accepted by the customer. If requested by the customer, intermediate materials will be stored for an additional period at additional charge. The provider is not liable for any loss or damage to stored material beyond what is recoverable by the provider's fire and extended insurance coverage. **22. TAXES.** All amounts due for taxes and assessments will be added to the customer's invoice and are the responsibility of the customer. No tax exemption will be granted unless the customer's "Exemption Certificate" (or other official proof of exemption) accompanies the purchase order. If, after the customer has paid the invoice, it is determined that more tax is due, then the customer must promptly remit the required taxes to the taxing authority, or immediately reimburse the provider for any additional taxes paid. **23. TELECOMMUNICATIONS.** Unless otherwise agreed, the customer will pay for all transmission charges. The provider is not responsible for any errors, omissions, or extra costs resulting from faults in the transmission.

The above are revisions adopted by the Printing Industries of America, the National Association of Printers and Lithographers, and the Graphic Arts Technical Foundation on behalf of their memberships. The previous update of Trade Practices was done in 1985.

Figure 5.10 The GCBP, revised in 1994 from the Printing Trade Customs. (Reproduced from the PINC 1995 Print Buyers Guide with permission of PIA, NAPL, and GATF.)

specific needs. The GCBP may be used as a framework to assist in writing these conditions. It is possible to develop different sets of terms and conditions which fit the various types of customers and products the printer serves and produces respectively. As with the GCBP, the customer must be informed of the specific terms and conditions that apply to her work prior to any production.

If either the Terms and Conditions of Sale or the GCBP are used, they are intended as a mechanism to smooth differences between the printer and the customer. They should promote good business practices and reduce the possibility of serious disagreements between printer and client. Their clauses are intended to be reasonable to both parties, thus reducing the potential conflict between them.

It is important that the printer carefully read and understand the customer's purchase order conditions, which can sometimes conflict with the GCBP. When such differences exist, or when the PO wording is questionable, it is wise for the printer to ask the customer for clarification or to consult a competent attorney before accepting the job. One example of a recurring problem in this area is the issue of sequential liability where a print buying organization denies payment to a printer (or other supplier) until the organization is paid by its supplier. This is most common with advertising agencies that sometimes purchase large quantities of printing and then refuse to pay for the printing until the advertising agencies are paid by their clients. Typically part of the PO agreement, this condition of sale holds the printer liable for paying his obligations without timely compensation by the customer.

5.11 The Order Entry Process

Order entry is completed once the job proposal or quotation is accepted by the customer. The purpose of a good order entry system is to successfully launch the job into the printing production cycle so that the job can be produced with minimum problems, on time, and within the quoted price.

The first step in the order entry process, which is taken before a job ticket is generated, is to review the original production plan and estimate, factoring in recent information about artwork, inventory on hand, buyouts, and scheduling issues so that a firm delivery date can be met. This review process can be simple or complex—it may take a few minutes or it may require extensive work—but it should be done carefully and include the most current information about the job. Too frequently the initial order entry review is incomplete or less thorough than it should be, which causes problems that could have been avoided if the review process had been more complete.

The review of the production plan should include the four following areas, which are critical to early decisions that directly affect production time, cost, and job quality:

1. review and evaluation of artwork for the job, including determining who will provide the artwork and the quality of art as it will affect production and overall product quality
2. availability of raw material inventory items for the job
3. availability of outside purchases necessary for the job
4. establishment of a complete production schedule which ties together all internal and external factors of the job and targets the promised delivery date

Once the production plan has been evaluated and the four key areas have been confirmed, the next step in the order entry process is to generate a job ticket or a job jacket like the one shown in Figure 5.11. The job ticket is typically a printed envelope or a sheet that provides the details of the order. If an integrated computer system is used, and the job was computer estimated, the job jacket can be quickly generated from the estimate, which saves time because much of the information is common to both the job jacket and the estimate. Some computer systems provide for the generation of an electronic job ticket, which can be used in place of the printed job ticket or envelope. Electronic job tickets require computer terminals situated throughout the plant. The ticket can be viewed from any terminal. Some companies use a combination of printed and electronic job tickets.

Large companies employ order entry personnel who exclusively complete order entry tasks, while smaller companies draw on estimating, CSR, and sales staff to complete order entry processing in addition to fulfilling their regular duties. Regardless of who completes the order entry tasks, attention to job details and a focus on meeting or beating the promised delivery date are critical elements.

5.12 Production and Delivery of the Job

When the printing company's production system is organized and uses effective order entry methods as previously described, production on most printing orders begins without fanfare. Early in the job all production elements are planned so that the job flows easily into the company's production system, much like a canoe calmly entering a stream. Good preplanning, teamwork, and a continuous focus on job details during production pay off as jobs smoothly move through the maze of production steps.

Even with a superior order entry system, skilled production employees, and the best equipment, production disruptions occur, and they tend to be hard to predict. Experienced printers work to minimize these disruptions by constantly evaluating and correcting internal production methods. Even so, the most

DATE: _____ ID# _____ JOB# _____

TIME IN: _____ CUSTOMER: _____ ☐ NEW

RANDOM PROOF _____ ADDRESS: _____

FINAL PROOF _____ CITY, STATE, ZIP _____

FILM/DISK _____ PHONE# ( ) _____ CONTACT _____

SALES _____ FAX# ( ) _____

PRODUCTION _____ P.O.# _____ OPEN ACCOUNT ☐ _____ ☐ COD

JOB DESCRIPTION: | **SHIP TO:** ☐ CUSTOMER ☐ OTHER

FINAL FILM:

☐ NEGATIVES ↓ ↑
☐ POSITIVES ↓ ↑
☐ LINE SCREEN _____ ☐ STRIPPING TINTS _____
☐ DUPE FILM
☐ MASTER FILMS TO FILE
☐ FILM W/PROOF
☐ RANDOM ONLY

RANDOMS OK'D BY ☐ CUSTOMER ☐ SALES ☐ SHOP
VARNISH ☐ OA ☐ SPOT ☐ OTHER
DIE VINYL ☐ CUSTOMER SUPPLIED
          ☐ ASG BUILD/SUBMIT FOR APPROVAL

NO. OF PAGES _____
NO. OF VERSIONS _____ BREIF DEC: _____
NO. OF COLORS: FRONT _____ BACK _____
☐ SCREEN TO PMS COLORS ____ ____ ____ ____
TRIM SIZE _____
TRIM SIZE _____
TRIM SIZE _____
TRIM SIZE _____
BLEED SIZE _____
FOLDED SIZE _____
OTHER _____
ARCHIVE ☐ YES ☐ NO   **MB** _____

CUSTOMER SUPPLIED:

35mm:_____	REF:_____	FLOPPY:_____
2x2:_____	B/W:_____	44MB:_____
4x5:_____	LINE ART:_____	88MB:_____
5x7:_____	KEYLINE:_____	OPTICAL:_____
8x10:_____	DUMMY:_____	CD ROM:_____

REQUESTS: ☐ MATCH TX ☐ MATCH SAMPLE ☐ PLEASING

CONFERENCE
☐ STRIP PER LAYOUT ☐ BOARD ☐ OTHER

PROOFING:

☐ WATERPROOF ☐ MATCHPRINT ☐ DIGITAL PROOF
☐ COLORTRAX ☐ OTHER _____

SPECIAL STOCK PROVIDED ☐ YES ☐ NO

☐ COMMERCIAL ☐ PUBLICATION ☐ SPECIAL
TONERS: PMS _____ PMS _____ PMS _____ PMS _____
COLOR ROTATION:____ ____ ____ ____ ____
☐ COLORKEY/CROMACHECK
☐ BRITELITE

_____ **PAPER PRINTS** ☐ BACKED-UP ☐ FLAT
                      ☐ HEAD TO HEAD ☐ HEAD TO FOOT

VARNISH ON PROOF ☐ COLOR PROOF ☐ PAPER PROOF
DIE VINYL ON PROOF ☐ COLOR PROOF ☐ PAPER PROOF

PRESS: ☐ WEB ☐ SHEET ☐ SWOP ☐ DENSITY
          ☐ COATED ☐ UNCOATED ☐ SPECIAL

| **VOLUME #** | **PRE-FLIGHT P/U INFO:** | **INTERNAL USE ONLY:** |

ADDTIONAL INFO: | **ASG SUPPLIED DISKS:**

PRICE $: _____

Figure 5.11 Computer-generated job ticket for a prepress company. (Reproduced with permission of AGS Sherman Graphics, Chicago, Illinois.)

frequent production problems for a typical printing company are the result of poorly prepared artwork, difficulties with outside vendor products and services, and customer misunderstandings. Experienced printers know that successful production comes from controlling all predictable elements of the job and monitoring for unexpected or unplanned problems that, when discovered, are resolved quickly and correctly.

Problematic Artwork

It is not unusual for artwork to be a problem, particularly when it is supplied by the customer. Customer-supplied artwork in printing has a history of inconsistency given the general inexperience of customers in preparing the art and the casualness with which printing companies accept less-than-ideal art as finished art.

In the past few years this problem has been complicated by DTP, which allows customers to provide artwork in digital form, usually via SyQuest cartridges or floppy disks. The problem is that the customer feels the artwork is finished when he gives it to the printer, but the printer finds upon reviewing it that the electronic files are incomplete or unfinished. If these shortcomings are communicated to the customer in a negative way, it opens a Pandora's box of issues that pits the printer against the customer. Such conflict can lead to misunderstandings between the two and potentially the printer's loss of the customer's future business. In sum, DTP has provided a technological environment where customer-supplied art has become problematic.

Production Tracking

The tracking of employee operations and activities, inventory, and chargeable time during the actual production of the job allows the company to maintain accurate production standards and BHRs. As discussed in Chapters 2 and 3, the process of collecting such data, which is the first step in the job costing process, may be done manually, by EFDC, or by a DMI system. While manual data collection tends to be laborious and is largely unused, EFDC is convenient and has become widely accepted in the industry.

Production Scheduling

Scheduling production can be done manually and by computer. Even with the fairly good CAS programs that are available, the process is complex and manual scheduling boards remain popular even in large printing and publishing companies. The objective of any good scheduling system is to arrange all work-in-process into the most efficient production sequence, whereby all job requirements, critical production factors, targeted delivery dates, and quality levels are met.

At the core of the CAS system is typically a database file containing factual information on every job to be scheduled. This information resides in the computer's memory by such identifiers as job number, cost center, estimated time, estimated material cost, and so on. The information is then sorted by the type of scheduling format desired, such as "due date backward to today," "today to due date," "a given production point to due date," or "due date backward to a given production point." After this step is completed, various reports can be generated by cost center, job number, or other criteria depending on the report generation software.

Figure 5.12 is a section of a CAS printout in graphic calendar form which shows jobs sorted by calendar day and by production center. Figure 5.13 is a segment of a CAS report sorted by job number which shows all work currently scheduled for the job by cost center. To use CAS systems, they must be interactive with real-time data collection so that tracking all jobs is done as the production activities occur.

General Production Rules

There are some general production rules designed to resolve problems before they occur. The first rule is that meeting the targeted delivery date is the number one priority for the printer. Every production option, including overtime, should be exercised to meet a committed deadline. In instances where delivery schedules are compressed, the production system should be geared to expedite production. No delivery commitments should be made that cannot be reasonably kept. For most customers, timely delivery of their products is among the top three reasons they return to the printer for future graphic needs.

Second, every attempt should be made to minimize errors throughout each production step of the job. Employees should verify the accuracy of their work on a constant basis. Easy and direct communication with the customer is essential. The customer should be consulted regarding artwork changes, proof approvals, press sheets, and any other areas where differences of opinion might occur. This is particularly true when the final graphic product has changed extensively from the beginning of the job.

Third, the customer should approve changes in the job specifications before they are incorporated into the job. For example, if the paper selected is no longer available or its cost has risen substantially, the customer should choose a substitute with the printer's assistance. If a modified or different production method has been substituted that may affect the product, the printer should inform the customer of the change. The printer should be careful in making job modifications but should also have some flexibility in this regard. Good production judgment should be exercised. The best practice is to discuss and resolve any modifications that affect the final product directly with the customer.

The fourth rule deals with the complex area of AAs, which are commonly defined as changes made during production of the job that are suggested by the

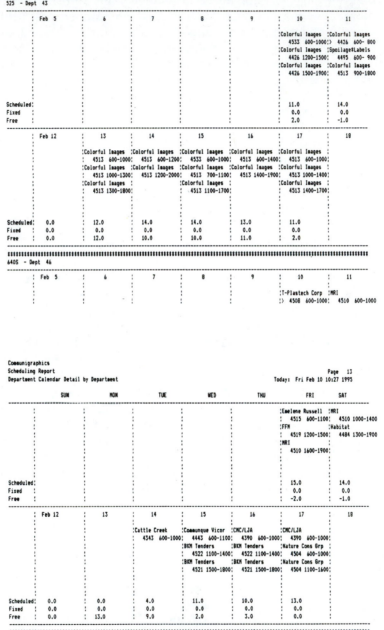

Figure 5.12 One page of a CAS printout: Department calendar details by department. (Reproduced with permission of Communigraphics, Denver, Colorado, with assistance from Logic Associates, White River Junction, Vermont.)

```
4494 Lifelines Newsletter              Cust: 29400 Design Directions
     Sman: 40 Tom Roling              Planner: 1 Dave Bascom
     Booked: 02/09/95                 Due:  03/03/95
     Planned Ship: 03/10/95           Priority:
     Quantity: 30000                  Job Status: SCHED
     Scheduling Notes:    Lifelines Newsletter
                          TRMS 0209 30m              2S
```

ST	FO	SJ	DEPT	HRS	START	END
D			10 COMMITMENT DUE IN	0.0	1000 02/09	
			Tx here 2/08			
S			21 SCANNER	2.0	1000 02/10	1200 02/10
S			27 CS PROOFING	1.0	1200 02/10	
S			28 CS PROOF OUT	0.0	1000 02/13	
			Scatter Color			
S			10 COMMITMENT DUE IN	0.0	1000 02/13	
			Disk due in 2/13			
S			29 CS PROOF IN	0.0	600 02/14	
			Scatter Color			
S		3	25 MAC	3.0	600 02/15	
			Rip and assemble original files			
S			27 CS PROOFING	1.0	1200 02/15	
			1st Page Proofs			
S			11 PROOF OUT	0.0	1000 02/16	
			1st Page Proofs			
S			12 PROOF IN	0.0	1000 02/20	
			1st Page Proofs			
S		3	25 MAC	1.0	600 02/21	
			Corrections			
S			27 CS PROOFING	0.5	1000 02/21	
			2nd Page Proofs			
S			11 PROOF OUT	0.0	1000 02/22	
			2nd Page Proofs			
S			12 PROOF IN	0.0	1000 02/24	
			2nd Page Proofs			
S		3	31 STRIPPING	4.0	600 02/25	
			Strip final film			
S		3	33 PROOFING	1.0	600 02/27	
			Production Blueline			
S		3	34 PLATEMAKING	2.0	600 02/28	
S		3	46 640S	9.0	600 03/02	1500 03/02
S		2	50 BOBST	7.0	600 03/06	1300 03/06
S		3	61 CUTTING	4.0	600 03/07	1000 03/07
S		3	62 FOLDERS	6.0	1200 03/07	
S			81 SHIPPING	4.0	1500 03/10	

```
              * * * * * * * * * * * * * * * * *

4495 ***Spoilage***Labels PO# 29378    Cust: 80001 Communi Spoilage
     Sman: 1 House Accounts           Planner: 1 Dave Bascom
     Booked: 01/25/95                 Due: 01/30/95
     Planned Ship: 01/30/95           Priority:
     Quantity: 7380                   Job Status: SCHED
     Last Work:   01/27/95 S/R-25" PLTS
     Scheduling Notes:    Labels PO# 29378
                          PMLW 0125 7.38m SS 5/0
```

ST	FO	SJ	DEPT	HRS	START	END
D			34 PLATEMAKING	1.0	600 01/28	
			1 set of plates			
S	10	10	43 525	3.0	600 02/11	900 02/11
			1 form - 24up Labels			

Figure 5.13 One page of a CAS printout: Job schedule detailed by job number. (Reproduced with permission of Communigraphics, Denver, Colorado, with assistance from Logic Associates, White River Junction, Vermont.)

customer and are therefore chargeable beyond the quoted price. There are two distinct categories of AAs: (1) job changes that are suggested by either the customer or the printer which are chargeable to the customer and are referenced in this text as chargeable author's alterations or CAAs, and (2) job changes suggested by either party which are nonchargeable to the customer and are referenced here as nonchargeable author's alterations or NAAs. Figure 5.14 is a sample form used to collect and track AAs in prepress, a production area where job changes frequently occur.

As a general industry practice, AAs are chargeable when the customer has initiated them or the printer has obtained prior permission to make them. However, two AA problems occur frequently. First, many printers waive charges on some—even many—alternations to maintain customer goodwill, to keep the customer's job within budget, or for other reasons. The problem is that printers are inconsistent as to which alterations are chargeable and which are "freebies." The second problem is that some printers make changes in customer's jobs on their own and without prior permission from the clients, such as modifying an electronic art file so that the job outputs faster or at a higher quality level. The manner used to resolve these two situations impacts whether alterations are CAAs or NAAs.

Successful printers track all AAs using EFDC or DMI and charge for AAs that are reasonable and authorized by the customer. For example, if the preflight of a customer-supplied electronic artwork file shows that a certain problem should be corrected, the customer is contacted, she gives her approval of the correction, and the correction is made as a CAA. If the printer makes a file correction that is not authorized by the customer, however, the issue becomes whether the change is chargeable or nonchargeable.

The AAs are summarized on the final invoice. Some printers invoice only CAAs, while others show all AAs and "zero out" the AAs that are not charged. It is clear that customers do not appreciate receiving invoices with CAAs that did not receive their prior authorization and frequently object to paying these extra charges. These disruptions slow payment and may require management intervention. In the extreme, and depending on the quantity and cost of the job, litigation may be initiated. Good business practice dictates that printing company management establish and implement rules as to how to approve alterations and how to handle CAAs and NAAs. Doing so provides an environment of consistency and fairness to all customers.

Additional Points Regarding Production

Two other points regarding production should be noted. First, shipping, delivery, fulfillment, and other postpress services are critical to some customers and are therefore important VA services the printer can provide. These include mailing through the United States Postal Service (USPS); streamlining delivery through

CONFIRMATION OF ALTERATIONS ☐
QUOTATION ☐

ASG

ASG SHERMAN GRAPHICS, INC.

CUSTOMER _____   AUTHORIZED _____

SUBJECT _____   RECEIVED BY _____

CUSTOMER ORDER NO. _____   LETTER   PHONE   DIRECT CONTACT

JOB NO. _____ DATE _____   _____

PAGE or REF	DESCRIPTION	

Figure 5.14 Alteration check sheet for a prepress house. (Reproduced with permission of ASG Sherman Graphics, Chicago, Illinois.)

UPS, Federal Express, and other express carriers; or arranging for alternative delivery methods. Some printers provide drop-ship services where the customer's products are counted and bundled or boxed directly after printing and finishing and are shipped from the printer to the customer. These postpress services can be complex and time consuming, but they are important VA services that cement the bond between customer and printer beyond the production of the graphic products.

Second is the area of customer storage, also known as finished goods storage. It is not unusual for customers to have limited space to store the products they have ordered. Because printers typically have access to inexpensive storage, either in their printing plants or at other sites, providing the customers with storage services for their finished goods can be a VA service the customers greatly appreciate. When printers provide finished goods storage, ownership of the job should be transferred to the customer even though the job is stored in the printer's facility. The printer, however, should maintain fire and sprinkler insurance on the finished goods. The GCBP No. 21 in Figure 5.10 covers finished goods storage to some degree.

Related to storage of finished goods is the ownership and storage of preparatory materials used to produce the printed product. Ownership issues are covered in GCBP No. 6 of Figure 5.10, which states that ownership of preparatory materials remains the exclusive property of the provider. Thus, if a printer provides full-service production of a printing order, as the provider he effectively retain rights to its film and related prepress materials. Despite this, many printers opt to return job materials to customers as a standard operating procedure. Sometimes, however, the printer has no choice because the customer's PO requires the return of these job materials.

If the printer does exert ownership and stores these materials, there is no minimum storage time limit set as trade practice. However, many printers store bulky production materials—stripped flats, plates, and mechanical artwork—for three years. The storage of magnetic media as archived files has no established length of time because little storage space is needed. When storing customer-owned materials at customer request, charging for storage is common. However, when the printer claims ownership of job materials, storage is done at the printer's expense.

5.13 Completing the Job Cost Summary

After the job is finished and is awaiting delivery, it is necessary to first review the actual time and materials data collected during the production process, then to compare these actual data to the estimated times and costs that were originally developed. This procedure, which is known as job costing, can be accomplished either manually or by computer, depending on how the data were collected and which computer tools are available to complete the process.

For example, if the company uses EFDC or DMI, data analysis can be completed entirely by computer. If the data were collected manually, it is possible to build a computer spreadsheet to analyze them. This is done by inputting the manually collected data into the spreadsheet program and then using available spreadsheet tools to complete the analysis. Spreadsheets are discussed in Chapters 2 and 3.

Job costing provides the company with feedback in the three following important areas:

1. Job costing highlights the differences between actual and estimated times and costs. The ultimate goal is to provide concrete data to modify existing production standards so that future estimating is more accurate. It can also show estimating errors.
2. Job costing shows deviations in the production of the job, including HEs and AAs that occurred during production. It allows for analysis of such problems and provides a feedback mechanism to charge for alterations and to determine the cost of HEs and the rework necessary to correct them.
3. Job costing shows job planning errors, which is valuable feedback to job planners and estimators for future jobs.

One outcome of job costing is a variance report that shows differences between actual and estimated times and costs. Although the job costing process is always completed at the conclusion of production, printers with EFDC and DMI are able to complete the process immediately after the job is finished and before the customer's invoice is generated. This allows for immediate feedback on job highlights and also allows the printer to evaluate the number and cost of AAs, which can be a significant source of lost revenue if they are not invoiced. Although it is prudent to obtain the customer's approval before an alteration is completed, sometimes alterations are done as simple matters of course and charging for them is necessary.

Figure 5.15 is a partial job costing production summary report showing estimated to actual times and costs for a sample job by a West Coast printer.

Some printers job cost only certain jobs, perhaps larger volume orders, a random selection of jobs, or only those jobs which appear to have many AAs or HEs. Regardless of whether job costing is completed before or after invoicing, the feedback relative to estimating standards is an important part of the job costing process.

5.14 Invoicing and Cash Flow

Efficient monitoring and use of money is a critical aspect of any printing company. It is essential that printing managers operate their companies on

```
Blueline per Sq In        4110     02/02    0.02/ea   1000.0    20.00

Total Direct Material                                          467.63
-----------------------------OUTSIDE PURCHASES-----------------------------


PO#:15379  Vendor#  2000  Kirk Paper Co., Inc. Ordered: 02/02/95
Item#    Qty     PO Item# Description                   Date      Cost
  1      3500 100# magno dl bk 17 1/2 x 22 1/2         02/09    209.16

PO#:15685  Vendor#  2554  Prepress Assembly    Ordered: 02/17/95
Item#    Qty     PO Item# Description                   Date      Cost
  1        1 halftones                                 02/17     30.00
Total Outside Purchases                                         239.16


--------------------------PRODUCTION SUMMARY--------------------------
                 Est   Act                 %
                 Hrs   Hrs   Est$  Act$  Var   AA$   OT$  Total$
Elec. Pre-Press  0.8   0.9    66    74   -13               74
Stripping        0.0   2.4         194                    194
Proofing         1.1   0.9    58    47    20               47
Platemaking      2.4   1.7   131    93    29               93
6/25 MR          3.5   4.1   830   984   -18              984
6/25 Run         1.2   1.5   281   367   -31              367
6/25 WU          1.3   0.3   300    72    76               72
Pressroom Feeder 0.0   0.5                                  0
Cutting          0.9   0.3    57    22    62               22
Folding          0.8   1.2    50    78   -55               78
```

```
Watermark Press Ltd.
 33188  ^Multiprotocal Inter:(Part#:A1        (continued)        page 3

--------------------------PRODUCTION SUMMARY--------------------------
                 Est   Act                 %
                 Hrs   Hrs   Est$  Act$  Var   AA$   OT$  Total$
Shipping/Receiving 0.2  0.3   10    17   -73               17
Total Labor      11.9  14.0  1783  1947   -9             1947

Outside Purchases 0.0   0.0         310                   310
Film / Proofing   0.0   0.0     7    24  -235              24
Plates            0.0   0.0    60   133  -122             133
Ink               0.0   0.0   184         100               0
Paper             0.0   0.0   244   239     2             239
Bindery/Shipping  0.0   0.0     8         100               0
Total Material    0.0   0.0   503   707   -41             707

TOTAL COST       11.9  14.0  2286  2654   -16            2654
```

Figure 5.15 Computer job cost production summary. (Reproduced with permission of Watermark Press, San Francisco, California, with assistance from Logic Associates, White River Junction, Vermont.)

sound financial bases to ensure stability and company survival over the long term.

Cash Flow Sequence

An important ingredient in the operation of any printing business is the manner by which money moves through the company. In elementary form, this sequence of cash flow events follows a circular pattern (Figure 5.16). It begins with cash-on-hand in the business (left side of figure). This cash is used to meet all out-of-pocket and fixed prepress expenses included in the preparation of the customer's printing order. In the next production step, press and bindery operations, additional variable costs such as labor and paper expenses, are incurred (top of figure). At this point, the cash outlay represents the total manufacturing cost for the job (right of figure). After the work is delivered, the customer is invoiced for payment, and the bill represents an account receivable to the printing company or an account payable by the customer (bottom of

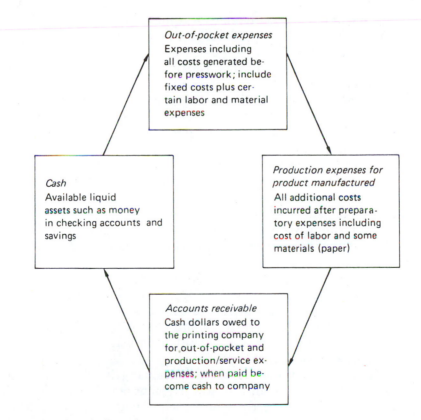

Figure 5.16 Diagram of cash flow for a printing company

figure). Once the customer pays this bill, usually by check, the cash cycle starts anew. The pattern is one of repetition.

The ideal situation is for the company to have enough money to meet all of its financial obligations, including anticipated growth, yet not have too much cash tied up in noninterest accounts like checking accounts where the money provides no financial return. In any given time period, the total cash received should be greater than the total disbursements. For example, if total cash received in the month of March was $100,000, and the disbursements (the total of all incurred expenses) for the same month totaled $110,000, the company would have to borrow or obtain from some other source an additional $10,000 to meet all of its March commitments. The cost of borrowing money can be high and is not usually a desirable solution for most businesses. Consistent borrowing inevitably leads to greater indebtedness and will, in the long term, force bankruptcy or liquidation of the business.

Accounts Receivable Collection Period

One major problem with many printing companies is that their cash flows are limited. Two key reasons contribute to this situation. First, printers do not bill quickly enough after their jobs are completed. Second, customers do not pay their bills in a timely manner, which is once the invoice is received.

For example, the average accounts receivable collection period (ARCP) in printing—the amount of time in days it takes from the date of invoice to the date of payment—is approximately fifty days, which is far too long. Slow billing practices help increase the lengthy receivable time. For example, if a company bills at the end of each month for all jobs, jobs delivered early in the month are given as much as four weeks' credit. The customer, upon receiving the bill, probably does not pay it immediately but may wait thirty or even sixty days before paying. The net result is that the customer is using the printed goods, which are paid for with the printer's capital, for perhaps two months or more without compensating the printer. This is the equivalent of the printer loaning the customer the money for the job, then waiting for the customer to pay off the loan.

On the accounts payable side, printers tend to pay their bills fairly quickly, usually within a one-month period. Typically credit requirements for graphic arts suppliers and paper retailers are tight, which means that the materials used for jobs must be paid for by the printers fairly quickly, usually within thirty days. In addition, the cost of labor for plant personnel must be paid a very short time after completion of work.

The net effect is that the printing company finances the customer's business through the loose credit and slow payment practices it allows the customer to use. At the same time, the printer incurs an unfavorable cash position by being forced to meet her own account payable obligations quickly. The net effect of this squeeze between accounts payable and accounts receivable can be devastating on the company.

Effective Cash Flow

The flow of cash is a very important aspect of the printing business for reasons already discussed. It is a matter with which the top management of the company must deal carefully and effectively.

The key to effective cash flow is twofold. First, the customer should be invoiced as soon as possible after delivery of the printed goods. One working day or sooner is recommended; on the day the job is shipped is ideal. Thus, the customer receives the goods and immediately thereafter the invoice, after which he has thirty days to make payment. Discounting for early payment, such as "2% net 10 days," which means the customer enjoys a 2 percent discount if the bill is paid within ten days, is sometimes used by the printers but has not proven to inspire quicker payment on the whole. Charging interest on the unpaid balance after thirty days also does not speed payment to any significant degree. Although these techniques may work sometimes, both receive varied reaction on the part of printing management and customers alike.

Besides cash discounting and adding interest charges to the customer's unpaid balance, the split invoice technique is used by the company to improve the cash situation of the business. Basically, the split invoice technique requires customers to pay a certain deposit against the quoted price of the job prior to any work being done on the order. The deposit can vary from 10 percent to full payment. Fifty percent is the most popular amount. This procedure allows the printers to pay some of their out-of-pocket costs of the work with the customers' money and to not tie up their own cash. Once the jobs are printed and delivered, the customers are invoiced immediately for the remaining amounts due, which they are obligated to pay within thirty days.

The split invoice technique is effective because it commits the customers to their work before any production is completed, reduces the final payment by the customers, and allows the printers to use less of their own capital in the production of the customers' orders. A problem with the split invoice technique is that given the intensely competitive nature of printing and the many printing companies vying for the customers' orders, sometimes customers take their printing work elsewhere when asked for deposits on their jobs. However, the split invoice technique can be implemented with certain types of customers and can be helpful when the company desires an improved cash position.

A second key to effective cash flow is for the printer to establish some type of cash forecasting system. Using such a procedure to project income and disbursements for a six-month or one-year period based on forecasted sales and anticipated collections of receivables is a good planning strategy. In effect, the printer can "road map" cash movement through the business for the selected time period, predicting months where excess cash will exist and other months where the cash balance will be unfavorable. Cash forecasting is desirable for printing firms wishing to tighten or define income and disbursement patterns or to project available excess cash for investment or other purposes.

Chapter 6

Estimating Paper

6.1   Introduction

6.2   Conventional Paper Manufacture and Terminology

Pulp Classifications

Cellulose Fiber Types and Fiber
   Length

Refining Paper

Papermaking

Paper Surfaces

Paper Grain

Paper Thickness

Sheeting and Wrapping Paper

Paper Supply and Demand

**6.3   Emerging Paper Products, Recycled Papers, and
Substitute Printing Substrates**

The Recycling Process

Synthetic Substrates

6.4   Printing Paper Classifications

Business Papers

Book Papers

Cover Papers

Paperboards

Miscellaneous

6.5   Printing Paper Sizes and Weights

Basic Size of Paper
Basis Weight of Paper
Standard Sizes of Paper

M Weight (1,000 Sheet Weight) of
  Paper
Comparative Weight of Paper
Bulk of Paper

6.6   Paper Metrication

Metric Paper Sizes (ISO Standards)

Metric Paper Weights

6.7   Ordering Paper for Sheetfed Printing Production

The Specified Form

Paper Catalogs and Paper Prices

6.8   Paper Planning for Sheetfed Production

Paper Sheet Sizes and Terms
Regular Paper Cutting

Stagger Cutting
Paper Waste from Cutting

6.9   Bookwork Impositions

Sheetwise Imposition Techniques
Side and Saddle-Stitching Procedures

Work-and-Turn Imposition Techniques

6.10   Press Spoilage for Sheetfed Production

Sheetfed Press Spoilage Data

6.1 Introduction

Paper is the most used material in the printing industry. Based on trends of PIA ratio studies over the past twenty-five years, paper accounts for between 20 percent and 30 percent of the cost of the average printing order. Because of paper's obvious importance, the estimator must thoroughly understand how to classify, order, and cost this material.

6.2 Conventional Paper Manufacture and Terminology

Paper is a thin mat of cellulose fibers, or a mat made of fibers from cotton, wood, or other vegetables. The principal machine used in paper manufacturing is called a Fourdrinier machine, named after the Fourdrinier brothers who held its patent. Papermaking generally involves converting logs or other fibrous substances into a watery pulp known as slurry, which is then placed on the revolving wire screen of the Fourdrinier machine. After the water is drained from the slurry, the remaining mat of overlapping fibers moves through a series of rollers on the machine that squeeze it dry and evaporate excess water.

Pulp Classifications

There are four classes of pulp in conventional papermaking: (1) groundwood, (2) old paper, (3) rag, and (4) chemical.

Groundwood pulp, which is normally used for newsprint, is produced by first grinding debarked logs into particle form, then refining the particles in water and pouring the solution onto the revolving Fourdrinier screen. Substances such as lignin and resins, which are considered impurities, are not removed in the process. Groundwood pulp is not strong and is usually quite inexpensive.

The second type of pulp is called old paper pulp and is made from old, previously manufactured paper. The paper can be unprinted, which is called either reclaimed paper or "broke" by paper manufacturers, and is preferred if available, but printed paper (postconsumer paper), which is called recycled paper, is used in greater quantity because it is more readily available. Normally, old paper is dissolved in a lye bath to be deinked and is then bleached for whiteness. Because of the popularity of recycled paper, it is discussed in more detail later in this chapter.

The third type of pulp is obtained from cotton and linen rags and is known as rag pulp. Sometimes nylon or rayon rags are also used. For the most part, unused white rags are preferred, especially in the production of rag-content papers. This type of paper stock is permanent and is popular for letterheads and legal documents that must last for many years. Pulp content varies from 25 percent to 100 percent. Paper with a pulp content of 25 percent has one-quarter rag content and three-fourths wood fiber, while paper with a rag content of 100 percent has no wood fiber content.

The last type of pulp, the one that is used for the majority of paper products, is chemical. There are several types of chemical pulps based on the kinds of wood and chemicals used. Basically, however, the chemical process begins with the arrival of cut logs at the mill yard. A debarking procedure is used initially, after which the barkless logs are chipped into small pieces. The chips are then transported to a large pressure-cooker tank, called a digester, where they are mixed with various chemicals such as lime, sulfurous acid, and caustic soda. Over a period of four or five hours the wood chips are "cooked" apart, which removes their lignin and resins and leaves their cellulose fibers. Following cooking, the fibers are washed to remove as much of the chemicals as possible and are then bleached if printing papers are being made. Both hardwoods and softwoods are used for making chemical pulp.

Cellulose Fibers Types and Fiber Length

The kind of wood that is used and the length of fiber contribute to the kind and type of paper that is manufactured. Softwoods, such as fir, pine, and spruce, provide the basic strength and durability for paper and are a major ingredient in most papers used for printing (as distinguished from papers that have industrial applications). Hardwoods, such as poplar, beech, and aspen, are also added to printing paper and serve to increase bulk and improve surface uniformity. The proper mix of softwoods and hardwoods is determined by the type of paper that is desired.

Fiber length is related to paper strength. Generally, the hardwoods have the shortest fibers (one to three millimeters), which contribute only slightly to strength. Softwood fibers are longer (one to eight millimeters) and usually provide the major strength component of papers used for printing. If cotton content is desired, which is accomplished by adding cotton fibers, the strength and durability of the stock that is produced, such as a rag-content bond, are significantly increased. Cotton fibers may be as long as thirty millimeters. Fiber length can be shortened prior to papermaking by using special machines that chop the fibers as the slurry passes through them.

Most papers used for printing have largely softwood compositions with added amounts of hardwood for improved printability. Different applications of paper require different strengths, so the fiber length of paper varies with respect to the end use of the paper product.

Refining Paper

All conventional pulps go through a refining stage prior to being made into paper. The refining technique is known as beating and is a very important step in pulp preparation. The pulp is put into a large tub with water and other ingredients, and the fibers are smashed against a metal or stone bed, which frays (fibrillates) and flattens the ends of the fibers so that they hold together more firmly in paper form. The type and amount of beating have a great deal to do with the character of the resultant paper, as do fiber length and the type of wood used. Additional fillers, sizing ingredients, and colorants may be added during the beating procedure. The slurry that is sent to the papermaking machine may be from two or three different beaters, each with a different type of wood and amount of beating activity. Proper slurry combinations are determined by manufacturing experience.

Papermaking

After beating the slurry is transported through a piping system to a flow box, or head box, at the beginning of the Fourdrinier papermaking machine. At this point, the mixture is distributed, or flowed, across a moving belt of wire screen mesh which allows the fibers to mat as the water drains off or is removed by vacuum. The speed of the moving belt, and the speed of the entire Fourdrinier machine, is extremely high. It can be as much as 2,000 linear feet per minute.

The width of paper that is made on the Fourdrinier ranges from four to ten feet, depending on machine design. After the paper forms on the screen belt, it moves into a long series of rollers that apply pressure and heat to squeeze the sheet smooth and compress it while evaporating residual water. The papermaking process is continuous where paper is made as one continuous ribbon. At the dry end of the Fourdrinier, the web or roll of paper stock is wound tightly to form a log of paper. Here, also, it is sometimes slit into narrower roll widths for immediate wrapping and shipping to web printing plants.

Additives. Sizing compounds are added to paper to provide resistance to rapid moisture penetration. Internal sizing materials for the paper stock, which are added to the slurry, are called engine or beater sizing compounds. If sizing compounds are added to the surface of the sheet after formation, the process is called external or surface sizing. Papers such as blotter and newsprint are poorly sized; they accept ink, but the ink spreads quickly. Papers for writing purposes are normally sized using both internal and external processes. Rosin is the most common chemical used for sizing, but modern technology has provided other sizing ingredients as substitutes.

Fillers are added to the slurry prior to papermaking normally to increase the opacity of the paper. Sometimes called loaders, fillers may be clay, calcium carbonate, talc, or titanium dioxide and generally constitute between 8 percent and 15 percent of the weight of uncoated offset book paper.

Coloring materials, or colorants, which may be mineral pigments or organic or synthetic dyes, are used to color many kinds of printing papers. Most pigments are added during the mixing process when the paper is in slurry form. Dyes are applied after the paper has been formed and sized. For whiteness, titanium dioxide is a common additive, although calcium carbonate, which is less expensive, is also used.

The use of calcium carbonate has shifted the pH of some printing papers from acid to alkaline, which has caused various lithographic printing and ink drying problems but benefits otherwise. The advantages of alkaline papers include less discoloration or yellowing with age, reduced whitening cost, a more environmentally friendly sheet (in contrast titanium dioxide is a metallic additive), and an overall lower manufacturing cost.

Additional special additives are also manufactured into paper for special considerations. Bleaches are added to increase brightness and vegetable starches are used to bind the fibers and increase surface smoothness. Resins may be added to increase the wet strength of lithographic printing papers.

Watermarks and Textures. Watermark images are put into the paper when it is wet. Immediately after the sheet is formed on the wire belt, a dandy roll riding on top of the screen impresses an image on the wet paper mat. This procedure causes the fibers to press tightly together and form a visible, translucent image that is evident when a sheet of watermarked paper is held up to the light.

The dandy roll is also used to manufacture "laid" and "wove" papers in a procedure very much like the watermark technique. Additional surface textures, such as linen, leather, and pebble-grain finishes, are produced using rotary embossing techniques after the paper is formed and dry.

Paper Surfaces

There are different types of paper surfaces that affect the visual quality of paper, the printability of the material, and the cost of paper. The following discussion covers these areas.

Coated and Uncoated Papers. Uncoated paper stock is paper as it is produced during the papermaking process. Coated paper has received a fine layer of mineral substance on its surface. Coatings may consist of clays, barium sulfate, calcium carbonate, or titanium dioxide clay, which is the most common. Coatings may be applied by blades, rollers, or by passing the web of paper through a vat of solution. Paper can be coated one side (C1S) or coated two sides (C2S). Coating may be done "on the machine" during initial manufacture or "off the machine" during a later stage of production.

Coated stocks represent the smoothest possible surfaces for the printing of halftones and process color images. Sometimes the coating is polished to impart an even shinier surface with greater reflectivity. Papers used for textbooks are usually dull to minimize glare and reflection of light. Papers used for other purposes may be glossy or enameled to provide increased light reflectance. Sometimes the term "enamel" is used when discussing either dull-coated or glossy-coated stocks.

Calendered Papers. Calendering is polishing the paper surface without adding chemicals or coatings to the paper. The result is a smooth surface without the expense of additional coating procedures. Calendered papers, with their smooth surfaces, minimize lithographic printing problems and give uniform bases for printing inks.

Calendering may be done on the machine or off the machine, just as with coated stocks. Paper that receives a normal, on-the-machine amount of calendering is called machine finished stock (sometimes abbreviated MF). Extremely smooth paper surfaces, such as supercalendered papers that are calendered by running the web of paper through a series of calendering stacks, are possible with off-the-machine calendering. In this process, brisk buffing action is provided to the paper with cotton and steel rollers. Sometimes paper that has been sized is highly calendered also to produce a very smooth sheet surface called sized and supercalendered (S&SC). In addition, some types of coated papers are calendered after coating, which provides a very polished, highly reflective surface with excellent printability. Other kinds of coated papers, such as antique papers, receive no calendering during manufacture.

Many printers refer to book papers, which are also commonly termed "offset" or "opaque" papers, and business papers by number, such as a "No. 1 offset (book)" or "No. 3 sulfite." The numbering system is an index of the overall quality of the paper relative to its ingredients and its amount of finish given during manufacturing. Better papers have lower numbers, while higher numbers represent less expensive stocks. The range for book papers is from No. 1 highly calendered, finely made book stock to No. 5, which is groundwood paper with limited calendering. The same numbering system is used to identify coated book stocks and bond papers, even though ingredients and finishing processes vary with these papers.

Paper Grain

As the screen belt on the Fourdrinier moves, the fibers tend to align in the direction of the movement. This tendency causes what is known as grain, which as noted in Figure 6.1 is the alignment of fibers in a common direction in a sheet of paper.

Paper grain has important production considerations. First, paper is stiffer in the direction of its grain. Thus, when paper must be folded in half against its grain (e.g., when the direction of the grain is parallel to the fold of the sheet), the paper cracks along that fold instead of folding sharply. However, when completing multiple folds in paper, perforation and scoring are sometimes used

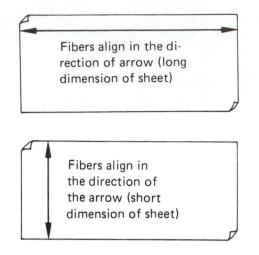

Figure 6.1 Examples of fiber direction in long- and short-grain papers

to ensure sharp folds against the grain. Second, paper tends to swell and shrink from humidity, and such changes are greater across the grain than in the direction of the grain. These problems can be significant when precise registration of images using the lithographic printing process is necessary. Third, paper tears more easily with the grain than against it. Fourth, papers used for lithographic production should, when possible, have their grains parallel to the axis of the printing cylinder. This is because lithographic dampening solution causes the paper to swell much more against the grain than in the direction the grain travels. The following five tests are methods by which the grain of paper can be easily determined:

Resistance Test. In heavier weights of paper, grain direction can be determined by curling the sheet in each direction and feeling the relative resistance to the curl. The curl with less resistance is the direction of the grain.

Fold Test. With all weights of paper, grain direction can be determined by folding the sheet in each direction. Paper folds easier, straighter, and with less cracking and buckling parallel to the grain.

Tear Test. Grain direction can be quickly determined by tearing the sheet in each direction. Paper tears straighter in the direction of the grain.

Moisture Test. Grain direction can easily be determined by moistening a piece of paper either with the tongue or a convenient water source. Paper curls parallel to the direction of the grain. This test is good for lighter weight papers.

Stiffness Test. Tear two 1 inch x 5 inch strips from opposite directions in a sheet of paper. Place the two strips together and hold them flat on one end between the thumb and forefinger. Observe that one strip sticks out almost straight while the other strip tends to droop and curl. Grain direction is long with the strip that tends to stick out and short with the one that droops.

Paper Thickness

Paper thickness is determined by the amount of fiber deposited on the moving screen belt during papermaking. Modern papers used for printing have fairly uniform thicknesses. That is, if a sheet of paper measures 0.002 inch thick, it is very close to 0.002 inch thick throughout the sheet. The thickness of paper is also referred to as the caliper.

While most printing papers measure between 0.001 inch and 0.008 inch in caliper, cardboards are traditionally measured in plies. Cardboards are used for point-of-purchase displays and in instances where very stiff paperboard is required. Use the following formula to convert ply thickness to caliper thickness:

caliper thickness = (number of plies x 0.003 in./ply) + 0.006 in.

Thus, a sheet of 6-ply board is 0.024 inch thick:

(6 plies x 0.003 in./ply) + 0.006 in. = 0.024 in.

Sometimes points are used in with such measurements. A point is the equivalent of 0.001 inch. Thus, 24-point board is 0.024 inch thick (24 points x 0.001 in).

Sheeting and Wrapping Paper

Once the paper has been completely manufactured, it moves to the sheeting area if it is going to be converted into sheets. Here, large sheeters, which feed as many as twenty rolls at one time, cut the web stock into exact sheet dimensions. Because many of the webs have already been slit to desired widths during papermaking, sheeting may determine only the length of the paper. Because sheeting is an additional manufacturing step, sheeted papers are more expensive than web stocks.

The final operation at the mill for both sheet and web paper is the wrapping and shipping of the paper products. Sheeted papers may be packaged in small amounts and then placed in cartons, or they may be cartoned without any separate packaging. Web papers are typically wrapped with kraft paper to protect the roll, although some web stocks are shipped without outside wrap. Sheeted stock ordered in larger quantities is usually placed on skids or pallets, which are typically wooden or metal bases upon which the paper is carefully stacked. Skids require paper-handling equipment in the printing plant, but they are a convenient method for shipping large quantities of paper in sheet form.

The final wrapping of skids and rolls and the cartoning of paper can be important, depending on the type of paper and the printing process that will be used. For fine printing papers to be printed by offset lithography, an airtight package is desired to maintain the proper moisture relationship of the paper to the outside during shipping to the warehouse and ultimately to the printing plant. If moisture content is not controlled, production problems may result during lithographic printing. The modern paper mill uses mechanized wrapping equipment with vacuum closure and excellent sealing compounds. Once paper is cartoned or wrapped, it is shipped by railroad or truck to the paper wholesaler, who in turn sells it to the printer.

Paper Supply and Demand

Paper is the most essential commodity to a printer, but over the long term it is becoming increasingly difficult to obtain. At various times in the 1970s and 1980s the demand for paper outstripped production capacity at United States mills, which forced the printing industry into unfortunate shortage situations. This problem was exacerbated by the export of printing papers and pulp to foreign countries beginning in the mid-1980s. This situation was alleviated somewhat in the late 1980s with imported papers from countries in Europe and the Pacific Rim.

Paper manufacturers respond that not only is the use of paper on the rise, particularly for printing, but that an expanding economy is responsible for this greater demand. A 1991 estimate indicates that the consumption of paper in the United States reached an estimated 720 pounds per person, compared with an estimated worldwide average of slightly over 90 pounds. The apparent total annual United States paper consumption (production plus imports minus exports) reached 82 million tons in 1988.

The American Paper Institute (API), surveying data covering the period from November 1987 through November 1988, found that United States paper mills produced 4.3 percent more paper than in the same period the previous year, but were still unable to meet demand. Manufacturers say that although there are new papermaking facilities going on line, this expansion is not enough to keep up with the continually escalating demand.

History has shown that paper shortages invariably result in higher paper prices, which usually remain somewhat escalated until after the shortages are over. At the same time, paper shortages have a tendency to force printers to stockpile the major kinds of paper they frequently use, which makes the shortages even more pronounced and causes the printers to have major cash outlays for excessive inventory.

6.3   Emerging Paper Products, Recycled Papers, and Substitute Printing Substrates

One of the most important movements affecting printing papers in the 1980s and 1990s was the shift by customers and printers alike to environmentally sensitive substrates. There were also parallel movements of customers and printers to "regular recycled" and "100 percent deinked recycled" papers and to kenaf fibers as substitutes for cellulose, synthetic paper substitutes, and chlorine-free papers. The environmental issues are driven by significant public interest in improving water and air quality, as well as the growing concern that the decomposition of paper takes many years, which makes landfill disposal of once-used paper unwise over the long term. Despite the increased costs of these types of papers, the purchase of recycled papers and substitute substrates continues to grow.

Recycled paper products, which were initially driven by newsprint recycling which began in the 1960s, have been available for many years. Newsprint wastepaper is bulky to store, highly flammable, and deteriorates rapidly. Thus, waste newsprint is turned around fast and with minimum storage. Although newsprint is the major source of cellulose fiber for recycled paper, public participation in recycling other types of paper products is increasing interest in other cellulose fiber sources. However, some types of papers cannot be easily recycled due to their coatings and other chemical ingredients.

The Recycling Process

Recycling paper requires removing ink, or deinking, which is a complex technical process given the numerous chemical ingredients in both papers and inks. In general, when deinking is only partially completed, which is common, the recycled product is less white and thus requires the addition of coloration products, bleaches, or both. Given this, some recycled papers are a mix of recycled pulp and new pulp and have additives that provide color, bulk, and strength to the final product. Technology and public interest have caused movement toward the production of 100 percent recycled paper, which is generally divided into recycled papers that have additives for coloration and are chlorine bleached and "recycled and deinked" papers that contain fewer coloration chemicals but may require some bleaching.

Recycled paper manufacturing has become a successful and profitable venture for paper companies, but it requires high investment and careful technical control. When the final recycled product is a mix of a small amount of recycled pulp and a great percentage of virgin (new) cellulose fiber, manufacturing problems are minimized. As the percentage of recycled fiber increases, however, coloration, strength, printability, and other problems emerge. Consistency of recycled paper products is keenly important to printers, particularly as it relates to lithographic production and an emerging class of inks that also fits the recycling environment. Thus, when recycled paper is going to be made, there must be a careful evaluation of its type and kind of recycled pulp early in the process. The manufacturing of 100 percent recycled, deinked paper requires even greater manufacturing care and control.

One trend of producing recycled paper has been to reduce the dependence on the virgin cellulose fibers that are added to the recycled pulp, which means fewer trees are harvested and used. Parallel to this "save-a-tree movement" is the emergence of kenaf-based papers. The kenaf plant is the result of cross-breeding cotton and okra plants. It has become a popular cellulose substitute for both practical and environmental reasons: Kenaf requires no pesticides, grows to maturity in less than six months, and yields three to five times more fiber per acre per year compared to the Southern pine. When used to make uncoated paper, the kenaf fiber is less dense, which means it requires fewer and less concentrated chemicals and therefore reduces toxic pollution, and it needs less energy and less water during manufacturing. Also, the final sheet, when printed with soya inks, is completely recyclable, which means deinking is simplified and less costly.

Related to the use of recycled papers is the issue of whiteness and how such whiteness is achieved. Generally papers are whitened during manufacturing either by adding whitening ingredients or by bleaching the fibers with chlorine bleach. Although both methods are used, recent changes in the Federal Water Pollution Control Act of 1972 have forced paper manufacturers to address their bleaching methods and water pollution as it relates to paper manufacturing. The result is a resurgence of interest in low-chlorine or totally chlorine-free (TCF) papers. Reducing or removing chlorine tends to have little effect on the printing, printability, or use of these types of papers by customers. Although TCF paper costs more, it contributes to significantly less water pollution because it adds no chlorine when it is used as recycling pulp.

Synthetic Substrates

Like the interest in TCF papers, the interest in synthetic substrates, which are primarily plastic products, is also increasing. Synthetic papers offer great durability through high wear-, water-, and tear-resistances, which affects both printing and the paper's ultimate use by the customer. This high durability also extends product life, which can save in reprint costs. Synthetics include polyethylene (Teslin and Polyart) and polypropylene (Kimdura) bases, which have no grain like conventional papers. Printing on these substrates typically requires increased technical control of ink drying, pH of fountain solutions, and printability factors. Although synthetic papers tend to be expensive, if they are properly fitted to match customer needs, they may save money in the long run.

The estimating procedures used for these substrates are largely the same as those used for sheeted paper stocks. The cost basis of cellulose or kenaf fiber products is in dollars per 100 pounds (CWT) or in cost per 1,000 sheets, while the cost basis of synthetic substrates is in dollars per 100 sheets or dollars per 1,000 sheets.

6.4 Printing Paper Classifications

There are five major classifications of printing papers: business papers, book papers, cover papers, paperboards, and miscellaneous. Each category has different physical characteristics that are designed to accommodate the types of products for which they are made. As shown in Figure 6.2, each major class has subgroups that relate to its specific end-use requirements.

It should be understood that whenever possible the paper sales representative aids the estimator or estimating trainee in understanding the paper to be purchased for any given order. Of course, the more the estimators work with the various categories of paper, the more familiar they become with the lesser-known differences between seemingly comparable paper stocks.

Business Papers

This classification includes bond, ledger, thin, mimeographic, and safety papers. All have a basic size of 17 inches x 22 inches, although substance numbers, which are also known as basis weights, vary with each classification of stock (see Figure 6.2). Business papers are subdivided into the following categories.

Bond. Bond papers are also called "sulfite bonds" or "sulfites" because they are manufactured using the sulfite chemical process. As a general rule, sulfite bonds are numbered with respect to their grade values. Sulfite Number 1, the top and most expensive grade, is readily recognized because it always bears a watermark. It is sized for excellent printing and writing qualities. Sulfite Numbers 2 and 3 are less expensive and of lesser quality. They are not watermarked and are normally not manufactured today. Numbers 4 and 5 sulfites are even less expensive and of commensurate quality, but they are suitable for many printing jobs, especially direct mail and other throwaway materials. The range of substance numbers for the business papers shown in Figure 6.2 applies to all sulfite bond levels.

Premium grade bond stocks are usually made with 25 percent, 50 percent, 75 percent, or 100 percent cotton fiber. Any remaining percentages are cellulose fiber. Thus, using this system, a 50 percent rag bond is 50 percent cotton fiber and 50 percent cellulose fiber; a 25 percent rag content paper is 25 percent cotton fiber and 75 percent cellulose fiber. The greater the cotton content, the more expensive the stock. Therefore, 100 percent cotton fiber stock is the most

Stock classifications	Basic size (in.)	Basis weight (lb.)
Business papers	17 × 22	
Bond		13, 16, 20, 24
Ledger		24, 28, 32, 26
Thin (manifold and onionskin)		7, 8, 9, 11, 12
Xerographic and Mimeographic		16, 20, 24
Safety		
Book papers	25 × 38	
Uncoated		40, 45, 50, 55, 60, 65, 70, 75, 80, 100
Coated		40, 45, 50, 55, 60, 65, 70, 75, 80, 100
Text		40, 45, 50, 55, 60, 65, 70, 75, 80, 100
Cover papers	20 × 26	60, 65, 80, and 100 are common
Paperboards		
Index bristol	25 1/2 × 30 1/2	90 and 110 are common
Tagboard	24 × 36	100, 125, 150, 175, 200
Blanks	22 × 28	2-ply to 6-ply
Printing bristol	22 1/2 × 28 1/2	75, 90, and 110 are common
Wedding bristol	22 1/2 × 28 1/2	75, 90, 100, and 110
Miscellaneous		
Blotter	19 × 24	100, 120
Label	25 × 38	60, 80
Newsprint	24 × 36	28, 30, 32, 36

Figure 6.2 Printing paper classifications, basic sizes, and basis weights

expensive. Usually, rag-content papers are used when permanence is desired, such as with letters, legal documents, and map products.

All grades of bonds have generally good writing properties; fair to excellent strength depending on the amount of cotton, sizing, and the cellulose fiber length; are sized to ensure good printability by offset or letterpress processes; and are available in a wide array of colors. Bond stock is used in large quantities for business forms printed by letterpress, lithographic web, and flexography. Bond papers may be purchased in either sheet or web form from the paper merchant.

Ledger. Ledger papers are available in both sulfite and rag-content types. Ledger stocks are strong and durable and are sized during manufacture to have excellent writing characteristics. Such papers are used for accounting and similar record-keeping functions. Ledgers are available in many varieties conforming to machine tabulations and computer processing.

Thin. Thin business papers may either be manifold, which is the sulfite grade, or onionskin, which is the cotton content body. Some thin papers are manufactured with thicker bulks yet maintain the same low-substance weights. Thin papers include substance 12, which is sometimes considered a bond paper. Owing to significant increases in mailing costs in recent years, perhaps the major use of thin papers is for direct mail. They are also popular as second sheets, which are the second copies or file copies of typed letters. Thin papers are used when weight or storage is an element in the product application.

Xerographic and Mimeographic. Xerographic paper is made specifically for use with copying machines that require high temperature fusing of carbon toner through a heat transfer process. Mimeographic paper is made specifically for use with mimeographic machines. The mimeographic process involves "cutting" a paper master through which ink is forced when the master is placed on the mimeographic machine.

Because the printing techniques used with each process are completely different, paper is manufactured for each process with different sizing compounds, fillers, and moisture-retaining ingredients. When purchasing either mimeographic or xerographic paper, be certain the correct stock is ordered. If the type of paper is switched, copies will appear poorly printed.

Both xerographic and mimeographic papers are commonly purchased as "cut papers," which are typically 8 1/2 inch x 11 inch letter size, 8 1/2 inch x 14 inch legal size, and 11 inch x 17 inch tabloid size. Most paper catalogs have a section labeled "cut paper" or "cut stock" where these papers are usually found.

Safety. Safety paper is manufactured with an impregnated background pattern and is generally used for documents involving financial exchange, such as checks and letters of credit. The reason for the name "safety" is that once the paper has been written on with ink, it is impossible to modify the document without removing the background pattern.

Book Papers

Book paper is used in the production of literally thousands of products: books, magazines, periodicals, trade journals, calendars, annual reports, advertising pieces, and labels, to mention only a few. It is commonly termed "offset" or "opaque" paper as well as being known formally as "book stock." Book paper is manufactured in the three following grade classifications:

1. Uncoated (or plain) book paper, which is very popular for less expensive books, textbooks, and other products.
2. Coated book paper, which is usually used when high-quality reproduction is desired, as in the printing of process color images.
3. Text papers, which are used in the production of books and other products when colored, special-finish paper is desired. Text papers generally have deckled (ragged) edges, are available in many fancy colors (including fluorescents), and have definite surface textures.

Cover Papers

Cover stocks are thicker papers designed to be used as wraps for many types of books and other published materials. The advent of perfect binding for paperback books, telephone directories, and many other products has heightened the use of cover papers in book manufacturing. Cover papers generally have excellent printability, may be coated or uncoated, and are typically available in colors and with surface characteristics matching those of the text paper (book) category.

Paperboards

There are five major divisions of paperboard stock, each with a number of different basic sizes (see Figure 6.2). All board stocks have high bulk and are used in the production of thousands of packaging products, as well as posters, announcements, point-of-purchase displays, and many other printed products. Index bristol is perhaps the largest single seller in this category and is used in the manufacture of index cards, business cards, and other similar products. Tagboard, another paperboard classification, is a generally inexpensive stock used in the making of tags and other products where strength is important. Blanks, which may be purchased C1S or C2S, are used in the production of many types of displays; they are exceptionally thick and strong and print well when coated. Printing bristols are sulfite board stocks used for less expensive board items, such as business cards. Wedding bristol is a rag-content paperboard stock used for wedding invitations and other announcements of important events.

Miscellaneous

The miscellaneous category includes three major types of paper. The first, blotter paper, is not used much today because of the popularity of ballpoint pens. However, blotter is still used in the production of checkbook backs and desk pads. Label paper, the second type of miscellaneous paper, is somewhat similar to uncoated book paper and is used in the production of many types of food canning labels and other label products. Perhaps the largest seller in the miscellaneous category is newsprint, which is used as the substrate for newspapers, paperback books, and many other less expensive published products. The majority of newsprint today is sold in web or roll form and is printed using rotary letterpress or web offset lithographic equipment. Sheet newsprint is not used to any great extent in the printing and publishing industry today.

Most paper merchants provide the printing plant with sample swatches and books to aid the sales representatives, estimators, and customers in making paper selections. These samples allow the customer and sales representative to discuss the different types of paper available for the job under consideration. The estimator also uses them to verify the stock selections made. Sample books are supplied to the printing company for free because they essentially stimulate sales of the paper merchant's products.

6.5   Printing Paper Sizes and Weights

The following information must be understood by the printing estimator or estimating trainee to effectively estimate paper. It should be noted that the size-and-weight system used for printing papers can be confusing to the novice. Careful attention should be given to learn as much as possible about the sizes and weights of papers. Although the metrication of printing papers may someday become a reality, for the present it appears that the system described here will prevail in the United States.

Basic Size of Paper

"Basic size" refers to the established size (in inches) of paper stock upon which the basis weight of the stock is calculated. (See the next section for the definition of "basis weight.") The basic size of most paper stocks is also recognized by buyers and sellers as the one size that has common use requirements.

For example, the basic size of business paper (Figure 6.2, middle column) is 17 inches x 22 inches. As Figure 6.3 shows, both an 8 1/2 inch x 11 inch letterhead and a 7 1/4 inch x 8 1/2 inch invoice can be cut efficiently from the basic size business sheet. As another example, consider the basic size of book paper, which is 25 inches x 38 inches (Figure 6.2, middle column). When producing books, a very common standard page size before final trimming and finishing is 6 1/4 inches x 9 1/2 inches. (This size provides for a 1/4 inch trim on three sides of the book.) When 6 1/4 inches x 9 1/2 inches is divided into the 25 inch x 38 inch basic book paper size (Figure 6.4), sixteen pages can be positioned on one side of the press sheet.

As shown in Figure 6.2, the classifications of cardboard and miscellaneous paper each have different types of stock with different basic sizes. However, the classifications of business, book, and cover papers each have one basic size that covers all types of paper offered in those categories. Because there are so few

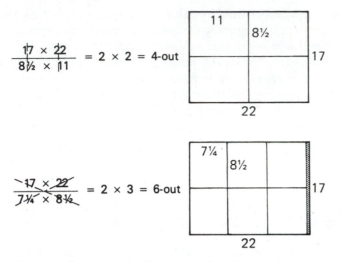

$$\frac{17 \times 22}{8\frac{1}{2} \times 11} = 2 \times 2 = \text{4-out}$$

$$\frac{17 \times 22}{7\frac{1}{4} \times 8\frac{1}{2}} = 2 \times 3 = \text{6-out}$$

Figure 6.3 Cutting diagrams for basic size bond measuring 17 inches x 22 inches

basic sizes and because the estimator works with them frequently, it is best for students and trainees to memorize them.

Basis Weight of Paper

By definition, the basic size of paper serves as the one size upon which basis weight is calculated. Basis weight, or substance weight, is defined as the weight of 500 sheets (one ream) of the basic size of a particular classification of paper. Figure 6.2 lists typical basis weights in its right-hand column. These weights

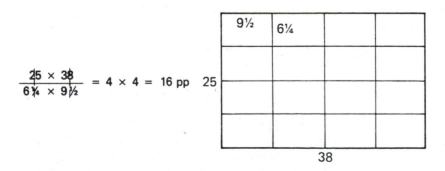

$$\frac{25 \times 38}{6\frac{1}{4} \times 9\frac{1}{2}} = 4 \times 4 = \text{16 pp}$$

Figure 6.4 Imposition diagram for basic size book paper measuring 25 inches x 38 inches

are the most common, but other, less typical weights are also available. It should be noted that basis or substance weight is not directly related to paper thickness. Basis weight, substance weight, and poundage or pounds all mean the same thing—the scale weight of 500 sheets of a particular type of paper in its basic size. Common industry terminology is to use the term "basis," "substance," or "pound" as the full word or in an abbreviated version; the addition of the word "weight" is optional as well. For example, book paper is frequently discussed as "substance 50," "sub 50," "basis 50," or "50 pound." It can also be referenced as "sub weight 50" or "basis weight 50."

Figure 6.2 indicates four basis weights for bond paper with a basic size of 17 inches x 22 inches: substance 13, substance 16, substance 20, and substance 24. Therefore, applying the basis weight definition, 500 sheets of 17 inch x 22 inch bond paper (basic size) of substances 13, 16, 20, and 24 have scale weights of 13, 16, 20, and 24 pounds respectively. Thus, if 500 sheets of substance 20 (sub 20) bond paper were purchased in the 17 inch x 22 inch size, they would weigh 20 pounds; if 5,000 of the same sheets were purchased in substance 16, they would weigh 160 pounds (5,000 sheets ÷ 500 sheets = 10; 10 x 16 = 160).

Standard Sizes of Paper

Sometimes the basic size of paper is not the most suitable nor the best for customer needs or printing production. For this reason, paper merchants sell paper in standard sizes, which are sizes other than the basic sizes that print, cut, or fold in manners that are advantageous to the customer and the printer. Thus, the paper merchant sells bond paper in the basic size (17 inches x 22 inches), as well as in numerous other standard sizes that conform to printing equipment requirements or to desired finish sizes.

Standard sizes of paper offered for sale vary in dimensions from one paper merchant to another. Three general rules that follow apply to the standard sizes offered:

1. The basic size of one type of paper is frequently offered as the standard size of another. For example, book paper (whose basic size is 25 inches x 38 inches) is also offered in 17 inch x 22 inch size, which is the basic size for bond papers. Conversely, bond may be sold in the 25 inch x 38 inch standard size.

2. Standard sizes of paper are many times offered in exact mathematical ratios of other sizes. For example, book paper (whose basic size is 25 inches x 38 inches) is also sold in 19 inch x 25 inch size, which is exactly one-half of the longer dimension of the basic size book paper. This same paper is also sold in 38 inch x 50 inch standard size, which is twice the shorter dimension of the basic size. Bond paper (whose basic size is 17 inches x 22 inches) is commonly sold in 22 inch x 34 inch size, which is twice the

shorter dimension of the basic size; in 34 inch x 44 inch size, which is twice as large as both dimensions of basic size; and in 11 inch x 17 inch size, which is one-half of the longer dimension of the basic size.

3. Some standard sizes are sold in unusual dimensions that fit well with various sizes of printing press equipment or that correspond to standard product sizes which are popular with customers. Some of the more common standard sizes following this rule are: 16 inches x 21 inches (government size), 17 1/2 inches x 22 1/2 inches, 17 inches x 28 inches, 23 inches x 29 inches, 23 inches x 35 inches, 24 inches x 38 inches, and 35 inches x 45 inches.

Basic and standard sizes are listed in any paper catalog, sometimes called a price catalog, which can be obtained from any paper merchant.

M Weight (1,000 Sheet Weight) of Paper

Although basis or substance weight is one key measurement of paper poundage, a second measurement is the M weight or 1,000 sheet weight. This weight is important for estimating paper, specifying paper, and dealing with paper during production. The M weight appears with the substance weight on labels of paper cartons in the printing plant. Thus, two paper poundage numbers are needed for ordering and specifying printing papers of all kinds: (1) the substance number or basis number, which by definition is the weight per 500 sheets of the basic size, and (2) the M weight or 1,000 sheet weight, which is defined as the weight of 1,000 (M) sheets of the size of paper in the carton.

For example, if 1,000 sheets of 17 inch x 22 inch (basic size) and substance 20 bond were delivered in one carton to the printing plant, the two weights on the carton label would be "substance 20," which in this case is the weight per 500 sheets of the basic size, and "40 M, " which is the weight per 1,000 sheets of 17 inch x 22 inch size, which is the basic size in this case.

Comparative Weight of Paper

The M weight system just described works easily for basic sizes. However, standard sizes of paper are also sold in large quantities, but their M weights must be calculated because they are not purchased in the basic size. To determine the M weight of any standard size of paper, which is known as the "comparative weight" or the "1,000 sheet equivalent weight," the following system is used.

Comparative weight is based on the development of a comparison ratio of paper size to the weight of the paper. The formula to determine comparative weight is:

comparative weight = (area of desired paper size ÷ area of basic paper size) x basis weight doubled

where area is measured in square inches.

Example 6.1. We want to purchase a substance 80 cover paper, basic size 20 inches x 26 inches, in the standard size of 17 inches x 22 inches. Determine the weight of 3,000 sheets.

Solution

Use the comparative weight formula and substitute to find the equivalent weight:

$$\frac{\text{area of desired paper size}}{\text{area of basic paper size}} \times \text{basis weight doubled}$$

$$\frac{17 \text{ in.} \times 22 \text{ in.}}{20 \text{ in.} \times 26 \text{ in.}} = \frac{374 \text{ sq. in.}}{520 \text{ sq. in.}} \times (\text{sub. } 80 \times 2)$$

$$= 0.7192 \text{ x } 160 \text{ M} = 115.08 \text{ M (or lbs./1,000 shts.)}$$

Then use the poundage result of the comparative weight calculation to find the weight of 3,000 17 inch x 22 inch sheets:

3,000 shts. x 115.08 M (lbs./1,000 shts) = 345.2 lbs. (scale weight of paper)

Example 6.2. We want to buy 8,000 sheets of 24 inch x 36 inch bond, substance 16. (Find the basic size for bond in Figure 6.2.) Determine the equivalent weight and the total weight of 8,000 sheets.

Solution

Use the formula and substitute:

$$\frac{\text{area of desired paper size}}{\text{area of basic paper size}} \times \text{basis weight doubled}$$

$$\frac{24 \text{ in.} \times 36 \text{ in.}}{17 \text{ in.} \times 22 \text{ in.}} = \frac{864 \text{ sq. in.}}{374 \text{ sq. in.}} \times (\text{sub. } 16 \times 2)$$

$$= 2.31 \text{ x } 32 \text{ M} = 73.92 \text{ M (or lbs./1,000 shts.)}$$

Use the poundage result of the comparative weight calculation to find the weight of 8,000 24 inch x 36 inch sheets:

8,000 shts. x 73.92 M (lbs./1,000 shts.) = 591.36 lbs. (scale weight of paper)

Figure 6.5 is an equivalent weight table reproduced from a paper catalog. Most paper catalogs contain similar tables. Such a table provides a handy and quick

EQUIVALENT WEIGHTS IN PAPER

While each type of paper uses a different basic size - book papers use 25x38, writings use 17x22, etc. - a chart like this brings out the fact that a 50# offset and 20# bond are the same weight, as are a 65# cover and an 80# vellum bristol. The finish, bulk and strength could vary from one type of sheet to another. But on some jobs because of size, availability or some other reason it might be advantageous to consider an equivalent sheet. **For a more detailed chart, see the General Information Section.**

	Bond 17 x 22	Book 25 x 38	Cover 20 x 26	Printing & Index Bristol 25½ x 30½	Kraft, News & Tag 24 x 36
Bond	**13**	33	18	27	30
Duplicator	**15**	38	21	31	35
Ledger	**16**	41	22	33	37
Mimeo	**20**	51	28	42	46
Writing	**24**	61	33	50	55
	28	71	39	58	65
	32	81	45	67	74
	36	91	50	75	83
Book	16	**40**	22	33	36
Offset	18	**45**	25	37	41
Text	20	**50**	27	41	45
	24	**60**	33	49	55
	28	**70**	38	57	64
	30	**75**	41	61	68
	31	**80**	44	65	73
	35	**90**	49	74	82
	39	**100**	55	82	91
	47	**120**	66	98	109
Cover &	36	91	**50**	75	83
Vellum	43	110	**60**	90	100
Bristol	47	119	**65**	97	108
	58	146	**80**	120	133
	65	164	**90**	135	150
	72	183	**100**	150	166
Index &	43	110	60	**90**	100
Printing	53	135	74	**110**	122
Bristol	67	170	93	**140**	156
Tag	43	110	60	90	**100**
	54	137	75	113	**125**
	65	165	90	135	**150**
	76	192	105	158	**175**
	87	220	120	180	**200**

Figure 6.5 Equivalent weight chart. (Reproduced with permission of Zellerbach, a Mead Company.

reference from which the estimator can determine equivalent weights without using the preceding mathematical formulas.

Because equivalent weights are necessary to calculate paper poundage during estimating, it is important that estimators understand how to complete this procedure. Also, when paper is purchased, as is explained later in this chapter, a specified form is used to detail all elements of the paper order. Both the substance weight of the basic size and the comparative weight are required.

To summarize, it is important to remember the following definitions:

- Basis weight is the weight per 500 sheets of the basic size.
- The M weight is the weight per 1,000 sheets of the size of paper purchased, which is not always the basic size.

These definitions hold throughout all discussions of paper weights in the printing industry.

Bulk of Paper

The thickness of paper, or caliper, is a measurement in thousandths of an inch of the bulk of the sheet. The bulk of paper is important for press and folding requirements, especially during book production, and is often a marketing concern for the book publisher.

Most printing estimators have a paper micrometer, which is a handheld device used to accurately determine paper thickness. A machinist's micrometer works for this purpose also. When measuring paper thickness, a half-dozen measurements should be taken and the average figure used. Even though modern technology has assured a very flat and even paper sheet, slight variations in thickness still occur.

Figure 6.6 is an average caliper bulking chart reproduced from a paper price book. It lists all classifications of paper, selects certain basis (substance) weights, and provides a caliper thickness measurement for these weights. It must be noted that such measurements are averages for many kinds of paper. Thus, the caliper of basis 70 regular offset, which has a caliper of 0.005 inch in Figure 6.6, varies with each manufacturer's basis 70 sheet. Some could average 0.0046 inch, others could be perhaps 0.0052 inch thick, and so on. The caliper of a sheet in a particular basis weight can vary but does not significantly affect the paper's weight.

6.6   Paper Metrication

Although various efforts have been made to move the United States to the metric measurement system, there seems to be little interest on the part of either the United States government or the American citizen to make the conversion. America is the only major industrialized nation in the world using nonmetric

AVERAGE CALIPER BULKING CHART

These are averages. Variations will be found if paper is run on light or heavy side of substance weight, depending on various mill runs. The thicker the caliper, the wider the variation.

	Basis	Thickness		Basis	Thickness
Bond, Cotton Fiber 17 x 22			**Cover 20 x 26**		
(Flat Finish)	13	.0025	(Antique)	50	.0065
	16	.003		65	.0095
	20	.0035		80	.0115
	24	.004		D.T.	.019
(Cockle Finish)	13	.003	(Coated)	60	.0055
	16	.0035		80	.008
	20	.004		100	.010
	24	.00475	**Index Bristol**	90	.007
Bond, Sulphite	13	.003	**25½ x 30½**	110	.0085
17 x 22	15	.0035	(Sulphite)	140	.011
	20	.004	**Printing Bristol 22½ x 28½**		
	24	.0045	(Antique)	100	.011
Ledger	24	.004		120	.014
17 x 22	28	.005	(Plate)	100	.009
	32	.0055		120	.011
	36	.006	**Tag**	100	.007
Coated Book 25 x 38			**24 x 36**	125	.009
Gloss	60	.003		150	.011
	70	.0035		175	.013
	80	.004		200	.015
	100	.005			
	120	.006			
Dull	70	.004			
	80	.0045		**Ply**	**Thickness**
	100	.0055	**Board**	3	.015
Offset	50	.00375	**22 x 28**	4	.018
25 x 38	60	.0045		5	.021
(Regular Finish)	70	.005		6	.024
	80	.0055		8	.030
	100	.007		10	.036
	120	.008			
	150	.010			

Figure 6.6 Average caliper bulking chart. (Reproduced with permission of Zellerbach, a Mead company.)

measurements. Britain, Canada, and Australia began the conversion process in the early 1970s and are completely metric now. In 1975 President Gerald Ford signed into law a metric conversion bill stating that the official policy of the United States is to "... coordinate and plan the increasing use of the metric system..." However, the bill provided little money for this process and did not establish a timetable or mechanism by which the metric changeover would occur.

In point of fact, however, it is slowly becoming a metric world in the United States. As America becomes more internationalized in its business dealings—as it imports German, Japanese, or Swedish printing equipment—it is being forced into dealing with metric measurements to the point that by the turn of the year 2000 it is likely to be at least partially into the conversion process. The American public may not yet feel comfortable with liters, grams, and meters, but the integration of metric measurements into the products they buy will force them slowly to begin working with this system.

To some, learning metric is like learning a second language. Just as people learn French by converting English words to their French versions with two-way dictionaries, they use conversion tables to convert metric figures to United States measurements. For example, 1 meter equals 39.37 inches, and one inch equals 2.54 centimeters. Others find the best way to learn metric measurements is to learn the values independent of any comparison measurements, thus learning metric "straight" without conversion values. Regardless of the way metric is learned, most educators agree it is best to move slowly into the subject and to avoid trying to learn the metrication all at once.

The metric system includes measurements in length (meters), solid weight (grams), liquid weight (liters), and temperature (Celsius). It is based on units of 10, 100, and 1,000, which allows metric measurement components to be easily calculated. For example, 1 millimeter is one-thousandth of a meter and equals 39.37/1,000 or 0.03937 inches. The following basic chart is provided to compare a few common product examples:

1 meter	=	39.37 inches (slightly more than 1 yard)
1 millimeter	=	0.001 meter or 0.03937 inches (about the diameter of a paper clip wire)
1 centimeter	=	0.01 meter or 0.3937 inches (about the thickness of a regular pencil)
2.54 centimeters	=	1 inch
1 kilometer	=	1,000 meters or about 3,281 feet (about 0.60 of 1 mile)
1 gram	=	0.0022 pounds (about the weight of 1 paper clip)
1 kilogram	=	2.2 pounds
1 liter	=	1.06 quarts
0° Celsius	=	32° Fahrenheit (the temperature at which water freezes)

Metric Paper Sizes (ISO Standards)

Unlike most of the lay public, the American paper industry began to convert to metric more than five years ago, and today observant production workers note metric unit measurements on the paper cartons delivered to the plant. Also, CAE vendors selling their systems worldwide have been required to convert their original American programs in nonmetric measurements to metric values, including calculations of paper and measurements in inches to millimeters, meters, and grams.

International paper sizes were first formalized in 1922 in Germany using that country's DIN standard, and continued in 1947 with the formation of the International Standards Organization (ISO), which was created to promote the development of standards throughout the world. Under the ISO system, paper dimensions are based on the area of a square meter in the rectangular form proportion of $1:\sqrt{2}$. The result of this proportion is that if one-half the longer side of the rectangle is halved or the shorter side is doubled, the proportion is still $1:\sqrt{2}$ and still equals one square meter or an exact ratio.

Out of the ISO Standards has developed the ISO-A series of paper sizes, commonly known as the "A-series," which is used for business papers and other popular paper stocks. The basic size is known as A0 and its area equals 1 square meter. From this basic size all other sizes are derived. For example, 2A is twice as big as the basic size in one dimension and two meters in area, while A1 is one-half of the longest dimension of the AO sheet and one-half square meter in dimension. Figure 6.7 graphically demonstrates this concept for the A series in millimeters, which includes A1 through A10 sizes, and lists exact measurements. The following chart represents the A-series paper sizes with their corresponding approximate inch dimensions:

International A sizes (in mm)				Approximate dimensions (in in.)		
2A	1,189	x	1,682	46.8	x	66.2
A0	841	x	1,189 (basic size)	33.1	x	46.8
A1	594	x	841	23.4	x	33.1
A2	420	x	594	16.5	x	23.4
A3	297	x	420	11.7	x	16.5
A4	210	x	297	8.3	x	11.7
A5	148	x	210	5.8	x	8.3
A6	105	x	148	4.1	x	5.8
A7	74	x	105	2.9	x	4.1
A8	52	x	74	2.0	x	2.9
A9	37	x	52	1.5	x	2.0
A10	26	x	37	1.0	x	1.5

There are also ISO-B and ISO-C series papers. The B-series paper stocks are intended for posters and other large-size paper goods and were developed because

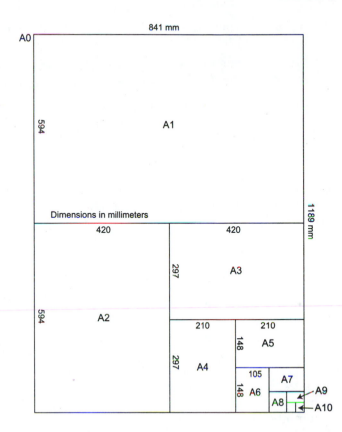

Figure 6.7 Diagram of ISO-A series with measurements in millimeters and A sizes indicated

the jump from the business papers of the A-series to these larger levels was impractical. The following chart represents most of the B-series sizes and their corresponding approximate inch dimensions:

International B sizes (in mm)				Approximate dimensions (in in.)		
B0	1,000	x	1,414	39.4	x	55.7
B1	707	x	1,000	27.8	x	39.3
B2	500	x	707	19.7	x	27.8
B3	353	x	500	13.9	x	19.7
B4	250	x	353	9.8	x	13.9
B5	176	x	250	6.9	x	9.8

International B sizes (in mm)   *Approximate dimensions (in in.)*
B6   125   x   176   4.9   x   6.9
B7   88   x   125   3.5   x   4.9
(chart continues through B10)

The C-series envelopes, postcards, and similar products were developed to accommodate the A-series products when the latter are folded or flat. The following chart represents the C-series sizes and their corresponding approximate inch dimensions:

International C sizes (in mm)   *Approximate dimensions (in in.)*
C4   229   x   324   9.0   x   12.8
C5   162   x   229   6.3   x   9.0
C6   114   x   162   4.5   x   6.3
DL   110   x   220   4.3   x   8.7

The C- and A-series products correlate by number. For example, the C4 envelopes are intended to allow A4 letters to be mailed unfolded, while the C5 envelopes allow the same with the A5 flat sheets. Because of the $1:\sqrt{2}$ ratio discussed earlier, the C4 envelope also accommodates A3 sheets folded in half, and the C5 envelope encloses an A4 sheet folded in half on its long dimension.

The DL category in the previous chart provides for two equally spaced parallel folds of an A4 sheet, which is regular folding of a business letter, or for the A5 sheet to be folded in half on its short dimension.

To accommodate bleeds and additional paper needed for folding and trimming, British printers use a group of sizes which include paper for normal trim (R) and extra trim (SR). For example, the finished A0 sheet (see Figure 6.7) measures 841 mm x 1,189 mm. The accepted normal trim (RA0) dimensions enlarge the sheet to 860 mm x 1,220 mm, and the extra trim (SRA0) dimensions expand the sheet dimensions to 900 mm x 1,280 mm. Suggested trims are available for most sheet sizes in the A, B, and C series when requested from the paper merchant.

Metric Paper Weights

The calculation of weights of paper in the metric system uses basis weight or substance as expressed in grams per square meter—g/m^2, gsm, or, most commonly, "grammage." This is the weight of 500 sheets of a defined type or kind of paper whose surface area is 1 square meter. As was noted earlier, the basic size of the A-series is 1 square meter.

Converting the basis weights (500-sheet weights) of the basic sizes of paper stocks from grammage to basis weights and from basis weights to grammage uses the factors in the following chart:

Paper type	Size (in in.)	Factor for grammage to ream weight	Factor for ream weight to grammage
Writing papers	17 x 22	0.266	3.760
Cover papers	20 x 26	0.370	2.704
Newsprint	24 x 36	0.614	1.627
Book papers	25 x 38	0.675	1.480

(Source: Based on TAPPI standard T410.)

Figure 6.8 presents some grammages for normal basis weights of basic sizes of paper stocks using the conversion system and formulas for such conversions. For anyone unfamiliar with metric paper weights, Figure 6.8 provides a good comparison of these data.

Two standard series of basis weights in grams per square meter (grammage), R20 and R40, have been developed to be used with the metric system. The R

Paper type	Size (in in.)	Size (in mm)	Ream weight (in lbs.)	Grammage (in gsm)
Bond	17 x 22	432 x 559	Sub 16	60
			20	75
Book	25 x 38	635 x 965	40	59
			50	74
			60	89
			70	104
Cover	20 x 26	508 x 660	60	162
			70	189
			80	216
Newsprint	24 x 36	610 x 914	28	46
			30	49

To convert any substance weight to grammage or vice versa, the following formulas can be used:

$$\text{Ream weight to grammage} = \frac{\text{ream weight} \times 1.406}{\text{sheet area in square inches}}$$

Grammage to sub weight = gsm × sheet area (sq. in.) × 0.000711

Figure 6.8 Comparison chart of basic sizes to metric sizes and ream weights to grammage

designates Colonel Charles Renard, who devised the systems. The numbers relate the systems' bases. For example, R20 is based on the geometric progression based on the twentieth root of 10, which equals a multiplier of 1.12 or 12 percent over the preceding step. R40, which is based on the fortieth root of 10, provides twice the number of intermediate grammage steps as does R20. The two have been combined as the R20/R40 range and paper mills have been asked to make their stock in the following grammages:

25.0	45.0	71.0	106.0	160.0
28.0	50.0	85.0	118.0	180.0
31.5	63.0	100.0	140.0	200.0

When calculating the weight in kilograms per 1,000 (M) sheets, the following formula applies:

$$\text{M sheet kg weight} = \frac{\text{length of sheet (mm)} \times \text{width of sheet (mm)} \times \text{gsm}}{1,000}$$

Example 6.3 that follows uses this formula.

Example 6.3. We have a skid of bond paper with a grammage of 75 gsm (20 lb.) and dimensions of 432 mm x 559 mm (17 inches x 22 inches). What is the weight of 1,000 sheets in kilograms (kg)?

Solution

$$\text{M sheet kg weight} = \frac{432 \text{ mm} \times 559 \text{ mm} \times 75 \text{ gsm}}{1,000,000} = 18.11 \text{ kg}$$

Because 1 kilogram weighs about 2.2 pounds, multiplying 18.11 kg by 2.2 equals 39.85 pounds, which is approximately the nominal poundage of 1,000 sheets of basis 20 or 40M bond in the basic size.

6.7   Ordering Paper for Sheetfed Printing Production

The process of correctly ordering paper is important since any error can lead to a missed deadline because the proper paper stock was not properly specified, the correct quantity of paper was not provided, or the cost of paper was incorrectly estimated.

The Specified Form

The specified form provides complete information from the estimator or the purchasing agent to the paper merchant when ordering paper in sheets. All criteria for the stock to be ordered are stated clearly, explicitly, and in the following order:

1. stock number (as specified by the paper merchant), if any
2. number of sheets requested
3. sheet size requested
4. basis weight and M weight (enclose the latter in parentheses)
5. color
6. specific brand name of the paper (may also be indicated as the first item)
7. other information, such as special finishes or grain direction, packing, loading, and shipping instructions

The following examples show exactly how to write the specified form.

Example 6.4. We want to order 5,550 sheets of orange Ticonderoga Text, stock number 003-221, grain long, 25 inches x $\underline{38}$ inches, substance 60.

Solution

Prepare an order form that reads:

003-221, 5,500 sht., 25 x $\underline{38}$, sub 60 (120 M), orange, Ticonderoga Text, grain long

Example 6.5. We want to order 6,800 sheets, Hammermill bond, 25 percent rag content, stock number 001-340, cockle finish, grain short, substance 20, $\underline{22}$ inches x 34 inches, white.

Solution

Prepare an order form that reads:

001-340, 6,800 sht., $\underline{22}$ x 34, sub 20 (80 M), white, Hammermill bond, 25% rag, cockle finish, grain short

Note that in Example 6.4 the M weight was determined by doubling the substance weight. This was possible because the stock was ordered in the basic size. The second example required the use of a conversion to determine the M weight because the stock was not ordered in the basic size. (Refer to Figure 6.2 to find the basic size for bond and calculate the correct M weight as described in Section 6.5.)

Specifying Paper Grain. Paper grain, which is the alignment of cellulose or other types of fibers in paper, may be either long or short depending upon the way the paper was sheeted during manufacture or cut later in the printing plant. Such grain may be indicated with a straight line either above or below the sheet dimension that applies. In Example 6.4, the grain is long and thus can be written 25 x <u>38</u> or 25 x 38. The line over or under the long dime<u>ns</u>ion indicates the grain direction. In Example 6.5, the grain is short; thus, <u>22</u> x 34 or 22 x 34 is the correct representation.

The grain line then makes the words "grain long" or "grain short" optional when writing the specified form. The grain line is important when grain is a critical factor in printing production. Further discussion of grain can be found in Section 6.8.

Paper Catalogs and Paper Prices

Most paper wholesalers supply the printing estimator with a large range of sample paper swatches and a paper price catalog. Together these items contain all of the information that is necessary to select appropriate paper stocks, determine prices, and aid in ordering precise kinds and sizes of paper.

The catalog may be a notebook that provides for the insertion of price changes in any section. The pages of the catalog are generally dated to indicate when the prices became effective. These catalogs are divided into sections by type of paper and may include additional sections for items such as envelopes, cut paper products, and industrial papers. See the index page from a pricing catalog in Figure 6.9 for such section divisions.

Printing papers are manufactured and costed by weight at the mill. Most catalogs list a price per 100 pounds (a CWT price) which is easily converted to a price per pound. A second pricing system used by most paper merchants involves converting the CWT price into a price per 1,000 (M) sheets. Because most estimators calculate paper in terms of sheets and not pounds, the M sheet price is easier to work with. It also saves computation time because, unlike in the CWT system, poundage is not required as part of the calculation of paper. A third pricing system, used for paperboards and other board stock, is a price per 100 sheets. The paper catalog usually lists CWT prices for most paper stocks, with accompanying M sheet or 100 sheet prices, depending upon the type of paper.

Figure 6.10 shows a page for Simpson Opaque book stock from a paper pricing catalog. "Price per CWT" is shown above all of the right-hand columns of the page, and "Price per 1,000 sheets" is set below it four rows as the main head of the set of tables occupying most of the page. In addition, prices are broken down into various carton levels. The columns are categorized across the page from left to right as follows: the first column, titled "Prod Code Stk" is a stock number. It is followed by the "Basis Wgt" column, the sheet sizes available column (titled "Size"), the weight per M sheets column (titled "M Wgt"), the number of sheets per carton column (titled "Ctn Qty"), and the "Caliper" column. The price per CWT and the price per 1,000 sheets vary depending upon the quantity being purchased. These price variations are in the last four columns on the far right side of the table: "1 Ctn," "4 Ctns," "16 Ctns," and "5,000 Lbs."

Main Index

Uncoated Book and Cover

Bond ● Writing

Text ● Cover

Coated Book and Cover

Bristol, Index and Tag

Carbonless

Pressure Sensitive and Gummed

Cut Size Papers

Envelopes and Announcements

Supplies/Packaging

Rolls

Recycled Papers

Specials

General Information

Figure 6.9 Index page for a paper catalog. (Reproduced with permission of Zellerbach, a Mead company.)

SIMPSON

Simpson

Simpson Opaque

#2 Offset Opaque Unwatermarked
High opacity, economical, bright finish. Offers significant postage savings.
For offset and letterpress.

Packaged: Unsealed Cartons
Unit of Measure: Sheet

	PRICE PER CWT			
	1 Ctn	4 Ctn	16 Ctn	5000 Lbs
White, 50lb	117.60	111.00	102.60	96.00
White, 60 & 70lb	114.65	108.25	100.05	93.60

							PRICE PER 1000 SHEETS			
Prod Code	Stk	Basis Wgt	Size	M Wgt	Ctn Qty	Caliper	1 Ctn	4 Ctn	16 Ctn	5000 Lbs
White, Smooth Finish										
453171 -2	50		17½ x 22½	41	3000	.0036	48.22	45.51	42.07	39.36
453172 -2			23 x 29	70	1500		82.32	77.70	71.82	67.20
452995 -2			23 x 35	85	1500		99.96	94.35	87.21	81.60
453173 -2			25 x 38	100	1500		117.60	111.00	102.60	96.00
452984 -2	60		17½ x 22½	50	2500	.0043	57.33	54.13	50.03	46.80
453174 -2			19 x 25	60	2400		68.79	64.95	60.03	56.16
453175 -2			23 x 29	84	1500		96.31	90.93	84.04	78.62
452977 -2			23 x 35	102	1500		116.94	110.42	102.05	95.47
453176 -2			25 x 38	120	1250		137.58	129.90	120.06	112.32
469165 -2			28 x 40	141	1000		161.66	152.63	141.07	131.98
452978 -2	70		17½ x 22½	58	2500	.0050	66.50	62.78	58.03	54.29
453177 -2			19 x 25	70	2000		80.25	75.78	70.04	65.52
453178 -2			23 x 29	98	1250		112.36	106.08	98.05	91.73
452979 -2			23 x 35	119	1000		136.43	128.82	119.06	111.38
453179 -2			25 x 38	140	1000		160.51	151.55	140.07	131.04

(Continued on next page)

Figure 6.10 Example page from a paper price catalog. (Reproduced with permission of Zellerbach, a Mead company.)

Example 6.6. We want to order 13,000 sheets of Simpson Opaque, white, smooth finish. Stock will be basis 60 and will be bought in the 25 inch x 38 inch size. (Stock size and quantity are determined based on production factors that have not as yet been explained; figures in this problem are for example only.) Determine the cost of this paper using both the price per 1,000 (M) sheets and the price per 100 pounds (CWT).

Solution

First refer to Figure 6.10, then take the following steps:

Step 1. Locate "basis 60" in the chart.

Step 2. Now locate the 25 inch x 38 inch size. Note that the M weight in the next column is 120 pounds (which is double the basis 60, the basic size) and that each carton contains 1,250 sheets.

Step 3. From the information in the initial problem, determine the carton level to be purchased and divide the total number of sheets needed by the number of sheets per carton (ctn.):

$$13,000 \text{ sht.} \div 1,250 \text{ sht./ctn.} = 10.40 \text{ ctn.}$$

The 4-carton price from Figure 6.10 then applies to this example because it represents a carton range between 4 and 16 cartons. Sometimes paper purchases are amalgamated, which allows for a higher carton level quantity and a greater cost savings. Amalgamation must be determined through discussions with the paper sales representative.

Step 4. Locate the 4-carton CWT and M sheet prices in the "4 Ctns" column of Figure 6.10. The CWT price is $108.25 and the M sheet price is $129.90.

Step 5. Determine the number of pounds of paper. Multiply the weight of 120 lbs./M shts. and multiply that by 13 M shts. (the number of sheets needed): 120 lbs./M shts. x 13.0 M shts. = 1,560 lbs.

Step 6. Find the cost using the CWT price:

$$1,560 \text{ lbs.} \times \$108.25/\text{CWT} = \$1,688.70$$

Step 7. Cross-check this answer using the M sheet price:

$$13.0 \text{ M shts.} \times \$129.90/\text{M shts.} = \$1,688.70$$

Formulas to Determine CWT and M Sheet Prices. The CWT and M sheet prices are interchangeable. The following formula is used to change the CWT price to the M sheet price:

M sheet price = (CWT price ÷ 100) x poundage per M sheets

To change the M sheet price to the CWT price, use this formula:

CWT price = (M sheet price ÷ poundage per M sheets) x 100

These formulas require that the 1,000 sheet weight or equivalent weight be calculated accurately.

Example 6.7. From Figure 6.10 we know that at the 16-carton rate, a basis 70 sheet costs $100.05 per CWT. Determine the price per M sheets in the 25 inch x <u>38</u> inch size and then check Figure 6.10 to see whether the calculated price is correct.

Solution

Step 1. Use the appropriate formula and substitute:

M sheet price = (CWT price ÷ 100) x poundage per M sheets

= ($100.05 ÷ 100) x 140 lbs./M shts = $140.07/M shts.

Step 2. Checking Figure 6.10 we see that basis 70, 25 inches x 38 inches has a 16-carton price of $140.07/M shts. The calculated price is therefore correct.

Example 6.8. Given a 16-carton price for basis 70 Simpson Opaque of $140.07 per M sheets, determine the price per CWT. Stock is 25 inches x <u>38</u> inches (see Figure 6.10).

Solution

Step 1. Use the appropriate formula and substitute:

CWT price = (M sheet price ÷ poundage per M sheets) x 100

= ($140.07/M shts. ÷ 140 lbs./M shts.) x 100

= $100.05/CWT

Step 2. Checking Figure 6.10 we see that basis 60 &70, 16-carton level is $100.05/CWT. Therefore the calculation is correct.

It is vital that estimators get to know their paper sales representatives or paper company representatives on personal bases as appropriate. These paper sales representatives are in a position to pass along information with regard to paper closeouts and other paper bargains. They may amalgamate certain stock purchases, which provides significant cost reductions to the printing company. Due to the high cost of paper, maintaining a good working relationship with paper sales representatives can save hundreds of dollars in paper costs yearly.

6.8   Paper Planning for Sheetfed Production

The intention of this section is to investigate and discuss various sheet sizes of paper used when completing sheetfed printing production techniques. Two types of cutting—regular and stagger—are covered and examples of each are presented. In addition, paper problems similar to those evident during printing production are solved in step-by-step form and, finally, calculating percentage of waste for paper stocks is explained.

Paper Sheet Sizes and Terms

The printing estimator must understand the various production sizes of paper and the relationships between them. The finish size sheet (fss) is defined as the final sheet size desired by the customer. Sometimes the term "finish size" is used. The press size sheet (pss) is the sheet size used during actual press work for the customer's order. If a job is produced "1-up"—that is, 1 fss per pss—the finish size and press size are often the same dimensions. However, production is not 1-up when the press sheet is slightly oversized to accommodate final trimming or images that print off the edge, called bleeds.

The last important term, the parent size sheet (pars) or stock size sheet (sss), is the sheet size that is purchased from the paper merchant and delivered to the plant. In many cases, printing production works this way: The pars (the largest sheet) is first cut to produce press sheets that are printed on the press. The press sheets are then cut to produce the finish sheet for the customer. It is possible that the fss has the same dimensions as the pss and that the pss has the same dimensions as the pars. Production circumstances dictate this interrelationship of sizes.

The term "up," which has already been introduced, is important to the pss. Essentially, the "number up" relates to the number of finish sheets positioned, or imposed, on the press sheet. Press sheets are produced with multiple images "up" so that fewer press sheets are used to print a job. The greater the number of images up on the press sheet (e.g., 2-up, 4-up, 6-up, 8-up, and so on), the fewer the press sheets that are needed to produce a given quantity for the customer.

Such production planning for the printing press saves considerable press time and allows more jobs to be run in any given time period. Of course, large printing presses require more money to purchase and have higher BHRs than do small presses. Basically, most printing plants acquire the largest press equipment possible and then maximize their numbers up accordingly. The overall effect is a reduced cost per unit produced because the large press is used far more efficiently than is the small press with a low sheet capacity.

Regular Paper Cutting

If, when a pss is cut to finish sheets, the grain of the paper goes in the same direction with all cut sheets, a regular cut was used. Consider Examples 6.9 and

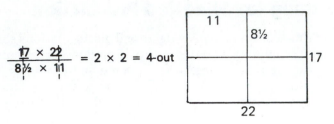

$$\frac{17 \times 22}{8\frac{1}{2} \times 11} = 2 \times 2 = \text{4-out}$$

Figure 6.11   Cutting diagram for Example 6.9

6.10 that follow which show both the mathematics and the diagrams of such regular cuts.

Example 6.9. We want to cut 8 1/2 inch x 11 inch letterheads from parent size 17 inch x 22 inch basic size bond. Grain can go either short or long, but the cut should be the most efficient-that is, the least wasteful possible.

Solution.

Cut the sheet as shown in Figure 6.11. This cut provides that four press sheets are cut from the 17 inch x 22 inch pars. The 8 1/2-inch sides of the letterheads are cut out of the 17-inch side of the pars and the 11-inch sides of the letterheads are cut out of the 22-inch side of the pars. Grain runs the short direction with all sheets and there is no paper waste.

Example 6.10. We want to cut 8 inch x 12 inch finish size flyers from parent 24 inch x 36 inch newsprint. Show cuts for both short and long grain directions and determine which is less wasteful.

Solution.

Step 1. Cut the pars as shown in Figure 6.12. This cut is an even cut, with the grain for each finish size piece running in the short (8 in.) direction. The 8-inch dimensions of the flyers cut evenly out of the 24-inch dimension of the parent sheet (three times) and the 12-inch dimensions of the flyers cut evenly out of the 36-inch dimension of the parent sheet (three times). With this solution each pars yields 9 finish sheets, all with the grain running in the short direction. There is no cutting waste with this solution.
Insert Figure 6.12

Step 2. Cut the sheet as shown in Figure 6.13. This cut provides that the grain in the finish sheets runs in the long (12 in.) direction. Note that there is some paper waste (see shaded area), which makes this cut undesirable. If the

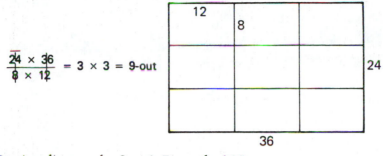

$$\frac{\overline{24} \times \overline{36}}{8 \times 12} = 3 \times 3 = 9\text{-out}$$

Figure 6.12 Cutting diagram for Step 1, Example 6.10

grain has to be long for some reason, the best solution is to order the pars with grain long.

It should be noted that the term "out" refers to the number of pieces that can be cut from a sheet of paper. As mentioned earlier, the term "up" relates to the number of finish sheets imposed on a press sheet. The two terms are not interchangeable.

Basic Sheetfed Paper Problem. The plan of production is very important to paper estimating. To demonstrate the importance, Example 6.11 that follows compares two sheetfed presses with different press size sheet capacities. Essentially, it compares a 1-up job to a 4-up job. Step-by-step directions for the solution are given.

Example 6.11. A customer wants 5,000 1-color letterheads printed. Finish size will be 8 1/2 inches x <u>11</u> inches, and substance 20 bond will be used. Plant

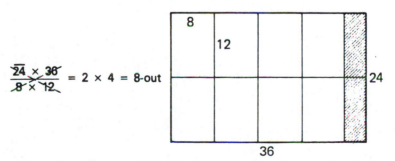

$$\frac{\overline{24} \times \overline{36}}{8 \times 12} = 2 \times 4 = 8\text{-out}$$

Figure 6.13 Cutting diagram for Step 2, Example 6.10

$$\frac{11 \times 15}{8\frac{1}{2} \times 11} = 1 \times 1 = \text{1-up}$$

Use pss $8\frac{1}{2} \times \underline{11}$.

Figure 6.14 Cutting diagram for Step 1, Example 6.11

production scheduling indicates that a Heidelberg TOM (maximum press size sheet 11 inches x 15 inches) and a Heidelberg MO (maximum press size sheet 19 inches x 25 1/2 inches) are both available.

Determine the number and size of press sheets needed for each press in order to produce the customer's 5,000 letterheads. Press spoilage, an extra amount of paper that is added to compensate for press setup and makeready throwaway, is not added in this problem.

Solution

Step 1. Determine the number up on the press sheet for the Heidelberg TOM and draw a diagram (see Figure 6.14). Use an 8 1/2 inch x <u>11</u> inch pss for this press printing the images 1-up.

Step 2. Determine the number up for the Heidelberg MO and draw a diagram (see Figure 6.15). Use a 17 inch x <u>22</u> inch pss that can be printed 4-up for this press.

Step 3. Divide the number up for the Heidelberg TOM into the number of finished pieces to determine the number of press sheets needed:

5,000 shts. ÷ 1-up = 5,000 pss

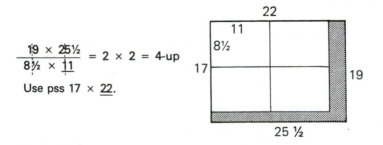

$$\frac{19 \times 25\frac{1}{2}}{8\frac{1}{2} \times 11} = 2 \times 2 = \text{4-up}$$

Use pss $17 \times \underline{22}$.

Figure 6.15 Cutting diagram for Step 2, Example 6.11

Step 4. Divide the number up for the Heidelberg MO into the number of finished pieces to determine the number of press sheets needed:

$$5,000 \text{ shts.} \div 4\text{-up} = 1,250 \text{ pss}$$

This far, the solution indicates that the Heidelberg TOM requires a 5,000 pss run, while the Heidelberg MO requires a press run of 1,250 pss. The Heidelberg TOM runs 1 image up on the 8 1/2 inch x 11 inch pss, and the Heidelberg MO runs 4 images up on the 17 inch x 22 inch pss. If both presses run at exactly the same production output, the Heidelberg TOM requires 4 times the press time of the Heidelberg MO. Because the BHR for each press is different (the Heidelberg TOM's BHR is less than the Heidelberg MO's BHR because it is smaller), costs for presswork for each is different also. Essentially, it is up to the estimator to choose the most expeditious, least expensive production method.

To continue this example with respect to the pars, assume that the Heidelberg MO has been selected to run the letterheads 4-up on a 17 inch x 22 inch pss. Checking a paper catalog under sub 20 bond and the desired type of paper reveals that the list of sizes for purchase includes 8 1/2 inches x 11 inches, 11 inches x 17 inches, 17 inches x 22 inches, 17 1/2 inches x 22 1/2 inches, 22 inches x 34 inches, and 34 inches x 44 inches.

Because minimizing cutting is desirable, the 17 inch x 22 inch size appears to be the most preferable purchase, which makes the press sheet and the pars the same size. In such a situation, the stock goes immediately to the pressroom upon arrival at the plant to be placed directly on the press. However, the stock requirement in this problem states that the grain of the finish sheet must go in the long direction, so the 17 inch x 22 inch short grain paper is not suitable. The pars that is purchased must be 22 inches x 34 inches to allow the press sheet and the finish sheet to meet the desired grain requirements.

To determine the number of 22 inch x 34 inch pars necessary, the following mathematics are completed:

Step 5. Divide the 17 inch x 22 inch pss (with grain long) into the 22 inch x 34 inch pars (with grain short) to determine the number out of the pars. Therefore:

$$\frac{22 \text{ in.} \times 34 \text{ in.}}{17 \text{ in.} \times 22 \text{ in.}} = \frac{2}{1} = 2\text{-out}$$

Step 6. Divide the number out into the indicated number of required press sheets to determine the number of 22 inch x 34 inch pars necessary to complete the order. Remember that no press spoilage is added for setup and printing of the job in this example (it is considered later in this chapter). Therefore:

$$1,250 \text{ pss} \div 2\text{-out} = 625 \text{ pars}$$

In summary, to produce the 5,000 8 1/2 inch x <u>11</u> inch letterheads for the customer, 1,250 pss (17 inches x <u>22</u> inches) must be cut 2-out from 625 pars (<u>22</u> inches x 34 inches) bond. The letterheads will print 4-up on the press sheet.

A Complete Paper Problem. Every estimator must know how to solve a complete paper problem, including knowing how to determine paper cost and poundage. A complete paper problem with its detailed solution follows in Example 6.12.

Example 6.12. A customer wants 40,000 handbills, <u>6</u> inch x 9 inch finish size, printed 1 color, 1 side, on basis 60 offset book. We have in inventory <u>24</u> inch x 36 inch stock for the order. The maximum press size sheet is 14 inches x 20 inches. Stock costs $105.00 per CWT. Determine the following:

- the suitable press size sheet (running as many images up as possible)
- the number of press size sheets needed
- the number of parent size sheets needed
- the cost and poundage of paper necessary to complete the order
- the number of total impressions required on the press

Do not add any paper spoilage for this problem.

Solution

Step 1. Divide the 6 inch x 9 inch fss into the maximum 14 inch x 20 inch pss to yield the number up to be printed on the press sheet and the size of the press sheet to be used. Therefore:

$$\frac{14 \text{ in.} \times 20 \text{ in.}}{6 \text{ in.} \times 9 \text{ in.}} = 2 \times 2* = 4\text{–up}$$

*Note: These values have been rounded to the nearest integers. They are a result of dividing 6 inches into 14 inches and 9 inches into 20 inches.

Use the following formula to determine the size of the pss:

$$\frac{6 \text{ in.} \times 9 \text{ in.}}{2 \times 2} = \underline{12} \text{ in.} \times 18 \text{ in. pss*}$$

*Note: These values are a result of multiplying 2 times 6 inches and 2 times 9 inches because the press sheet will be imposed 2 images across by 2 images deep.

Step 2. Divide the number up into the total number of fss desired by the customer to determine the number of <u>12</u> inch x 18 inch pss necessary to

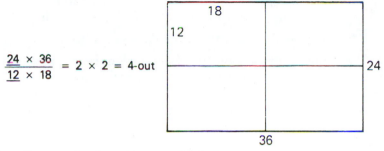

$$\frac{24 \times 36}{12 \times 18} = 2 \times 2 = \text{4-out}$$

Figure 6.16 Cutting diagram for Step 3, Example 6.12

complete the order. (Press spoilage is normally added to this figure.) Calculate as follows:

$$40,000 \text{ fss} \div \text{4-up} = 10,000 \text{ pss}$$

Step 3. Divide the pss into the pars to determine the number out that can be cut from the pars (see Figure 6.16).

Step 4. Divide the number cut out of the pars into the number of pss to determine the number of 24 inch x 36 inch pars necessary.

$$10,000 \text{ pss} \div \text{4-out} = 2,500 \text{ pars}$$

Step 5. Because the paper is not the basic size, complete a comparative weight conversion to determine the new M weight of the 24 inch x 36 inch book stock.

$$\frac{24 \text{ in.} \times 36 \text{ in.}}{25 \text{ in.} \times 38 \text{ in.}} \times 120 \text{ lbs./M} = \frac{864}{950} \times 120 \text{ lbs./M}$$

$$= 0.91 \times 120 \text{ lbs./M} = 109 \text{ lbs./M}$$

Step 6. Multiply the calculated new M weight by the number of pars (in thousands) to determine the poundage of paper (24 inch x 36 inch) to be used:

$$109 \text{ lbs./M} \times 2.5 \text{ M} = 272.5 \text{ lbs.}$$

Step 7. Multiply the number of pounds by the cost of the paper per pound to determine the cost of the required stock. This stock at $105.00/CWT has a per-pound cost of $1.05 ($105.00 ÷ 100 lbs. = $1.05/lb.). Therefore:

$$272.5 \text{ lbs.} \times \$1.05/\text{lb.} = \$286.13$$

Step 8. The number of forms (fms.) or colors times the number of pss equals the number of impressions (imps.) necessary on the press. Because the order in this example is for 1 color, 1 side, 1 form is needed:

$$1 \text{ fm.} \times 10,000 \text{ pss} = 10,000 \text{ imps.}$$

It is important to follow the steps indicated here as precisely as possible. Doing so helps alleviate any confusion on the part of the estimator with respect to the sizes of the sheets required, helps in ascertaining the quantities printed up and cut out of the sheets used, and aids in adding press spoilage (which is covered in Section 6.10).

Stagger Cutting

Regular cutting, as previously described, provides for the grain for all cut sheets to go in the same direction. Stagger cutting, also called "dutch cutting" or "bastard cutting," does not give this result. While the grain goes the short way with some of the stock cut in stagger cutting, it goes the long way with other sheets. The primary reason for stagger cutting is to maximize the number of press sheets cut from a pars. It is also possible with stagger cutting to maximize the use of a press sheet by staggering the imposed images to be printed on the press sheet, which subsequently requires a stagger cut after printing. Consider Example 6.13 that follows:

Example 6.13. We have an order for 3,000 8 1/2 inch x 13 inch legal-size memo sheets to be printed 2-up on substance 6 bond. Our inventory shows that we have a large amount of 17 inch x 22 inch bond on hand that would be suitable for this job, and we therefore do not care to order other stock. Our customer indicates that grain is not a problem with the final use of this product. Draw a diagram showing what this cut will look like and then determine the number of 17 inch x 22 inch pars that will be needed.

Solution

Step 1. Divide 8 1/2 inches x 13 inches into 17 inches x 22 inches to cut 2-out; then divide 8 1/2 inches x 13 inches into the remaining 9 inches x 17 inches of paper (see Figure 6.17). This calculation provides for 3 pss out of the pars. Two pieces from each sheet will have grain long, and one piece will have grain short. Shaded areas in the diagram represent paper that will be thrown away.

Calculate as follows:

$$\frac{17 \text{ in.} \times 22 \text{ in.}}{8\frac{1}{2} \times 13 \text{ in.}} = 2 \times 1 = 2\text{-out}$$

$$\frac{9 \text{ in.} \times 17 \text{ in.}}{8\frac{1}{2} \text{ in.} \times 13 \text{ in.}} = 1 \times 1 = 1\text{-out}$$

$$2 \text{ pss} + 1 \text{ pss} = 3 \text{ pss}$$

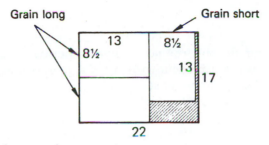

Figure 6.17   Cutting diagram for Example 6.13

Step 2. Because we can cut 3-out of the 17 inch x <u>22</u> inch pars, we are required to use 1,000 pars for this job from our inventory:

$$3,000 \text{ pss} \div 3\text{-out} = 1,000 \text{ pars}$$

Especially with stagger cutting, the completion of an accurate diagram is necessary to be certain that the cut will work out correctly. This diagram should become part of the job ticket to aid employees during the production of the job.

There is a quick check to determine the approximate number that can be cut from a pars. It involves maximizing the number to be cut out by using the following formula:

$$\text{maximum number out} = \text{area of the pars} \div \text{area of the pss}$$

where area is measured in square inches. In Example 6.13, 17 inches x 22 inches (374 square inches) is divided by 8 1/2 inches x 13 inches (110.5 square inches) to produce a figure of 3.38 finish size sheets (8 1/2 inches x 13 inches) that are cut from the pars. The final result is 3-out, and the remaining fraction of the sheet is considered waste.

Stagger cutting minimizes paper waste when cutting odd sheet sizes from parent sheets that are not well suited to the production of the work. Stagger cuts require more time in cutting production and generally more cutting machine adjustments. Also, stagger cuts require that the first cut that is made does not affect the number out of the pars.

Because the grain direction changes with a certain amount of the cut paper, many printers find stagger cuts undesirable. To avoid such problems, these printers order specific stock sizes for specific jobs to be produced, which also allows them to maintain lower inventories of paper stock, a situation that is usually desirable. Nonetheless, every estimator should understand how to complete a stagger cut and how to maximize the number of sheets to be cut out.

Paper Waste from Cutting

When plants purchase only certain sizes of paper stock and attempt to use these limited sizes for all jobs, the possibility of increased paper waste becomes a problem. Such waste can occur with either regular or stagger cuts but is almost certain with a large number of stagger cuts.

Stock waste is calculated as the ratio of the unused area of the paper sheet (in square inches) to the total sheet area (in square inches) and is expressed as a percentage. In the preceding stagger cutting problem, Example 6.13, 3 pieces, each measuring 8 1/2 inches x 13 inches, were cut from the 17 inch x 22 inch pars. The area of the three sheets totals 331.5 square inches (110.5 x 3). The 17 inch x 22 inch pars is 374 square inches. The difference between 374 square inches and 331.5 square inches is 42.5 square inches. Dividing 42.5 square inches by 374 square inches determines a paper waste of 11.4 percent. Generally, any waste greater than 5 percent of the parent sheet is considered undesirable and should be avoided. A simple formula to calculate paper waste percentage is:

paper waste percentage = 1 – (area of sheet used ÷ total area of sheet) x 100

where area is measured in square inches.

It must be noted that "percentage waste" is a comparison of unused paper to the total sheet size. The term should not be confused with "paper spoilage," which is the amount of paper added to the job prior to production to compensate for production problems, production setup, registration of the job on the press, and throwaway stock in the bindery. Lithographic press spoilage is presented in the last section of this chapter, Section 6.10.

6.9 Bookwork Impositions

The printing of books and booklets involves what are known as impositions. An imposition is the exact position or lay of book pages on a press sheet that, after printing, is folded and trimmed to produce a signature. While a signature is printed in flat sheet form, it is typically defined as a collection of printed pages imposed in a defined, prearranged sequence and folded to become part of a book or booklet. For books and booklets that contain a limited number of pages, it may be necessary to produce only one signature to complete the order; for larger books, more than one signature is usually required.

Keep in mind that imposition techniques may be used with either sheeted or webfed presses. However, for simplicity, this discussion centers around imposition procedures for sheetfed presses. The initial planning of such press sheets is a key ingredient when estimating books and booklets to be produced in a printing plant. Every estimator should understand basic bookwork impositions thoroughly.

Sheetwise Imposition Techniques

Sheetwise (SW) impositions, also called work-and-back (W&B) impositions, are easy to understand and produce. In an SW imposition, one-half of the pages of the signature are printed on one side of the press sheet, and the other half are printed on the opposite side of the press sheet and back up the pages that are printed on the first side. As a result, SW impositions require two different forms: one for the front of the press sheet and one for the back. A form is the imposition of pages for one side of the press sheet. It uses one lithographic plate. The same press gripper edge, or the front edge of the press sheet, is used during all press runs for both sides of the sheet. However, the side guide, which is used for aligning the press sheet left to right, changes from side to side as the sheet is flipped over to back up the other form.

Consider the diagram in Figure 6.18, which represents the production of a 4-page booklet using an SW imposition. The imposition shown is termed "1-4 SW" to indicate that there is 1 signature which contains 4 pages and is produced with an SW page lay. The SW technique allows for the production of signatures with pages in geometric multiples. That is, the signatures contain 2, 4, 8, 16, 32, 64, or 128 pages. It is possible to produce a 24-page booklet by combining a 16-page signature and an 8-page signature. Such combinations are discussed later in this chapter.

To see how the SW imposition can be applied, consider Examples 6.14 and 6.15 that follow. These examples involve a 32-page booklet. For this booklet, only two procedures follow printing: folding and stitching. They are considered here only as they relate to the imposition technique. Stitching is a binding procedure that follows folding. However, for the purposes of these examples, stitching is discussed first. It is important to bear in mind that for books and other types of booklets, there are other procedures involved, including different binding procedures. For more discussion of these procedures, see Chapter 11.

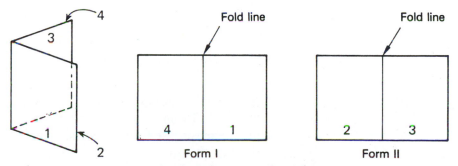

Figure 6.18 Sheetwise imposition diagram for 4-page booklet

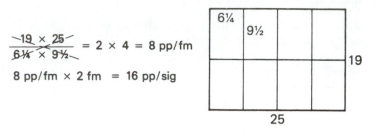

$$\frac{\cancel{19} \times \cancel{25}}{\cancel{6\frac{1}{4}} \times \cancel{9\frac{1}{2}}} = 2 \times 4 = 8 \text{ pp/fm}$$

$$8 \text{ pp/fm} \times 2 \text{ fm} = 16 \text{ pp/sig}$$

Figure 6.19 Sheetwise imposition for diagram for Step 1, Example 6.14

Example 6.14. An advertising agency wants 10,000 copies of a 32-page booklet produced. Its untrimmed page size is 6 1/4 inches x 9 1/2 inches. (Later in production, trimming will make the finish size of the booklet 6 inches x 9 inches.) There will be no duplicate pages produced—there will be only one Page 1, one Page 2, and so on. There are two presses available to produce this job: a Komori 19 inch x 25 inch (maximum pss) and a MAN Roland 25 inch x 38 inch (maximum pss). The booklet will be type matter only printed in black ink. Using the SW imposition technique, we will investigate the possible production procedures. We will do so by determining the number of press sheets needed for each press.

Solution

Step 1. Just as with the cutting calculations, divide the 6 1/4 inch x 9 1/2 inch untrimmed page size into the 19 inch x 25 inch pss of the Komori press. Note that the 6 1/4 inch and 9 1/2 inch dimensions divide evenly into their respective dimensions of the pss, thus allowing for 8 pages to be placed in each form, front and back (see Figure 6.19). Therefore, each signature contains 16 pages.

Step 2. Divide the 6 1/4 inch x 9 1/2 inch untrimmed page size into the 25 inch x 38 inch pss of the MAN Roland press. Because the 25 inch x 38 inch pss is double that of the 19 inch x 25 inch pss, the number of pages positioned on one side of the press is doubled (see Figure 6.20). Thus, each signature contains 32 pages.

Step 3. Dividing the number of pages per booklet (bkt.) by the number of pages per signature (sig.), we find that it will take 2 (19 inch x 25 inch) signatures to produce the booklet on the Komori press. Therefore, we must run 2-16 SW. The calculation is as follows:

$$32 \text{ pp./bkt.} \div 16 \text{ pp./sig.} = 2 \text{ sigs.}$$

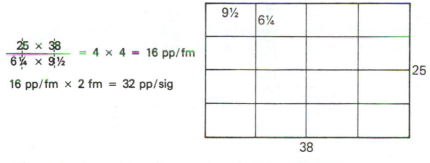

$$\frac{25 \times 38}{6\frac{1}{4} \times 9\frac{1}{2}} = 4 \times 4 = 16 \text{ pp/fm}$$

$$16 \text{ pp/fm} \times 2 \text{ fm} = 32 \text{ pp/sig}$$

Figure 6.20 Sheetwise imposition diagram for Step 2, Example 6.14

Step 4. With the 25 inch x 38 inch pss of the MAN Roland press, we note that we are able to impose 16 pages on each side of the press sheet and are therefore able to put all 32 pages of the booklet on the pss. Thus, running 1-32 SW on this press allows the booklet to be imposed in one complete press sheet:

$$32 \text{ pp./bkt.} \div 32 \text{ pp./sig.} = 1 \text{ sig.}$$

Therefore, we will run 1-32 SW.

Side and Saddle-Stitching Procedures

In Example 6.14, the 1-32 SW imposition produces one large signature on the press sheet, which requires some form of stitching after it is folded to hold all of its pages together. The 2-16 SW procedure requires gathering and stitching because two press sheets—two signatures—are needed to make the 32-page booklet this way.

There are two stitching procedures that can be used in bookwork, and they apply to either the 1-32 SW or the 2-16 SW. The first is side stitching, which involves holding all pages securely together by placing wire stitches through the binding edge of the signature, from top to bottom. The second method, saddle stitching, involves inserting the signatures inside each other and then placing wire stitches along the fold of the book, or the saddle as it is sometimes called. The diagrams in Figure 6.21 illustrate each of these stitching techniques for the 2-16 SW.

In the case of the 1-32 SW, either stitching method can be applied. Because no gathering of signatures is involved in this method, the imposition of pages is not affected by either type of stitching procedure. However, for the 2-16 SW, gathering of all signatures is necessary and must be coordinated with the type of stitching procedure to be used. As Figure 6.21 shows, side stitching produces

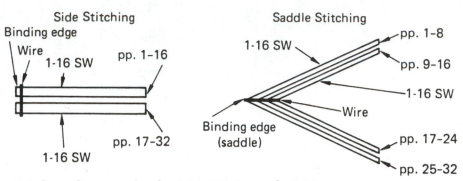

Figure 6.21   Stitching diagrams for the 2-16 SW, Example 6.14

one signature containing pages 1 through 16 and a second signature with pages 17 through 32. Saddle stitching, in contrast, requires one signature for pages 1 through 8 and 25 through 32 and a second signature for pages 9 through 24. Thus, the sequence of pages in the side stitching diagram differs from the sequence of pages in the saddle stitching diagram and different impositions are required for the two binding procedures.

It should be understood that when small presses are used in the production of books and booklets, the number of signatures and the amount of gathering and stitching in the bindery increases considerably. Such situations may be undesirable when producing books in large quantities.

One tool that helps to determine the method of stitching and aids in the overall production planning of bookwork is the form chart. Form charts divide pages into outside and inside types, which by definition impose on opposite sides of the press sheet. Form charts indicate different page impositions depending on the type of stitching to be used. Consider the following sample 4-page form chart that follows the "outside-inside-inside-outside" pattern:

Outside	*Inside*
Page 1	Page 2
Page 4	Page 3

Thus, if Page 1 of a booklet is an outside page, Page 2, which is printed on the back of Page 1, is an inside page. It follows then that Page 3, which faces Page 2, is also an inside page, and that Page 4, which backs up Page 3, is an outside page. This sequence is the basis for all form chart development, regardless of the number of pages in the signature.

Example 6.15. From Example 6.14 we know that the 1-32 SW requires 2 forms, each of which contains 16 pages imposed on a 25 inch x 38 inch pss, and that the 2-16 SW requires 4 forms, each of which contains 8 pages imposed on a 19 inch x 25 inch pss. Now we will consider both side and saddle stitching for the booklet.

As noted previously, the 1-32 SW does not require gathering because all pages are imposed in 1 signature. Stitching, however, is required to hold the signature together. The 2-16 SW requires both gathering and stitching because 2 signatures are necessary to produce the 32-page booklet. Knowing that the customer needs 10,000 copies of this booklet allows determination of the amount of paper (without press spoilage) and the number of impressions required to complete the order. Continue to investigate the production procedures with the additional information.

Solution

Step 1. Figure 6.22 shows the form chart for the 2-16 SW with side stitching. Note that Form I contains pages 1, 4, 5, 8, 9, 12, 13, and 16 for a total of 8 pages and that Form backs up Form I and contain pages 2, 3, 6, 7, 10, 11, 14, and 15, also for a total of 8 pages. Forms III and IV back up each other and contain 8 different pages, as illustrated. Because the pages are ordered sequentially, this solution is the only one possible for binding using side stitching procedures.

	Outside	Inside	
	1	2	
	4	3	
	5	6	
Form I	8	7	Form II
	9	10	
	12	11	
	13	14	
	16	15	
	17	18	
	20	19	
	21	22	
	24	23	
Form III	25	26	Form IV
	28	27	
	29	30	
	32	31	

Figure 6.22 Form chart for the 2-16 SW with side stitching, Example 6.15

	Outside	Inside	
	1	2	
Form I	4	3	Form II
	5	6	
	8	7	
	9	10	
	12	11	
	13	14	
	16	15	
Form III	17	18	Form IV
	20	19	
	21	22	
	24	23	
	25	26	
Form I	28	27	Form II
	29	30	
	32	31	

Figure 6.23 Form chart for the 2-16 SW with saddle stitching, Example 6.15

Step 2. Figure 6.23 shows the form chart for the 2-16 SW with saddle stitching. The chart indicates that Form I contains pages 1, 4, 5, 8 and 25, 28, 29, and 32 for a total of 8 pages. Form II backs up Form I and contain pages 2, 3, 6, 7, and 26, 27, 30, and 31, also for a total of 8 pages. Forms III and IV back up each other and each contains 8 different pages, as illustrated. Because of the way the pages are ordered, saddle stitching must be used to bind the booklet.

Step 3. Figure 6.24 indicates form charts and pages in those form charts for the 1-32 SW. As with the other form charts, the exact lay of pages on the press sheet is not as important as determining the basic setup of the imposition. (Exact page lay is covered when dummying of the signatures is discussed later in this chapter.)

Step 4. The quantity of 19 inch x 25 inch paper necessary to produce the customer's 10,000 booklets using the 2-16 SW imposition is found by multiplying the number of signatures per copy by the number of required copies. The type of stitching used has no direct bearing on the number of sheets required. If weight and poundage data had been provided, it would be possible to determine the weight and cost of paper necessary for the order. Calculate the needed quantity of paper as follows:

	Outside	Inside	
	1	2	
	4	3	
	5	6	
	8	7	
	9	10	
	12	11	
Form I	13	14	Form II
	16	15	
	17	18	
	20	19	
	21	22	
	24	23	
	25	26	
	28	27	
	29	30	
	32	31	

Figure 6.24   Form chart for the 1-32 SW, Example 6.15

2 sigs./bkt. x 10,000 bkts. = 20,000 sigs. = 20,000 pss

Step 5. The amount of 25 inch x 38 inch paper required to produce the customer's 10,000 booklets is determined by multiplying the number of signatures by the number of required copies. Even though this answer is one-half of the number required using the 19 inch x 25 inch pss, remember that the 25 inch x 38 inch pss is twice the size of the 19 inch x 25 inch pss. Thus, the same amount of paper is needed with either solution, but there will be half as many sheets of 25 inch x 38 inch paper required:

1 sig./bkt. x 10,000 bkts. = 10,000 sigs. = 10,000 pss

Step 6. Total impressions are determined by multiplying the number of required forms by the number of copies needed. The solution here is for the 19 inch x 25 inch pss, which requires 40,000 impressions total (without spoilage):

4 fms. x 10,000 bkts. = 40,000 imps.

Step 7. The solution indicated here represents total impressions (without spoilage) for the 25 inch x 35 inch pss. Note that this solution saves 20,000 impressions over the 19 inch x 25 inch pss impressions. That is, press time is halved with this solution. Remember, however, that the larger MAN Roland

25 inch x 38 inch press costs significantly more per hour to operate than does the smaller press. The total number of impressions is determined as follows:

$$2 \text{ fms. x } 10,000 \text{ bkts. } = 20,000 \text{ imps.}$$

The Folded Dummy. The folding of a dummy, which is a model indicating how the press sheet will be folded and how the pages of the signature will be numbered, must be completed to finish this example. The dummy accompanies the job order throughout production and indicates specific page positions for printing and finishing operations. Any size of paper may be used for the dummy. Some estimators prefer to use the untrimmed press sheet, but it is not necessary. For this example, begin with a 14 inch x 20 inch sheet.

The initial folding sequence for the SW imposition is shown in Figure 6.25 and is described in the following steps:

Step 1:   Secure an unfolded sheet measuring 14 inches x 20 inches.
Step 2:   Fold the sheet in half to produce a 4-page signature measuring 14 inches x 10 inches.
Step 3:   Turn the sheet so the folded edge is at the top and make a second fold by aligning the left edge of the folded sheet with the right edge to produce an 8-page signature measuring 7 inches x 10 inches.
Step 4:   Again turn the sheet so the folded edge is at the top.
Step 5:   Make a third fold by aligning the left edge of the doubly folded sheet and aligning it with the right edge to produce a 16-page signature measuring 5 inches x 7 inches.
Step 6:   Notch the top edge (the folded edge) to ensure that each page is in the proper direction.
Step 7:   Number the pages consecutively using the directions in the text that follows.
Step 8:   Unfold the signature to full press size and check the lay of the pages.

Page numbering of the signature should be completed after the signature is folded. Begin by placing the binding edge of the signature to the left side, then tear the bottom right-hand corners of the pages in the last half of the signature. Next, beginning with the front page of the signature, number each page in the bottom right- or left-hand corner. Start with *1* and end with *16*.

When numbering is completed, set aside the signature and fold another sheet of paper following the same procedure. Number this second signature from *17* to *32* consecutively to complete the numbering of the side-stitched dummy for the 2-16 SW. Unfold each sheet and compare the pages of the sheet to the pages of the form chart. The pages on each sheet should match the pages in the form chart. Remember, the dummy provides exact page lay for the press sheet. The

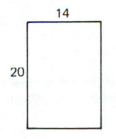

Step 1

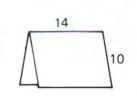

Step 2

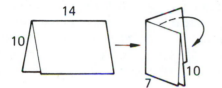

Step 3

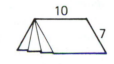

Step 4

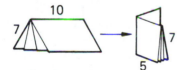

Step 5

Step 6

Step 7

Outside form		Inside form	
8 ◇ 1		2 ◇ 7	
9 ◇ 16		15 ◇ 10	
12 ◇ 13		14 ◇ 11	
5 ◇ 4		3 ◇ 6	

Step 8

Figure 6.25 Folding a dummy for a 16-page sheetwise imposition. (A similar procedure used for work-and-turn impositions also.)

form chart is a useful planning tool but it does not provide exact placement information.

Follow the exact folding procedure just described with two more sheets of 14 inch x 20 inch (or any size) paper. Take the first signature and number the pages *1* through *8* consecutively, then number the remaining pages *25* through *32* consecutively. Number the second folded dummy from *9* to *24* consecutively to complete the numbering of the saddle-stitched dummy for the 2-16 SW. Finally, insert the signatures inside one another to represent the required 32-page booklet. Unfold the signatures and compare them to the appropriate form chart.

Still working with the 14 inch x 20 inch paper, fold it as previously described until a 16-page signature with a page size of 5 inches x 7 inches is produced. After the last fold is completed, turn the signature 90 degrees clockwise and fold it in half again, thus halving the page size to 3 1/2 inch x 5 inches and doubling the number of pages. Tear the appropriate corners to facilitate the numbering of pages and number the signature from 1 to 32 consecutively. This dummy represents the 1-32 SW and should be compared to the appropriate form chart.

Folding Techniques. A word of caution is necessary when discussing the folding of bookwork signatures. The preceding folding example and the example that follows utilize the right-angle folding technique in which the sheet is turned 90 degrees with each fold. It is also possible to use other folding techniques, such as parallel folds or mixtures of right-angle and parallel folds, when folding book signatures. Many printing and publishing operations standardize signature production with respect to the sizes of the book page and the press sheet and the types of folding and stitching, but there are no specific standards that apply for all companies. Thus, it is vital that the estimator plan the size, folding, and stitching for each book or booklet individually using the appropriate company standards of production. In doing so, a dummy and form chart should be prepared.

One common technique is for the estimator to request a folded dummy from the bindery department, thus ensuring imposition accuracy. Also, with some types of folding procedures, the form chart technique as described will not work precisely as indicated. For various folds common to bookwork, refer to Chapter 11, which covers various bookbinding and finishing aspects.

Work-and-Turn Imposition Techniques

Work-and-turn (W&T or WT) is another popular imposition technique for books and booklets. In W&T impositions, all pages of the signature are printed on one form so that all pages of the signature can be printed on one side of the press sheet instead of one-half on one side and one-half on the other. Using W&T thus reduces by one-half the number of pages that can be printed on a press sheet if

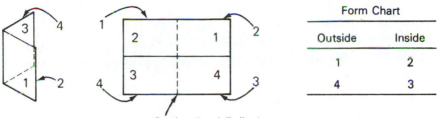

Figure 6.26 Work-and-turn imposition diagram and form chart for a 4-page booklet

the sheet size is the same as with an SW imposition. In addition, W&T requires only one form per signature instead of the two forms necessitated by SW impositions.

With W&T, presswork involves first printing one-half of the required number of copies and then backing up these printed sheets with the same form by running the sheets through the press a second time. Following this procedure, the W&T press sheets, which contain two identical signatures, are transported to the bindery area where they are cut in half before folding, thereby separating the two matching signatures. If production procedure permits, slitting the W&T signatures in half on the press or during folding is sometimes completed.

The production of a 4-page booklet by W&T methods is completed as indicated in Figure 6.26, which is accompanied by a form chart. Note that the form chart has no vertical center line, which means that both the outside and the inside pages are imposed on the same side of the press sheet. Compare this imposition to an SW imposition, where outside pages are in one form and inside pages are in a second form that backs up the first. Example 6.16 that follows illustrates the W&T imposition technique.

Example 6.16. Again assume that we want to produce a 32-page booklet as we did in Example 6.14. Recall that the untrimmed page size is 6 1/4 inches x 9 1/2 inches, 10,000 copies are needed, the presses available are a Komori 19 inch x 25 inch (maximum pss) and a MAN Roland 25 inch x 38 inch (maximum pss), all typematter will be printed in black ink, and no duplicate pages will be produced or used. All impositions utilized for this problem will be W&T. Describe the production procedures to be used.

Solution

Step 1. Begin by dividing the untrimmed page size of 6 1/4 inches x 9 1/2 inches into the 19 inch x 25 inch pss of the Komori press. This calculation indicates that it is possible to impose 8 pages per side of the press sheet.

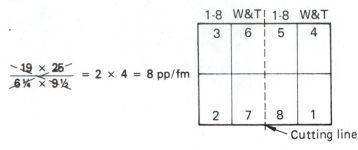

$$\frac{19 \times 25}{6\frac{1}{4} \times 9\frac{1}{2}} = 2 \times 4 = 8 \text{ pp/fm}$$

Figure 6.27 Work-and-turn imposition chart for Step 2, Example 6.16

Step 2. Because the W&T press sheet is cut in half after printing, the imposition requires that each press sheet produce 2 signatures that are exactly alike. Thus, the 19 inch x 25 inch pss will have 8 pages per form: 4 outside pages and 4 inside pages imposed on the same side of the sheet (see Figure 6.27). The press sheet then produces 2 (8-page) signatures, each with 19 inch x 25 inch pss (one on each side).

Step 3. Dividing 8 pp./sig. into the total number of pages in the booklet shows that a 4-8 W&T (4 signatures of 8 pages each) must be produced with the 19 inch x 25 inch pss:

32 pp./bkt. ÷ 8 pp./sig. = 4 sigs./bkt. = 4-8 W&T

Step 4. Divide the 6 1/4 inch x 9 1/2 inch untrimmed page size into the 25 inch x 38 inch pss of the MAN Roland press. This calculation shows that it is possible to impose 16 pages per side—double the number of pages possible with the 19 inch x 25 inch pss.

Step 5. The 25 inch x 38 inch pss will have 16 pages per form: 8 outside pages and 8 inside pages imposed on the same side of the sheet on opposite sides of the cutting line on the press sheet (see Figure 6.28). Thus, each press sheet will produce 2 (16-page) signatures that are exactly alike.

Step 6. Dividing 16 pp./sig. into the total number of pages in the booklet indicates that 2-16 W&T (2 signatures of 16 pages each) is necessary to complete this order using the 25 inch x 38 inch pss:

32 pp./bkt. ÷ 16 pp./sig. = 2 sigs./bkt. = 2-16 W&T

Step 7. Figure 6.29 shows the completed form charts for the 4-8 W&T (19 inch x 25 inch pss), both for side stitching and saddle stitching. Compare these

1-16	W&T	1-16	W&T
6	3	4	5
11	14	13	12
10	15	16	9
7	2	1	8

Cutting line

$$\frac{25 \times 38}{6\frac{1}{4} \times 9\frac{1}{2}} = 4 \times 4 = 16 \text{ pp/fm}$$

Figure 6.28 Work-and-turn imposition chart for Step 5, Example 6.16

charts to the form charts for the SW example (see Figures 6.22 and 6.23). Note that 4 forms are needed, each containing 8 pages.

Step 8. Figure 6.30 shows the completed form charts for both side stitching and saddle stitching for the 2-16 W&T (25 inch x 38 inch pss). The solutions presented cover all of the possibilities; no other solutions exist. Note that two

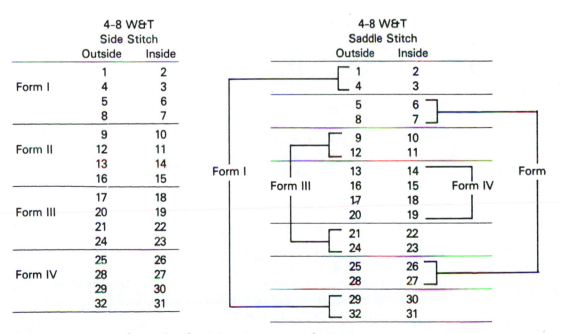

Figure 6.29 Form charts for the 4-8 W&T, Example 6.16

| | 2-16 W&T Side Stitch | |
	Outside	Inside
	1	2
	4	3
	5	6
Form I	8	7
	9	10
	12	11
	13	14
	16	15
	17	18
	20	19
	21	22
Form II	24	23
	25	26
	28	27
	29	30
	32	31

| | 2-16 W&T Saddle Stitch | | |
	Outside	Inside	
	1	2	
	4	3	
	5	6	
	8	7	
	9	10	
	12	11	
	13	14	
Form I	16	15	Form II
	17	18	
	20	19	
	21	22	
	24	23	
	25	26	
	28	27	
	29	30	
	32	31	

Figure 6.30 Form charts for the 2-16 W&T, Example 6.16

forms are needed, each containing 16 pages. Compare these form charts to the SW solutions presented in Example 6.15 (see Figure 6.24).

Step 9. The total amount of stock sheets needed (without spoilage) is determined by multiplying the number of signatures required in that press sheet size first by 1/2 (a constant representing one press sheet containing two signatures) and then by the number of copies required:
For 4-8 W&T (19 inch x 25 inch pss):

$$4 \text{ sigs./bkt. x } 1/2 \text{ pss/sig. x } 10,000 \text{ bkts.} = 20,000 \text{ pss}$$

For 2-16 W&T (25 inch x 38 inch pss):

$$2 \text{ sigs./bkt. x } 1/2 \text{ pss/sig. x } 10,000 \text{ bkts.} = 10,000 \text{ pss}$$

Step 10. The total number of impressions is determined by multiplying the number of forms required by the number of booklets needed:
For 4-8 W&T (19 inch x 25 inch pss):

$$4 \text{ fms. x } 10,000 \text{ bkts.} = 40,000 \text{ imps.}$$

For 2-16 W&T (25 inch x 38 inch pss):

2 fms. x 10,000 bkts. = 20,000 imps.

Note that when the press sheets are the same size, the total number of forms and impressions is the same as with the SW impositions. Thus, even though different imposition techniques are used, the press time and stock that are used are the same.

The initial folding sequence of the dummy is the same for the W&T as it is for the SW (see Figure 6.25). Because each W&T press sheet is printed with the same form on both sides, each press sheet contains two copies of each page of the signature. Numbering of the W&T signature is completed as follows: Number the first sheet of the dummy *1*, followed with *2* on the reverse side. Then progress to the next page of the dummy and repeat the Page 1–Page 2 sequence. Now go to the third page of the dummy and number it *3* and its back side *4*. Then do the same for the next page of the dummy. This sequence, 1-2, 1-2, 3-4, 3-4, 5-6, 5-6, and so on, should be followed whenever the dummy of a W&T is made. After numbering, the sheet should be unfolded and compared to the form chart. Note that pages 1, 4, 5, and 8 fall on one side of the cutting line, and pages 2, 3, 6, and 7 fall on the opposite side. If the sheet is turned over, the page positions in the form compare exactly to the first side.

Comparison of the results of the 32-page booklet using SW and W&T imposition techniques is found in Figure 6.31. Review of Figure 6.31 shows that when the pss and the quantity are the same, the number of press sheets, the number of forms, and the total impressions compare exactly, regardless of the type of imposition. It also indicates that the W&T imposition requires extra cutting time prior to folding and requires greater gathering time in the bindery because more signatures are required. Of course, the use of slitting equipment and automated saddle-binding and gathering equipment minimizes such problems

	2-16 SW	4-8 W&T	1-32 SW	2-16 W&T
Size of press sheet	19 × 25	19 × 25	25 × 38	25 × 38
Number of copies needed	10M	10M	10M	10M
Total pss needed	20M	20M	10M	10M
Number of forms needed	4	4	2	2
Total impressions	40M	40M	20M	20M
Number of signatures to fold	2	4	1	2
Add'l operations	None	pss cut before folding	None	pss cut before folding
Form charts stitching	Compare separately			

Figure 6.31 Comparison of sheetwise and work-and-turn imposition techniques

in the modern printing plant. Comparisons should also be made between the various types of stitching procedures in order to be aware of the array of solutions available in the production of such a booklet.

Combinations of SW and W&T impositions are used in the production of books that contain even numbers of pages. As an example, the production of a 24-page booklet might be completed using 1-16 SW and 1-8 W&T that have the same pss or 3-8 W&T. The difference is that the former combination produces two signatures in the bindery while the latter produces three. It is possible to produce a 56-page book run in 1-32 SW, 1-16 W&T, 1-8 W&T, or other alternatives. It also is possible to utilize duplicate pages with film contacting techniques, thus providing for consistent maximization of press sheets and lower per-page production cost.

Most successful publishing houses utilize other types of imposition techniques also, such as the work-and-tumble (w&t), which is similar to W&T but which turns the sheet sideways for second side and cuts lengthwise. This technique allows the publishers to produce on the press sheet signatures containing 6, 12, 18, 24 pages, and so on. The form chart technique works well with these sizes of signatures also. The major contingency, however, is that folding and stitching must be coordinated to yield exact page placement and must be carefully checked before such w&t impositions are attempted.

It is important to note that the folding sequence when making the dummy should be consistent. If not, certain pages will lay differently or shift on the press sheet from one position to another. Normally, most printing operations follow a prescribed folding sequence to which all production is geared. Of course, if folding departures are considered, they should be thoroughly investigated prior to use. If web presses are used for bookwork, they have fixed cutoff and folding procedures as well as standard webbing conditions, which are webbing patterns that produce a defined signature with an appropriate page layout. When producing books with this type of equipment, any departures from normal operations must also be thoroughly considered.

The form chart is a very useful tool when planning color impositions. Normally, once the size of the book (the total number of pages to be produced) is known but prior to stitching completion, pages where color will be used may be circled or otherwise marked on each page of the chart where they will run. Stitching may then be completed with these color pages included, which allows all color to be printed in the fewest number of forms and thus minimizes production costs.

6.10 Press Spoilage for Sheetfed Production

The addition of spoilage to the number of base press sheets required for a job is necessary if the customer is to receive the number of finished pieces that have been ordered. Spoilage is the additional paper included at the beginning of the press production of a job to compensate for throwaways and unusable sheets produced during presswork, binding, and finishing operations.

The sheetfed lithographic press spoilage schedule in Figure 6.32 contains example data for normal printing, binding, and finishing operations. This information is presented for example only and is not necessarily reflective of any printing company. It is desirable for such data to be developed and tailored for each printing firm. It is important to note that some printing firms develop separate spoilage data for press and finishing operations, as opposed to building schedules that combine the two. This is typical where the production relationship between press and finishing varies from job to job. Some jobs require significant presswork and little finishing while other jobs require little presswork and much finishing.

The two most popular techniques for adding press spoilage are the straight-percentage method and the sheet-plus-percentage procedure. With the straight-percentage technique, the number of press sheets for the base run is multiplied by the indicated percentage, thereby calculating the number of extra sheets needed to compensate for throwaways during printing and finishing. Using this method requires that spoilage schedules be built with both makeready and running percentages summed as one percentage figure. In some plants, the straight-percentage technique is used when press makeready is completed with already printed press sheets that are used multiple times for press makeready.

The sheet-plus-percentage method, which is used in Figure 6.32, requires that the estimator begin by adding a certain number of preparation/makeready spoilage sheets to be spoiled during that phase of press setup, then adding an additional percentage to cover running spoilage.

It is important to point out that accuracy in spoilage data is vital to reducing manufacturing costs. Progressive printing companies work diligently to ensure that estimated spoilage additions reflect, as closely as possible, the actual spoilage required when producing an order. Such companies also strive to reduce spoilage additions to the lowest point, thereby reducing paper cost and making their product costs more competitive. Of course, paper spoilage data must be carefully gathered and compared using job cost summaries to allow these companies to maintain such precise control over paper spoilage in their plants.

Sheetfed Press Spoilage Data

A significant amount of printing and publishing is produced using sheetfed lithographic presses. Figure 6.32 provides spoilage figures for 1-, 2-, 4-, 5-, 6-, 7-, and 8-color sheetfed presses. Schedule data are for example only because it is best for these data to be tailored to each printing company's equipment, manning, and other key factors that affect spoilage. Figure 6.32 also provides averaged data covering lithographic presses that utilize generally available

			1st color	Add'l color	Run %
1-color press	Ordinary	Flat sheet work (per form)	50	25	1.0%
		Work and turn (both sides)	75	50	2.0
		Sheetwise (both sides)	100	75	2.0
	Premium	Flat sheet work (per form)	75	25	1.5
		Work and turn (both sides)	100	50	2.5
		Sheetwise (both sides)	125	75	2.5
	Process	Flat sheet work (per form)	100	50	2.0
		Work and turn (both sides)	125	75	3.0
		Sheetwise (both sides)	150	100	3.0
2-color press	Ordinary	Flat sheet work (per form pair)	125		1.5%
		Work and turn (both sides)	150		2.5
		Sheetwise (both sides)	175		2.5
	Premium	Flat sheet work (per form pair)	150		2.0
		Work and turn (both sides)	175		3.0
		Sheetwise (both sides)	200		3.0
	Process	Flat sheet work (per form pair)	175		2.5
		Work and turn (both sides)	200		3.5
		Sheetwise (both sides)	225		3.5
4-color press	Ordinary	Flat sheet work (per form set)	150		2.0%
		Work and turn (both sides)	175		3.0
		Sheetwise (both sides)	200		3.0
	Premium	Flat sheet work (per form set)	175		2.5
		Work and turn (both sides)	200		3.5
		Sheetwise (both sides)	225		3.5
	Process	Flat sheet work (per form set)	200		3.0
		Work and turn (both sides)	225		4.0
		Sheetwise (both sides)	250		4.0
5-color press	Ordinary	Flat sheet work (per form set)	175		2.5%
		Work and turn (both sides)	200		3.5
		Sheetwise (both sides)	225		3.5
	Premium	Flat sheet work (per form set)	200		3.0
		Work and turn (both sides)	225		4.0
		Sheetwise (both sides)	250		4.0
	Process	Flat sheet work (per form set)	225		3.0
		Work and turn (both sides)	250		4.0
		Sheetwise (both sides)	275		4.0
6-color press	Ordinary	Flat sheet work (per form set)	200		2.5%
		Work and turn (both sides)	225		3.5
		Sheetwise (both sides)	250		3.5
	Premium	Flat sheet work (per form set)	225		3.0
		Work and turn (both sides)	250		4.0
		Sheetwise (both sides)	275		4.0
	Process	Flat sheet work (per form set)	250		3.0
		Work and turn (both sides)	275		4.0
		Sheetwise (both sides)	300		4.0
7-color press	Ordinary	Flat sheet work (per form set)	225		2.5%
		Work and turn (both sides)	250		3.5
		Sheetwise (both sides)	275		3.5
	Premium	Flat sheet work (per form set)	250		3.0
		Work and turn (both sides)	275		4.0
		Sheetwise (both sides)	300		4.0
	Process	Flat sheet work (per form set)	275		3.0
		Work and turn (both sides)	300		4.0
		Sheetwise (both sides)	325		4.0
8-color press	Ordinary	Flat sheet work (per form set)	250		2.5%
		Work and turn (both sides)	275		3.5
		Sheetwise (both sides)	300		3.5
	Premium	Flat sheet work (per form set)	275		3.0
		Work and turn (both sides)	300		4.0
		Sheetwise (both sides)	325		4.0
	Process	Flat sheet work (per form set)	300		3.0
		Work and turn (both sides)	325		4.0
		Sheetwise (both sides)	350		4.0

ADJUSTMENTS: For multicolor presses, deduct 10% from total spoilage quantity for each unit which does not print. Deduct 20% from total if fully waterless production, assuming crew is experienced.

Figure 6.32 Offset press spoilage schedule. Data provided for example only and may not reflect actual production. Includes paper for folding and other finishing operations.

on-press and peripheral devices which reduce makeready times, an important production fixed cost. The schedule must be adjusted for waterless offset production, perfecting production, and for presses that do not utilize devices that reduce makeready and running times.

The decision as to the appropriate level of quality must be made and referenced to the company. "Ordinary" is intended to cover normal plant quality, "premium" covers the types of work where some amount of critical adjustment and registration is necessary, and "process" covers signatures and press sheets that contain full-color images and dot-for-dot registration. Additional press sheets are added as quality level improves.

Press preparation and makeready spoilage figures are given in the chart on the basis of the number of press sheets to be added per form for flat sheet work (per form, form pair, or form set) and for W&T and SW imposition spoilage additions (both sides). Flat sheet work data represent nonbook impositions including advertising work, letterheads, flyers, and so on. The W&T and SW figures are used for specific imposition methods to produce book signatures and booklets where forms are matched by the imposition process.

Press running spoilage is calculated as a percentage of the base number of total press sheets required and is not intended to be an accumulating procedure wherein makeready is included in that base figure. The added press spoilage figures also serve as bindery spoilage to cover the setup and running of folding and stitching equipment. When estimating multicolor presswork, the figures in the chart include the amount of sheets for printing all colors in one press pass, per form group.

The use of 6-, 7-, and 8-color sheetfed presses for greatly enhanced color production output is reflected in the schedule. This has been driven by recent technological advances in electronic prepress where Hi-Fi and other types of color output, which print seven colors (CMYK plus RGB) in one press pass, have emerged. This shift to extensive color production is linked to a growing interest and willingness to pay for such technology on the part of printing company customers, who find the vivid color appealing to their own customers.

Waterless offset production has also emerged as a potentially major participant in sheetfed production. Toray Industries of Japan has perfected the waterless plate, waterless inks are easily available, and the technology has been shifted to daily production in a growing number of printing companies. Because waterless inks heat as they are worked on press, ink cooling methods have been developed to accurately maintain proper ink temperatures. Waterless printing is available in three ways:

1. purchasing a new press which is fully waterless upon delivery
2. retrofitting a lithographic press with ink chilling and other necessary hardware
3. purchasing a Heidelberg DI or Heidelberg QM press with digital laser plate imaging equipment

With experience and a trained press crew, waterless printing saves paper both in makeready and running production. Figure 6.32 indicates that when waterless production is completed with experienced press personnel, a 20 percent deduction from both makeready and run spoilage should be taken although this percentage can vary in actual production.

Example 6.17. A customer has requested us to print 15,000 letterheads, finish size 8 1/2 inches x <u>11</u> inches, to run 3/0 (or "three over zero" meaning three colors one side, no colors on the other, or back, side). The job will print 4-up on a single-color offset press, premium quality. We will buy <u>22</u> inch x 34 inch substance 20 bond that costs $78.60 per M sheet. Determine the number of press size sheets needed, the amount and cost of the stock, and the total impressions, including spoilage.

Solution

Step 1. Begin by determining the size of the press sheet using the finish size and 4-up information (see Figure 6.33).

Step 2. Divide the number up into the total number of copies (cps.) to be delivered to the customer to find the number of 17 inch x <u>22</u> inch pss required:

15,000 cps. ÷ 4-up = 3,750 pss

Step 3. Referring to Figure 6.32 information for 1-color press, premium quality, flat sheet work, locate preparation and makeready figures for "1st color," "Add'l color," and "Run %," and apply as indicated. (Note: The run spoilage is found by multiplying the 1.5 percent listed in Figure 6.32 by 3,750 pss by 3 forms, one for each color.) Determine spoilage figures.
Total press sheets: 3,750 pss
First color preparation and makeready: 75 pss
Second and third colors preparation and makeready (25 x 2): 50 pss
Run spoilage (57 pss x 3 fm): 171 pss
Total press sheets with spoilage: 4,046 pss

(8½ × 11) × 4-up = (8½ × 11) × (2 × 2) = 17 × <u>22</u> pss

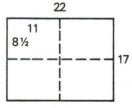

Figure 6.33 Press sheet size for Example 6.17

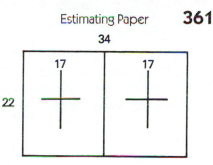

$(\underline{22} \times 34)/(\underline{22} \times 17) = 2 \times 1 = 2\text{-out}$

Figure 6.34 Number-out diagram for Example 6.17

Step 4. Divide 17 inch x $\underline{22}$ inch pss into the $\underline{22}$ inch x 34 inch pars to yield 2-out (see Figure 6.34).

Step 5. Divide the number out into the total number of press sheets required (found in Step 3) to determine the number of 22 inch x 34 inch pars required:

$$4{,}046 \text{ pss} \div 2\text{-out} = 2{,}023 \text{ pars}$$

Step 6. Determine a new M weight for the parent size 22 inch x 34 inch bond:

$$\frac{22 \text{ in} \times 34 \text{ in.}}{17 \text{ in.} \times 22 \text{ in}} \times 40 \text{ lbs./M} = 80 \text{ lbs./M}$$

Step 7. Determine the poundage:

$$2.023 \text{ M pars x } 80 \text{ lbs./M} = 161.84 \text{ lbs.}$$

Step 8. Determine the stock cost:

$$2.023 \text{ M pars x } \$78.60/\text{M} = \$159.01$$

Step 9. There are three different forms printing in register on one side of the press size sheet. Maximum total impressions to be used for scheduling the job during production will be 12,138, which is determined as follows:
3 fms. x 4,046 pss = 12,138 max. imps.

Example 6.18. In the Example 6.16 imposition problem, the customer wanted 10,000 copies of a 32-page booklet, 6 1/4 inch x 9 1/2 inch untrimmed page size. After completing and reviewing all solutions, we decided to produce the booklets using 2-16 W&T and to saddle stitch them in the bindery. The 1-color, 25 inch x 38 inch MAN Roland will be used with makeready and running spoilage at the ordinary levels. We will buy 25 inch x 38 inch substance 50 book paper costing $116.50 per M sheet. All pages will print in black ink with no additional colors. Determine the amount and cost of stock and total impressions, including spoilage. A form chart showing stitching should also be provided.

Solution

Step 1. Review previous calculations with respect to size of forms, number of signatures per book, and base number of press size sheets needed:

$$\frac{25 \text{ in} \times 38 \text{ in.}}{6 \text{ in.} \times 9 \text{ in}} = 4 \times 4 = 16 \text{ pp./fm.}$$

$$\frac{32 \text{ pp/bkt.}}{16 \text{ pp./sig.}} = 2 \text{ sigs./bkt.}$$

2 sigs./bkt. x 1/2 pss/sig. x 10,000 bkts. = 10,000 pss

Step 2. Prepare a form chart (see Figure 6.35) showing the imposition and saddle stitching of 2-16 W&T. Each form contains 16 pages.

Step 3. Press spoilage is based on the number of initial sheets needed, which in this case is 10,000 sheets of 25 inch x 38 inch. Using the 1-color press, ordinary level, 150 sheets are added for press preparation because there are 2 plates and hence 2 preparations. An additional 2 percent (200 sheets) is then added to cover all running spoilage. Total press sheets needed will be 10,350:

Total press sheets: 10,000 pss

Preparation and makeready: 150 pss (2 sigs. x 75 pss/sig.)

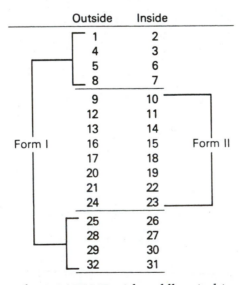

Figure 6.35 Form chart for 2-16 W&T with saddle stitching, Example 6.18

Run spoilage: 200 pss
Total press sheets with spoilage: 10,350 pss (and pars)

Step 4. Calculate the poundage:

$$10.35 \text{ M pars} \div 100 \text{ lbs./M shts.} = 1,035 \text{ lbs.}$$

Step 5. Determine the stock cost:

$$10.35 \text{ M pars} \times \$116.50/M = \$1,205.78$$

Step 6. Because each press sheet must be printed on both sides, total impressions may be determined by doubling the number of total press sheets, including spoilage. As shown, a total of 20,700 impressions will be required to complete the specified order:

$$10,350 \text{ pss} \times 2 \text{ sides/sht.} = 20,700 \text{ max. imps.}$$

Example 6.19. A customer wants us to print 45,000 4-color inserts on our Heidelberg MOVP 4/C press with a maximum press size sheet of 19 inches x 25 1/2 inches. The inserts will print 4/4 (four colors each side) with a finish size of 9 1/2 inches x 12 1/2 inches, no bleeds. Stock in inventory is basic size book, grain short, substance 60 which costs $131.60/M sheets. Determine the number of press size sheets needed without spoilage, the number of press size sheets with spoilage, the number of parent sheets, the cost and poundage of the parent sheets, and the number of impressions including spoilage. Use process level, flat sheet work data because this is not a bookwork job. Use 4/C press spoilage data from Figure 6.32.

Solution

Step 1. Begin by determining the size of the press sheet using the finish size and 4-up information (see Figure 6.36).

Step 2. Divide the number up into the total number of copies to be delivered to the customer to find the number of 19 inch x 25 inch pss required:

$$45,000 \text{ copies} \div 4\text{-up} = 11,250 \text{ pss}$$

Step 3. Referring to the Figure 6.32 information for a 4-color press, process quality, flat sheet work, locate preparation/makeready figures for "4-color press" and "Run %," and apply as indicated. As with the previous examples, the run spoilage is found by multiplying the 3.0 percent figure listed in Figure 6. 32 by the 11,250 pss by the 2 sets of forms. Determine spoilage figures as follows:
Total base number press sheets: 11,250 pss
First 4/C form prep: 200 pss
Second 4/C form prep: 200 pss

9 1/2 x 12 1/2 divided into a max pss of 19 x 25 1/2 = 2 x 2 = 4 up

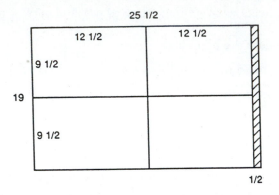

Figure 6.36   Press sheet size for Example 6.19

Run spoilage, first form set (4/C): 338 pss
Run spoilage, second form set (4/C): 338 pss
Total pss with spoilage: 12,326 pss

Step 4. Divide 19 inch x 25 inch pss into the 25 x 38 pars to yield 2-out (see Figure 6.37):

19 inch x 25 inch divided into a maximum pars of 25 inch x 38 inch =
2 x 1 = 2-out

Step 5. Divide the number out into the total number of press sheets required (found in Step 3) to determine the number of 25 inch x 38 inch par required:

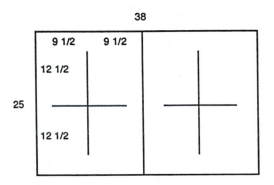

Figure 6.37   Press sheet size for Example 6.19

$$12{,}326 \div 2\text{-out} = 6{,}163 \text{ pars}$$

Step 6. Determine the M weight for the 25 inch x 38 inch pars:

$$\frac{25 \text{ in.} \times 38 \text{ in. (parent size)}}{25 \text{ in.} \times 38 \text{ in. (basic size)}} \times 120 \text{ lbs./M} = 120 \text{ lbs./M}$$

Step 7. Determine the poundage:

$$6.163 \text{ pars} \times 120 \text{ lbs./M} = 739.56 \text{ lbs.}$$

Step 8. Determine the stock cost:

$$6.163 \text{ pars} \times \$131.60/M = \$811.05$$

Step 9. There are two different sets of forms to print on the press sheet: one 4-color set on one side and a different 4-color set on the other side. Maximum total impressions to be used for scheduling the job during production will be 24,652, which is determined as follows:

2 passes (2 sets of 4/C forms each) x 12,326 pss = 24,652 max. imps.

Chapter 7

Estimating Ink

7.1   Introduction

7.2   Overview of Ink Components
Pigments   Additives
Vehicles

7.3   Ink Mileage Schedule for Estimating Lithographic Ink Quantity

7.4   Variables When Estimating Lithographic Ink Consumption
Type of Substrate   Number of Copies and Impressions
Color and Type of Ink   Percentage of Ink Waste
Coverage of the Form to Be Printed

7.5   Estimating Lithographic Ink Quantity

7.6   Estimating the Cost of Ink

7.1 Introduction

Ink is a vital material in the printing manufacturing process, but it generally does not represent a significant expense compared to other job costs—usually from 2 percent to 5 percent of the average cost of a printing order. Ink estimating, however, still must be completed during cost estimating for two reasons. First, because profits in printing tend to be marginal, all definable cost factors for any printing job must be identified, and it is reasonably easy to estimate ink costs as a portion of the total job cost. Second, the ink estimating procedure allows for the determination of approximate quantities of ink. This determination is important when inks must be specially mixed or require special ordering or formulation. Should too little ink be ordered under such circumstances, a production bottleneck could result.

The focus of this chapter is on lithographic paste inks, which are among the largest groups of ink sold in the United States. However, it should be noted that recent shifts in printing technology toward nonlithographic production are causing a shift in the types of inks used. There are three parallel movements in this area:

1. Toward the perfection of the waterless printing process, which requires waterless plates, waterless inks, and waterless presses. Waterless printing is an ink-on-paper printing process that excludes the use of water, or fountain solution, from lithographic production. Its benefits are numerous, including less paper waste, brighter colors, and faster makereadies. Although waterless production is limited at this writing, industry predictions cite probable extensive use of this process by the year 2000.

2. Toward the emergence of Xerography for on-demand printing, which uses carbon toners in place of printing inks. The most popular form for this type of production is the Xerox DocuTech system. Production is typically from electronic or digital files with output using a toner-to-paper system.

3. Toward the emergence of full-color digital presses, which use carefully manufactured ink products developed exclusively for digital imaging system reproduction processes.

The method described in this chapter to estimate ink quantity and cost for sheetfed offset production can be used for estimating ink quantity and cost for these emerging printing technologies as well. This method requires the development of ink mileage data for each process that are based on actual ink consumption during production.

Ink estimating for web lithography is covered in Chapter 12, but the basic ink ingredients described in this chapter are largely the same for lithographic sheetfed and web production.

7.2 Overview of Ink Components

There are three categories of ingredients in lithographic printing ink: (1) pigments, or solid matter which imparts the color to the ink; (2) vehicles, or the liquids which carry the pigments and assist in binding the pigments to the substrates; and (3) additives, which tailor the ink to the specific substrate, printing process, and ultimate use factors. The discussion that follows is intended to provide the estimator with a general knowledge of ink ingredients. Varying the basic ingredients in ink can affect performance during production, end-use factors, and the cost of ink.

Pigments

Pigments in inks are very finely ground solid materials that provide coloration and opacity and establish the life of the product relative to color permanence and light fastness. Light fastness is the ability of a pigment to retain the specific coloration value when exposed to oxygen, sunlight, and other naturally occurring conditions. Characteristics defining pigments include particle size, specific gravity, refractive index, texture, and wettability. Each of these characteristics is controlled during ink manufacture so the final result is an ink product that meets printing production and end-use requirements. Printing ink pigment technology has been largely unchanged in the past thirty years, although some experimentation has been given to pigment substitutes so that deinking during paper recycling can be done more completely, more quickly, and with greater environmental sensitivity.

Vehicles

Essentially, the vehicle in lithographic printing ink carries the pigment and the additives, which modify the ink for special use. Vehicles, which provide the tack and flow characteristics of ink, are made from petroleum, synthetic, or vegetable oils that dry to a solid after printing. The type of vehicle is a primary determinant for ink drying, but drying is also affected by certain additives. Ink drying is a key factor for ink production and use. In general, drying is accomplished by a variety of chemical reactions that are sometimes used in combination. These reactions may involve absorption of the vehicle into the substrate, oxidation of the vehicle by air, polymerization or cross-linking of the vehicle and pigment, evaporation of the vehicle, or radiation of the vehicle and pigment using ultraviolet (UV) or infrared curing methods.

Vehicles for ink have seen significant study and change in recent years, primarily because of environmental issues. Vehicles have undergone significant research also because they tend to be the largest component of ink products and are the most environmentally sensitive of the ingredients. For years the de facto ink vehicle standard for paste inks was petroleum oil (such as news ink and lithographic ink). Petroleum oil was inexpensive, it was a known ingredient with an established technology, and it was easily obtained. However, problems with petroleum vehicles mounted: They had high solvent emissions (which were measured as volatile organic compounds or VOCs), gave off toxic waste, were harder to deink (completely remove dried ink pigment) when recycling printed paper materials, and were not a renewable resource.

Experimentation with vegetable oil substitutes, including soya, corn, hardwood, and canola products, has resulted in some success, but evidence of significant environmental savings is unclear. Nevertheless, many paste inks now contain a large part of soya or some other vegetable oil and a small part of petroleum oil. When an ink is sold as "100 percent soya," it means that soya is the only vegetable oil product used, not that the ink vehicle is made completely of soya.

It should be noted that the more fluid, nonpaste gravure and flexographic inks, which are also used in large quantities for graphic reproduction, have been reformulated from petroleum-based to water- or vegetable-based vehicles to meet VOC and other environmental standards.

Additives

Ink additives, the third component of ink, are used to tailor the ink to meet production and end-use requirements. Additives include driers, antiskinning agents, antioxidants, waxes, plasticizers, lubricants, solvents, body gums, reducing oils, and binding varnishes. Driers, the most common additive, are primarily used to reduce the time needed for the ink to set, which allows for faster backup printing or finishing of the product. Waxes, also a frequent additive, are used to prevent setoff and facilitate scratch resistance by making the dry ink film more slippery.

Additives can be manufactured into the ink before purchase, or they are frequently added during production as needed. Care must be taken with additives because each contributes another set of chemical conditions to the ink product that may affect follow-up printing, binding, end-use factors, permanence, or stringent environmental factors such as air quality.

Modifying ink ingredients, particularly ink vehicles (which are receiving the most experimental activity), changes how much ink is required to print a given job. This amount of ink is known as the ink mileage. Thus, it is wise for each printing company to develop its own ink estimating data that are tailored to the company's own equipment and production. In addition, the cost of ink is generally rising because ingredients are more expensive and funding for research and development is needed so that inks can meet important environmental standards.

7.3   Ink Mileage Schedule for Estimating Lithographic Ink Quantity

The offset ink mileage schedule in Figure 7.1 is provided to estimate ink quantities. Chart data represent the approximate number of thousand square inches that one pound of ink covers. Thus, when printing on a No. 1 enamel using the lithographic process, one pound of regular black ink has a mileage of approximately 425,000 square inches.

Chart data are cross-referenced by the color of ink and the type of stock that are to be printed. Also included are tint base, mixing white, varnish, and process color coverage information.

There are no allowances for leftover ink or ink lost from production and press washup. Such losses usually amount to between 2 percent and 10 percent of the total volume of ink for the job. For example, a 10 percent ink loss might be allowed on a 5-pound can and a 5-percent loss might be allowed for a 100-pound can. It should be clear that the chart data presented in Figure 7.1 are approximations owing to the many variables occurring during production. Differences exist in what seem to be the same types and kinds of paper in stock, ink absorbency factors, climatic conditions, and various production differences in the pressroom. Waterless inks, carbon toners, and digital press inks are not included in the schedule data.

7.4   Variables When Estimating Lithographic Ink Consumption

The discussion that follows details the variables necessary for estimating lithographic ink quantities. Figure 7.1 demonstrates the relationships of some of these variables.

Type of Substrate

The smoother the surface of the paper stock or substrate, the less the amount of ink that is required. Thus, a top-grade enamel, which is exceptionally smooth, requires less ink during printing than does a rougher-coated stock. For example, Figure 7.1 shows the regular black ink mileage for a No. 1 enamel to be 425,000 square inches per pound, while the black ink mileage of antique (uncoated and uncalendered) paper is at 275,000 square inches per pound. Thus, printing on an antique paper stock requires almost twice the amount of regular black ink necessary for printing on a No. 1 enamel. It should be noted that litho coated, dull coated, and MF papers have approximately the same mileage requirements.

Matching substrates and inks relative to drying factors may affect ink mileage,

Color of Ink

Type of Stock	Regular Black	Base Black	Purple	Transparent Blue	Transparent Green	Transparent Yellow	Chrome Yellow	Persian Orange	Transparent Red
No. 1 enamel	425	445	360	355	360	355	285	345	350
No. 2 enamel	400	435	355	345	355	355	270	335	345
Litho coated	380	425	350	340	350	355	260	325	345
Dull coated	375	415	320	335	335	340	250	310	340
M.F. book	400	435	350	340	350	340	250	325	340
Newsprint	290	350	250	230	250	235	165	240	240
Antique	275	335	235	220	235	220	150	225	225

Color of Ink

Type of Stock	Opaque Red	Brown	Overprint Varnish	Opaque White	Tint Base	Process Colors		
						Cyan	Magenta	Yellow
No. 1 enamel	350	345	450	200	400	355	350	355
No. 2 enamel	345	340	435	185	390	350	347	355
Litho coated	340	335	425	175	380	340	345	355
Dull coated	325	325	415	165	375	335	340	340
M.F. book	340	335	425	175	385	340	340	340
Newsprint	190	240	—	150	265	235	240	235
Antique	175	225	—	135	250	220	225	220

Color of Ink

Type of Stock	Silver	Mettallics	Fluorescent
No. 1 enamel	335	215	270
No. 2 enamel	—	—	—
Litho coated	300	200	240
Dull coated	285	200	240
M.F. book	-	-	-
Newsprint	-	-	-
Antique	220	130	160

Note: Numbers given indicate thousands of square inches of coverage per pound of ink

Figure 7.1 Lithographic ink mileage schedule, by color of ink and type of substrate. (Reproduced with permission of Gans Ink and Supply Company, Los Angeles, California.)

too. For this reason, inks and paper stocks should be carefully matched to ensure desired drying relative to maximum mileage and optimum coverage. Orders that require large estimated quantities of inks on unique or unfamiliar substrates should have the ink product formulated specifically for the type of paper or substrate. This ensures the best combination of ink and paper and expedites production during press and bindery manufacturing.

Color and Type of Ink

Two general rules apply to the color and type of ink used. First, the darker the ink color, the greater the ink mileage per pound. Thus, black inks require less ink per pound than do colored inks, and darker colors provide greater ink mileage pound for pound than do lighter inks. The second general rule is that the more opaque the ink, the lower its mileage, and the more transparent the ink, the greater its mileage per pound. On the lithographic ink mileage schedule in Figure 7.1, one pound of transparent yellow printed on No. 1 enamel has a mileage value of 355,000 square inches. On the same type of paper, chrome yellow, which is an opaque ink, has a mileage factor of 285,000 square inches per pound. Process colors, because they are transparent inks lacking in hiding power, provide reasonably high mileage values per pound when compared to more opaque colors.

As noted previously, the specific ingredients in printing ink relate to mileage during press production. Most lithographic inks contain various amounts of pigment, vehicle, drier, resin, and wax. Because the combination of these ingredients varies with respect to the desired type of ink product, it is difficult to provide specifics regarding mileage. Most printing companies purchase a certain brand of ink or an ink made by a certain manufacturer and consistently use it for most stocks they print. With a limited amount of study, it is possible for estimators to determine specific mileages based on the standard brands of ink used in their plants. These data ensure estimating accuracy with these identified paper-and-ink combinations.

Coverage of the Form to Be Printed

Ink estimating requires knowledge of the size of the form to be printed in square inches and the approximate coverage of ink on the form. A form, also known as a plate or a printer, is one image or a collection of images printed in the same color. Ink coverage, which is expressed as a percentage, relates to the amount of area on the page over which the ink will be printed. Thus, the smaller the percentage of ink coverage, the lighter the coverage, and the larger the percentage, the heavier the coverage. Such coverage data relate directly to the quantity of ink and should be determined as accurately as possible during estimating. The type of composition matter, halftones, screen tints, type reverses, solids,

Type of form	Percent of coverage
Very light composition, no halftones	15
Normal composition, no halftones	20
Normal composition, bold paragraph heads	25
Medium composition, no halftones	35
Heavy composition, no halftones	50
Halftones	50
Screen tints*	—
Solids	100
Reverses	60–90
Process color separations:	
Magenta and cyan	40
Yellow	50
Black	20

*Approximate screen percentage

Figure 7.2 General guidelines to estimate ink coverage

and process color separations can all be evaluated at various percentages. Figure 7.2 provides some general coverage values when estimating ink coverage.

To simplify the coverage estimating procedure, a page is first measured in square inches. Then a percentage of coverage is determined for the aggregate of all images on that page. Finally, the page size is multiplied by the percentage of coverage to determine the square inch area of the paper that will be covered by ink.

For example, we have a 1-page flyer with a type page measuring 6 inches by 10 inches, or 60 square inches in area. Black ink coverage for this page, which includes both type matter and halftones, is estimated at 35 percent. Therefore,

$$60 \text{ sq. in.} \times 0.35 = 21 \text{ sq. in.}$$

which represents the amount of area covered with ink on the page when it is printed. Approximately one-third of each page will be covered with black ink.

Determination of coverage tends to be an estimate. A significant majority of printed material contains combinations of type and tonal matter, as in the previous example, and the usual procedure for determining coverage is to arrive at an aggregate coverage percentage. Whenever possible, visual samples should be used, and every attempt should be made to be precise.

Estimating ink coverage is not a complicated process, and it is not intended to be burdensome. However, pinning down ink coverage remains a problem when estimating ink because the process is frequently done before a product is visually conceived. This makes it difficult to determine the coverage factors specific to the graphic product. Given this problem—but understanding that ink may be an important job cost that should be included in the estimate—many printers develop a process by which coverages are averaged based on similar other jobs done by the company.

Number of Copies and Impressions

Naturally, the quantity of printed material directly relates to the amount of ink required for any given job. Whenever possible, ink consumption should include all press sheet setup and running spoilage additions because ink is also required for these operations. Of course, the volume of ink increases or decreases proportionately to the quantity of printing ordered.

Percentage of Ink Waste

Waste of ink is one aspect of production that is difficult to pin down precisely. Normally, such waste comes from ink that has been poorly stored, residual ink that is difficult to remove from the container, ink in the press fountain that has been color contaminated by a previous color (this ink must be discarded), and ink that is normally lost from press washups. For the most part, such ink loss does not amount to more than 10 percent of the total required amount for any given job. Of course, many factors enter into how much ink is actually wasted during production, and only individual plant study can accurately determine this figure. Nonetheless, this slight additional amount should be planned and estimated in order to be certain that quantities of ink are above, and not below, minimum needed amounts to complete the printing order.

7.5   Estimating Lithographic Ink Quantity

The preceding discussion covered all of the variables when estimating ink. The following incorporates all such variables into a formula used to estimate ink quantities:

number of pounds of ink = (total form area x percentage of coverage x total number of copies x anticipated percentage of ink waste) ÷ ink mileage factor

where total form area is measured in square inches, the total number of copies includes press spoilage, and the ink mileage factor is determined from Figure 7.1. Once the actual poundage of ink has been determined, that value is multiplied by the cost per pound to find the job cost for ink.

Each time any variable in the formula changes, a new ink formula must be built to reflect that change. In a typical commercial printing job, the two most common changes are in color of ink, which is reflected as a change in ink mileage, and in the coverage percentage. For example, a 2-color job (red and black) prints with one-half of its black pages at 40 percent coverage and the other half of its black pages at 25 percent. All of the red pages print at 35 percent. Three formulas are thus needed to estimate ink for this example: one for black at 40 percent, one for black at 25 percent, and one for red at 35 percent. Total form area (the sum of the type page areas), the total number of copies including spoilage, and the anticipated ink waste and loss remain unchanged for all colors and all coverage percentages in this example.

The following list provides pointers for using the ink poundage formula:

1. The total form area is determined by multiplying the area (square inch value) of one type page by the number of pages to be printed in that color at the same percentage coverage. For example, a 16-page booklet with a type page measuring 40 square inches prints in black ink with 30 percent coverage for 8 pages and 50 percent coverage for the other 8 pages. Total form area is then 8 pages x 40 square inches per page = 320 square inches to be used at each coverage percentage (30 percent and 50 percent) when the formulas are built.

2. The coverage percentage figure is expressed in the formula in decimal form. For example, 45 percent becomes 0.45 and 25 percent becomes 0.25.

3. The number of copies including press spoilage can be calculated in one step by adding 1.00 to the percentage spoilage figure, which is then multiplied by the base number of copies. For example, for a 10,000 run with 5 percent spoilage, the percentage figure in the formula is (1.00 + 0.05) x 10,000 copies = 10,500 total press sheets. The same result is achieved if 10,000 is first multiplied by 5 percent, which equals 500 press sheets, and then the base 10,000 copies are added back to total 10,500 sheets to be printed, including spoilage.

4. The anticipated ink waste and loss percentage is handled the same way as press spoilage: Add 1.00 to the percentage of ink waste and loss. For example, if the anticipated ink waste and loss is 2 percent, then the formula figure is 1.00 + 0.02 = 1.02.

5. The ink mileage factor, which is taken from the schedule in Figure 7.1, varies by ink color and substrate used, as previously discussed. The schedule is based on the number of thousand square inches per pound of ink. Thus, if the schedule figure for a particular color is 385, it translates to 385,000 square inches of mileage per pound of ink for that color.

6. Any coverage of ink poundage at a thousandth of a pound is rounded up to the next hundredth of a pound. Similarly, any fraction of a cent is rounded up to the next whole penny.

7.6 Estimating the Cost of Ink

Once the quantity of ink has been estimated, the cost of ink can be determined by multiplying the poundage by the dollar cost paid by the printer. The cost is typically on a per pound basis, but other bases are sometimes used.

It is almost uniformly agreed that the cost of ink is secondary to its performance during printing production. Every production manager at one time or another has faced poor ink performance during printing or as a related follow-up problem when drying, chalking, or some other technical difficulty arises. Two common causes are cited here. First, lower-priced inks tend to cause production problems, so buying cheaper inks is unwise. Second, inks and substrates should be matched for compatibility, so it is prudent to evaluate compatibility during the estimating stage. This could save considerable production time and cost later. When printers do not consider these two issues—perhaps for a modest initial cost savings to the printing company by buying a less expensive ink—the total job cost increases significantly because of the additional materials, time, and rescheduling necessary to redo all or part of the ruined order.

Purchasing inks in large quantities reduces the cost per pound, but of course ties up valuable capital that might be used in other areas more effectively. When ink is purchased in small cans, waste is usually high, thus inflating the poundage cost actually paid. Most plants prefer to buy inks in 5-pound cans or larger to reduce such waste and thereby cut production costs.

Example 7.1. We are to print 25,000 copies of a 16-page booklet on a lithographic offset press. Type page size is 5 inches x 8 inches. All 16 pages will print with black ink at 30 percent coverage; 8 pages will print with a second color, opaque red, at 25 percent coverage, and 6 more pages will run in Persian orange at 20 percent coverage. Add 5 percent per color for press spoilage (for a total of 15 percent) and an additional 5 percent to compensate for ink waste and loss during production. The job will be printed on dull-coated stock. The black ink costs $7.20 per pound, the red ink costs $14.05 per pound, and the orange ink costs $15.35 per pound. Determine the cost and quantity of each color of ink necessary to complete this order.

Solution

Step 1. Find the page size in square inches:

$$5 \text{ in. x } 8 \text{ in.} = 40 \text{ sq. in./p.}$$

Step 2. Find the number of copies including spoilage:

$$25{,}000 \text{ cps. x } 1.15 = 28{,}750 \text{ cps.}$$

Step 3. Find the poundage for the black ink:

$$\frac{40 \text{ sq. in.} \times 16 \text{ pp.} \times 0.30 \times 28{,}750 \times 1.05}{375{,}000} \text{ sq. in./lb.} =$$

$$\frac{5{,}796{,}000 \text{ sq. in.}}{375{,}000 \text{ sq. in./lb.}} = 15.46 \text{ lbs.}$$

Step 4. Find the cost of the black ink:

$$15.46 \text{ lbs.} \times \$7.20/\text{lb.} = \$111.31$$

Step 5. Find the poundage for the red ink:

$$\frac{40 \text{ sq. in.} \times 8 \text{ pp.} \times 0.25 \times 28{,}750 \times 1.05}{325{,}000} \text{ sq. in./lb.} =$$

$$\frac{2{,}415{,}000 \text{ sq. in.}}{325{,}000 \text{ sq. in./lb.}} = 7.43 \text{ lbs.}$$

Step 6. Find the cost of the red ink:

$$7.43 \text{ lbs.} \times \$14.05/\text{lb.} = \$104.39$$

Step 7. Find the poundage for the orange ink:

$$\frac{40 \text{ sq. in.} \times 6 \text{ pp.} \times 0.20 \times 28{,}750 \times 1.05}{310{,}000} \text{ sq. in./lb.} =$$

$$\frac{1{,}449{,}000 \text{ sq. in.}}{310{,}000 \text{ sq. in./lb.}} = 4.68 \text{ lbs.}$$

Step 8. Find the cost of the orange ink:

$$4.68 \text{ lbs.} \times \$15.35/\text{lb.} = \$71.84$$

Step 9. Summarize the poundage findings:
Black ink: 15.46 lbs.
Red ink: 7.43 lbs.
Orange ink: 4.68 lbs.

Step 10. Summarize the cost findings:
Black ink: $111.31
Red ink: $104.39
Orange ink: $71.84
Total cost: $287.54

Example 7.2. We have an order for a 4-color poster measuring 18 inches x 24 inches finish size, with a form size of 16 inches x 22 inches (there is a 1-inch white margin on all sides). Based on an evaluation of the color photo to be printed, coverages are anticipated to be as follows: magenta, 45 percent; cyan,

65 percent; yellow, 40 percent; and black, 15 percent. Add 3 percent per form for paper spoilage and 4 percent for ink waste and loss during production. Stock will be litho coated offset book, substance 70. The customer wants 7,500 copies delivered. Ink costs are: magenta, $10.35 per pound; cyan, $15.20 per pound; yellow, $9.75 per pound; and black, $7.80 per pound. Determine ink poundage and cost for the job.

Solution

Step 1. Determine the form size of the poster in square inches:

$$16 \text{ in. x } 22 \text{ in. } = 352 \text{ sq. in.}$$

Step 2. Determine the number of copies including spoilage. (Each color of ink requires 1 form. Therefore, 3 percent/form x 4 forms = 12 percent.):

$$7,500 \text{ cps. x } 1.12 = 8,400 \text{ cps.}$$

Step 3. Find the poundage for the magenta ink:

$$\frac{352 \text{ sq. in.} \times 0.45 \times 8,400 \times 1.04}{345,000 \text{ sq. in/lb.}} = \frac{1,282,782 \text{ sq. in.}}{345,000 \text{ sq. in./lb.}} = 4.02 \text{ lbs.}$$

Step 4. Determine the cost for the magenta ink:

$$4.02 \text{ lbs. x } \$10.35/\text{lb.} = \$41.61$$

Step 5. Find the poundage for the cyan ink:

$$\frac{352 \text{ sq. in.} \times 0.65 \times 8,400 \times 1.04}{340,000 \text{ sq. in/lb.}} = \frac{1,998,797 \text{ sq. in.}}{340,000 \text{ sq. in./lb.}} = 5.88 \text{ lbs.}$$

Step 6. Find the cost for the cyan ink:

$$5.88 \text{ lbs. x } \$15.20/\text{lb.} = \$89.38$$

Step 7. Determine the poundage for the yellow ink:

$$\frac{352 \text{ sq. in.} \times 0.40 \times 8,400 \times 1.04}{355,000 \text{ sq. in/lb.}} = \frac{1,230,029 \text{ sq. in.}}{355,000 \text{ sq. in./lb.}} = 3.46 \text{ lbs.}$$

Step 8. Find the cost for the yellow ink:

$$3.46 \text{ lbs. x } \$9.75/\text{lb.} = \$33.74$$

Step 9. Determine the poundage for the black ink:

$$\frac{352 \text{ sq. in.} \times 0.15 \times 8,400 \times 1.04}{380,000 \text{ sq. in/lb.}} = \frac{461,261 \text{ sq. in.}}{380,000 \text{ sq. in./lb.}} = 1.21 \text{ lbs.}$$

Step 10. Find the cost for the black ink:

$$1.21 \text{ lbs. x } \$7.80/\text{lbs.} = \$9.44$$

Step 11. Summarize the poundage findings:
Magenta ink: 4.02 lbs.
Cyan ink: 5.88 lbs.
Yellow ink: 3.46 lbs.
Black ink: 1.21 lbs.

Step 12. Summarize the cost findings:
Magenta ink: $41.61
Cyan ink: $89.38
Yellow ink: $33.74
Black ink: $9.44
Total cost: $174.17

Chapter 8

Estimating Electronic Prepress and Desktop Publishing Production

8.5   Overview of Cost Estimating Digital Prepress Production

8.6   Benchmarking Electronic Prepress Times and Costs

Setting Benchmarks for Production Activities

Benchmarking Production Times and Material Costs

8.7   Cost Estimating Desktop Publishing and Electronic Prepress Production

8.8   Cost Estimating Specific Electronic Prepress Production Operations

Schedule Format Description

Estimating Job Setup: File Acquisition, File Transfer, and Cost of Removable Media

Estimating Desktop Scanning Production

Estimating Page Layout and Illustration Production

Estimating Electronic Trapping and Image Manipulation

Estimating Electronic Imposition Production

Overview of Digital Output Technology

Estimating Black-and-White Laser Printing Production

Estimating Film Imagesetting and Computer-to-Plate Output

Estimating Low-Cost Digital Color Proofing Production

Estimating Dye Sublimation Digital Proofing Production

Estimating Laser Color Proofing Production

Estimating Iris Color Proofing Production

8.9   Developing a Template Spreadsheet Cost Estimating System for Electronic Prepress

8.10   Business and Production Aspects of Electronic Prepress

Observations on Success for Digital Prepress Providers

Preflighting: Computer-Ready Electronic Files 2 and Other Preflight Information

File-Checking Software

Terms and Conditions for Electronic Prepress

8.1 Introduction

A new paradigm based on proven digital imaging technology has shifted the printing industry from long-standing photomechanical production methods to electronic processes. The prepress segment has been affected at all production levels. It is clear that the future will continue to bring digital changes in prepress, as well as pronounced digital shifts affecting press and postpress technologies. The products and services provided by a graphic arts enterprise have become inextricably linked using digital technology.

This chapter provides estimating methods for digital prepress technology. Estimating image design and creation, including creative digital design services, begins the chapter. Estimating film and digital photographic services is then discussed. Because digital prepress production data should be tailored to fit a given company's equipment, software, and employees, benchmarking production times are covered. Numerous schedules containing production data for estimating a range of electronic prepress production operations are provided. The process of building spreadsheet templates for prepress estimating is also covered. The chapter concludes with a discussion of important production and business aspects of a typical electronic prepress enterprise.

8.2 Background and Terminology

Electronic imaging methods in prepress began with the development of drum scanning more than thirty years ago. Then, in 1984, Apple Computer introduced the Macintosh, and, in 1985, Aldus PageMaker software and laser printing were introduced. Initially this new technology appeared innovative and unique but limited to uncomplicated graphic imaging. However, the seed had been planted and the paradigm shift to digital imaging had begun.

By the late 1980s electronic imaging methods were revolutionizing printing production everywhere. Hardware platforms became faster, better, and less costly, and continuing software enhancements offered ever-increasing simplicity and power. Although by the mid-1990s the transition from conventional prepress to electronic prepress methods for many printers and their customers had entered adulthood, a certain amount of discomfort remained because the technology had not yet been fully perfected.

Electronic prepress has affected how printers do business at the most basic, core level. Using conventional prepress methods, printers controlled literally all aspects of prepress production with the exception of mechanical art production. Printers provided numerous VA services, including typesetting, process camera imaging and film contacting, stripping, proofing, and platemaking. These areas were tightly controlled by the printer as part of the manufacturing process, and customers could not easily intervene in them. However, DTP and digital imaging have changed this. Today any skilled digital file creator—a graphic designer or artist, a secretary or an executive, a student or a teacher—has much of this prepress power through the inexpensive software she conveniently uses on the stand-alone Macintosh or PC in her home or office.

This change has forced printers into maintaining a high degree of expertise in both conventional prepress technology and digital production methods. It has also effectively shifted control of important graphic decisions from the printer to the customer, putting the customer in a powerful position when preparing artwork for jobs. On the whole customers have reacted positively. While some customers continue their extensive use of conventional photomechanical technology, other customers have shifted entirely to digital prepress. In fact, proficiency in electronic image generation for some customers has become quite high, to the point that it sometimes exceeds the printer's knowledge and experience.

For many printers it has been an uncomfortable, topsy-turvy experience that has been complicated by high investment costs for electronic equipment, disruptive production flow, a distinct loss of control as customers were handed these prepress tools via complex computer software, and marginal profits. Ultimately printers who have made the paradigm shift to digital technology have been better off, but it has been difficult for them to maintain a sense of perspective given the struggles and risks involved.

Certain digital terminology should be clarified. In this book, desktop publishing (DTP), electronic prepress (EPP), and digital prepress (DPP) are used interchangeably. So, too, are the terms "digital" and "electronic" in that both require the use of a computer platform, appropriate software, and related input and output devices. The term "analog" means any process done parallel to another process or technique, such as photomechanical proofing methods that are substituted for digital proofing procedures. A digital file creator (DFC) is anyone—from a very skilled digital imager to a novice—with a computer and appropriate software who produces electronic files ranging from excellent to poor. These DFCs include graphic designers, printing company employees, secretaries, teachers, executives, students, housewives—people of all ages, genders, and ethnic boundaries. A final output provider (FOP) is the company or person responsible for generating the end product or final output from the digital file. Because this output is frequently imaged film ready for platemaking, the term final (or finished) film provider (FFP) is sometimes substituted for FOP. When a client or a customer provides the printing company with film for his job, it is known as "customer-furnished film," also commonly termed "final film" or "furnished film."

8.3 Image Creation and Execution: Graphic Design and Artwork Production

In light of the rapid shift to DTP and EPP methods, it is important to distinguish the role of the graphic designer or graphic artist relative to the creation and execution of the finished art for a client. To do this, it is best to separate the process into two distinct operations: (1) the creative process of graphic design, which is termed "image creation" in this text, and (2) the production of the graphic concept, which is termed "image execution" and follows image creation.

Image Creation

It is generally agreed that developing a unique, creative graphic design is a process that remains much the same regardless of whether the job is executed using conventional or digital production methods. The image creation process usually begins with an idea that is developed using proven graphic design fundamentals, paper and pencil, and concept exploration. However, it is possible that emerging digital technology may assist the graphic designer even in these earliest stages of design development. For example, digital design using a "pick and click" image assembly process and development of prepackaged designs for certain products and services are already available in various forms. However, today creative image development remains a transference of ideas from concept to reality—from brain to paper—to meet the needs and conditions of the client.

A typical graphic design commission requires that the graphic designer or graphic artist determine a clear description of what the client desires. Then, after she explores the parameters creatively, the designer comes up with various ideas and concepts to resolve the client's problem. The best graphic art solutions begin with a design plan that takes into account the practical steps necessary to achieve the finished graphic product.

The graphic design process typically requires four sequenced steps: thumbnail sketches, followed by rough art renditions of selected thumbnails, after which comes comprehensive artwork, and finally finished artwork. The process typically requires many thumbnails, which are simple, quick sketches, with the client and designer working together to narrow concepts and ideas as the process moves toward one final graphic product.

Generally thumbnails and rough art are manually produced using the artist's sketching and drawing abilities, while comprehensive art and finished art may be done either manually or electronically depending on various factors in the client-designer relationship. When the design process is shortcut, production problems tend to be more frequent and cost more money later. For example, producing only a few thumbnails, or skipping or shortcutting either the rough or comprehensive artwork stages, bypasses important concept issues at each of these junctures. Frequently, too little time is spent at the thumbnail stage, where the creative imaging process sets the tone and image dynamics for the final product.

The design of a graphic product should meet two key conditions. First, it should achieve the objectives the customer or the ultimate product user has established. Second, it should incorporate imaging concepts to ensure that the job can be produced within the customer's budget and time requirements. Professional, experienced graphic designers constantly evaluate their work in light of these two issues.

Thumbnail sketches should be a "no holds barred" exploration of graphic images within product design to meet customer's end-use requirements. This exploration is typically done through one or more meetings between the customer and the graphic designer. At this genesis stage, less attention should be paid to the details of production and cost and more should be paid to meeting the customer's graphic imaging objectives. As the design is narrowed through thumbnail exploration, a group of the best images is selected for the production of rough artwork. At this time the thumbnails are enhanced to more accurate renditions and frequently are made in actual size.

Production methods, the customer's budget requirements, and time factors enter at the rough art stage. As the choices are narrowed to one or two final images, comprehensive artwork, which should be a working model of the final product as it is intended to look and work, is prepared. Once the comprehensive art is reviewed (the customer's budget and production costs are important considerations here), a final choice is made and the production of finished graphic art commences.

The customer's input at all design stages is critical to the success of the final printed product. Because the customer is the purchaser and frequently the ultimate consumer of the printing, design form and function are key considerations. It is the customer's responsibility to explain the purpose and use of the graphic product to the designer beginning at the thumbnail stage. This is usually done through interviews and discussion between the two parties and is supplemented by samples if available. In turn, it is the designer's job to provide the customer with ideas and graphic images to meet or exceed the purpose and use conditions that are indicated.

Image Execution

Once the design process has narrowed to a reasonable number of possible graphic images, usually at the comprehensive stage of image development, the graphic designer begins to develop the images digitally. Because this process tends to be time consuming, only the best final images should move to the comprehensive stage. Many artists prefer to complete the comprehensive art as illustrations, fine art images, or drawings on paper, then scan these images to produce digital files. Once the files are in digital form, they are corrected and modified to produce final art. The point at which an image moves from paper to digital form is not fixed, so some graphic artists work digitally at the rough art stage, while others complete their final art on paper and then scan the image and make minimum corrections using digital methods.

As DTP has become accepted and available to anyone at a reasonable cost, a growing number of customers are attempting to save money by designing and producing their own graphic products. This decision can sometimes cost the customer more money in the long run, however, because it is not unusual for the customer to incorrectly evaluate the functions his graphic product must fulfill. The product thus misses its targeted needs, which costs the customer valuable market share. In addition, given a wide range of options for mechanical and electronic art production, and the frequent inattention to detail paid to completing the artwork, the art may be improperly prepared. A simple mistake, such as leaving out what appears to be an unimportant artwork detail, can be expensive later to correct either during production or, worse, when the job is printed with the error.

The earlier errors in artwork are discovered the better. Preflighting a file, which is checking the artwork for errors before the job enters production, is frequently done too late. Error reduction is achieved when the artist has a thorough knowledge of how electronic artwork is prepared. Repairing artwork should be completed by a person who is thoroughly knowledgeable in this area and is focused on achieving the desired job quality with minimum final output problems. Corrections are usually completed by the FOP, who is also frequently the printer, but a service bureau or trade shop may also complete this work. Artwork corrections can be costly, time consuming, and may cause significant scheduling problems.

Artwork for Graphic Production

Graphic artwork is prepared using conventional (e.g., mechanical or pasteup methods) or electronic (e.g., digital) procedures or a mix of the two. Although the movement of a growing number of printers is toward 100 percent electronic artwork from all customers, many printers routinely accept both. Flexibility on the part of the printer in accommodating either type of artwork is important because many customers submit electronic art using various types of DTP hardware and software.

The flowchart in Figure 8.1 shows the steps a printing order follows when conventional mechanical artwork is used. Although electronic art is quickly replacing mechanical art, printers continue to receive mechanical art from customers or art that is mixed between electronic and mechanical. As shown in Figure 8.1, photomechanical artwork is typically rendered into high-contrast line, halftone, and color-separated film images from typeset materials, pre-

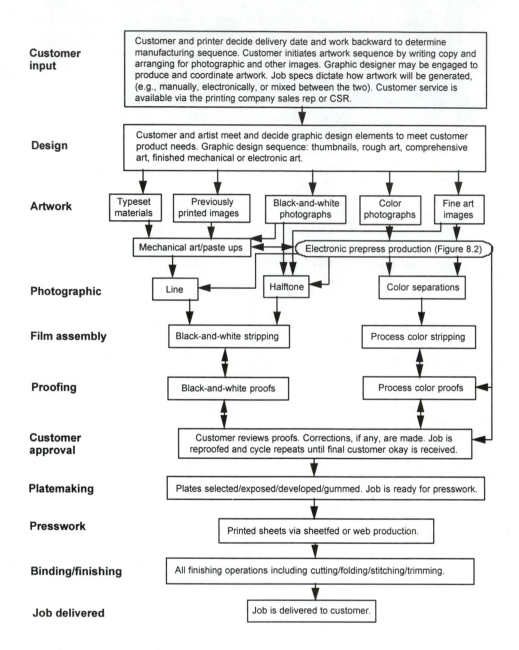

Figure 8.1 Flowchart showing steps for producing a printing order using typical photomechanical prepress methods and the lithographic printing process

viously printed images, black-and-white photographs, color photographs, and fine art images. Depending on the image elements, these components make up the parts that go together to produce mechanical art "boards," which are also known as pasteup art. The prepress production sequence then sequentially utilizes photographic methods using a process camera, followed by manual film assembly, then proofing, customer approval, and finally platemaking. Chapter 9 provides details regarding the estimating of these photomechanical production methods.

Figure 8.2 is a flowchart showing color EPP operations and is referenced in the "Electronic color production" bubble of Figure 8.1 under the "Color photographs" and "Fine art images" boxes. The production methods shown in Figure 8.2 insert into the production routine illustrated in Figure 8.1, adding complexity to available imaging options and cross-linking production methods between digital and photomechanical methods.

Figure 8.2 is divided into three distinct segments: image capture, image assembly, and image output production (illustrated on the left side of the figure). The image capture segment begins with original art at photographic transparencies, color prints (c-prints), or pieces of original artwork that are electronically scanned or input using digital photography. Kodak's Photo-CD process is popular for transferring color images into digital form. The scanning process outputs either film separations or digital separations, both of which are proofed and corrected and then either manually or electronically assembled in the second segment, image assembly.

Following the image assembly process, proofing is completed and the job moves to platemaking, where either photomechanical or computer-to-plate (CTP) imaging methods are employed.

As shown in Figure 8.2, it is possible to mix conventional and digital techniques at a number of points during production. As mentioned earlier, this is commonly termed "analog production." For example, analog proofs are proofs made using conventional photomechanical technology, even though digital proofing methods may have already been used. Thus, analog production is a parallel production operation that produces results that are similar to, but not precisely like, the results of the digital process used. Analog proofs are the most common analog production operation because they are precise replicas of the filmset images and are exceptionally high in color quality. However, because they are photomechanical and require manual production, they are usually more expensive than digital proofs.

Profitable graphic imaging companies attempt to maintain smooth job flows and thus provide production sequences that are predictable. To accomplish this, jobs are carefully preflighted before production begins and are followed with careful monitoring and maintenance of global and detailed production issues. Even with these controls, however, some jobs bounce between conventional and digital methods and do not follow their anticipated production patterns. The

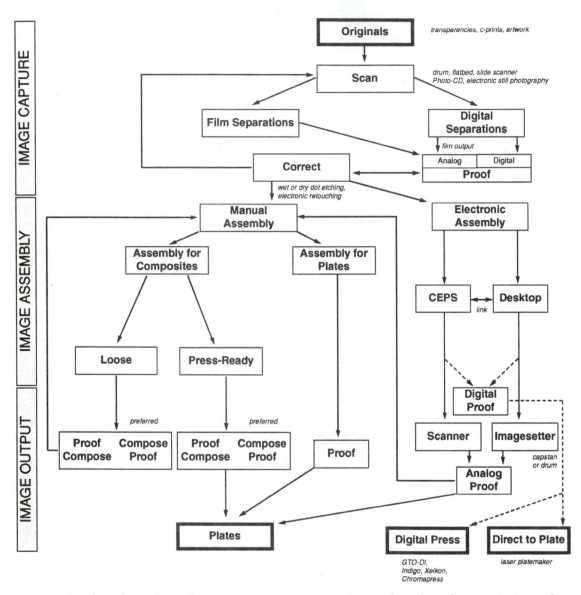

Figure 8.2 Flowchart for color prepress operations. (Reproduced with permission of Professor Michael Blum, California Polytechnic State University, San Luis Obispo, California.)

point at which a job crosses over between conventional and digital production is generally dictated on an as-needed basis that takes into consideration job cycle time, job due date, ease of production, employee skills, equipment and software, quality desired, and cost.

The methods used to prepare mechanical artwork have become routine and straightforward through years of experience. However, the transition from conventional to electronic art has been occurring rapidly, driven primarily by aggressive DTP technology enhancements and the inherent flexibility of digital processes. This rapid transition from mechanical art to electronic art has caused numerous problems for printers, who are frequently the end-users of the electronic art products. This is evident upon review of Figure 8.2. Certainly the rapidity of the transition, along with the complex technical problems that have been difficult to resolve, are key issues. In addition, there have been few computer hardware and software standards that printers and customers have shared. All of this shifting artwork technology has occurred in an environment of increased customer demand for color in their printed products, which adds another level of complexity to the process.

One result of DTP technology is that it is increasingly important for printers to assist the originator of the electronic art—the digital file creator or DFC—in preparing all artwork related to her jobs, either through training or on-line assistance during the design and art production stages. Successful printers have embraced this partnership, effectively growing their businesses through close DFC interaction. Preflighting, which was defined earlier as checking electronic artwork before the job is committed to production, has become a routine step to ensure minimum production problems. Service bureaus, many of which are former trade typesetters, are frequently either the DFC or are involved in the art production sequence. Service bureaus are popular because of the range of digital services they provide to artists, designers, customers, and printers.

From the printing estimator's vantage point, the key consideration of DTP technology is the kind and quality of artwork that enters production, whether it is mechanical, electronic, or mixed. This is because of the increased costs and time that are needed when artwork is improperly prepared. As DTP has become less expensive and available to everyone from the novice designer to the skilled professional, customer-supplied artwork has increased in frequency. The DTP technology has shifted many critical prepress operations that were performed in conventional photomechanical and film assembly departments of a printing company (e.g., imposition, trapping, tints, color production, bleeds, and trims) to the designer's desktop system. This has given important printing production decisions to artists and designers who are sometimes inexperienced or unable to assimilate these key details into their artwork. Thus, electronic artwork can either be properly prepared and flow smoothly into production, or it can cause extensive problems that require expensive rework, usually in a time-compressed situation.

During the job specification process, when the details upon which an estimate is based are obtained, the customer indicates whether he will furnish the artwork for his job. If the art is mechanical and camera ready, and the artist or designer is experienced, it is likely that little additional work will be necessary prior to photomechanical production. With increasing frequency, however, the customer will indicate that the art will be supplied digitally (e.g., by floppy disk, SyQuest disk, or other electronic medium). From these digital files the printer will be expected to generate all stages from electronic files to finished film, which, as explained earlier, means the film is fully imaged and ready for platemaking. Problems in the transitory stages between customer-supplied electronic art files and final film can result in major cost increases to the customer.

Some customers want their printers to provide full graphic services. In such cases the customer authorizes the printing company to procure artwork from sources available to the printer. Typically the printer engages an experienced graphic designer who may work independently from the printer, or the printer may work in cooperation with other artists or a service bureau. Instead of exercising these options, sometimes the printer prepares the art in house using company designers, staff artists, and company EPP equipment.

Estimators and production planners know that the design and preparation of artwork for printing—regardless of whether the art is mechanical or electronic—are vital planning elements. A cardinal rule in printing is, "As goes the artwork, so goes the job," which means that if artwork is prepared incorrectly, the production of the printing order is likely to be problematic as well. Thus, if the art is poorly designed or the design is poorly prepared, the printer will undoubtedly experience production problems. For example, if bleeds, folds, and trims are not built into the job; if colors are improperly trapped or out of register; if the design is creative but simply cannot be executed economically, the job was poorly planned and coordinated during its initial copy preparation stages. The better the initial planning of the job and the more skilled the execution of the artwork, the more expeditiously the job moves through production.

Experienced graphic artists understand the importance of their art products on printing production. The more experience a graphic designer has with respect to printing production—that is, the more she understands and can deal with the technology of printing as it relates to the artwork she produces—the lower the cost and the less time that is needed during printing production. With the aggressive shift to electronic art and the incorporation of prepress production into the DTP software used to generate this art, it is not possible to generate high-quality artwork for printing without the artist or designer having a suitable working knowledge of printing concepts.

Sources of Graphic Image Production

Artwork for printing can come from a number of sources, each of which may have an effect on the quality, reproducibility, and effectiveness of the graphic image. The following discusses these sources and some of the important issues with each source.

Artwork Prepared by the Customer. With increasing frequency, print customers, who include businesses of all types and sizes, including corporations and publishers, are insisting on generating artwork for their jobs. When this happens, one of the four following options is typical:

1. The customer will provide finished, camera-ready mechanical art.
2. The customer will provide a combination of mechanical and electronic artwork that represents art for the entire job.
3. The customer will provide a disk or other magnetic media containing the art for the job in electronic form.
4. The customer will provide final film ready for platemaking.

Each of these options requires a different production sequence, and the sequence is unpredictable because of the critical details included as each job is created. Thus, artwork details drive the downstream production processes for every job. This flow is complicated when the customer-supplied artwork is improperly prepared.

When the customer provides camera-ready mechanical art, the production sequence shown in Figure 8.1 is typical. When the customer provides a combination of mechanical and electronic art, production requires matching the supplied artwork to the conventional and electronic processes necessary, which follows the production sequences in Figure 8.2. When the customer provides a disk containing the job in full electronic format, the printer must first RIP or output the electronic files to final film, then proof, correct, give final approval to, then print the artwork. When the customer provides final film, the printing production sequence bypasses the photographic and electronic processes. The film arrives, is quickly stripped and plated, and the job is printed.

Printers should be careful with customers who are trying to save money on their jobs but who lack in-depth knowledge of the imaging processes involved. This is because the costs associated with correcting customer-supplied artwork that is improperly prepared can be excessive as well as time consuming. To avoid this, when a new or potentially inexperienced customer insists on providing his own artwork and the printer does not wish to provide these services, the printer should recommend a knowledgeable graphic designer, service bureau, or trade shop to work with the customer. Sometimes the customer on his own will engage a desktop-literate graphic artist, service bureau, or trade shop without the printer's knowledge.

When an order is generated from a print buyer who has a good knowledge of the imaging processes required for the job, the buyer may prepare the art in house or may go through a service bureau or trade shop for finished film for the job. The buyer's decision is typically based on the complexity of the job relative to the in-house equipment and employee skills. Because trade shops and service bureaus are engaged in business to handle print buyers, publishers, and corporate accounts, competition among them is intense.

Artwork Prepared by an In-Plant Artist. Depending on the type of customer served by the printer, some printing companies provide design and art services using their own skilled personnel and company equipment. Having a resident artist is particularly desirable when streamlining and standardizing production or when the majority of products the company prints require unique graphic design elements. Such products might include posters, packaging items, and annual reports. Most printing plants that produce a significant amount of business forms have in-plant artists to complete form design. Based on the skill and experience of the in-plant artist, both electronic and conventional artwork is generated.

An in-plant artist offers a number of advantages which include control of both the quality of design and the mechanical art, thereby streamlining production of the job after art, and control of the timeliness of production of art, so rush or special jobs can be more easily accommodated. An in-house artist also improves company profitability because the art is produced in house and is thus a value-added profit center. Finally, in-house art staff increase security to the printer because, under the Printing Trade Customs discussed in Chapter 5, the artwork is owned by the printer when it is produced as part of the customer's order unless otherwise agreed.

Artwork Prepared by a Service Bureau or Trade Shop. Given the complexities of electronic artwork, printers, corporate customers, publishers, and print buyers sometimes use service bureaus and trade shops to provide finished film or to assist in art production. Service bureaus, which in many cases are former trade typesetting or trade composition houses, offer a range of electronic graphic design and related services, in addition to conventional mechanical art production if it is requested by customers. Most service bureaus and trade shops provide a range of digital products, from final film to proofs to on-demand printing services using the Xerox DocuTech or other system.

When artwork is purchased from a service bureau or trade house, the prepared material is usually of high quality. This high-quality material flows easily and with minimum alteration into print production. Trade houses and services bureaus tend to work closely with printing companies and build their reputations on the reproducibility of their graphic products and services. Frequently the customer selects and works with one or two trade shops or service bureaus by applying the purchasing objectives of quality, service, and experience while deemphasizing price. Printers also tend to follow these objectives when working closely with a chosen group of service bureaus or trade shops. Doing this ensures smoother production and saves money in the long term through fewer production problems.

Artwork Prepared by a Freelance Graphic Artist or Graphic Designer. Freelance graphic artists and designers can be excellent sources of artwork for the printer, provided that the graphic designers are aware of printing processes and technical printing requirements in depth. Many freelance designers charge flat rates for their services, which may include creative idea development, research, thumbnail sketches, rough art, comprehensive art, and the completion of finished mechanical or electronic art or final film. Fees vary according to the reputation of the artist; the artist's special skills, such as calligraphic work; the type of work under consideration; the size of the job; the general availability of the graphic artist; and the relative amount of electronic typesetting and design capacity the artist can provide.

Freelance graphic artists are hired by the customer either prior to contacting the printer, at the printer's suggestion, or by the printer as an outside purchase for the customer's job. Frequently a freelance designer works for more than one customer at the same time, so meeting deadlines can be a problem. For this reason, it is advisable that each printing company has a list of freelancers to contact. Being able to call on a variety of designers also provides a variety of design ideas for the company because each graphic artist produces a different range of visual images.

As the skill and reputation of the freelance artist grows, her services may become harder to arrange and higher in price. It is therefore necessary that an estimate for the freelancer's services is secured on a job-by-job basis or that the printing estimator is provided with some method to determine the cost of artwork. Of course, the availability of the artist also must be determined. Charts for estimating the relative costs of certain creative art services provided by the freelance artist are presented later in this chapter.

Artwork Prepared by a Studio. The art studio is essentially a group of artists working together and sharing common facilities. Sometimes each member of the studio represents a different discipline and is called upon when his particular services are needed. The art studio is like any other business: It is concerned about sales, production, billing, and internal business matters.

The person in charge of art studio projects is called an art director and is versed in both the business and the creative aspects of art and design. Most art directors determine which projects will be accepted, assign people to work on certain jobs, and generally serve as coordinator for such efforts. The art director may work closely with the printing company in determining the specifics of design for a customer's order.

Art studios, because they have more personnel than does the independent freelance artist, have the capacity to undertake reasonably large projects. They also have the ability to develop creative graphic ideas and then produce mechanical or electronic art, frequently as final film to the printing company. They have the skills to coordinate all elements of art and any intermediate artwork steps, including design, type input, conventional or digital photographic studio services, and preparation of unique, original art. An experienced art studio can offer the printing plant an entire array of art and copy preparation services so that all art elements of the customer's order can be produced for efficient printing production.

Artwork Prepared by an Agency. Advertising agencies and public relations firms—or other companies established to meet the corporate client's graphic and media needs—can be important buyers of printed products, and frequently in large quantities. Although agency operations vary, agency-supplied mechanical or electronic artwork, or final film in some cases, may be provided to the printer. Many agencies engage a variety of sources for graphic art production depending on the complexity of the job, delivery and scheduling issues, and the level of skill and equipment capability within the agency. Thus, agency artwork can be generated by the agency's internal art staff, freelancers hired by the agency, trade shops or service bureaus, full-service printers, or any mix of this group. For example, artwork from an agency can be originated by an in-house agency artist at the first stage, then go to a trade shop or service bureau for further work before final film is sent to the printer.

The relationship between the advertising agency or public relations firm and the printer runs the gamut from cooperative and open to strained and problematic. In recent years centralized advertising agency operations have shifted to decentralized environments, so control by a single national advertising agency office is now less common. Printers have generally embraced this decentralization process. Even so, agencies recognize that they maintain control over the printers because the volume of printing these agencies purchase may be in the millions of dollars with only one or two jobs. These jobs may, in turn, be very profitable to the printing companies.

Because many agencies tend toward tight schedules and desire to control prepress production at all stages, printers are sometimes asked to compromise printing schedules to accommodate what they may consider unreasonable job changes or modifications by the agencies. Also, the printers may sometimes be asked to cut corners during production to meet agency budgets, while at the same time the agencies are unwilling to bend on their design concepts, such as the size or style of product. For printers, these are frustrating but anticipated realities of dealing with agency clients.

One of the areas where the conflict between agency and printer becomes most noticeable is in the quality and timeliness of artwork for the job. When agencies provide final film that is ready for platemaking, artwork problems tend to be minimized. Sometimes, however, agencies provide substandard artwork to the printer but expect a high-quality final product. The art may be the wrong size, poorly prepared for final film output, or piecemeal instead of as a unified whole. While it is fair to say that advertising agencies and public relations firms represent customer demands that sometimes strain the printer's goodwill, it is also understood that the volume of work these agencies purchase is so high that it encourages significant printer interest.

8.4 Estimating Creative Prepress Services

Estimating the costs of creative prepress services, including graphic design and related artwork production, has always been difficult. The reasons are varied. Frequently artwork is not prepared nor even conceived when the estimate is requested, in which cases specifying artwork details is next to impossible. These details have major impact on the production methods and cost of the job. Also, the method of art preparation, which initiates a production plan that is critical to job cost, is subject to wide variation from artist to artist.

Today most graphic artists choose between conventional and electronic artwork preparation methods or mix them with the extensive additional choices of artwork production within the electronic or conventional method chosen. Although the range of art production choices when artwork is prepared electronically, which is driven by available software choices and the designer's skill in using the software, may have a significant effect on job cost, the choices made by the artist do not usually include this cost dimension.

Even when artwork is prepared before the estimate is requested, estimating is difficult because many production problems are not evident until the job actually begins production. As discussed previously, the development and acceptance of preflighting electronic artwork is an important step to ensure that the job will flow properly into the production sequence. This step is also of great help in keeping production costs in line and the job within the customer's budget. It should be clear that the preflighting concept, although it has not always been specifically termed "preflighting," has been practiced with mechanical artwork by successful printing companies for many years.

Estimating Creative Art Services

Figure 8.3 provides one method for estimating the dollar amount of creative art services provided by an experienced graphic designer or graphic artist. It is a price-driven process as noted. The dollar amounts indicated are intended as guidelines because many different elements go into the creative processes by which original artwork is produced. Generally there are no standard prices and the environment in which they are developed is usually quite competitive.

Service or activity	Rate
Initial consultation fee	$60/hr.
Research, concept development, client meetings	$40/hr.
Artist preparation of thumbnails and/or rough drawings	$40/hr.
Artist preparation of comprehensive or final mechanical art*	$50/hr.
Artist preparation of comprehensive or final electronic art**	$60/hr.

Special design services**
  Illustrations
  Fine art
  Cover art (books and magazines)
  Calligraphic services
	Price by image, page, or job

Dollar figures in this schedule are provided for example only. Rates include designer's computer and software, but proofs and other materials are extra.

* See Chapter 9 to cost estimate mechanical artwork time and cost.

**See Figure 8.5 and other data in this chapter to cost estimate digital production including keyboarding input, graphic image creation, graphic image modification, and output.

Figure 8.3 Price estimating schedule for graphic design and creative artwork production

Issues such as royalties for the use of a creative design and licensing agreements for first-time and reuse of images are important. Prices can be developed based on the use of the image, on a page-rate situation (if the job is a book, magazine, newsletter, or so on), or on hourly or daily rates. Typically the rate quoted includes the artist's equipment. When an artist establishes her prices, subjective factors such as the artist's reputation, experience, skill, capital investment in equipment and software, and scheduling availability are normally factored in.

Because comprehensive art is sometimes the first electronic art produced, the schedule in Figure 8.3 links to Figure 8.5 and other related schedules in this chapter that are used for estimating DTP and EPP. Example 8.1 that follows demonstrates the use of Figure 8.3 for estimating a typical graphic design project.

Example 8.1. We want to estimate the time and cost for our in-plant graphic artist to prepare a new logo for a client's corporation letterheads, business cards, and other business communication materials. The customer wants a full-color logo with calligraphic type designed specifically to portray the image of the company. The artist plans to spend 1 hour of initial consultation, 1 hour in research, 2 hours completing thumbnails and rough art, 2 hours in client meetings for concept approval and review, and 3 hours preparing comprehensive and final electronic art. We estimate it will cost a flat $120.00 for the development of calligraphic imagery and that digital proofs and other materials will cost $150.00.

Solution

Refer to the schedule in Figure 8.3 for hourly costs.

Step 1. Determine the cost of initial consultation:

$$1 \text{ hr. x } \$60.00/\text{hr.} = \$60.00$$

Step 2. Determine the cost of research:

$$1 \text{ hr. x } \$40.00/\text{hr.} = \$40.00$$

Step 3. Determine the cost of preparing thumbnails and rough art:

$$2 \text{ hr. x } \$40.00/\text{hr.} = \$80.00$$

Step 4. Determine the cost for client meetings:

$$2 \text{ hr. x } \$40.00/\text{hr.} = \$80.00$$

Step 5. Determine the cost for preparing comprehensive and finished electronic art:

$$3 \text{ hr. x } \$60.00 = \$180.00$$

Step 6. List the cost to prepare calligraphic imagery:

$$\text{Flat fee of } \$120.00$$

Step 7. List the cost for digital proofs and other materials:

$$\text{Estimated cost of } \$150.00$$

Step 8. Determine the total estimated time:

$$1 \text{ hr.} + 1 \text{ hr.} + 2 \text{ hr.} + 2 \text{ hr.} + 3 \text{ hr.} = 9 \text{ hr.}$$

Step 9. Determine the total estimated cost of artwork for this job:

$$\$60.00 + \$40.00 + \$80.00 + \$80.00 + \$180.00 +$$
$$\$120.00 + \$150.00 = \$710.00$$

Estimating Film and Digital Photographic Services

Photographic imaging can be done using either conventional film-based methods or digital cameras that capture images into a computer system. When conventional film images are generated, and the final image is to be digitized so that it can be included in electronic art or other digital files, two conversion methods are common: scanning and Photo-CD. Estimating scanning times are detailed later in this chapter, while almost all Photo-CD conversion is done by outsourcing the film to a local company that provides the conversion service. Cost per image in Photo-CD is very low and the turnaround for this conversion is usually overnight. The digitized images are provided to the DFC in CD format and are color separated for immediate use.

The technology of digital photography is yet to be fully realized because it is currently limited to studio situations where images remain still. The typical, basic digital photographic equipment configuration includes a digital camera, which must be connected to a computer system with sufficient random-access memory (RAM) to hold the captured image; a high-quality monitor for accurate color viewing; digital archiving equipment; appropriate computer software for image capture; and peripheral lighting and other equipment. High-quality digital image capture requires expensive equipment and employees who are technically skilled in both photographic and digital methods. Digital photographic applications, although limited to still photography, are numerous and include image capture for advertising such items as canned goods, prepared foods, glassware, jewelry, and numerous other products. The full application of digital photography will be realized as technology enhancements allow images in motion to be captured with the same simplicity and level of quality as still images.

Figure 8.4 provides a price-driven schedule for estimating conventional and digital photographic services. Dollar amounts shown are for example only. As with the prices for creative design and artwork services, prices for conventional and digital photographic services should be established based on the skill of the photographer, the photographer's reputation, the quality of work desired, the capital investment in equipment and software, and scheduling availability. Some art studios and full-service printers have resident photographers perform these duties; others subcontract this service. Freelance designers sometimes provide conventional and digital photographic services, while others contract them out to professional photographic freelancers depending on the difficulty of the work and other factors.

Similar to their graphic design colleagues, professional photographers are concerned about the royalties paid on their images, licensing agreements, and first-time use and reuse rights. Because of this, the client is sometimes asked to sign an agreement which provides details in these areas. Examples 8.2 and 8.3 that follow show how to apply schedule data in Figure 8.4 for estimating conventional and digital photography production.

Example 8.2. Our photographic department will shoot a series of photographs for a 16-page fashion brochure using our in-house studio facilities. The job will require 4 models at a total cost of $1,200.00. An estimated 12 rolls of color 35-mm Kodachrome at $12.00 per roll and 4 rolls of black-and-white film at a cost of $6.00 per roll will be used. We estimate it will take 6 hours

Service or activity	Rate
Stage setting, product preparation	$20 per hr.
Model fee	Apply model fee

Image capture to photographic film

Setup cost: Photo equipment in studio setting	$50 per job
Setup cost: Photo equipment in remote setting (on location)	$100 per job + mileage or travel fee
Photographic services: Image capture production to film	$40 per hr.
Film development: Color transparencies or prints	$20 + material cost
Film development: Black and white	$20 + material cost
Film conversion: Film to Photo-CD	$20 + material cost

Digital image capture

Setup cost: Digital photo equipment in studio setting	$70 per job
Setup cost: Digital photo equipment in remote setting (on location)	$120 per job + mileage or travel fee
Photographic services: Image capture to digital medium (incl. archiving)	$50 per hr.
Digital image correction, manipulation, or image modification*	$60 per hr.
Digital proof for customer review*	$10 per proof

Figures in this schedule are provided for example only.

* See Figure 8.5 and other schedules in this chapter to cost estimate digital production including image modification and proofing output.

Figure 8.4 Price estimating schedule for conventional and digital image capture and related services

to shoot the photos with concurrent stage setting throughout the shoot. Determine the estimated price for this job.

Solution

Refer to Figure 8.4 to price estimate this job.

Step 1. Determine the setup cost:

Flat fee of $50.00 per job

Step 2. Determine the stage setting fee:

6 hr. x $20.00 per hr. = $120.00

Step 3. Determine the model fee:

Flat fee of $1,200.00

Step 4. Determine the cost for capturing images to film:

$$6 \text{ hr. x } \$40.00 \text{ per hr.} = \$240.00$$

Step 5. Determine the cost of color transparency film and development:

$$\$20.00 \text{ fee} + [\$12.00 \text{ per roll x } 12 \text{ rolls}] = \$164.00$$

Step 6. Determine the cost of black-and-white film and development:

$$\$20.00 \text{ fee} + [\$6.00 \text{ per roll x } 4 \text{ rolls}] = \$44.00$$

Step 7. Determine the total estimated cost:

$$\$50.00 + \$120.00 + \$1,200.00 + \$240.00 + \$164.00 + \$44.00 = \$1,818.00$$

Example 8.3. We want to price estimate the digital photographic production of a 24-page cook book. The job will take 2 full days (16 hours) of studio time to shoot and will require 30 hours of product preparation using our kitchen facilities and cooking staff. Food products will be provided by the client and will not be included in the estimate. We have determined there will be 1 half-day (4 hours) of image correction completed as part of the job; any other correction included as prepress production will be done later. We anticipate 20 color proofs for customer review. Determine the estimated price for this job.

Solution

Refer to Figure 8.4 to price estimate this job.

Step 1. Determine the setup cost:

$$\text{Flat fee of } \$70.00 \text{ per job}$$

Step 2. Determine the product preparation fee:

$$30 \text{ hr. x } \$20.00 \text{ per hr.} = \$600.00$$

Step 3. Determine the cost for capturing images to film:

$$16 \text{ hr. x } \$50.00 \text{ per hr.} = \$800.00$$

Step 4. Determine the cost of image modification and correction:

$$4 \text{ hr. x } \$60.00 \text{ per hr.} = \$240.00$$

Step 5. Determine the cost of color proofing:

$$20 \text{ proofs x } \$10.00 \text{ ea.} = \$200.00$$

Step 6. Determine the total estimated price:

$$\$70.00 + \$600.00 + \$800.00 + \$240.00 + \$200.00 = \$1,910.00$$

8.5 Overview of Cost Estimating Digital Prepress Production

It would be ideal if a "cookbook" solution were available for accurately estimating digital prepress (DPP) production. Unfortunately, with the complexity of digital technology and the numerous production choices available, there is no "one-system-for-all" estimating method if accuracy is desired. Consider the following reasons:

1. Establishing an accurate DPP cost estimating system requires the identification of numerous specific digital production operations, known as component tasks, which, when summed, drive the production times and costs of the job. Developing this list of component tasks requires time and effort, and many companies are unwilling to make this commitment. Component task identification and use is discussed in detail later in this chapter.

2. Even if a company has developed a complete list of component tasks, identifying which tasks apply to each job as the job is being estimated can be difficult. This is because the electronic files generated by the DFC can vary extensively.

3. Many customers request estimates before production on their jobs begins. Because the electronic art is frequently not completed at this point of the job—the job may be early in the design stage or perhaps not even that far along—a "best guess" must be made as to the final digital art files and how output ready these files will be. Because many important costs are driven by the details of how the electronic artwork is prepared, estimating accuracy can be easily compromised.

4. Even when the component tasks are identified, digital production times are mixed between computer processing times and the electronic skills of company employees, neither of which is completely predictable.

5. Although customer files are frequently problematic—even with a good preflight system—the customers want their estimates to cover such unpredictable situations. When the printer attempts to charge for file corrections and repairs necessary to produce finished film for a customer's job, a strained relationship between company and customer sometimes occurs, which leads to unhappy customers.

6. There is frequently misalignment between the estimated times for digital production and the actual times needed to complete the job. For this reason, data collection systems and job costing are important tools for tracking EPP jobs. However, many FOPs do not take the time or the effort to complete these tasks. Data collection and job cost reviews are important information feedback tools that should be used to track digital production times.

7. Estimating and scheduling DPP requires a thorough knowledge of electronic technology and digital production methods. Unfortunately, too many estimators, CSRs, sales representatives, schedulers, and other employees do not understand this technology. This lack of knowledge is one of the reasons that price estimating has emerged as a common way to estimate EPP.

8. Given the unpredictability of production, scheduling EPP is inconsistent. Also, scheduling larger blocks of time is easy, while scheduling the small, incremental pieces of time that are typical of DTP is more difficult.

9. Price lists have emerged as the de facto standard for estimating and quoting DTP. However, price lists can be inaccurate because they are driven by key points that differ from company to company. For example, Company A may stress product availability and fast turnaround, while Company B may stress high product quality and volume discounts. Thus, price list estimating is frequently not an "apples-to-apples" comparison between companies, but instead addresses those factors each company has determined are important to its prices. Unfortunately, the resulting prices on the company's price list may not represent the true costs incurred.

10. The DFCs take different approaches to completing jobs, which affects downstream production on the part of the FOP or the printer. In addition, a DFC may use his current software version for a given job, but this version may be too old or not compatible with the version at the printing company. Font suitcases are another detail that may become a potential problem. These are important details that tend to cause production disruptions even with a good preflighting review.

11. There is currently no commercially available, reasonably priced computer software program specifically developed for cost estimating DPP. This means that graphic imaging companies are first forced to develop their own approaches, then their own software—frequently using spreadsheets—and finally they must monitor their home-grown processes so that they accurately reflect their digital production processes. For many printers, developing a desktop estimating system is too time consuming and complex.

On a daily basis the process of cost estimating DPP jobs can be problematic. Job specifications are frequently unknown or unclear when the estimate is requested, and the time available to complete the estimate may be only a day or a few hours. In addition, once an estimate, which is driven by either the cost estimating methods described here or the price estimating methods discussed in Chapter 4, is provided to the customer, the profitability of the job is largely in executing the details of the order.

These details and nuances are difficult to determine unless the digital files are prepared and preflighted before the estimate is completed. This is a key reason for insisting that, before the electronic artwork is produced, the customers become trained and knowledgeable in specific digital software applications, as well as in the use of accurate job preflighting to check important electronic art details. Although it distresses customers, many FFPs protect the printers by stating in their quotes or bids that their prices are not firm or committed until the jobs have been preflighted.

Finally, it should be emphasized that detailed cost estimating of EPP should be an energized, fast-paced process with a focus on accuracy. Successful estimators balance accuracy and estimating time. When estimating is done with computer assistance, the "what-if" scenarios that focus on saving both the company and the customer money and time can be quickly evaluated.

8.6   Benchmarking Electronic Prepress Times and Costs

As a printer, service bureau, trade shop, or FOP becomes familiar with digital production, she should look for similarities that allow for the development of her own predictable estimating standards. She should train sales representatives, CSRs, and estimators in electronic technology, and she should develop tailor-made methods to gather accurate digital job specifications. The more the process is standardized and predictable, the greater is the accuracy of estimate and the less chaotic are production planning and scheduling.

Ideally the company should develop its own production standards and BHRs. The concept and methods to do this are discussed in Chapters 2 and 3 and require a knowledge of data collection, spreadsheet programs, and MISs, as well as a keen interest on the part of employees in taking complex procedures and simplifying them without losing the essence of accuracy for both time and cost components. For companies wishing to do this, benchmarking has become an important tool.

Benchmarking is the determination of a specific point or mark that remains fixed and secure, from which deviations may be measured. The process of benchmarking digital imaging requires two sequenced benchmark actions: (1) establishing a set of production activities and, (2) establishing production times that reflect the activities completed using the production operations identified in Step 1.

Setting Benchmarks for Production Activities

Benchmarking EPP production methods requires a knowledge of each piece of equipment and how the equipment relates to other equipment. This knowledge should also take employee skills into account, particularly when skill level drives certain production decisions, which equipment will be used, and which software will be chosen.

Setting benchmarks for digital production operations requires the careful identification of three ingredients: (1) the specific operations needed to complete the task, (2) the specific production components to accomplish the operation, and (3) the production pathways or production sequence by which electronic jobs are produced. Production in many DPP operations is fairly predictable in that certain types of jobs tend to move through the EPP maze in a defined manner. Many digital jobs require the same production activities and components and follow perhaps one of six or seven production pathways. Only a few jobs are unpredictable or deviate from one of the pathways. A high level of employee skill and good preflighting methods are of considerable help in limiting the number of production pathways available, as are the specific choices of activities and software within each of these pathways.

Benchmarking Production Times and Material Costs

Once the production operations and specific components are benchmarked in light of the normal job pathways, specific production times and material costs must be studied and benchmarked. For example, benchmarking page layout and editing production using QuarkXPress or PageMaker requires two sequential steps: (1) establishing a representative unit basis for the production operation, such as minutes per page, minutes per image, or minutes per megabyte (Mb), and (2) establishing a time that represents the production component. In many cases the simplest way to establish a time is to time the production operation using a stopwatch or a clock. When timing any production operation that requires an employee, it is wise to obtain the employee's permission prior to completing the time measurements. Figure 8.9, which appears later in this chapter, is an example of the result of such benchmarking activity for page layout and editing. The times and costs in this schedule are provided for example only and do not represent any specific company's production.

Any company's existing or current benchmarked production methods and production standards should be reviewed at least one time per year, but more frequent review may be necessary. When this review indicates that the benchmark may no longer be valid, care should be taken because a key point of the benchmark concept is that the benchmark provides a fixed, unchanging point from which deviations are measured. Two choices for revising benchmarks are possible: (1) establish a completely new benchmark, or (2) keep the existing benchmark and modify or evaluate the deviation range to cover the new variations.

In general, a new benchmark should not be established unless there are clear, pronounced reasons to undertake this activity. Establishing a new benchmark takes time and careful study. The following are some of the cases in which a new benchmark should be established:

1. when the method of production changes in any major way
2. when employee skills change through training or experience or when new employees bring different skill levels that clearly shift productivity
3. when new electronic equipment becomes fully functional
4. when equipment upgrades that are related to new electronic equipment change the primary production sequence
5. when software revisions result in major changes in production

Keeping an existing benchmark and revising the deviation scale is typically less work than establishing a new benchmark. However, the revising option should not be used as a patch in instances where a new benchmark is clearly warranted.

All benchmarked production methods and production times and costs should be kept in written form in a secure place. The background information with which each benchmark has been established should also be noted in writing so that the benchmark can be revised or changed easily.

The production times, material costs, and BHRs contained in the schedules and example problems in this chapter and in this book are presented for example only. They are not benchmarked times or costs. Also, because digital production methods vary widely, no attempt has been made to benchmark these either. In sum, benchmarking must be focused to address a company's specific production environment and specific activities.

8.7 Cost Estimating Desktop Publishing and Electronic Prepress Production

DTP is a process whereby text and graphic images are input into a microcomputer, then are manipulated and massaged to produce an integrated, final graphic product. Hardware requirements of an EPP system center on a microcomputer platform, such as a Macintosh or an IBM-PC, with a hard disk providing 200 Mb or more of immediately accessible storage and a minimum of eight Mb of RAM. Input peripherals include flatbed or drum scanners, digitizing tablets, magnetic drives for transferring digital files, and a keyboard for text input. Output peripherals include numerous PostScript-driven devices, which are generally segmented into laser printers for paper-based images, film output devices, digital proofing equipment, and CTP hardware that bypasses film output devices.

The hardware platform for graphic imaging is most frequently the Macintosh, which has become the accepted standard for graphic artists, service bureaus, trade shops, and printers. The IBM-compatible platforms with DOS and Microsoft Windows are also used, as are operating systems that are UNIX based. Major software vendors tailor versions of their products to each type of hardware configuration and operating system. Interconnectedness between computers that use the same operating system is achieved using various network arrangements, as well as telecommunication methods. Local area networks (LANs) provide smooth, fast file or data transfer between computers that are close to one another, while wide area networks (WANs) and telecommunication systems provide speedy digital file exchange to remote sites. Cross-platform environments, where operating systems and hardware are different, are used as well. This allows the Macintosh PowerPC, IBM compatibles with DOS-Windows, and DEC-VAX with UNIX to share digital files.

The chosen hardware/operating system tends to lock the job into that hardware/operating system for the entire life of the job. This is important to remember because cross-platform environments are not always desirable. The choices of hardware and software for a given job are normally made by the DFC when the job is created. Hardware choices are limited to Macintosh, IBM compatible, and UNIX-based platforms and establish the operating system for the prepared files. As just mentioned, the Macintosh is generally recognized as the system of choice for graphic production.

Like hardware and operating system choices, most software choices, once they are made, represent a permanent selection and usually lock the user into using that software. However, the range of software program options has some variability. This is because there is intense competition between software vendors in many software areas, and no single program has emerged as the de facto standard. Software programs for DTP and EPP are divided into six general categories. Some of the more popular programs are noted in the following:

Category	*Software*
Word processing:	Microsoft Word, WordPerfect, T/Maker WriteNow
Painting:	BrushStrokes, Claris MacDraw/MacPaint, ZSoft Paintbrush, Painter, Studio 32, Aldus SuperPaint
Illustration:	Deneba Software Canvas, Adobe FreeHand, Adobe Illustrator, Corel Draw
Image processing:	Fractal Design ColorStudio, EFI Cachet, Kodak PhotoEdge, Adobe Photoshop, Adobe Streamline
Page layout:	Corel Ventura, Frame Technology FrameMaker, Kodak Renaissance, Adobe PageMaker, Personal Press, Timeworks Publish It! Easy, Quark Inc. QuarkXPress
Imposition:	Farrukh Imposition Publisher, Ultimate Technologies Impostrip, DK&A INposition, ScenicSoft PREPS, Adobe PressWise

Which software is used and how it is applied as the electronic art is created are both critical elements in assuring smooth production and proper final film. Software drives the ease with which art is designed and executed, the way files are connected, the production time for digital output devices being used (e.g., digital proofer and filmsetter), the quality of the job, and the simplicity of file structure, which affects numerous production issues. The compatibility of software programs between the DFC and the FOP can be a significant problem affecting the cost of prepress production.

A copy of the software chosen by the DFC must reside at the site where final film is generated. This site may be the DFC's office, the printing company, or a service bureau or trade shop. Because there is no standard software program or set of programs that is recognized by all DFCs in any given software category, and because the FOP accepts jobs from many DFCs, file incompatibility problems from job to job are common.

There are compatibility problems within software versions, too. This is because most software vendors revise and upgrade their products on a frequent basis. When this is done, the new software version replaces the previous version. The version is denoted by a number after the name of the software. For example, QuarkXPress was first released as QuarkXPress 1.0 (commonly referenced as "Quark 1.0"), but over time new versions were released. "Quark 3.3" is a recent version.

Generally the notation system works like this: A major revision receives a full integer, while a modified revision receives a decimal equivalent. For example, when QuarkXPress released a major revision of its then-current 2.2 version, it was retitled "Quark 3.0." Then, some months later after Quark completed various minor revisions of its 3.0 version, it released "Quark 3.1." The term "backward compatible" describes a new software version that is compatible with previous versions, but the term does not imply that the compatibility covers every past version back to the original release.

The preceding is important to estimators in that incompatibility between files, for whatever reasons, may result in inaccurate estimates. However, it is difficult to predict incompatibility problems because DFCs frequently do not know the exact version of software to be used on a given job, or the version is not identified when the job details are determined. Another complication arises when the FOP, who accepts files from numerous DFCs and should have all versions of each software program available, does not have all versions. An example of this is when a job is created in PageMaker 2.0, while the FOP has from versions 3.0 to the current PageMaker version. The problem here is that there is no backward compatibility in the PageMaker version 2.0.

Figure 8.5 provides a schedule for estimating DTP and EPP production. The schedule is divided into two separate production functions: imaging production (top) and output production (bottom). Imaging production has five activity groups: (1) job setup and preliminary activities, (2) text processing, (3) image creation, (4) image processing, and (5) image manipulation or graphic image modification. These five imaging production operations are done at a BHR representative of the fixed and variable costs, including the computer platform, software, labor rates, and so on.

Activity	Task or production component and basic time unit			
Job setup and preliminary activities (applies to all jobs)	Preflight review (1 per job unless otherwise specified) 0.50 hr. Initiate production on job (1 per job unless otherwise specified) 0.30 hr. Archiving, file storage (1 per job unless otherwise specified) 0.20 hr. Handling or transferring files/fonts (per file based on file size) 0.20 hr. (under 3 Mb) 0.40 hr. (over 3 Mb)			

Activity		Text keyboarding input	Proofreading
Text processing	Straight text matter	0.1000 hr./M characters	0.0222 hr./M characters
	Complex text matter	0.1667 hr./M characters	0.0350 hr./M characters
	Technical text including equations and symbols	0.2000 hr./M characters	0.0444 hr./M characters
	Foreign text	0.1250 hr./M characters	0.0222 hr./M characters
	Formatting ASCI text	0.0300 hr./M characters	

Activity		Simple*	Average*	Difficult*
Image creation	Illustration and drawing	0.30 hr./image	0.75 hr./image	1.00 hr./image
	Painting	0.20 hr./image	0.25 hr./image	0.40 hr./image
	Scanning (line)	0.15 hr./image	0.25 hr./image	0.35 hr./image
	Scanning (grayscale)	0.20 hr./image	0.30 hr./image	0.40 hr./image
	Scanning (color: RGB/CMYK)	0.40 hr./image	0.60 hr./image	0.80 hr./image
Image processing	Page layout & editing	0.15 hr./p.	0.20 hr./p.	0.25 hr./p.
	Electronic imposition (template)	0.05 hr./p.	0.15 hr./p.	0.20 hr./p.
	*Time shown is for the first image. Use 70% of the scheduled time for each additional image or page at the same category, the same level, in the same job.			

Activity	Simple	Average	Difficult	Very difficult
Image manipulation	0.20 hr./p. or image	0.30 hr./p. or image	0.50 hr./p. or image	0.80 hr./p. or image

Activity		Simple	Average	Difficult
Output Note: Time covers first output product only with no addition for rerunning corrected or additional output.	Laser (paper)	0.05 hr./p.	0.10 hr./p.	0.30 hr./p.
	All-inclusive consumable cost = $0.006/sq. in.			
	Digital proof (color)	0.10 hr./p.	0.20 hr./p.	0.30 hr./p.
	All-inclusive consumable cost = $0.040/sq. in.			
	Filmsetter or CTP	0.15 hr./p.	0.25 hr./p.	0.35 hr./p.
	All-inclusive consumable cost = $0.020/sq. in.			

Times and costs in this schedule are for example only. Two budgeted hour rates are typically required - an hourly cost for imaging production and a separate hourly cost for the appropriate output device(s) used. See Chapter 9 for estimating conventional (analog) proofing.

Figure 8.5 Schedule for cost estimating desktop publishing and electronic prepress production

Output production, which is separated from the image production activities groups by a double line in Figure 8.5, is segmented into laser, proof, and filmsetter output. Output times include RIPping, imaging, and processing operations. Output is completed using a BHR that covers the necessary output devices needed for the job.

Figure 8.5 can be used to estimate EPP production for any combination of activities. For example, it is possible that imaging production is completed with no output, or that output is completed with no imaging production. Although all jobs have setup activities, perhaps only a few will have text processing, but many are likely to have a mix of image creation, image processing, and image manipulation components. It is likely that most jobs will have some type of final output, from imaging to paper on a laser printer to color proofs to final film. Accuracy requires that the job specifications provide clear and sufficient information for estimating. If specifications are inaccurate, incomplete, or not given, accurately estimating production is not possible.

Production times are presented here for example only and require modification based on a specific company's system digital production system and employees. The skills of the operator in image creation, image processing, and image manipulation activities are key issues relative to benchmarking the time units used for estimating. To ensure estimating accuracy, care should be taken to review, benchmark, and job cost this area as needed.

The BHRs for imaging production should include the costs of an appropriate computer platform and necessary software, plus all other fixed and variable costs. For example, if a job requires a specific software package that must be purchased for that job and that will have a one-time use only, or if there are additional material costs that are directly related to a specific job or customer, these dollar amounts are added with appropriate markups. The all-inclusive cost of materials for final output materials are provided for example only and should be tailored to the company's specific output costs as identified by the FOP. Example 8.4 that follows demonstrates the application of Figure 8.5 data.

It should be noted that the BHRs here do not include any profit markup, nor do the material costs include markups for handling or inventory. Profit markup can be added as a percentage of total job cost or by using the specified markup procedure indicated by company management.

To calculate DTP production time and cost, use the following formulas:

total time for imaging production = time for job setup + time for text processing + [time for first image created + time for additional images created at 70 percent] + [time for first image processed + time for additional images processed at 70 percent] + [time for first image manipulated + time for additional images manipulated at 70 percent]

time for output production = time for laser output + time for proof output + time for film output total cost for DTP production = [total time for job setup + text processing + image creation + image processing + image manipulation x BHR cost] + [total time for output production x BHR cost] + output consumable costs

Apply the profit markup percentage or use another profit markup method.

Example 8.4. We have been asked to estimate the time and cost required to produce an 8-page brochure using our Macintosh Power PC (PPC) platform and necessary output equipment. The following provides the details of this job:

Preliminary activity:	Initiate production with preflighting and archiving. We estimate there will be 4 files under 3 Mb and 2 files over 3 Mb.
Text processing:	There are an estimated 13,200 manuscript characters to be input as straight text matter. Proofreading should be included.
Image creation:	Adobe Illustrator will be used to generate 4 images at simple and 5 images at average. The job will have 8 line scans at simple and 6 grayscale scans at average.
Image processing:	The 8 pages at average will require page layout and editing in PageMaker.
Image manipulation:	Four Illustrator images will require touchup and the generation of a spot (second) color at moderate level. Three of the 6 grayscale images will require cropping, touchup, and vignetting at complex level.
Output:	We estimate there will be a total of sixteen 8 1/2 inch x 11 inch pages output to our laser printer to check at average level, and 12 sheets of film 10 inches x 12 inches output at average level to our filmsetter as final film.
Cost and profit markup:	The BHR for our PPC platform and appropriate software is $45.70, for the laser printer is $12.75, and for the filmsetter is $38.40. We will mark up the total estimated job cost by 40 percent to determine our targeted selling price for this job.

Solution

Refer to Figure 8.5 for production standards and material costs.

Step 1. Determine the job setup time:

Initiate production: 0.30 hr.

Preflight review: 0.50 hr.
Archiving and file storage: 0.20 hr.
Files/font cost: [4 files x 0.20 hr.] + [2 files x 0.40 hr.] = 0.80 hr. + 0.80 hr. = 1.60 hr.
Total time for job setup: 0.30 hr. + 0.50 hr. + 0.20 hr. + 1.60 hr. = 2.60 hr.

Step 2. Determine the text processing time:

Typesetting: 13.2 M char. x 0.1000 hr./M char. = 1.32 hr.
Proofreading: 13.2 M char. x 0.0222 hr./M char. = 0.29 hr.
Total time for typesetting and proofreading: 1.32 hr. + 0.29 hr. = 1.61 hr.

Step 3. Determine the image creation time:

Illustration, 4 images @ simple: [1st x 0.30 hr.] + [3 add'l. x 0.30 hr. @ 70%] = 0.30 hr. + 0.63 hr. = 0.93 hr.
Illustration, 5 images @ average: [1st x 0.75 hr.] + [4 add'l. x 0.75 hr. @ 70%] = 0.75 hr. + 2.10 hr. = 2.85 hr.
Scan, 8 line @ simple: [1st x 0.15 hr.] + [7 add'l. x 0.15 hr. @ 70%] = 0.15 hr. + 0.74 hr. = 0.89 hr.
Scans, 6 grayscale @ average: [1st x 0.30 hr.] + [5 add'l. x .30 hr. @ 70%] = 0.30 hr. + 1.05 hr. = 1.35 hr.
Total image creation time: 0.93 hr. + 2.85 hr. + 0.89 hr. + 1.35 hr. = 6.02 hr.

Step 4. Determine the image processing time:

Page layout & editing, 8 pp. @ average: [1st x 0.20 hr.] + [7 add'l. x .20 hr. @ 70%] = 0.20 hr. + 0.98 hr. = 1.18 hr.
Total page layout & editing time: 1.18 hr.

Step 5. Determine the image manipulation time:

Illustration, 4 images @ moderate: 4 x 0.30 hr. = 1.20 hr.
Scans, 3 images @ complex: 3 x 0.50 hr. = 1.50 hr.
Total image manipulation time: 1.20 hr. + 1.50 hr. = 2.70 hr.

Step 6. Determine the imaging production time:

Total time for job setup, text processing, image creation, image processing, and image manipulation: 2.60 hr. + 1.61 hr. + 6.02 hr. + 1.18 hr. + 2.70 hr. = 14.11 hr.

Step 7. Determine the imaging production cost:

Cost: 14.11 hr. x $45.70 = $644.82

Step 8. Determine the output production time:

Laser output, 16 pp. @ average: 16 pp. x 0.10 hr. = 1.60 hr.
Filmsetter output, 12 pp. @ average: 12 pp. x 0.25 hr. = 3.00 hr.

Total time for output: 1.60 hr. + 3.00 hr. = 4.60 hr.

Step 9. Determine the output production cost (without materials):

Laser output: 1.6 hr. x $12.75 = $20.40
Filmsetter output: 3.00 hr. x $38.40 = $115.20
Cost of output (without materials): $20.40 + $115.20 = $135.60

Step 10. Determine the output material cost:

Laser, 16 shts. of 8 1/2 inch x 11 inch paper: 16 shts. x [8.5 inches x 11 inches]
x $0.006 sq. in. = $8.98
Filmsetter, 12 shts. of 10 inch x 12 inch film: 12 shts. x [10 inches x 12
inches] x $0.02 sq. in = $28.80
Total output material cost: $8.98 + $28.80 = $37.78

Step 11. Determine the total estimated time for this job:

Imaging production + output production: 14.11 hr. + 4.60 hr. = 18.71 hr.

Step 12. Determine the total estimated cost for this job, including materials:

Cost of imaging production + cost of output production + cost of output
materials: $644.82 + $135.60 + $37.78 = $818.20

Step 13. Determine the targeted selling price using a 40 percent markup
over cost:

Total estimated cost + 40 percent markup: $818.20 x 1.40 = $1,145.48

8.8 Cost Estimating Specific Electronic Prepress Production Operations

Accurately cost estimating DPP requires the identification of specific prepress production operations, followed with the development of standard production times and consumable material costs. Obtaining accurate production times and material costs is difficult for many EPP providers given the continuously changing technology and the complexities of electronic production. The use of benchmarking procedures as previously discussed can be helpful when developing these standards.

The schedules that appear in this segment provide example production times and consumable material costs for detailed estimating of certain EPP operations. The schedules have been arranged in the order that follows typical electronic production: file acquisition/management, input production operations, and output production. Data contained in these schedules may not represent the production times and costs for a given company, but they provide the framework for the initiation of such a schedule. Discussion of how these standards are benchmarked was provided earlier, and the process to build template spreadsheets so they can be used interactively is detailed later in this chapter.

Two key ingredients are necessary to properly use these EPP cost estimating schedules. First, the estimator must have a working knowledge of DTP and EPP production methods. Although the estimator does not need to be able to complete the production operation, understanding the production techniques and procedures is essential. Second, accurate cost estimating is based on a set of job specifications that describes the electronic and other production tasks. As noted elsewhere in this text, gathering complete job specifications can be difficult when estimates are requested before or during the development of digital files or when the sales representative does not understand EPP procedures.

As a printer, service bureau, trade shop, or an FOP becomes familiar with digital production, he should look for similarities that allow for the development of his own predictable digital estimating standards. He should train sales representatives, CSRs, and estimators in electronic technology, and he should develop tailor-made methods to gather accurate digital job specifications. The more the process is standardized and predictable, the greater is the accuracy of the estimates and the less chaotic production planning and scheduling become.

The development of any cost estimating method covering sophisticated, complex technology requires a balance of simplicity on one hand and accuracy on the other. This is not an easy balance to achieve.

Schedule Format Description

A standard format has been used to keep these EPP cost estimating schedules easy to use. Figure 8.6, which represents the format used for all schedules, consists of seven columns that define the production components and provide the production times and consumable cost data. The following briefly describes the schedule's development and use for estimating purposes.

Column 1   Operation or activity: This is the production operation or activity to be estimated.

Column 2   Production task or component: This is the specific job task or production component to be performed or that is required as part of job production.

Column 3   1st production unit: This is the time, in minutes, necessary to perform the task the first time.

Column 4   Follow-up production unit: This is the production time necessary to perform the task each time after the first time. Frequently the follow-up production takes less time than the initial operation.

Column 5   Unit basis: This defines the basis of the production unit, usually in minutes per production task or component.

1	2	3	4	5	6	7
Operation or activity	**Production task or component**	**1st production unit**	**Follow-up production unit**	**Unit basis**	**Production adjustment factor (PAF) range**	**PAF adjustment notes**
File acquisition and management	Job preflight & prelim. review	30		min./job	50-200%	Based on size and complexity of job
	File setup and management	5	1	min./Mb	50-200%	Based on media type, data decompress.
	Loading fonts	5	2	min./font	50-200%	
	Archiving files	1	1	min./Mb	50-200%	
Remote file transfer	9600 bps modem	22	17	min./Mb	75-150%	Based on compressability of data and quality of data connection
	14.4 kbps modem	14	9	min./Mb	75-150%	
	28.8 kbps modem	9	4	min./Mb	75-150%	
	ISDN	6	1	min./Mb	75-150%	
	T1	4	0.08	min./Mb	75-150%	
Consumables: Media	5.25" SyQuest 44 Mb	$60	$60	$/unit	100%	
	5.25" SyQuest 88 Mb	$65	$65	$/unit	100%	
	5.25" SyQuest 200 Mb	$90	$90	$/unit	100%	
	3.5" SyQuest 105	$70	$70	$/unit	100%	
	3.5" SyQuest 270	$80	$80	$/unit	100%	
	Bernoulli 230	$110	$110	$/unit	100%	
	Zip drive 100 Mb	$20	$20	$/unit	100%	
	DAT	$15	$15	$/unit	100%	
	CD	$20	$20	$/unit	100%	

Figure 8.6   Schedule for estimating electronic job setup: File acquisition, file transfer, and cost of consumable media. Times and costs are for example only.

Column 6   Production adjustment factor (PAF) range: This is the range of adjustment of the production time that might be applied if desired. For example, preliminary file review is targeted to take 30 minutes per job, but the review for some jobs may take half of that time or twice that time. Thus, the PAF for this example is a range from 50 percent to 200 percent, or from 15 minutes to 60 minutes. The intention of the PAF range is to provide flexibility in applying the data.

Column 7   PAF adjustment notes: This provides information relative to when the PAF might be applied to modify the production times.

Estimating Job Setup: File Acquisition, File Transfer, and Cost of Removable Media

Figure 8.6 provides data for estimating job setup, which include file acquisition, file transfer of data between remote sites, and the cost of media consumable. As noted, file acquisition production components (first row) include job preflighting and preliminary file review, file setup and management, loading fonts, and archiving files. Times and costs are for example only.

Figure 8.6 also provides production data for estimating remote file transfer (second row), including modem, ISDN, and T1 data exchange methods. Consumable media (third row) costs cover SyQuest cartridges, Bernoulli and ZIP media, DAT tapes, and CDs for Photo-CD.

Following are formulas for estimating the total time and total cost of job setup:

total time for job setup production = [minutes for job preflight and preliminary review + file setup and management + loading fonts + archiving files ÷ 60 min./hr.] + [minutes for remote file transfer ÷ 60 min./hr]. Apply PAF as needed.

total cost for job setup production = [total time for file acquisition and management production x BHR]+ [total time for remote transfer x BHR] + [media consumable costs]

Example 8.5 that follows is provided to demonstrate the application of Figure 8.6.

Example 8.5. We want to estimate the time and cost of job setup, including file acquisition and related costs. The job has been prepared electronically and exists as a 30-Mb file. There are 5 font suitcases included in the job. One 10-Mb file will be transferred using our ISDN line. We will charge for one 44-Mb SyQuest cartridge that will be used to transfer and archive the job. A $50 BHR will apply which includes all computer hardware and software to complete the job.

Solution

Refer to the schedule in Figure 8.6 for hourly production standards.

Step 1. Determine the file acquisition and management time:

1 unit job preflight & preliminary job review x 30 min./job = 30 min.
File setup: 1 unit @ 5 min./Mb + 29 units @ 1 min./Mb = 34 min.
Loading fonts: 1 unit @ 5 min./font + 4 units @ 2 min./font = 9 min.
Archiving files: 1 unit @ 5 min./Mb + 29 units @ 1 min./Mb = 34 min.
Total file acquisition and management time: 30 min. + 34 min. + 9 min. + 34 min. = 107 min. ÷ 60 min./hr. = 1.78 hr.

Step 2. Determine the remote file transfer time:

ISDN: 1 unit @ 6 min./Mb + 9 units @ 1 min./Mb. = 15 min. ÷ 60 min./hr. = 0.25 hr.

Step 3. Determine the total job setup time:

1.78 hr. + 0.25 hr. = 2.03 hr.

Step 4. Determine the total hourly cost for this job:

$$2.03 \text{ hr. x } \$50.00/\text{hr.} = \$101.50$$

Step 5. Determine the cost of consumable materials:

$$1 \text{ SyQuest 44-Mb cartridge} = \$60.00$$

Step 6. Determine the total cost for job setup:

$$\$101.50 + \$60.00 = \$161.50$$

Estimating Desktop Scanning Production

Desktop scanning is an important digital image capture process. Scanners are divided into drum (photomultiplier tube or PMT) and flatbed (charge-coupled device or CCD) units. In recent years sales of both types of scanners have soared as all segments of the DTP industry—printers, publishers, advertising agencies, graphic designers, service bureaus, trade shops, businesses, and home enthusiasts—have begun utilizing digital production for many graphic uses. This trend is due to the fact that the production of a high-quality black-and-white or full-color image no longer requires the extensive scanner training or detailed knowledge that was necessary with older scanner units. In addition, scanner prices have continuously dropped while scanning power—and the computer platforms to which they are linked—have continuously improved. Desktop digital scanning for both PMT and CCD scanners provide operator simplicity in the foreground, supported by sophisticated hardware and software technology in the background.

Estimating scanning production requires a general knowledge of scanner technology. Figure 8.7 provides estimating data for both drum (PMT) and flatbed (CCD) scanners. Scanning production for either type of unit is segmented into four parts: prescan production, scanning time, postscan production, and additional time penalties which apply as indicated. Production times are for example only. It must be noted that both types of scanners vary extensively relative to their maximum input sizes, levels of automation, output qualities, speed of operation, and prices.

The smoother scanning production is completed the less costly this important image capture process becomes. It is far better to complete a scan correctly the first time than to repair a poorly scanned image using Photoshop or other software. Image mounting, prescan benchmarking, and software features that allow for ease of use all have a bearing on scanning production. One important factor in scanning productivity is the amount of computer RAM available. The general rule is that available RAM should exceed the anticipated file size of the image by at least two times. Production output is affected by how automated the scanning process is, gang scanning methods (grouping similar types of images from different jobs for a scanning session), and operator knowledge and skill.

Operation or activity	Production task or component	1st production unit	Follow-up production unit	Unit basis	Production adjustment factor (PAF) range	PAF adjustment notes
DRUM (PMT) SCANNING						
Prescan production	Small original (35mm)	10	7	min./image	50-150%	
	Medium original (4x5)	14	11	min./image	50-150%	
	Large original (8x10)	21	16	min./image	50-150%	
Scanning time production	Scan time calculation = desired output size (across drum) x desired dpi ÷ rpm of drum plus 1 minute for carriage travel and computation time.					
Postscan production	Small file (3Mb or less)	4	4	min./image	50-150%	
	Medium file (3.1-12 Mb)	6	6	min./image	50-150%	
	Large file (Over 12 Mb)	9	9	min./image	50-150%	
Additional time penalties	Over 400% enlargement	15	15	min./image	50-250%	
	Negative image	20	20	min./image	50-250%	
	Original artwork	20	20	min./image	50-250%	
	Critical color match	30	30	min./image	50-250%	
FLATBED (CCD) SCANNING						
Prescan production	Small original (35mm)	5	4	min./image	50-150%	
	Medium original (4x5)	7	6	min./image	50-150%	
	Large orignial (8x10)	10	8	min./image	50-150%	
Scanning time production	Scan time (lineart)=output size (length) x desired dpi ÷ pixels per minute x 1.5 (for carriage travel & computation time)					
	Scan time (grayscale)=output size (length) x desired dpi ÷ pixels per minute x 2 (for carriage travel & computation time)					
	Scan time (RGB)=output size (length) x desired dpi ÷ pixels per minute x 4 (for carriage travel & computation time)					
Postscan production	Small file (3Mb or less)	4	4	min./image	50-150%	
	Medium file (3.1-12Mb)	6	6	min./image	50-150%	
	Large file (Over 12 Mb)	9	9	min./image	50-150%	
RGB to CMYK conversion and sharpening	Small file (3Mb or less)	4	4	min./image	50-150%	Adjust time if automated conversion
	Medium file (3.1-12 Mb)	6	6	min./image	50-150%	Adjust time if automated conversion
	Large file (Over 12 Mb)	9	9	min./image	50-150%	Adjust time if automated conversion
Additional time penalties	Over 400% enlargement	15	15	min./image	50-250%	
	Original artwork	20	20	min./image	50-250%	
	Critical color match	30	30	min./image	50-250%	
	Negative/trans. attachment	20	20	min./image	50-250%	

Figure 8.7 Schedule for estimating scanning time for drum and flatbed desktop scanners. Times are for example only.

Drum (PMT) Scanners. Drum scanners first entered the printing plant more than twenty years ago as very expensive technology requiring sophisticated operator knowledge. They were first used for producing color separations to film and then as a digital imaging sources for high-end color electronic prepress systems (CEPS). Their image quality was, and continues to be, excellent.

In those earlier years, production was evaluated against the cost of completing color separations using more expensive and finicky photomechanical methods. Although these larger drum scanning units, which are known as high-end scanners, continue to be used, smaller desktop drum scanners are quickly replacing them. The reasons are clear and pronounced. Desktop PMT scanners do not require the proprietary complications evident with high-end scanners, and they interface directly into a desktop computer platform, which makes them convenient and readily accessible. Also, software enhancements coupled with hardware improvements have made desktop drum scanners easy to operate. "On-the-fly" (during the scanning cycle) RGB-to-CMYK (separating primary colors red, blue, and green to subtractive printing colors cyan, magenta, yellow, and black) conversion, selective color correction, and batch scanning are a few of the many features of PMT desktop scanners.

Drum scanning is easier to estimate than flatbed scanning because the drum scanner operates at a constant speed and many of its functions, such as RGB-to-CMYK conversion and image sharpening, are completed real time in the scanner hardware. The following clarifies each of the four production steps for drum scanning using Figure 8.7. Schedule times are provided for example only.

Step 1 Prescan production: This covers the time needed to read the job instructions, evaluate the image, dust and mount the image, position the scanning head, focus the image, perform a prescan benchmark, and adjust cropping, sizing, exposure, color balance, and image sharpening. Time is based on the size of the original image.

Step 2 Scanning time production: This is calculated by the formula noted in Figure 8.7. The longer dimension of the output size is used. For example, the total time to scan a 4 inch x 5 inch original positive image to an 8 inch x 10 inch positive at 600 dots per inch (dpi) with a scanning speed of 1,500 revolutions per minute (rpm) is [(10 in. x 600 dpi) ÷ 1,500 rpm] + 1 min. = 5 min.

Step 3 Postscan production: This covers time to double-check and verify the results, remove and properly store the original, and save the file. Postscan production time is based on the estimated size of the file generated in Mb.

Step 4 Additional time penalties: The addition of time penalties applies as appropriate and should be developed to fit a specific company's typical production methods. The list appearing in Figure 8.7 provides example penalties and times.

Flatbed (CCD) Scanners. Flatbed (CCD) scanners are available in a wide range of types and kinds, with no clear de facto standard model or unit. This makes estimating difficult. The CCD scanners are available in small or large size, come in one-pass or three-pass (trilinear) versions, operate at different scanning speeds for varying image capture procedures, and vary widely relative to purchase price. Although drum scanners generally offer higher resolution, greater dynamic range, and a greater price-to-performance ratio compared to flatbeds, technological improvements are moving CCD scanners ahead in both quality and productivity.

In sum, flatbed scanner improvements are quickly approaching the image capture quality of drum scanners, such as on-the-fly RGB-to-CMYK color conversion, selective color correction, and batch scanning, largely through software improvements competed by the scanner operator on the desktop. Thus, while drum scanners have built-in hardware functions that make them generally superior, flatbed scanner improvements in both hardware and software are moderating the differences. Experts predict that by the year 2000 it is likely CCD scanners and desktop drum scanners will be evenly matched in quality, productivity, and purchase price.

Establishing an estimating method for flatbed scanners is related to how the scanner operates. Generally lower cost CCDs have limited automation, while more costly flatbeds offer automatic exposure settings, color correction, RGB-to-CMYK conversion, and image sharpening. Some flatbed scanners take one pass to complete an RGB scan, others take three. Scanning time is based on the number of pixels captured per minute in the direction of travel of the CCD head, but different flatbeds scan at different rates. Thus, the development of an estimating schedule for flatbed scanning requires first determining the pixels per minute for color (RGB), grayscale (tonal), and bitmap (line art) image capture, then establishing a factor that adjusts for the scanner's various peripheral operations, including carriage travel and software computation time.

The following clarifies each of the five production steps for flatbed scanning using Figure 8.7. Schedule times are provided for example only.

Step 1 Prescan production: This covers the time needed to read the job instructions, evaluate the image, dust and mount the image, position the scanning head, focus the image, perform a prescan benchmark, and adjust cropping, sizing, exposure, color balance, and image sharpening. Time is based on the size of the original image.

Step 2 Scanning time production: This is calculated by the formula noted in Figure 8.7. Scan time depends on the type of image capture completed, which is segmented into line art, grayscale, and RGB production. Time is driven by output size of the final image, desired dpi, image capture (in pixels per minute or ppm), and an adjustment factor for carriage travel and computer computation time. The longer dimension of the output size is used. For example, the total time to scan a 4 inch x 5 inch original color print to produce an 8 inch x 10 inch

RGB file at 600 dpi using a 1,200 ppm CCD scanner is [(10 in. x 600 dpi) ÷ 1,200 ppm] x 4 = 20 min.

Step 3 Postscan production: This covers time to check and verify the results, remove and properly store the original, and save the file. Postscan production time is based on the estimated size of the file generated in Mb.

Step 4 RGB-to-CMYK conversion and sharpening: For CCD scanners that do not provide this conversion automatically, or when this conversion is semiautomatic or takes additional effort, time must be added to complete this operation.

Step 5 Additional time penalties: The addition of time penalties applies as appropriate and should be developed to fit a specific company's typical production methods. The list appearing in Figure 8.7 provides example penalties and times.

Figure 8.8 is provided to demonstrate how a table for estimating scanning would be developed to facilitate the process. In this example, the schedule was based on drum scanning 4 inch x 5 inch and 35-mm originals at 300 dpi, with a scan capture rate of 1,500 rpm. Other scenarios could also be completed based on a given company's production output, type of scanner, and the variables that affect scanning output for the scanners used. As noted in Figure 8.8, the first 4 inch x 5 inch original scanned to 8 inch x 10 inches would take 23 minutes, and each additional image to follow would require 20 minutes. A 35-mm original scanned to 8 inches x 10 inches, which is more than a 400 percent enlargement, would take an estimated 34 minutes for the first image and 31 minutes for each follow-up image of similar size and type.

Operation or activity	Production task or component	1st production unit	Follow-up production unit	Unit basis	Production adjustment factor (PAF) range	Explanation of time calculations (see Fig 8.7)
Drum scanning 35mm original, 300dpi, scanning at 1500 rpm	2x2.5 (small file)	30.5	27.5	min./image	75-150%	Pre@10+Scan@1.5+Post@4+Enlr@15=30.5 min
	4x5 (small file)	31	28	min./image	75-150%	Pre@10+Scan@2+Post@4+Enlr@15=31 min
	6x7.5 (medium file)	33.5	30.5	min./image	75-150%	Pre@10+Scan@2.5+Post@6+Enlr@15=33.5 min
	8x10 (medium file)	34	31	min./image	75-150%	Pre@10+Scan@6+Post@6+Enlr@15=34 min
	10x12.5 (large file)	37.5	34.5	min./image	75-150%	Pre@10+Scan@3.5+Post@9+Enlr@15=37.5 min
	12x15 (large file)	38	35	min./image	75-150%	Pre@10+Scan@4+Post@9+Enlr@15=38 min
Drum scanning 4x5 original, 300dpi, scanning at 1500 rpm	2x2.5 (small file)	19.5	16.5	min./image	75-150%	Pre@14+Scan@1.5+Post@4=19.5 min
	4x5 (small file)	20	17	min./image	75-150%	Pre@14+Scan@2+Post@4=20 min
	6x7.5 (medium file)	22.5	19.5	min./image	75-150%	Pre@14+Scan@2.5+Post@6=22.5 min
	8x10 (medium file)	23	20	min./image	75-150%	Pre@14+Scan@3+Post@6=23 min
	10x12.5 (large file)	41.5	38.5	min./image	75-150%	Pre@14+Scan@3.5+Post@9+Enlr@15=41.5 min
	12x15 (large file)	42	39	min./image	75-150%	Pre@14+Scan@4+Post@9+Enlr@15=42 min

Figure 8.8 Example of how an estimating schedule for scanning would be developed based on Figure 8.7 data. Times are for example only.

Estimating Page Layout and Illustration Production

Figure 8.9 is provided to estimate page layout production, page editing, illustration creation, and illustration editing. These production operations are common to many desktop jobs. Although what is presented in Figure 8.9 appears to be a connected group of activities, each of the four production operations is not necessarily linked to the others and may be estimated separately if the job specifications indicate this.

Typically, page layout production is completed early in the development of the electronic artwork. Page editing follows the layout process to adjust, correct, or provide image modifications. Sometimes the work is staged in that page layout production is completed by one employee and page editing is done later by another individual. Illustration creation and illustration editing may also follow this pattern. Thus, original illustrations may be created by a skilled illustrator, and follow-up editing may be done later by another employee. Production combinations may vary. For example, one employee may do all of the page layout and illustration work and another person may complete all of the editing, or the same employee may do all four production activities.

It should be noted that although some page layout software can be used to

Operation or activity	Production task or component	1st production unit	Follow-up production unit	Unit basis	Production adjustment factor (PAF) range	PAF adjustment notes
Page layout **One- and spot color**	1/C: Small (5x7, under 90 sq. in.)	6	4	min./p.	75-300%	Based on page complexity, operator skill, and creativity required
	1/C: Medium (8.5x11, 91-150 sq. in.)	9	7	min./p.	75-300%	
	1/C: Large (11x17, over 150 sq. in.)	16	14	min./p.	75-300%	
	Time for each spot color after 1st color	5	3	min./p.	75-300%	
Page layout **Four or more colors**	Small (5x7, under 90 sq. in.)	20	15	min./p.	75-300%	Based on page complexity, operator skill, creativity required, and use of color
	Medium (8.5x11, 91-150 sq. in.)	25	20	min./p.	75-300%	
	Large (11x17, over 150 sq. in.)	30	25	min./p.	75-300%	
Page editing **using digital methods**	One-color pages	6	4	min./p.	75-300%	Based on job or page complexity, extensiveness of anticipated editing; time indicated covers single edit round
	Additional spot colors	4	3	min./p.	75-300%	
	Four-color pages	12	10	min./p.	75-300%	
Illustration creation **Manual or digital image** **creation, incl. scanning input**	One-color illustration	30	30	min./image	75-300%	Based on illustration complexity, illustrator skill, creativity, and use of color
	Additional spot colors	10	10	min./image	75-300%	
	Four-color illustration	60	60	min./image	75-300%	
Illustration editing **using digital methods**	One- and spot-color illustration	15	15	min./image	75-300%	Based on illustration complexity, extensiveness of anticipated editing; time indicated covers single edit round
	Four-color illustration	20	20	min./image	75-300%	

Figure 8.9 Schedule for estimating page layout, page editing, illustration creation, and illustration editing production. Times are for example only.

generate illustrative materials, frequently the illustrator prefers to use stand-alone illustration software because it provides greater image flexibility. Illustration editing is done to enhance a specific illustration. Illustration editing is not to be confused with image manipulation, where created images are extensively modified beyond routine image editing. Image manipulation is covered in Figure 8.10 which follows.

Some types of graphic production require multiple editing rounds whereby the page layout or illustrative artwork is improved and enhanced at different editorial levels and by different people. Sometimes this editing is completed at different remote sites using transportable media or telecommunication methods to transfer images. When multiple editing is expected—and it is usually predictable based on the client and the project—editing production times should be increased accordingly.

Estimating Page Layout and Page Editing. Page layout and page editing are common production activities performed with many electronic jobs. Popular page layout programs include QuarkXPress, Adobe PageMaker, and FrameMaker, which all share similar software attributes but also vary in terms of how they execute the desired graphic image or effect. The choice of which software program to use for a job is frequently made by the DFC when the job is started. There tends to be little shifting between page layout software once this initial choice is made.

Page layout begins with the customer or client choosing a format and style of page that properly addresses her graphic need. This format is then developed into a master page image, which is basically a master page template with digital text, illustrations, and other graphic images imported into each page in the forms of Tagged Image File Format (TIFF), Encapsulated PostScript (EPS), PICT, or other formats. File compression and decompression, file size, and other issues affect production times and output.

While page layout covers the importing and arrangement of images on the page, page editing covers desktop operations that enhance the images as they relate to each other on a single page, as well as to the overall graphic balance of the product. This includes establishing gray balance for tonal images, sharpening images, adding and rotating tints, setting trim and bleed marks, and completing necessary image sharpening. When images must be manipulated or modified extensively beyond normal editing, additional time should be added using Figure 8.10, which is discussed next.

As indicated in Figure 8.9, page layout is segmented into one, two, and four or more colors by approximate page size. Production times, published here for example only, are in minutes per page with a production adjustment factor of 75 percent to 300 percent, which applies based on page complexity, operator skill, and operator creativity. Page editing covers the production time for one-

and two-color pages, as well as four or more colors and is adjusted based on the job or page complexity and the extensiveness of the editing that is anticipated.

Estimating Illustration Creation and Illustration Editing. Accurately estimating illustration creation and illustration editing can be difficult because these processes are a mix of creative and electronic skills which may be unpredictable in terms of the time required. Also, the time necessary to produce an illustration or a group of illustrations may not correlate to the artist's asking price for the work. It is not unusual for illustrative artwork to be priced according to a mixture of factors, including the total number of illustrations in the job, job scheduling relative to the artist's time availability, who the client is, the artist's reputation, and the desirability of the job on behalf of either the artist or the client.

Even with a high level of electronic skill and knowledge, many illustrators do their initial drawings or renderings on paper and then scan the renderings for digital use. Original art is created on paper because many graphic artists do not feel comfortable with electronic drawing tablets or mouse-driven digitizing tools. Also, most illustrators do not work under time conditions or time constraints. Therefore, actual times for producing original illustrations may not correlate with estimated times. Editing illustrations, which is usually done once the images are in electronic form, can also be difficult to estimate because the time needed to modify an image is hard to predict.

Figure 8.9 provides production times for creating one-color, spot-color, and four-color illustrations, as well as production times for editing illustrations. Production adjustment, which ranges from 75 percent to 300 percent, is based on the complexity of the illustration, the skill of the illustrator, the creativity required, and the use of color.

The following formulas are used for estimating total time and total cost for page layout and illustration:

total time for page layout and illustration production = [minutes for page layout ÷ 60 min./hr.] + [minutes for editing pages ÷ 60 min./hr.] + [minutes for illustration creation ÷ 60 min./hr.] + [minutes for illustration editing ÷ 60 min./hr.]. Apply PAF as needed.

total cost for page layout and illustration production = [total time for page layout production x BHR] + [total time for editing pages x BHR] + [total time for illustration production x BHR] + [total time for illustration editing x BHR]. Add material costs if required.

Note: The BHR value could differ for any production operation because the computer platform and software may vary.

Example 8.6 that follows is provided to demonstrate the application of Figure 8.9 data.

Example 8.6. We want to estimate the time and cost to produce a 24-page booklet using QuarkXPress. Page size is 8 1/2 inches x 11 inches. Eight pages will be prepared in 4 colors; the remainder will be black with a spot red. Client review necessitates that one round of editing will be included. The job will require four 2-color illustrations and three 4-color illustrations be produced digitally from previously scanned materials which require no editing. A $55.00 BHR, which includes all computer hardware and software to complete the job, will apply to all production.

Solution

Refer to the schedule in Figure 8.9 for hourly production standards.

Step 1. Determine the 2-color page layout time:

1/C: 1st p. @ 9 min. + 15 pp. @ 7 min. = 9 min. + 105 min. =
114 min. ÷ 60 min./hr. = 1.90 hr.
Spot color: 1st p. @ 5 min. + 15 pp. @ 3 min. = 5 min. + 45 min. = 50 min.
÷ 60 min./hr. = 0.83 hr.
Total time for 16 2-color pages = 1.90 hr. + 0.83 hr. = 2.73 hr.

Step 2. Determine the 4-color layout time:

1st p. @ 25 min. + 7 pp. @ 20 min. = 25 min. + 140 min. = 165 min. ÷ 60
min./hr. = 2.75 hr.

Step 3. Determine the page editing time:

2/C (black and red):
1st color = 1st p. @ 6 min. + 15 pp. @ 4 min. = 66 min. ÷ 60 min./hr. = 1.10 hr.
Spot 2nd color = 1st p. @ 4 min. + 15 pp. @ 3 min. = 49 min. ÷ 60 min./hr. =
0.82 hr.
8 pp. 4/c: 1st pp. @ 12 min. + 7 pp. @ 10 min. = 82 min. ÷ 60 min./hr. = 1.37 hr.
Total page editing production time: 1.10 hr. + 0.82 hr. + 1.37 hr. = 3.29 hr.

Step 4. Determine the illustration creation time:

2/C:
1st color = 1st @ 30 min. + 3 @ 30 min. = 120 min. ÷ 60 min./hr. = 2.0 hr.
Spot 2nd color = 1st @ 10 min. + 3 @ 10 min. = 40 min. ÷ 60 min./hr. = 0.67 hr.
4/C: 1st image @ 60 min. + 2 @ 60 min. = 180 min. ÷ 60 min./hr. = 3.0 hr.
Total illustration creation time: 2.0 hr. + 0.67 hr. + 3.0 hr. = 5.67 hr.

Step 5. Determine the total time for page layout, editing, and illustration production:

2.73 hr. + 2.75 hr. + 3.29 hr. + 5.67 hr. = 14.44 hr.

Step 6. Determine the total cost for page layout, editing, and illustration production:

14.44 hr. x $55.00 BHR = $794.20

Estimating Electronic Trapping and Image Manipulation

Electronic trapping and image manipulation are image modification procedures that are completed once the job has been digitized and exists as an electronic file. These procedures require that the computer platform and software used when the job was created are used again. Although trapping and image modification are different procedures, they are presented together here because both activities follow the initial digitization of the image.

Estimating Electronic Trapping. Electronic trapping, where images are carefully and accurately overlapped using digital methods, can be completed either manually or automatically. Manual trapping is done using FreeHand or Illustrator software and is executed by careful image processing on the part of a skilled employee. Automatic trapping, termed autotrapping, requires the use of software such as TrapWise or Island Trapper, which are specifically designed for this purpose.

Autotrapping is typically done in one of two ways. One way is like an autopilot process where the operator identifies certain pages and the program applies preset trapping rules to all images on the page. The other way to autotrap requires the operator to apply specific traps to specific elements on a page, such as screen overlaps, type, and similar complex items, which are then automatically trapped by the program. It should be noted that using autotrapping software is completely different from trapping using a drawing or an illustration program.

Estimating electronic trapping, as noted in the first row of Figure 8.10, is divided into manual and autotrapping operations. The unit basis for manual trapping is minutes per image. Its PAF is between 50 percent and 400 percent because image complexity may cause substantial deviation from established production times. Autotrapping images are segmented into simple and complex types with a unit basis of minutes per page. Because autotrapping tends to be less cumbersome than manual trapping, its PAF is less extreme—from 50 percent to 200 percent.

Trapping productivity is linked to the size and complexity of the file. Simple images usually trap more easily. Image complexity tends to increase time. How the image was originally drawn and layered could make a difference in trapping time, from perhaps 20 minutes to 2 hours. Some companies apply a minimum cost or estimate a standard minimum time for each trap they anticipate in a job.

Operation or activity	Production task or component	1st production unit	Follow-up production unit	Unit basis	Production adjustment factor (PAF) range	PAF adjustment notes
Electronic trapping	Manual via drawing program	15	12	min./image	50-400%	Based on image complexity
	Autotrapping (simple)	7	3	min./p.	50-200%	Based on image complexity
	Autotrapping (complex)	11	7	min./p.	50-200%	Based on image complexity
Image manipulation: Color correction, tone and contrast adjustment	Small (3 Mb or less)	8	6	min./image	50-200%	Based on image quality, size, desired quality level, complexity, and the level of creativity required
	Medium: (3.1-12 Mb)	11	8	min./image	50-200%	
	Large (12.1-25 Mb)	17	13	min./image	50-200%	
	X-large (25.1-40 Mb)	23	17	min./image	50-200%	
Image manipulation: cropping & resizing	Small (3 Mb or less)	4	4	min./image	50-200%	Based on image size and amount of change required
	Medium: (3.1-12 Mb)	7	6	min./image	50-200%	
	Large (12.1-25 Mb)	12	10	min./image	50-200%	
	X-large (25.1-40 Mb)	20	16	min./image	50-200%	
Image manipulation: sharpening	Small (3 Mb or less)	4	3	min./image	50-200%	Based on image quality, size, desired quality level, complexity, and the level of creativity required
	Medium: (3.1-12 Mb)	7	5	min./image	50-200%	
	Large (12.1-25 Mb)	12	10	min./image	50-200%	
	X-large (25.1-40 Mb)	20	16	min./image	50-200%	
Image manipulation: airbrushing & cloning	Small (3 Mb or less)	10	10	min./image	50-200%	Based on image quality, size, desired quality level, complexity, and the level of creativity required
	Medium: (3.1-12 Mb)	15	15	min./image	50-200%	
	Large (12.1-25 Mb)	22	22	min./image	50-200%	
	X-large (25.1-40 Mb)	34	34	min./image	50-200%	
Image manipulation: duotones	Small (3 Mb or less)	10	5	min./image	50-200%	Based on image quality, desired quality level, and the level of creativity required
	Medium: (3.1-12 Mb)	10	5	min./image	50-200%	
	Large (12.1-25 Mb)	10	5	min./image	50-200%	
	X-large (25.1-40 Mb)	10	5	min./image	50-200%	
Image manipulation: filters and special effects	Small (3 Mb or less)	4	3	min./image	50-400%	Based on image quality, size, desired quality level, complexity, and the level of creativity required
	Medium: (3.1-12 Mb)	7	5	min./image	50-400%	
	Large (12.1-25 Mb)	12	10	min./image	50-400%	
	X-large (25.1-40 Mb)	20	16	min./image	50-400%	

Figure 8.10 Schedule for estimating electronic trapping and image manipulation. Times are for example only.

Estimating Electronic Image Manipulation. Image manipulation is a group of production operations that are completed on digitized black-and-white (grayscale) and color (RGB-to-CMYK) images to enhance the quality of the images and to tailor each image to the needs of the client. Production is completed on the images after they are scanned and input in continuous-tone form. High-quality original artwork and good scanning procedures using a high-quality scanner minimize the time needed to complete these operations. Image manipulation procedures, which are typically completed using Photoshop, Live Picture, QuarkXPosure, and similar software, tend to be technically complex and are not considered editing operations as previously described and estimated in Figure 8.9.

Figure 8.10 covers six image manipulation operations. Other image manipulation activities are possible and should be included as appropriate to a given company's production. As noted in Figure 8.10, the production component (second column) is file size and the unit basis (fifth column) is minutes per image. File sizes are segmented into small, medium, large, and extra large and are bracketed from 3 Mb or fewer (small size) to up to 40 Mb (extra-large size). Files over 40 Mb require development of individual times based on study of a specific company's production methods.

Production times can vary extensively in this area, so the times presented in Figure 8.10 are for example only. When estimating, it is likely that the job specifications will show that certain image manipulation production procedures, such as the production of duotones or airbrushing, will be necessary, while the need for other image manipulation operations may not be predictable until the files are initially digitized.

In general, estimating duotone production is fairly easy (fifth row of image manipulation schedule in Figure 8.10). In contrast, the use of filters and special effects (bottom row of Figure 8.10) may have extreme variation, from instantaneous results to results in 20 or more minutes, based on such key factors as available RAM and operator skill. Because of this unpredictability, some companies apply minimum dollar charges or estimate standard minimum time blocks to cover image manipulation or image rework.

The best way for a company to accurately estimate image manipulation is for it to (1) develop its own data, and (2) gather accurate job specifications from its customers. A company develops its own data by first identifying its specific image manipulation production operations and then developing production times for these operations. To do this, each image manipulation operation should be evaluated to address the company's electronic production. Hardware, software, quality of image desired, image complexity, creativity, and employee skill should all be taken into account during the evaluation. Gathering accurate job details in this area can be difficult unless the job has been designed and image selection and production have begun.

The following formulas are used for estimating the total time and total cost of trapping and image manipulation production:

estimated total time for electronic trapping and image manipulation production = [minutes for electronic trapping ÷ 60 min./hr.] + [minutes for image manipulation Operation 1 ÷ 60 min./hr.] + [minutes for image manipulation Operation 2 ÷ 60 min./hr.] + [minutes for image manipulation Operation 3 ÷ 60 min./hr.], and so on. Apply PAF as needed.

total cost for electronic trapping and image manipulation production = [total time for electronic trapping x BHR] + [total time for image manipulation Operation 1 x BHR] + [total time for image manipulation Operation 2 x BHR] + [total time for image manipulation Operation 3 x BHR], and so on. Add material costs if any are incurred.

Note: The BHR could differ for electronic trapping or image manipulation because various computer platforms and software may be used.

Example 8.7 that follows is provided to demonstrate the application of the Figure 8.10 data.

Example 8.7. We want to estimate the time and cost to electronically trap and image manipulate the following digital files as part of a job we are expecting to receive:
- manually trap 3 spot-color images using drawing program software
- autotrap 4 complex process-color pages
- color correct and tone adjust 4 files of approximately 5 Mb each
- crop and resize 6 files, all 2 Mb or less
- airbrush 3 files: the first is 2 Mb, the second is 8 Mb, the third is 13 Mb
- prepare 3 duotones from scanned files: 2 are 1-Mb files, the other is a 3.6-Mb file

No PAFs will be used. A $48.00 BHR, which includes all computer hardware and software to complete the job, will apply to this production.

Solution

Refer to the schedule in Figure 8.10 for hourly production standards.
Step 1. Determine the cost to manually trap and autotrap all images:

Manual trap: 1st image @ 15 min. + 2 follow-up images @ 12 min. = 15 min. + 24 min. = 39 min. ÷ 60 min./hr. = 0.65 hr.
Auto trap: 1st color image @ 11 min. + 3 follow-up images @ 7 min. = 11 min. + 21 min. = 32 min. ÷ 60 min./hr. = 0.53 hr.
Total trapping time for all images = 0.65 hr. + 0.53 hr. = 1.18 hr.

Step 2. Determine the color correction and tone adjustment time:

1st file @ 11 min. + 3 follow-up files @ 8 min. = 11 min. + 24 min. = 35 min. ÷ 60 min./hr. = 0.58 hr.

Step 3. Determine the crop and resize time:

1st file @ 4 min. + 5 follow-up files @ 4 min. = 4 min. + 20 min. = 24 min. ÷ 60 min./hr. = 0.40 hr.
Step 4. Determine the airbrushing time:

1st file @ 10 min. + 2nd file @ 15 min. + 3rd file @ 22 min. = 10 min. + 15 min. + 22 min. = 47 min. ÷ 60 min./hr. = 0.78 hr.

Step 5. Determine the duotone production time:

1st file @ 10 min. + 1 follow-up file @ 5 min. + 1st file @ 10 min. =
10 min. + 5 min. + 10 min. = 25 min. ÷ 60 min./hr. = 0.42 hr.

Step 6. Determine the total time for image manipulation production:

1.18 hr. + 0.58 hr. + 0.40 hr. + 0.78 hr. + 0.42 hr. = 3.36 hr.

Step 7. Determine the total cost for image manipulation production:

3.36 hr. x $48.00 BHR = $161.28

Estimating Electronic Imposition Production

Electronic imposition is the accurate placement of fully prepared digital pages, images, or files into a predefined electronic matrix prior to film imagesetting, proofing, or platemaking. The term "electronic imposition" has generally been applied in reference to the production of signatures as they relate to the manufacture of books and booklets, but electronic imposition methods can be used for accurately generating any desired configuration of images, including multiples of the same image up on the page. Typical output formats are proofs for image review or approval or fully imposed film that is ready for platemaking. Electronic imposition technology is an ideal CTP application and will be of significant use as this technology becomes perfected.

There are two approaches to completing electronic imposition. The first is to use plug-in software that interfaces with page layout programs such as QuarkXPress and PageMaker. In general these plug-in software modules have been developed to provide basic imposition production, such as printer's spreads, and other types of page-related functions. Generally they are limited in what they can do.

The second and more common electronic imposition procedure requires the purchase and use of software developed specifically for this imposition purpose, such as PressWise, INposition, PREPS, or Impostrip. These stand-alone electronic imposition programs typically require the five following production steps to produce a book or booklet:

1. The pages are created and fully imaged in a page layout program.
2. The fully imaged pages are PostScripted (converted to a PostScript file) so they are identified as digital files.
3. The imposition program is used to create the book or booklet relative to signature and form size, page position, type of signature, stitching configuration, shingling (also known as "creep," which is where page positions shift in a book due to paper bulk), marks (for cutting, folding, and positioning), and other important details.

4. The PostScripted pages created in Step 2 are imported or digitally transferred into the imposition format created in Step 3.
5. The imposed forms, which contain fully imaged pages, are output to film or to a CTP unit.

When the same types of books using the same type of signature configuration are common and frequently produced, production time is reduced by using a template system at Step 3. These standing imposition templates are developed in a preformatted manner and are used over and over, which saves time because numerous production choices are bypassed.

Figure 8.11 provides estimating data for the second, third, and fourth steps just described. (Step 1 is estimated using Figure 8.9 when the file is originally created, and Step 5 is estimated as a film output using Figure 8.13, which is discussed later in the chapter.) Schedule times are for example only. The type of imposition software used, the page size, the use of a preformatted template, the available RAM, the job complexity, and operator skill have a bearing on production time, and adjustments should be made to compensate as needed.

The following formulas are used for estimating the total time and total cost of electronic imposition production:

Operation or activity	Production task or component	1st production unit	Follow-up production unit	Unit basis	Production adjustment factor (PAF) range	PAF adjustment notes
Page layout and editing	See Figure 8.9 to estimate.					
Electronic imposition: Generate PostScript pages or files	Small (4x6, under 50 sq. in./p.)	1	0.5	min./p.	50-400%	Based on software, file size, and complexity
	Medium (6.5x9.5, 51-100 sq. in./p.)	2	0.8	min./p.	50-400%	Based on software, file size, and complexity
	Large (9x11, 100-200 sq. in./p.)	3	1	min./p.	50-400%	Based on software, file size, and complexity
	X-large (12x16, over 200 sq. in./p.)	4	1.5	min./p.	50-400%	Based on software, file size, and complexity
Electronic imposition: Define imposition and marks	Using preformatted/standing template	1	0.5	min./p.	50-200%	Based on size and complexity of job
	New format: Simple	3	1	min./p.	50-200%	Based on size and complexity of job
	New format: Average	5	2	min./p.	50-200%	Based on size and complexity of job
	New format: Complex	8	3	min./p.	50-200%	Based on size and complexity of job
Electronic imposition: Importing pages	Pages or files	1	0.5	min./p. or file	100%	
Film or direct-to-plate output	See Figure 8.13 to estimate.					

Figure 8.11 Schedule for estimating electronic imposition. Times are for example only.

total time for electronic imposition production (assuming page files are properly prepared and edited in a page layout program) = [minutes to generate PostScript pp./files ÷ 60 min./hr.] + [minutes to define imposition and marks ÷ 60 min./hr.] + [minutes to import PostScript pp. or files ÷ 60 min./hr.].
Apply PAF as needed.

total cost for electronic imposition production = total time for electronic imposition x BHR

Example 8.8 that follows is provided to demonstrate the application of Figure 8.11 data.

Example 8.8. We want to estimate the time and cost to prepare an output-ready electronic imposition for a 24-page, self-cover, saddle-stitched booklet, measuring 6 1/4 inches x 9 1/2 inches untrimmed page size. The pages will be fully prepared by our customer's graphic designer in PageMaker 5.0 and it is expected that the pages will be of average complexity. No PAFs will be used. A $52.00 BHR, which includes all computer hardware and software to complete the job, will apply to this production.

Solution

Refer to the schedule in Figure 8.11 for hourly production standards.

Step 1. Determine the time to generate PostScript pages:

1st file @ 2 min. + 23 follow-up files @ 0.80 min. = 2 min. + 18.4 min. = 20.4 min. ÷ 60 min./hr. = 0.34 hr.

Step 2. Determine the time to define imposition and marks:

1st file @ 5 min. + 23 follow-up pages @ 2 min. = 5 min. + 46 min. = 51 min. ÷ 60 min./hr. = 0.85 hr.

Step 3. Determine the time to import pages:

1st file @ 1 min. + 23 follow-up pages @ 0.50 min. = 1 min. + 11.5 min. = 12.5 min. ÷ 60 min./hr. = 0.21 hr.

Step 4. Determine the total time for electronic imposition production:

0.34 hr. + 0.85 hr. + 0.21 hr. = 1.40 hr.

Step 5. Determine the total cost for electronic imposition production:

1.40 hr. x $52.00 BHR = $72.80

Overview of Digital Output Technology

Digital output is the generation of a fully imaged product that represents all or part of a digital file residing on the EPP platform. Output hardware includes the computer monitor, which is directly connected to the desktop platform where the image is viewed, laser-driven imaging devices, film setting equipment, dye sublimation equipment, ink jet devices, and CTP equipment. Output to the computer monitor is known as a "soft proof," while substrate materials include paper (for hard proofs), photographic and emerging silverless films, and lithographic and waterless printing plates.

The technology supporting all output devices is complex and varies relative to the type of device. For example, computer monitors appear similar from one to the next, but they vary widely in color range and value of color, both of which are critical when color matches must be precise. The maximum size of most output devices is also an important consideration. Larger imagesetters generally have greater production output, but this advantage must be balanced with the high investment cost and memory required. In addition, the cost of first-generation output technology is typically very high, but it undergoes a considerable reduction as the unit is sold and used over time. An example of this is the black-and-white laser printer, which was originally limited in its dpi quality, image density, and output speed, and which cost thousands of dollars. Today, a black-and-white laser printer is available for a few hundred dollars and both its quality and its performance have improved substantially over earlier models. This same scenario is true of filmsetters and most digital and laser color proofing devices.

The process of outputting an image, sometimes termed "printing" or "printing out an image," can be segmented into three sequential steps. The first step, which is done on the desktop platform, is to convert the completed digital file to an output language, of which Adobe PostScript Level 2 is by far the most common. This PostScript conversion is done internally, automatically, and quickly on the computer platform when the operator requests imageset output. Once the PostScript file is generated, it is automatically transferred in the second step to a raster image processor (RIP) where the PostScript commands are translated into pixels, or tiny defined areas, that are then transferred to the output device to produce a fully imaged page. This second step, which is known as "RIPping" the file, can be completed quickly or slowly depending on the amount of memory the RIP contains, the size of the file and the dpi level of the device (which together generally establish the number of pixels), and other technical issues. The third step is to generate the final image on the selected output device. This step may be completed quickly or slowly relative to the RIP configuration built into the unit. It should be noted that less complex output devices, such as black-and-white laser printers, provide both RIP and printing as one seamless operation, while more complex output units, such as dye sublimation proofing equipment or film output devices, usually separate RIP and imagesetting as distinct operations.

Accurately estimating output time can be difficult because both RIP and printing times are hard to determine and are not necessarily correlated. The RIP time is dictated in part by the amount of memory contained in the RIP. Because a high-resolution color file may contain millions of pixels, an RIP that has limited memory will be slow, which in turn may tie up the computer platform that requested the output. Thus, a slow RIP frequently becomes a critical production bottleneck. Choices to increase output speed include the purchase and installation of RIP memory upgrades; the use of file servers, which provide intermediate file storage to free the working computer platform; the use of hardware that supports multiple RIPs to one imaging device; or the use of emerging software-based RIPs. In general, the purchase of RIP upgrades that are linked with the use of file servers is a frequent solution for this production bottleneck.

Because the RIP-output technology using PostScript Level 2 has established a de facto standard for image output, it represents a key paradigm shift as the printing industry moves to the twenty-first century. This is because any output device can be standardized to this technology, and therefore a focus on output speed and level of quality relative to any output device becomes the engine driving the industry. This standardized output technology drives any proofing device, any filmsetter for lithographic production, any computer-to-plate (CTP) device (an emerging technology which bypasses conventional film production), any digital press (another emerging technology that is discussed in Chapter 10), or any electronic communication via CD-ROM, the Internet, and the World Wide Web. In sum, as faster and better output devices are developed, the printing industry will change from heavily lithographic printing production to a mix of digital and lithographic production. In addition, it is likely that the customer's choice of digital versus lithographic product will be based on many of the same issues facing the current printing industry, namely fast job turnaround, print quality, related services provided in addition to printing, and selling price for the products and services provided.

The area of color proofing is a critical crossover between digital and conventional technology. One reason is that digital color proofing systems, which are classified as thermal wax, laser, dye sublimation, or ink jet, are sometimes unable to provide the high level of quality that is desired relative to the desired color resolution and color match. Digital color proofing equipment is also limited in size, which is another disadvantage. In addition, the cost of digital proofing equipment, in light of the quality it provides, is high. Other issues such as the permanence of digital proofs and their lack of consistency in image and color remain problems.

For these reasons, photomechanical or analog off-press proofing methods are used for final film that has been output. When corrections are needed, the correction process first typically requires the digital file to be changed, then for the corrected film to be output and the job to be reproofed. Thus there is a common production pathway between digital and photomechanical production methods.

As detailed in Chapter 9, two categories of photomechanical or analog color proofs are currently used in the industry: press proofs and off-press proofs. Press proofs require that color images be stripped, plated, and produced using conventional lithographic presswork. This process is expensive and time consuming, but it provides extremely accurate proof results. Off-press proofs are subdivided into overlay proofs and laminated or single-sheet proofs.

The digital output of large proofs, known as wide format or large format printing, is done using electrostatic or ink-jet technology. Chapter 10 covers this subject as part of the print production area, while Figure 8.17, which is discussed later in this chapter, provides estimating data for wide format printing using various sizes of Iris ink-jet printers.

Estimating Black-and-White Laser Printing Production

Black-and-white laser printers are the least complex of all output devices because they have been technically improved over their more than ten years of use in production. Most of these printers combine RIP and output into a seamless, single operation. Speed is driven by the complexity of image to be output and the dpi built into the unit, so a grayscale image produced as a halftone and output at 1,200 dpi would take more time to output than a simple line image at 300 dpi. Generally black-and-white laser printers are available at very reasonable cost, and the quality of image is usually at least 300 dpi. Equipment cost goes up as the dpi increases and as the maximum output size the unit can produce increases.

Figure 8.12 is provided to estimate black-and-white laser printing. Times and material costs are for example only. RIPping and printing are one continuous operation. Letter and tabloid sizes are provided and the unit basis is minutes per page produced. The PAF applies to reduced or increased times based on file complexity, file size, and software used to generate the image. Material costs, which use a unit basis of dollars per page, are also specified and include the cost of both paper and toner.

For example, we want to estimate the cost of 20 letter-size laser pages to send to a customer for image approval. Due to the complexity of the images, we will apply a PAF of 150 percent. As indicated in Figure 8.12, base production is 2 minutes for the first page, plus 0.20 minute x 19 pages or 3.8 minutes, totals 5.8 minutes. Using the 150 percent adjustment, the time for black-and-white laser printing production of the 20 prints in this example multiplies out to 8.7 minutes (1.5 x 5.8 min.) or 0.15 hour (8.7 min. ÷ 60 min./hr.). If the BHR for this output device were $25.00 per hour, the estimated production cost would be

Operation or activity	Production task or component	1st production unit	Follow-up production unit	Unit basis	Production adjustment factor (PAF) range	PAF adjustment notes
B&W laser printer: **RIPping & printing**	Letter (8.5x11) Tabloid (11x17)	2 5	0.20 0.30	min./p. min./p.	50-400% 50-400%	Based on job complexity, file size, software used, and likelihood of rerunning the file more than once
B&W laser printer: **Consumable cost**	Paper and toner (8.5x11) Paper and toner (11x17)	$0.04 $0.07	$0.04 $0.07	$/p. $/p.	100% 100%	

Figure 8.12 Schedule for estimating black-and-white laser printing. Times and costs are for example only. Schedule data cover first imagesetting output only, so time or cost for rerunning second or additional output is not included.

$3.75 (0.15 hr. x $25.00). The cost of paper and toner is $0.04 for each of the 20 sheets, which totals $0.80. Therefore, the total estimated cost for the 20 prints is $4.55 ($3.75 + $0.80).

Estimating Film Imagesetting and Computer-to-Plate Output

Although film output devices have become technically sophisticated over the ten or more years they have been in use, CTP imaging is an emerging technology that has yet to be perfected. However, CTP holds great promise to increase output productivity for jobs that are printed using conventional lithographic or waterless processes.

Both film imagesetting and CTP output require RIP and imagesetting as sequenced but separate operations, and the production steps for both are very much alike. While film output is a common production operation for most versions of DTP software, CTP relies heavily on electronic imposition and the automating trapping applications discussed earlier in this chapter.

Film imagesetters, or filmsetters, are available to be imaged from a roll of film or from sheets of film which are mounted on a revolving drum. For sheetfed or drum-based units, the size of the drum dictates the maximum output size. Small-drum imagesetters are older units and large-drum imagesetters are more recently introduced. Both small- and large-drum equipment RIP and imageset in similar manners, but a major advantage of large-drum equipment is that it can output fully punched and imposed film as one complete flat or as a set of film images. Small-drum units are limited in that they can output only sections of an imposed flat or image area. Therefore, larger images on small-drum units must first be RIPped and output in sections, then manually stripped together as pieces. This can be time consuming and may cause a production bottleneck.

Film processing after imaging can be done in line or off line. In-line processing provides for film processing as an integral part of filmsetting production, while off-line processing requires the film to be transported by the operator to a film processor in another room. In-line processing is convenient but can sometimes slow film output because speed of film throughput is slow. Off-line processing is less convenient due to the separateness of its operation but it may be faster than the in-line process overall. The decision to process in line or off line is made when the equipment is purchased. Printers who have already invested in rapid-access film processing for photomechanical use, and who will continue to complete some of their prepress production using photomechanical methods, may opt to purchase their filmsetters with off-line processing and realize dual use of one processor.

Factors affecting filmsetting and CTP imaging time include file size, image resolution, complexity of image, and the mechanical speed of the filmsetter or CTP unit. For a typical printing company, accurately estimating filmsetting or CTP production is a process of first identifying the key factors for the types of work to be output, then developing a set of production times that reflect these types of filmset products. The process should include RIPping the image, imagesetting, and processing the film or plate.

Figure 8.13 is provided for estimating filmsetting or CTP imagesetting for single- and spot-color and color-separation production. Estimating requires determining the time for RIPping the image plus the time for imaging and processing the image. The unit basis for single- and spot-color production is minutes per page, while the unit basis for CMYK production is for the 4-color set. Production time adjustment ranges from 50 percent to 400 percent based on file complexity, file size, the software used to create the image, and the likelihood of rerunning the job a second or an additional time. Film cost is $0.02 per square inch of film required.

The following formulas are used for estimating total time and total cost for film output:

total time for film output (assuming page files are properly prepared and edited in a page layout program) = [minutes to RIP page ÷ 60 min./hr.] + [minutes to image and process film ÷ 60 min./hr.]. Apply PAF as needed.

total cost for film output = total time for electronic imposition x BHR. Add material cost as needed.

Example 8.9 that follows is provided to demonstrate the application of Figure 8.13 data.

Example 8.9. We want to estimate the film output time and cost for a 48-page annual report consisting of 32 pages of black-and-white work with a spot second color (which is 64 pieces of film at 32 pages x 2 colors) and 16 pages of

Operation or activity	Production task or component	1st production unit	Follow-up production unit	Unit basis	Production adjustment factor (PAF) range	PAF adjustment notes
Film output: RIPing (single and spot color)	Small (6x9, under 100 sq. in.)	5	4	min./p.	50-400%	Based on job complexity, file size, software used, and likelihood of rerunning the job due to imaging problems
	Medium (10x12, 101-200 sq. in.)	8	7	min./p.	50-400%	
	Large (14x18, 201-400 sq. in.)	12	10	min./p.	50-400%	
	X-large (20x24, over 400 sq. in.)	15	13	min./p.	50-400%	
Film output: Imaging and processing (single and spot color)	Small (6x9, under 100 sq. in.)	2	2	min./p.	100%	
	Medium (10x12, 101-200 sq. in.)	3	3	min./p.	100%	
	Large (14x18, 201-400 sq. in.)	5	5	min./p.	100%	
	X-large (20x24, over 400 sq. in.)	6	6	min./p.	100%	
Film output: RIPping (CMYK seps)	Small (6x9, under 100 sq. in.)	20	17	min./4c set	50-400%	Based on job complexity, file size, software used, and likelihood of rerunning the job due to imaging problems
	Medium (10x12, 101-200 sq. in.)	32	27	min./4c set	50-400%	
	Large (14x18, 201-400 sq. in.)	48	11	min./4c set	50-400%	
	X-large (20x24, over 400 sq. in.)	60	51	min./4c set	50-400%	
Film output: Imaging and processing (CMYK seps)	Small (6x9, under 100 sq. in.)	8	8	min./4c set	100%	
	Medium (10x12, 101-200 sq. in.)	12	12	min./4c set	100%	
	Large (14x18, 201-400 sq. in.)	18	18	min./4c set	100%	
	X-large (20x24, over 400 sq. in.)	24	24	min./4c set	100%	
Film output: Consumable cost	Film	$0.02	$0.02	$/sq. in.	100%	

Figure 8.13   Schedule for estimating film and CTP imagesetting. Times and costs are for example only. Time covers first imagesetting output only, so time or cost for rerunning second or additional output is not included.

4-color process with bleeds (which is 64 pieces of film at 16 pages x 4 colors). The job is fully prepared in QuarkXPress and no PAFs apply. Print page size is 8 1/2 inches x 11 inches (trimmed), and the job is imaged as one-up pages on 10 inch x 12 inch film. A $55.00 BHR, which covers the filmsetter, the computer platform and software to process the files and output the film, and the film processor, will apply to this production.

Solution

Refer to the schedule in Figure 8.13 for hourly production standards and film cost.

Step 1. Determine the time to RIP 32 pages to print in black and spot color: Black: 1 p. @ 5 min. + 31 follow-up files @ 4 min. = 5 min. + 124 min. = 129 min. ÷ 60 min./hr. = 2.15 hr. x 2 colors = 4.30 hr.

Step 2. Determine the time to image and process 32 pages of black and spot color:

1 p. @ 2 min. + 31 follow-up files @ 2 min. = 2 min. + 62 min. =
64 min. ÷ 60 min./hr. = 1.07 hr. x 2 colors = 2.14 hr.

Step 3. Determine the time to RIP 16 pages of 4 colors:

1 p. @ 20 min. + 15 follow-up files @ 17 min. = 20 min. + 255 min. =
275 min. ÷ 60 min./hr. = 4.58 hr.

Step 4. Determine the time to image and process the 4-color film:

1 p. @ 8 min. + 15 follow-up files @ 8 min. = 8 min. + 120 min. =
128 min. ÷ 60 min./hr. = 2.13 hr.

Step 5. Determine the total time for electronic imposition production:

4.30 hr. + 2.14 hr. + 4.58 hr. + 2.13 hr. = 13.15 hr.

Step 6. Determine the total cost for film output production:

13.15 hr. x $55.00 BHR = $723.25

Step 7. Determine the film cost:
Black and spot color film: 64 pc. x [10 in. x 12 in.] x $0.02 sq. in. = $153.60
4/c film: 16 color images x 4 seps. each = 64 pc. film x [10 in. x 12 in.] x
$0.02 sq. in. = $153.60
Total film cost: $153.60 + $153.60 = $307.20

Step 8. Determine the total cost of film output:

$723.25 + $307.20 = $1,030.45

Estimating Low-Cost Digital Color Proofing Production

Low-cost digital color proofing units are similar to black-and-white laser printers except that the low-cost digital color units proof in full color on plain paper. This group of tabletop printers, which range in price from $1,500 to $10,000, have self-contained RIPs and imagesetting processors and can be purchased and installed on a "plug-and-play" basis. This means that they have fairly simple installation and calibration requirements and can be put into use quickly and with minimum technical difficulty. Low-cost digital color proofing units have become popular for providing approximate color. Their affordable pricing assists in their wide range of use. Generally the digital color imaging system uses ink jet or thermal wax, and its resulting image and color quality varies from good to marginal.

Figure 8.14 is provided for estimating low-cost digital color printing. Times

Operation or activity	Production task or component	1st Production Unit	Follow-up Production Unit	Unit Basis	Production adjustment factor (PAF) range	PAF adjustment notes
Low cost color printer: RIPping & printing	Letter (8.5x11) Tabloid (11x17)	6.5 11	0.5 2	min./p. min./p.	50-400% 50-400%	Based on job complexity, file size, software used, and likelihood of rerunning the file more than once
Low cost color printer: consumable cost	Paper and toner (8.5x11) Paper and toner (11x17)	$0.08 $0.14	$0.08 $0.14	$/p. $/p.	100% 100%	

Figure 8.14 Schedule for estimating low-cost digital color printing. Times and costs are for example only. Time covers first imagesetting output only, so time for rerunning second or additional output is not included.

are for letter and tabloid sizes based on minutes per page. The PAF varies from 50 percent to 400 percent based on the complexity of the job, file size, software used, and the potential of rerunning the file more than one time. The cost of materials, which includes both paper and toner, is $0.08 per page for letter size and $0.14 for 11 inch x 14 inch size.

Estimating Dye Sublimation Digital Proofing Production

Dye sublimation proofs, such as the 3M Rainbow, are one of the most popular digital color proofs when speed and quality are important. The proof is a continuous-tone image that is approximately 300 dpi, and proof quality, which includes color value and color range, is generally very good. Although the cost of the substrate and the ribbon of dye which provides the color is high, RIPping and imaging is fast and the overall cost compared to outputting film and producing an analog MatchPrint or other type of proof is low.

Figure 8.15 is provided for estimating dye sublimation proofing output. Schedule times are for example only. To determine an estimated total time, RIP time and imaging time must be added. For example, to produce a letter size (A4) color proof would take a total of 12 minutes, which is broken down into 8 minutes for RIPping the file and 4 minutes for imaging the substrate. Although some time is saved for each follow-up RIP of the same image (about 2 minutes), no time is saved in the imaging operation, so a second proof of the same A4 image would take an estimated 10 minutes to produce (12 min. - 10 min.). Production adjustments to these times should be made when the job is complex, when the file is particularly large, when the software is not proven, or when the proof may have to be rerun.

The costs of materials shown in Figure 8.15 are based on a cost per page

Operation or activity	Production task or component	1st production unit	Follow-up production unit	Unit basis	Production adjustment factor (PAF) range	PAF adjustment notes
Dye sublimation output: RIPping	Letter (8.5x11/A4)	8	6	min./p.	50-400%	Based on job complexity, file size, software used, and likelihood of rerunning the file more than once
	Tabloid (11x17)	12	9	min./p.	50-400%	
Dye sublimation output: Imaging	Letter (8.5x11/A4)	4	4	min./p.	100%	
	Tabloid (11x17)	5	5	min./p.	100%	
Dye sublimation output: Consumable cost	Paper and ribbon (8.5x11)	$6.00	$6.00	$/p.	100%	
	Paper and ribbon (11x17)	$9.00	$9.00	$/p.	100%	

Figure 8.15 Schedule for estimating dye sublimation digital output. Times and costs are for example only. Time covers first imagesetting output only, so time or cost for rerunning second or additional output is not included.

produced unit. Although material costs for dye sublimation proofing tend to be high, the quality and speed of production is good. Because changing the dye ribbon between sizes of prints is not a simple task, some providers of dye sublimation proofs offer only one size on a continuous basis.

Estimating Laser Color Proofing Production

Laser color copiers, such as the Fiery/Canon CLC system, are basically color scanners that are linked to a color printing engine and have computerized imaging and paper automation. These units, which provide quick and generally good color results, are used frequently during the creative imaging process for demonstrating color in comprehensive art. Advertising agencies use color copiers for clients who wish to see color proofs quickly and inexpensively. Printers sometimes use color copies to intermediately look at color in a job, prior to using more time-consuming analog proofing methods. Color copiers are also used to provide a limited number of copies of a color image, in what amounts to short-run digital color, which can save considerable time and money compared to other digital color processes. Most color copiers provide 300 or higher dpi continuous-tone images with good resolution, but small type and image details do not tend to reproduce well. Duplexing, or printing on both sides, is possible with some color laser copiers.

Figure 8.16 is provided for estimating color laser copier production. Images must be RIPped separate from being output. All production units are in minutes per page, and pages are in letter and tabloid dimensions. Production adjustment

Operation or activity	Production task or component	1st production unit	Follow-up production unit	Unit basis	Production adjustment factor (PAF) range	PAF adjustment notes
Color copier: RIPing	Letter (8.5x11)	7	4	min./p.	50-400%	Based on job complexity, file size, software used, and likelihood of rerunning the file more than once
	Tabloid (11x17)	10	6	min./p.	50-400%	
Color copier: Imaging output	Letter (8.5x11)	0.5	0.15	min./p.	100%	
	Tabloid (11x17)	0.75	0.3	min./p.	100%	
Color copier output: Consumable cost	Paper and toner (8.5x11)	$0.50	$0.50	$/p.	100%	
	Paper and toner (11x17)	$0.90	$0.90	$/p.	100%	
	Card stock and toner (8.5x11)	$0.70	$0.70	$/p.	100%	
	Card stock and toner (11x17)	$1.10	$1.10	$/p.	100%	

Figure 8.16 Estimating laser color digital proofing output. Times and costs are for example only. Time covers first imagesetting output only, so time or cost for rerunning second or additional output is not included. Use follow-up production unit for multiple copies of same image or for the second image when duplexing different images.

ranges from 50 percent to 400 percent based on job complexity, file size, software used, and the likelihood of rerunning the file more than once. Times are for example only and do not provide for rerunning images if the first result is not acceptable. Paper stocks include bond and book or card stock. Consumable cost is provided on a cost per page basis for both letter and tabloid sizes. If duplexing (printing on both sides of the substrate) and the images are different for each side, the RIP and imaging times are doubled but consumable costs are not.

Using Figure 8.16, an estimate of the time and cost to produce 4 copies of 1 letter-size color photograph on bond paper with no PAF would require the following:

RIPping: 7 minutes for imaging (1 image with no follow-up images) = 7 minutes

Color copier output: 0.50 min. for the first page + (0.15 min. x 3 more images) = 0.50 min. + 0.45 min. = 0.95 min.

Therefore, the total time for the 4 copies is 7.95 minutes or approximately 8 minutes.

Consumable cost of total materials: $0.50 x 4 shts. = $2.00

Estimating Iris Color Proofing Production

Iris printers are high-resolution color proofing systems using ink jet technology. The quality of their output is very good—they produce images from between

Operation or activity	Production task or component	1st production unit	Follow-up production unit	Unit basis	Production adjustment factor (PAF) range	PAF adjustment notes
Iris proofing: RIPping	Small (8x10)	20	17	min./p.	50-400%	
	Medium (10x12)	32	27	min./p.	50-400%	Based on job complexity, file size,
	Large (14x18)	48	11	min./p.	50-400%	software used, and likelihood of
	X-large (18x24)	60	51	min./p.	50-400%	re-running the file more than once.
	XX-large (30x45)	100	85	min./p.	50-400%	
Iris proofing: Iris 3012 output	Setup	3.5	3.5	min./form	75-125%	Based on operator efficiency, paper used
	Imaging	3.1	3.1	lateral inches/min.	50-200%	Based on resolution and drum speed
Iris proofing: Iris 3024 output	Setup	7.5	7.5	min./form	75-125%	Based on operator efficiency, paper used
	Imaging	1.6	1.6	lateral inches/min.	50-200%	Based on resolution and drum speed
Iris proofing: Iris 3047 output	Setup	10	10	min./form	75-125%	Based on operator efficiency, paper used
	Imaging	0.8	0.8	lateral inches/min.	50-200%	Based on resolution and drum speed
Iris proofing: Consumable cost	Paper and ink	$0.07	$0.07	$/sq. in.	100%	

Figure 8.17 Schedule for estimating Iris proofing output. Times and costs are for example only. Time covers first imagesetting output only, so time or cost for rerunning second or additional output is not included.

150 dpi and 300 dpi and the visual resolution of the images is significantly higher than similar color output devices because each dot can vary on a 32-step scale. Thus, Iris proofs appear as continuous-tone images.

All Iris printers are drum based, which allows them good overall productivity. Although various technical issues are involved in the speed versus quality relationship, output is generally at 300 dpi with a drum speed of 190 inches per second (ips). Lower speeds do not necessarily provide greater quality, however. Output requires that four ink jet nozzles deliver CMYK, vegetable-based inks to the substrate.

Figure 8.17 is provided to estimate Iris proofing time and cost. Figures are for example only. The schedule covers three Iris models, which are delineated by the circumferences of their imaging drums: the 3012 or 12-inch unit, the 3024 or 24-inch unit, and the 3047 or 47-inch unit. The 3012 unit, which is fully automatic in sheet feed and ejection, is designed for outputting 11 inch x 17 inch pages quickly, while the 3024 and 3047 units are manually operated. Producing an Iris print is a separate RIP and output process. The RIP time is the same for any model. Output is segmented into setup and imaging operations. The setup time is based on minutes per sheet, while the imaging time is based on the travel of the ink jet head in lateral inches. The cost for materials includes the cost for paper and ink and is calculated using a cost per square inch basis.

For example, to produce 1 10 inch x 12 inch proof on a 3012 Iris proofer would require 32 minutes for RIPping, plus 3.5 minutes for setup and 3.2 minutes for imaging (10 inches ÷ 3.1 inches per minute), which totals 38.7 minutes. The cost for paper and ink would be 120 sq. in. (10 inches x 12 inches) at $0.07 per sq. in. = $8.40.

8.9 Developing a Template Spreadsheet Cost Estimating System for Electronic Prepress

Cost estimating EPP can be quickly and accurately completed through the establishment and use of a template or pro forma estimating system. As discussed in Chapter 5, template estimating is a process by which a master estimating worksheet (or template) is developed to represent anticipated production in a specified area. Frequently a computer spreadsheet program is used for this purpose, which allows the master to be copied quickly and accurately. Estimating a job is then completed quickly using a copy of the master worksheet as a base and changing those areas that differ from one job to the next. Computerized template estimating for EPP is fast and precise as long as the job specifications can be accurately identified.

Establishing a pro forma estimating system for EPP requires the identification of four groups of data as indicated by the columns in Figure 8.18, which is a blank master template spreadsheet. These are: (1) the component production operations that are possible (Column 1), (2) the operation code that identifies each component (Column 2), (3) the hourly base production units that represent one unit of work, grouped by component (Column 4), and (4) the BHR for each production operation (Column 6).

Completing the template requires that the estimator review each job component listed in Column 1 by determining or estimating the number of units required (Column 3). The estimator must also determine the probable material cost (Column 8) and assign a penalty markup or PAF (Column 9) if applicable. In this example, a profit markup of 35 percent has been included (Column 11), which can be changed by changing the percentage at the top of the column. Figure 8.19 is a completed spreadsheet showing a template estimate for a typical DTP job.

The template estimating process requires that the estimator have a thorough set of job specifications and that he understand the component production operations that will be necessary to complete the job. In cases where the estimator is unfamiliar with the production components, the estimate can be completed by his supervisor or another person working in the EPP department.

Customer name: _____   Date: _____

Address: _____

Telephone: _____   Estimator: _____

35.00%

1	2	3	4	5	6	7	8	9	10	11	12
Component production operation	Operation code	Estimated units required	Prod. unit (hr)	Estimated prod. time (hr)	BHR	Production cost (hr x BHR)	Estimated material cost	Production adjustment factor (100%=none)	Estimated total job cost	Profit markup (35%)	Suggested selling price
Design plan/roughs	600		0.50		$35						
Image planning	601		0.50		$35						
Job routing plan	602		0.30		$35						
File setup	610		0.30		$25						
Typesetting-straight text	620		0.20		$25						
Typesetting-complex text	621		0.30		$35						
Typesetting-technical text	622		0.30		$40						
Typesetting-foreign text	623		0.20		$40						
Typesetting-ASCII text	624		0.20		$25						
Scanning-position	630		0.20		$35						
Scanning-OPI/APR	631		0.20		$35						
Scanning-high resolution	632		0.20		$50						
Scanning-B/W	633		0.20		$30						
Scanning-other	634										
Desktop drawing	640		0.25		$40						
Desktop painting	641		0.25		$40						
Desktop illustration	642		0.25		$40						
Desktop image processing	642		0.25		$40						
Desktop page layout	644		0.25		$40						
Desktop imposition	645		0.25		$40						
Image modification 1	650		0.20		$50						
Image modification 2	651		0.30		$50						
Image modification 3	652		0.40		$50						
Image modification 4	653		0.50		$50						
Proofing-thermal	660		0.10		$40						
Proofing-dye sublimation	661		0.10		$60						
Proofing-ink jet	662		0.10		$50						
Proofing-analog	663		0.10		$35						
RIP-imagesetter (paper)	670		0.10		$25						
RIP-imagesetter (film)	671		0.10		$50						
RIP-to CEPS (Scitex)	672		0.10		$40						
Customer training/support	680		0.50		$30						
System work & archiving	690		0.25		$40						

Estimated total production time	Estimated total production cost / Estimated total material cost	Estimated total job cost / Profit markup @ 35% / *SUGGESTED SELLING PRICE*

Figure 8.18 Blank master template spreadsheet used for estimating a DTP job

Customer name: James M. Carrow & Company

Date: July 28, 1995

Address: 355 W. Newton Road, Chicago, IL 60611

Telephone: 312/555-1234

Estimator: Victoria Chen

35.00%

1	2	3	4	5	6	7	8	9	10	11	12
Component production operation	Operation code	Estimated units required	Prod. unit (hr)	Estimated prod. time (hr)	BHR	Production cost (hr x BHR)	Estimated material cost	Production adjustment factor (100%=none)	Estimated total job cost	Profit markup (35%)	Suggested selling price
Design plan/roughs	600	4	0.50	2.00	$35	$70.00		100%	$70.00	$24.50	$94.50
Image planning	601	2	0.50	1.00	$35	$35.00		100%	$35.00	$12.25	$47.25
Job routing plan	602	2	0.30	0.60	$35	$21.00		100%	$21.00	$7.35	$28.35
File setup	610	4	0.30	1.20	$25	$30.00		100%	$30.00	$10.50	$40.50
Typesetting-straight text	620		0.20	0.00	$25	$0.00		100%	$0.00	$0.00	$0.00
Typesetting-complex text	621	10	0.30	3.00	$35	$105.00		133%	$139.65	$48.88	$188.53
Typesetting-technical text	622		0.30	0.00	$40	$0.00		100%	$0.00	$0.00	$0.00
Typesetting-foreign text	623		0.20	0.00	$40	$0.00		100%	$0.00	$0.00	$0.00
Typesetting-ASCII text	624	5	0.20	1.00	$25	$25.00		100%	$25.00	$8.75	$33.75
Scanning-position	630	8	0.20	1.60	$35	$56.00		100%	$56.00	$19.60	$75.60
Scanning-OPI/APR	631		0.20	0.00	$35	$0.00		133%	$0.00	$0.00	$0.00
Scanning-high resolution	632	4	0.20	0.80	$50	$40.00		150%	$60.00	$21.00	$81.00
Scanning-B/W	633	4	0.20	0.80	$30	$24.00		100%	$24.00	$8.40	$32.40
Scanning-other	634										
Desktop drawing	640		0.25	0.00	$40	$0.00		100%	$0.00	$0.00	$0.00
Desktop painting	641		0.25	0.00	$40	$0.00		100%	$0.00	$0.00	$0.00
Desktop illustration	642	6	0.25	1.50	$40	$60.00		100%	$60.00	$21.00	$81.00
Desktop image processing	642		0.25	0.00	$40	$0.00		100%	$0.00	$0.00	$0.00
Desktop page layout	644		0.25	0.00	$40	$0.00		100%	$0.00	$0.00	$0.00
Desktop imposition	645		0.25	0.00	$40	$0.00		100%	$0.00	$0.00	$0.00
Image modification 1	650		0.20	0.00	$50	$0.00		100%	$0.00	$0.00	$0.00
Image modification 2	651	3	0.30	0.90	$50	$45.00		133%	$59.85	$20.95	$80.80
Image modification 3	652	4	0.40	1.60	$50	$80.00		150%	$120.00	$42.00	$162.00
Image modification 4	653		0.50	0.00	$50	$0.00		100%	$0.00	$0.00	$0.00
Proofing-thermal	660		0.10	0.00	$40	$0.00		100%	$0.00	$0.00	$0.00
Proofing-dye sublimation	661	5	0.10	0.50	$60	$30.00	$125.00	100%	$155.00	$54.25	$209.25
Proofing-ink jet	662		0.10	0.00	$50	$0.00		100%	$0.00	$0.00	$0.00
Proofing-analog	663	10	0.10	1.00	$35	$35.00	$175.00	100%	$210.00	$73.50	$283.50
RIP-imagesetter (paper)	670	8	0.10	0.80	$25	$20.00	$8.00	100%	$28.00	$9.80	$37.80
RIP-imagesetter (film)	671	8	0.10	0.80	$50	$40.00	$160.00	100%	$200.00	$70.00	$270.00
RIP-to CEPS (Scitex)	672		0.10	0.00	$40	$0.00		100%	$0.00	$0.00	$0.00
Customer training/support	680	2	0.50	1.00	$30	$30.00		100%	$30.00	$10.50	$40.50
System work & archiving	690	2	0.25	0.50	$40	$20.00		100%	$20.00	$7.00	$27.00
				20.60		$766.00	$468.00		$1,343.50	$470.23	$1,813.73
				Estimated total production time		Estimated total production cost	Estimated total material cost		Estimated total job cost	Profit markup @ 35%	SUGGESTED SELLING PRICE

Figure 8.19 Completed spreadsheet showing a template estimate for a DTP job

When a template estimating system like those shown in Figures 8.18 and 8.19 is developed from scratch, the two primary objectives should be superior accuracy and quick estimating output. Compromises of accuracy and speed should be carefully evaluated and honestly noted. Policy guidelines that might slow the estimating process, particularly those for the less defined areas of penalties and profit markup, should be developed to expedite estimating output.

Columns 3 and 4 of Figures 8.18 and 8.19 are critical to the accuracy of the estimating process. The estimator must be able to evaluate jobs by carefully assigning units needed (Column 3) with the base production hours (Column 4) as the key. Although Column 3 units change with each estimate, the base production units in Column 4 should be carefully established using job costing methods (see Chapters 2, 3 and 5) or benchmark review (discussed earlier in this chapter). These base production units should reflect real-time changes in production so that estimating and scheduling information is as accurate as possible.

The estimator's evaluation of the job specifications is the primary source for assigning units in Column 3. The development of job specifications that accurately reflect the job remains a problem with cost estimating EPP. Because this is an area where accuracy may be compromised, company policy should be developed regarding methods and ways that job specification accuracy can be assured.

Estimating in a printing company should be completed quickly and without fanfare. While it is difficult to establish the average time needed to complete a complex cost estimate, the process should take no more than fifteen or twenty minutes. A good cost estimate provides an accurate view of the time and cost values, including material costs, for a proposed job. An accurate estimate also provides a valuable source of information upon which production decisions can be made. Spreadsheets and computer estimating systems, which are discussed in Chapters 2 and 3, are valuable tools to speed estimating output and should be used with this goal in mind.

8.10   Business and Production Aspects of Electronic Prepress

Digital prepress technology has forever changed the way customers and printers work together. Software, production methods, hardware, and desktop skills of customers and employees is constantly changing. Success requires that DPP purchase electronic equipment, learn how to use it, modify it to fit their specific needs, and perfect it so that production is fast and error free. Nothing stands still as the digital revolution moves forward.

Observations on Success for Digital Prepress Providers

The following is a list of factors common to printing companies, trade shops, and service bureaus that have experienced success in DPP. The acronym SDPPPs means "successful digital prepress providers."

1. Successful digital prepress providers strategically market and sell to targeted desktop clients. By all accounts it is clear that success in EPP means organizing the company to market and sell digital products and services around identified customer needs. SDPPPs do not attempt to sell EPP products and services to every potential customer, but instead organize the company around electronic products and services that strategically fit selected client needs. SDPPPs develop cohesive strategies and marketing plans for selling and producing EPP products and services.

2. Successful DPP providers reduce customer-supplied electronic art problems by developing digital guidelines and providing good preflight feedback. SDPPPs know that considerable time and money is lost—and frustrations are high—when client files are, for whatever reason, unable to output properly. To resolve this problem, SDPPPs take the following two-pronged approach: First, they establish digital guidelines for all work to be submitted electronically, and second, they preflight each job carefully before it enters production. Because of their crucial importance to DPP success, both of these steps are detailed later in this chapter.

3. Successful DPP providers develop a defined process or method for costing, estimating, and pricing EPP jobs. SDPPPs understand the importance of knowing their costs and relating these costs to their proposals/quotes and to prices for their clients. They quantify desktop production through capturing real-time production times and interfacing these times with BHRs. There is a clear understanding that costs must be monitored through some type of job costing process, and that these costs mirror the production efficiencies of desktop. SDPPPs relate cost to price and understand that the more cost and price are equal in value, the less profitable the job will be. Successful DPP providers offer desktop products and services at competitive prices which are based on identified cost and production components.

4. Successful DPP providers establish a policy whereby customers pay for all the work performed, either directly or indirectly. It is clear a significant profit in DPP is impossible to achieve when desktop products and services are given away or provided free to customers on a continuous basis. SDPPPs understand this basic business tenet and thus build cost recovery systems where customers directly or indirectly pay for all of the work done on their files. For example, if a client file does not output properly to film, it is common to spend some amount of production time correcting the file so that it does output. Many FOPs tend to limit the time—to perhaps 60 minutes—in which they attempt file correction, and they typically do this at no charge to the customer. Over a period of time, however, customers tend to expect this no-charge repair policy, and thus tend to provide files that require some rework.

Unlike the FOPs, SDPPPs set their prices with a certain amount of file correction time built in, and they also establish a chargeback policy for file corrections they make beyond a reasonable time period. They typically charge these file corrections as AAs. Very few services are provided for free by the SDPPPs, even though some services may appear to be free. As digital files become less problematic and require less correction through customer training and effective guideline checklists, price discounts are provided. The discount rebates correction time dollars and appears to the client to be the result of enhanced knowledge and skill.

5. Successful DPP providers develop and use good output order forms or job control forms and require fully marked-up laser proofs for every job entering production. Successful DPP providers develop functional output order forms (see Figure 8.20) and require each customer to complete this document when submitting her job for production. SDPPPs also require that each job be submitted with laser proofs representative of expected output for all electronic artwork. At the preflight stage these documents provide guidance and input as to how the job was electronically constructed. Missing items can be quickly noted, file software versions can be checked, and final output can be clarified. Output order forms and laser prints give both the customer and the SDPPP a point of reference relative to file problems and necessary corrections.

6. If files are not output ready, successful DPP providers establish and hold to cutoff times for rebuilding them. Even though SDPPPs diligently work with customers to reduce problems with file output, such problems still occur. When this happens, SDPPPs work to repair files for an established time (with cost recovery built into their hourly rates). If a file is unable to be fully corrected, the client may choose to complete the repairs himself, or he may opt to have the FOP finish the repair for an estimated dollar amount. Frequently scheduling and job turnaround factor into the client's decision.

7. Successful DPP providers offer training to both customers and employees, with a focus on continuous self-improvement. As printing manufacturing methods have become increasingly electronic and technology driven, employee and customer training have shifted from an option to a necessity. Training provides knowledge, and knowledge is essential for effectively producing the desired digital and printed products in minimum time and with no defects.

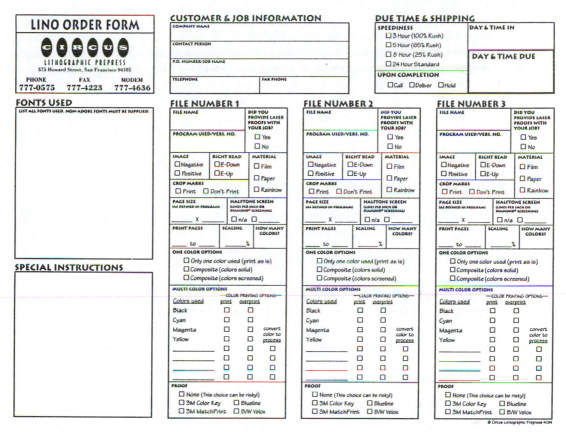

Figure 8.20 Example output order form. (Reproduced with permission of Circus Lithographic Prepress, San Francisco, California.)

Friendly feedback systems are part of the education process for customers and miniseminars during evenings and weekends are common.

8. Successful DPP providers understand the critical interaction between prices, customer needs, and company profitability. Successful DPP providers recognize that the prices they charge for their digital goods and services must meet competitive requirements. They also recognize that prices are the most essential component of profit generation for the company. Thus, despite intense competition, SDPPPs minimize price cutting and focus on providing the customer clear VA benefits. Providing high quality customer service is a key ingredient in this process, as is the practice of TQM.

9. Successful DPP providers recruit and hire the best employees they can find and build them into self-reliant teams. Success in any technology-driven business enterprise begins with knowledgeable employees as new hires, and continues only when the employees are provided continuous training and are empowered to work as team members who produce quality products. Intelligent recruitment is a key component in success, and SDPPPs use techniques such as preemployment testing and team interviews to ensure that only the "best and brightest" become serious candidates for a position. Development of self-reliant teams is also a critical component of success because employees ultimately work together on a range of complex and intricate jobs that require cooperation.

10. When purchasing EPP equipment, the best companies study their options carefully and get professional advice when needed. Purchasing EPP equipment and software is risky and complicated. Capitalization cost, production efficiency, training, maintenance, interfaces with current and future customer demands, interfaces with current and future equipment, and quality level are but a few of the issues facing companies purchasing digital equipment. SDPPP input begins with a continuous monitoring of emerging technology through trade shows, magazines, vendors' information sessions, and customer input. Employee input and feedback are welcome and encouraged. SDPPPs engage the input of competent professional consultants in this process as well, because they realize that the consultants' costs are marginal when compared to a poor purchase decision that could effectively cost the company thousands of dollars in lost time and materials.

11. Successful DPP providers continuously seek the most efficient production methods and time-saving procedures to meet the time-compressed needs of their customers. As customers have moved to EPP production, they have also come to expect reduced cycle-time turnaround at all phases of graphic production. Job turnaround is minimized because customers are better trained and able to produce better files. Production decisions are made quickly and immediately; they are not put off for higher authority. Written company communication is reduced to a minimum and communication is done by voice as much as possible. Employees team up to work on jobs, and the skills of each team member are maximized. Employees feel trusted and are unafraid to make on-the-spot, critical decisions if necessary, even if those decisions represent commitments that could place the company at financial risk. In addition, SDPPPs continuously seek new and better ways to compress time using both technology and practical resources.

12. Successful DPP providers establish and work in a TQM environment that is focused on continuous improvement. The convergence of technology-driven manufacturing methods and TQM is a key component for successful DPP providers. TQM integrates knowledge, technology, and people in a positive business environment. Elements of TQM include employee empowerment, continuous improvement, SPC, and the building of self-reliant teams and individuals. Numerous books and information sources are available on TQM at most bookstores and libraries.

Preflighting: Computer-Ready Electronic Files 2 and Other Preflight Information

Poor preparation of electronic artwork is a continuing problem that FOPs inherit from DFCs. Badly constructed electronic artwork forces the FOP into the frequently uncomfortable role of parent to the client's child persona. It opens a group of issues that, if improperly handled, threaten the positive relationship between the two parties. Some questions that arise from these issues are: who will repair the files, who will pay for the rework costs, can the FOP indicate the errors in a nonhostile manner so the DFC remains a positive participant in the process, and does the DFC desire to improve her skills or does she simply want to have the file repaired at minimum cost and job interruption?

Successful FOPs use the following four-step process to achieve harmonious relationships with DFCs once a job has been committed to the company:

1. They provide a set of guidelines or procedures showing clearly how files should be correctly prepared.
2. They offer assistance during the preparation of the files through telephone and other contact.
3. They preflight submitted electronic art quickly.
4. They encourage the client or DFC to avoid making mistakes by providing written feedback. In addition, some FOPs encourage new or inexperienced DFCs to provide pro forma or test files before building extensive electronic art. The FOPs then review these files to reduce problems when preparing live jobs.

It is generally agreed that the best set of guidelines for preparing electronic files is the *Computer Ready Electronic Files 2* guidelines. First published in 1993 by the Scitex Graphic Arts Users Association (SGAUA) and revised in 1995, these guidelines have become widely accepted as the most comprehensive set of working guidelines for preparing digital files. Figure 8.21 shows sample pages from the 1995 book. The SGAUA encourages the reproduction and distribution of its guidelines for the good of the industry. It also encourages each FOP to modify the *Computer Ready Electronic Files 2* guidelines to more accurately fit his own company's work flows, processes, and methods. To obtain a copy of the guidelines, contact the SGAUA at 800/858-0489.

Providing a source of assistance when building files is essential to reducing file problems. For this reason many successful FOPs offer telephone hotlines or drop-in assistance for the DFCs. The DFCs' questions are handled in a direct

Limitations and Discussion *Checklist*

Information needs to be available to the designer about the limits that define the "playing field." If discussed early in the creative process, a designer will not knowingly build a design beyond attainable limits. Following are some of the parameters that need to be discussed between a service provider and their customer. These may vary from provider to provider and may also vary from project to project. Designers can use this form to collect pertinent information from each of their service providers.

Transport
☐ Types and capacities of storage media available for transporting files.
☐ Who provides the media for transported files, particularly for files being returned to the customers?
☐ If telecommunications is an option, has the connection already been established?

Software Compatibilities
☐ What kinds of computers are used at both sites? If they are not the same, discuss how this might be resolved and what limitations exist.
☐ Fonts: Are names, manufacturers and versions compatible with those the designer needs?
☐ Are the designers' programs (and versions) compatible with those used by their provider?
☐ Which compression schemes and versions are preferred?

Prepress Process
☐ Maximum size of film output with bleed and trim.
☐ How much bleed and trim is required?
☐ Will the designer provide trim and bleed marks? Are other special marks needed?

Limitations and Discussion *Checklist*

☐ Who is doing the trapping? Are there limitations the designer should be aware of?
☐ If the designer is trapping, how much does the vendor require?
☐ Should FPO files be included with the files being submitted?
☐ Is imposition software used by the service provider? If so, what considerations should the designer be aware of while preparing files?
☐ Are die lines needed? Can the designer get an electronic file of the die line? In what format? Is it print side up or down?
☐ Are UPC codes needed? What is the most accurate way to get this done?

Workflow
☐ Are "Saved as PostScript" files to be submitted? What does the designer need to know to do this properly? Does the designer have the correct printer driver?
☐ If an image substitution workflow is to be used, discuss what can and cannot be done to the images given to the customer.
☐ Is the client's workstation(s) capable of working with large or complex files? How many Mb (approx.) will a 4-color high-res image be at $8\frac{1}{2}$x11? 5x7? 4x6? How many Mb (approx.) will a 4-color low-res image be at $8\frac{1}{2}$x11? 5x7? 4x6?
☐ What resolution should a LIVE image be for a 133, 150, 175 and 200 line screen?

Page 8   CREF   CREF   Page 9

Figure 8.21 Sample pages from *Computer Ready Electronic Files 2* guidelines. (Reproduced with permission of Scitex Graphic Arts Users Association from their 1995 *Computer Ready Electronic Files 2* book.)

and positive manner and suggestions are freely made to the DFCs regarding how jobs can be improved.

Once the DFC has completed the electronic art, she should carefully evaluate her job using a self-directed preflight checklist. Sometimes the FOP will use an output order form or job control form for this purpose. The self-directed preflight checklist, which is obtained from the FOP, is intended as a guide for the DFC to double-check her work before submitting it to the FOP. Figure 8.22 is a preflight checklist developed by members of PINC's group known as Digital PINC. Further information on this preflight checklist can be obtained by calling PINC at 415/495-8242.

D T P   E L E C T R O N I C

Preflight Checklist

*A few things to check over while you and your file
are both still on the ground.*

**Questions BEFORE you prepare
the file...**

- Is your service provider's hardware and software (including versions) compatible with yours?

- Does the output that can be provided meet your needs?

- What different types of media can the service provider support?

- What modem protocols does the service provider support if files are transmitted?

- What compression programs does the service provider support?

- What font libraries does the service provider support?

- Should the service provider or I do trapping on files?

- Should the file be prepared as printer or reader spreads?

Proofs

- Supply a composite proof (either laser or color) of the FINAL file provided for output.

- For color jobs, in addition to a composite proof, also supply separated laser proofs of each color and indicate color identification on each sheet created by the application.

Acceptable graphic formats

- Submit only TIFF or EPS file formats regardless of platform.

- Convert color graphics files from RGB to CMYK including any nested or embedded elements.

- Unacceptable file formats for imagesetter output: PICT, PAINT, RGB TIFF, RGB EPS, Quick Time, Single file CMYK EPS.

  Note: Embedding unacceptable formats in an OK format does not make the resulting file OK. Also, duotones and files with clipping paths must be supplied as EPS.

**Am I sure the file for output is
complete and correct? Have I...**

- Included all the application files and source files including EPS files?

- Included all display and printer fonts used in the file?

- Removed any extraneous versions or files from the medium that don't pertain to the job being output?

- Included complete fonts for type faces I've modified from library faces and given them a different name from the library font?

- Named all FPO images for APR with the *same names* as the scanned images?

Have I forgotten anything?

- The service provider's job sheet with the submitted file showing...
  - applications used (including version number)?
  - file names?
  - directories?
  - fonts used?
  - due date?
  - contact name including the business AND after hours phone numbers

- Do I have the rights on all the copyrightable material I've used in the file?

- Did I make a backup copy of the file and retain it?

Figure 8.22 Preflight checklist. (Reproduced with permission of Printing Industries of Northern California, San Francisco, Calif.)

File preparation considerations...

◆ In draw programs have I limited anchor points to the smallest number possible to minimize RIPping problems?

◆ Have I incorrectly used the "Style" menu for type styles (bold, italic, etc.), rather than correctly using the actual font in "Font" menu?

◆ Have I established crop marks correctly from the page setup or preferences and not placed them manually?

◆ Have I included overwork for bleeds outside of crop area?

Some things that don't always appear as they seem

◆ Laser proofs of the same file do not always output the same way on an imagesetter.

◆ Monitor images do not match hard proof images.

◆ All digital proofing devices do not output color hues and values the same way.

Responsibilities: File Originator

◆ Provide complete files that can be run within acceptable RIPping times.

◆ Provide all necessary information that permits efficient running of files.

◆ Provide ease of contact with originator and service provider or printer should problems arise.

Responsibilities: Service Provider

◆ Establish norms for RIPping times for various jobs as a benchmark.

◆ Establish costs for author's alterations done at the customer's request.

◆ Establish procedures for calling customer promptly when problems are discovered.

What is usually included in the Service Provider's base costs?

◆ Installing fonts listed on order form and included with job.

◆ Setting up applications to run customer file based on client supplied information.

◆ Cursory file examination (look for obvious problems that show up when file is viewed on the monitor).

◆ Quality control to meet printing requirements.

◆ Final image output.

◆ Redo due to vendor error.

What is not usually included in the Service Provider's base costs?

◆ Trapping

◆ Scanning

◆ File Editing including conversion of RGB to CMYK.

◆ Creating laser proofs if not supplied with file.

◆ Additional time associated with jobs containing incomplete or missing elements.

◆ Color proofing of final film or output.

This Preflight Checklist was developed through a consensus of Digital PINC members — people who deal with electronic mechanicals on a daily basis.

Figure 8.22 *(continued)*

Preflighting the electronic art is the FOP's review of the digital artwork before it enters production. During this review the FOP looks for missing parts, improperly prepared images, or other difficulties that may cause production problems. Preflighting is most successful when the following conditions are met:

1. The preflight process is done quickly, within one working day of submission of the job to the FOP.
2. Based on the preflight review, the client is permitted to make the necessary file corrections by getting the file back and completing the modifications. Feedback for these modifications is typically provided by the FOP as a free customer service.
3. The FOP assists the client or DFC so that the DFC does not feel uncomfortable, awkward, or intimidated.

Opinion varies as to which outside provider employee should complete the preflight review. Some FOPs use a preflight coordinator or a preflight administrator who is roughly the equivalent of the CSR who evaluates mechanical artwork as jobs enter production. Although other companies allow only their skilled digital technicians to complete their preflight checks, this tends to slow the preflight process because the technicians are frequently too busy to turn around the preflight reviews in one day or sooner. Still other FOPs use a "whoever is available" method to complete their preflight checks, which provides staffing flexibility but may compromise results if less experienced employees are too frequently available.

The preflight review should be a thorough evaluation of all parts of the job, including media format, fonts, colors, and graphic components. The result of the preflight process is a written checklist from the FOP to the client or DFC which indicates areas of the job that need correction, revision, or rework. Figure 8.23 is a sample digital imaging preflight checklist used by Bay State Press of Framingham, Massachusetts. Space is provided at the bottom of the form for listing all file problems and necessary corrections, with time and cost estimates.

Completing file repairs can be a sensitive area between client and FOP. A number of important issues require evaluation. For example, are the repairs too technically complex to be completed by the DFC, who did them incorrectly in the first place? Would it be less time consuming to have the FOP make the corrections? If the schedule for the project is tight, should the file repair be done by the FOP, who has more skill but who may charge for this service? How much will the file correction cost in terms of dollars and lost time if it is done incorrectly the first time?

Many FOPs include time in their job estimates for preflight review and some file corrections. The amount of time varies from company to company, but sixty minutes is not an unusual amount of preflight and correction time for a typical electronic job. Thus, if preflight took twenty minutes, forty minutes would re-

BAY STATE PRESS

DIGITAL IMAGING PREFLIGHT

Job Number _____
Client _____
Salesman/CSR _____
Date In _____ Time _____
Delivery Date _____
Composite Lasers Supplied   ❑ Y   ❑ N
Color-broken Lasers Supplied   ❑ Y   ❑ N
Color Lasers Supplied   ❑ Y   ❑ N
Document Size: a) _____
       b) _____
Folds to: a) _____ b) _____
Number of Pages: a) _____ b) _____
Bleeds: a) ❑ Yes ❑ No   b) ❑ Yes ❑ No

File Information

1. _____
   size _____ pages _____
2. _____
   size _____ pages _____
3. _____
   size _____ pages _____
4. _____
   size _____ pages _____
5. _____
   size _____ pages _____
6. _____
   size _____ pages _____
7. _____
   size _____ pages _____

Colors on Ticket:

❑ Process only   ❑ Process plus Spot   ❑ Spot only

1. _____	❑ Process	❑ Spot
2. _____	❑ Process	❑ Spot
3. _____	❑ Process	❑ Spot
4. _____	❑ Process	❑ Spot
5. _____	❑ Process	❑ Spot
6. _____	❑ Process	❑ Spot

Preflight Operator: _____

Disk Format:

❑ **Windows**   ❑ **Macintosh**

❑ 3¼ disk _____   ❑ Magneto Optical _____
❑ Syquest _____   ❑ Bernoulli _____
❑ Modem Upload   ❑ Other _____

Applications Used:

_____
_____
_____

Composite Lasers Printed	❑ Y	❑ N
Color-Broken Lasers Printed	❑ Y	❑ N
Color Lasers Printed	❑ Y	❑ N
Bleeds in File	❑ Y	❑ N
Proper Folding Setup	❑ Y	❑ N
Varnish Plate in File	❑ Y	❑ N

Fonts:

Missing		Supplied
❑	_____	❑
❑	_____	❑
❑	_____	❑
❑	_____	❑
❑	_____	❑
❑	_____	❑
❑	_____	❑
❑	_____	❑
❑	_____	❑
❑	_____	❑
❑	_____	❑
❑	_____	❑

Colors in File:

1. _____	❑ Process	❑ Spot
2. _____	❑ Process	❑ Spot
3. _____	❑ Process	❑ Spot
4. _____	❑ Process	❑ Spot
5. _____	❑ Process	❑ Spot
6. _____	❑ Process	❑ Spot

Imported Graphics:

Missing

❑
   Application _____
   Resolution _____ Scale _____
❑
   Application _____
   Resolution _____ Scale _____
❑
   Application _____
   Resolution _____ Scale _____
❑
   Application _____
   Resolution _____ Scale _____
❑
   Application _____
   Resolution _____ Scale _____
❑
   Application _____
   Resolution _____ Scale _____
❑
   Application _____
   Resolution _____ Scale _____
❑
   Application _____
   Resolution _____ Scale _____
❑
   Application _____
   Resolution _____ Scale _____
❑
   Application _____
   Resolution _____ Scale _____
❑
   Application _____
   Resolution _____ Scale _____
❑
   Application _____
   Resolution _____ Scale _____
❑
   Application _____
   Resolution _____ Scale _____

Description of Problem:	Work to be done:	Time:	Cost:
❑ _____	❑ _____	___	___
❑ _____	❑ _____	___	___
❑ _____	❑ _____	___	___
❑ _____	❑ _____	___	___
❑ _____	❑ _____	___	___
❑ _____	❑ _____	___	___
❑ _____	❑ _____	___	___
❑ _____	❑ _____	___	___
❑ _____	❑ _____	___	___
❑ _____	❑ _____	___	___
❑ _____	❑ _____	___	___
❑ _____	❑ _____	___	___
❑ _____	❑ _____	___	___
❑ _____	❑ _____	___	___
❑ _____	❑ _____		

Comments:

Figure 8.23 Digital imaging preflight checklist. (Reproduced with permission of Bay State Press, Framington, Massachusetts.)

main for "free" file corrections. In general, when the digital artwork can be corrected within the estimated time allotment, the file corrections appear on the invoice as a gratis service to the DFC. However, when the corrections are extensive—beyond the estimated time or the time-available repair window—the DFC should be given the option of making the changes himself at no cost. If the DFC declines the option, the FOP can make the changes as chargeable alterations.

As mentioned earlier, sometimes new clients are asked by the FOP to prepare pro forma or test files that represent the specific job or type of job they will be creating. This test file should represent the levels of complexity and difficulty the job is likely to have. The preparation of this test file should provide an opportunity for the FOP to work with the client and evaluate the client's skills. Once the pro forma file has been evaluated and deemed acceptable, the customer should be encouraged to create the full job.

File-Checking Software

A group of software packages has emerged that provides either the DFC or the FOP with a quick method to check files for various missing fonts, linked graphics, screen previews, and colors. Figure 8.24 lists these nine file-checking software packages. As noted, font and linked graphics checking is available from Adobe System's CheckList 2.5.1, Shawk's Roundup 2.0, Download Mechanic 1.5, and PStiMate from Graphic Systems Technology. PostScript errors and related PostScript problems can be checked using Systems of Merritt's LaserCheck 1.0 and Advanced PostScript Error Handler and Cheshire Group's PinPoint Error Reporter and PinPoint-XT. Screen page previews can be checked using PantherProof 1.1 from Prepress Solutions and Adobe System's Acrobat 2.0.

Graphic Systems Technology's PStiMate 2.0 (for PageMaker) and PStiMate-XT (for QuarkXPress) are used to predict the amount of RIP time a PostScript page will require. These are useful estimating tools for evaluating film and proofing RIP times, but they require that files be fully prepared and output ready if accuracy is to be achieved.

File-checking software is an emerging DPP area. It is likely that the future will bring additional software products that provide improved digital file checking. In addition, the development of DMI data collection for EPP will be of great assistance in monitoring DTP at all levels, which will allow for improved predictability for most DPP operations.

Terms and Conditions for Electronic Prepress

The emergence of EPP production has been rapid and chaotic. It has occurred in an environment where the customer or DFC has gained significant control over numerous imaging procedures that were previously controlled by the printer or

Software	Publisher	Features	Cost
CheckList 2.5.1	Adobe Systems, Inc. (formerly Aldus Corp.) 411 First Ave. South Seattle, WA 98104-2871 800/828-2320	fonts linked graphics	distributed free with PageMaker 5.0
RoundUp PS 2.0	Shawk, Inc. Client Services Group 1695 River Rd. Des Plaines, IL 60018 800/621-1909	fonts linked graphics colors	$99.00
Download Mechanic 1.5	Acquired Knowledge, Inc. 3655 Nober DR. - Ste. 380 San Diego, CA 92122 819/587-4558	fonts linked graphics colors	$249.00
PStiMate 2.0 PStiMate-XT	Graphic Systems Technology, Inc. South Park 1 1973 International Wy. Hebron, KY 41048	fonts linked graphics colors RIP time estimate	$349.00
LaserCheck 1.0	Systems of Merritt, Inc. 2551 Old Dobbin Dr. E. Mobile, AL 38895 205/660-1240	laser mockup with fonts and PostScript calls	$149.00
Advanced PostScript Error Handler	Systems of Merritt [address above]	PostScript stack contents	$295.00
PinPoint Error Reporter PinPoint-XT	Chesire Group 321 S. Main St. - Ste. 36 Sabastopol, CA 95472 707/887-7510	coordinates of PostScript errors printed on output; can be combined with LaserCheck	$89.50
Panther Proof 1.1v7	Prepress Solutions, Inc. 11 Mt. Pleasant Ave. East Hanover, NJ 07936 800/443-6600	screen page preview	$195.00
Acrobat 2.0	Adobe Systems, Inc. 1545 Charleston Rd. P. O. Box 7900 Mountain View, CA 94039 415/961-4400	screen page preview	$195.00

Figure 8.24 File-checking software for EPP. (Reproduced with permission of Graphic Arts Technical Foundation, Pittsburgh, Pennsylvania.)

Terms and Conditions
for Electronic Prepress

Definitions

The Client is the party who orders electronic prepress output (film, reproduction-quality paper, plates). The Client may or may not be the creator of the electronic files used to generate this output. The Vendor is the seller of electronic prepress output and may also be the creator of some or all of the electronic files. The Printer is the printing facility that uses the output to reproduce the Client's project.

Purpose

To define responsibilities of Clients and Vendors in the production of electronic prepress output.

Preliminary Work

Production of design layouts, software templates, comps or output samples prior to actual production is billable work. Client may not use such materials for production purposes without mutually agreed upon compensation to the Vendor.

Client Specifications

Client shall provide all information required by Vendor regarding file information and output requirements before work may proceed. Any service required by Vendor resulting from incomplete or incorrect information supplied by Client is billable work. Regardless of method of transfer (magnetic, optical, network or modem), Client is responsible for correctness of supplied data.

Acceptance of Work

The client agrees to pay for all acceptable work, defined here as output which meets predefined project specifications. The Client does not pay for unacceptable work. Any work put to use by the Client cannot be deemed to have been unacceptable. The Vendor's responsibility for unacceptable work is limited to replacement of the work. If work is cancelled prior to completion, Client is obligated to pay for time and materials charges already accrued.

Hard Copy and Proofing

Proofs are the industry-standard method of ensuring agreement among Client, Vendor and Printer as to the correctness of the job. Required proofs must be signed, dated and any changes clearly indicated before work continues.

Client will provide Vendor with low resolution proof prints of all electronic files. PostScript application and print files must be proofed on an Adobe-licensed PostScript laser printer. Proofs will be generated from files identical to those supplied to Vendor, and must match as closely as possible the specifications requested from Vendor for high-resolution output. If appropriate proofs are not submitted, Vendor will generate proofs as billable work. If client waives proofs, Vendor accepts no responsibility for the correctness of the output.

Client will provide Printer with appropriate proofs of supplied film (blueline, velox, color overlay or laminated proof). Printer will specify which proofing method is appropriate. If such proof is not provided, Printer will provide the proof as billable work. If client waives proofs, Printer assumes no responsibility for correctness of print.

Color Separation and Trapping

If Client provides color files and orders color separation of those files, Client is responsible for how those colors separate and how the colors trap. If Client asks Vendor to check for separation or trapping, it is billable work over and above any agreed-upon page imaging charges.

Fonts

The Client may provide any screen or printer fonts the Vendor does not own for use only on the Client's job, provided that installing these fonts does not violate laws regulating illegal copying of software. These laws generally stipulate Vendor may not archive or otherwise retain printer fonts provided by Client. Client must resupply Vendor with these screen and printer fonts each time they are required for imaging. Vendor may use supplied printer fonts only on the Client's current job.

Printer's Specifications

It is the Client's responsibility to ensure that Vendor receives written instructions from Printer regarding line screens, bleed specifications, separation requirements, trapping and other considerations unique to the printing process but controlled during electronic imaging. Vendor's time and materials required to meet these specifications is considered billable work. If the Client does not provide Printer specifications, and the Printer consequently rejects the output, Client remains financially liable for Vendor's charges. If specifications are provided but Vendor does not comply, Vendor assumes financial liability for the output.

File Preparation

If Vendor deems it necessary to perform additional work on the Client's files in order to fulfill the Client's requirements, this is billable work. Changes to the Client's files may require additional proofing before work continues. This additional work may result from Printer's requirements not specified by Client. In this case, Vendor should estimate the cost of such work and Client shall approve this estimate before work continues.

Alterations, Corrections and Estimates

Requests for and responses to estimates shall be written and itemized to include all billable expenses relating to the job. Any variations Client introduces that change the scope of a project's parameters or specifications beyond itemized estimates constitute Alterations, and are considered billable work beyond any estimated amounts. Changes made because of Vendor's failure to follow instructions or to make agreed changes from proofs are considered Corrections and do not add to Client's costs. Client errors requiring correction due to incomplete, inaccurate, or poorly prepared copy; handwritten copy; verbally submitted text or changes, incorrectly prepared files or mismarked proofs will be considered Alterations and will be billed accordingly.

Scheduling and Job Completion

Neither Client, Vendor nor Printer is responsible for meeting any schedule requirements about which they have not previously and specifically agreed. Vendor cannot guarantee scheduled delivery until receipt and inspection of final electronic files. Printer cannot guarantee press schedules until Client approves final proofs. Tentative schedules are contingent on a Client's estimated deadlines. If the Client postpones or advances the deadline, Vendor may review and adjust fees accordingly. If the Client puts a project on hold or suspends work pending proof approvals, schedules should be renegotiated.

A job shall be considered completed when Client, Vendor or Printer accept or approve any itemized service. Client will pay for all acceptable job work in a given project, whether or not that project is subsequently accepted, delayed, cancelled or rejected. Neither Client, Vendor nor Printer shall be held responsible for delays beyond their control, such as power outages, flood, fire or other calamities.

Ownership of Materials

Ownership of all materials (photographs, illustrations, computer data, computer media and other requirements of production) shall be determined at the outset of a project. Estimates and billings must accurately reflect and should clearly itemize specific ownership agreements. Regardless of that determination, no ownership is confirmed until final payment is made. Ownership is negotiable, but unless otherwise specified:

Client owns all materials, including computer data and media, provided to the Vendor. The Client owns final film and reproduction-quality output after invoices for the same are paid, even if these materials are stored by the Vendor or Printer.

Vendor owns any data files altered in the course of the work, and all media not specifically supplied by Client for the purpose of storing this data. If ownership of data is transferred to the Client, Vendor may charge for data, media, storage, disclosure of expertise and documentation of changes made to Client's files.

Printer owns all materials (duplicates, composites, intermediates, flats, plates) necessary to convert Client's materials into a format suitable for offset printing.

Copyright and Trademark

It is client's sole responsibility to ensure all materials supplied for reproduction do not violate copyright or trademark restrictions. This includes, but is not limited to, installation of software in violation of licensing agreements, excerpted text, electronically-generated illustrations, photos and transparencies supplied for scanning, and digitized photographs supplied on disk or other media. Vendor assumes no liability whatsoever for Client's use or misuse of copyrighted materials.

Figure 8.25 Terms and conditions for EPP. (Reproduced with permission of Pacific Printing & Imaging Association, Boise Chapter.)

FOP. Thus, the roles of each party have been redefined which, in turn, has changed the business and operational practices that have been used in the printing industry for years.

As noted in Chapter 5, GCBP, also known as the 1994 Printing Trade Customs, were revised to reflect the extensive changes in digital imaging that were not evident when the 1985 revision was completed. The 1994 GCBP were written to reflect the common business practices of the printing industry by defining the working parameters between customer and printer.

Some companies wish to develop their own "Terms and Conditions of Sale" whereby they establish their own contractual provisions that are tailored to meet the specific products and services they provide. The GCBP may be used as a framework to assist in developing these written conditions. It is possible to develop more than one set of terms and conditions, each tailored to a targeted customer group or desktop product. As with the GCBP, prior to any production on a job, the customer must be informed of the specific terms and conditions that apply to her job.

Figure 8.25 is an example of "Terms and Conditions of Sale for EPP" which covers fourteen issues from "Definitions" of the parties to "Copyright and Trademark" factors. This document can be used by any FOP, including DPP imaging service bureaus, trade shops, and printing companies who deal extensively with digital files and who desire to use their own terms and conditions and not the Printing Trade Customs.

Care should be taken when drafting any set of terms and conditions so that there are no contradictory statements that might lead to misinterpretation or misunderstanding by the customer or client. In order to reduce this problem it is wise to have a lawyer who is familiar with contract wording and DPP technology review any terms and conditions of the document before it is used.

Chapter 9

Estimating Photomechanical Prepress Production

9.1 Introduction

9.2 Photomechanical Production Methods

Process Cameras

Graphic Arts Enlargers

Opti-Copy

Film Contacting and Duplicating

Photomechanical Proofing Systems
and Materials

9.3 Photomechanical Production Planning

Artwork Specifications and Job Preflighting

Specific Job Requirements

Plant Production Details

Cost to Customer and Company

9.4 Estimating Mechanical Art Production
Developing Page Rates for
Estimating Art Production

9.5 Estimating Phototypesetting Production

9.6 Estimating Line, Halftone, and PMT Production Time and Cost

9.7 Estimating Film Contacting and Duplicating Production Time and Cost

9.8 Estimating Photographic Proofing Time and Cost

9.9 Estimating Color Separation Production Time and Cost

9.10 Film Assembly Methods
General Table Stripping Techniques
Pin Registration Procedures
Multicolor Stripping Procedures
   (Table Stripping Process Color)

Complex Color Film Assembly Procedures

9.11 Estimating Film Assembly Time and Cost

9.12 Photomechanical Platemaking and Proofing Methods
Categories of Offset Plates
Overview of Bases and Coatings
Working Parameters of Lithographic
   Plates

Automatic Plate Processing
Photomechanical Proofing Systems
   and Materials

9.13 Estimating Platemaking and Proofing Time and Cost

9.1 Introduction

Graphic images can be produced using fully photomechanical (or conventional) methods, fully electronic (or digital) technology, or a mix of the two. For jobs manufactured using exclusively photomechanical operations, which are now fairly uncommon with the growth of digital imaging, the production sequence begins with mechanical artwork, followed in order with process camera production, film contacting, table stripping, proofing, job corrections, platemaking, and, finally, presswork on an offset press. For jobs done using exclusively electronic production, which are discussed in detail in Chapter 8, images are digitized by scanner or other input means, modified, electronically assembled into pages using page layout software, and then output to paper, digital proof, film, or mass produced on a digital press.

The dilemma facing many printing companies is that production for most printed products is a mixture of conventional and electronic manufacturing methods. However, determining the best mix between the two is frequently unpredictable because that mix is dictated by the way the job was originally designed as well as by various cost and production issues.

To many printers, using digital production up to the film output stage has become easy, fast, and convenient. In fact, most designers enjoy producing electronic artwork using DTP technology. However, electronic imposition software remains cumbersome and slow, and large-scale film output devices to RIP large, fully imposed film flats remains expensive. Thus, many printers use digital production to obtain final film in small film size, then quickly and accurately table strip this finished film. Once the film is stripped, conventional (analog) proofing methods, which have been technologically simplified and streamlined and improved environmentally, are used. These analog color proofs tend to have higher quality color range, resolution, and longevity when compared to the time and money digital proofs require. Job corrections, if needed, are made using a mix of conventional and digital production. Once the job is approved for printing, conventional platemaking technology is used to produce lithographic or waterless plates for press because computer-to-plate technology is as yet unperfected.

The mix of conventional and digital production is driven by designer choice, production time (or delivery date) to be met, cost, and job quality. In some cases, conventional production may simply be faster. Sometimes employees are not familiar or are not experienced with specific digital production methods to achieve a particular result, but they can achieve the result easily using conventional methods. Frequently, too, the printing company does not have the electronic equipment to produce the product digitally, but it does have the equipment to produce it photomechanically.

This chapter provides estimating information for photomechanical production, including estimating data for process camera, film assembly, proofing, and platemaking methods. Although these conventional methods have been reduced in use or phased out by emerging digital production processes in some areas of the printing industry, they remain integral production methods for many printing companies both in the United States and abroad. This is particularly true in the areas of film assembly, proofing, and platemaking where conventional or analog production remains strong.

9.2   Photomechanical Production Methods

It is safe to say that any printing company today can quickly and reliably produce high-quality photographic film images both photomechanically and digitally. Suppliers and equipment manufacturers to the graphic arts have technologically advanced their products and services so that any printer can produce high-quality graphic products in a quick and reliable manner.

Although the movement from photomechanical or conventional production to electronic imaging has been occurring at an ever-accelerating pace, conventional photographic processes remain a integral part of prepress production. As time passes and digital imaging becomes less costly, more user friendly, and more accepted by designers, customers, and printers, many of these conventional photomechanical techniques are likely to be abandoned. How long this will take is impossible to predict.

Process Cameras

Process cameras are used to photographically render mechanical art to the exact size desired for final production. Such cameras photograph two-dimensional images and reduce or enlarge the images by moving their copy and lens planes while keeping their focal planes stationary. (The focal planes, also called vacuum backs, are where the vacuum suction holds the film securely during exposure.) Although equipment varies, most process cameras can reduce the copyboard image to as small as one-fourth the original size (25 percent) and enlarge it up to three times the original size (300 percent). Same-size images are exposed at 100 percent. Small plants generally use gallery cameras, which are totally enclosed in the plants' darkrooms and are limited with respect to copyboard and film sizes. Large plants may use either floor or overhead process cameras, which have their focal planes (vacuum backs) built into the darkrooms and their remaining parts in adjoining areas. These overhead cameras are classified as darkroom cameras and generally have large copyboard and film size capabilities.

Process cameras may be purchased with various types of light sources, including pulsed xenon, quartz, and incandescent. Artwork may be either reflection mechanicals or transmission (film) copy when the cameras are able to handle both types. Usually, however, reflection copy is used. Process cameras are excellent for the production of both line and halftone images. Halftones arc commonly screened with contact screens that contain many continuous-tone dots into which the original photograph is broken. Process cameras may also be used to produce color separations using either direct or indirect separation techniques and color filters, but this is not common today.

Graphic Arts Enlargers

Graphic arts photographic enlargers were at one time very popular for completing color separation production. Each separation exposure required careful control and considerable operator skill. Over the past twenty years, however, as both analog and digital color scanning have emerged to provide fast and accurate production, enlargers have played a significantly reduced role, to the point that today they are infrequently used.

Still, enlargers can still be found when production of black-and-white halftones are needed because these halftones can be exposed directly from original continuous-tone film images in one step. Enlargers are also still used as a controllable light source for exposing orthochromatic film materials during the contacting process.

Opti-Copy

Opti-copy is a photographic projection technique by which an image can be reduced or enlarged and then exposed directly to film in the desired size. Opti-copy systems are commonly found in printing firms that photocompose multiple images on one sheet of film, such as labels to run 24-up or coupons to run 16-up. To do this, one image, or an accurately related group of images (4-up), is used to project multiples directly to film.

The major advantages of the Opti-copy system, when compared to the conventional step-and-repeat systems found in platemaking, are its accuracy of image and its high production output.

Film Contacting and Duplicating

Film contacting is the production process of reproducing existing film images using a vacuum contacting unit, a specialized light source, a timer to control exposure, and contact or duplicating film materials. Contact film provides a film image that has opposite tonality from the original. Thus, a film negative is contacted to produce a positive, or a positive is contacted to negative form. Film duplicating, which uses positive acting duplicating or "dupe" film, provides for the production of images that have the same tonality as the originals. For example, a film negative in this process is used to make another negative or a positive is used to make another positive.

Film contacting procedures are found in both the photographic and film assembly areas of printing companies. Because many commercial printers specialize in multicolor production jobs that are tailored to customers, completing contacting and duplicating procedures in film assembly has become common.

For printing companies doing a significant amount of complex color work using table stripping procedures, fitting images together precisely becomes a critical matter. To accomplish this fit, photographic spreads and chokes are completed by contacting so that images fit—or trap—properly. A spread is a slightly enlarged image that is photomechanically made from the film negative of the original image, while a choke is a slightly smaller image that is made from the film positive of the original. The slight enlargement or reduction provides the overlap, or trap, of the two images.

Contacting is also used to produce film composites, whereby many film images are photocomposed onto one piece of film. These composites primarily save time during the stripping and platemaking processes which follow. This photocomposed film is sometimes termed "composed film" or "composited film" and is referenced on live jobs in the industry as "composed film furnished." This means that the final film given to the printer has the fewest number of pieces for film assembly, which saves time both in film assembly and platemaking and proofing.

As mentioned earlier, equipment for accurate contacting consists of a vacuum frame, a suitable light source, and an accurate timing mechanism. The vacuum frame ensures positive, direct contact between the previously imaged film and the raw (unimaged) film. Generally a large vacuum frame setup can be obtained fairly inexpensively compared to the cost of obtaining other imaging equipment, such as a process camera or an electronic color scanner.

Both darkroom and daylight film products are available. Darkroom films are orthochromatic (red blind) and require that the contact setup be placed in a safelighted, controlled environment. Daylight film products, which are popular in stripping departments, allow the contact frame and associated equipment to be situated in a fairly bright—but spectrally controlled—environment. Both daylight and darkroom films are available as contact films (which, as discussed earlier, reverse polarity from negative to positive to negative, and so on, with each photographic step) and duplicating films (which keep the same polarity, negative to negative to negative, or positive to positive to positive, with each photographic step). Film processing with both contact and duplicating films can be completed manually or automatically. Automatic rapid-access processing systems are fast, reliable, and popular today.

In sum, film duplicating and contacting procedures can be used to do the following:

1. make duplicates of existing film images
2. make reverses of existing film images

3. produce spreads from existing negative film images
4. produce chokes from existing positive film images
5. make composite film images by collecting many same-color images on one piece of film

The usual procedure for film duplicating (or contacting) begins after the pasteup or halftone has been reduced or enlarged to the desired size and reproduced in film form. Because this procedure requires contact between films, sizing of the image must be completed prior to contacting. Working at the vacuum frame and under the appropriate safelight for the film, the unimaged film is placed on the open frame with the imaged original over it. The frame is then closed and the vacuum drawdown is applied. When the vacuum pressure reaches the desired level, thus ensuring intimate contact, a timed exposure is given. When the exposure is completed, the exposed film sheet is processed and the resultant duplicate or contact negative should be identical to the original negative.

It is possible to contact films either emulsion to emulsion (e-e) or emulsion to base (e-b). Photographic film consists of a clear base, which is typically from 0.004 inch to 0.007 inch thick, and a light-sensitive emulsion coated on one side. This emulsion is essentially a photographic gelatin holding light-sensitive silver salts in suspension. The problem with contacting is that the thickness of the film's base can change the size of very fine dots and lines in images, or it may cause image loss altogether.

The e-e contacting procedure requires all film emulsions to be touching each other during each of two contact steps, keeping image loss to a minimum. The e-e process thus requires the generation of an intermediate film image during the first step of the contacting process. (This intermediate is a film image that physically is emulsion up [e-up] with a right-reading orientation and is not typically stripped as part of a job.) The e-e contact method requires two steps. In the first step, the original film image is first placed e-e to a piece of raw film, then it is exposed and processed to produce the intermediate film image. The second step requires the intermediate to first be placed e-e in contact with a second piece of raw film, then it is exposed and processed to produce a duplicate film image. A disadvantage of e-e contacting is that the intermediate film image ultimately is discarded and plays no part in future production operations of the job, which is costly.

The e-b contacting process is perhaps more popular because no intermediate negative is required. However, e-b contacts usually require longer exposures and may slightly change fine halftone dots and line images because exposure is completed through the film base. When estimating contacting and duplicating procedures, plant production generally dictates the technical specifics that apply.

Film contacting has important applications in printing production. For example, if a job is to be imaged on a lithographic plate 16-up, film duplicating could be used to take one negative and make the remaining fifteen. This might provide some economic benefit to the customer who currently uses step-and-repeat techniques whereby one film image is moved about during platemaking to produce the 16-up result. Another example: If a line of type were to reverse in a black background and then be printed with a second color (sometimes termed a Pantone Matching System or PMS color), this would be a trap. A trap requires the production of a spread film image of the overprint type or a choke of the reverse type. A third example: Film contacting is also used to photographically combine numerous film images onto one sheet of film, saving stripping and platemaking production time. This technique is known as "compositing" and the final product is known as "composite film."

Because of the profound economic effect that film contacting has on job quality and printing production, it is vital that the estimator has a clear understanding of this process. Of all the conventional photographic procedures available, contacting is the most versatile and dynamic, and it is therefore somewhat difficult to estimate.

Photomechanical Proofing Systems and Materials

There are three main reasons for proofing a job: (1) to check the job at intermediate stages of production for registration or other production problems, (2) as a final internal production check on the job for quality and related imaging issues, or (3) for customer or client approval of the job before production continues. The discussion that follows is limited to manual or analog proofing methods, which are distinguished from the digital proofing methods covered in Chapter 8. Even as the digital proofing methods enjoy success, they tend to be limited in size, high in cost, and provide sometimes inaccurate color results. For these reasons, analog color proofing methods continue to be used extensively for film that is generated from digital files.

Proofing is divided into monochromatic (single color) and multicolor proofing categories. The most popular monochromatic proof is DuPont's negative-acting Dylux or blueline proof. Exposure of the Dylux proof to an intense UV light breaks open an encapsulated imaging chemical, which immediately begins to turn blue in the image areas. Because no contact with water or other processing chemistry is needed, Dylux proofs are very dimensionally stable. Dylux is available in single-faced (C1S) versions for proofing single-sided material and double-faced (C2S) versions for proofing double-sided materials such as bookwork impositions. Various exposure levels provide different levels of blue density. As a result, Dylux can be used to check multicolor registration and alignment.

There are essentially two categories of photomechanical (or analog) color proofs currently used in the industry: press proofs and off-press proofs. Press proofs require that color images be stripped, plated, and produced using conventional lithographic presswork. This production is expensive and time consuming, but it provides extremely accurate proof results.

Off-press proofs are subdivided into overlay proofs and laminated, or single-sheet, proofs. Overlay proofs, which have been popular for many years, consist of acetate carrier sheets coated with a pigmented diazo emulsion. They are available in both negative-working and positive-working varieties. When the negative-acting type is exposed with UV light, its coating becomes insoluble to the solvent-based developer, and the image remains on the acetate carrier after development. Overlay proofs include 3M Color-Key and Enco NAPS/PAPS; DuPont's Chromacheck is an example of another category of overlay proofs that use dry materials and a peel-apart system.

Single-sheet proofs require the lamination of their carrier sheets to a substrate. The proof colors here "build" on the substrate in a superimposed fashion. One clear advantage of laminated proofs is their accuracy of color because the colors are trapped in direct contact over one another and are not on separate carriers as with overlay proofs. However, a major disadvantage of single-sheet proofs is that a lamination or an imaging mistake on any superimposed layer requires the entire proof be remade, which is costly and time consuming.

It should be noted that the area of color proofing is a critical digital imaging cross-over point. One reason is that digital color proofing systems, which are classified into thermal wax, laser, dye sublimation, and ink jet categories and are covered Chapter 8, are sometimes unable to provide the high level of quality that is desired relative to the color resolution and color match that are desired. In light of its quality, the cost of digital proofing equipment is high. In addition, digital color proofing equipment is also limited in its size, which is another disadvantage. Other issues, such as the lack of permanence of digital proofs and their lack of consistency in image and color, remain problems. For these reasons, the use of photomechanical (analog) off-press proofing methods are used from when final film has been output. When corrections are needed, the digital file must first be changed, then the corrected film must be output, the new film stripped, and finally the job must be reproofed. Thus there are common production pathways between digital and photomechanical production methods.

9.3   Photomechanical Production Planning

Estimating prepress requires the estimator to have a good knowledge of both conventional and EPP operations. It is essential that the estimator understand the processes used in his plant to be able to produce the images required, whether they are conventional, digital, or a mix of the two. The estimator must also be familiar with the types of artwork provided to initiate the job, the important job requirements, and the specific production details that are critical to the job. The estimator must be able to evaluate various production plans in light of the cost to both the customer and the company and suggest modifications that reduce costs to both parties.

Even when the estimator has this knowledge, obtaining accurate job specifications from the customer remains a frequent problem. This subject is addressed in Chapter 5 of this book in depth, but the importance of clear job specifications cannot be overstated, because the accuracy of job specifications correlates to the accuracy of the production plan and the cost estimate produced.

Artwork Specifications and Job Preflighting

If there is an area where the job specification process breaks down, it is in the details relative to how artwork will be prepared for a given job. This area is important because the details of the artwork establish many of the key factors that affect production time and cost.

Obtaining accurate artwork specifications has been problematic for many years, and the emergence of intermixed digital and mechanical artwork has increased the inaccuracy significantly. Many factors enter into this problem, among them the fact that customers increasingly insist on preparing their own artwork but are inexperienced in the complexity of preparing this task or frequently deviate from their original specifications for various reasons. Thus, because the original estimate was completed using job specifications were not representative of the final artwork, the customer is liable for any alterations that must be made to produce the job.

Because this problem of inaccurate artwork specifications recurs frequently, the standard operating procedure (SOP) for many printing companies is to estimate the job assuming the customer will provide final film that is ready for stripping. Final film bypasses photographic processes and some stripping operations. Sometimes, too, printers utilize the job preflight process, where the artwork is reviewed and evaluated in light of how smoothly it will enter production. This preflighting can be done by a CSR, a production staff member, or an estimator. When the preflight review indicates that the job will be problematic, the customer is contacted and arrangements are made to correct the problems. In general, the better the artwork preflights, the more smoothly the job will be produced.

Specific Job Requirements

Sometime during the review process, each job should be broken into its component parts, and the production planner should develop an itemized list or log covering anticipated prepress materials, including line, halftone, color separation, contact, finished film, and other prepress items. The job should be laid out and dummied, and the estimator or production planner should carefully analyze how the print order will move through the manufacturing sequence. Dozens of factors are important here, such as camera copyboard size, contact frame size, digital output device speed and size, press speed and size, the availability of equipment, the anticipated quality level of product, employee skills, and the likelihood of trade vendors meeting their turnaround requirements.

Plant Production Details

Manufacturing and production requirements vary from job to job. It has been said that no job in a printing company is produced exactly like any other.

The estimator must be thoroughly familiar with the specific production opportunities that are available using the company's current equipment and personnel and should work toward the most economical manufacturing sequence for both the customer and the printer. For example, it may be desirable to produce the job 1-up on the press sheet, or perhaps 4-up or 8-up is desirable. The latter choices would necessitate multiple image production during design and art production or perhaps additional film exposures in the photographic area or step-and-repeat techniques when the job moves into image assembly. It is essential that the estimator consider all production possibilities, factoring in both conventional and EPP operations, presswork configurations, and finishing procedures.

Cost to Customer and Company

Certainly one of the most important jobs of the estimator is to evaluate each manufacturing step in light of the cost variations between production plans. Such cost determinations are affected by the BHR of the plant center where the work will be done, the productivity of the employees doing the work, the complexity of the job, and the relative time required to complete the job. Such cost evaluations should include fair assessments of all materials required, including anticipated additional charges to be paid by the customer for AAs, which are customer-requested job changes. Of course, any errors made by company employees during the production of the job, which are commonly known as HEs, must be borne by the company and should not be charged to the customer.

9.4   Estimating Mechanical Art Production

Figure 9.1 can be used to determine the time necessary to make up mechanicals as camera-ready art. The size (format size) of the mechanical artwork in square inches must be known in order to locate the correct time in the schedule. Chart times should be adjusted according to the artist's skills. It is assumed that all copy that is ready for pasteup is clean, crisp, and sharp. As noted in Figure 9.1, initial base art that is pasted to illustration board (I-board) includes the following

	Under 100 sq. in.	101-200 sq. in.	201-300 sq. in.	301-400 sq. in.	Over 400 sq. in.
Base art prep time	0.15 hr.	0.20 hr.	0.25 hr.	0.30 hr.	0.40 hr.
Paste: Hr. per piece	0.03 hr. per piece pasted				
Overlay prep time	0.08 hr.	0.12 hr.	0.16 hr.	0.20 hr.	0.25 hr.
Paste: Hr. per piece	0.03 hr. per piece pasted				

Preparation of mechanical art is determined by adding preparation times and paste up times together. Use the appropriate square inch value for the format size of the job. Determine the number of pieces pasted. Additional colors/overlays are extra and apply as indicated. Use the appropriate BHR. Production times in decimal hours.

Figure 9.1 Schedule for estimating mechanical art and pasteup production. Schedule data for example only.

production operations: preparing the board to the correct size; measuring and laying out the illustration board for image placement; marking the board for proper sheet size, trim, and fold marks; and adding registration marks if needed. Tissue and kraft paper overlays are included as part of the base art layout time. If the artwork is multicolor and mechanically separated using acetate overlays, additional time must be added for each overlay used and for each piece to be pasted to the overlay. Schedule times for overlays include the attachment of register marks, page corner marks, and any other production or quality devices used.

The following formulas are used in Example 9.1:

total time for mechanical production = (board layout time x number of boards) + (number of pieces to be pasted x production time per piece) + (overlay attachment production time x number of boards) + (number of pieces to be pasted per overlay x production time per piece)

total production cost for mechanical art = (mechanical production time x artist BHR) + cost of materials used

Example 9.1. A customer requests an estimate for a 4-page brochure, untrimmed page size 8 3/4 inches x 11 1/4 inches, to be printed in black with a second spot color throughout. Each pasteup will be completed at 100 percent (same size) on artist illustration board. An overlay will be used for the second spot color. Our artist has indicated that there will be 6 pieces (pcs.) to paste for each black page and 4 pieces for each overlay. The BHR for the artist is

$37.90. Determine the time and cost to produce the 4 pages of mechanicals for camera.

Solution

Refer to the schedule in Figure 9.1.

Step 1. Calculate the layout time:

8 3/4 in. x 11 1/4 in. = 98 sq. in. (rounded to nearest whole number)

0.15 hr./p. x 4 pp. = 0.60 hr.

Step 2. Determine the number of black pieces pasted:

6 pcs/p. x 4 pp. = 24 pcs.

Step 3. Determine the black pasteup time:

24 pcs. x 0.03 hr./pc. = 0.72 hr.

Step 4. Determine the time required for overlay attachments:

1 overlay/mechanical x 4 mechanicals = 4 overlays

4 overlays x 0.08 hr./overlay = 0. 32 hr.

Step 5. Determine the overlay pasteup:

4 pcs/overlay x 4 overlays = 16 pcs.

16 pcs. x 0.03 hr./pc. = 0.48 hr.

Step 6. Determine the total time for pasteup:

0.60 hr. + 0.72 hr. + 0.32 hr. + 0.48 hr. = 2.12 hr.

Step 7. Calculate the total cost (without materials):

2.12 hr. x $37.90/hr. = $80.35

Developing Page Rates for Estimating Art Production

In some cases, estimators prefer to estimate artwork using "per page" time and cost rates. This can be done quite simply by manually cost estimating the time and cost of art production for one job or a cross section of jobs, then dividing both time and cost figures by the number of pages included in the estimate.

For example, for the 4-page brochure estimated in Example 9.1, the total cost of the job is $80.35 and it will take 2.12 hours to produce. Developing a per-page rate for this job is accomplished by dividing $80.35 by 4 pages, which equals $20.09 per page. Similarly, dividing 2.12 hours by 4 pages yields an estimated production time of 0.53 hours per page. These page rates, when averaged with other, similar 2-color jobs, could be used to estimate any type of 2-color work (e.g., black type with a second PMS or flat color) assuming the number of pieces to paste totals ten in any combination between the base art and overlay (the example has six pieces to paste to the base art and four pieces to the overlay).

When developing any type of cost or hourly standard for a finished product, such as a piece of mechanical art in the previous example, it is important that the product be clearly identified and that the figures be used only for similar types of work. Also, because the original per-page rates were built on an identified cost estimating process, revision of the per-page standards should be done using the same cost estimating model. Averaging the data by cost estimating a number of jobs that share similar production requirements (e.g., jobs that all have two colors, a black keyline and one overlay PMS color, and about the same size) provides a result that is generally more accurate than simply using one job the estimator believes to represent the finished product.

Establishing hourly mechanical art page production time and cost uses the following formulas:

hourly page production time = total production time for preparing similar mechanical art ÷ number of pages of finished mechanical art)

hourly page production cost = (total production time for preparing similar mechanical art x employee BHR) + cost of materials used ÷ number of pages of finished mechanical art

9.5   Estimating Phototypesetting Production

Phototypesetting technology has been largely replaced by the DTP and EPP production methods that were discussed in Chapter 8. Figure 9.2 is provided to demonstrate the process of estimating phototypesetting production where applicable. This schedule covers four kinds of phototypesetting equipment, but there are other keyboarding and typesetting units in production.

The data in Figure 9.2 are based on hours per 1,000 characters. This unit is also termed the "keystroke measure of production." Estimating the production of the phototypesetting output is based on a percentage of keyboarding time because the greatest amount of time in phototypesetting production is spent keyboarding. Figure 9.2 divides the type of manuscript copy into five categories: straight text matter with a mix of italics and boldface, capital and small capital letters with text, tabular forms, foreign text matter, and technical material with mixed text and symbols. These classifications are the most common, but others can be developed to fit individual manuscript and typesetting circumstances. Text processing using DTP methods is covered in Figure 9.2 and uses largely the same procedure described for estimating phototypesetting production.

To estimate using Figure 9.2 involves three steps. The first step is to determine the total keyboard production time using the number of characters (in thou-

| | Phototypesetting unit production - Multiplier of keyboard production | | | | | | | | | |
| Keyboard production (hr./M char.) | Mergenthaler VIP | | APS Micro 5 | | Mergenthaler 202 | | | Compugraphic 8400 | | Proofreading production (hr./M char.) |
	5-18 pt.	Over 18 pt.	5-30 pt.	31-120 pt.	6-12 pt.	13-72 pt.	73-120 pt.	6-24 pt.	25-72 pt.	
Straight text matter with mix of bold face and italic — 0.0952	0.12	0.18	0.01	0.01	0.01	0.01	0.02	0.01	0.01	0.0222
Capital and small capital letters with text — 0.1190	0.14	0.21	0.01	0.01	0.01	0.01	0.02	0.01	0.01	0.0222
Tabular matter — 0.1818	0.11	0.17	0.01	0.02	0.01	0.02	0.03	0.01	0.02	0.0333
Foreign text matter — 0.1250	0.13	0.20	0.01	0.02	0.01	0.02	0.03	0.01	0.02	0.0222
Technical matter with mixed text and symbols — 0.2000	0.11	0.17	0.01	0.02	0.01	0.02	0.03	0.01	0.02	0.0444

Figure 9.2 Production schedule for estimating phototypesetting composition. Schedule data are for example only.

sands) times the production standard for the type of manuscript indicated. The second step, which is determining phototypesetting production time, requires locating the phototypesetting unit production multiplier (referenced to the selected phototypesetting equipment, at the specified point value, by the type of manuscript) times the keyboard production time. The third step is to estimate proofreading time, which is calculated by multiplying the number of characters (in thousands) by the production standard for proofreading from Figure 9.2. The total phototypesetting time is the sum of the three figures.

The following formulas are used to estimate phototypesetting time and cost:

$$\text{keyboard production time} = (\text{number of characters} \div 1{,}000) \times \text{keyboard hours per M characters}$$

$$\text{keyboard production cost} = \text{keyboard production time} \times \text{keyboarding BHR}$$

$$\text{phototypesetting unit production time} = \text{keyboard production time} \times \text{phototypesetting unit multiplier}$$

$$\text{phototypesetting unit production cost} = \text{phototypesetting unit production time} \times \text{phototypesetting BHR}$$

$$\text{proofreading production time} = (\text{number of characters} \div 1{,}000) \times \text{proofreading hours per M characters}$$

$$\text{proofreading production cost} = \text{proofreading production time} \times \text{proofreading BHR}$$

total production time = keyboard production time + phototypesetting
production time + proofreading production time

Phototypeset output is produced in either film or photographic paper high-contrast images. Resin-coated photographic papers are popular because of their excellent dimensional stability and their cost savings over film. The paper-set material is used in the preparation of mechanical art as discussed earlier in this chapter. If photographic film positives are produced from the phototypesetter, they can move directly to platemaking with positive-acting plates or they can be converted to film negatives using common film contacting procedures.

Example 9.2. A customer has provided us with a manuscript to be typeset that totals 218,400 characters. The material will be set on a Mergenthaler 202, 9 point on 10, in Times Roman in straight text matter with italics. Keyboard and phototypesetting BHR is $56.70; proofreading BHR is $22.40. Determine the production time and cost for typesetting.

Solution

Refer to Figure 9.2.

Step 1. Calculate the keyboard production time:

218.4 M char. x 0.0952 hr./M char. = 20.79 hr.

Step 2. Calculate the phototypesetting unit production time:

20.79 hr. x 0.01 = 0.21 hr.

Step 3. Calculate the phototypesetting production time and cost:

20.79 hr. + 0.21 hr. = 21.0 hr. x $56.70/hr. = $1,190.70

Step 4. Calculate the proofreading production time:

218.4 M char. x 0.0222 hr./M char. = 4.85 hr.

Step 5. Calculate the proofreading production cost:

4.85 hr. x $22.40/hr. = $108.64

Step 6. Summarize the findings:

Total production time required: 21.0 hr. + 4.85 hr. = 25.85 hr.

Total production cost: $1,190.70 + $108.64 = $1,299.34

9.6   Estimating Line, Halftone, and PMT Production Time and Cost

Figure 9.3 is provided for estimating line, halftone, and PMT production. Schecule times are presented in decimal hours per exposure for both manual and automatic film processing. To the right side of the schedule is the standard production time for the exposure and processing of diffusion-transfer materials such as PMTs. These products also require automatic processing, which is completed using a specialized tabletop unit, not the processor unit used for film products. PMTs have become a popular intermediate photographic step in the preparation of pasteups and mechanicals.

Schedule times include placement of the copy in the copyboard, adjustment of the camera for reduction or enlargement, normal exposure, and processing with the applicable tray or automatic unit. Schedule data assume that the artwork to be used is of good quality. Adjustments in production times are to be made for poor-quality artwork and filter exposure operations. Time and cost

	Production time in hours		
	Line (per piece)	Halftone (contact screen, per piece)	PMT
Automatic processing	0.12 hr.	0.15 hr.	0.07 hr.
Manual processing	0.15 hr.	0.20 hr.	N/A

Note: Time and cost for remakes are not included. Schedule times and costs cover film products of all sizes

Adjustments: For poor quality artwork, increase time 25%. For filter exposures, increase time 20%. Consider duotones as two halftones.

Material and processing costs based on square inches of film material used:
Line film (plastic-base materials): $0.016 per sq. in.
Halftone film (polyester-base materials): $0.021 per sq. in.
PMT (negative and receiver paper): $0.012 per sq. in. (includes both pieces)

Figure 9.3 Schedule for estimating line and halftone production time and cost using a process camera. Schedule data are for example only.

for remakes of film images that are not usable during job production have not been included in the schedule data. Film and chemistry costs have been summed and calculated on a basis of cost per square inch of processed film. Costing data for plastic-base line film, polyester-base "lith" halftoning film, and PMT products are provided. Such costs should be adjusted for each individual plant, as should the indicated chart times.

Example 9.3. A customer requests an estimate for a 16-page booklet with cover, untrimmed page size 6 1/4 inches x 9 1/2 inches. Job specifications indicate that all 16 pages will be pasteup typematter to be shot same size. They will be gang-shot 4-up on the copyboard and exposed to standard 16 inch x 20 inch plastic-base line film. In addition, there will be 10 halftones to fit with the line work, and they will be shot individually on 5 inch x 7 inch halftoning film. The 2 outside cover pages will print in black and red, in register, and will be prepared as mechanicals with overlays; they will be exposed separately on 8 inch x 10 inch polyester film. The inside front and back covers will be blank. All film processing will be manual. The BHR for the process camera, including film processor, is $64.50. Estimate production time and cost for the camera including material costs.

Solution

Refer to Figure 9.3.

Step 1. Use the following formula to determine the camera production time required to shoot the booklet line work when 16 pieces are shot 4-up on 16 inch x 20 inch line film and the manual processing time for each exposure is 0.15 hour:

(number of pieces of art to be photographed ÷ number up on copyboard) x production time per piece = production time

(16 pcs. ÷ 4-up) x 0.15 hr./pc. = 4 pcs. x 0.15 hr./pc. = 0.60 hr.

Step 2. Determine the camera production time required to shoot 10 half-tones separately

(1-up) on 5 inch x 7 inch film at 0.20 hr. each:

10 pcs. x 0.20 hr./pc. = 2 hr.

Step 3. Determine the camera production time required to shoot the cover line work. Because the front and back cover images print in two colors each, both covers require two negatives—one for each color—for a total of four negatives. The negatives will be shot separately on 8 inch x 10 inch polyester halftoning film and will require 0.15 hour each to shoot.):

$$4 \text{ pcs.} \times 0.15 \text{ hr./pc.} = 0.60 \text{ hr.}$$

Step 4. Determine the total camera production time:

$$0.60 \text{ hr.} + 2 \text{ hr.} + 0.60 \text{ hr.} = 3.20 \text{ hr.}$$

Step 5. Use the following formula to determine total camera production time cost (not including materials):

$$\text{total production time} \times \text{BHR} = \text{production time cost}$$

$$3.20 \text{ hr.} \times \$64.50/\text{hr.} = \$206.40$$

Step 6. Use the following formula to determine material and film cost:

$$\text{material and film cost} = \text{number of pieces of material and film}$$
$$\times \text{ number of square inches per piece} \times \text{material}$$
$$\text{and film cost per square inch}$$

For line film:

$$4 \text{ pcs.} \times (16 \text{ in.} \times 20 \text{ in.})/\text{pc.} \times \$0.016/\text{sq. in.} = \$20.48$$

For halftones:

$$10 \text{ pcs.} \times (5 \text{ in.} \times 7 \text{ in.})/\text{pc.} \times \$0.021/\text{sq. in.} = \$7.35$$

For the cover:

$$4 \text{ pcs.} \times (8 \text{ in.} \times 10 \text{ in.})/\text{pc.} \times \$0.021/\text{sq. in.} = \$6.72$$

Total material and film cost:

$$\$20.48 + \$7.35 + \$6.72 = \$34.55$$

Step 7. Use the following formula to determine the total cost for process camera production:

$$\text{total production cost} = \text{production time cost} + \text{material cost}$$

$$\$206.40 + \$34.55 = \$240.95$$

Step 8. Summarize the findings:
Total production time: 3.20 hr.
Total production time cost: $206.40
Total material cost: $34.55
Total production cost: $240.95

9.7 Estimating Film Contacting and Duplicating Production Time and Cost

Figure 9.4 is provided for estimating film contacting and duplicating production time and cost. To do this, the estimator should identify the following:

1. the size of the vacuum frame to be used
2. the type of processing to be used
3. the number of film images to be contacted at one time (the number up)
4. whether the contacting process will be e-b or e-e
5. whether film compositing or spreads or chokes will be required
6. the type of imaging material to be used

The data in Figure 9.4 assume that the original film materials are dry and suitable for contact exposure. The schedule is organized in a step-by-step

---

Preparation and setup

Small contact frame (20 x 30 inches or under): 0.05 hr.
Large contact frame (over 20 x 30 inches): 0.10 hr.

Contacting film production

Note: Schedule times below provide for direct contact and processing of raw film to imaged film, such as e-b contacting. Double times and material costs for e-e contacting to provide for both intermediate and final film images.

Automatic processing	1-up*	2-up	3-up	4-up	Each add'l. over 4-up
Small frame (20 x 30 inches or under)	0.10 hr.	0.12 hr.	0.14 hr.	0.16 hr.	0.02 hr.
Large frame (over 20 x 30 inches)	0.12 hr.	0.14 hr.	0.16 hr.	0.18 hr.	0.02 hr.
Manual processing					
Small frame (20 x 30 inches or under)	0.14 hr.	0.16 hr.	0.18 hr.	0.20 hr.	0.04 hr.
Large frame (over 20 x 30 inches)	0.16 hr.	0.18 hr.	0.20 hr.	0.22 hr.	0.04 hr.

* Number up refers to the number of pieces of film contacted and exposed at one time and not the number of images contacted on one piece of film.

Adjustments

Compositing	Count exposures and add 0.02 hr. for each additional exposure of working films after the first expousre, which is provided in the above schedule.
Step-and-repeat	Count exposures and add 0.02 hr. for each exposure of working films after the first exposure, whicich is provided in the above schedule.
Spreads and chokes	For each spread or choke, add 0.08 hr. to the above schedule time.

Material costs

Contact film:	$0.015 per sq. in.	
Duplicating film:	$0.019 per sq. in.	(includes all processing costs)
Dylux paper:	$0.002 per sq. in. (C1S) $0.003 per sq. in. (C2S)	

Note: Time and cost for remakes are not included.

Figure 9.4 Production schedule for estimating film contacting and duplicating. Schedule data are for example only.

fashion, beginning with preparation and setup, moving to contacting production time, and then making adjustments as they apply. Materials costs are added based on square inches of required products. Remakes are not included. The appropriate BHR for the contacting center will be used.

Just as when determining the number of line and tonal exposures using the process camera, estimating contacting and duplicating procedures require that the estimator or production planner develop a system for breaking each job into its basic production operations. This is typically done by identifying the number of contacts or duplicates that is required, as well as the number of composites, spreads, or chokes that are needed. If an estimator is unfamiliar with film contacting/duplicating techniques and materials, she should spend time learning the essentials by observing production.

The following formulas are used to estimate film contacting and duplicating time and cost:

production time = preparation and setup + contacting production time + adjustments (as required)

production cost = production time x BHR

material and film cost = number of pieces of film or paper x number of square inches per piece x film cost per square inch

total production cost = production cost + material cost

Example 9.4. Our job log for an important customer indicates that we have to produce the following materials using contacting procedures: sixteen 10 inch x 12 inch duplicate negatives (e-b) to be completed 4-up, 8 duplicate halftones (e-e, 2-up) on 8 inch x 10 inch dupe film, and 4 composite negatives (e-b, 1-up) that are each to receive 6 exposures (from a total of 24 negatives) on 11 inch x 14 inch dupe film. The vacuum frame measures 22 inches x 34 inches with a BHR of $47.70. Add for one setup because all of this work will be done at one time. There is automatic film processing.

Solution

Use Figure 9.4.

Step 1. Determine the preparation and setup time:

1 setup (large frame) x 0.10 hr. = 0.10 hr.

Step 2. Determine the production time required to dupe the 16 negatives, 4-up on 10 inch x 12 inch dupe film using e-b procedures:

(16 pcs. ÷ 4-up) x 0.18 hr. ea. = 0.72 hr.

Step 3. Determine the production time required to produce 8 halftones using e-e procedures, 2-up on 8 inch x 10 inch dupe film:

$$\text{(8 pcs.} \div \text{2-up) x 0.14 hr.} = 0.56 \text{ hr. x 2.0 (e-e times are doubled)}$$
$$= 1.12 \text{ hr.}$$

Step 4. Determine the production time required to dupe-composite 24 individual negatives to 4 final composites using e-b procedures on 11 inch x 14 inch dupe film:

$$\text{(4 pcs.} \div \text{1-up) x 0.12 hr.} = 0.48 + (0.02 \text{ x 20 additional exposures)}$$
$$= 0.88 \text{ hr.}$$

Step 5. Determine the total production time:

$$0.10 \text{ hr.} + 0.72 \text{ hr.} + 1.12 \text{ hr.} + 0.88 \text{ hr.} = 2.82 \text{ hr.}$$

Step 6. Determine the production cost (not including materials):

$$2.82 \text{ hr x \$47.70} = \$134.51$$

Step 7. Determine the total material cost for duplicating film:

$$\text{16 pcs. x (10 in. x 12 in.)/pc. x \$0.019} = \$36.48$$

$$\text{8 pcs. x (8 in. x 10 in.)/pc. x \$0.019} = \$12.16 \text{ x 2} = \$24.32$$

$$\text{4 pcs. x (11 in. x 14 in.)/pc. x \$0.019} = \$11.70$$

Total material cost:

$$\$36.48 + \$24.32 + \$11.70 = \$72.50$$

Step 8. Determine the total production cost:

$$\$134.51 + \$72.50 = \$207.01$$

Step 9. Summarize the findings:
Total production time: 2.82 hr.
Total production time cost: $134.51
Total material cost: $72.50
Total production cost: $207.01

9.8   Estimating Photographic Proofing Time and Cost

Figure 9.5 is provided for estimating graphic arts photographic proofing procedures. Proofing techniques in Figure 9.5 are divided into five major types. The first two types utilize safelighted darkroom materials with appropriate contact frames, process cameras, or enlargers, while the latter three involve the use of the UV light sources typically used for lithographic platemaking and daylight

	Exposure and processing time (apply adjustments as needed) Up to 20 x 24 inch proofs	Material and processing costs (per square inch)
Type 1: Darkroom proofing papers Includes all types of orthochromatic, lith, velox, and polycontrast photo papers. Time for exposure and processing under normal conditions.	0.15 hr.	$0.012 sq. in.
Type 2: Stabilization papers Covers all types of stabilization papers including Kodak Ektamatic and Fotorite products. Time for normal exposure and machine processing.	0.10 hr.	$0.01 sq. in.
Type 3: Dylux papers Exposure and related production of one-sided and two-sided Dylux.	0.015 hr (first exposure) 0.04 hr. (each add'l exposure)	C1S: $0.003 sq. in. C2S: $0. 004 sq. in.
Type 4: Overlay proofing Exposure and processing of Color-Key, NAPS/PAPS and similar overlay materials. Includes mounting time on selected substrate.	Automatic processing (per color) 0.15 hr. (first exposure) 0.04 hr. (each add'l exposure) Manual processing (per color) 0.20 hr. (first exposure) 0.04 hr. (each add'l exposure)	Color-Key Process colors: $0.014 sq. in. PMS Colors: $ 0.016 sq. in. NAPS/PAPS Process colors: $0.013 sq. in. Flat colors:$0.015 sq. in.
Type 5: Single-sheet (laminated) proofing Exposure and processing of DuPont Cromalin and 3M Matchprint III materials. Times include laminating film to substrate, exposure, and processing for one layer; add for each proof layer as needed. Material costs include base substrate. (See Fig. 9.8 for related information.)	Automatic processing (per color) 0.20 (each exposure) Manual processing (per color) 0.15 (each exposure)	Matchprint III* Process colors: $0.021 sq. in. PMS colors: $0.022 sq. in. Cromalin* $0.020 (film and toner) * per laminated and fully toned layer, including all materials
Note: Time and cost for remakes not included.		

Figure 9.5 Schedule for estimating proofing production. Schedule data are for example only.

contacting. Proofing done using this schedule goes to a maximum of 24 inches x 30 inches. Larger proofs, covered by Types 3, 4, and 5 in the schedule, utilize large vacuum contact frame and are sometimes completed with platemaking, which is covered in Figure 9.8 later in this chapter.

It is important to note that exposure data and material and processing costs are presented here for example only and are best developed carefully for each individual printing plant. All costs are on a dollar-per-square-inch basis. Schedule times include all operations necessary to set up, position, expose, and process the applicable proofing material. Time and costs for remakes are not included and must be added separately if needed. Example 9.5 utilizes Figure 9.5 data and is presented here to demonstrate how the schedule would be used.

Example 9.5. We have a job that requires estimating the following segments based on our production analysis: 30 velox (halftone) proofs, 8 inches x 10 inches each; 15 continuous-tone prints on Ektamatic SC paper, 9 prints on 8 inch x 10 inch paper and 6 prints on 16 inch x 20 inch paper; and 6 4-color process separations on 10 inch x 12 inch Enco NAPS. The BHR for the veloxes and continuous-tone proofs is $38.70. The contact frame BHR for the NAPS overlay proofs is $49.75. Determine the production time and cost for this job, including material cost.

Solution

Use Figure 9.5.

Step 1. Determine the production time required for the 30 veloxes (Type 1):

$$30 \text{ pcs. x } 0.15 \text{ hr./pc.} = 4.50 \text{ hr.}$$

Step 2. Determine the production time required for the 15 Ektamatic proofs (Type 2):

$$15 \text{ pcs. x } 0.10 \text{ hr./pc.} = 1.50 \text{ hr.}$$

Step 3. Determine the production time required for the process color separation proofs (6 sets with 4 pieces/set is a total of 24 pieces) (Type 4):

$$24 \text{ pcs. x } 0.20 \text{ hr./pc.} = 4.8 \text{ hr.}$$

Step 4. Determine the total production time:

$$4.50 \text{ hr.} + 1.50 \text{ hr.} + 4.8 \text{ hr.} = 10.8 \text{ hr.}$$

Step 5. Determine the total production time cost (not including materials): For the veloxes and Ektamatic proofs:

$$4.50 \text{ hr.} + 1.50 \text{ hr.} = 6 \text{ hr.}$$

$$6 \text{ hr. x } \$38.70/\text{hr.} = \$232.20$$

For the color separations:

$$4.8 \text{ hr. x } \$49.75/\text{hr.} = \$238.80$$

Total production time cost:

$$\$232.20 + \$238.80 = \$471.00$$

Step 6. Determine the total material cost:
For the veloxes:

$$30 \text{ pcs. x } (8 \text{ in. x } 10 \text{ in.})/\text{pc. x } \$0.012/\text{sq. in.} = \$28.80$$

For the Ektamatics:

$$9 \text{ pcs. x } (8 \text{ in. x } 10 \text{ in.})/\text{pc. x } \$0.010/\text{sq. in.} = \$7.20$$

$$6 \text{ pcs. x } (16 \text{ in. x } 20 \text{ in.})/\text{pc. x } \$0.010/\text{sq. in.} = \$19.20$$

For the NAPS:

$$24 \text{ pcs. x } (10 \text{ in. x } 12 \text{ in.})/\text{pc. x } \$0.013/\text{sq. in.} = \$37.44$$

Total material cost:

$$\$28.80 + \$7.20 + \$19.20 + \$37.44 = \$92.64$$

Step 7. Determine the total production cost:

$$\$471.00 + \$92.64 = \$563.64$$

Step 8. Summarize the findings:
Total production time: 10.8 hr.
Total production time cost: $471.00
Total material cost: $92.64
Total production cost: $563.64

9.9   Estimating Color Separation Production Time and Cost

Figure 9.6 provides data for estimating color scanning production using digital and analog-digital scanning equipment. As is noted later, this schedule uses a step-by-step procedure beginning with image review and check, then image mounting, followed by scanner setup and prescan adjustment, scanning time where the separation is actually exposed or digitized, and, finally, automatic film processing. Digital scanning equipment is sometimes used for digital image capture only, without direct film output, in which case the scanned image is electronically stored as a high-resolution file for EPP use. In such instances, there would be no film output at the conclusion of scanning, and automatic

	Digital scanner	Analog-digital scanner
1. Image review and check (each image)	0.10	0.10
2. Image mounting (each image)	0.05	0.05
3. Scanner setup and prescan adjustment (each image)	0.10	0.20
4. Scanning time (per 4/C set) Small format: Medium format: Large format:	0.20 0.30 0.40	0.40
5. Auto processing (per 4/C set)	0.10	0.10

Material costs: (includes all processing costs)	Halftone scanner film (used with contact screen): $0.018 sq. in. Continuous-tone film: $0.015 sq. in. Laser film (Helium Neon): $0.014 sq. in. Laser film (Argon Ion): $0.011 sq. in.

Note: Time and cost for rescans or remakes are not included.

Figure 9.6 Schedule for estimating high-resolution scanning production. Schedule data for example only.

processing (Step 5) would not be included in the estimate. The application of Figure 9.6 data is demonstrated in Example 9.6 that follows.

Schedule data for Figure 9.6 assumes there are high-quality original transparencies or reflection art. Using either production process, times and costs for remakes or rescans is not included. Chart times and costs are presented here for example only. The following formulas are used to calculate digital scanner production time and cost:

digital scanner production time = image review (per image) + image mounting (per image) + scanner setup and prescan adjustment (per image) + scanning time (per scanned set) + automatic processing (per scanned set)

digital scanner production cost = digital scanner production time x digital scanner BHR

material and film cost = number of pieces of film or paper x number
of square inches per piece x film cost per square inch

total digital scanner production cost = digital scanner production
cost + film and material cost

Example 9.6. We have a job that consists of 44 transparencies to be color
separated using our Crosfield Magnascan 645 digital scanner. Based on our
production review, we have the following breakdown by scan group: 6 scans
with 6-up mounted on the scanner copy drum (total of 36 separations), 2 scans
with 3-up (total of 6 separations), and 2 scans with 1-up (total of 2 separations).
Argon Ion laser film will be used in the 20 inch x 24 inch size for all output.
Automatic film processing will be used. Scanning time is at medium format.
Add 10 percent additional time and materials for anticipated rescans. Scanner
BHR is $153.50. Also estimate the cost to proof using Cromalin materials and
our automatic toning machine (ATM). Proofs will be ganged onto 5 22 inch x
26 inch Cromalin proof sheets. Use Figure 9.5 and a contact frame/ATM
combined BHR of $47.90.

Solution

Use Figure 9.6 (color scanning production) and Figure 9.5 (proofing).

Step 1. Determine the scanner production time:
Image review:

$$44 \text{ images x } 0.10 \text{ hr. ea. } = 4.4 \text{ hr.}$$

Image mounting:

$$44 \text{ images x } 0.05 \text{ hr. ea. } = 2.2 \text{ hr.}$$

Scanner setup and prescan adjustment:

$$44 \text{ images x } 0.10 \text{ hr. } = 4.4 \text{ hr.}$$

Scanning time:

$$11 \text{ scan groups x } 0.30 \text{ hr. ea. } = 3.3 \text{ hr.}$$

Automatic processing:

$$11 \text{ scan groups x } 0.10 \text{ hr. ea. } = 1.1 \text{ hr.}$$

Step 2. Determine the total scanner production time:

$$4.4 \text{ hr. } + 2.2 \text{ hr. } + 4.4 \text{ hr. } + 3.3 \text{ hr } + 1.1 \text{ hr. } = 15.4 \text{ hr.}$$

Step 3. Calculate the 10 percent additional production time:

$$15.4 \text{ hr. x } 1.10 = 16.94 \text{ hr.}$$

Step 4. Determine the total scanner time cost:

$$16.94 \text{ hr. x } \$153.50/\text{hr.} = \$2,600.29$$

Step 5. Determine the scanner film cost:

$$10 \text{ pcs. x } (20 \text{ in. x } 24 \text{ in.}) \text{ x } \$0.011/\text{sq. in.} = \$52.80$$

Step 6. Calculate the 10 percent additional materials:

$$\$52.80 \text{ x } 1.10 = \$58.08$$

Step 7. Determine the proofing time (see Figure 9.5, Type 5 Cromalin proofing):

$$4 \text{ colors x } 5 \text{ Cromalin proofs} = 20 \text{ exposures x } 0.15 \text{ hr.} = 3.00 \text{ hr.}$$

Step 8. Calculate the total proof production cost:

$$3.00 \text{ hr. x } \$47.90 = \$143.70$$

Step 9. Determine the Cromalin material cost (see Figure 9.5, Type 5 Cromalin proofing)

$$20 \text{ laminations x } (22 \text{ in. x } 26 \text{ in.}) \text{ x } \$0.020/\text{sq. in.} = \$228.80$$

Step 10. Summarize the findings:
Total production time: 16.94 hr. + 3.0 hr. = 19.94 hr.
Total production time cost: $2,600.29 + $143.70 = $2,743.99
Total material cost: $58.08 + $228.80 = $286.88
Total production cost: $2,743.99 + $286.88 = $3,030.87

9.10 Film Assembly Methods

Film assembly, proofing, and platemaking are vital prepress functions in the lithographic sequence, and they also carry over to digital production. At this time, it is common for digitally produced final film to be assembled manually, then proofed and followed with digital corrections to new final film. When the job is ultimately approved for printing, photomechanical platemaking production is completed from stripped final film. These photomechanical production operations are frequently termed "analog methods" because they parallel digital production operations. Thus, analog stripping replaces digital stripping, just as analog proofing or platemaking replaces its respective parallel digital counterpart.

Film assembly, also commonly termed "stripping" or "table stripping," is a procedure by which images on film are assembled in an ordered fashion to produce the desired graphic results. Stripping precedes proofing and photomechanical platemaking production. Film assembly can be done manually or with the assistance of computerized stripping devices such as the Gerber AutoPrep. Manual film assembly is completed using various types of masking bases and requires accurate measurements and exact alignment of film images. The process is labor intensive and requires considerable skill for many of the operations performed. For jobs that have final film provided, and which will be plated photomechanically, stripping is a process of accurately positioning these film images in relation to one another. Computer-assisted stripping incorporates the use of an electronic device for precise placement of images.

Proofing and platemaking follow film assembly and are controlled, precise manufacturing methods. Proofing is the rendering of the imaged materials into a form that allows for visual review by the customer and printer, and it is an important step for customer approval before platemaking can be completed. Platemaking is the exposure and development of metal image carriers representing the final graphic images the customer desires. These metal plates are used with an offset press to produce multiple copies of the graphic image on paper or some other substrate.

Stripping, proofing, and platemaking are labor-intensive operations that are frequently sources of job errors. Automatic plate and proof processing, improved consistency of platemaking and proofing emulsions to provide greater exposure latitude, and the adoption of fully anodized plate bases and dimensionally stable proofing materials have made the platemaking and proofing area largely a troublefree, expeditious production area.

Film assembly resembles mechanical artwork production to a considerable degree. Both processes deal with exact measurements, precise layout, defined image registration, and a resultant visual product. However, copy preparation is a prephotographic procedure that is normally completed by a pasteup artist, while film assembly deals almost exclusively with line and halftone film images in either positive or negative form. Because the majority of art for conventional prepress is prepared in positive form as reflection copy, the assembly of negative film materials represents the usual practice in most manual stripping departments in the United States. European printers tend to work more with positive film images.

General Table Stripping Techniques

Film images to be stripped originate from digital output devices or photomechanical production or a mix of the two. Initially, the stripper, the individual who assembles these film pieces, visually evaluates the images for quality, density, sizing, and other production requirements. In conjunction with this initial review, the stripper analyzes the artwork, digital proofs, or laser output and reads all pertinent instructions regarding the positioning of the images on the plate (and ultimately the press sheet). He checks to be certain that all film elements required for the job are provided. The stripper also evaluates the job relative to special film requirements, such as spreads, chokes, compositing, special proofing needs, or any other extraordinary consideration.

Once the materials have been verified as accurate and complete, the stripper selects the proper masking base to be used for the job. These base materials are sometimes called "flat materials" or "stripping supports." There are three types of base materials commonly used for table stripping: goldenrod masking base; clear acetate, which is better known as clearbase; and cut-and-peel or peelcoat materials. Goldenrod and peelcoat masking materials are sheets of orange, yellow, or amber; goldenrod is made of either paper or vinyl, while peelcoat materials consist of clear acetate with a gelatin membrane layer of colored material. The goldenrod color allows the light from the light table to be seen but protects covered areas of the offset plate from being exposed during plate-making so that they remain nonimage areas. Most plants stock masking base precut to the sizes of offset plates that fit company presses. Typically, a job is stripped to be printed on a specific press because there are variations between presses relative to image placement. Thus, stripping requires production planning before the process is initiated.

Stripping can be done with the film either emulsion up or emulsion down, which are referenced as e-up stripping and e-down stripping respectively. E-down stripping is commonly done when stripping to a goldenrod support, while e-up stripping is used when stripping to clearbase or peelcoat materials. A typical film product provided to the stripper is e-down film, which means that the film is right reading when the emulsion of the film is down (or away) from the stripper. E-up film is identified as film that has its emulsion up when the image is right reading.

Assume we want to strip a 1-color (1C) job that has one film negative. The following procedures describe the two ways this probably would be done in a typical commercial printing plant.

Stripping a 1-Color Job to Goldenrod Masking Material. Working at a light table with a T-square and triangle or at a line-up table, the stripper, by drawing on the goldenrod sheet with a pencil or a pen, accurately draws position marks for precise placement of the image. It is important that this work be done accurately because little image movement is possible once the job has been plated and goes to press. The film to be stripped is e-down film.

The stripper, while still at the light table, slides the film negative under the goldenrod sheet and positions the negative image relative to the marks drawn in pen or pencil. This is the e-down stripping method. Holding the film securely, two or three small goldenrod areas are cut away where the negative is located and tape is used to secure the negative to the goldenrod sheet. The flat, which is an assemblage of film and masking base, is now turned over on its back (the image is now wrong reading) and the negative is taped securely to the back of the masking base. The final step is to cut the goldenrod masking material from the image areas of the negative to allow white light to pass through during platemaking and proofing.

Stripping a 1-Color Job to Clearbase Masking Material. Working at a light table with a T-square and a triangle or at a line-up table, the stripper, by drawing on the clearbase sheet with an acetate pen, accurately draws position marks for precise placement of the image. Again, it is important that this work be done accurately because little image movement is possible once the job has been plated and goes to press. The film to be stripped is e-down film.

The stripper, still working at the light table, turns the clearbase upside down and positions the film negative e-up with the image wrong reading over the marks made in pen. Taping of the film image to the clearbase material (the negative is still e-up) is now completed. Once the film negative has been securely taped to the clearbase support, the clearbase is flipped over so that the film negative is e-down and closest to the light table. At this point, the stripper secures a sheet of goldenrod masking material that is the same size as the clearbase and positions it over the entire clearbase sheet containing the e-down, stripped negative. Now, at a light table with the film image right reading, the stripper cuts away the goldenrod where the right-reading film negative appears to allow white light to pass through during platemaking and proofing. When the plates and proofs are made, the clearbase flat and goldenrod are superimposed, blocking light in all areas but those where the windows appear in the goldenrod mask.

Pin Registration Procedures

Many jobs require more than one color, as in the preceding example. To effectively and economically strip multicolor work using conventional methods, pin registration is used.

Pin registration is a process by which masking base materials are punched or positioned before stripping so that the relationship between the flats and the film images positioned on the flats remain fixed. The pins are usually made of metal (plastic is also used) and come in two styles: 1/4-inch round hole and slotted pins (pins with rectangular slot that are approximately 1/4-inch x 3/8-inch and have two parallel flat sides).

There are two common ways pin registration is accomplished during image assembly: stripping tabs and commercial pin registration punches with matching pin bars. A stripping tab is a nylon or acetate strip approximately 1 inch x 3 inches with a round hole or slot hole punched in one end. To use stripping tabs, masking sheets that are to be registered, which is a process that is normally done before stripping, are carefully aligned on the light table. Two tabs are then taped along one side of the masking sheet, roughly equidistant from the center and at least one-half the distance to the corner of the masking material. The tabs hang out from the edge of the sheet. If a 3-color job required three flats, there would be three masking sheets prepared in this manner, and each would be stripped to hold the appropriate images for the color to be represented. Stripping would be done on the table using pins and exposures to plates, and proofs would also use pins suitable for insertion into the platemaking or proofing vacuum frame.

Commercial pin registration systems are available for purchase and use in table stripping, and they have two essential parts: a punching unit and associated pin bars used on the light table and in the vacuum frame for platemaking and proofing. The punching unit, which is usually a tabletop device, allows one side of a sheet of unpunched masking base to be inserted into it (about 2 inches) via manual depression of a bar or a handle that punches a fixed group of round and slot holes along the sheet's edge. Because the same punch is used over and over, the system becomes standardized throughout the stripping area and ensures consistency from job to job and day to day. Pin bars, which are normally made of metal for heavy-duty, continuous use, exactly match the pin positions in the punching unit. These bars are placed both on the light table and in the various vacuum frames for platemaking and proofing.

Commercial pin registration systems, because of their consistency, reliability, speed of use, and accuracy, are very popular today. Most of the systems are not considered expensive compared to the hours required to restrip a poorly registered job. Manufacturers of commercial pin registration equipment provide standard pin placement arrangements instead of designing different pin positions for each printer. Tailor-made systems are also available. The holes are a combination of round hole and slot types along the masking sheet edge to allow for the slight dimensional changes that inevitably occur in masking materials.

Multicolor Stripping Procedures (Table Stripping Process Color)

Although single-color stripping is fairly easy to understand and do, the majority of work done in the commercial printing industry is multicolor, or many colors printed in precise registration to each other. Multicolor production is divided into two categories: flat color work and process color work. Flat color production is simply different pigment colors of ink (commonly PMS colors are used) prepared and printed in relation to one another. Process color work involves printing four colors—cyan, magenta, yellow, and black (CMYK)—in precise registration to each other to reproduce a full-color photograph.

Multicolor work, if it is completed using conventional table stripping and mechanical art, begins with mechanical artwork that has been preseparated into color layers, called overlays. Each overlay represents a different ink color of the final image. Photographic imaging using a process camera or scanner is then completed to translate each overlay into negative film form, and the film negatives are sent to the stripping department for placement on masking sheets so that proofing and platemaking can be completed. Assume, for example, that we want to strip a 4-color (4/C) process poster that measures 16 inches x 20 inches and has black type. The film negative containing type would be imaged from reflection mechanical art and photographed to one negative, called a black type printer, while the four color separation film negatives (CMYK film) would be produced from a color scanner.

Working on the light table and using a commercial pin registration system, the stripper would do the following to strip the job:

1. Check the line negative and four separations film negatives for quality. This is a visual check to be certain the materials are properly sized and suitable for stripping.
2. Obtain four sheets of clearbase and two sheets of goldenrod masking material and punch each using the commercial pin punch.
3. Use the black type mechanical art, which is sometimes called a keyline, and one of the goldenrod sheets on pins at the light table to accurately mark the location of the black type printer in pencil or pen. The stripper also marks this masking sheet with required production measurements, such as the press center line, press sheet gripper, and plate gripper. This goldenrod sheet is now a key (or master) flat to which all other images will ultimately register.
4. After all measurements and positioning marks have been carefully determined, the black type negative is stripped to the goldenrod masking base. This is done using e-down stripping by sliding the negative image under the goldenrod base (which is on pins), lining it up to the hand-drawn image position marks on the goldenrod, then taping the negative to the goldenrod sheet securely. Once this is done, a window is opened in the goldenrod material so that everything on the masking sheet but the type to print is covered with goldenrod. This process is called "laying and cutting" because the negative has been laid in (or positioned) and followed with the opening (or cutting) away of goldenrod.
5. With the black type negative on pins and flipped over to be e-up (or wrong reading), the stripper now takes a clearbase masking sheet and positions it over the stripped material. The cyan film negative is now turned wrong reading (e-up) and positioned carefully to marks on the black keyline, thus registering the separated image to the black type. When it is located exactly, the cyan printer is taped to the clearbase material and serves as a key to which all of the remaining process color separations are stripped. Because this flat was registered to the black keyline (master) flat, it is typically considered complementary to the black flat.
6. The black type flat is removed from the pins and placed aside, and the stripped cyan printer is repositioned on the pins, wrong reading. Over this the second sheet of clearbase is positioned on the pins, and the magenta separation is accurately registered and taped to the cyan image using e-up

stripping methods. This requires careful alignment using a magnifying device. It is important to note that this alignment process can be slow and tedious work. Most separations are imaged with register marks so that the stripper can "lay in" the separations fairly quickly, which speeds production. The magenta image stripped to clearbase is a complementary flat.

7. The process of laying in the yellow and black separations is repeated, each to a different sheet of clearbase material. Each flat is complementary to the black type master. All separation stripping described thus far is done to the cyan flat as the master, stripping e-up. At this point, the black type master flat on goldenrod is stripped and all four color separations have been laid in to four clearbase supports.

8. The stripper now puts the black type flat on pins, e-down (right reading), and positions a new goldenrod sheet over it on pins. Using the keyline black type flat, the stripper cuts open a window representative of the precise area to be covered by the color image, thus creating the edge of the image area. When this is done, this goldenrod sheet has one area—or window—cut in it, which is called a "common window" or "CW flat." It will be used with each clearbase separation during proofing and platemaking to provide a precise border and thus define the process color image size. It is common to use peelcoat materials for the common window flat because they are a tougher, more stable product than goldenrod paper.

9. In order to control quality on press, many printing companies strip additional flats that include color bars and marks for positioning, cutting, and folding. Color bars, which are stripped to each clearbase separation with an accompanying window in the CW flat, allow for accurate ink density control during printing. The "marks flat," which can be incorporated into the black type flat (with an appropriate mask to block the type images) or stripped as a separate flat to double-expose to all four plates with other images, has become fairly common for faster makeready on press and when follow-up bindery operations are needed.

10. The final group of flats, called a flat file, represents the complete collection of images for this poster job. The following describes each:
    *   black (K) type (keyline) flat on goldenrod, which is the master flat
    *   cyan (C) separation flat on clearbase, which is a complementary flat with cyan color bars along its tail edge
    *   magenta (M) separation flat on clearbase, which is a complementary flat with magenta color bars along its tail edge
    *   yellow (Y) separation flat on clearbase, which is a complementary flat with yellow color bars along its tail edge
    *   black (K) separation flat on clearbase, which is a complementary flat with black color bars along its tail edge
    *   CW flat on goldenrod, which is a complementary flat
    *   marks flat, if desired

The process described previously represents the most common table stripping procedure for color separation in the printing industry. It should be noted that there are other methods that can be employed, such as stripping the separations to blueline (Dylux) materials.

Complex Color Film Assembly Procedures

It is important to note that many printing orders consist of five, six, or more colors. Although the 4-color process requires the printing of CMYK (as described), customers sometimes wish to varnish (add gloss) or add flat colors (PMS colors) to their conventional process color images. To allow such printing to be done in one pass, printers purchase 6-, 7-, and 8-color presses, which are the most productive. Stripping a 6-color job thus involves the film assembly of the 4-color process as just described and the addition of varnishing flats and PMS flats.

Stripping complex color jobs or multicolor work can be done using conventional photomechanical production methods where jobs are "built" on the table, or completed from final (or furnished) film generated by electronic prepress filmsetting devices. While both production methods are used, there has been a major and pronounced movement to stripping digitally-generated final film since electronic production is ideally suited to meet the demands of complex multicolor imaging. Thus, table stripping remains an integral part of printing production even as digital output has gained in popularity, although the stripping operations performed using final film are much less complex and substantially reduced in labor-intensiveness. As computer-to-plate (CTP) digital output devices and systems become technically viable, it is clear that stripping will be less important in the production cycle.

The following describes important materials and techniques commonly used for table stripping, which also have some application to electronic imaging production.

Screen Tints. Screen tints provide for even toning of an area that would otherwise print as a solid. Sometimes called "plate screens," these screen tints are pieces of film that contain overall dot patterns. Screen tints are purchased by their numbers of lines and percentages of printable dot. For example, "200-30" indicates that the screen tint is a 200-line screen with a 30 percent printable dot. The commercially available tints usually range in 10 percent increments from 10 percent to 90 percent and in values from 85 lines to 300 lines, which are increment standards in the industry. Digital production allows tinting to be easily completed on the desktop and incorporated into the final film product.

The general procedure to tint an image in a stripped flat is as follows. First, identify the negative or the area of the negative to be tinted. Then turn the flat over so that the image is e-up (wrong reading). The tint screen is then cut slightly larger that the image area and is taped e-up over it so that the emulsion is up for both the image and the tint. When the flat is turned over, the emulsion of the screen tint will directly contact the plate or proof, as will the rest of the image. This technique minimizes dot gain, or the spread of the image, which can affect the printed result.

Flat color, as previously discussed, is a special pigment mix or black. Thus, adding a screen tint to an image printing in black or a PMS color simply tones that color down to a lesser value. However, process colors can combine to produce a fairly accurate spectrum or rainbow of all colors in reproducing color separations—screen tints and process colors can produce color matches of hundreds of colors. These are known as "fake colors." The advantage of fake color is that when magenta, cyan, yellow, and black are printed on the press sheet, literally hundreds of other colors can be manufactured using screen tints to print using the same four process colors.

For example, combining a 30 percent cyan tint and a 40 percent magenta tint in one image produces a purple color that is somewhat toned down from solid purple because tints are used and the whiteness of the stock blends into the colors. Color selecting, or tint matching, is commonly done from standard tint mixing charts that are either developed by printing firms for internal use or by various sources such as ink suppliers. One popular color tool is Pantone's Process Color Simulator, which allows the printer to reproduce a selected PMS color using fake color or to reproduce a fake color using PMS color.

It is important to note that fake color stripping requires that tints be laid into flats so that they do not cause a moiré pattern, which is an undesirable optical effect caused by two or more screen tints angled such that they interfere with each other. Different devices, such as GATF's Screen Angle Guide, have been developed to aid the stripper in angling such tints. Some strippers, to save time, simply lay in matching tints for fake color work by eye, which involves rotating the tints until no undesirable pattern is visually evident.

Fake color techniques are easily achieved with various software programs when producing jobs on the desktop. This involves first selecting the proper screen percentages, then rotating the screens to minimize the moiré pattern.

Trapping Techniques. A trap is a slight overlap between two related graphic images. Traps are completed so that images can fit together precisely and in an unobtrusive manner. A trap is completed by slightly reducing or enlarging one of the two images, which allows one image to overprint or underprint the second image. Traps are common between screen tint areas and are frequently found with color imaging. When traps are required in a job, they can either be built into the artwork (either with mechanical art or electronic art), or they can be produced during the stripping of the job using spread and choke techniques.

When artwork is produced electronically, trapping production may be included as part of the software used to generate or manipulate the image (commonly an automatic trapping procedure) or as separate program designed exclusively for trapping. Chapter 8 covers electronic trapping in more detail.

Producing Spreads and Chokes. The following discussion relates to the production of spreads and chokes using photomechanical methods and light diffusion techniques. A spread, which is also commonly termed a "fatty," begins with an imaged film negative original that can be contacted to either duplicating or contacting film. Clear acetate spacers are used between the imaged film negative and the raw (unimaged) film to cause the image to become slightly larger. Greater amounts of spread increase as the quantity of spacers increases. If contact film is used, the resultant spread film image is positive, and if duplicating film is used, the resultant image is a fatty negative. Diffusion sheets that resemble frosted acetate are used to scatter light during the exposure process.

A choke, also known as a "shrink" or "squeeze," requires an imaged film positive original that can be contacted to either duplicating or contacting film. Again, clear acetate spacers are used between the imaged positive (on top) and the raw film, which cause the choked image to be reduced in size. The greater the number of spacers, the greater the resultant image shrinks. Diffusion sheets are used to scatter light during the exposure process. If contact film is used, the resultant choked image is a squeezed negative, and if duplicating film is used, the resultant choked image is positive.

The primary problem with spreads and chokes done using acetate spacers and diffusion sheets, as previously described, is that fine type, sharp image edges, corners, and other fine-image details tend to quickly close up or plug. Increasing the amount of spacers used, which in turn increases the amount of image trap, worsens this plugging problem.

To resolve this problem with the diffusion method, some companies purchase and use orbital equipment to produce the image fit. This orbital equipment provides for greater clarity of image edges and adjacent images, which makes traps clean and sharp. Orbital technology does away with spacers and diffusion sheets.

Basically the system works as follows: A negative (for a spread) or a positive (for a choke) is mounted on a stable, clear-plastic platform, and a piece of raw (unimaged) contact or duplicating film is secured to an orbital bed directly below the imaged negative or positive. Rotation of the orbital plate during exposure provides even imaging to the raw film. Greater rotation yields a fatter spread or a thinner choke. Very fine image detail is maintained by precisely controlling the rotation. This allows for traps to be generated precisely, accurately, and quickly, instead of by a more "hit-or-miss" approach. The orbit is precise and adjustable to control the trap thickness accurately. The most popular orbital machine is the Byers MicroModifier. As with conventional spread and choke procedures, daylight contacting or duplicating film and rapid-access processing are most typically used.

Figure 9.4 provides estimating data for spreads and chokes using conventional spacers and diffusion exposure processes.

Film Compositing Procedures. Film compositing procedures may be completed either in the photographic or image assembly departments during production of the complex color job. It is a process by which numerous images that would print in the same ink color (on the same offset plate) are photomechanically combined onto one piece of film. The result are generally known as "composite film" or "final composites."

Producing composite film materials is done for the following reasons:

1. To reduce or minimize plate and proof exposures by collecting all of the same images that go on one plate onto film. This saves production time because film exposures take significantly less time than individual exposures of images to plates. This also has a side benefit in that a plate remake for a job "on press" is substantially less using composed film.
2. To gather images that are most easily or best produced in film form, which makes follow-up stripping production easier.
3. As a check for image quality, image fit, or image combinations.

Photocomposing negative film materials to duplicating film, which maintains negative image polarity, is the most common composition process. However, producing composite negatives can also be done from film positives using contact film. Raw materials needed to composite images include contact or duplicating daylight film, rapid-access silver halide paper, or Dylux. Pin registration procedures should be common to both the imaged film materials and the raw film or paper that is receiving the compositing exposures.

Consider the following example: We have a 4/C poster to strip. The black printer contains four different black separations and three black lines of type, each on a separate piece of film. We want to produce a composite black printer containing all of these images on one piece of negative film for one exposure to a lithographic plate.

To do this, we would begin with a sheet of daylight duplicating film. Rapid-access processing will be used. E-e contacting will also be used to minimize dot spread, which means that all compositing exposures will be made to an intermediate piece of raw dupe film that will be processed and then contacted e-e to a second sheet of raw dupe film to produce a final, strippable duplicate negative. (Careful planning is usually required to ensure that the final working film composites used for stripping have emulsions on the desired sides.) The following steps would be taken to do this:

1. Begin by punching two pieces of raw film with the pin registration punch used for registration of the negatives to be composited.

2. Place one piece of raw film e-up (light side up) in the vacuum frame and place the first black separation in direct emulsion contact with the raw film. Close the frame, engage the vacuum, and allow suitable drawdown time to complete the exposure.

3. Remove the first separation, place the second separation over the raw film, and complete the exposure for the second image.

4. Remove the second separation, place the third separation over the raw images, and complete the exposure for the third image.

5. Remove the third separation, place the fourth separation over the raw film, and complete the exposure for the fourth image.

6. Remove the fourth separation, place the first Type 1 image over the raw film, and complete the exposure.

7. Remove the first Type 1 image, place the second Type 1 image over the raw film, and complete the exposure.

8. Remove the second Type 1 image, place the third Type 1 image over the raw film, and complete the exposure.

9. At this point the film sheet has received seven exposures, each containing a different negative image. Processing of this fully exposed (raw film), intermediate negative is now completed.

10. When processing is done, the intermediate negative, which contains four separations and three lines of black type, is contacted e-e to the second sheet of raw duplicating film using the standard pin registration system, vacuum frame, and exposure.

Once processed, the result is a duplicate film negative ready for stripping. Figure 9.4 provides estimating data for film compositing production.

Step-and-Repeat Techniques. Step-and-repeat techniques allow for maximizing the same image on an offset plate many times. Thus, one film negative or a group of negatives can be exposed to a plate numerous times. Each exposure increases the number of images on the plate and thereby reduces the number of press sheets required during printing. Although step-and-repeat techniques reduce photographic and image assembly production times, they can increase plate-making exposure times extensively.

The step-and-repeat sequence can be executed in a number of different ways. There are manual techniques that utilize wedges and butterflies but that are not particularly accurate with large plates and many exposures. The use of pin registration for step-and-repeat is popular in most printing plants, and, as mentioned earlier, many different individual pin registration systems are available. Accuracy is extremely good when using pin registration for step and repeat.

The pin registration step-and-repeat technique begins with a row or column of images that are to be repeated. For example, four of the same image are received by the stripper from the photographic area. She then assembles the images in a row across the top of the masking sheet, four across. Then she prepares a pin registration system along one or both sides of this flat. During plate exposure, this row of images is exposed along the top of the plate, which provides four images across. Then that row is moved down the distance of the pins, and a second exposure is given for the next row. (Extra masking paper is used to cover adjacent plate areas.) This sequence is repeated until the four images have been moved the length of the printing plate. If four exposures were made of the row of four images, the plate would print 16-up with all images positioned in precise and exact relation to one another.

Large-volume printing plants have generally investigated, if not purchased, modern step-and-repeat machines. Although equipment configurations and models vary, as does the cost, many models provide for vertical mounting of the plate on the plate bed. The film negative, which is carefully imaged and prepared for this technique, is placed in a film carrier, behind which a UV light source is provided. Carefully machined gear tracks along all four sides of the perimeter of the unit then allow the film carrier to be positioned exactly where desired on the printing plate, normally within 0.001 inch.

Although step-and-repeat machines represent the ultimate in equipment cost and although multiple exposures are required for each plate, the cost savings in press time that results because images are maximized on every printing plate can be significant. In addition, because only a limited number of film images are necessary and very little image assembly is required, time and cost savings can be high in camera work and image assembly operations. For large presses and high-volume printing operations, the purchase and use of step-and-repeat equipment can be readily justified.

Opti-copy represents another way to step-and-repeat images. As discussed earlier in this chapter, Opti-copy is an accurate photographic projection system used to project one or more images directly to film or an offset plate. Because Opti-copy units are fairly expensive, and because other, more conventional step-and-repeat units are already installed and operational, their use in the printing industry is limited to companies that have significant production capacity for Opti-copy work.

Figure 9.4 provides estimating data for step-and-repeat production.

Manual Peelcoat and Photographic Etch-and-Peel Materials. Peelcoat materials, also termed mechanical masking films, are masking products that are used extensively for both table stripping and mechanical art production. Peelcoat material is a thin, transparent, lacquer-based membrane coated on an acetate carrier. To use this material, the artist or stripper places it lacquer side up over the image and gently and carefully cuts and peels the desired areas away, which lets white light from the light table show through. These white areas represent the image areas on the plate or proof. Popularly known as "Rubylith" or "Amberlith," peelcoats are used to produce knockouts whereby the background area of a photograph or other image is dropped out or masked away. They are also used in place of conventional goldenrod masking base when producing CW flats for process color stripping. Peelcoat materials can be punched or have tabs attached if used with pin registration.

Photographic peelcoat material is also a popular product for certain types of manual stripping. Commonly known as etch-and-peel products, their application is valuable when traps meet at extremely fine points or when stripping very fine line work that requires knockouts or image masking of any type. Essentially photographic peelcoat materials are exposed to the film image, which may be a choke or a spread providing the necessary trap, using an intense UV light source. Immersion in a special developing bath for approximately three minutes follows, and then the image is carefully washed in a water bath. Once the peelcoat material is fully dry, it is workable for peeling.

Film Correction Techniques. Opaquing of line negatives is perhaps the most common film correction technique. This technique involves the application of a clay material over pin holes and other film areas that are transparent but should be opaque. Although some strippers use small artist's brushes and jars of opaque material, other strippers prefer to use opaquing pens that are similar to felt-tip markers. It is also possible to image the film with opaque material, especially when working with film positives. However, actual image generation by the stripper is considered an awkward procedure because final artwork is best prepared by artists during the copy preparation stage. Any film area that lacks density—that is, does not have a suitable blackness—requires opaquing prior to the platemaking operation. Opaquing line images is done frequently, but opaquing halftones is not a usual practice because it is very difficult to correct individual dots.

The cutting of line and tonal film images into other pieces of film is a reasonably simple technique. Basically, the procedure involves cutting out and removing a film image that is not desired and simultaneously inserting the correction or halftone. Lith tape, which is red and does not allow the plate to be exposed along the cut line, is then used to secure the cut-in into the fitted area.

Film scribing is another common correction technique, especially with line work. Basically, the stripper is able to create a line image, or a single line, through the removal of the film emulsion. Scribing is the normal correction process when fine lines have filed in from poor copy preparation or photographic development problems. The technique is usually completed using special scribing tools that are available to the stripper.

9.11 Estimating Film Assembly Time and Cost

Accurately estimating film assembly is dependent on the completeness of the film materials which arrive at the stripping area, linked to the overall complexity of the job. Generally the more flats a job requires, the more pieces of film that the stripper must handle to strip the flats, and the more pieces of film which require individual production work, the more difficult it is to estimate stripping accurately.

For jobs that must be completed using traditional film assembly operations where jobs are "built" on the table during stripping, estimating can be difficult for the following reasons:

1. Stripping techniques and procedures vary from one employee to another. There are many ways that a given job might be stripped, even with image assembly employees working next to each other in the same company.
2. Many small operations are required to complete table stripping, particularly when completing complex color work. Some jobs may require spreads and chokes, others knockouts or composites, still others special effects such as drop shadow boxes. Also, how these jobs are produced can vary, because more than one procedure can yield the same result.
3. Because table stripping is largely a manual skill, establishing accurate production standards is difficult.
4. Many estimators do not know how even a simple job is stripped because they have never worked in the film assembly area before. It is difficult to accurately estimate any area of printing production with which one is unfamiliar.
5. Estimating many jobs is done without looking at the artwork, which requires the estimator to take a "best guess." The image assembly area is where most of the repair and correction procedures occur for improperly prepared art.
6. Jobs moving through film assembly are subject to a significant level of AAs, perhaps more than any other production area in printing manufacturing. Some jobs may be stripped and proofed, then changed to meet shifting customer demands and restripped and reproofed, then changed again to meet customer needs, restripped, and reproofed a third time. Some customers require a "proof to satisfaction" condition when the job is begun, which requires the printer to produce as many proofs—with changes—as it takes to secure customer approval.

When the stripper is provided with final film which is fully and accurately imaged using digital filmsetting equipment, stripping is straightforward and estimating is simplified since final film provides a complete image. However, the size of the final film product, which is dictated by the size of the filmsetter, is important. For example, when a small-output filmsetter is used to generate final film, pages may be output one at a time or perhaps two-up, so a job which consists of many pages will consist of many pieces of final film to be stripped. Such a job will require the stripper to manually impose and then strip the job page by page, so table stripping time (and cost) will be high. One production alternative—which would save substantial table stripping time—would be to electronically impose the job on a digital platform and then filmset it on a large-output filmsetter in fully imposed 16-page forms, ready for platemaking. With this alternative there are minimum stripping costs, but higher output costs because the final film has been generated in the larger size.

Figure 9.7 is provided for estimating production stripping. It has been divided into three sections: (1) time for flat preparation, (2) time for laying and cutting, and (3) time for additional or special operations performed during the table stripping process. Each production time segment should be determined and then the times should be added, with adjustments applied as appropriate. The BHRs are applied as determined, based on the estimated hours of production and the addition of material costs that apply.

It is essential that a flat configuration production plan be developed prior to applying the schedule data in Figure 9.7. Normally this plan, which is completed by the estimator, breaks the job into the required component parts as it will likely be stripped during production. Such a flat configuration plan should succinctly detail the number of master and complementary flats to be stripped, the number of pieces of film to be laid in and the windows to be cut, and any special or additional operations that will be required. The more knowledge the estimator has about table stripping, the more quickly and accurately the flat configuration plan can be developed.

Once the flat configuration plan is completed, schedule data (see Figure 9.7) are applied to determine production times. The following provides information related to applying that data in a step-by-step format:

Step 1

Flat preparation time includes time for the employee to read all work order instructions, review film materials, plan the stripping procedure, organize the work, punch flats for pin registration, and lay out the flats, which includes making image position marks. The key/master flat time represents the production time needed for each master flat to be stripped. As defined previously, master flat is one to which all other flats in the flat file register. Complementary flats are all flats that register to a given master flat. They have reduced production times because the master flat covers most of the job complexity.

Certain jobs require that a flat be stripped detail the folding, cutting, and other marks that will be needed for the press and bindery manufacturing operations, or both, of the job. The "Marks flat" column at the top of Figure 9.7 provides times for the addition of such a flat. Times cover all flat preparation and stripping production. The typical printing order in production requires one marks flat per job.

Step 2

Laying and cutting time in hours per piece is referenced by the size of the film and the type of stripping that is required. The latter is categorized as simple,

Flat preparation, marks flat production, and flat material cost

Approx press size in inches (sq. in.)	Flat preparation time (hrs. per flat)		Marks flat (hrs. each)	Flat material cost*	
	Key/master flat	Complementary flat (each add'l. per same flat set)		Vinyl goldenrod and clearbase	Peelcoat
10 x 15 (150)	0.10	0.04	0.06	$0.30	$0.45
14 x 20 (280)	0.15	0.05	0.08	$0.55	$0.85
17 x 22 (374)	0.18	0.08	0.10	$0.75	$1.15
19 x 25 (475)	0.20	0.10	0.12	$0.95	$1.45
23 x 29 (667)	0.25	0.12	0.14	$1.35	$2.00
24 x 36 (864)	0.30	0.14	0.18	$1.75	$2.60
25 x 38 (950)	0.35	0.16	0.20	$1.90	$2.85
38 x 50 (1900)	0.40	0.20	0.24	$3.80	$5.70
44 x 60 (2640)	0.45	0.22	0.28	$5.30	$7.90
52 x 77 (4004)	0.50	0.25	0.32	$8.00	$12.00

*Cost of goldenrod paper and marks flat stripping materials recovered through the BHR.

Laying and cutting time (in hours per piece stripped)

Film size for stripping in sq.inches (typical film size)	Simple			Average			Difficult		
	Lay Only	Cut Only	Lay & Cut	Lay Only	Cut Only	Lay & Cut	Lay Only	Cut Only	Lay & Cut
Up to 35 sq . in. (5x7 or less)	0.05	0.02	0.07	0.07	0.03	0.10	0.08	0.04	0.12
36 to 80 sq. in. (8x10)	0.07	0.02	0.09	0.10	0.03	0.13	0.10	0.04	0.14
81 to 120 sq. in. (10x12)	0.08	0.03	0.11	0.13	0.04	0.17	0.13	0.05	0.18
121 to 200 sq. in (11x17)	0.10	0.03	0.13	0.15	0.04	0.19	0.17.	0.05	0.22
201 to 300 sq. in. (15x20)	0.11	0.04	0.15	0.18	0.05	0.23	0.21	0.06	0.27
301 to 400 sq. in (17x22)	0.13	0.04	0.17	0.22	0.05	0.27	0.24	0.06	0.30
Over 400 sq. in. (20x24)	0.16	0.04	0.20	0.25	0.05	0.30	0.29	0.06	0.35

Additions

Chokes & spreads	Use Figure 9.4 to estimate.
Composites	Use Figure 9.4 to estimate.
Dupes & contacts	Use Figure 9.4 to estimate.
Tints	0.03 hr. per each black-and-white tint laid (any size)
	0.05 hr. per each matched process color tint laid (any size)
Color bars	0.08 hr. per color bar stripped to clearbase (incl. cutting goldenrod window)
Knockouts	0.15 hr. (simple cut), 0.20 (average cut), 0.30 (difficult cut)
Cut-ins	0.10 hr. per each cut-in completed (includes taping)
Scribing	0.15 hr. per each 100 linear in. of scribed line on film emulsion

Note: Time and cost for restripping or reworking jobs are not included.

Figure 9.7 Film assembly production schedule. Schedule data are for example only.

average, or difficult. Each of these three categories is divided into three divisions: lay only, cut only, and lay and cut. The following describes the application of this part of the schedule:

Goldenrod Stripping. Goldenrod stripping (e-down technique) is popular among many printers for quickly assembling line or halftone negatives. This process requires first that the film image be laid in and taped to the goldenrod masking support, and then that a window be cut in that same goldenrod support for that negative. These steps are typically completed by the stripper as sequential production operations and utilize the "Lay & Cut" portion of the schedule in Figure 9.7 because both the laying in of the film image and the cutting the window are done as sequential production operations.

Clearbase Stripping. Clearbase stripping (e-up technique) is done when assembling color separations, book impositions, and numerous other products. It requires that the separations first be carefully laid in (registered to another separation) and taped to the clearbase support. They are then followed up by "cutting only" of CWs in a separate sheet of peelcoat or goldenrod masking material. Table stripping of a typical 4-color separation requires careful registration or "laying only" of four printers, with "cutting only" of one window per color separation. When stripping color separations to clearbase, the stripper completes all "laying-in" operations for all film separations of all printers e-up before cutting the CW flat using goldenrod or peelcoat materials.

Some strippers, instead of stripping line or halftone negatives directly to goldenrod as described in the previous Goldenrod Stripping section, prefer to strip these film materials to clearbase and cut windows in separate peelcoat or goldenrod base. If this were the common production practice in a company, the "Lay only" and "Cut only" data in Figure 9.7 would be used instead of the "Lay & Cut" data for stripping line and halftone work, as well as for color separation production. Stripping to clearbase with an accompanying goldenrod or peelcoat knockout mask is frequently faster but also increases the material cost because both clearbase and goldenrod masking materials are required.

Step 3

The additions segment of the schedule in Figure 9.7 is to add for any special operations or other production activities completed on the job. These may include scribing, cut-ins of film materials for correction purposes, the addition of color tints, the addition of color bars to color separation clearbase flats, and knockout production using Rubylith or Amberlith peelcoat materials. If traps are required using conventional choke and spread contacting procedures, the film contacting and duplication covered in Figure 9.4 would be used.

The following formulas summarize how manual image assembly production time and cost are estimated using Figure 9.7:

total table stripping production time = flat preparation time (key flats + master flats + marks flats) + laying and cutting time (see following formulas) + additions (as applicable)

laying and cutting time for goldenrod stripping = number of pieces of film to be laid in and cut x production time per piece

laying and cutting time for clearbase stripping = number of separations film images to be laid in x production time per piece + number of windows to be cut (in CW flat) x the production time per window

total table stripping production cost = total table stripping production time x table stripping BHR + material cost for stripping base

The cost of base materials for stripping can be recovered two ways: through the company BHR cost recovery process or as a stand-alone material cost. The costs for vinyl mask, clearbase, and peelcoat products—the most expensive stripping base materials-are provided in Figure 9.7 and should be added when stripping methods necessitate the extensive use of these materials. When the base material is goldenrod paper, which is a small cost compared to these other flat base products, it can be recovered as part of the BHR process as a department supply (see Line 35 of any BHR sheet in Chapter 3 where costs for miscellaneous department supplies are covered). In the examples that follow, if goldenrod materials are not mentioned as a base product, it is assumed that the material is goldenrod paper.

Example 9.7. We want to estimate the table stripping production time and cost to produce a 7 1/4 inch x 8 1/2 inch announcement, to run 6-up and print black and red, two sides (2/2) on a Heidelberg MOZP (maximum press size sheet 19 inches x 25 1/4 inches). The BHR for the table stripper who will do this job is $57.90. Use 19 inch x 25 inch flat data for stripping.

Film supplied: 6 duplicate line negatives each of 4 images (12 black type and 12 red line drawings) so that stripping can be completed 6-up. There will also be 1 black and red duotone per finished image, or a total of 12 duotones (12 black and 12 red film images). The duotones will strip to clearbase 6-up, with separate CWs on peelcoat; each plate will double-burn the duotone images.

Stripping details: Stoesser pin registration system. Vinyl goldenrod for all line work, clearbase and peelcoat for duotones. Windows 8 inches x 10 inches for line work and 5 inches x 7 inches for duotones, all at simple level. Use 19 inch x 25 inch flat data. There will be 12 black-and-white tints for the black type flats (40 percent) and 12 20-percent tints for the red line flats. The first black flat will be a master flat; all others will register to that flat as complements. Add for one marks flat for registration and as a trim-out guide to burn to each black plate.

Flat Configuration Plan

Side 1 (2 plates: 1 Black 6-Up Plate and 1 Red 6-Up Plate)

Flat 1   Black type (master) with 6 pcs. film, vinyl goldenrod

Flat 2   Black duotone (complement) with 6 pcs. film, clearbase

Flat 3   Red line work (complement) with 6 pcs. film, vinyl goldenrod

Flat 4   Red duotone (complement) with 6 pcs. film, clearbase

Flat 5   Common-window (complement) for duotones, cut 6 windows, peelcoat

Side 2 (2 Plates: 1 Black 6-Up Plate and 1 Red 6-Up Plate)

Flat 6   Black type (complement) with 6 pcs. film, vinyl goldenrod

Flat 7   Black duotone (complement) with 6 pcs. film, clearbase

Flat 8   Red line work (complement) with 6 pcs. film, vinyl goldenrod

Flat 9   Red duotone (complement) with 6 pcs. film, clearbase

Flat 10 CW (complement) for duotones, cut 6 windows, peelcoat

Flat 11 Marks flat (complement) to burn with one black plate, vinyl goldenrod

Total number of pieces of stripping base material needed: 5 pcs. vinyl goldenrod, 4 pcs. clearbase, 2 pcs. peelcoat

Solution

Use Figure 9.7.

Step 1. Determine the flat preparation and marks flat production time:

1 master flat (19 inches x 25 inches) x 0.20 hr. ea. = 0.20 hr.

9 complements (19 inches x 25 inches) x 0.10 hr. ea. = 0.90 hr.

1 marks flat (19 inches x 25 inches) x 0.12 hr. ea. = 0.12 hr.

Total preparation/startup production time:

0.20 hr. + 0.90 hr. + 0.12 hr. = 1.22 hr.

Step 2. Determine the laying and cutting time:

24 pcs. (8 inches x 10 inches, lay & cut to goldenrod, simple) x 0.09 hr. ea. = 2.16 hr.

24 pcs. (5 inches x 7 inches, lay to clearbase, simple) x 0.05 hr. ea. = 1.20 hr.

12 windows (5 inches x 7 inches, cut to peelcoat, simple) x 0.02 hr. ca. = 0.24 hr.

Total laying and cutting time:

2.16 hr. + 1.20 hr. + 0.24 hr. = 3.60 hr.

Step 3. Determine the additional time:

$$24 \text{ tints (black-and-white) x } 0.03 \text{ hr. ea.} = 0.72 \text{ hr.}$$

Step 4. Determine the total image assembly time:

$$1.22 \text{ hr.} + 3.60 \text{ hr.} + 0.72 \text{ hr.} = 5.54 \text{ hr.}$$

Step 5. Determine the total image assembly production cost:

$$5.54 \text{ hr. x } \$57.90/\text{hr.} = \$320.77$$

Step 6. Calculate the flat material cost:
Goldenrod vinyl: 5 pcs. x $0.95 ea. = $4.75
Clearbase: 4 pcs. x $0.95 ea. = $3.80
Peelcoat: 2 pcs. x $1.45 ea. = $2.90
Total film assembly material cost: $4.75 + $3.80 + $2.90 = $11.45

Step 7. Summarize the findings:
Total production time: 5.54 hr.
Total production time cost: $320.77
Total material cost: $11.45
Total production cost: $332.22

Example 9.8. We want to estimate the image assembly time and cost to table strip a 4-color process art flyer for a local college. It will run 4/4 on a Komori Lithrone 426 (maximum press size sheet 20 inches x 26 inches) on an 18 inch x 24 inch pss. The front side of the flyer will have 8 separations to strip and the back side will have 6 more. Each side will also have a black type printer (1 negative) to be stripped as a keyline master and will be double-burned to the black process color plate. The BHR for the table stripper who will do this job is $61.75.

Stripping details: Stoesser pin registration system. Vinyl goldenrod for black line work, clearbase and peelcoats for separations. Windows 17 inches x 22 inches for black line and 5 inches x 7 inches for laying in all separations at average level. Cutting for CW flat windows at simple, 5 inches x 7 inches. Use 17 inch x 22 inch flat data. Add for one color bar per each stripped separation, or for a total of 8 for the job. Each black type flat will be a master flat for that side, and all others flats—including the process color flats—will register to that flat as complements. Add for one marks flat for registration and as a trim-out guide to burn to each black plate.

Flat Configuration Plan

Side 1 (4 Plates: 1 Black, 1 Magenta, 1 Cyan, 1 Yellow)

Flat 1   Black type (master) with 1 film negative, vinyl goldenrod

Flat 2   Black separation flat (complement) with 8 film negatives, clearbase

Flat 3   Magenta separation flat (complement) with 8 film negatives, clearbase

Flat 4   Cyan separation flat (complement) with 8 film negatives, clearbase

Flat 5   Yellow separation flat (complement) with 8 film negatives, clearbase

Flat 6   CW (complement) for separations, cut 8 windows, peelcoat

Side 2 (4 Plates: 1 Black, 1 Magenta, 1 Cyan, 1 Yellow)

Flat 7   Black type (master) with 1 film negative, vinyl goldenrod

Flat 8   Black separation flat (complement) with 6 film negatives, clearbase

Flat 9   Magenta separation flat (complement) with 6 film negatives, clearbase

Flat 10 Cyan separation flat (complement) with 6 film negatives, clearbase

Flat 11 Yellow separation flat (complement) with 6 film negatives, clearbase

Flat 12 CW (complement) for separations, cut 6 windows, peelcoat

Flat 13 Marks flat to burn with one black plate, for trim-out information

Total number of pieces of stripping base material needed: 2 pcs. vinyl goldenrod, 8 pcs. clearbase, 2 pcs. peelcoat

Solution

Use Figure 9.7.

Step 1. Determine the flat preparation and marks flat production time:

2 master flat (17 inches x 22 inches) x 0.18 hr. ea. = 0.36 hr.

10 complements (17 inches x 22 inches) x 0.08 hr. ea. = 0.80 hr.

1 marks flat (17 inches x 22 inches) x 0.10 hr. ea. = 0.10 hr.

Total preparation/startup production time: 0.36 hr. + 0.80 hr. + 0.10 hr. = 1.26 hr.

Step 2. Determine the laying and cutting time:

2 pcs. (17 inches x 22 inches, lay & cut to goldenrod, average) x 0.27 hr. ea. = 0.54 hr.

56 pcs. (5 inches x 7 inches, lay to clearbase, average) x 0.07 hr. ea. = 3.92 hr.

14 windows (5 inches x 7 inches, cut to peelcoat, simple) x 0.02 hr. ea. = 0.28 hr.

Total laying and cutting time: 0.54 hr. + 3.92 hr. + 0.28 hr. = 4.74 hr.

Step 3. Determine the additional time:

8 color bars x 0.08 hr. ea. = 0.64 hr.

Step 4. Determine the total image assembly time:

1.26 hr. + 4.74 hr. + 0.64 hr. = 6.64 hr.

Step 5. Determine the total image assembly production cost:

6.64 hr. x $61.75/hr. = $410.02

Step 6. Determine the flat material cost:
Vinyl goldenrod: 2 pcs. x $0.75 ea. = $1.50
Clearbase: 10 pcs. x $0.75 ea. = $7.50
Peelcoat: 2 pcs. x $1.15 ea. = $2.30
Total film assembly material cost: $1.50 + $7.50 + $2.30 = $11.30

Step 7. Summarize the findings:
Total production time: 6.64 hr
Total production time cost: $410.02
Total material cost: $11.30
Total production cost: $421.32

9.12 Photomechanical Platemaking and Proofing Methods

Platemaking and proofing follow the stripping process. Using traditional lithographic or waterless printing, every job must be imaged to one or more photomechanical plates, from which presswork is completed to produce the correct number of printed sheets. However, while all jobs must be plated, not all jobs are proofed. For example, proofing would be completed if the customer wished to carefully review his job one final time for accuracy, quality, or image reproduction. However, sometimes customers bypass the proofing process when deadlines are pressing or when the job simply does not warrant a close check. The following discussion provides information on platemaking and proofing technology and processes with which the estimator should be familiar.

Categories of Offset Plates

There are two types of printing plates commonly available today: lithographic and waterless. Both are used with the offset printing process. Lithographic plates, which have ink-receptive coatings adhered to their surfaces, work on the principle that ink (or grease) and water (or fountain solution) do not mix. The lithographic method has been the production process of choice for the past forty or more years and currently holds a significant lead as the process of choice for most printed products.

As its name implies, waterless offset printing is the graphic reproduction of images without water. Originally developed and released by the 3M Company in the 1960s under the name "driography," the patent rights of this process were sold to Toray Industries of Japan in the mid-1980s. Toray perfected the technology and reintroduced it as the waterless process. Offset presses using the waterless process require waterless plates and specially formulated inks. The plates that are used consist of ink-repelling silicone rubber layers and ink-adhering aluminum layers. The inks must be chilled during production so that they maintain their viscosity and body. This chilling is done by rollers that can either be retrofitted to the lithographic press or purchased with a press that is manufactured to run waterless exclusively. Waterless is also used exclusively with the Heidelberg DI and QM printing equipment. This is discussed further in Chapter 10.

Although the benefits of waterless plates are pronounced and the quality of this emerging technology is high, lithographic production, and therefore lithographic plates, far outsell waterless plates. Lithographic plates a may be divided into two major categories: surface and etched. Surface plates, which have ink-receptive coatings adhered to their surfaces, are further divided into presensitized and wipe-on groups. Etched plates are categorized into deep-etch and multimetal divisions.

Presensitized plates, which are purchased ready for exposure to a flat, represent the largest category of all lithographic plates in terms of total sales dollars. They are popular because of their ease of use during production, excellent image quality, and good consistency of image from plate to plate. Even though they are more expensive than the wipe-on plate (described in the following), they do not require preliminary coating during production, which saves time. Presensitized plates are used in thousands of commercial printing and publishing operations throughout the world. There are many manufacturers of presensitized plates, including Enco (Hoechst Celanese), 3M, DuPont, Fuji, Polychrome, Kodak, and Western.

As just mentioned, wipe-on plates are the second type of surface lithographic plate. These plates require that the platemaker wipe a light-sensitive coating on the aluminum base and then dry it thoroughly. Exposure and attendant processing are then completed. The most significant advantage of wipe-on plates is that they are far less expensive than the presensitized type because coating is done in the plant prior to use. In addition, wipe-on plates are generally good image carriers on the press and can be readily obtained in large quantities. Disadvantages include the additional time necessary during production for the coating and drying steps and the fact that the wipe-ons have a tendency to be inconsistent from time to time, especially when defined production techniques for coating and development are not followed carefully. Wipe-on plates are used in large quantities in the newspaper industry and in many web printing and publishing operations.

Of the two major categories of etched plates, the deep-etch type has excellent image-reproducing capability and good mileage during printing. The major disadvantage of the deep-etch plates is that they require many intricate steps in production, which makes them costly and sometimes inconsistent. The acceptance of presensitized plates, which are easy to obtain and provide for fast exposures and simple processing with high mileage capability, has eroded the deep-etch plate market. Very few printing companies use deep-etch plates today.

Multimetal plates represent the longest-running plate for the printing and publishing industry. Sometimes called trimetals, these image carriers have bases of aluminum or steel to which copper (an ink-receptive metal) and chromium or stainless steel (water-receptive) are electroplated. Etching is also part of the manufacturing procedure. Multimetals generally run 2 million impressions or more when press conditions are carefully controlled. Special equipment is required for their production, which makes them expensive initially. They are popular in the packaging industry and for long-run magazines and other publications where circulation is in the millions.

Overview of Bases and Coatings

A surface lithographic plate is a combination of a metal base and a light-sensitive coating or emulsion. Various metals, such as zinc, have been used as bases in past years, but today aluminum serves as the base metal for all lithographic plates. The thickness of the aluminum sheet may very depending upon the size of the press, and many plates are grained because the roughened surface provides better coating adhesion and improved water-carrying capability. In addition to graining, aluminum plates are also passivated (silicated or anodized) to reduce the chemical reaction that sometimes occurs between the base and certain coatings. Passivation also helps to improve plate performance on the press.

Once the base has been grained and passivated, it is ready to be coated. There are three major types of coating products used for presensitized plates: diazo, photopolymer, and silver halide compounds. Diazo coatings are by far the most frequently used because they are readily obtained, inexpensive, and easy to store and use. Various additional chemical ingredients are used with the diazo sensitizer to allow for different mileage results.

Photopolymer coatings are popular today because they offer increased run lengths over diazo products, easy exposure and processing, and faster roll-up on the press. Polymer coatings are more expensive than diazos because they are synthetic and must be carefully manufactured. However, their increased plate mileage and excellent press performance make them very popular.

Silver halide coatings are used for short-run lithographic surface plates when limited quantities are desired. These coatings resemble photographic emulsions but they are applied to metal or plastic bases instead of paper or polyester. Kodak PMT (diffusion-transfer) and Itek plates are both examples of silver halide image carriers. Another short-run lithographic plate is the electrostatic master. However, the ink-receptive carbon toner used for this plate is not a photographic coating but rather a product fused to the base material during the making of the plate.

Working Parameters of Lithographic Plates

All surface lithographic plates may be categorized with respect to exposure and processing orientation. Lithographic plates that expose from negatives to produce positive images, called negative-acting or negative-working plates, reverse image tonality. Plates that produce the same tonality are called positive acting or positive working. Because negative film images are the usual output from the photographic area in most printing plants, negative-acting plates, which reproduce a positive image, represent the majority of image carriers used in the printing industry today.

The processing of surface plates is either additive or subtractive. Additive surface plates require the addition of a developing lacquer to harden the plate image and make it visible. Subtractive surface plates are purchased in pre-lacquered form and require removal of the lacquer from the nonimage areas during processing. Subtractives outsell additives because they are easier to develop and seem more consistent from plate to plate.

Prior to 1985, most lithographic plates were processed using solvent-based chemicals, which included alcohol and other somewhat toxic ingredients. Due to pressure from various sources, lithographic plate manufacturers introduced aqueous-based chemicals for processing plates as direct substitutes for the solvent-based products. Although chemical changes were necessary in the photographic plate coatings, the shift to aqueous-based products is currently in transition. At this writing, both solvent-based and aqueous-based products are available and are purchased by most lithographic plate manufacturers.

There is little noticeable difference between solvent-based and aqueous-based lithographic plates in terms of their physical appearances. There is also little difference in exposure or processing times or productivity issues during plate-making. Chemical products for processing plates are not interchangeable between brands of plates, even though their coating ingredients may be similar.

An automatic plate processor cannot process both additive and subtractive varieties, again because of the differences in processing chemistry and development techniques.

When a lithographic plate is made, it initially receives all exposures required from either negative or positive film images. Manual or automatic film processing then follows using the appropriate developing agents and rub-up procedures. With negative-acting plates, the clear film areas allow the intense UV light to pass through, which renders these areas insoluble to developing agents and produces the plate image. Areas covered by black film or masking material stop the UV light and thus are soluble to developing chemistry and are removed during plate processing to create the nonimage areas of the plate. Following development, gum arabic is applied to protect the plate surface and enhance performance during the press run. Normally, the platemaking employee completes both the exposure and the processing operations.

Automatic Plate Processing

Automatic plate processing is found in most printing companies today, largely for the same reasons as automatic film processing: Automatic plate processing is productive, fast, provides assured consistency of developed image, controls processing variables, reduces manpower, saves space, and reduces plate remakes. Processors using solvent-based chemicals cannot process aqueous-based plates, and vice versa. Changing the processor from solvent-based to aqueous-based chemistry is a fairly simple procedure and affects primarily the development area of the processor; the gumming and finishing processor units remain largely unchanged.

Plate processors vary in cost depending on the size of the unit and the type of plate to be processed. Additive processors are used for wipe-on plates and are common in newspaper and publishing plants. Subtractive processors are more popular in the commercial printing segment because they can develop two-sided plates simultaneously or one-sided plates placed back to back after exposure. In addition, subtractive processors utilize a recirculating bath system, which allows for the reuse of developer chemicals and therefore saves on developer material cost. Both additive and subtractive processor models provide plate gumming as their final processing steps.

Some of the major lithographic plate manufacturers sell standardized lines of subtractive plates that use the mileage of the plate as the variable for selecting which plate is best for a given job. All of the plates in the series expose and develop using the same times and methods. Thus, Job A may require a plate that requires 25,000 impressions, while Job B requires a different plate in the series that must produce 100,000 impressions. Using one supplier's brand of plate, which has a range of plates available in the series, streamlines platemaking production and allows the company to use one plate processor for all of the plates needed in the company.

Photomechanical Proofing Systems and Materials

The equipment used for platemaking is also used in parallel fashion for the exposure of proofing materials because both products are sensitive to UV light. Photographic proofing serves one or more of the following purposes:

- as an intermediate visual look at a job-in-process (or a segment of a job-in-process)
- as a portion of a job requiring photographic work as a segment of art preparation where the photographic work being proofed will become a part of the mechanical pasteup
- as a final visual look at a job for internal plant approval or for customer review and approval

Monochromatic Proofs. The most popular black-and-white or monochromatic proofing material is DuPont Dylux, which is a paper substrate manufactured with an encapsulated imaging material that is broken by exposure to actinic light. Because no contact with any liquid is necessary for processing this material, Dylux proofs, also known as bluelines or blueline proofs, are extremely dimensionally stable. Exposure requires a UV light source that is typical of the platemaking equipment found in most printing companies. Once the Dylux proof is fully imaged, exposing it to a clearing filter neutralizes the remaining encapsulated photosensitive emulsion and renders the image permanent.

Other monochromatic proofs include brownline or silverprint materials, rapid-access silver halide products such as DuPont's Bright Light Papers (BLPs) and 3M's Lights On Papers (LOPs), various azo products, and stabilization proofs such as Ektamatic and Fotorite materials. Certain monochromatic proofing materials are available in single-faced (C1S) or double-faced (C2S) versions for proofing two-sided jobs and bookwork impositions to check backup positions.

Color Proofing Materials. Photomechanical color proofs are categorized into two types: off-press and press (or on-press). Off-press proofs are further subdivided into overlay proofs and laminated (or single-sheet) proof classifications.

It should be noted that the area of color proofing is a critical digital imaging cross-over point. One reason is that color digital proofing systems, which are classified into thermal wax, laser, dye sublimation, and ink jet types and are covered in Chapter 8, are sometimes unable to provide the high level of quality that is desired relative to the level of quality desired for color resolution and color match. In light of its quality, the cost of digital color proofing equipment is high. Digital color proofing equipment is also limited in size, which is another disadvantage. Other issues, such as the lack of permanence of digital proofs and their lack of consistency in image and color, remain problems. For these reasons, the use of photomechanical or analog off-press proofing methods are used from when final film has been output. The correction process typically requires first that the digital file is changed, then that the corrected film is output, and finally that the job is reproofed. Thus, there is a common production pathway between digital and photomechanical production methods.

Estimating color proofing, whether by conventional or analog production, is important because it is both labor and materials intensive. Color proofing requires a high level of operator skill and knowledge and continuous employee involvement. Both overlay and laminated proofing products tend to be expensive, and their labor costs are high because their production requires constant employee interaction. Also, color proofing is an unpredictable production area where cycling is common—some jobs may be proofed only once or twice, while other jobs may have ten or more proofing cycles before they secure final job approval. For these reasons, proofing can be a significant job cost that may not always be estimated accurately.

Off-Press Proofs. This popular category of photomechanical proofs is divided into overlay and laminated (or single-sheet) products. Each is discussed relative to information needed for estimating and production planning.

Overlay Proofs. These proofs consist of single acetate sheets of color pigment which, when exposed, processed, and superimposed over one another, provide a composite image of the final print. Overlay proofs are relatively low in cost and can be produced quickly and easily in most printing plants. Color specification standards such as Standard Web Offset Publications (SWOP) can be matched. Opinion on the quality of the proofs varies among industry users, particularly when related to the fact that pigment lots vary from box to box and that the clear carrier sheets impart an undesirable grayness to the final image and thus render the accuracy of the proof questionable to some customers.

The 3M Color-Key, Hoechst Negative-Acting Proofing System (NAPS) and Positive-Acting Proofing System (PAPS), and DuPont Chromacheck are products in the overlay proofing group. These materials, which are pigmented diazo products, are exposed to the appropriate film image using UV light and are then developed manually or automatically using the required processing chemicals. Color-Key is available in the standard process colors plus twenty-six PMS color choices, while NAPS/PAPS are available in process colors plus a variety of standard flat colors. There are differences between Color-Key and Hoechst overlay products, but their final physical proofing results appear much the same.

DuPont's Chromacheck is an overlay negative-acting proofing system that produces images using a postexposure peel-apart system. No processing is required and the process is completely dry. The colored pigment is an adhesive photopolymer material. Exposure to UV light adheres the image areas to the base, and the proof image is produced when the two films are peeled apart using a vacuum easel or an autopeeler system that can be purchased from DuPont.

Laminated (or Single-Sheet) Proofs. Laminated proofs are made by Agfa, Du-Pont, Fuji, 3M, and Hoechst. Although they vary in their photoemulsion characteristics, they all require three steps to produce one imaged layer: lamination, exposure, and development. These steps are repeated to superimpose each new laminated layer over all of the previous layers and colors, which produces full-color images. Thus, the single base substrate is laminated, exposed, and developed multiple times.

Making an off-press laminated proof begins when the base substrate is passed through the laminator. A thin sheet of photosensitive film is securely adhered to the base sheet in this process. Following this, a photographic film negative or positive is registered to the laminated material and is given an exposure. In the next step, the laminated sheet is passed through a toning or developing unit where the image is developed and finished. The cycle then is repeated—the substrate receives a second laminated layer over the first finished image, a companion film negative or positive is registered to the visible first image, then exposure is done, and finally the second color is developed or toned. Therefore, a 4-color proof requires four lamination steps, four exposures, and four developing steps.

Laminated proofs are exceptionally accurate in color resolution and yield very high image quality. They can be produced in large sizes, which makes them popular for proofing digital images beyond the smaller size range of most digital proofing equipment. Laminated proofs are available in either positive-acting and negative-acting versions. Typically the exposures vary from one color to another, so they require benchmark exposure testing from color to color and box to box. The movement is toward environmentally friendly aqueous-based or water-based systems and away from solvent-based products. DuPont WaterProof is an example of a fully water-processed, environmentally safe proofing product.

Four popular laminated proof products are covered in Figure 9.8: DuPont Cromalin, Fuji Color-Art, 3M Matchprint III, and DuPont WaterProof.

Press Proofs. Color press proofs, or on-press proofs, are still used when a large quantity of proofs is desired, particularly for advertising and packaging purposes. Such proofs first require the manual stripping of separated materials, then platemaking and printing on a press. To economize, the press sheets are normally ganged with many images, usually a collection of jobs proofed on one sheet. After the presswork is complete, the flats are torn apart and the color separations are separated by job for restripping.

Press proofs are expensive because all of the work is done for review and the work is nonproductive in terms of delivering finished copies to the customer.

Press proofs are time consuming and can be done only when the job schedule allows sufficient time to complete such production. The primary advantage of press proofs, and the main reason for their popularity in light of their high cost and time requirements, is that they most closely approach the final printed version of the color image. Even so, as analog and digital proofing technology improves in quality and reduced cycle time, press proofs are expected to be phased out.

9.13 Estimating Platemaking and Proofing Time and Cost

Figure 9.8 contains schedules for estimating lithographic platemaking and proofing production time and cost of materials. Chart data are divided into manual plate and proof processing and automatic plate and proof processing, which are further divided into manual and automatic (step-and-repeat) exposures. First, the plate size or maximum press size for the press should be located. Use higher square inch values for plates and sheets that do not fit exactly a listed size. The cost of plate and proofing materials is a separate part of the schedule and is oriented around the square inch value of the proof or the size of the plate. Processing chemicals have been included in the plate and proofing costs indicated in the schedule. Examples 9.9 and 9.10 that follow demonstrate how to apply Figure 9.8 data.

As with estimating image assembly, a plate and proofing configuration plan should be developed to frame out the production that will be done during the manufacturing sequence. There are links between image assembly and platemaking/proofing, which necessitates that planning be considered early when estimating both areas. Use the following formulas with the data in Figure 9.8 to estimate platemaking and proofing time and cost:

platemaking and proofing production time = (number of first exposure flats x first exposure production time) + (number of additional exposure flats x additional exposure production time)

platemaking and proofing production cost = platemaking and proofing production time x platemaking and proofing BHR

plate cost = number of plates x cost per plate

proof cost = number of proofs x size of proof in square inches x cost per square inch

total cost for platemaking and proofing = production cost + platemaking and proofing material cost

Manual plate and proof processing time (hrs.)				Maximum press size sheet or plate size (sq. in.)	Automatic plate and proof processing time (hrs.)			
Manual exposure		Automatic exposure*			Manual exposure		Automatic exposure*	
First	Each add'l	First	Each add'l		First	Each add'l	First	Each add'l
0.11	0.03	0.06	0.02	10 x 15 (150)	0.08	0.03	0.05	0.02
0.16	0.05	0.08	0.03	14 x 20 (280)	0.12	0.05	0.06	0.03
0.19	0.06	0.11	0.04	17 x 22 (374)	0.14	0.06	0.08	0.04
0.24	0.07	0.14	0.04	19 x 25 (475)	0.18	0.07	0.11	0.04
0.27	0.08	0.15	0.04	23 x 29 (667)	0.20	0.08	0.12	0.04
0.32	0.10	0.16	0.04	24 x 36 (864)	0.22	0.10	0.13	0.04
0.35	1.10	0.18	0.04	25 x 38 (950)	0.26	1.10	0.14	0.04
0.37	0.10	0.20	0.04	38 x 50 (1900)	0.30	0.10	0.15	0.04
0.41	0.10	0.21	0.04	44 x 60 (2640)	0.35	0.10	0.16	0.04
0.45	0.10	0.22	0.04	52 x 77 (4004)	0.37	0.10	0.17	0.04

*Step-and-repeat machines

Plate size	Sq. Inches	Enco SF	Kodak KNA4	3M Viking G1	3M Viking G2	Western Aqualith	DuPont Howson HPN	Fuji FNS	Toray Waterless
10x15	150	$1.58	$1.77	$1.27	$2.02	$1.43	$1.75	$1.37	$3.38
14x20	280	$2.94	$3.30	$2.37	$3.77	$2.67	$3.27	$2.56	$6.30
17x22	374	$3.93	$4.41	$3.17	$5.04	$3.56	$4.36	$3.43	$8.42
19x25	475	$4.99	$5.61	$4.02	$6.40	$4.52	$5.54	$4.35	$10.69
23x29	667	$7.00	$7.87	$5.65	$8.98	$6.35	$7.78	$6.11	$15.01
24x36	864	$9.07	$10.20	$7.32	$11.64	$8.23	$10.08	$7.91	$19.44
25x38	950	$9.98	$11.21	$8.05	$12.80	$9.04	$11.09	$8.70	$21.38
38x50	1900	$19.95	$22.42	$16.09	$25.59	$18.09	$22.17	$17.40	$42.75
44x60	2640	$27.72	$31.15	$22.36	$35.56	$25.13	$30.81	$24.18	$59.40
52x77	4004	$42.04	$47.25	$33.91	$53.93	$38.12	$46.73	$36.68	$90.09

Overlay proofs	Laminated (single-sheet) proofs	Monochrome proofs
3M Color-Key Process colors: $0.014/sq. in. PMS colors: $0.016/sq. in. **Hoechst (Enco) NAPS/PAPS** Process colors: $0.013/sq. in. Flat colors:$0.015/sq. in. **DuPont Chromacheck** Process colors: $0.016/sq. in. Flat colors:$0.018/sq. in.	**DuPont Cromalin: **** $0.020/sq. in. (film + toner) **Fuji Color-Art**** Process colors: $0.017/sq. in. PMS colors: $0.019/sq. in. **3M Matchprint III **** Process colors: $0.021/sq. in. PMS colors: $0.022/sq. in. **DuPont WaterProof **** Process colors: $0.022/sq. in. PMS colors: $0.023/sq. in. ** per laminated and fully toned layer	**Dylux** C1S: $0.003/sq. in. C2S: $0.004/sq. in. For all proofing, use platemaking exposure times indicated above. Proofing costs include processing materials.

Note: Time and cost for plate or proof remakes are not included.

Figure 9.8 Photomechanical platemaking and proofing schedule, including plate and proofing material costs. Schedule data are for example only.

Example 9.9. We want to estimate the proofing and platemaking time for Example 9.7 previously presented. To review, the products are 7 1/2 inch x 8 1/2 inch announcements, stripped to run 6-up, printed black and red, both sides (2/2), on a Heidelberg MOZP. There are duotones to print in red and black, as well as separate red and black line images. The stripped job requires 4 plates, 2 black and 2 red, with each plate receiving exposures from 2 different flats.

Platemaking and proofing details: Stoesser pin registration system. 19 inch x 25 inch Enco SF aqueous plates will be made. Manual exposure and automatic plate processing. 3M Color-Key overlay proofs, manually exposed and automatically processed, will also be made in the plate size to check registration and will be imaged with the marks flat (on one black proof) to check trim-out and other production marks. PMS colors will be used. The BHR for platemaking/proofing is $54.90.

Platemaking and Proofing Configuration Plan
Side 1 (2 Plates: 1 Black 6-Up Plate and 1 Red 6-Up Plate)
Plate 1 Black type + black duotone (with CW flat) + marks flat
Plate 2 Red line work + red duotone (with CW flat)

Side 2 (2 Plates: 1 Black 6-Up Plate and 1 Red 6-Up Plate)
Plate 3 Black type + black duotone (with CW flat)
Plate 4 Red line work + red duotone (with CW flat)

Solution

Use Figure 9.8.

Step 1. Determine the platemaking production time:
Plate 1
(black printer, 19 inches x 25 inches, auto processing, manual exposure):

> 1 first exposure (black type) x 0.18 hr. ea. = 0.18 hr.

> 2 additional exposures (black duotones and marks flat) x 0.07 hr. ea. = 0. 14 hr.

Production time for Plate 1: 0.32 hr.

Plate 2
(red printer, 19 inches x 25 inches, auto processing, manual exposure):

> 1 first exposure (red line work) x 0. 18 hr. ea. = 0.18 hr.

> 1 additional exposure (red duotones) x 0.07 hr. ea. = 0.07 hr.

Production time for Plate 2: 0.25 hr.

Plate 3
(black printer, 19 inches x 25 inches, auto processing, manual exposure):

1 first exposure (black type) x 0. 18 hr. ea. = 0.18 hr.

1 additional exposure (black duotones) x 0.07 hr. ea. = 0.07 hr.

Production time for Plate 3: 0.25 hr.

Plate 4
(red printer, 19 inches x 25 inches, auto processing, manual exposure):

1 first exposure (red line work) x 0.18 hr. ea. = 0.18 hr.

1 additional exposure (red duotones) x 0.07 hr. ea. = 0.07 hr.

Production time for Plate 4: 0.25 hr.

Total platemaking production time: 0.32 hr. + 0.25 hr. + 0.25 hr. + 0.25 hr. = 1.07 hr.

Step 2. Determine the proofing production time:

Proof 1
(black printer, 19 inches x 25 inches, auto processing, manual exposure):

1 first exposure (black type) x 0.18 hr. ea. = 0.18 hr.

2 additional exposures (black duotones and marks flat) x 0.07 hr. ea. = 0.14 hr.

Production time for Proof 1: 0.32 hr.

Proof 2
(red printer, 19 inches x 25 inches, auto processing, manual exposure):

1 first exposure (red line work) x 0.18 hr. ea. = 0.18 hr.

1 additional exposure (red duotones) x 0.07 hr. ea. = 0.07 hr.

Production time for Proof 2: 0.25 hr.

Proof 3
(black printer, 19 inches x 25 inches, auto processing, manual exposure):

1 first exposure (black type) x 0.18 hr. ea. = 0.18 hr.

1 additional exposure (black duotones) x 0.07 hr. ea. = 0.07 hr.

Production time for Proof 3: 0.25 hr.

Proof 4
(red printer, 19 inches x 25 inches, auto processing, manual exposure):

1 first exposure (red line work) x 0.18 hr. ea. = 0.18 hr.

1 additional exposure (red duotones) x 0.07 hr. ea. = 0.07 hr.

Production time for Proof 4: 0.25 hr.

Total proofing production time: 0.32 hr. + 0.25 hr. + 0.25 hr. + 0.25 hr. = 1.07 hr.

Step 3. Determine the total platemaking and proofing production time:

1.07 hr. + 1.07 hr. = 2.14 hr.

Step 4. Determine the total platemaking and proofing production cost:

2.14 hr. x $54.90/hr. = $117.49

Step 5. Determine the platemaking and proofing material cost:

4 plates (Enco SF, 19 inches x 25 inches) x $4.99 ea. = $19.96

4 proofs x (19 inches x 25 inches) x 0.016/sq. in. = $30.40

Total plate and proof materials: $19.96 + $30.40 = $50.36

Step 6. Summarize the findings:
Total production time: 2.14 hr.
Total production time cost: $117.49
Total material cost: $50.36
Total production cost: $167.85

Example 9.10. We want to estimate the proofing and platemaking time for Example 9.8. To review, the product is a 4/4 color art flyer for local college, stripped for a Komori Lithrone 426 (maximum press size sheet 20 inches x 26 inches). There are a total of 14 separations, 8 on the front side and 6 on the back. A total of eight plates are required.

Platemaking and proofing details: Stoesser pin registration system. Use the 19 inch x 25 inch plate data for 3M Viking G-2 plates. Manual exposure and manual processing. Proofing will be done with DuPont WaterProof using process colors, manually exposed and automatically processed for customer approval and internal registration check. The marks flat will be proofed (on one black proof) to check trim-out and other production marks. The BHR for platemaking/proofing is $57.40.

Platemaking and Proofing Configuration Plan

Side 1 (4 Plates: One Black, One Magenta, One Cyan, and One Yellow)

Plate 1 Black type + black separations (with CW flat) + marks flat

Plate 2 Magenta separations (with CW flat)

Plate 3 Cyan separations (with CW flat)

Plate 4 Yellow separations (with CW flat)

Side 2 (4 Plates: One Black, One Magenta, One Cyan, and One Yellow)

Plate 5 Black type + black separations (with CW flat)

Plate 6 Magenta separations (with CW flat)

Plate 7 Cyan separations (with CW flat)

Plate 8 Yellow separations (with CW flat)

Solution

Use Figure 9.8.

Step 1. Determine the platemaking production time:

Plate 1
(black printer, 19 inches x 25 inches, manual processing, manual exposure):

1 first exposure (black type) x 0.24 hr. ea. = 0.24 hr.

2 additional exposures (black separations and marks flat) x
0.07 hr. ea. = 0.14 hr.

Production time for Plate 1: 0.38 hr.

Plate 2
(magenta printer, 19 inches x 25 inches, manual processing, manual exposure):

1 first exposure (magenta separations) x 0.24 hr. ea. = 0.24 hr.

Production time for Plate 2: 0.24 hr.

Plate 3
(cyan printer, 19 inches x 25 inches, manual processing, manual exposure):

1 first exposure (cyan separations) x 0.24 hr. ea. = 0.24 hr.

Production time for Plate 3: 0.24 hr.

Plate 4
(yellow printer, 19 inches x 25 inches, manual processing, manual exposure):

    1 first exposure (yellow separations) x 0.24 hr. ea. = 0.24 hr.

Production time for Plate 4: 0.24 hr.

Plate 5
(black printer, 19 inches x 25 inches, manual processing, manual exposure):

    1 first exposure (black type) x 0.24 hr. ea. = 0.24 hr.

    1 additional exposure (black separations and marks flat) x 0.07 hr. ea. = 0.07 hr.

Production time for Plate 5: 0.31 hr.

Plate 6
(magenta printer, 19 inches x 25 inches, manual processing, manual exposure):

    1 first exposure (magenta separations) x 0.24 hr. ea. = 0.24 hr.

Production time for Plate 6: 0.24 hr.

Plate 7
(cyan printer, 19 inches x 25 inches, manual processing, manual exposure):

    1 first exposure (cyan separations) x 0.24 hr. ea. = 0.24 hr.

Production time for Plate 7: 0.24 hr.

Plate 8
(yellow printer, 19 inches x 25 inches, manual processing, manual exposure):

    1 first exposure (yellow separations) x 0.24 hr. ea. = 0.24 hr.

Production time for Plate 8: 0.24 hr.

Total platemaking production time: 0.38 hr. + 0.24 hr. + 0.24 hr. + 0.24 hr. + 0.31 hr. + 0.24 hr. + 0.24 hr. + 0.24 hr. = 2.13 hr.

Step 2. Determine the proofing production time:

Side One

Proof layer 1

(black printer, 19 inches x 25 inches, auto processing, manual exposure):

> 1 first exposure (black type) x 0.18 hr. ea. = 0.18 hr.

> 2 additional exposures (black separations and marks flat) x 0.07 hr. ea. = 0.14 hr.

Production time for proof Layer 1: 0.32 hr.

Proof layer 2

(magenta printer, 19 inches x 25 inches, auto processing, manual exposure):

> 1 first exposure (magenta separations) x 0.18 hr. ea. = 0.18 hr.

Production time for proof Layer 2: 0.18 hr.

Proof layer 3

(cyan printer, 19 inches x 25 inches, auto processing, manual exposure):

> 1 first exposure (cyan separations) x 0.18 hr. ea. = 0.18 hr.

Production time for proof Layer 3: 0.18 hr.

Proof layer 4

(yellow printer, 19 inches x 25 inches, auto processing, manual exposure):

> 1 first exposure (yellow separations) x 0.18 hr. ea. = 0.18 hr.

Production time for proof Layer 4: 0.18 hr.

Side Two

Proof layer 1

(black printer, 19 inches x 25 inches, auto processing, manual exposure):

> 1 first exposure (black type) x 0.18 hr. ea. = 0.18 hr.

> 1 additional exposure (black separations) x 0.07 hr. ea. = 0.07 hr.

Production time for proof Layer 1: 0.25 hr.

Proof layer 2

(magenta printer, 19 inches x 25 inches, auto processing, manual exposure):

> 1 first exposure (magenta separations) x 0.18 hr. ea. = 0.18 hr.

Production time for proof Layer 2: 0.18 hr.

Proof layer 3
(cyan printer, 19 inches x 25 inches, auto processing, manual exposure):

1 first exposure (cyan separations) x 0.18 hr. ea. = 0.18 hr.

Production time for proof Layer 3: 0.18 hr.

Proof layer 4
(yellow printer, 19 inches x 25 inches, auto processing, manual exposure):

1 first exposure (yellow separations) x 0.18 hr. ea. = 0.18 hr.

Production time for proof Layer 4: 0.18 hr.

Total WaterProof production time: 0.32 hr. + 0.18 hr. + 0.18 hr. + 0.18 hr. + 0.25 hr. + 0.18 hr. + 0.18 hr. + 0.18 hr. = 1.65 hr.

Step 3. Determine the total platemaking and proofing production time:

2.13 hr. + 1.65 hr. = 3.78 hr.

Step 4. Determine the total platemaking and proofing production cost:

3.78 hr. x $57.40/hr. = $216.97

Step 5. Determine the platemaking and proofing material cost:

8 plates (Viking G-2, 19 inches x 25 inches) x $6.40 ea. = $51.20

8 proof layers (WaterProof, 19 inches x 25 inches) x
0.022/sq. in. = $83.60

Total plate and proof materials: $51.20 + $83.60 = $134.80

Step 6. Summarize the findings:
Total production time: 3.78 hr.
Total production cost: $216.97
Total material cost: $134.80
Total production cost: $351.77

Chapter 10

Estimating Sheetfed Offset and Digital Press Production

10.4 Increasing Sheetfed Pressroom Productivity

Maximize Press Sheet Usage   Increase Press Efficiency
Schedule Production Efficiently   Modify Job Specifications

10.5 Changeover Points for Estimating Offset Presswork

10.6 Estimating Sheetfed Offset Presswork

Makeready and Press Preparation   Washup
Press Running

10.7 Sheetfed Presswork Estimating Tips

10.8 Print-on-Demand and Digital Press Technology

Overview of Print-on-Demand   Digital Printing Production
Defining Print-on-Demand Run   Wide Format Imaging Technology
   Length Quantities   for Proofing and Small Print Runs
Size and Scope of the Print-on-De-   Evaluating Costs of Digital Presses
   mand Market   and Print-on-Demand
Direct Digital Output at the Desktop Cost Comparisons of Four Digital
   for up to Ten Copies   Presses to Conventional Printing
Very Short-Run Black-and-White and
   Color Printing
High-Speed Document Production

Appendix: Presswork Estimating Schedules

10.1 Introduction

Although estimating prepress offers the estimator a challenge given the numerous production choices possible, estimating pressroom production—as long as the offset process is used—remains a fairly straightforward procedure.

This chapter covers a range of subjects related to the costing and pricing of traditional sheetfed press production. Estimating methods for offset lithographic production remain largely unchanged, but newer model sheetfed presses that print up to eight colors in one pass require less makeready and washup times and run at higher production speeds.

Discussion of viable, emerging print-on-demand (POD) systems, such as copying, document processing, digital presses, and related technological advances including waterless printing, are covered in this chapter when defining these emerging processes. At this time these systems are generally limited when compared to the extensive use of lithographic printing, but it is likely that this situation will change as these systems are perfected to meet specific customer needs.

10.2 New Paradigms in Printing Processes

Today's print orders are completed using one of two general approaches: (1) prepress production using either photomechanical or electronic methods followed with traditional press and postpress production, or (2) on-demand printing systems where jobs are printed as needed in a JIT format.

Print production using prepress, press, and binding—the traditional production methods—remains the way many jobs are processed. However, emerging POD and digital printing systems are changing the way printing is manufactured, and the pressroom is at the center of this revolution. Considered a generally safe harbor during the DTP revolution that began in the mid-1980s, the sheetfed pressroom is now receiving major research and development activity. Digital output technology, which is discussed in Chapter 8 as a method for proofing and producing limited image output, has shifted to address the on-demand production of multiple copies.

To many industry experts and observers, the status of offset lithography, which is the "ink-and-water don't mix" image reproduction process, is changing. Digital imaging in the forms of electrostatic methods, laser systems, ink-jet methods, and thermal wax are among the processes now competing with lithography. For some printers, there is a return to a feeling of unpredictable chaos, which is similar to the feeling they experienced as DPP was emerging in the late 1980s and early 1990s.

Revolution in Printing Process Choice Is Underway

Press production is in the early stages of an energized and significant state of change. Emerging printing processes offering new print production choices are a reality. Customers and markets are changing. Economically feasible short-run color products using digital technology—not lithography—are available through the Heidelberg, Xeikon, Indigo, and Agfa ChromaPress systems. Document production, which was first revolutionized by Xerox with the introduction of commercial electrostatic copying in the 1960s, was again changed in the early 1990s with the emergence of Xerox's DocuTech Publishing System. DocuTech, and the previously mentioned digital printing methods, have created a print-on-demand market that threatens conventional lithographic printing production at its core. Lithography also faces growing challenges as the development of waterless printing proves both viable and cost effective, because existing lithographic press equipment can be retrofitted to capitalize on this process. In addition, the Heidelberg DI and QM presses have merged DPP technology and waterless printing to provide high-quality color reproduction in a quick turnaround environment.

The revolution in how printed products are mass produced is driven by the four following key issues, each of which must be addressed if a printing company is to survive into the twenty-first century.

Customer-Driven Needs. The customer's desire for imaged products that meet his immediate graphic needs in terms of quantity, quality, price, and delivery is at the core of this paradigm shift. Printed products can be generally segmented into the following categories: commercial, document-based, color, publications and catalogs, and specialty. Overlap between these products and the processes by which they are economically produced is evident, which is causing considerable confusion and chaos for many printers. Other areas of this chapter address these issues as appropriate.

Industry Segmentation. There is an emerging segmentation separating printers, service bureaus, trade shops, and other graphic image providers. In past years, mass production of imaged products was the essential difference separating printers from their industry colleagues in service bureaus, trade shops, and related service companies. However, many of the emerging on-demand and digital printing systems are being sold and installed with these affiliated service providers or to new companies using exclusively digital production methods. Thus, full-service printers now must compete at different levels, using different technology to produce a range of products based on customer need. In addition, all of this is occurring in an area of printing production that has a high level of capital intensiveness. Survival into the twenty-first century will require printers to identify "who they are" by process and product because halting this segmentation is not possible.

Competitive Cost Issues. To remain competitive, there is a pressing need on the part of all printers to control costs. Globally speaking, costs in a printing company can be categorized as either fixed or variable, and both are receiving great scrutiny relative to cost impact on the job. Many press equipment manufacturers, responding to industry pressure, have worked diligently to lower fixed costs because they are easily identified. Key among press fixed cost are the costs of makeready prior to printing the job and washup after the pressrun. Given this cost-saving focus, new sheetfed presses are equipped with electronic and mechanical devices that significantly speed both makeready and washup activities, save minutes per job, and add up to savings of many hours per year. Such cost savings are passed on the customer, which keeps the printer more competitive.

The most significant variable cost in printing production is the cost of labor, which is being reduced through equipment automation, waterless printing, and other changes. While it is clear that revenue or profit in printing is driven primarily by selling price and not by internal plant cost, it is also clear that cost issues have a significant bearing on establishing price. Thus, survival in printing requires caution and careful management scrutiny of cost issues affecting all aspects of the company.

Meeting the Demand for Reduced Cycle Time. In the past ten years, printing production has been increasingly affected by the customer's demand for faster delivery of her product. This time compression, which translates to reduced cycle times in production, has shifted lead times from weeks to a few days. Given the prepress chaos and related time increases in EPP because of unfamiliar technology, meeting deadlines for printers means saving time in the pressroom. The push for faster press makeready systems, higher speed presses, digital printing for short runs, and fewer errors during production are examples of how this time compression is being met.

Shift in Buyer Patterns and Print Needs

For years it was not unusual for printers to offer their products and services without considering what the customers or print buyers wanted or needed. When the customer needed a job printed, the printer sent a sales representative to the customer, the job was specified, then it was estimated and sold and the job was manufactured using the printer's typical production cycle. The CSRs coordinated job details, handled customer complaints, and worked to expedite the job and manage any damage that arose. Although some printers developed marketing plans and encouraged more than minimum customer support, others were in a position to practice "wait-and-see" attitudes with their customers.

In the 1980s things began to change, and printers began to lose their dominance over customers. The emergence of DTP allowed customers to make important prepress production decisions, so jobs were no longer under the exclusive control of the printers. Parallel to this trend was the recognition of TQM as a viable business practice. This model emphasizes world-class customer service, continuous improvement, employee empowerment, and scientific process control methods, among many important aspects. While some printers willingly became customer sensitive as a tenet of TQM, others were forced into following this pattern or risk losing important jobs. Customers and print buyers quickly recognized these changes and began to exert more control as they dealt with the printers. Responses of the printers varied widely: Some printers gladly developed partnerships with customers, some became price driven to encourage customers, some continued in their old patterns, and still others tried to balance service, price, and quality.

Recent print buyer surveys show that buyers want quality printing produced on time, good communication, responsive support services, and competitive prices. The average time in which printers have to produce most jobs has shifted to from weeks to days, but not all jobs are time compressed. Customers in the survey showed that they expected accurate estimates, accurate and timely billing, and responsive, dignified treatment overall.

An increasing number of print buyers are seeking printers who will become their sole source providers. This way, the buyer only has to deal with one printing company to meet all of his printing needs. A printer who becomes a sole source provider may produce only a fraction of the customer's printing work in house and will instead act primarily as the customer's purchasing agent by arranging the remainder through outside suppliers.

Prepress Issues, Print Production Run Length, Quality, and Service

The growth of DTP and the customers' insistence on providing their own electronic artwork have played important roles in changing the customer-printer relationship. This is because many prepress production decisions are now made by the customer when she creates the job on the desktop. When these decisions are poorly made or improperly executed digitally, the customer and the printer must jointly resolve the problems before the job can be produced. It is not unusual for customers to err in constructing their digital files, but they tend to balk at paying for repairing their electronic files, even if the errors are attributable to them. This has led printers to provide customer training, job preflighting, and standardized DPP so that jobs flow without expensive and time-consuming corrections.

Depending on their graphic needs, DTP has effectively allowed many print buyers to lower their initial order quantities and thereby increase the frequency of their orders to meet the same printing volume. For example, prior to DTP, a customer might place an order for 10,000 postcards that he anticipated would last one year. Today that same order might be for 2,500 postcards that are expected to last three months. After the postcards are gone, they may be redesigned with a different image. This means that, in general, print order quantities today tend to be lower and the number of jobs-in-process for a given printing company tend to be higher to maintain the same level of pressroom volume.

One result of this shift to more jobs with lower quantities per job is that printing company staff, especially sales representatives, CSRs, and estimators, must process more jobs to maintain similar volume. Another result is that the number of straight reprint orders, which are jobs that are printed a second or an additional time with little or no change from the first printing, have generally been reduced to a small percentage of a typical printing company's total volume. This phenomenon is discussed in detail in Chapter 5.

DTP has generally shifted the quality expectations of customers upward in both image resolution and color reproduction. Customers now expect higher quality without asking for it. Many have become knowledgeable about how quality is achieved on the desktop and expect such quality to carry through on related print manufacturing steps. In cases where the image quality of customer digital files is compromised through inexperience, some customers have come to expect the printers to rebuild their files to the level of quality they originally envisioned. This may sometimes be difficult to for the printer to do, but customer expectations remain high. Overall, the level of print quality, driven by technological advances in digital imaging and printing methods, has improved with many products. When the quality issue is important, the printer and the customer must address it directly and openly so that misunderstandings in this area do not arise.

For successful printers, world-class customer service has become essential. These printers treat their customers with dignity regardless of the sizes of their jobs. Promises are always kept. Customers are treated as the only thing that matters and printing company employees take a personal interest in each customer's order so that communication is effective. This emphasis on communication minimizes problems and rework with the job. Customer inquiries are answered within the day they are asked, and customer suggestions to improve product service and quality are taken seriously. The successful printer encourages partnerships with customers and assists in technical and nontechnical areas of customer involvement. With the successful printer, no reasonable area of customer graphic need is left to chance.

The Stability of Offset Lithography

Manufacturing a printed product is divided into three sequenced operations: prepress, press, and postpress production. Although digital imaging has reconfigured the prepress area so extensively that EPP production is now the method of choice for initially imaging the job, press and postpress have, until now, remained less affected. In fact, in the past ten years, there has been only a slight shift relative to the choice of printing process, and it is generally acknowledged that lithography has lost little ground and remains the printing process of choice.

A number of reasons can be advanced for this slower digital transition in the pressroom. First, there is the momentum by which offset lithographic printing has remained the process of choice because no other process has yet proven continually superior in cost, quality, and image control. Offset lithography has been perfected over years of use—the process is controlled, printers understand how it works, and their collective experience with it is extensive. Offset lithography is predictable, dependable, and printers are comfortable with it.

The second reason, which is linked to the momentum offset lithography enjoys, is that collectively United States printers have invested billions of dollars in lithographic printing equipment. This huge investment base cannot be put aside on the chance that an emerging printing technology might be better. It is the rare printing manager who would risk abandoning a known printing process in which her company has invested heavily, regardless of how glamorous or sophisticated any new or emerging process might appear.

Third, technological change tends to be focused on resolving basic customer needs, which are then piggybacked to meet new demands in a spiraling pattern of development. Although DTP has faced this "customer-needs-drive-improvements" issue squarely, it is just beginning to be addressed in the press area. For example, early laser printers were slow and their quality was not very good. Over time, however, technical improvements were made to them, PostScript Level 2 became the accepted output language, and color imaging systems emerged. For a while customers were happy. However, happy customers can be happier, so these changes were followed by further technical improvements in color imaging and faster RIPping and by the concept that mass production of graphic images might be possible using exclusively digital production and not a lithographic printing press. Only in the past few years have basic customer needs and emerging digital technology been tied together in the press area, and lithographic press production has remained largely unaffected by this connection.

The fourth reason that digital transition has been slower in the pressroom is that significant changes that affect the structure of printing production tend to be moderated by the environment in which the changes occur. The ten-year paradigm shift of photomechanical prepress methods to DPP (from the mid-1980s to the mid-1990s) occurred in a production segment of the industry that was already chaotic and somewhat unstable. History has shown that press and postpress production have been more stable than prepress in process control, investment, payback, and similar quantitative measures. Thus, structural change in press and postpress have been slowed because their environment—the customers, employees, investment, payback time, energy, and motivation to change—has not forced extensive new paradigm shifts until recently.

Finally, it should be clear that important technological change in offset lithographic printing has occurred with regularity over the past ten years. This change has allowed offset lithographic production to compress time and maintain quality. Presses have been continuously enhanced using computer systems and microprocessors. The shift to centralized, electronic console systems for press operation has reduced the number of press operators and facilitated instantaneous image control during pressruns, which in turn has significantly cut press spoilage and other downtime losses. Makeready time has been reduced using digital plate scanning equipment, semiautomatic plate changing equipment, easier perfector changeover, quick plate cocking, and automatic washup systems. Electronic print monitoring devices have been developed to provide closed-loop process control throughout printing production and to facilitate troubleshooting and print problem resolution. The perfection and use of waterless printing has enhanced quality and has proven to be a responsive, controllable addition in the use of conventional press equipment. Positive sheet flow systems are used with most presses. Sheet output, which is measured in impressions per hour (iph), has increased significantly and cut costly press time during pressruns. Lithographic chemicals, plates, inks, and associated materials have improved and the quality of lithographically printed products remains excellent.

It is anticipated that emerging digital printing methods and waterless printing will erode various lithographic printing markets over time. This will not occur overnight, nor will it relegate offset lithographic printing to an unimportant or minor position in the printing production sequence for many years.

Waterless Printing

Waterless printing is the removal of water as a component in lithographic printing, and it is for this reason it is sometimes termed "waterless lithography." The perfection of waterless imaging in the mid-1980s by Toray Industries of Japan and the growing use of waterless printing throughout the world together represent a significant technology shift in the way images are mass produced. This is because the water in conventional printing, which is actually a mixture of water, gum arabic, acid, and alcohol or an alcohol substitute, either causes or contributes to a number of difficulties that have a bearing on image quality, press output, and material cost. Waterless technology is based on the simple principle that a specially formulated ink does not adhere to the silicone rubber areas of a printing plate but instead adheres to the nonsilicone areas of the plate. The process works this way: A waterless printing plate (or image carrier) is manufactured with an aluminum base coated with a photopolymer silicone rubber emulsion. After exposure to a film image, the plate is developed whereby the image areas have their silicone rubber removed and are blue-etched to make them more oleophilic. The areas where there are no images retain their silicone rubber coating. Once the plate is mounted on the press, the ink adheres to the blue-etched areas, which do not contain silicone, and thus become the image areas, while the silicone areas repel the ink and do not generate images.

The advantages of waterless printing are numerous and impressive. The problems of paper expansion, wrinkling, buckling, registration, ink adhesion, and ink drying are eliminated with this process. Reductions of these paper problems in turn reduce press makeready time and the cost of makeready, as well as the additional paper needed to make ready and run an order. Waterless inks, which are available through a number of United States ink companies, print sharply and cleanly, dry faster than conventional inks, and cause no chemical problems, such as emulsification, which inhibits drying. Printing problems such as ghosting, picking, glazing, dot gain, and color washout are all but eliminated with waterless printing. The correlation of color proofs to waterless press sheets has been largely reconciled. Waterless experience in Japan, where it was perfected, Australia, and Europe (where it has been used in some companies for ten years), provides proof of the quality of image reproduction time after time and job after job. Advantages of waterless printing include:

- Fountain solution is eliminated, which removes the need for mixing, monitoring, and related support.
- There is faster makeready with corresponding reductions of ink and paper spoilage.
- There is improved print definition and image clarity.
- Less ink is required to achieve desired densities.
- Ink/water balance problems are eliminated.
- Ink drying is faster.
- There is less dot gain and better image resolution.
- Finer screens can be printed with no related image problems.
- Color consistency is more easily maintained.
- Image removal as a plate correction is easily accomplished on press.
- Because the process is less complex to control, less experienced employees can be operate the equipment without significant loss of image quality or production output.
- There are possible new markets where high-quality printing is expected.

Among the important purposes of water in lithography is to serve as a coolant during the printing process. Because waterless printing removes this coolant, waterless inks must be cooled during printing or the process does not work. Two methods are used to cool inks in waterless printing. The more popular of the two is ink roller cooling, which requires a temperature-controlled mixture of water and ethylene glycol to be circulated through the rollers of the ink train. Each ink color is controlled separately; darker inks generally run at higher temperatures. The second method, air cooling, requires the installation of a fan at the plate-mounting location on the press. Cool air is blown on the plate and the warm air is extracted, thus providing a temperature-controlled environment. The air recirculation process is generally more energy efficient than roller cooling.

Both types of heat exchange require installing new pieces on the older lithographic presses or retrofitting the presses, which can be expensive. However, waterless printing is not possible without an ink temperature control system. Also, once a lithographic press has been converted to waterless production, it still can be used for lithographic printing if needed. All lithographic presses manufactured after 1994 are waterless capable without retrofitting. In addition to the ink-cooling problems of waterless printing, disadvantages include:

- Plates can be easily scratched, and plate scratching can lead to higher plate remakes.
- Press retrofitting for ink cooling can be expensive.
- The life of waterless plates may be shorter than the life of lithographic plates. (The mileage of Toray waterless plates is capped at approximately 150,000 impressions.)
- Waterless plates cost two to three times more than lithographic plates.
- Waterless inks cost approximately 35 percent more than lithographic inks.
- Press crews must be trained in a different technology.
- There is a risk in that successful waterless printing requires a complete commitment by management and employees.

Waterless production is effective for both sheetfed and web printing, but there are fewer web installations than sheetfed installations in the United States. The only waterless plate currently available is made by Toray Industries, which perfected the process that was first introduced by 3M in the 1960s. The cost of the plate is roughly two and one-half times higher than a conventional lithographic plate. The Heidelberg-DI and QM presses, which are discussed later in the chapter, operate exclusively using waterless technology.

Once the learning curve for waterless production is complete and crews are experienced with it, there are typically press production time savings. As noted in Figures 10.A2 through 10.A6 in the appendix to this chapter, assuming there is an experienced waterless press crew, there is a range of 10 percent to 30 percent time reduction in makeready and a 5 percent to 20 percent reduction in running hours. Additional cost savings from reduced paper needed for spoilage are also common and can be substantial over time because jobs make ready faster and run with fewer printing problems. Other cost savings result from reduced dampening maintenance time and faster job turnaround. It should be noted that any adjustment percentage should be based on the company's specific level of experience with waterless production. Such time and cost adjustments should be determined once the company has had sufficient experience with the process.

Cost increases for waterless production include higher costs for waterless plates and inks. Ink mileage, however, is approximately the same. Because the process has a learning curve that carries a cost burden, this cost should not be missed. The BHR cost system should be adjusted to recover for the additional investment cost if retrofitting for ink temperature control equipment is needed. However, there will be a corresponding savings from retrofitting in that there will be no lithographic dampening system or related system maintenance. Many newer multicolor presses are manufactured to be waterless compatible at little additional cost. These newer presses can run either with either lithographic or waterless processes.

Computer-to-Plate Technology

CTP systems, also termed direct-to-plate systems, provide for the generation of press-ready plates without intermediate materials or production steps. The emergence of CTP requires the convergence of, and skill in, four important prepress areas: digital file production, electronic imposition software, digital proofing, and digital/laser platemaking technology. A key ingredient to the success of CTP systems is the research and development of a new category of digitally imaged plates at a print quality level and cost value that are acceptable to printers.

The advantages of CTP systems are impressive and include the elimination of film imaging production and film materials, the elimination of table stripping, the elimination of conventional platemaking production and plate materials, the elimination of conventional proofing production and materials, and, because numerous prepress production steps have been automated, the expedited production of jobs. As these systems are perfected, the cost savings to printers is expected to be significant.

The four general types of plates that are the best digital plate emulsion or image carriers in CTP systems are: (1) silver halide plates, (2) electrophotographic plates, (3) high-speed photopolymer plates, and (4) spark discharge plates. Although various base materials have been researched, including plastic, aluminum remains the base substrate of choice. It is likely that the CTP systems most likely to emerge will implement one of these four types of plates and will use an imaging engine matched to the emulsion or type of image carrier.

Spark discharge CTP technology, which uses the fourth type of plate just mentioned, was successfully introduced in 1991 by Presstek in conjunction with the Heidelberg-DI press. Although the initial system was limited in image size and its quality was not very good, by 1993 Presstek's Pearl laser-diode ablation imaging technology improved in both quality and clarity for larger images. The link was also made from this technology to waterless printing, which has moved the Heidelberg-DI press into a major position relative to the POD technology discussed later in this chapter.

The printing and publishing industry eagerly awaits CTP technology as it is perfected. It is expected that CTP equipment will be positioned next to a printing press and that when the job is digitally ready it will be RIPped, plates will be generated and positioned on the press, a quick makeready will be necessary for image approval, and finally the job will be printed. The CTP system will be fully digital and changes will be made using digital methods only. One problem yet to be resolved is the development of a digital proofing system that can accurately correlate with the image quality produced using computer-generated plates. Of concern, too, is the cost of CTP equipment and its consumable materials compared to conventional photomechanical methods, because it is likely that this new technology will be expensive.

10.3   The Changing Environment of Traditional Sheetfed Print Production

Offset sheetfed press production, as with numerous other production centers in the emerging digital printing plant, is undergoing structural changes that point to significant long-term shifts for the industry.

Specific Areas Where Sheetfed Press Is Changing

Up through the mid-1980s, many printing managers emphasized the importance of the pressroom over other areas of printing production and focused much of their attention on pressroom performance as it related to job profitability. After all, the pressroom was both labor intensive and capital intensive, and it provided the company with a focused printed product as output, not as parts or segments of products as did prepress and finishing production. Maintaining pressroom efficiency was considered by some as the critical, controlling factor relative to job and company profitability, and many managers believed the pressroom was the area where the company "made or lost money."

However, changes are occurring that require the press manufacturing area of a printing plant to be viewed differently than in the past. These changes are briefly summarized as follows:

1. In many printing firms, there has been a noticeable philosophical shift in management focus away from production and toward marketing and customer service. Many progressive printing firms have moved away from past decades of being production driven and have been forced, largely by competitive pressures, to become both customer sensitive and market driven. An increasing number of company owners and managers realize that the true key to profitability in printing is not in precisely controlling production costs—even though cost control is important—but in serving customers and focusing on markets and clients that fit into the printers'

products and process orientations. The pressroom has become recognized as one key—but not the only key—to achieving true customer satisfaction and generating profits to continue in business.

2. The smoothing of EPP production and the interconnectedness to digital presses is an important emerging trend. A growing number of printers are evaluating the purchase of digital presses to handle fast-turnaround, short-run volume while continuing to use their existing press equipment for longer runs. Digital press production is discussed later in this chapter.

3. Along with the philosophical movement from production to marketing and customer service, many printing managers have become aware of the true meaning of the concept of value added (VA), whereby all productive work done on a given job should directly increase the value of that product to the customer. Thus, the actual presswork of the job is but one of many job ingredients that adds value to the customer's final product. Today, prepress and postpress operations have become recognized as important contributors that add value to a customer's product. For example, selling creative design skills for a job, doing the color separations required, completing sophisticated typesetting, foil stamping, die cutting, and special bindery operations are critical to giving the final printed product more value to the customer, and thus they contribute more profit to the printer. In sum, the pressroom is recognized as an important component of the VA process, but it is certainly not the only one.

4. The pressroom is no longer the production area with the greatest capital or labor intensity. Through the mid-1990s, there has been continuous and unabated change in prepress, including the addition of expensive electronic equipment of all kinds. Postpress equipment, too, has become more specialized, and printers have realized they need to install selected bindery equipment if they wish to offer such services for VA purposes. Also, to compete and survive, which means producing quality printing in faster response to customer demand, managers have been forced into installing this sophisticated prepress and bindery equipment in their manufacturing plants. Not only is much of this electronic equipment expensive, but it also requires considerable labor and training efforts, which increase the need for skilled, trained, and knowledgeable employees. In effect, both labor intensiveness and equipment costs have required printing management to take a broader, more encompassing view of the numerous profit centers in any printing plant.

5. Automation has reduced labor intensity everywhere in the pressroom. Linked to the labor demands brought on by prepress and bindery, press equipment manufacturers and vendors of pressroom supplies have worked to streamline production activities on the printing press. These efforts have allowed offset lithographic production to compress time yet maintain

quality. Consider the following important technological changes in sheet-fed press over the past few years:

- Makeready time has been reduced using digital plate scanning equipment, semiautomatic plate changing equipment, easier perfector changeover, quick plate cocking, and automatic washup systems.
- Feeder and delivery units have been redesigned to reduce paper waste and setup times, thereby further reducing press preparatory costs.
- Presses and press peripherals have been continuously enhanced using computer systems and microprocessors; positive sheet flow systems are standard equipment on all new presses and are retrofitted to older models.
- The shift to centralized, electronic console systems for press operation has reduced the number of press operators and facilitated instantaneous image control during pressruns, which has significantly cut press spoilage and other downtime losses and allowed for faster overall production.
- The electronic print monitoring devices built into the electronic console systems have been developed to provide closed-loop process control throughout printing production to facilitate troubleshooting and print problem resolution on the fly.
- Waterless printing has been perfected and is emerging as the process of choice for a growing number of printers, for both sheetfed and web production.
- Vendors of lithographic chemicals, plates, inks, and associated materials have worked to constantly improve their products and services.
- Press speeds, which are measured in iph, have increased significantly, cutting costly press time during pressruns.
- The emergence of employee empowerment, teamwork, and press crew training has improved the level of skill for pressroom employees.
- All of these advances have led to a net reduction in the number of pressroom employees, which has left the pressroom with fewer yet more highly skilled craftspeople/technicians.

6. Since the mid-1980s, there has been an increased focus on improving the productivity of the high-volume sheetfed pressroom, not only through technical press improvements but through the installation of 6-, 7-, and 8-unit multicolor printing presses. These large-unit multicolor presses improve productivity significantly because they require less press time by reducing the number of passes for the complex color work now demanded by customers. Presses printing seven or more colors allow for one-pass printing of hi-fi color, which prints process color CMYK plus three (or more) special accent colors to enrich color fidelity, and other emerging new color processes.

In some printing companies, the strategy of using multicolor press purchases has streamlined the production management process as well. As an example, purchasing all sheetfed presses in the same size, with variable numbers of printing units on each press, provides great scheduling flexibility. A 6-color, 1-sided order could be run on a 6-color press in one pass or, if that press were occupied, on 4-color and 2-color presses in two passes. Stripping is standardized to one size of press equipment and finishing is unchanged regardless of press choice.

Such improvements—scheduling efficiency, reduced prices through improved productivity, and controlled job delivery so fast-turnaround work can be more easily accommodated—are all essential keys to satisfying customers. They also ensure long-term profitability in the pressroom and, more globally, to the printing company over the long term.

The previous six points are not intended to reduce the importance of the press area. The importance of excellent presswork—producing the needed quantity and quality of product for the customer—cannot be overemphasized. The pressroom yields a critical graphic product that the customer will see and use, even though prepress and finishing contribute to the product's VA as well. In sum, there is no doubt that the pressroom represents a vital, critical area of printing production and is an important control point upon which the company may build its reputation.

The Issue of Press Overcapacity

Of major importance to both sheetfed and web press production is the ever-present issue of pressroom overcapacity. To put this issue another way, is there too much press time available within the press industry compared to the press time needed by the customers? If the answer is yes, will the situation change in the next few years as digital presses go on line to capture the short-run (under 2,000 copies) market?

Some experts argue that the significant increase of multicolor sheetfed presses, when coupled with faster and wider web presses and a group of emerging digital presses for shorter run color printing, has set up a situation whereby there is far more press capacity than there is existing printing volume from customers. Other experts say that there is no overcapacity because the sale of conventional sheetfed, web, and digital presses by equipment manufacturers has not yet shown any sign of reduction, and this is the key measure of overcapacity in their opinion.

Whether or not there is an inherent overcapacity in the printing industry is an issue that remains unclear. However, in light of the increasing number of multicolor sheetfed presses, faster and multiwide web presses, and short-run digital presses being sold, and in light of the higher costs of this highly sophisticated equipment, there is no question that profitable management for existing pressroom equipment is a vital issue for printing managers everywhere.

10.4   Increasing Sheetfed Pressroom Productivity

Productivity in the pressroom is an essential issue for most printers, particularly in light of the intense competition for printing jobs, the movement of customers to increasingly complex multicolor work, the substantially compressed delivery dates, and the investment cost of press equipment. The printing estimator or production planner should consider the recommendations discussed in the following sections to improve pressroom productivity.

Maximize Press Sheet Usage

No pressroom can be considered efficient unless equipment use is maximized. Every revolution of every press provides the capacity to print the maximum surface area of a press sheet. Efficient plants work diligently to maximize their pss using the following general approaches:

1. Images are maximized on the press sheet using EPP duplicating methods, film duplication/stripping techniques, or step-and-repeat platemaking procedures.
2. Press sheets are imposed using ganging techniques where different customer's jobs are combined. Here quality level, quantity, ink color, type of paper, and other job particulars must be matched.
3. When completing bookwork production, press sheets are imposed with the maximum number of pages per sheet, or signatures are ganged on a larger press sheet. Also, customers are informed when ordering bookwork products that smaller page sizes will require less paper, which saves the customer money and may also allow more pages per press sheet and fewer signatures per book.

Schedule Production Efficiently

Efficient production scheduling is important to profitability in the pressroom and can be streamlined by the CAS systems discussed in Chapter 2. A good CAS system should interface with the order entry, production planning, estimating, and inventory modules. The following scheduling points also deserve consideration:

1. Consistently identify and correct pressroom bottlenecks. This may require an extreme solution such as the purchase of a new press or a simple solution such as a revised imposition method or approach. Certain jobs

that consistently represent bottlenecks in the pressroom might be better purchased from a printer more suited to the work.

2. Press selection should be carefully made as early in the scheduling process as possible, taking into account key job factors such as run length, quality, and delivery date. The estimate typically provides these key production data regarding press production. The use of changeover points (COP), which are discussed later in this chapter, may also be of assistance in selecting the press.

3. Multicolor jobs should be scheduled in the most effective pattern. One way to ensure this is to buy all presses in the same size, but vary the number of printing units among the array of presses. For example, a company would purchase all 40-inch Komori presses broken out between 2-color presses, 4-color presses, and 6-color presses. Given this situation, prepress and stripping procedures could be standardized to the 40-inch size, and a 4-color job could be scheduled to run in one pass on one of the 4-color presses, or, if either press were unavailable, in two passes on the 2-color press. Such standardization of production allows greatly enhanced flexibility to meet delivery dates and the freedom to schedule multicolor work in the most effective, cost-saving manner.

Increase Press Efficiency

Increasing press efficiency is a key pressroom issue and of great concern to most printers because it deals with both cost and time issues. The four following ways are commonly used to increase press efficiency: (1) purchase and use automated press peripherals, (2) provide effective training for press employees, (3) focus on reducing press makeready times and costs, and (4) achieve maximum press speed during the pressrun.

There are numerous automated peripherals for sheetfed presses, including plate scanning equipment that provides ink density programming, semiautomatic plate changing systems, automatic blanket and ink washup systems, systems for precisely hanging and cocking plates, automated fountain solution monitoring devices, ink agitation systems, and many more. The test as to whether or not to purchase a peripheral is to determine the likelihood of its use on a daily, consistent, or frequent basis and the amount of time it will save over the long term. Thus, if the attachment will only be used in very special instances or its time savings will not be significant over a one-year period, it may be an unwise purchase.

There is no question that when pressroom employees are properly trained, considerable time and money is saved. It is best when training is administered in a condensed, concise form and is focused on quick trainee application of the material covered. Modular training methods where the subjects are broken up into building blocks of information are usually very effective for pressroom employees. Training should include information on how to work effectively in a team environment, and it should provide each employee with a sense of empowerment for making production decisions.

The more quickly a job moves from the makeready stage to the production of salable press sheets, the less the cost to the printer and the customer. This is a key point in keeping press costs down and being more competitive. Makeready time can be reduced by automating key makeready functions and by effectively training press employees in procedures to reduce makeready, both of which were previously discussed. New sheetfed presses are manufactured to allow minimum makeready time. Waterless production, when it is used by skilled employees, reduces makeready time as well.

Most newer presses are operated from master consoles and most image modifications during printing are quickly executed and controlled using closed-loop feedback systems. Console monitoring allows a skilled press operator to carefully establish a top running speed for the job while evaluating print quality on the fly. This type of monitoring also ensures maximum productivity during the press run and provides the most effective process control environment possible.

Modify Job Specifications

A number of changes can be suggested to the customer that will reduce job cost while increasing pressroom output. Customer approval should be obtained where approriate. The following list summarizes some alterations that might be offered:

1. Reduce the finish size (trimmed size) of the job, thereby allowing for an increase in the number of images imposed on the press sheet. Also consider reducing the amount of trim margin built into the press sheet.
2. Standardize paper stock so that only stocks that provide for efficient press output are used. Avoid paper that is too thick or too thin and stocks that are not suited to the selected printing process.
3. Make it plant policy to put all color to be printed in the fewest possible forms, but maximize color in the forms that are selected.
4. Modify the quality level of the job, perhaps from excellent to good, which may allow for increased press speeds and reduced makeready time. This consideration is especially important for customers who consistently purchase higher quality products than their use requirements dictate.
5. Produce work at quantity levels that are most suited to the individual production flow and press equipment of a given plant. Such work may involve short-run work for Plant A and long-run jobs for Plant B. Because of the high speeds that are achieved using web offset and gravure, consider

sending longer run work out or shifting it from sheetfed to in-plant webs after reviewing all related production factors.

10.5 Changeover Points for Estimating Offset Presswork

Changeover points (COPs), sometimes termed break-even points (BEPs), allow the estimator or production planner to compare different press outputs and thereby select the least costly press for the job under consideration. To accurately establish such a system, the estimator must identify prepress, makeready, and washup production costs (fixed costs); the BHR and production output rate for the presses to be compared; and a basic unit (BU) of output represented by a product common to all presses.

Figure 10.1 demonstrates how unit cost (UC) diminishes as volume increases, a situation that is typical of printing manufacturing. Fixed cost (FC), also called setup cost, includes those costs incurred during printing production that do not

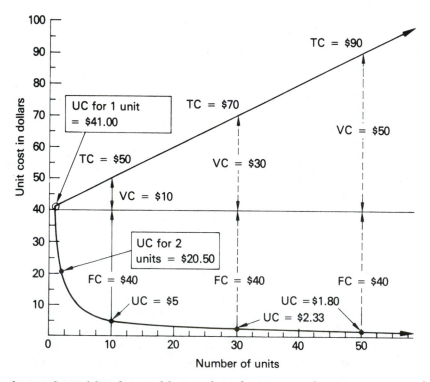

Figure 10.1 Relationship of fixed, variable, total, and unit costs for printing manufacturing.

change, such as taxes, depreciation, insurance, and preparatory presswork costs. Variable cost (VC) includes costs that increase as production continues, such as the cost of paper and presswork. Total cost (TC) represents the sum of FC and VC at a given quantity, and unit cost (UC) is determined by dividing TC by the number of units produced.

The following formulas and number substitutions clearly illustrate the relationship between FC, VC, TC, and UC. In Figure 10.1, the FC is $40.00 and the VC is $1.00 per unit, but these dollar figures are for illustrative purposes only.

$$TC = FC + (VC \text{ per unit x number of units produced})$$

$$UC = TC \div \text{number of units produced}$$

Thus, at 1 unit in Figure 10.1:

$$TC = \$40.00 + (\$1.00/\text{unit x 1 unit}) = \$41.00$$

$$UC = \$41.00 \div 1 \text{ unit} = \$41.00$$

At 10 units:

$$TC = \$40.00 + (\$1.00/\text{unit x 10 units}) = \$50.00$$

$$UC = \$50.00 \div 10 \text{ units} = \$5.00$$

At 30 units:

$$TC = \$40.00 + (\$1.00/\text{unit x 30 units}) = \$70.00$$

$$UC = \$70.00 \div 30 \text{ units} = \$2.33$$

As can be seen in Figure 10.1 and the previous number substitutions, the UC diminishes rapidly as the number of units increases. The reason is that while VC increases, the constant FC is spread out over a larger number of units produced, which diminishes the cost per unit. The conclusion is that the greater the quantity that is produced and sold for any given printing order, the less the UC, even though the TC increases as the quantity increases. Understanding this concept of diminishing UC and the definitions of FC and VC is necessary to better understand COP development.

As previously indicated, COP analysis requires the identification of three specific data: (1) the FC for the presses to be compared, (2) the applicable BHR, and (3) the appropriate production output in impressions per hour (imp./hr.). The BU of production, which is a specific size or type of product common to all presses under consideration, must also be carefully identified.

Example 10.1 that follows illustrates how to calculate a COP. The following formulas should be used for the calculations:

$$\text{dollars per M basic units} = \frac{\text{BHR} \div \text{impressions per hour (imp. /hr.)}}{\text{number up on press sheet}} \times 1,000 \text{ units}$$

$$\text{COP*} = \frac{\text{FC}^1 - \text{FC}^2}{\text{dollars per M basic units}^2 - \text{dollars per M basic units}^1}$$

*The COP formula is derived algebraically from $y = mx + b$, a formula used for linear graphing.

$$\text{TC} = \text{FC} + (\text{dollars per M basic units} \times \text{number of units})$$

Example 10.1. We want to determine the COP to compare a Komori S26 1-color (1/C) press and a Komori S226P perfecting 2-color (2/C) press. The BU for this comparison will be signatures printed one over one or one color on each side (1/1). Both presses will produce these signatures using a 1-16 SW configuration in two 8-page forms with an untrimmed page size of 8 1/2 inches x 11 inches. Both presses will print a 20 inch x 26 inch press sheet. Because the Komori S226P 2/C perfects, press sheets will require one pass, while printing on the S26 1/C will require two passes, one color for each side of the sheet. The 1/C press will also require 2 makereadies and 2 washups (there are 2 plates), while the Komori 2/C perfector will require 1 makeready that covers both printing units.

The table that follows represents current FC and VC data for each press. Figure 10.A2 in the appendix to this chapter has been used to provide data for each press. Schedule data for makeready and washup for both presses will be at average level. We have estimated that it will cost $46.00 to prepare the two plates needed for the job, and the plates are interchangeable to either press. The dollar figures used are for example only: A company developing its COP should use its most current FC and VC. Determine the COP for these two presses both mathematically and graphically.

	Fixed cost	
Prepress Production	**Komori S26 (1/C) (FC)**	**Komori 226P (2/C perfector)**
Preparatory	$ 46.00 (2 plates, 20 in. x 26 in.)	$ 46.00 (2 plates, 20 in. x 26 in.)
Makeready	$ 80.44 (0.5 hr. x 2 plates x BHR)	$121.41 (1.0 hr. x BHR for both plates)
Washup	$ 80.44 (0.5 hr. x 2 plates x BHR)	$ 78.92 (0.65 hr. x BHR for both plates)
Total setup cost	$206.88	$246.33

Presswork	Variable cost (VC)	
BHR	$80.44	$121.41
Production output	6,600 imp./hr.	6,600 imp./hr.

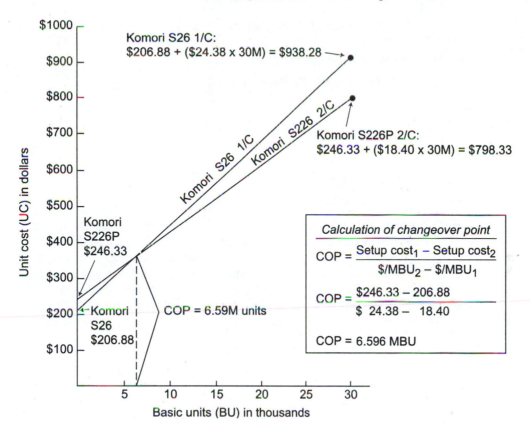

Figure 10.2 Changeover (or break-even) graph comparing a Komori S26 1/C press to a Komori S226P 2/C perfecting press producing 16-page signatures printed 1/1.

Solution

Use the formulas that precede the example in the text.

Step 1. Calculate the dollars per 1,000 basic units ($/MBU) for each press using the appropriate formula:

For the Komori S26:

$$[(\$80.44 \div 6,600 \text{ imp./hr.}) \div 1 \text{ sig.}] \times 1,000 \text{ units} \times$$
$$2 \text{ passes} = \$24.38/\text{MBU}$$

For the Komori 226P:

$$[(\$121.41 \div 6,600 \text{ imp./hr.}) \div 1 \text{ sig.}] \times 1,000 \text{ units} \times$$
$$1 \text{ pass} = \$18.40/\text{MBU}$$

Step 2. Determine the TC for each press at 30 M signatures using the appropriate formula:

For the Komori S26:

$$\$206.88 + (\$24.38/MBU \times 30 \text{ M sigs.}) = \$938.28$$

For the Komori 226P:

$$\$246.33 + (\$18.40/MBU \times 30 \text{ M sigs.}) = \$798.33$$

Step 3. Calculate the COP using the appropriate formula:

$$[\$246.33 - \$206.88] \div [\$24.38 - \$18.40] =$$
$$6.59 \text{ MBU sigs. (approximately)}$$

The COP of 6.59 MBU means that the 1/C Komori S26 is the more cost-effective press up to 6,590 BU (16-page signatures printing 1/1, requiring two passes to complete the job), after which the 2/C Komori 226P (printing 16-page signatures 1/1, but perfecting and printing finished sigs in one pass) provides a better cost advantage. Thus, at 6,590 signatures, the costs are the same with either press. The greater the number away from 6,590 basic units—either more than or less than 6,590 BU—the greater the cost savings for the respective printing press.

Step 4. Using graph paper, label the vertical axis "UC in dollars" and the horizontal axis "BU in thousands." First plot the 1/C Komori S26 and Komori 226 FCs along the cost axis (which is FC only, at 0 quantity), and then plot the TC for each press at the 30,000 quantity level. (See Step 2 for TC calculations for each press.) Once these pairs of points are located accurately, use a ruler to connect the Komori S26 points, and then connect the Komori 226P points. The lines should cross at approximately 6.59 MBU, as noted in Figure 10.2.

It is most important to note that COPs are affected by slight changes in FC or VC factors, by modification of equipment output, or by a change in the BU. The system can be used to compare sheetfed presses to sheetfed presses, sheetfed presses to web presses, or web presses to web presses. As long as the BU is the same, any number of presses can be plotted on the same graph to compare multiple press outputs.

Estimators use the COP system to enable them to make quick production and press cost comparisons for standard company product lines. Of course, all input data should be accurate and updated to reflect the most current costs incurred during production.

When a computer system is asked to make a cost comparison and to pick a press or other piece of equipment automatically, which are common requests made of the CGE systems discussed in Chapter 2, the use of the COP process is usually employed. This requires generating FC and VC data as demonstrated in

Example 10.1 and processing these data using the COP formula shown in Step 3 of Example 10.1. Graphing procedures are not frequently used because the formula provides the same result automatically.

10.6 Estimating Sheetfed Offset Presswork

Even though emerging digital presses and webfed presses have begun to compete with sheetfed presses in certain short-run and long-run markets, sheetfed offset still represents a major force in producing the bulk of printed goods in the United States. Figures 10.A1 to 10.A6 in the appendix to this chapter are provided for estimating sheetfed lithographic times and costs. The indicated cost rates and standard production times are likely to change from plant to plant and should be developed on an individual plant basis for accuracy. Chapters 2 and 3 discuss data collection and the methods to develop these standards.

The following clarifies industry terminology when estimating press and discussing printing orders. Sheetfed presses are referenced by the number of printing units they have using the following notation: 1/C (1-color), 2/C (2-color), 4/C (4-color), 5/C (5-color), 6/C (6-color), and so on. A job to be printed is typically referenced by the number of colors printed on each side, such as "4 over 2," which is also written 4/2. This means that the job will print four colors on one side and two on the back side, and it will therefore require six plates.

The term "pass" means that a sheet goes through a press and is printed for the number of units (colors) that have been arranged. If a sheet were passed through a 4/C press, it would print four colors on one side and no colors on the back of the sheet, or 4/0. This is known as a straight mode. All presses print in the straight mode, but some multicolor presses can print in a perfecting mode as well. "Perfecting' means that the sheet is printed on both sides during one press pass. Sometimes the term "simplex" or "simplexing" is used to describe printing on one side of the sheet, and the term "duplex" or "duplexing" is used to describe printing on both sides.

If a 2/C press is a perfector, it can be set up to print in two different modes: 2/0, which is not perfecting (straight mode), or 1/1, which is perfecting. If a 4/C press perfects, it can print 4/0 (straight mode) or 2/2 (perfecting mode). Sometimes a multicolor press perfects in more than one mode. For example, a 6/C press may perfect in 4/2 or 5/1 depending on the job requirements. The switching of presses between modes is a function of makeready time for multicolor presses. Some estimators use a higher makeready level, such as difficult instead of average, to adjust for the extra time needed to complete the mode change, while other estimators simply add time to the regular makeready hours based on established plant data on changeover times.

When an estimate is being prepared, the job under consideration must be carefully analyzed and broken down in detail. This analysis ensures that the proper categories of makeready and press preparation, running, and washup are used. As is noted later, both the makeready and press preparation category and the running category are subdivided into simple, average, and difficult levels; washup is either single or double depending upon the next color on the press. Sometimes makeready is estimated at average level while running is assessed at difficult or simple.

Each job must be analyzed and categorized individually during estimating. Most printing companies establish standard operating procedures (SOPs) for assigning their levels of makeready, running, and washup so that most jobs can be quickly estimated. Some companies develop specific categories to cover their types of presswork and do not use the catchall categories of simple, average, and difficult.

The following defines the parameters by which the schedule data can be applied:

Makeready and Press Preparation

Simple: These jobs are not complex and do not require special paper stocks.

Average: These are more complex jobs with more intricate images and multicolor printing that will take more time to make ready.

Difficult: These are the most difficult jobs the company does. These typically include high-quality, process color, and multicolor printing jobs that require precise registration. Also, unusual paper stocks and jobs with heavy ink coverage, varnishes, and coatings are covered here.

Press Running

Simple: These are jobs that run without feeding, image transfer, or other problems. The stock here is 0.003 inch to 0.006 inch thick.

Average: These are more complex jobs with more intricate images and multicolor printing that take more time to run because press speed must be reduced. The paper stock in this category is between 0.002 inch to 0.003 inch and 0.006 inch to 0.008 inch thick.

Difficult: These jobs typically include high-quality, process color, and multicolor printing that requires precise registration and thus lower press speeds. Also, unusual paper stocks and jobs with heavy ink coverage, varnishes, and coatings are covered in this classification. Stock is thinner than 0.002 inch or thicker than 0.008 inch.

Washup

Single: This is used in the case when a like ink color is used for the next job, such as when a light ink is to be changed to a similar light ink or when a dark ink is to be changed to another dark ink (use the single chart figure because one washup is required).

Double: This covers dark ink to be changed to a lighter ink for the next job (double the chart figure because two washups are required).

The following formulas are used with the offset presswork estimating schedules to estimate sheetfed production time and cost:

total number of press sheets required = (total number of finished pieces up on the press sheet) x (spoilage percentage + 100 percent)

makeready and press preparation production time = number of forms per job x hours per form for makeready and press preparation

hours of press time per form = total number of press sheets required ÷ number of impressions per hour per form

press running time = hours of press time per form x number of forms per job

number of washups per form = hours of press time per form ÷ hours of press time per form per washup

production time for washups = number of washups per form x hours of washup time per form x number of forms per job

total production time per job = makeready and preparation production time + press running time + production time for washups

total production cost per job = total production time per job x press BHR

Note: All rounding is up to the nearest whole digit (see Step 4 of Example 10.2 that follows.)

Example 10.2. A customer wants an estimate for 26,000 3-color letterheads to be printed in black, red, and blue. Letterheads will run 4-up on a Heidelberg MO 1-color press on a press sheet measuring 17 1/2 inches x 22 1/2 inches (which is smaller than the maximum size press sheet of 20 inches x 26 inches). Finish size for the product will be 8 1/2 inches x 11 inches. Makeready and press preparation will be at the average level with the press running at difficult level. One washup will be done for each 5 hours of press time per form and per color. Use a single wash for black and blue and a double wash for red. Add 9 percent spoilage to the base number of press sheets required (3 percent per color). Determine the press time and total press cost using schedule data and a BHR at 70 percent.

Solution

Use Figure 10.A2 in the appendix to this chapter and the preceding formulas.

Step 1. Determine the number of press size sheets required:

(26,000 pcs. ÷ 4-up) x (0.09 + 1.00) = 6,500 pss x 1.09 = 7,085 pss

Step 2. Determine the total time for makeready and press preparation of 3 forms (black, red, and blue):

$$3 \text{ fm. x } 0.5 \text{ hr./fm.} = 1.50 \text{ hr.}$$

Step 3. Determine the total press running time:
Hours of press time per form:

$$7,085 \text{ pss} \div 6,000 \text{ imp./hr.} = 1.18 \text{ hr./fm.}$$

Press running time:

$$1.18 \text{ hr./fm. x } 3 \text{ fm.} = 3.54 \text{ hr.}$$

Step 4. Determine the total time for washups (wu) using the following formula. Round decimal answers to the next whole number and use the resulting value to locate the hours of washup time per form in the appropriate estimating schedule.
Number of washups per form:

$$1.18 \text{ hr./fm.} \div 5 \text{ hr./fm./wu.} = 0.24 \text{ wu./fm. (which}$$
$$\text{rounds up to } 1 \text{ wu./fm.)}$$

Time for 2 washups at single rate (black and blue):

$$0.50 \text{ hr./wu. x } 2 \text{ wu./fm.} = 1.00 \text{ hr.}$$

Time for 1 washup at double rate (red):

$$0.50 \text{ hr./wu. x } 2 \text{ x } 1 \text{ wu.} = 1.00 \text{ hr.}$$

Total washup time:

$$1.00 \text{ hr.} + 1.00 \text{ hr.} = 2.00 \text{ hr.}$$

Step 5. Determine the total production time and cost:
Total production time:

$$1.50 \text{ hr.} + 3.54 \text{ hr.} + 2.00 \text{ hr.} = 7.04 \text{ hr.}$$

Total production cost:

$$7.04 \text{ hr. x } \$83.77 = \$589.74$$

Example 10.3. We have an order for 260,000 postcards (4 inch x 6 1/2 inch finish size) to print 5/2 on a 5-color press and a 2-color press in our plant. A Komori 540 Lithrone (28 inch x 40 inch press, 5-color, BHR $411.93) will be used for the process run, and a 2/C Heidelberg SORSZ for the 2-color black. Add a flat 12 percent spoilage to the base number of press sheets to cover all passes on both presses. Average level will be used for preparation, difficult level will be used for running, and there will be one washup per each 4 hours of presswork per form set or pair. The 5-color press has an additional feeder operator to be added. Determine the press time and total press cost using schedule data and a BHR at 70 percent.

Solution

Use Figures 10.A2 and 10.A4 in the appendix to this chapter and the appropriate formulas.

Step 1. Determine the number of pss required:

$$(260,000 \text{ pcs.} \div 40\text{-up}) \times (0.12 + 1.00) = 6,500 \text{ pss} \times 1.12 = 7,280 \text{ pss}$$

Step 2. Determine the total time for makeready and press preparation on the Komori 540 Lithrone for 1 form set of 5 colors:

$$1 \text{ fm. set} \times 2.00 \text{ hr./fm. set} = 2.00 \text{ hr.}$$

Step 3. Determine the total press running time for the Komori 540 Lithrone: Hours of press time per form set:

$$7,280 \text{ pss} + 6,500 \text{ imp./hr.} = 1.12 \text{ hr.}$$

Total hours of press time for 1 form set (5 colors):

$$1 \text{ fm. set} \times 1.12 \text{ hr./fm. set} = 1.12 \text{ hr.}$$

Step 4. Determine the total washup time for the Komori 540 Lithrone: Number of washups per form set:

$$1.12 \text{ hr./fm. set} \div 4 \text{ hr./fm. set/wu.} = 0.28 \text{ wu./fm. set (which} \\ \text{rounds up to 1 wu./fm. set)}$$

Total time for washups:

$$1 \text{ wu./fm. set} \times 1 \text{ fm. set.} \times 1.50 \text{ hr./wu.} = 1.50 \text{ hr.}$$

Step 5. Determine the total production time and cost for the Komori 540 Lithrone:
Total production time:

$$2.00 \text{ hr.} + 1.12 \text{ hr.} + 1.50 \text{ hr.} = 4.62 \text{ hr.}$$

Total production cost:

$$4.62 \text{ hr.} \times (\$411.93 + \$37.42)/\text{hr.} = \$2,076.00$$

Step 6. Determine the total time for makeready and press preparation on the Heidelberg SORS:

$$1 \text{ fm. pr.} \times 1.20 \text{ hr./fm.} = 1.20 \text{ hr.}$$

Step 7. Determine the total press running time for the Heidelberg SORSZ:

Hours of press time per form:

$$7{,}280 \text{ pss} \div 6{,}000 \text{ imp./hr.} = 1.21 \text{ hr.}$$

Total hours of press time for 1 form:

$$1 \text{ fm. pr.} \times 1.21 \text{ hr./fm.} = 1.21 \text{ hr.}$$

Step 8. Determine the total washup time for the Heidelberg SORSZ:
Number of washups per form:

$$1.21 \text{ hr./fm.} \div 4 \text{ hr./fm./wu.} = 0.30 \text{ wu./fm. (which}$$
$$\text{rounds up to 1 wu./fm.)}$$

Total time for washups:

$$1 \text{ wu./fm.} \times 1 \text{ fm.} \times 0.90 \text{ hr./wu.} = 0.90 \text{ hr.}$$

Step 9. Determine the total production time and cost for the Heidelberg SORS:
Total production time:

$$1.20 \text{ hr.} + 1.21 \text{ hr.} + 0.90 \text{ hr.} = 3.31 \text{ hr.}$$

Total production cost:

$$3.31 \text{ hr.} \times \$147.60/\text{hr.} = \$488.56$$

Step 10. Determine the total production time and cost for both presses:
Total production time:

$$4.62 \text{ hr.} + 3.31 \text{ hr.} = 7.93 \text{ hr.}$$

Total production cost:

$$\$2{,}076.00 + \$488.56 = \$2{,}564.56$$

Example 10.4. A local church group wants 24,000 16-page booklets printed to detail its church's 100-year history. Untrimmed page size is 8 3/4 inches x 11 3/4 inches, which trims to an 8 1/2 inch x 11 inch final page size. The booklets will print on a 440 Akiyama (28 inch x 40 inch) perfecting console press with a BHR of $330.90, running waterless. The job will run in 1-16 SW with black text and a spot red PMS second color throughout for paragraph heads and duotones (to register to black halftones). Use average level for makeready/press preparation and running and single washups with one wash per each 4 hours of press time per form or any fraction thereof. Add 2 percent per plate to the base number of press sheets for spoilage (for a total of 8 percent), which includes reduced spoilage for waterless. The job will perfect to print 2/2 and be completed in one press pass. Waterless production will allow a 20 percent deduction from total makeready time and a 15 percent deduction from total running time. Determine the press time and total press cost using schedule data and a BHR at 70 percent.

Solution

Use Figure 10.A3 in the appendix to this chapter and the appropriate formulas.

The booklet will run in 1-16 SW with 2 black and 2 spot red PMS plates. Each form will contain 8 pages and the untrimmed press sheet will be 22 1/2 inches x 35 inches.

	Outside	Inside	
	1	2	
	4	3	
	5	6	
Form I (black)	8	7	Form II (black)
Form III (red)	9	10	Form IV (red)
	12	11	
	13	14	
	16	15	

Step 1. Determine the press size sheet and form chart data confirmation:

$$\frac{28 \text{ in.} \times 40 \text{ in.}}{8\frac{3}{4} \text{ in.} \times 11\frac{1}{4} \text{ in.}} = 4 \times 2 = 8 \text{ pp./fm.}$$

$$8 \text{ 3/4 in. x 11 1/4 in.}$$

$$8 \text{ pp./fm x 2 fm.} = 16 \text{ pp./sig. on a 22 1/2 in. x 35 in. pss}$$

Therefore, for production, 1 pss = 1 sig. of 16 pp.

Step 2. Determine the total number of press sheets (signatures) required:

$$24,000 \text{ pcs. x } (0.08 + 1.00) = 25,920 \text{ pss}$$

Step 3. Determine the total time for makeready and press preparation:

$$2.25 \text{ hr./fm. set x 1 fm. set} = 2.25 \text{ hr.}$$

$$2.25 \text{ hr.} - (0.20 \text{ x } 2.25) \text{ for waterless} = 1.8 \text{ hr.}$$

Step 4. Determine the press running time:
Hours of press time per form:

$$25,920 \text{ pss} \div 7,800 \text{ imp./hr.} = 3.32 \text{ hr. x 1 pass} = 3.32 \text{ hr.}$$

$$3.32 \text{ hr.} - (0.15 \text{ x } 3.32) \text{ for waterless} = 2.82 \text{ hr.}$$

Step 5. Determine the total washup time:
Number of washups per form set:

$$2.82 \text{ hr./fm. set} \div 4 \text{ hr./fm./wu.} = 0.71 \text{ wu./fm. (which rounds up to 1 wu./fm. set)}$$

Total time for washups:

$$1 \text{ wu./fm. set x 1 fm. set x 1.00 hr./wu.} = 1.00 \text{ hr.}$$

Step 6. Determine the total production time and cost:
Total production time:

$$1.80 \text{ hr.} + 2.82 \text{ hr.} + 1.00 \text{ hr.} = 5.62 \text{ hr.}$$

Total production cost:

$$5.62 \text{ hr. x } \$330.90/\text{hr.} = \$1,859.66$$

Example 10.5. We want to compare the church booklet job in Example 10.4, which ran 2/2 on our waterless 4-color perfector, with printing that same job on our new waterless 8-color perfecting Komori 840 Lithrone (BHR $564.42). The job will still run in 1-16 SW on a press size sheet of 22 1/2 inches x 35 inches and print in one pass, but it will run 4/4. Use average level for makeready/press preparation and running and single washups with one wash per each 4 hours of press time per form set or any fraction thereof. Add 10 percent to the base number of press sheets for spoilage using 1.25 percent per form. Waterless production will allow a 20 percent deduction from total makeready time and a 15 percent deduction from total running time. Add for one floor help person and one feeder operator. Determine the press time and total press cost using schedule data and a BHR at 70 percent.

Solution

Use Figure 10.A6 in the appendix to this chapter and the appropriate formulas.

Step 1. The booklet will run in 1-16 SW on a 22 1/2 inch x 35 inch press sheet. Each form will contain 8 pages. The press will print one side of the sheet with CMYK and then flip to print the other side with CMYK, so one pass will print the entire job.

Step 2. Determine the number of press size sheets required:

$$24,000 \text{ pcs. x } (0.10 + 1.00) = 26,400 \text{ pss}$$

Step 3. Determine the total time for makeready and press preparation for 1 form set (8 plates):

$$2 \text{ fm. sets x } 2.20 \text{ hr./fm. set} = 2.20 \text{ hr.}$$

$$2.20 \text{ hr.} - (0.20 \times 2.20) \text{ for waterless} = 1.76 \text{ hr.}$$

Step 4. Determine the total press running time:
Hours of press time per form set (8 plates):

$$26,400 \text{ pss} \div 7,800 \text{ imp./hr.} = 3.38 \text{ hr. x 1 pass} = 3.38 \text{ hr.}$$

$$3.38 \text{ hr.} - (0.15 \times 3.38) \text{ for waterless} = 2.87 \text{ hr.}$$

Step 5. Determine the total washup time:
Number of washups per form set:

$$2.87 \text{ hr./fm. set} \div 4 \text{ hr./fm. set/wu.} = 0.72 \text{ wu./fm. set (which}$$
$$\text{rounds up to 1 wu./fm. set)}$$

Total time for washups:

$$1 \text{ wu./fm. set x 1 fm. set x } 1.80 \text{ hr./wu.} = 1.80 \text{ hr.}$$

Step 6. Determine the total production time and cost:
Total production time:

$$1.76 \text{ hr.} + 2.87 \text{ hr.} + 1.80 \text{ hr.} = 6.43 \text{ hr.}$$

Total production cost:

$$6.43 \text{ hr. x } (\$564.42 + \$29.69 + \$41.87)/\text{hr.} = \$4,089.35$$

10.7 Sheetfed Presswork Estimating Tips

Because of the capital and labor intensiveness of the pressrooms in most printing plants, estimating presswork may be a make-or-break proposition for even the most cautious estimator. The following pointers are offered to aid the estimator when dealing with presswork estimating:

1. Whenever possible, try to fill the press sheet completely with salable images. This reduces expensive press time per image printed. When production costs are decreased, the company becomes more cost competitive and is likely to experience a volume increase. Be aware, however, that filling the press sheet may increase certain prepress costs for film duplication, additional digital film output, or step-and-repeat procedures.
2. Throughout the plant, and especially in the pressroom, lock production into standard operating procedures (SOPs). This production ingredient is

common to most high-profit printers. Standardization allows for easy development of COP data because the BU for production comparison is the same.

3. Develop pressroom changeover charts using your own specific production data and costs.

4. Constantly monitor existing production standards and costs, especially in the capital-intensive press area. Develop a standard production manual with BHRs and hourly production standards using an accurate collection of historic production data.

5. When estimating with the applicable presswork charts and schedules, be careful to categorize each job into the appropriate section. Remember that it is possible to develop additional categories of data, such as "very simple" or "super difficult," for types of work that do not fit into existing divisions.

6. Investigate the profitability of specialized products, including black-and-white printing, multicolor work, and specific niches or markets that fit press equipment capacity and process. Gear sales toward the type of work that is most profitable at quantity and quality levels most appropriate for your company.

7. Consider buying out press sheets from other printers when presswork is not typical of your usual production. Carefully investigate cost differences by comparing minimal production charges against buyouts from other printers. As production becomes more specialized, which is an important key to company profitability, cost savings on buyouts of printed press sheets may become substantial.

8. During the estimating process, check the job under consideration with pressroom production scheduling. If the job is awarded to your company, production and delivery aspects will have already been given an initial review. Meeting the customer's delivery date is among the most important areas of customer VA.

9. As an estimator, be able to identify common printing problems, bottlenecks that occur in the pressroom, and related pressroom activities. When a pattern can be identified, modify presswork estimating schedules to compensate.

10. Develop an understanding of the integrated duties and responsibilities of pressroom personnel and the presses they use. Attempt to learn how they work on a daily basis. Learn how they approach each job, the shortcuts they might take, and the working styles they use that affects production time and cost.

10.8 Print-on-Demand and Digital Press Technology

POD and DPP technology have converged to provide print buyers reduced job turnaround time, a flexible imaging environment, and lower high inventory costs because quantities are limited to immediate need only. Although run lengths are short and job turnaround is fast, however, the quality of the printed image can vary, and the price can fluctuate widely. The following provides information regarding this important paradigm shift that affects many buyers of print media and the printers who serve them.

Overview of Print-on-Demand

POD, also known as on-demand or JIT printing, is the most important paradigm shift to affect the printing industry since the development of photomechanical offset lithographic technology in the early 1950s. The POD system affects all aspects of a printing company—customers, sales, production, employees, suppliers, and the management methods that bind these company activities. Furthermore, there is no area of the printing industry that will be untouched as POD systems are enhanced and perfected. There will be very few United States printers—commercial or specialized, large or small, in a big city or a small town—who will be able to ignore the impact of POD on their businesses.

POD is the graphic reproduction of a customer's order to meet the product demands and quantity requirements the customer has established. Its advantages are fast production turnaround, the option of limited quantities at reasonable cost, the ability to print from desktop files, and generally good quality. Typically POD lead time is short and quantities are carefully established by the customer to meet immediate inventory needs. POD is not a "while-you-wait" printing system, although that is possible, but is instead mass reproduction of images to paper to meet an immediate customer graphic need.

Image input for POD can be by mechanical art as reflection copy or by electronic file transmitted via network or magnetic media. Because POD is typically geared to meet the customer's immediate graphic imaging need and not the customer's long-term graphic need unless desired, the customer can order precisely the quantity needed to meet the event or condition of the time. This means that there are no print-to-inventory issues, which allows customers to utilize JIT inventory systems for their printing needs and therefore save money and warehouse space. Because most POD systems integrate DTP, they accept electronic art or mechanical art. As a result, changing images between printing orders can be easily done by the customer on her DTP equipment, which provides unparalleled imaging flexibility. Some POD systems allow variable imaging on each sheet printed, thus making it possible to personalize each sheet for an identified person or group.

POD methods have branched into separate process areas: direct digital output at the desktop, short-run black-and-white and color copying, document production, digital press production, and large format imaging. Supporting these process areas are emerging technology enhancements that include CTP technology and waterless production.

The advantages of limited-run digital printing are numerous. Jobs can be produced with minimum FC because they are generated from DTP files and bypass photomechanical film, plates, and stripping operations. Digital files can be easily corrected and files can be customized quickly. There is very little paper spoilage in this process and generally the imaging materials are environmentally friendly. Disadvantages of limited-run digital printing include high initial investment cost and a technology that is not yet fully perfected. Print quality is not always as bright, crisp, and clarified as customers can obtain with conventional printing. Because the systems are digital and not mechanically driven as offset presses are, essential equipment maintenance must be completed by trained technicians from the manufacturer of the equipment. Finally, there is an inherent inflexibility of paper sizes and types of paper that can be successfully printed in limited runs, while sheetfed offset presses do not have this problem.

Defining Print-on-Demand Run Length Quantities

For the purposes of this discussion, "very short run" is defined as a job with from 10 to 100 copies of the same image, "short run" is any job with from 101 to 500 copies, "medium run" covers from 501 to 2,000 copies, and "long-run" jobs are over 2,000 copies. The term "limited run" covers quantities from 10 to 1,000 copies. These quantity levels are suggested because there is no quantity standard currently accepted throughout the printing and publishing industry by which POD data are evaluated.

Size and Scope of the Print-on-Demand Market

Based on 1993 data from Charles A. Pesko Ventures, the printing industry-including electrostatic, sheetfed, and web printing—was an $83 billion market. Of this total, Pesko Ventures indicates that $38 billion was linked to jobs that were 5,000 copies or fewer. Jeffrey Hayes, of Pesko Ventures, indicated that "short-run printing is the single fastest growing segment of commercial and quick printing, growing two to three times faster than the rest of the industry." It appears likely that the market share of limited quantity printing is likely to increase at the expense of longer run jobs.

In general, the market demand for limited-run printing is being met by service bureaus and commercial printers. However, trade shops and large corporation in-plants are poised to purchase this equipment and provide these products on fast-turnaround bases. As the technology is improved and becomes more popular and available, advertising, specialized product promotion, narrow-market catalogs, and short-run color publications are likely to be prime purchasers.

Direct Digital Output at the Desktop for up to Ten Copies

There have been significant improvements in the quality, speed, and reliability of digital output devices used with DTP. In general, these units are used to produce single or limited copies of digital files for proofing purposes. Both monochromatic and color output devices are in wide use. Chapter 8 provides details on these systems and how they are estimated with EPP production.

Very Short-Run Black-and-White and Color Printing

Despite their generally low ranking in the hierarchy of printing methods, black-and-white and color copiers are projected to produce an increasing volume through the year 2000, particularly in the very short-run range of ten to 100 copies. An important issue is defining the line between proofing output and printing/copying production. This issue remains cloudy and will likely be decided by vendor competition as it relates to cost and quality, and especially as it relates to the short-run color imaging market.

Given the movement to DTP and the considerable interest in digital output for more than a few copies to meet proof or review purposes, short-run printing/copying equipment has emerged as a frontline POD method. It is likely that this segment of the printing industry will experience significant growth in the next few years as systems become available and costs become reduced with volume increases.

Black-and white units include the Xerox 5090 and numerous other plain paper copiers, while short-run color systems include the Canon CLC Color Copier and an emerging group of color copying systems. Chapter 8 covers estimating data for low-cost digital color proofing and digital color laser proofing output.

High-Speed Document Production

The expedited production of documents to meet the demands of government, education, the military, and the commercial graphics industry is an important and large target market. High-speed copiers such as the Xerox 5090 have long been used to meet this demand, and the emergence of the Xerox DocuTech in 1991 has moved this demand into the system of choice for longer run, high-speed document production.

The DocuTech is an extremely fast, in-line graphic imaging system. It provides complete digital imaging, printing, and finishing capability in line and at very high speed. Because the unit is self-contained and interconnected between prepress, printing, and finishing, one trained operator can produce numerous jobs and thousands of properly imaged sheets in a single shift.

Two DocuTech models are available: the DocuTech 90 and the DocuTech 135, which produce 90 copies per minute and 135 copies per minute respectively. Each DocuTech unit consists of a dual computer front end, an electronic scanner, a printing unit, and a finishing unit. Scanning is fast and allows for flexible digital imaging of many types of copy; a connection to any digital network provides an input source of digital files from remote computer locations. Printing is extremely fast using a laser-driven imaging system patented by Xerox. In-line stapling and hot glue binding capabilities are standard equipment on these machines. Peripheral equipment includes web in-feeding and a range of binding options that allow the in-line production of perfect-bound books and manuals with separately printed covers.

DocuTech production is extremely fast once the images are digitally available to the printing unit. Paper can be imaged either in simplex (printed one side) or duplex (printed two sides) mode at very high speed. Image quality is generally good, especially given the high speed capacity, but current models only provide monochromatic (black-and-white) output. Any type of paper substrate can be printed on these machines, but size is limited to a maximum of 11 inches x 17 inches. The 8 1/2 inch x 11 inch size is the most popular.

The DocuTech is a high-capacity printing unit that is marketed and sold to replace traditional single-color offset presses. Customers and markets are fairly easy to identify, which makes commercial application very competitive. DocuTech installations are typically governments, large corporations, and educational institutions throughout the world. The cost of the equipment begins at about $250,000, so DocuTech requires a customer base with high-volume needs to be justified. The DocuTech 135 is targeted to produce 3 million copies per month on a one-shift basis, and multiple shifts allow for even greater production output. Because maintenance of a DocuTech is essential and can be costly, a maintenance contract is prudent if the machine will be used heavily.

The DocuTech has redefined single-color imaging methods. It is expected that a large portion of single-color offset printing will move to the DocuTech or similar competing POD systems by the year 2000.

Digital Printing Production

Digital printing, also known as direct-to-press printing, is considered by many printing industry and digital imaging experts as the core area of technological revolution in the pressroom. Digital presses are the result of a clear need for high-quality printed products that avoid the time and expense of photomechanical production and that can be imaged directly from desktop digital files. For purposes of this discussion, the run length of digital presses typically ranges from 51 to 500 copies, although larger quantities are sometimes produced. Digital presses include Agfa's ChromaPress, the Heidelberg-DI and Heidelberg QM presses, Indigo E-Print 1000, Scitex Spontane, Xeikon DCP-1, and digital duplicators. Each is discussed briefly in the following.

Agfa ChromaPress. The Agfa ChromaPress and the Xeikon DCP-1 (discussed later) utilize the same printing engine (the same imaging system from which printing to a substrate is completed), but the front end of the ChromaPress is very different from that utilized in its prepress technology. The ChromaPress is centered around a workflow management system that integrates and automates production steps. Input software titled ChromaPost provides designer control over the color management of the job, while ChromaWatch tracks and prepares jobs using Ultimate Technologies ImpoStrip. Once jobs are imposed and output ready, Agfa's ChromaWrite inserts the job into the print queue, passes files to the RIP, and monitors the status of the printing process. Initial cost, including Agfa's proprietary, integrated software, is $300,000.

Heidelberg-DI and Heidelberg QM. The Heidelberg-DI press and the companion Heidelberg QM are a marriage of conventional offset technology, digital imaging methods, and waterless printing. Both the DI and QM systems have three component segments: (1) the Presstek Pearl spark discharge laser imaging system for imaging plates directly on the press, (2) a press computer to manage the process, and (3) the Heidelberg offset press with waterless ink temperature controls. To use the press, each of the four printing cylinders is first prepared with a new (unimaged) waterless aluminum plate, then the images are RIPped from digital files to the Presstek's Pearl laser imaging system, which in turn images all four plates simultaneously at up to 2,540 dpi in thirty minutes or less.

Both presses can economically print from 50 to 20,000 copies on coated or uncoated papers. The DI press handles stock up to 14 inches x 20 inches in size, while the QM has a maximum sheet capability of 13 3/8 inches x 18 1/8 inches. The DI operates at a top speed of 8,000 single-sided iph, while the QM is faster at a maximum of 10,000 iph.

Indigo E-Print 1000. Indigo's E-Print 1000 is capable of producing 6-color work on both sides of an 11 inch x 17 inch maximum sheet size at 800 dpi. Scitex-native or PostScript Level 2 are used to drive Indigo's proprietary software, from which images are generated. During printing, pages are digitally imaged to an electrically charged cylinder, which is then inked with Indigo's ElectroInk. After inking the image is transferred to a blanket, then to an impression cylinder, and finally to the substrate. The imaging process is then repeated again and again. Indigo output is 2,000 letter-size sheets per hour printed four colors on one side, and 1,000 letter-size sheets per hour when duplexing 4-color images. Cost of an Indigo is in the vicinity of $300,000.

Scitex Spontane. This printer accepts PS and Scitex data from Macintoshes, PCs, or UNIX workstations. It prints 400 dpi at a production rate of 900 tabloid-size pages per hour, duplexed four colors on each side.

Xeikon DCP-1. Xeikon's DCP-1 is made in Belgium and distributed in the United States by AM Multigraphics. Introduced in June 1993 in Antwerp, Belgium, the Xeikon is a digital color web press that perfects to print ten colors in a five over five (5/5) duplexed configuration using electrophotographic technology. Imaging at 600 dpi provides for the printing of 2,000 four-color, 8 1/2 inch x 11 inch images per hour. The DCP-1 fully supports PostScript Level 2, as well as Harlequin's ScriptWorks RIP software. Spooling capability is driven by a 486DX2/66 Windows-based PC that allows multitasking, which means the RIP can rasterize images for one job while printing another. Each of the ten printing units exposes an image to the web of paper and toner is applied and permanently fused to the paper using heat to the substrate. Primary stocks used are coated and uncoated book, basis 50 through 130. Base cost of the DCP-1 is around $200,000.

Digital Duplicators. These units require the production of a digital master that is automatically made on the press using a digital scanning system. An original image is scanned and the press produces a thermally made, perforated master which becomes the printing image carrier. Printing is a process by which ink is fed through the perforations of the master onto the substrate. After printing the master is discarded. Although quality may be an issue with these units, their copy costs are very inexpensive at fractions of a cent each.

Riso Incorporated has marketed the digital copier heavily, although A.B. Dick, Gestetner, Ricoh, and others also have digital duplicator models. Riso has recently introduced a number of enhancements to its system, including an image editing system for design enhancements and a computer interface system for Macintosh and PC computers.

Wide Format Imaging Technology for Proofing and Small Print Runs

Large format electrostatic plotters, which are available in both monochromatic and color systems, are used for computer-aided design (CAD) and engineering output such as maps. They are able to print up to 54 inches wide, have a resolution from 200 dpi to 300 dpi, and require special papers. In addition, temperature and humidity can adversely affect their quality. Complete systems from Xerox or CalComp may cost as much as $300,000.

Ink-jet plotters, such the Iris ink-jet printer, are much more popular for large format output and are used for prepress proofing, design comprehensives, and very short-run printing (up to fifty copies). Generally, however, ink-jet production remains too expensive for high-volume, multiple copy color production. The biggest of the wide-format Iris ink-jet printers, which has a maximum image output width of 47 inches and prints vibrant, high-quality color, costs over $100,000. Chapter 8 covers estimating for Iris output as a color proofing device.

LaserMaster also provides a wide-format ink-jet DisplayMaker Professional which prints up to 36 inches wide with good color quality. Its cost is approximately $25,000.

Another method for printing (or proofing) large format images is to first digitally output the image to a large drum filmsetter, then to use analog proofing methods to produce the proof from the film images. This process tends to be slow and expensive for both time and materials, although the quality of the proof is excellent. It is also possible to first output the image in patchwork pieces to a small filmsetter and manually strip the film to produce a full image, then make an analog proof. Generating a patchwork digital proof is another way to produce large-format images in the absence of the previously noted options.

It should be noted that most digital proofing and printing devices can output images no larger than 11 inches x 17 inches (tabloid size), and some go no larger than the standard letter size of 8 1/2 inches x 11 inches (A4 size). This means that printing large images is not common. The development of wide (or large) format imaging represents an emerging technology, but the process remains generally limited to proofing output or very small print runs. Because large format devices print from a roll of paper, the width of the machine dictates one of the two finished dimensions possible.

Although wide format printing is not found in most commercial printing companies, it has become a market niche for some service bureaus and quick printers. Technology improvements will likely reduce the cost of this process and more volume will be printed using these devices.

Evaluating Costs of Digital Presses and Print-on-Demand

Given the newness of digital press technology and the intensely competitive environment found throughout the printing industry, the decision to buy a digital press is difficult. There are a number of issues that are important when evaluating POD from the printer's perspective. The following briefly discusses some of these issues and provides information relative to establishing costs for this emerging technology.

Points on Buying a Digital Press. As with any new technology, those who buy and use the equipment first pay more than those who wait. This money contributes to the substantial research and development efforts of the vendor. The decision to purchase and use a digital press rests on many important issues, including the following:

- the business owner's overall passion and belief in digital press technology meeting customer needs
- the owner's comparative risk-taking nature
- the owner's ability to put forward the initial capital resources for the purchase, as well as his ability to meet the related costs needed to establish a functioning environment for the press
- the owner's view of her overall financial requirements, including equip-

ment depreciation, setup costs, production output as a revenue generator, and the payback on the investment over a reasonable period of time

- the ability to locate customers or markets willing to pay for the products and services at the level of quality the digital press equipment can produce
- the ability to staff the press by locating or training employees quickly to properly use the equipment.

There are no easy or quick answers to the previous points. As with any new technology, the digital press that is purchased locks the vendor and the printer together as partners—it is a marriage from which both partners desire financial success. Thus, before the purchase is made it is prudent to evaluate each system carefully and to weigh the advantages and disadvantages of the technology. The details of each system, such as the specific maintenance cost items, become critical because overlooking one aspect or detail may be the difference between profit and loss over the long term. There is no simplified system or cookbook process to compare digital presses, and there is as yet no digital press that can be considered the de facto standard to which all other presses can be evaluated.

Gearing up to Sell Digital Press Sheets. Key areas to research when considering the purchase of a digital press are the markets and customers willing to pay for the goods and services the press will produce. The capacity to produce sheets in the POD environment does not ensure success without customers who are willing to buy what the press will produce. There should be no purchase of a digital press without the careful evaluation of customers and markets and the development of a strategy to generate volume for the press.

Selling POD is unlike selling commercial printing, because POD is driven completely from desktop files, has defined quality parameters, and changes the buyer's inventory paradigm from "in stock" to "JIT." Many commercial printing customers are not immediately aware of how POD can be applied to meet their needs. They should begin applying the process by segmenting out current customers who are likely to need the POD technology, and then they should identify new possible markets. Because digital presses require the generation of digital files using DTP technology, customers must be familiar with DTP. In general, customers who purchase longer print runs are less likely to need or want digital press production because the cost per sheet is substantially higher. Finally, because digital presses are not typically capable of producing the vibrant color that is available through conventional and waterless printing, this is a likely area of concern.

As previously discussed, each digital press differs from the others in terms of quality and operation. Thus, the market assessment should be done with the exact press type and model already identified. One practical guideline for completing the market assessment are the factors that affect the pricing of the

1. Market demand for the product
2. Manufacturing costs
3. Product mix
4. Competition
5. Quality of product
6. Services provided to the customer
7. Quantity of work to be printed
8. Volume of work in the plant
9. Customer's willingness and ability to pay for the job
10. Potential future business from the customer
11. Value added
12. Profit desired by top management
13. Location of the printing company to the customer
14. The customer's or print buyer's general attitude
15. The technical difficulty of the job in terms of the printer meeting the service or quality requirements desired by the customer
16. The ego satisfaction gained by the printer desiring the customer or customer wanting exclusive printer services
17. Printer's exclusive production capability
18. Customer's resale value of the printed product

Figure 10.3 Factors that influence prices for graphic products and services.

specific digital press products that are likely to be offered. These factors are noted in Figure 10.3 and are discussed in depth in Chapter 4.

Cost Comparisons of Four Digital Presses to Conventional Printing.

Purchasing a digital press must include an assessment of all known cost factors that affect both the investment and the day-to-day operation. There should be every attempt to present the costs in a balanced way so that the final comparison between presses is accurate. The evaluation should be done using the same types of products and equivalent cost figures that are honestly determined.

Figure 10.4 is a cost comparison between conventional lithographic printing using a Heidelberg GTO 4-color press (GTO 4C) and a Heidelberg GTO 2/C (GTO 2C) with six digitally driven presses: the Heidelberg GTO-DI (with Presstek Pearl laser plate imaging and printing waterless), the Indigo E-Print 1000 digital press, the Xeikon DCP-1 digital press, the Canon CLC800 (including RIP), the Heidelberg QM (referenced as the QM-DI), and the Scitex Spontane. As its caption indicates, Figure 10.4 was revised in September 1995. It first appeared in *NEPP Digital Printing Report* (Vol. 1, No. 2) in February 1994.

Cost Factors - 1-page flyer	GTO 4C	GTO 2C	GTO-DI (Prt)	Indigo	Xeikon	CLC800&RIP	QM-DI	Spontane
Operator(s)	1.00	1.00	1.00	0.50	0.50	0.30	1.00	0.50
Operator base salary	24960.00	20960.00	24960.00	15000.00	15000.00	7000.00	21000.00	15000.00
Equipment capital cost	466100.00	230000.00	603400.00	425000.00	350000.00	80000.00	495000.00	200000.00
Estimated maintenance	9322.00	4500.00	12066.00	42500.00	35000.00	9600.00	15000.00	24000.00
Overage charges						0.06		
Technical Considerations								
Speed (11x17 units per Hour)	8000	7000	6000	1000	2100	240	5000	1800
Sides at one time	1.00	1.00	1.00	2.00	2.00	1.00	1.00	2.00
Budgeted Hourly Rates								
Manned Hours	1920.00	1920.00	1920.00	1920.00	1920.00	1920.00	1920.00	1920.00
Fixed Costs								
Depreciation	58262.50	28750.00	75425.00	53125.00	43750.00	10000.00	61875.00	25000.00
Rent	1050.00	1050.00	1050.00	1050.00	1050.00	1050.00	1050.00	1050.00
Fire insurance	1399.70	690.69	1812.01	1276.28	1051.05	240.24	1486.49	600.60
Variable Costs								
Direct labor	24960.00	20960.00	24960.00	15000.00	15000.00	7000.00	21000.00	15000.00
Fringes (25%)	6240.00	5240.00	6240.00	3750.00	3750.00	1750.00	5250.00	3750.00
Supervision (15%)	3744.00	3144.00	3744.00	2250.00	2250.00	1050.00	3150.00	2250.00
Direct supplies	1900.00	950.00	1700.00	2125.00	1750.00	400.00	1700.00	1000.00
Repairs & Maintenance	9322.00	4500.00	12066.00	42500.00	35000.00	9600.00	15000.00	24000.00
TOTAL Direct Costs	106878.20	65284.69	126997.01	121076.28	103601.05	31090.24	110511.49	72650.60
General Factory (15%)	16031.73	9792.70	19049.55	18161.44	15540.16	4663.54	16576.72	10897.59
TOTAL Manufacturing								
Administrative (42%)	44888.84	27419.57	53338.75	50852.04	43512.44	13057.90	46414.82	30513.25
TOTAL ALL-INCLUSIVE	167798.77	102496.96	199385.31	190089.75	162653.65	48811.68	173503.03	114061.44
Costs Per Hour								
85% Productivity	102.82	62.80	122.17	116.48	99.67	29.91	106.31	69.89
80% Productivity	109.24	66.73	129.81	123.76	105.89	31.78	112.96	74.26
75% Productivity	116.53	71.18	138.46	132.01	112.95	33.90	120.49	79.21
Time and Cost Factors								
Makeready (% of Hour)	0.80	0.40	0.50	0.00	0.00	0.00	0.40	0.00
Separated film negatives	96.00	96.00	0.00	0.00	0.00	0.00	0.00	0.00
Proofing	50.00	50.00	0.00	0.00	0.00	0.00	0.00	0.00
Stripping	40.00	40.00	0.00	0.00	0.00	0.00	0.00	0.00
Platemaking	40.00	40.00	0.00	0.00	0.00	0.00	0.00	0.00
Plates	18.00	9.00	38.00	0.00	0.00	0.00	40.00	0.00
Ink (per copy)	0.003	0.003	0.003	0.23	0.00	0.00	0.003	0.00
Press makeready	87.40	53.38	64.90	0.00	0.00	0.00	45.18	0.00
Toner (per copy)	0.00	0.00	0.00	0.00	0.21	0.30	0.00	0.2
Blanket/plate/drum/oil (per copy)	0.003	0.003	0.003	0.22	0.15	0.00	0.003	0.14
Maintenance (per copy)	0.00	0.00	0.00	0.00	0.00	0.06	0.00	0.00
Bindery - trim, fold or cut (per unit)	0.01	0.01	0.01	0.01	0.00	0.01	0.01	0.00
Bindery - collate, bind (per unit)	0.00	0.00	0.00	0.00	0.00	0.00	0.00	0.00
Pack (carton, shrinkwrap)	0.00	0.00	0.00	0.00	0.00	0.00	0.00	0.00
Warehouse	0.00	0.00	0.00	0.00	0.00	0.00	0.00	0.00
TOTAL Costs excluding paper	332.20	288.79	103.41	0.46	0.36	0.37	85.59	0.34
TOTAL Consumables/services	0.016	0.016	0.016	0.46	0.36	0.37	0.016	0.34
Comparison Costs								
11x17/4c/1s								
50	333.68	377.08	105.29	29.19	20.52	25.12	87.52	19.06
100	335.16	378.74	107.17	58.38	41.04	50.24	89.45	38.13
500	347.03	392.02	122.22	291.88	205.21	251.21	104.88	190.63
1000	361.05	408.62	141.04	583.76	410.43	502.41	124.18	381.25
5000	476.46	541.39	291.58	2918.78	2052.13	2512.05	278.54	1906.27
11x17/4c/2s								
50	667.36	754.17	210.58	58.38	41.04	50.24	175.03	38.13
100	670.33	757.48	214.34	116.75	82.09	100.48	178.89	76.25
500	694.05	784.04	244.45	583.76	410.43	502.41	209.76	381.25
1000	722.10	817.23	282.08	1167.51	820.85	1004.82	248.36	762.51
5000	952.92	1082.77	583.16	5837.56	4104.26	5024.10	557.09	3812.55
PER UNIT 11x17/4c/2s								
50	13.35	15.08	4.21	1.17	0.82	2.02	3.50	0.76
100	6.70	7.57	2.14	1.17	0.82	2.02	1.79	0.76
500	1.44	1.63	0.49	1.17	0.82	2.02	0.42	0.76
1000	0.72	0.82	0.28	1.17	0.82	2.02	0.25	0.76
PER UNIT 8.5x11/4c/2s								
50	6.67	7.54	2.11	0.58	0.41	1.01	1.75	0.38
100	3.35	3.79	1.07	0.58	0.41	1.01	0.89	0.38
500	0.72	0.82	0.24	0.58	0.41	1.01	0.21	0.38
1000	0.36	0.41	0.14	0.58	0.41	1.01	0.12	0.38

Figure 10.4 Chart comparing printing costs for various digital presses to traditional printing. Figures do not include the cost of paper or RIP time. Revised version, July 1995. (Reproduced with permission of *NEPP Digital Printing Report.* Based on research by Professor Frank Romano, Rochester Institute of Technology, Rochester, New York.)

As noted in Figure 10.4, the cost analysis process begins by identifying cost factors and technical considerations, after which BHRs are established, which provide the cost per hour data. Time and cost factors for each machine are then determined, with the conventional GTO 4C press showing high fixed costs ($332.20) and the GTO-DI has substantially reduced fixed costs ($103.41). The Indigo, Xeikon, Canon, QM-DI, and Spontane show very low fixed costs because they are imaged directly from digital files and require no prepress production.

Based on these data, per sheet comparison costs at 50, 100, 500, 1,000, and 5,000 quantities are shown for a product printing at 11 inches x 17 inches at 4/0 and a product printing at 11 inches x 17 inches 4/4. For all comparisons the cost of paper and the cost of RIP time were not included. For example, 500 copies of a 4/4 job printed 11 inches x 17 inches on a Xeikon has a total cost of $410.43, while the same job would cost $583.76 on an Indigo and $209.76 on a Heidelberg QM-DI.

These figures allow the generation of a cost per printed sheet, shown as "Per Unit 11x17/4C/2s" and "Per Unit 8.5x11/4C/2s" on Figure 10.4. Analysis of the 8 1/2 inch x 11 inch product printed 4/4 (8.5x11/4C/2s) shows a cost per unit at the 500 quantity for a traditional GTO 4/C press is $0.72, while the same GTO-DI price drops to $0.24. The Indigo per copy price is at $0.58, Xeikon is at $0.41, Canon is at $1.01, the QM-DI is at $0.21, and the Scitex Spontane is at $0.38. Figure 10.5 is a graph comparing the costs curves generated from the data in Figure 10.5.

A number of conclusions can be drawn form Figures 10.4 and 10.5. First, it is clear that the Indigo, Xeikon, Canon, and Spontane systems do not provide any cost advantage to the buyer as quantities increase because their costs per copy are the same at any quantity. The costs are the same because there are no makeready or preliminary costs for these systems. Second, both the Heidelberg GTO-DI and the QM-DI press print this product less expensively than conventional lithographic presses and are also less costly than Indigo, Xeikon, Canon, or Spontane. Third, when comparing the Xeikon, Indigo, Canon, and Spontane systems, Spontane appears to have a slight per copy cost advantage over Xeikon, with Indigo in third place and Canon in fourth. Finally, neither 4-color nor 2-color conventional printing is cost effective against any digital system at quantities below 450. A declining per unit cost achieves a close cost value with Spontane, Xeikon, and Indigo at the 1,000 quantity level. Projections beyond 1,000 copies were not made with this study, although conventional printing should become very competitive with all digital systems at approximately 2,500 copies.

Figure 10.4 and the graph generated from it in Figure 10.5 were strictly based on cost data. No attempt was made to evaluate or compare systems relative to image or print quality, ease of production, complexities related to digital file structure, or nuances of operation that could be important to certain customers or certain types of products.

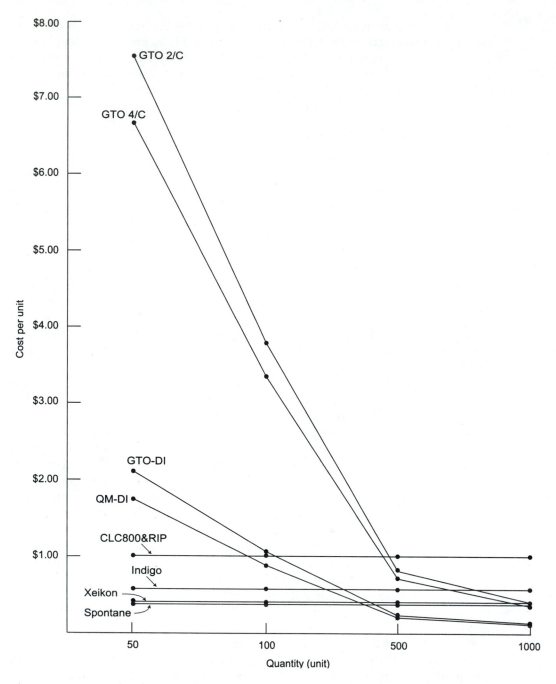

Figure 10.5 Graph of Figure 10.4 that compares various digital press unit costs for an 8 1/2 inch x 11 inch, 4/C, 2 sides (4/4) product at quantities of 50, 100, 500, and 1,000.

Estimating Digital Press Production. How digital press production will be estimated should also be considered before the press is purchased. Typically emerging technology is initially estimated using the price estimating methods discussed in Chapter 4, because prices are market driven and not cost driven. Although costs are essential to understand and control, volume to initiate work for the press generally begins by meeting the market price against other POD providers. Most printers experienced in implementing new technology expect to lose money at the outset, but strategically anticipate positive financial results once the technology is stable, employees are trained and have experience on the press, and the predesigned marketing/sales plan has been implemented.

Cost estimating digital press production requires the identification of the production operations or activities, the establishment of an accurate BHR, careful calculation of consumable materials, and assessment of other cost factors. As noted in Chapter 8 (Figures 8.18 and 8.19), building a spreadsheet template to complete the cost estimating process is the best way to initiate the process.

Appendix to Chapter 10

Presswork Estimating Schedules

The figures in this appendix were reproduced with permission of Printing Industries Association, Inc., of Southern California from its *1994-95 Blue Book of Production Standards and Costs for the Printing Industry.*

PRESSWORK SCHEDULE—OFFSET

(Time given represents machine hours on the decimal system)

DUPLICATORS & SMALL PRESSES

PRESS NAME	SIZE	RATED SHEETS PER HOUR	HOUR RATE AT 70% Productivity	PREPARATION/MAKE-READY TIME			AVG. IMPRESSION PER RUN HR.			WASH-UP TIME
				SIMPLE TIME	AVERAGE TIME	DIFFICULT TIME	SIMPLE	AVERAGE	DIFFICULT	
Multi, 1250, chute del.	10 x 15	9000	44.57	0.20	0.25	0.30	6750	5400	4500	0.25
Multi, 1250, chain del.	10 x 15	9000	45.29	0.20	0.25	0.30	6750	5400	4500	0.25
Hamada 500CDA	11 x 15	9000	45.04	0.20	0.25	0.30	6750	5400	4500	0.25
Multi, 1650, chute del.	12 x 16	11000	45.05	0.20	0.25	0.30	8250	6600	5500	0.25
Multi, 1650, chain del.	12 x 16	10000	45.74	0.20	0.25	0.30	7500	6000	5000	0.25
Heidelberg TOM	11 x 15	10000	49.85	0.20	0.25	0.30	7500	6000	5000	0.25
Heidelberg TOK	11 x 15	10000	50.08	0.20	0.25	0.30	7500	6000	5000	0.25
AB Dick 8820	11 x 17	10000	45.01	0.30	0.40	0.50	7500	6000	5000	0.40
AB Dick 1-8855S, 2/c	11 x 17	10000	46.87	0.30	0.40	0.50	7500	5400	5000	0.50
Ryobi 2800 CD	11 x 17	9000	45.75	0.30	0.40	0.50	6750	5400	4500	0.40
Hamada 600 CD	11 x 17	9000	45.42	0.30	0.40	0.50	6750	5400	4500	0.40
Ryobi 3200 CD	12 x 17	9000	46.87	0.30	0.40	0.50	6750	5400	4500	0.40
Embassy Super Maxim	12 x 18	10000	52.29	0.30	0.40	0.50	7500	6000	5000	0.40
AB Dick 9810	13 x 17	10000	50.91	0.30	0.40	0.50	7500	6000	5000	0.40
AB Dick 9810, 2/c	13 x 17	10000	52.64	0.30	0.40	0.50	7500	6000	5000	0.40
Multi 1960, chute del.	18 x 15	8500	51.47	0.30	0.40	0.50	6375	5100	4250	0.40
Multi 1960, chain del.	18 x 15	8500	52.44	0.30	0.40	0.50	6375	5100	4250	0.40
Multi 3650 Auto, chute del.	12 x 16	10000	47.17	0.30	0.40	0.50	7500	6000	5000	0.40
Multi 3650 Auto, chain del.	12 x 16	10000	48.13	0.30	0.40	0.50	7500	6000	5000	0.40
Multi 1650, 2/c, chain del.	12 x 16	10000	51.95	0.40	0.50	0.60	7500	6000	5000	0.50
Multi 1962, 2/c, chain del.	18 x 15	8500	54.31	0.40	0.50	0.60	6375	5100	4250	0.50
Multi 3875 Auto	12 x 18	9000	60.95	0.40	0.50	0.50	6750	5400	4500	0.40
Hamada 700 CD	18 x 14	9000	52.13	0.30	0.40	0.50	6750	5400	4500	0.40
Ryobi 500N	14 x 18	8000	53.56	0.30	0.40	0.50	6000	4800	4000	0.40
Ryobi 500N-NP	14 x 18	8000	56.56	0.40	0.50	0.60	6000	4800	4000	0.50
Davidson 702PJ	14 x 17	8000	55.71	0.40	0.50	0.60	6000	4800	4000	0.50
Ryobi 3200PFA, 2/c	12 x 17	9000	58.15	0.40	0.50	0.60	6750	5400	4500	0.50
Ryobi 3302M	12 x 17	9000	60.59	0.30	0.40	0.50	6750	5400	4500	0.40
Hamada 800 CDX	14 x 20	9000	54.54	0.30	0.40	0.50	6750	5400	4500	0.40
Multi Eagle	15 x 20	10000	60.40	0.30	0.40	0.50	7500	6000	5000	0.40
Davidson 901, chain del.	15 x 20	9000	53.20	0.30	0.40	0.50	6750	5400	4500	0.40
A.B. Dick 9890	17 x 22	10000	58.87	0.30	0.40	0.50	7500	6000	5000	0.40
A.B. Dick 9890, 2/c	17 x 22	10000	61.02	0.40	0.50	0.60	7500	6000	5000	0.50

Figure 10.A1 Offset presswork estimating schedule: Duplicators and small presses.

PRESSWORK SCHEDULE—OFFSET

(Time given represents machine hours on the decimal system)

ONE COLOR PRESSES

PRESS NAME	SIZE	RATED SHEETS PER HOUR	HOUR RATE AT 70% Productivity	PREPARATION/MAKE-READY TIME			AVG. IMPRESSION PER RUN HR			WASH-UP TIME
				SIMPLE TIME	AVERAGE TIME	DIFFICULT TIME	SIMPLE	AVERAGE	DIFFICULT	
Heidelberg GTO52	14 x 20	8000	63.02	0.30	0.40	0.50	6000	4800	4000	0.40
Heidelberg MO	19 x 25	12000	83.77	0.40	0.50	0.60	9000	7200	6000	0.50
Komori S26	20 x 26	11000	80.44	0.40	0.50	0.60	8250	6600	5500	0.50
MAN Roland 201	20 x 29	12000	89.64	0.50	0.60	0.70	9000	7200	6000	0.50
Heidelberg SORM	20 x 29	12000	87.40	0.50	0.60	0.70	9000	7200	6000	0.50
Heidelberg SORS	28 x 40	12000	113.99	0.60	0.70	0.80	9000	7200	6000	0.60

INCLUDES ONLY ONE PRESSMAN

You must compute your own cost figures for two-, four-, five-, six-, seven-, and eight-color presses. The hour rate for the second pressman, feeder, and floor help must be added to the cost center hour rate where applicable before computing the hourly cost for makeready, impressions per thousand, or wash-up.

Floor help	$27.49
Feeder	$36.69
Second pressman	$52.06

TWO COLOR PRESSES

PRESS NAME	SIZE	RATED SHEETS PER HOUR	HOUR RATE AT 70% Productivity	PREPARATION/MAKE-READY TIME			AVG. IMPRESSION PER RUN HR			WASH-UP TIME
				SIMPLE TIME	AVERAGE TIME	DIFFICULT TIME	SIMPLE	AVERAGE	DIFFICULT	
Heidelberg GTOZP*	14 x 20	8000	94.09	0.65	0.90	1.20	6000	4800	4000	0.65
Heidelberg MOZP*	19 x 25	12000	125.68	0.65	0.90	1.20	9000	7200	6000	0.65
Komori S226	20 x 26	11000	110.76	0.65	1.00	1.30	8250	6600	5500	0.65
Komori S226P *	20 x 26	11000	121.41	0.65	1.00	1.30	8250	6600	5500	0.65
Komori Lithrone 226-II	20 x 26	13000	138.88	0.65	1.00	1.30	9750	7800	6500	0.65
Akiyama BT228	20 x 28	13000	145.63	0.75	1.00	1.30	9750	7800	6500	0.75
Komori Lithrone 228-II	20 x 28	13000	157.36	0.75	1.00	1.30	9750	7800	6500	0.75
MAN Roland 202	20 x 29	12000	121.53	0.75	1.00	1.30	9000	7200	6000	0.75
Heidelberg SORMZ	20 x 29	12000	120.79	0.75	1.00	1.30	9000	7200	6000	0.75
MAN Roland MP104*	28 x 40	13000	207.79	0.90	1.20	1.50	9750	7800	6500	0.90
MAN Roland 702	28 x 40	15000	258.98	0.90	1.20	1.50	11250	9000	7500	0.90
Heidelberg SORSZ	28 x 40	12000	147.60	0.90	1.20	1.50	9000	7200	6000	0.90
Komori Lithrone 240P*	28 x 40	11000	196.44	0.90	1.20	1.50	8250	6600	5500	0.90
Komori Lithrone 240-III	28 x 40	13000	212.83	0.90	1.20	1.50	9750	7800	6500	0.90
Akiyama 240	28 x 40	13000	203.28	0.90	1.20	1.50	9750	7800	6500	0.90
Komori Lithrone 244-III	32 x 44	13000	261.66	1.20	1.40	1.90	9750	7800	6500	1.00
Komori Lithrone 250-III	38 x 50	13000	396.02	1.20	1.40	1.90	9750	7800	6500	1.00
MAN Roland 800 55	39 x 55	10000	314.46	1.20	1.40	1.90	7500	6000	5000	1.00
MAN Roland 800 55C	39 x 55	10000	405.99	1.20	1.40	1.90	7500	6000	5000	1.00
MAN Roland 800 63	47 x 63	10000	358.39	1.20	1.40	1.90	7500	6000	5000	1.00
MAN Roland 800 63C	47 x 63	10000	450.18	1.20	1.40	1.90	7500	6000	5000	1.00

* denotes Perfector
C denotes Coater

Waterless production adjustment with experienced crew
Makeready time reduction range 10-30%
Press running time reduction range 5-25%
Adjustment % will vary based on experience.

Figure 10.A2 Offset presswork estimating schedule: One- and two-color presses.

PRESSWORK SCHEDULE—OFFSET

(Time given represents machine hours on the decimal system)

INCLUDES ONLY ONE PRESSMAN

You must compute your own cost figures for two, four, five, six, seven, and eight-color presses. The hour rate for the second pressman, feeder, and floor help must be added to the cost center hour rate where applicable before computing the hourly cost for makeready, impressions per thousand, or wash-up.

Floor help $28.63
Feeder $37.42
Second pressman $57.33

FOUR COLOR PRESSES

PRESS NAME	SIZE	RATED SHEETS PER HOUR	HOUR RATE AT 70% Productivity	PREPARATION/MAKE-READY TIME SIMPLE TIME	AVERAGE TIME	DIFFICULT TIME	AVG. IMPRESSION PER RUN HR. SIMPLE	AVERAGE	DIFFICULT	WASH-UP TIME
Basic Model	14 x 20	8000	135.85	1.15	1.65	1.90	6000	4800	4000	0.80
Perfector	14 x 20	8000	143.52	1.15	1.65	1.90	6000	4800	4000	0.80
Console	14 x 20	10000	164.30	1.15	1.65	1.90	7500	6000	5000	0.80
Console, Hi Pile Feed	19 x 25	12000	227.23	1.40	1.90	2.10	9000	7200	6000	0.80
Console, Hi Pile, Perfector	19 x 25	12000	235.10	1.40	1.90	2.10	9000	7200	6000	0.80
Console	20 x 26	13000	223.62	1.50	2.00	2.20	9750	7800	6500	0.80
Console, Coater	20 x 26	13000	260.15	1.50	2.00	2.20	9750	7800	6500	0.80
Console,	20 x 28	13000	201.47	1.50	2.00	2.20	9750	7800	6500	0.80
Console, Coater	20 x 28	13000	284.04	1.50	2.00	2.20	9750	7800	6500	0.80
Console	20 x 28	13000	286.10	1.50	2.00	2.20	9750	7800	6500	0.80
Console	20 x 28	13000	247.56	1.50	2.00	2.20	9750	7800	6500	0.80
Console	20 x 29	12000	254.69	1.50	2.00	2.20	9000	7200	6000	0.80
Console, Coater	20 x 29	12000	278.75	1.50	2.00	2.20	9000	7200	6000	0.80
Console, Coater	28 x 40	13000	340.38	1.80	2.25	2.50	9750	7800	6500	1.00
Console, Perfector	28 x 40	13000	330.90	1.80	2.25	2.50	9750	7800	6500	1.00
Console, Coater, Perfector	28 x 40	13000	389.76	1.80	2.25	2.50	9750	7800	6500	1.00
Console	28 x 40	13000	349.92	1.80	2.25	2.50	9750	7800	6500	1.00
Console, Coater	28 x 40	15000	456.69	1.80	2.25	2.50	11250	9000	7500	1.00
Console, Coater	28 x 40	13000	398.01	1.80	2.25	2.50	9750	7800	6500	1.00
Console, Coater	28 x 40	13000	323.95	1.80	2.25	2.50	9750	7800	6500	1.00
Console, Coater	28 x 40	13000	373.67	1.80	2.25	2.50	9750	7800	6500	1.00
Console, Coater	32 x 44	13000	430.33	2.00	2.40	2.70	9750	7800	6500	1.20
Console, Coater	32 x 44	13000	512.46	2.00	2.40	2.70	9750	7800	6500	1.20
Console	38 x 50	13000	682.97	2.20	2.60	2.90	9750	7800	6500	1.20
Console, Coater	38 x 50	13000	783.43	2.20	2.60	2.90	9750	7800	6500	1.20
Console	39 x 50	10000	506.10	2.20	2.60	2.90	7500	6000	5000	1.20
Console	39 x 55	10000	531.77	2.50	2.75	3.00	7500	6000	5000	1.20
Console, Coater	39 x 55	10000	624.08	2.50	2.75	3.00	7500	6000	5000	1.20
Console, Coater	47 x 63	10000	569.67	2.50	2.75	3.00	7500	6000	5000	1.20
Console, Coater	47 x 63	10000	661.43	2.50	2.75	3.00	7500	6000	5000	1.20

Waterless production adjustment with experienced crew
Makeready time reduction range 10-30%
Press running time reduction range 5-25%
Adjustment % will vary based on experience.

Console has remote inking, dampening and registration controls.

Figure 10.A3 Offset presswork estimating schedule: Four-color presses.

PRESSWORK SCHEDULE—OFFSET

(Time given represents machine hours on the decimal system)

INCLUDES ONLY ONE PRESSMAN

You must compute your own cost figures for two-, four-, five-, six-, seven-, and eight-color presses. The hour rate for the second pressman, feeder, and floor help must be added to the cost center hour rate where applicable before computing the hourly cost for makeready, impressions per thousand, or wash-up.

Floor help	$28.63
Feeder	$37.42
Second pressman	$57.33

FIVE COLOR PRESSES

PRESS NAME	SIZE	RATED SHEETS PER HOUR	HOUR RATE AT 70% Productivity	PREPARATION/MAKE-READY TIME			AVG. IMPRESSION PER RUN HR.			WASH-UP TIME
				SIMPLE TIME	AVERAGE TIME	DIFFICULT TIME	SIMPLE	AVERAGE	DIFFICULT	
Basic Model	14 x 20	8000	165.12	1.30	1.80	2.00	6000	4800	4000	1.00
Console	14 x 20	10000	176.86	1.30	1.80	2.00	7500	6000	5000	1.00
Console, High Pile Feed	19 x 25	12000	265.06	1.30	1.80	2.00	9000	7200	6000	1.00
Console, High Pile, Perfector	19 x 25	12000	289.70	1.30	1.80	2.00	9000	7200	6000	1.00
Console	20 x 26	13000	258.08	1.30	1.80	2.00	9750	7800	6500	1.00
Console, Coater	20 x 26	13000	297.97	1.30	1.80	2.00	9750	7800	6500	1.00
Console	20 x 28	13000	282.63	1.30	1.80	2.00	9750	7800	6500	1.00
Console, Coater	20 x 28	13000	322.01	1.30	1.80	2.00	9750	7800	6500	1.00
Console	20 x 28	13000	240.56	1.30	1.80	2.00	9750	7800	6500	1.00
Console, Coater	20 x 28	12000	300.68	1.30	1.80	2.00	9000	7200	6000	1.00
Console	20 x 29	12000	276.31	1.30	1.80	2.00	9000	7200	6000	1.00
Console	28 x 40	13000	349.33	1.50	2.00	2.30	9750	7800	6500	1.50
Console	28 x 40	13000	411.93	1.50	2.00	2.30	9750	7800	6500	1.50
Console, Coater	28 x 40	13000	468.62	1.50	2.00	2.30	9750	7800	6500	1.50
Console	28 x 40	13000	414.96	1.50	2.00	2.30	9750	7800	6500	1.50
Console, Coater	28 x 40	13000	433.66	1.50	2.00	2.30	9750	7800	6500	1.50
Console	28 x 44	13000	383.45	1.50	2.00	2.30	9750	7800	6500	1.50
Console	32 x 44	13000	488.91	1.50	2.00	2.30	9750	7800	6500	1.50
Console, Coater	32 x 44	13000	569.78	1.50	2.00	2.30	9750	7800	6500	1.50
Console	38 x 50	13000	743.38	1.70	2.20	2.50	9750	7800	6500	1.70
Console, Coater	38 x 50	13000	841.52	1.70	2.20	2.50	9750	7800	6500	1.70
Console	39 x 50	10000	643.96	1.70	2.20	2.50	7500	6000	5000	1.70
Console, Coater	39 x 50	10000	735.97	1.70	2.20	2.50	7500	6000	5000	1.70
Console	39 x 55	10000	646.26	1.70	2.20	2.50	7500	6000	5000	1.70
Console, Coater	39 x 55	10000	738.03	1.70	2.20	2.50	7500	6000	5000	1.70
Console	47 x 63	10000	709.52	1.70	2.20	2.50	7500	6000	5000	1.70
Console, Coater	47 x 63	10000	802.23	1.70	2.20	2.50	7500	6000	5000	1.70

> **Waterless production adjustment with experienced crew**
> Makeready time reduction range 10-30%
> Press running time reduction range 5-25%
> Adjustment % will vary based on experience.

Console has remote inking, dampering and registration controls.

Figure 10.A4 Offset presswork estimating schedule: Five-color presses.

PRESSWORK SCHEDULE—OFFSET

(Time given represents machine hours on the decimal system)

INCLUDES ONLY ONE PRESSMAN

You must compute your own cost figures for two-, four-, five-, six-, seven-, and eight-color presses. The hour rate for the second pressman, feeder, and floor help must be added to the cost center hour rate where applicable before computing the hourly cost for makeready, impressions per thousand, or wash-up.

Floor help	$20.63
Feeder	$41.25
Second pressman	$57.33

PRESS NAME	SIZE	RATED SHEETS PER HOUR	HOUR RATE AT 70% Productivity	PREPARATION/MAKE-READY TIME SIMPLE TIME	AVERAGE TIME	DIFFICULT TIME	AVG. IMPRESSION PER RUN HR. SIMPLE	AVERAGE	DIFFICULT	WASH-UP TIME
Console	14 x 20	10000	229.54	1.30	1.80	2.00	7500	6000	5000	1.00
Console	20 x 26	13000	291.89	1.30	1.80	2.00	9750	7800	6500	1.00
Console, Coater	20 x 26	13000	321.99	1.30	1.80	2.00	9750	7800	6500	1.00
Console	20 x 28	13000	267.16	1.30	1.80	2.00	9750	7800	6500	1.00
Console	20 x 28	13000	354.77	1.30	1.80	2.00	9750	7800	6500	1.00
Console, Coater	20 x 28	13000	409.40	1.30	1.80	2.00	9750	7800	6500	1.00
Console	20 x 29	12000	303.76	1.30	2.00	2.30	9000	7200	6000	1.00
Console, Coater	20 x 29	12000	329.03	1.30	2.00	2.30	9000	7200	6000	1.00
Console, Perfector	28 x 40	13000	446.45	1.50	2.00	2.30	9750	7800	6500	1.20
Console, Coater, Perfector	28 x 40	13000	504.31	1.50	2.00	2.30	9750	7800	6500	1.20
Console	28 x 40	13000	460.01	1.50	2.00	2.30	9750	7800	6500	1.20
Console, Coater	28 x 40	13000	516.93	1.50	2.00	2.30	9750	7800	6500	1.20
Console	28 x 40	13000	480.28	1.50	2.00	2.30	9750	7800	6500	1.20
Console, Coater	28 x 40	13000	528.08	1.50	2.00	2.30	9750	7800	6500	1.20
Console	28 x 40	13000	384.91	1.50	2.00	2.30	9750	7800	6500	1.20
Console, Coater.	28 x 40	13000	484.20	1.50	2.00	2.30	9750	7800	6500	1.20
Console	28 x 40	15000	538.47	1.50	2.00	2.30	11250	9000	7500	1.20
Console, Coater	28 x 40	15000	596.64	1.50	2.00	2.30	11250	9000	7500	1.20
Console	32 x 44	13000	523.95	1.50	2.00	2.30	9750	7800	6500	1.20
Console, Coater	32 x 44	13000	613.20	1.70	2.20	2.50	9750	7800	6500	1.50
Console	38 x 50	13000	806.70	1.70	2.20	2.50	9750	7800	6500	1.50
Console, Coater	38 x 50	13000	905.05	1.70	2.20	2.50	9750	7800	6500	1.50
Console	39 x 50	10000	729.60	1.70	2.20	2.50	7500	6000	5000	1.50
Console, Coater	39 x 50	10000	822.16	1.70	2.20	2.50	7500	6000	5000	1.50
Console	39 x 55	10000	747.36	1.80	2.30	2.60	7500	6000	5000	1.60
Console, Coater	39 x 55	10000	840.22	1.80	2.30	2.60	7500	6000	5000	1.60
Console	47 x 63	10000	793.99	2.00	2.50	2.80	7500	6000	5000	1.80
Console, Coater	47 x 63	10000	890.28	2.00	2.50	2.80	7500	6000	5000	1.80

Waterless production adjustment with experienced crew
Makeready time reduction range 10-30%
Press running time reduction range 5-25%
Adjustment % will vary based on experience

Console has remote inking, dampening and registration controls.

Figure 10.A5 Offset presswork estimating schedule: Six-color presses.

PRESSWORK SCHEDULE—OFFSET

(Time given represents machine hours on the decimal system)

INCLUDES ONLY ONE PRESSMAN

You must compute your own cost figures for two-, four-, five-, six-, seven-, and eight-color presses. The hour rate for the second pressman, feeder, and floor help must be added to the cost center hour rate where applicable before computing the hourly cost for makeready, impressions per thousand, or wash-up.

				Floor help	$29.69
				Feeder	$41.87
				Second pressman	$63.19

SEVEN COLOR PRESSES

PRESS NAME	SIZE	RATED SHEETS PER HOUR	HOUR RATE AT 70% Productivity	PREPARATION/MAKE-READY TIME			AVG. IMPRESSION PER RUN HR.			WASH-UP TIME
				SIMPLE TIME	AVERAGE TIME	DIFFICULT TIME	SIMPLE	AVERAGE	DIFFICULT	
Console	28 x 40	13000	537.58	1.40	1.80	2.00	9750	7800	6500	1.40
Console, Coater	28 x 40	13000	595.63	1.40	1.80	2.00	9750	7800	6500	1.40
Console	28 x 40	13000	546.83	1.60	2.00	2.20	9750	7800	6500	1.60
Console, Coater	28 x 40	13000	596.95	1.60	2.00	2.20	9750	7800	6500	1.80
Console, Perfector	28 x 40	13000	506.49	1.60	2.00	2.20	9750	7800	6500	1.60
Console, Coater, Perfector	28 x 40	13000	564.99	1.60	2.00	2.20	9750	7800	6500	1.60
Console	28 x 40	13000	491.40	1.60	2.00	2.20	9750	7800	6500	1.80
Console, Coater	28 x 40	13000	543.06	1.60	2.00	2.20	9750	7800	6500	1.60
Console, Coater	28 x 40	15000	656.57	1.60	2.00	2.20	11250	9000	7500	1.80
Console	28 x 40	15000	598.52	1.60	2.00	2.20	11250	9000	7500	1.60

Console has remote inking, dampening and registration controls.

EIGHT COLOR PRESSES

PRESS NAME	SIZE	RATED SHEETS PER HOUR	HOUR RATE AT 70% Productivity	SIMPLE TIME	AVERAGE TIME	DIFFICULT TIME	SIMPLE	AVERAGE	DIFFICULT	WASH-UP TIME
Console	28 x 40	13000	613.30	1.80	2.20	2.40	9750	7800	6500	1.80
Console, Coater	28 x 40	13000	662.36	1.80	2.20	2.40	9750	7800	6500	2.00
Console, Perfector	28 x 40	13000	564.42	1.80	2.20	2.40	9750	7800	6500	1.80
Console, Coater, Perfector	28 x 40	13000	623.06	1.80	2.20	2.40	9750	7800	6500	1.80
Console, Coater	28 x 40	13000	605.07	1.80	2.20	2.40	9750	7800	6500	2.00
Console	28 x 40	13000	551.10	1.80	2.20	2.40	9750	7800	6500	1.80
Console, Coater	28 x 40	15000	739.02	1.80	2.20	2.40	11250	9000	7500	1.80
Console	28 x 40	15000	680.85	1.80	2.20	2.40	11250	9000	7500	1.80

Console has remote inking, dampening and registration controls.

> Waterless production adjustment with experienced crew
> Makeready time reduction range 10-30%
> Press running time reduction range 5-25%
> Adjustment % will vary based on experience.

Figure 10.A6 Offset presswork estimating schedule: Seven- and eight-color presses.

PRESSWORK SCHEDULE—LETTERPRESS
(Time given represents machine hours on the decimal system)

Note: You must add for floor help if required at $32.29 per person per hour.

LETTERPRESS

PRESS NAME	SIZE	RATED SHEETS PER HOUR	HOUR RATE AT 70% Productivity	PREPARATION/MAKE-READY TIME			AVG. IMPRESSION PER RUN HR.			WASH-UP TIME
				SIMPLE TIME	AVERAGE TIME	DIFFICULT TIME	SIMPLE	AVERAGE	DIFFICULT	
Heidelberg, Stamp & Emboss.	10 x 15	5500	53.42	0.75	1.00	2.00	4125	3300	2750	0.10
Heidelberg, Stamp & Emboss.	13 x 18	4000	56.63	0.75	1.00	2.00	3000	2400	2000	0.10
Kluge, Stamp & Emboss.	14 x 22	4000	55.83	0.75	1.00	2.00	3000	2400	2000	0.10
Platen, Hand-fed*	8 x 12	1800	42.88	0.75	1.00	2.00	1350	1080	900	0.15
Platen, Hand-fed*	10 x 15	1800	42.89	0.75	1.00	2.00	1350	1080	900	0.15
PLaten, Hand-fed*	12 x 18	1800	47.18	0.75	1.00	2.00	1350	1080	900	0.15
Heidelberg Platen	10 x 15	5500	52.45	0.75	1.00	2.00	4125	3300	2750	0.15
Kluge Automatic	11 x 17	4500	50.42	0.75	1.00	2.00	3375	2700	2250	0.15
Heidelberg	13 x 18	5500	56.05	0.75	1.00	2.00	4125	3300	2750	0.15
Kluge Automatic	13 x 19	5000	49.55	0.75	1.00	2.00	3750	3000	2500	0.15
Heidelberg*	15 x 20	5000	48.41	0.75	1.00	2.00	3750	3000	2500	0.15
Cylinder Press*	14 x 20	5000	50.12	0.75	1.00	2.00	3750	3000	2500	0.15

*Reconditioned Equipment

Figure 10.A7 Letterpress presswork estimating schedule.

Chapter 11

Estimating Postpress Production

11.1 Introduction

11.2 Value Added Postpress Production and Services

11.3 Estimating Flat Sheet Production

11.4 Estimating Commercial Booklet and Pamphlet Binding Operations

Hand Gathering Folded Signatures
Side-Wire Stitching
Saddle-Wire Stitching
Semiautomatic Saddle Stitching

Automatic Saddle-Wire Stitching Equipment
Perfect Binding for Books and Booklets
Pamphlet and Book Trimming

11.5 Estimating Banding, Wrapping, Mailing, and Shipping Operations

Banding, Boxing, and Paper Wrapping
Shrink-Wrapping Production

Mailing Operations

11.1   **Introduction**

Postpress production covers both manufacturing and service activities that occur after the job is printed. Postpress manufacturing, which is sometimes called binding and finishing production, represents the final manufacturing step for most printed work. During this step, the printed sheets are cut apart and/or trimmed, folded, gathered, jogged, and padded, or they are converted to the final product format and prepared for shipment. Because these operations are the last step in the manufacturing sequence, the high quality of the job can easily be destroyed if care is not taken at this point. While presswork establishes the quality of the printed images, postpress operations puts the finishing touches on the product as an entire package. A beautifully printed job can be ruined by poor finishing.

Postpress services, which are sometimes linked to postpress manufacturing, cover an array of options the printer provides. For example, affordable electronic ink-jet addressing systems allow printers to customize graphic materials for their clients. The selective binding methods that are available to small printing companies allows these printers to offer their customers the targeted marketing advantages formerly available only to very large printers and publishers. Lay-flat perfect binding for perfect bound books that have fast-cure adhesives are also available. Various postpress services, such as order fulfillment, shipping and distribution options, and packaging choices, are important to customers. In sum, the bindery has emerged as an equal player to prepress and press in terms of product valued added (VA).

However, postpress manufacturing has long been considered a stepchild of the pressroom, and with the recent focus on DPP, postpress has remained to many printers a second-class citizen. This feeling has been driven in part by the fact that historically a number of postpress activities were available only to very large printers. However, the success of these large companies has demonstrated over time that postpress is an equal partner in printing manufacturing because it contributes substantially to the VA the printer provides his customers. Today the success of postpress is recognized by a growing contingent of printers as a key VA component in their profitability formulas.

This chapter segments postpress estimating into three categories: (1) flat sheet production, (2) commercial booklet and pamphlet production, and (3) wrapping and mailing operations. Flat sheet production involves finishing operations performed while a job is in sheet form and includes cutting, trimming, folding, jogging, counting, padding, gathering, and drilling. Commercial booklet and pamphlet binding details the binding and finishing operations that result in folded, stitched, and finished booklets and pamphlets. Wrapping and mailing operations are performed to complete the job and prepare it for shipping.

11.2 Value Added Postpress Production and Services

For many printers, postpress represents the final manufacturing step in delivering a job. Postpress production includes cutting, folding, and trimming a job; producing finished books from signatures; and wrapping, boxing, and preparing a job for delivery to the customer. Postpress manufacturing operations are a collective group of activities that puts the final touches on a customer's product.

Today postpress is being redefined. Customers seek printers who offer enhanced postpress products and services. Like prepress and press technologies, postpress technology has been continually improving. A few years ago only large printers had the ability to offer a range of postpress options. Today a growing number of small printers are also providing these same VA postpress products and services at an equal or lower cost.

Even though more and more small printers are providing postpress production and services, some small and medium-sized printing plants still tend to buy out their postpress production contingent upon their production and equipment availabilities. The quantity of postpress outsourcing varies extensively. Some printers have little bindery equipment and send all of the work to their local trade binderies; others send only jobs that require special finishing operations or use trade binderies only when their own postpress facilities are filled to capacity.

Most large printing and publishing operations continue to offer specialized, high-speed equipment for high-volume postpress production. Customers seek these companies when they have large jobs that require extensive postpress activity. Today, however, because reduced quantities and POD require no inventory, reducing print run quantities and moving jobs to the digital arena are common practices.

Print Buyers Increasingly Select Printers Based on Postpress Systems and Services

While prepress and press have received considerable technological emphasis and have been of consuming interest to customers and printers alike, postpress has been a sleeping giant. Successful printers have come to recognize postpress as an important area of customer interest and an important reason customers place their orders with their companies instead of with other printers. In fact, because sophisticated prepress and press technology are successfully offered by many printers, a growing number of buyers consider postpress as the area to investigate when choosing a printer.

The emergence of postpress as a deciding factor in the customer selection process can be divided into four VA areas:

1. the ability of postpress to target market the customer's graphic product to select audiences or groups

2. the ability of postpress to provide enhanced differentiation of the customer's graphic products
3. the distribution, delivery, and other options available at the postpress stage
4. the printer's ability to provide postpress services in a rapid-response mode without losing quality or compromising accuracy

The discussion that follows provides insight into these four areas. It should be noted that for a printer or a publisher to provide these postpress products and services, she must purchase the appropriate equipment, have sufficient staff and floor space, and also become proficient at tailoring her postpress environment to meet each customer's desired outcome. There is no simple, single way to meet the customer's postpress needs. Instead, there are a variety of approaches.

Target or Selective Marketing Assisted by Postpress

Print buyers are always looking for ways to target their markets accurately. Cable television has expanded into hundreds of channels, newspapers print extensive color and different editions that are tailored to different surrounding communities, and radio has segmented audiences using talk radio, political topics, and financial subjects as targeting points. The competition between all of these media is intense and budgets are very large.

Selective marketing of graphic products is largely a function of postpress manufacturing and service. It is achieved in different ways, including through the use of selective insertion methods when collating products, computerized shipping systems, and ink-jet personalization of products. For example, a customer publishes a medical newsletter which is sent to 3,000 subscribers, but the subscribers are mixed between hospital administrators, physicians, pharmacists, nurses, and miscellaneous health-care professionals. The customer wants to advertise a new video, but he also wishes to segment advertising so that each subscriber group receives information specific to how this video addresses its needs and not the needs of the other subscribers. To do this, the subscriber list would be sorted from the electronic address file and collated so that each subscriber group received its copy of the newsletter with the appropriate video advertisement.

There are many such examples of target marketing programs using postpress manufacturing and service components. Some involve the use of electronic addressing methods, data management, sorting, and collating controls. Others involve postpress production that modifies a product enough that it is effectively a different product and appeals to new or different markets. Although postpress target marketing systems have been used by large printers for years, they require extensive investments and tend to be labor intensive. Today Muller-Martini and other postpress equipment vendors are developing equipment that allows this type of selective postpress production to also be done by small printers.

Product Differentiation

If there is an area of intense interest to print buyers, it is how their graphic products—their advertisements, magazines, books, menus, and so on—can be made different, unique, or quickly distinguishable from all of the competing products on the market. Postpress production is an important way to provide such differentiation.

Changing the size, shape, texture, feel, smell, weight, visual effect, audio output, or other characteristic of a product are some ways that this differentiation is accomplished. For example, a book might be designed to have a special insert of die-cut illustrations. This book would therefore require the production of the die-cut product and then the insertion of the illustrations as a postpress operation. Another customer may want to include a small sample of her product in a publication to selected markets or groups that receive the publication. To do so would require sorting these groups, then inserting the sample into the publication during postpress production. In another example, a book may be created with a special type of binding, a unique cover, or unusual dimensions that allows it to be quickly distinguished from all the other books with which it competes.

There is no cookbook method or planned procedure as to how to differentiate a product. The process requires ingenuity, creativity, and a focus on uniqueness coupled with a good knowledge of postpress equipment capacities and limitations. This means that sales staff must understand postpress production and relate it to the customer's needs, in a manner similar to the way they sell prepress and press technologies. So that there is benefit to the company, a key ingredient when assisting customers with ways to differentiate their products is to be certain that the postpress operations can be performed in house.

Distribution and Delivery Services

There is no question that an increasing number of customers desire additional services once their printed products have been produced and are ready for distribution. Some of these VA services are detailed in the following.

Storage of Finished Goods and Intermediate Job Materials. The storage of a customer's finished goods is an obvious service, but many printing companies offer it only on a temporary basis. Short-term finished goods storage, such as one or two days, is a reasonable service to provide at no charge, although the finished goods are considered the printer's property until the title has transferred from the printer to the customer. The GCBP (see Chapter 5), which are also known as the Printing Trade Customs, state that the title (ownership) shifts to the customer when one of three following conditions occurs: (1) when the job is shipped, (2) when the invoice is mailed, or (3) when the job is paid for.

Some customers do not have access to long-term storage and take advantage of the printer's reasonably priced finished goods storage. Typically storage is charged based on the area occupied by the customer's product, either in square feet or cubic feet. Because the printer is liable for damages that occur to the finished goods, it is prudent for him to have a good insurance policy that covers such unlikely occurrences.

Storage of the customer-supplied intermediate materials that are used to produce a customer's job, such as finished film or electronic media, are normally kept until the customer has accepted the job, then they are returned to the customer. As with finished goods storage, a VA service is to provide long-term storage for these customer-supplied materials. When extended-time storage is requested by the customer, the printer remains liable for keeping the materials usable. As with long-term finished goods storage, having a good insurance policy to cover damage to the materials is prudent.

Order Fulfillment Services. Order fulfillment is effective when the customer wants the printer to fill orders from the range of products the printer either produces or warehouses for the customer. For example, a short-run book manufacturer produces a range of titles by self-publishing authors. The manufacturer warehouses and fulfills small or single-book orders based on the publisher's advertising by providing such services as 800 number ordering, fast shipping, and credit card purchasing capability. The author is provided purchaser information from the manufacturer on each order fulfilled for her marketing purposes.

Although order fulfillment can be done as a postpress service where the products and services involved are not printed, most printers who complete the order fulfillment process provide some graphic services or printed products. Order fulfillment can be labor intensive, and it requires extensive warehouse space and materials handling equipment that allows for expedited and accurate filling of orders.

Packaging and Pick-Pack Services. Packaging is an important postpress service to many customers and can be a valuable revenue stream. Typically printers quote job delivery based on a specified standard packaging unit, which may vary from cardboard boxes to tied packages to skids of printed materials. Given the option, some customers prefer to select from a variety of packaging methods and styles, which range from simple boxing to gift-wrapped products to shrink-wrapped packages. Some printers offer a number of packaging options from which the customer can choose, which is known as a "pick-pack" system. Some customers want package content to vary for each customer, which is then part of order fulfillment process as briefly discussed.

The 800 Number Telemarketing. Although telemarketing is not specifically a postpress service, it can be provided to customers who do not have the ability or the experience to telemarket. Pricing methods, which are somewhat dictated by the type of products being sold or communicated, vary from hourly rates to per-call bases.

Kit or Display Assembly. Although kits and displays are an infrequent postpress operation for most printers, certain products require the assembly or gathering of many parts, sometimes in various mixtures or combinations. Kit assembly may also include order fulfillment because customers must order the finished product from a list of possible combinations and the customer may want the printer to provide all services.

Mailing Consultation and Services. This is a frequent and important postpress service for customers who use the post office for product delivery. Driven by the complexities of the postal system, including the need for intimate knowledge of different classes of mail, complicated cost structure, and delivery effectiveness, some printers become mailing experts as a service to their customers. This service must include all aspects of mailing and begin when the job is sold because product addressing, weight, size, and other issues are critical to classifying mail.

Mail List Management and Buyer Information Services. Because some postpress services, such as order fulfillment and mailing, involve the printer in the customer's business, some printers provide the collateral service of managing the customer's information, including his mailing lists. This service can be labor intensive and time consuming because updating requires constant attention and must be accurate. Linked to this mail list management and other postpress services is the development of related buyer information that can be used to target the buyer's future needs. For example, one or two questions asked of each 800-number caller when she places an order may lead to a new targeted audience, new products, and business expansion for the customer and printer alike.

Product Shipment Options. Providing various delivery options is a valuable service to a growing number of printing company customers. Delivery options can be segmented into two general categories: (1) product shipment by air transport, train, semitruck, small truck, van, or a combination of these carriers, or (2) the arrangement for alternative delivery services in place of the United States Post Office or other traditional carrier.

Product shipment options require the printer to have detailed knowledge of product size and weight, and targeted dates of delivery for the planned cities, as well as available carriers, their costs, and reliability patterns. For example, it may be possible to save considerable money by shipping a very large job by train to a select distribution site where it would then be sent by van carrier, as opposed to shipping the whole job by truck, which would require that each of the numerous rigs be sent to a specific drop point. It may also be possible to save money by using one truck carrier over another. The most cost-saving shipping method may be to ship individual customer orders directly from the printing company using an order fulfillment process.

When considering product shipment options, the time and reliability of delivery are almost always important issues. Also, because the cost, service, and reliability options change between types of carriers and within carrier groups, and because numerous combinations of delivery options are possible, this postpress service requires constant monitoring and evaluation.

Alternative Delivery Systems. The alternative delivery option is growing given the inflexibility, ever-rising per unit cost, lack of on-time arrival, lack of 100 percent delivery reliability, and other problems of the United States Postal Service. Established alternative delivery providers such as Federal Express and UPS are international and exceptionally reliable, but they tend to be expensive.

The emergence of entrepreneurial alternative delivery systems for specific cities and towns is growing. These systems use door-to-door canvassing for certain mass marketed products and targeted delivery for more specialized products. Although targeted delivery in a given city or town is expensive compared to sorting and delivery using the postal system, alternative systems are expected to grow as they develop integrated delivery networks in each city or town where they are used.

Electronic Production of Documents. Although electronic production of documents is not a postpress service per se, it is frequently part of the sales effort and does have inventory and storage conditions that may affect postpress products and services.

Digital on-demand printing systems provide a JIT environment for delivering products to customers. These systems can be located within a printing company and connected to postpress equipment that provides fast delivery of finished products, or they can be located at remote locations to provide close-to-the-customer delivery. Some POD systems include in-line finishing, but fancy finishing must be done off line.

Digital files for printing can be handled by shipping SyQuest or floppy disks using overnight carrier, electronic transmission of documents via commercial electronic networks or the Internet, or modem transmission using Switched 56, ISDN, or T-1 telecommunication.

Rapid Response of Postpress Activities

It is essential that postpress production and related postpress services are completed in a time-compressed manner. While prepress and press production have both seen significant reduction in cycle time, postpress production must meet or exceed these preceding manufacturing activities so that timely delivery can be assured. Speeding postpress manufacturing can be done by streamlining production using mechanical and electronic devices, automating production using robotic technology, or increasing the number of employees working on a particular job or in a particular production area. Combinations of these are also used.

Streamlining production using mechanical and electronic equipment is perhaps the method most used to speed postpress output. In general, reduced makeready and fast changeover methods that are engineered into new printing press equipment are also incorporated into postpress equipment. Materials handling equipment of all kinds—from fork lifts to conveyor systems to air-lift tables on cutting machines—are important time and energy savers. Connecting postpress equipment to press equipment to deliver a product using in-line manufacturing is also growing in popularity, especially with POD systems. Materials flow analysis and the use of sophisticated micromotion analysis provides feedback as to how postpress production can be speeded without losing quality.

Many postpress equipment manufacturers have aggressively begun to standardize binding and finishing processes through the development of robotic units that can perform certain postpress operations faster and more precisely than human workers. In the past, these systems required major investments in time and money and were available only to the largest printers. Today, however, a growing number of postpress equipment models have been downsized to meet the needs of medium and small printing companies and trade binderies. Mueller-Martini's Automated Bindery Controller System and its Trendbinder perfect binding unit are examples of this technology.

Even with increasing automation and robotics, it is sometimes necessary to employ part-time or temporary workers to speed production output. For most printers this is the least desirable option, but it is done when postpress production is bottlenecked and deadlines are likely to be missed.

Technological Advances to Support Postpress Value Added

The following is a brief description of emerging technological changes that have had significant effect on postpress VA.

Adhesive Binding Developments. The growth of perfect-bound books for many uses has led to the development and growing acceptance of lay-flat technology. Books bound using lay-flat methods are able to be opened to any page and remain open and laying flat without pressure. This allows the reader to use both hands for other activities while maintaining a specific page location. It is ideal when the book is used for cooking or any similar application where stable page location is required. Technical computer manuals, which are produced by the millions, are usually manufactured using lay-flat technology.

The lay-flat process is accomplished with the use of specialized perfect binding equipment and different types of adhesive products, including polyvinyl acetate (PVA) and polyurethane reactive (PUR) hotmelt adhesives. Although both products work well, recent advances in technology have reduced the toxicity and improved the effectiveness of PUR so that bound books can be briskly handled almost immediately after binding.

Process Improvement through Customer Feedback and Vendor Partnerships. The flurry of postpress activity has been encouraged by a group of emerging high-quality managers who recognize the need for employee training, maintenance of technical skills, and continuous improvement. While prepress and press areas have long had their share of this type of positive activity, postpress operations have been too scattered and too labor intensive to take full advantage of such efforts.

The encouragement of such process improvement in postpress has been greatly assisted by two key, collateral sources: (1) the customers who purchase the postpress service and (2) the vendors who develop, manufacture, and sell postpress equipment. Customers provide essential and important feedback that should not be ignored but instead should be used to improve postpress products and services. Postpress equipment vendors, working as partners with printers to resolve technical problems and develop new and better products, have also greatly assisted in the improvement of postpress products.

Selective Binding and Ink-Jet Technologies Help to Target Markets. The more the printer can assist the customer in targeting his client's needs, the more valuable the printer is to the customer. Selective binding and ink-jet technology are two important ways these objectives can be achieved. Muller-Martini's Automated Bindery Controller system was developed to assist bindery operators in data management, selective insertion, postal zone selection, and other operations so that products can be tailored to different audiences in one production run. This equipment is affordable to medium-size printers and is fairly easy to operate.

Ink-jet systems can provide product customization whereby each product can be personalized. This can be done in line during other postpress production and is valuable for certain types of target markets. Another important application of ink-jet technology is the development and use of moderately priced ink-jet addressing systems, such as Domino Amjet's Jet Address System. Original address input is done on a microcomputer by either the client or the printer; purchased mailing lists can be merged easily, which requires little additional digital work. The actual addressing process is done in line with other postpress operations. Sorting functions by name, zip code, or other function provide additional targeting opportunities.

Connection with Print-on-Demand. As noted in Chapter 10, the emergence of POD represents significant VA for companies that perfect the technology for their customers. When postpress operations, which are also termed "postprinting" when they are done in line immediately following imaging on a digital press, are effectively linked to POD, they form a potent combination. For example, the production of a product catalog would begin with high-speed printing followed with in-line collating, perfect binding, image personalization of the product cover using ink jet technology, and high-speed addressing. This would be done on a JIT basis at 20,000 finished copies per hour.

Activity has already begun in this area. Xerox DocuTech provides high-speed black-and-white graphic imaging coupled with stapling and hotmelt tape saddle binding. Xeikon and Indigo have limited postprinting capacity, which will be significantly enhanced as the process is perfected. As digital printing systems are developed, postprinting and postpress production will become an important VA connection that customers will be happy to pay for.

Maintaining Quality in Postpress Manufacturing and Services

Quality in postpress manufacturing is a critical issue and one that customers monitor closely. Assuming the job has been produced at the customer's desired level of imaging quality using prepress and press manufacturing, postpress must maintain this quality level. Because postpress production is sometimes a collection of steps that varies from job to job, quality is best built into the job as it is produced. It is better to build in quality than to discover a quality defect after the job has been completed because this defect would necessitate expensive rework to correct or, as sometimes happens, an entire remanufacturing of the job under rushed and costly overtime conditions.

Maintaining quality in postpress manufacturing is typically accomplished using the same methods as other manufacturing steps in printing production. For most successful printers, this involves frequent product inspection while the job is in process, as well as spot checking the job after it is done. When postpress operations require the tailoring of each item or a group of products in a job, such as with ink-jet personalization or ink-jet addressing, quality monitoring during production is even more critical.

An increasing number of successful printers have established company-wide quality assurance programs that cover all aspects of quality as it relates to the company's products and services. The TQM concepts, which empower employees to monitor quality at all times, and ISO 9000, which establishes quality guidelines, are both used to implement and monitor quality. An increasing number of customers are insisting that the printer provide a specific set of quantifiable quality standards in writing as part of the contract and before the job is awarded. This assures the customer that the quality of her product will be consistent and within an established level of variance.

Estimating and Pricing Postpress

Cost estimating postpress manufacturing is done in a manner similar to estimating prepress and press manufacturing methods. Estimating many of the routine production operations are detailed, with examples, in the remaining parts of this chapter.

The development of production standards and BHRs for emerging or new postpress technology is conditional upon the type of equipment and peripheral devices. As such equipment is purchased and installed, production activities must first be identified, after which benchmark production standards and BHRs are established. The general procedure to do this is described in Chapter 8.

Postpress services such as packaging options, delivery and shipping choices, ink-jet personalization and addressing, order fulfillment, and long-term storage should be priced so that the specific costs of the company are included. Details on establishing prices are provided in Chapter 4.

11.3   Estimating Flat Sheet Production

Flat sheet production includes all operations that are completed when the job is completed on paper in flat sheet form. This includes cutting and trimming, folding, hand gathering, jogging, counting, padding, and drilling production. Each of these operations is discussed in the following and is accompanied by estimating schedules and example problems to show how estimating would be completed.

Cutting and Trimming Production

The operations of cutting and trimming are common to a large number of jobs moving through any printing facility. The term "cutting" may be defined as the separation of a large sheet of paper stock or other substrate into smaller sheets. For example, a pars (stock sheet) is cut into press sheets in a cutting operation. "Trimming" is a final operation in which small amounts of paper are removed from the edges of the product. This operation ensures exact dimensions for all pieces, it squares the paper stock, and/or it provides for a neater product. Cutting may be either a prepress or postpress operation, while trimming is usually completed as a concluding, postpress technique.

A cutting machine is used for both cutting and trimming paper stock as a prepress or postpress operation. This piece of equipment consists of a flat, polished steel working base upon which the paper stock is slid; a cutting blade that is razor sharp; a clamp to hold the paper securely during cutting; and a back gauge that establishes the length of sheet to be cut. Paper stock is divided into handheld lifts and slid under the cutting blade until it fits securely against the back gauge, which has been preset for the specified distance or length of cut.

Table 1

Kind of Paper	Approx. Caliper (Thickness)	Approx. Sheets per load
13# Bond, 50# Coated Book	.0025″	1600
16# Bond, 60# Coated Book, 50# Offset Book	.0033″	1300
70# Coated Book	.0035″	1200
20# Bond, 80# Coated Book, 60# Offset Book	.0040″	1000
24# Bond, 100# Coated Book, 70# Offset Book	.0050″	800
80# Offset Book	.0060″	700
100# Tagboard	.0070″	600
80# Coated Cover, 50# Antique Finish Cover, 90# Index	.0080″	500
125# Tagboard, 110# Index	.0093″	400
65# Antique Finish Cover, 150# Tagboard, 140# Index	.0110″	400
4-Ply Board	.0180″	200

1. The number of sheets per load are based on normal production work of 4″ per load. If less, decrease proportionately— such as 50% if 2″ loads are used.
2. Caliper or thickness of the stock will vary by different manufacturers, and the above figures are approximate.

Table 2

Approx. Size of Paper	Setup Time		0.10	0.15		0.20		0.25		0.1	0.15
	Number of Sheets Cut From 1 Sheet of Load Size									Trim Out Bleeds & Gutters	
	2	3	4	5–8	9–12	13–16	17–20	21–24	25–28	29–32	1–2 Sides	3–4 Sides
8.5 × 11	.03	.05	.06	.07	.08	.09					.03	.05
19 × 25	.04	.07	.09	.10	.11	.13	.15	.18			.04	.06
23 × 29	.08	.11	.12	.14	.14	.16	.18	.20	.22		.04	.06
25 × 38	.10	.13	.13	.16	.15	.18	.20	.22	.24	.27	.05	.07
26 × 40	.10	.15	.18	.20	.21	.25	.28	.32	.35	.39	.06	.08
35 × 45	.14	.20	.22	.26	.27	.31	.35	.39	.43	.48	.07	.09

Note: Schedule data are decimal hours per lift cut. Add penalities as they apply. For intermediate sheet sizes, round up to the next highest value based on square inches.

Penalties: Add 20% to total time for cutting perforated or scored stocks. Add 15% to total time for cutting laminated or highly polished stocks. Add 10% total time for cutting stocks that caliper over 0.010 inch/sheet. Add 10% to total time for cutting stocks under 0.0015 inch/sheet.

Figure 11.1 Flat sheet cutting and trimming schedule. (Reproduced with permission of Printing Industries Association of Southern California from its *1994-95 Blue Book of Production Standards and Costs.*)

The hydraulic clamp is then dropped down (either manually with a foot pedal or automatically just before the blade begins its travel), thus holding the paper securely during the slicing action of the blade. This process is repeated continuously, with changes in the back gauge corresponding to changes in sheet length. Modern cutting equipment is manufactured with electronic safety devices ensuring that the sharp cutting blade does not repeat. In addition, most sophisticated cutters are now manufactured with electronic computer "spacing," which allows the operator to preset into processor memory certain desired cutting lengths. During the cutting procedure, the operator may move the back gauge to an established preset distance by engaging the computer unit. The unit saves considerable operator time in adjustment of the back gauge between cuts and ensures precisely the same length because it provides exact repeatability of back gauge setting.

Figure 11.1 is provided for estimating both cutting and trimming operations. The figure is divided into two segments: Table 1 is a lift schedule and Table 2 is a standard production time schedule that is presented as cutting time per lift. These tables must be used with each other.

To use Figure 11.1, the estimator begins with the lift schedule (Table 1) and identifies the kind of paper stock, weight (per 500 sheets of the basic size), and the caliper (thickness), thereby determining the approximate number of sheets per load (or lift). Essentially, a lift is a stack (pile) of paper or other material to be cut or trimmed in a height, size, or weight most easily handled by the cutter operator. Usually, a lift height of approximately 4 inches is considered a productive value. This lift value, or approximate number of sheets per lift, is divided into the total number of sheets to be cut or trimmed to yield the number of total lifts (or loads) to be cut. That is:

$$\text{total number of lifts to be cut or trimmed} = \text{number of sheets to be cut or trimmed} \div \text{number of sheets per lift}$$

Any fraction of a lift should be rounded to the next highest lift value.

The cutting and trimming schedule in Figure 11.1 is based on the number of cuts or trims out of the pss or pars and the size of the uncut or untrimmed sheet. The cutting and trimming schedule provides a cutting time per lift, which is used to determine cutting production time as follows:

$$\text{cutting production time} = \text{total number of lifts to be cut} \times \text{cutting time per lift}$$

If an intermediate size of sheet is to be cut, use the next higher size. The setup time is added to the cutting time to calculate the total production time.

In instances where trimming is a separate operation from cutting, such as the trimming of a 1-up job on four sides, only that portion of the schedule should be used. When trimming operations accompany cutting, the rates can be added because they apply to all lifts.

The addition of setup time should be made at least one time per job. Setup time includes time for reading the job ticket, making preliminary cutting calculations, moving (or programming) the back gauge, and performing any other operations required as preliminary work. Schedule data are based on a cutting crew of one person, but it is possible that more than one operator will be utilized. In such a case, the BHR will allow for cost recovery of this additional employee. Cutting and trimming production times include a reasonable amount for jogging into the cutter back gauge. Penalties, which are indicated at the bottom of the schedule in Figure 11.1, should be applied as appropriate.

In addition to those formulas just mentioned, the following formulas are used for estimating cutting and trimming production time and cost:

$$\text{total number of pss required} = (\text{number of fss required} \div \text{number up on the pss}) \times (\text{percentage of spoilage} + 100 \text{ percent})$$

$$\text{total number of pars required} = (\text{number of pss required including spoilage} + \text{number out of pars})$$

$$\text{total prepress cutting production time} = [(\text{number of pars required} \div \text{number of sheets per lift}) \times \text{cutting time per lift}] + \text{cutter setup time (Note: In this formula, the division portion of the equation yields the number of lifts to be cut and the ``cutting time per lift'' portion yields the cutting production time.)}$$

$$\text{total postpress cutting production time} = [(\text{total number of press size sheets required} \div \text{number of sheets per lift}) \times \text{cutting time left}] + \text{cutter setup time}$$

$$\text{total cutting production time} = \text{prepress cutting production time} + \text{postpress cutting production time}$$

$$\text{total production cost} = \text{total cutting production time} \times \text{cutter BHR}$$

Example 11.1. We want to determine cutting time and cost for 56,000 announcements, fss of 6 inches x 8 inches, run on basis 100 tagboard. The pars stock is 36 inches x 48 inches; the pss is 24 inches x 36 inches. The job will run 18-up on the press and cut 2-out of the pars. Add 6 percent of base pss for press spoilage. No trimming is required. The cutter is a 54-inch Polar 137 Monitor with a BHR of $68.50.

Solution

Use Figure 11.1.

Step 1. Determine the number of 24 inch x 36 inch pss and 36 inch x 48 inch pars to be cut:

$$(56,000 \text{ fss} \div 18\text{-up}) \times (0.06 + 1.00) = 3,111 \text{ pss} \times 1.06 = 3,298 \text{ pss}$$

$$3,298 \text{ pss} \div 2\text{-out} = 1,649 \text{ pars}$$

Step 2. For prepress cutting, cut 2 out of a 36 inch x 48 inch pars to produce 24 inch x 36 inch pss. Determine the following:
Number of lifts:

$$1,649 \text{ pars} \div 600 \text{ shts./lift} = 2.75 \text{ lifts} = 3 \text{ lifts}$$

Cutting time:

$$3 \text{ lifts} \times 0.14 \text{ hr/lift} = 0.42 \text{ hr.}$$

Prepress cutting time:

$$0.42 \text{ hr.} + 0.10 \text{ hr. setup} = 0.52 \text{ hr.}$$

Step 3. For postpress cutting, cut 18 out of a 24 inch x 36 inch pss to produce the total number of 6 inch x 8 inch fss. Determine the following:
Number of lifts:

$$3,298 \text{ pss} \div 600 \text{ shts./lift.} = 5.5 \text{ lifts} = 6 \text{ lifts}$$

Cutting time:

$$6 \text{ lifts} \times 0.20 \text{ hr./lift} = 1.20 \text{ hr.}$$

Postpress cutting time:

$$1.20 \text{ hr.} + 0.20 \text{ hr. setup} = 1.40 \text{ hr.}$$

Step 4. Determine the total cutting production time and cost:
Total cutting time:

$$0.52 \text{ hr.} + 1.40 \text{ hr.} = 1.92 \text{ hr.}$$

Total cutting cost:

$$1.92 \text{ hr.} \times \$68.50/\text{hr.} = \$131.52$$

Example 11.2. Determine the cutting time and cost for 35,000 letterheads, 2 colors, to run on substance 20 rag bond. Stock in inventory is 35 inches x 45 inches, to cut 4-out yielding 17 1/2 inch x 22 1/2 inch pss. Add 10 percent spoilage to base pss. After cutting to approximate finish size, trim finish pieces to 8 1/2 inches x 11 inches. The cutter is an Itoh 115 FC with a BHR of $64.60.

Solution

Use Figure 11.1.

Step 1. Determine number of 17 1/2 inch x 22 1/2 inch pss and 35 inch x 45 inch pars to be cut:

$$35,000 \text{ fss} \div 4\text{-up} \times (0.10 + 1.00) = 8,750 \text{ pss} \times 1.10 = 9,625 \text{ pss}$$

$$9,625 \text{ pss} \div 4\text{-out} = 2,406 \text{ pars}$$

Step 2. For prepress cutting, cut 4 out of a 35 inch x 45 inch pars to produce 17 1/2 inch x 22 1/2 inch pss. Determine the following:
Number of lifts:

$$2,406 \text{ pars} \div 1,000 \text{ shts./lift.} = 2.4 \text{ lifts} = 3 \text{ lifts}$$

Cutting time:

$$3 \text{ lifts} \times 0.22 \text{ hr./lift} = 0.66 \text{ hr.}$$

Prepress cutting time:

$$0.66 \text{ hr.} + 0.10 \text{ hr. setup} = 0.76 \text{ hr.}$$

Step 3. For postpress cutting, cut 4 out of 17 1/2 inch x 22 1/2 inch pss and then trim all cutout sheets to 8 1/2 inches x 11 inches (trim on four sides). Determine the following:
Number of lifts to be cut:

$$9,625 \text{ shts.} \div 1,000 \text{ shts./lift.} = 9.6 \text{ lifts} = 10 \text{ lifts}$$

Cutting time:

$$10 \text{ lifts} \times 0.09 \text{ hr./lift} = 0.90 \text{ hr.}$$

Number of lifts to be trimmed:

$$35,000 \text{ shts.} \div 1,000 \text{ shts./lift} = 35 \text{ lifts}$$

Trimming time:

$$35 \text{ lifts} \times 0.05 \text{ hr./lift} = 1.75 \text{ hr.}$$

Setups:
Add 0.10 hr. for cutting and 0.15 hr. for trim out setup.
Postpress cutting and trimming time:

$$0.90 \text{ hr.} + 1.75 \text{ hr.} + 0.25 \text{ hr.} = 2.90 \text{ hr.}$$

Step 4. Determine the total cutting production time and cost:
Total cutting time:

$$0.76 \text{ hr.} + 2.90 \text{ hr.} = 3.66 \text{ hr.}$$

Total cutting cost:

$$3.66 \text{ hr.} \times \$64.60/\text{hr.} = \$236.44$$

Folding Production

Paper stock may be folded using either knife or buckle folding equipment. Knife folders crease the sheet between two knurled rollers and are used with many web presses at the converting end of the presses. Buckle folders are far more common then knife folders in most printing and publishing operations because they are flexible in the manner by which they can fold, score, perforate, and slit in varying combinations. In addition, they are consistently high-output equipment items.

Buckle folders consist of a feeder, much like a press feeder, and folding units where parallel folds are put in the sheets as they bump against the folding plates of the folding units. As the sheets travel down the feedboard of the buckle folding machine, they are closely spaced but not overlapped when they enter the first folding unit. Knurled rollers in this unit drive a sheet into the first plate, which has been adjusted for the length of fold desired. Once the sheet bumps against the plate, it stops momentarily. The knurled rollers then grab it and move it out of the first unit, creasing it at the fold point and placing a fold parallel to the edge of the sheet. In the same folding unit, but with a different plate, additional parallel folds may be administered to the sheet in sequence. When all parallel folds have been completed, the creased sheet leaves the first folder unit and, if required, enters the second unit for additional folds. This second folder unit may be positioned at right angles to the first to provide folds that are parallel to and at right angles to the folds from the first unit. A large number of folding combinations are possible using the buckle folder, and it is important that folding considerations be carefully reviewed during the production planning and estimating phases of any job.

Buckle folding is essentially the same for both flat sheet and bookwork (booklet and pamphlet) operations. The combinations of parallel and right angle folds are planned and carefully executed in sequence with both operations. It should be noted that folder production speeds may vary with respect to the type of folding sequence required, the type of paper stock, and the thickness and grain of paper, among major factors. Figure 11.2 illustrates some of the more common folding configurations that apply to both flat sheet and bookwork impositions. Because equipment size and folding configuration vary considerably, these diagrams do not cover all of the folding possibilities.

It must be stressed that production planning should consider folding as one of the principal production factors. In fact, in some instances, all other job planning must be oriented around folding requirements. Practically every experienced estimator has had the unfortunate experience of planning and estimating an entire job, only to find during production that folding could not be properly completed. In some cases, the job might be salvaged; in others, the expensive task of redoing the entire job (perhaps at company expense) might be the only reasonable alternative. It does not take too many such episodes until the estimator or production planner carefully plans folding as a major element in job execution.

The parallel folding schedule in Figure 11.3 is divided into two segments: makeready/setup and running time. Penalties for stock caliper, slitting, gluing,

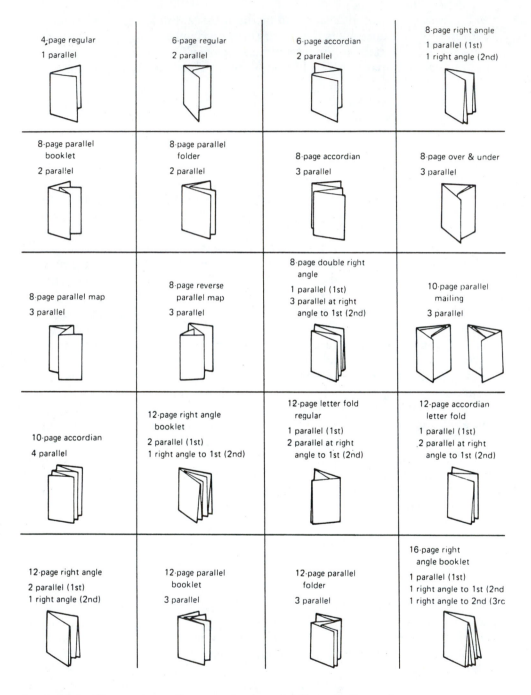

Figure 11.2 Illustrations of some common folding configurations.

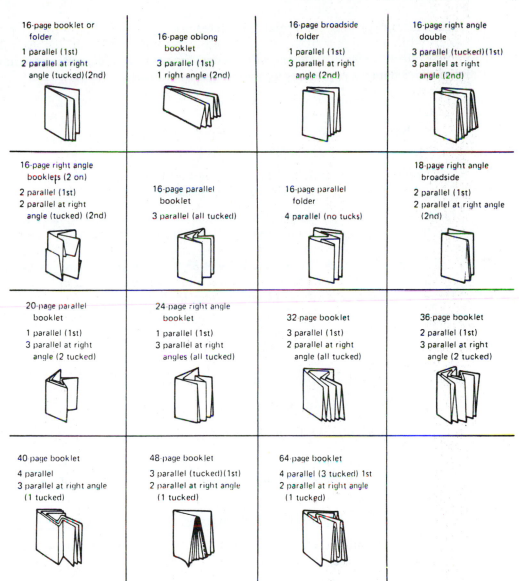

16-page booklet or folder

1 parallel (1st)
2 parallel at right angle (tucked)(2nd)

16-page oblong booklet

3 parallel (1st)
1 right angle (2nd)

16-page broadside folder

1 parallel (1st)
3 parallel at right angle (2nd)

16-page right angle double

3 parallel (tucked)(1st)
3 parallel at right angle (2nd)

16-page right angle booklets (2 on)

2 parallel (1st)
2 parallel at right angle (tucked) (2nd)

16-page parallel booklet

3 parallel (all tucked)

16-page parallel folder

4 parallel (no tucks)

18-page right angle broadside

2 parallel (1st)
2 parallel at right angle (2nd)

20-page parallel booklet

1 parallel (1st)
3 parallel at right angle (2 tucked)

24-page right angle booklet

1 parallel (1st)
3 parallel at right angles (all tucked)

32-page booklet

3 parallel (1st)
2 parallel at right angle (all tucked)

36-page booklet

2 parallel (1st)
3 parallel at right angle (2 tucked)

40-page booklet

4 parallel
3 parallel at right angle (1 tucked)

48-page booklet

3 parallel (tucked)(1st)
2 parallel at right angle (1 tucked)

64-page booklet

4 parallel (3 tucked) 1st
2 parallel at right angle (1 tucked)

Figure 11.2 *(continued)*

or perforating apply as appropriate. Makeready/setup times apply to any size folder, while running times are segmented into folders under 20 inches x 26 inches and those over 20 inches x 26 inches. Example 11.3 demonstrates how Figure 11.3 data are applied using the following formulas:

parallel folder production time = [setup time + running time
(where running time is calculated by the number of sheets to
be folded ÷ folder output in sheets per hour from schedule)]
x applicable penalties

total parallel folding production cost = total folding production
time x folder BHR

Example 11.3. Using the 6-page regular fold (see Figure 11.2), we have to fold 14,000 pieces (including spoilage and extras). Unfolded size is 24 1/2 inches x 11 inches, to be folded to 8 1/2 inches x 11 inches. A Stahl B23 (23 inch x 35 inch maximum sheet size) with a BHR of $58.50 will be used. Stock caliper is 0.005 inch. There will be no additional folds and no perforation or scoring. Determine the production time and cost for folding.

Solution

Use Figure 11.3.

Step 1. Determine the setup time for 2 folds:

0.30 hr. (first fold) + 0.10 hr. = 0.40 hr.

Step 2. Determine the running time for the folder (parallel fold section of schedule):
Folder output:
22 in. x 28 in. folder and 26 in. sheet length yield 5,000 shts./hr.
Running time:

14,000 pcs. ÷ 5,000 pcs./hr. = 2.80 hr.

Step 3. Determine the total parallel folding production time and cost:
Total folding time:

0.40 hr. + 2.80 hr. = 3.20 hr.

Total folding cost:

3.20 hr. x $58.50/hr. = $187.20

The signature or right-angle folding schedule shown Figure 11.4 is also divided into two segments: makeready/setup and running time. Penalties for stock caliper, slitting, gluing, or perforating apply when completed as part of the job. Makeready/setup times apply to any size folder, while running times are

Makeready/Setup

First Fold	.30 hour
Each Additional Fold	.10 hour
Each Slitter	.15 hour
Each Perforator	.15 hour
Each Scorer	.15 hour

Running Time (1–4 Folds, Makeready Not Included)

Sheet Length Through Machine	Machine Size—< 20 × 26	Machine Size—> 20 × 26
	Sheets Per Hour	Sheets Per Hour
6	15,000	
8	15,000	
10	13,000	13,000
12	13,000	13,000
14	9,000	7,000
16	9,000	7,000
18	7,500	6,500
20	7,500	6,500
22	6,500	6,000
24	6,000	5,500
26	5,500	5,000
28		5,000
30		4,500
32		4,500
34		4,000
36		4,000
38		4,000
40		3,500
42		3,500
44		3,500

NOTE: Add charges for additional personnel for banding, slitting, cartoning, etc.

Setup times indicated in schedule. Schedule basis sheets per hour.

Penalties: Add 25% to total time if stock calipers less than 0.003 inches or more than 0.006 inches. Add 50% to total time if foldig bible or manifold paper. Add 10% to total time if slitting, perforating, or gluing is completed during folding.

Figure 11.3 Schedule for estimating parallel folding machine production. (Reproduced with permission of Printing Industries Association of Southern California from its *1994-95 Blue Book of Production Standards and Costs.*)

Makeready/Setup

First Fold	.40 hour
Each Additional Fold	.10 hour

Running Time (Makeready Not Included)

	Signatures Per Hour	
	Up to 10 × 7 Inches	**Up to 12 × 9 Inches**
2 Folds	5,500	5,000
3 Folds	4,500	4,000
4 Folds	4,000	3,500

NOTE: Add charges for additional personnel for banding, slitting, cartoning, etc.

Setup times indicated in schedule. Schedule basis sheets per hour.

Penalties: Add 25% to total time if stock calipers less than 0.003 inches or more than 0.006 inches. Add 50% to total time if folding bible or manifold paper. Add 10% to total time if slitting, perforating, or gluing is completed during folding.

Figure 11.4 Schedule for estimating right-angle (signature) folding machine production. (Reproduced with permission of Printing Industries Association of Southern California from its *1994-95 Blue Book of Production Standards and Costs*.)

segmented by folded page size, with the first dimension indicating the binding edge of the signature. Example 11.4 is provided to demonstrate how Figure 11.4 would be used for estimating right-angle folder production using the following formulas:

signature (right-angle) folder running time = [setup time + running time (where running time is calculated by the total number of signatures to be folded ÷ number of signatures per hour from schedule)] x applicable penalties

total signature folding production cost = total folding production time x folder BHR

Example 11.4. Determine the time and cost to fold 21,000 16-page brochures, printed in a 1-16 SW. (See the 16-page right-angle booklet in Figure 11.2.) Untrimmed page size is 6 1/4 inches x 9 1/2 inches, and the press sheet/folder sheet measures 19 inches x 25 inches. Our folding dummy indicates there will be 3 folds at right angles to each other. Stock is basis 70 book that calipers at 0.0055 inch. No slitting, scoring, or perforating will be completed. Folding will be done on an MBO-B123 (23 inch x 36 inch maximum sheet size) with a BHR of $53.10.

Solution

Use Figure 11.4.

Step 1. Determine the setup time for 3 folds:

$$0.40 \text{ hr.} + 0.10 \text{ hr.} + 0.10 \text{ hr.} = 0.60 \text{ hr.}$$

Step 2. Determine the running time (see the right-angle folding section of schedule):

Folder output:

$$\text{Page size 6 1/4 in. x 9.50 in. (under 10 in. x 7 in.) and}$$
$$\text{3 folds yield 4,500 sig./hr.}$$

Running time:

$$21,000 \text{ pcs.} \div 4,500 \text{ sig./hr.} = 4.67 \text{ hr.}$$

Step 3. Determine the total folding production time and cost:
Total folding time:

$$0.60 \text{ hr.} + 4.67 \text{ hr.} = 5.27 \text{ hr.}$$

Total folding cost:

$$5.27 \text{ hr.} \times \$53.10/\text{hr.} = \$279.84$$

Hand Gathering Flat Sheets

Hand gathering is a procedure by which forms and other printed material are assembled. Perhaps the most common operation is the gathering of printed forms, which may be numbered and interleaved with carbon paper or printed on carbonless paper. The term "collating" has become synonymous with gathering procedures. The collating of printed signatures, either by hand or by machine, is also common.

Figure 11.5 provides for estimating production of hand-gathered materials. Schedule basis is the number of sets per hour broken out by size of sheet gathered. When used for estimating, the number of pieces to be gathered, also

Operation	8.5 × 11 Sheets Sets Per Hour	11 × 17 Sheets Sets Per Hour	17 × 22 Sheets Sets Per Hour
2 Pickups	600	500	350
3 Pickups	400	330	210
4 Pickups	300	225	120
5 Pickups	220	190	75
6 Pickups	185	160	
7 Pickups	160		
8 Pickups	135		

Setup time 0.10 hr. Schedule basis number of sets per hour gathered.

Penalties: Add 20% to total time if stock calipers less than 0.025 inches. Add 20% to total time for gathering odd sizes of paper. Add 30% to total time for gathering carbon interleaved forms.

Figure 11.5 Schedule for estimating hand gathering production. (Reproduced with permission of Printing Industries Association of Southern California from its *1994-95 Blue Book of Production Standards and Costs*.)

termed "pickups," and the size of the sheets to be collated must be identified. Penalties at the bottom of the schedule apply as indicated. The schedule data are used with the following formulas to estimate gathering production time and cost:

total gathering production time = [(number of sets to be gathered x number of pieces per set) ÷ number of gathered sets per hour] + penalty additions + setup time

total gathering production cost = total gathering production time x gathering BHR

The collating of folded signatures is detailed in the booklet and pamphlet section of this chapter (Section 11.4).

Example 11.5. We have printed 2,500 copies of a 4-part purchase order (white, canary, blue, and pink) on basis 50 book, caliper 0.004 inch, 8 1/2 inches x 11 inches. These copies must be hand gathered. Include time for carbon interleaving between each page of each 4-part set. The job has been numbered consecutively and must be gathered sequentially. The BHR for hand gathering is $29.80.

Solution

Use Figure 11.5.

Step 1. Determine the total production time to gather sets:
Time to gather (need 4 pickups):

$$2,500 \text{ sets} \div 300 \text{ sets/hr.} = 8.33 \text{ hr.}$$

Step 2. Add the appropriate penalties:
Penalty for numbering:

$$8.33 \text{ hr. x } 0.20 = 1.67 \text{ hr.}$$

Penalty for carbon interleaving:

$$8.33 \text{ hr. x } 0.30 = 2.50 \text{ hr.}$$

Step 3. Total the gathering production time:

$$8.33 \text{ hr.} + 1.67 \text{ hr.} + 2.50 \text{ hr.} = 12.50 \text{ hr.}$$

Step 4. Determine the total production cost to gather sets:

$$12.50 \text{ hr. x } \$29.80/\text{hr.} = \$372.50$$

Step 5. Summarize the findings:
Total gathering time: 12.50 hr.
Total gathering cost: $372.50

Jogging

The jogging of paper, the procedure by which paper stock is aligned in very even piles using manual operations or a vibrating jogger, is important throughout binding and finishing operations because it ensures perfect alignment of sheets as they are worked through various pieces of equipment. Jogging is also important when counting stock is required because aligned sheets allow faster and more accurate counting operations.

The jogging schedule in Figure 11.6 is based on the production output per 1,000 sheets of hand- or machine-jogged materials. The schedule is based on normal stock thickness (0.0025 inch to 0.008 inch) and approximate sheet size in inches. Penalties are added as they apply, especially for hard-to-handle stocks such as thin paper and gummed substrates.

For some operations performed in the bindery, such as folding and cutting, a small amount of production time has been built into the schedules for preliminary jogging operations. This jogging schedule should be used only when special jogging operations must be performed or when additional jogging is anticipated. (See Appendix B for formulas for jogging production time and costs.)

| | Time in Hours per (M) Sheets | |
Sheet Size in Inches	Hand	Machine
9½ × 12½ and under	0.06	0.04
12½ × 19 and under	0.13	0.09
19 × 25 and under	0.26	0.17
25 × 38 and under	0.39	
35 × 45 and under	0.52	
38 × 50 and under	0.65	
Over 38 × 50	0.78	

Setup time 0.10 hr. Schedule basis is hours per 1,000 sheets.

Penalties: Add 20% to total time if stock calipers less than 0.0025 inches. Add 20% to total time for gathering odd sizes of paper. Add 30% to total time for gathering carbon interleaved forms.

Figure 11.6 Schedule for estimating jogging production by hand or machine. (Reproduced with permission of Printing Industries Association of Southern California from its *1994-95 Blue Book of Production Standards and Costs*.)

Example 11.6. We must hand jog 6,500 sheets of onionskin to be used as second sheets for a legal agreement we have printed. Stock measures 8 1/2 inches x 14 inches and caliper at 0.0020 inch. The BHR for hand jogging is $29.80.

Solution

Use Figure 11.6.

Step 1. Determine the total production time to hand jog:
Time to jog:

$$(6,500 \text{ shts.} \div 1,000) \times 0.13 \text{ hr./M shts.} = 0.85 \text{ hr.}$$

Penalty for stock under 0.0025 inch:

$$0.85 \text{ hr.} \times 0.20 = 0.17 \text{ hr.}$$

Time for preparation: 0.10 hr.
Total jogging production time:

$$0.85 \text{ hr.} + 0.17 \text{ hr.} + 0.10 \text{ hr.} = 1.12 \text{ hr.}$$

Step 2. Determine the total production cost to hand jog:

$$1.12 \text{ hr.} \times \$29.80/\text{hr.} = \$33.38$$

Step 3. Summarize the findings:
Total jogging time: 1.12 hr.
Total jogging cost: $33.38

Counting

The counting of sheets and finished products in the bindery ensures that the quantity of finished products is accurate. Counting typically is completed either using manual techniques for small quantities or by inserting a metal gauge into a stack of jogged paper. The gauge divides the paper according to the number of sheets for which it has been preset. Gauge procedures are used for counting large quantities of paper. Regardless of the method used, the counting operations should be completed carefully yet quickly by bindery personnel.

The accompanying schedule in Figure 11.7 provides for estimating sheet production time on the basis of hours per 1,000 sheets or pieces counted. The size of paper or the finish size of the product must be known, as well as the thickness of paper (0.008 inch or less for thin or normal paper and over 0.008 inch for board), whether hand or gauge procedures will be used, and if dividers (such as chipboard), markers, or flags are to be inserted during the counting operation. Schedule times should be adjusted for individual production operations and personnel. (See Appendix B for formulas for counting production time and costs.)

Example 11.7. We have a job almost ready to be sent to the trade binders of 16-page signatures on a 19 inch x 25 inch pss in flat sheet form. Because the job is a "no less than" order, we must be certain that we send 12,500 sheets,

Sheet Size in Inches	Time in Hours per (M) Sheets or Pieces				Insert Dividers, Markers, or Flags
	Thin and Normal (0.008 in. thick or less)		Board (over 0.008 in. thick)		
	Hand	Gauge	Hand	Gauge	
20 × 26 or less	0.167	0.100	0.208	0.154	0.004 ea.
Over 20 × 26	0.250	0.154	0.357	0.250	0.006 ea.

Setup time is 0.10 hr. Schedule basis is hours per 1,000 sheets or pieces.

Penalties: Add 20% to scheduled time for counting scored, perforated, or hard-to-handle stocks.

Figure 11.7 Schedule for estimating sheet counting production by hand or gauge.

plus 3 percent for folder and stitcher waste. We will use a gauge for counting. Stock is basis 60 book, 0.0045 inch. The gauge-coating BHR is $29.80.

Solution

Use Figure 11.7.

Step 1. Determine the number of sheets to be counted:

$$12,500 \text{ shts. x } (0.03 + 1.00) = 12,875 \text{ shts.}$$

Step 2. Determine the total production time to count sheets:
Time to count:

$$12.9 \text{ M shts. x } 0.10 \text{ hr./M sht.} = 1.29 \text{ hr.}$$

Time for preparation: 0.10 hr.
Total production time:

$$1.29 \text{ hr.} + 0.10 \text{ hr.} = 1.39 \text{ hr.}$$

Step 3. Determine the total production cost to count sheets:

$$1.39 \text{ hr. x } \$29.80/\text{hr.} = \$41.42$$

Step 4. Summarize the findings:
Total counting time: 1.39 hr.
Total counting cost: $41.42

Padding

Padding operations involve the application of a glue material to temporarily bind paper stock. Padding is generally a hand operation in most binderies.

Figure 11.8, which is based on hours per 1,000 sheets padded, requires that the estimator know the number of sheets per pad, the number of total sheets to be padded, and the size of the sheets. Production time includes jogging of pads, counting and inserting chipboard, jogging piles of pads, the positioning for gluing, the application of glue, and the slicing apart of the pads when the adhesive is dry. (See Appendix B for formulas for padding production time and cost.)

Example 11.8. We must determine the time and cost to pad 3,500 4-part invoices that have been printed on collated NCR paper, 8 1/2 inches x 11 inches. There will be 25 sets per pad, or 100 sheets per pad. The BHR for padding is $29.80.

Solution

Use Figure 11.8.

Bindery*	8.5 × 11 or Smaller	9 × 12, 14 × 17 12 × 19	17 × 22, 17 × 28 19 × 24
100 Sheets to Pad	.20	.30	.40
50 Sheets to Pad	.30	.40	.50
25 Sheets to Pad	.35	.45	.55
10 Sheets to Pad	.40	.50	.60

* Includes stabbing, jogging, inserting chipboard, jogging piles, placing on table, putting on glue, and slicing pads apart.

To Determine Amount of Padding Time:
1. Determine the time per 1,000 sheets in the column for the appropriate sheet size.
2. Multiply the time per 1,000 sheets by the number of thousand sheets and add the prep time.

Setup time is 0.10 hr. Schedule time per 1000 sheets which includes stabbing, inserting chipboard, jogging piles, placing on table, putting on glue, and slicing pads apart when dry.

Figure 11.8 Schedule for estimating padding protection. (Reproduced with permission of Printing Industries Association of Southern California from its *1994-95 Blue Book of Production Standards and Costs.*)

Step 1. Determine the total production time to pad:
Number of sheets:

$$3,500 \text{ sets x 4 shts./set} = 14,000 \text{ shts.}$$

Time to pad:

$$14 \text{ M shts. x } 0.20 \text{ hr./M sht.} = 2.8 \text{ hr.}$$

Time for preparation: 0.10 hr.
Total production time:

$$2.8 \text{ hr.} + 0.10 \text{ hr.} = 2.9 \text{ hr.}$$

Step 2. Determine the total production cost to pad:

$$2.9 \text{ hr. x } \$29.80/\text{hr.} = \$86.42$$

Step 3. Summarize the findings:
Total production time: 2.9 hr.
Total production cost: $86.42

Drilling

Paper drilling equipment is used to drill holes in precise positions in the finished product. A single-spindle drill, also called a single-head drill, provides for the drilling of one hole at a time. The three-spindle drill, which has three revolving bits, is used for high-volume production and drills three holes in one operation. Most paper drills have semiautomatic paper-guiding mechanisms and are operated using a foot pedal for the actual drilling operation.

Figure 11.9 can be used for estimating drilling time with either single-spindle or three-spindle drilling equipment. Production output is measured in hours per 1,000 sheets drilled. Production time includes handling of already jogged sheets and drilling the required number of holes. The estimator must know the number of drilling heads on the equipment, the number of holes required, and the size and kind of paper stock. Schedule data should be adjusted for individual drilling operations and equipment and the skill of personnel. (See Appendix B for formulas for drilling production time and cost.)

Example 11.9. We must determine the time and cost to drill 150,000 notebook inserts using our 3-spindle drill. Stock is basis 50 book that calipers 0.0048 inch. Stock is properly jogged and ready for drilling. The BHR for drilling is $29.80.

Size	11 × 17 or Smaller		
Paper	**Single Spindle Drill**		**Three Spindle Drill**
	One Hole	**Each Addt'l. Hole**	**Three Holes**
Light Weight Paper 13# Bond, 50# Coated Book Stocks Calipering Less than .003"	.05	.02	.05
Average Weight Paper 16–24# Bond, 60–100# Coated Book 50–70# Wove Book Stocks Calipering .003"–.005"	.04	.02	.04
Heavier Weight Paper Stocks Calipering .0051"–.008"	.06	.02	.06

Setup time is 0.10 hr per drilling head. Schedule time per 1,000 sheets of paper drilled. Figures are based on properly jogged flat sheets.

Penalties: For stitched booklets, convert to sheets and add 20% to time shown. For 8 and 12 page booklets, add 50% to the schedule time due to the buildup of stitches.

Figure 11.9 Schedule for estimating paper drilling production. (Reproduced with permission of Printing Industries Association of Southern California from its *1994-95 Blue Book of Production Standards and Costs.*)

Solution

Use Figure 11.9.

Step 1. Determine the total production time to drill:
Time to drill:

$$(150,000 \text{ pcs.} \div 1,000) \times 0.04 \text{ hr./M pcs.} = 6.00 \text{ hr.}$$

Time for preparation:

$$0.10 \text{ hr.} \times 3 \text{ heads} = 0.30 \text{ hr.}$$

Total production time:

$$6.00 \text{ hr.} + 0.30 \text{ hr.} = 6.30 \text{ hr.}$$

Step 2. Determine the total production cost to drill:

$$6.3 \text{ hr.} \times \$29.80/\text{hr.} = \$187.74$$

Step 3. Summarize the findings:
Total drilling time: 6.30 hr.
Total drilling cost: $187.74

11.4   Estimating Commercial Booklet and Pamphlet Binding Operations

Booklets and pamphlets are typically products that contain sixty-four or fewer pages. Some small and medium-sized printing companies complete such types of work infrequently, while others specialize in booklet and pamphlet work. However, only one or two book or pamphlet jobs annually is not sufficient to warrant the purchase of some of the equipment covered here. Typically, when the volume of pamphlets or booklets is not high, finishing and binding will be completed at a trade bindery after the printer has produced the press sheets.

It should be made clear that the production of books, or works containing more than sixty-four pages, is not covered in this section. Generally, hardbound (casebound) and perfect-bound books are manufactured using complex book-binding equipment that is geared to operate at volumes suitable to justify such costly equipment. Casebound books require sewing, rounding, casing in, and other operations that are generally limited to specialized finishing lines in large book-publishing plants. Typically, a high-speed binding line is coordinated directly with sheetfed or web production to provide a complete manufacturing process for such book production. Equipment and facilities are specialized and usually tailored to the types of books produced.

This pamphlet binding and finishing section deals primarily with the gathering, wire stitching, and trimming of signatured materials. Some of the operations are manually performed, while others use automated or semiautomated equipment. As with all estimating data and equipment, such standards should be carefully reviewed before direct application to an individual plant or facility.

Hand Gathering Folded Signatures

Figure 11.10 is presented for estimating the time required to collate folded signatures into loose booklets. Schedule basis is gathering time per 1,000 booklets. The estimator must identify the untrimmed page size of the booklet, the number of signatures to be gathered, and whether the booklet is imposed upright or oblong. Preparatory time and penalties should be added as they apply.

It should be noted that the first dimension given with respect to the size of the booklet represents the binding edge dimension. For example, in the schedule, "10 x 7 and Under" indicates that the 10-inch dimension is the binding edge, which makes the booklet imposed in an upright page format. This notation method is common when estimating all areas of booklet and pamphlet finishing. (See Appendix B for formulas for signature gathering production time and cost.)

Side-Wire Stitching

Side-wire stitching is used for books and booklets that may be up to 1 inch thick. The procedure involves the insertion of wire stitches through the side of collated

No. of Signatures	Untrimmed Page Sizes					
	10 × 7 and Under		12 × 9 and Under		Over 12 × 9	
	Upright	Oblong	Upright	Oblong	Upright	Oblong
2	1.5	1.7	1.7	2.0	2.0	2.1
3	2.4	2.7	2.7	3.2	3.4	3.6
4	3.7	4.2	4.2	5.0	5.1	5.4
5	4.8	5.4	5.3	6.2	6.4	6.8
6	6.3	7.2	7.0	8.0	8.2	8.7

Setup time: 0.10 hr (2-3 signatures), 0.20 hr (4-6 signatures). Schedule basis is gathering time per 1,000 booklets

Penalties: For stitched booklets, convert to sheets and add 20% to time shown. For 8 and 12 page booklets, add 50% to the schedule time due to the buildup of stitches.

Figure 11.10 Schedule for estimating hand gathering of folded signatures. (Reproduced with permission of Printing Industries Association of Southern California from its *1994-95 Blue Book of Production Standards and Costs.*)

Number of Folded Signatures	Stitching Time in Hours per M Booklets (12 × 9 in. and under; 2 stitches)
3	1.70
4	1.80
5	1.90
6	1.95
7	2.00
8	2.05
9	2.10
10	2.20

Setup time is 0.20 hr. Stitching time in hours per 1,000 booklets.

Penalties: Add 10% to schedule time for each additional stitch over two. Add 15% to schedule time if untrimmed page size is over 12x9 inches.

Figure 11.11 Schedule for estimating side-wire stitching. (Reproduced with permission of Printing Industries Association of Southern California from its *1994-95 Blue Book of Production Standards and Costs.*)

signatures at the binding edge (see Chapter 6). Side-wire stitching does not provide the ease of opening offered by saddle-wire stitching or lay-flat binding, but it is used for books and booklets that are printed on bulkier stocks and where a rugged, sturdy binding is desired. While the covers of saddle-stitched books and booklets are stitched simultaneously with the signatures, side stitching allows for different cover attachment methods. For example, a cover may be side stitched with the signatures in a way that allows the wire stitches to show; or covers may be attached with glue after stitching to cover the side-wire material so it does not show.

Estimating side-wire stitching is done using Figure 11.11 and is based on hours per 1,000 books or booklets stitched with two stitches. The estimator must identify the number of signatures contained in the book and the untrimmed page size of the product. Preparatory time must also be added. Penalties apply for each stitch over the first two and when the book size is larger than the untrimmed 12 inch x 9 inch dimensions. (See Appendix B for formulas for side-wire stitching production time and cost.)

Example 11.10. We want to estimate the time and cost to gather and side-wire stitch a self-cover summary of court findings. The customer wants 2,200 summaries delivered. Each summary is an upright publication with an untrimmed page size of 9 1/2 inches x 6 1/4 inches (upright format), and there are 6 16-page signatures to be side stitched to make a 96-page product. The customer wants 3 stitches per booklet instead of the usual 2 stitches. The BHR for gathering is $29.80 and is $59.20 for the stitcher.

Solution

Use Figures 11.10 and 11.11.

Step 1. Determine the total production time to gather signatures:
Time to gather:

$$2.2 \text{ M bkts. x } 6.3 \text{ hr./bkt.} = 13.86 \text{ hr.}$$

Time for preparation: 0.20 hr.
Total gathering production time:

$$13.86 \text{ hr.} + 0.20 \text{ hr.} = 14.06 \text{ hr.}$$

Step 2. Determine the total production cost to gather signatures:

$$14.06 \text{ hr. x } \$29.80/\text{hr.} = \$418.99$$

Step 3. Determine the total production time to side-wire stitch signatures:
Time to stitch:

$$2.2 \text{ M bkts. x } 1.95 \text{ hr./M bkt.} = 4.29 \text{ hr.}$$

Time for preparation: 0.20 hr.
Total stitching production time:

$$4.29 \text{ hr. x } 0.20 \text{ hr.} = 4.49 \text{ hr.}$$

Penalty for third stitch:

$$4.49 \text{ hr. x } 0.10 = 0.45 \text{ hr.}$$

Total production time:

$$4.49 \text{ hr.} + 0.45 \text{ hr.} = 4.94 \text{ hr.}$$

Step 4. Determine the total production cost to side-wire stitch signatures:

$$4.94 \text{ hr. x } \$59.20/\text{hr.} = \$292.45$$

Step 5. Determine the total production time and cost to gather and stitch the booklets:
Total production time:

$$14.06 \text{ hr.} + 4.94 \text{ hr.} = 19.0 \text{ hr.}$$

Total production cost:

$$\$418.99 + \$292.45 = \$711.44$$

Saddle-Wire Stitching

Saddle-wire stitching can be done using manual, semiautomated, or fully automated methods. Figure 11.12 provides data for estimating manual (foot-operated) Rosback stitching, while Figures 11.13 and 11.14 cover semiautomated and fully automated saddle stitching equipment respectively.

Manual saddle-stitching equipment is popular for printing companies that do saddle-wire stitching infrequently but want to do the production in house with their own equipment. The gathering of signatures is completed separately from the stitching process. Saddle-wire stitching is common for booklets containing sixty-four or fewer pages, but it can be used for books up to 1/2 inch thick. As noted in Chapter 6, saddle-stitched products require different imposition treatment than do books and booklets that will be side stitched during binding. Of course, such imposition decisions must be made far in advance of such stitching procedures.

The basis of Figure 11.12 is the number of booklets stitched with two wire stitches per hour. The data apply to untrimmed sizes between 4 inches x 6 inches and 9 inches x 12 inches. A cover or an insert counts as a signature. Penalties apply for each additional stitch (over two), for extended covers, and for stitching booklets over 12 inches x 9 inches in untrimmed size. Add preparatory time as applicable. (See Appendix B for formulas for saddle-wire stitching production time and cost.)

> *Example 11.11.* We want to estimate the time and cost to hand gather and saddle-wire stitch a 48-page self-cover booklet in our plant. The booklet was printed and folded with 3 16-page signatures in an upright format and with an untrimmed page size of 11 1/4 inches x 8 3/4 inches. It will require 3 stitches. The BHR for gathering is $29.80 and $38.70 for saddle-wire stitching. We must deliver 5,200 copies.

No. of Sections	1	2	3	4	5
Quantity Per Hour	900	850	800	750	700

Setup time 0.10 hr. Schedule basis number of books saddle stitched per hour.

Penalities: Add 10% to schedule time for each additional stitch over two. Add 20% to total time if untrimmed page size is over 12x9 inches.

Figure 11.12 Schedule for estimating saddle-wire stitching production (foot-operated machine). (Reproduced with permission of Printing Industries Association of Southern California from its *1994-95 Blue Book of Production Standards and Costs*.)

Solution

Use Figures 11.10 and 11.12.

Step 1. Determine the total production time to gather signatures:
Time to gather:

$$5.2 \text{ M bkts. x } 2.7 \text{ hr./M bkt.} = 14.04 \text{ hr.}$$

Time for preparation: 0.10 hr.
Total gathering production time:

$$14.04 \text{ hr.} + 0.10 \text{ hr.} = 14.14 \text{ hr.}$$

Step 2. Determine the total production cost to gather signatures:

$$14.14 \text{ hr. x } \$29.80/\text{hr.} = \$421.37$$

Step 3. Determine the total production time to saddle-wire stitch signatures:
Time to stitch 3 signatures:

$$5,200 \text{ bkts.} \div 800 \text{ bkts./hr.} = 6.50 \text{ hr.}$$

Time for preparation: 0.10 hr.
Production time:

$$6.50 \text{ hr.} + 0.10 \text{ hr.} = 6.60 \text{ hr.}$$

Penalty for third stitch:

$$6.60 \text{ hr. x } 0.10 = 0.66 \text{ hr.}$$

Total stitching production time:

$$6.60 \text{ hr.} + 0.66 \text{ hr.} = 7.26 \text{ hr.}$$

Step 4. Determine the total production cost to saddle-wire stitch signatures:

$$7.26 \text{ hr. x } \$38.70/\text{hr.} = \$280.96$$

Step 5. Determine the total production time and cost to gather and stitch the booklets:
Total production time:

$$14.14 \text{ hr.} + 7.26 \text{ hr.} = 21.40 \text{ hr.}$$

Total production cost:

$$\$421.37 + \$280.96 = \$702.33$$

No. of Signatures	1	2	3	4	5
Quantity Per Hour	3,500	2,800	2,400	2,200	1,700

Setup time 0.30 hr for the first section and 0.10 for each additional section. Schedule basis number of books stitched per hour.

Penalities: Add 10% to schedule time for each additional stitch over two. Add 20% to schedule time if untrimmed page size is over 12x9 inches.

Figure 11.13 Schedule for estimating semiautomatic saddle-wire stitching production (Christensen or Rosback). (Reproduced with permission of Printing Industries Association of Southern California from its *1994-95 Blue Book of Production Standards and Costs*.)

Semiautomatic Saddle Stitching

Semiautomated Christensen and Rosback equipment combine the gathering and saddle stitching phases of booklet and pamphlet production as one in-line process. Final booklet trimming, however, is a separate operation. Semiautomated equipment is popular because its cost is moderate yet its production output is good. Usually a split-back gauge cutting machine is used for trimming.

The basis of the schedule data in Figure 11.13 is the number of signatures gathered and stitched with two stitches per hour; the trimming of stitched products is completed separately as just mentioned. The estimator must determine the number of signatures gathered to determine the production quantity per hour. Preparatory time is added as applicable. A booklet cover or tip-in insert is counted as a signature because either requires separate handling during production.

Automatic Saddle-Wire Stitching Equipment

Figure 11.14 is provided for estimating fully automated saddle stitching equipment. All gathering of signatures, stitching, and trimming is completed automatically as one in-line operation. Even though equipment configurations vary, this type of equipment is found in most large trade binderies and book manufacturing plants. This equipment is expensive to purchase so production is usually maintained at a high level. Schedule basis is the number of signatures gathered, stitched, and trimmed, cross-referenced by the quantity level of the

Quantity	Books Per Hour					
	No. of Signatures					
	1	2	3	4	5	6–8
1,000–5,000	6,000	5,500	5,000	4,500	4,000	3,500
5,100–25,000	7,000	6,000	5,500	5,000	4,500	4,000
25,000+	7,500	6,500	6,000	5,500	5,000	4,500

Setup time 1.00 hr for the first pocket and 0.20 for each additional pocket. Schedule basis number of books stitched and trimmed per hour.

Figure 11.14 Schedule for estimating fully automatic saddle-wire stitching production (Mueller, Macy, McCain, and so on). (Reproduced with permission of Printing Industries Association of Southern California from its *1994-95 Blue Book of Production Standards and Costs*.)

job. (See Appendix B for formulas for automatic saddle-wire stitching production time and cost.)

Example 11.12. We want to estimate the time and cost to automatically gather, stitch, and trim a 48-page self-cover booklet in our plant using our McCain saddle binding system, which includes 3-knife trimming. The booklet was printed and folded with three 16-page signatures in an upright format, with an untrimmed page size of 11 1/4 inches x 8 3/4 inches. Quantity is 5,200 copies and the booklet will require 3 stitches. The BHR for the unit is $72.20.

Solution

Use Figure 11.14.

Step 1. Determine the total production time to complete job: Gathering and stitching time:

$$5,200 \text{ bks.} \div 5,500 \text{ bks./hr.} = 0.95 \text{ hr.}$$

Time for setup/preparation:

$$1.0 \text{ hr. (1st)} + 0.20 \text{ hr. (2nd)} + 0.20 \text{ hr. (3rd)} = 1.40 \text{ hr.}$$

Total production time:

$$0.95 \text{ hr.} + 1.40 \text{ hr.} = 2.35 \text{ hr.}$$

Step 2. Determine the total production cost to complete the job:

$$2.35 \text{ hr. x } \$72.20 = \$169.67$$

Perfect Binding for Books and Booklets

Perfect binding is a bookbinding procedure using glue and preprinted flexible covers to bind a publication. Telephone directories, catalogs, and paperback books are examples of perfect-bound publications.

The perfect binding process is an in-line finishing operation that completes collating, gluing, and trimming. Pockets, or stations, hold prefolded signatures that are typically perforated during folding. All of the signatures for one finished booklet are collated automatically and then held tightly by a moving clamp system through a saw unit that cuts off from 1/16 inch to 1/4 inch of the spine (binding edge) of the signatures. Immediately after the sawing procedure is completed, while the booklet still tightly clamped, the signature moves across a gluing section (or wheels) that applies a glue mixture, after which a cover is wrapped to the glued area. Thus, the glue holds together all of the pages of the publication and the cover to the outside of the book as well. Three-knife trimming is typically done in line following cover attachment, and the book or booklet is completely finished and ready to be wrapped.

Perfect binding equipment is available with from four pockets to more than twenty pockets for signature collating and can typically handle books or booklets from 6 inches x 4 inches x 1/8 inch to those 20 inches x 12 inches x 4 inches. If a cover scoring unit is purchased, it can two-score (place two scored lines directly where the edges of the cover meet the spine) or four-score (place four scored lines so that the outer scored lines hinge the cover away from the spine). Signatures must be properly imposed and folded with their perforations along the binding edge to remove air easily during the binding process. Typically, signatures are from four to thirty-two pages on book stock of normal caliper. Covers, which are preprinted, are cut to the untrimmed size of the booklet and must be prescored if no scoring unit attachment is purchased with the perfect binder. Production problems and slowdowns during production generally relate to signature collating when signatures are too thin, when the type of stock is hard to feed, or when the printed stock has been varnished or is too glossy. Cover insertion and registration may be a problem when the varnish or gloss coating does not permit good control.

The schedule in Figure 11.15 is provided to estimate perfect binding production time. As with all schedules in this book, the indicated times are for example only and should be adjusted for individual plant production. (See Appendix B for formulas for perfect binding production time and cost.)

Example 11.13. Using our Muller-Martini Panda perfect binding machine, we must determine the production time and cost to perfect bind 9,500 chemistry books. They have been run on basis 50 book in 4 32-page signatures with an untrimmed page size of 11 1/4 inches x 8 3/4 inches. The cover is varnished,

Number of Sections (sig)	Binding Time in Hours per M Books or Booklets
1–3	0.14
4–6	0.15
7–10	0.17
11–14	0.18
15–17	0.20
17–20	0.22

Setup time 0.10 hr for the first pocket and 0.20 for cover insertion unit if used. Schedule basis is hours per 1,000 books which are perfect bound.

Penalities: Add 25% to schedule time for signatures under 16 pages. Add 20% to schedule time if cover is exceptionally glossy or varnished which may lead to insertion problems. As 15% to total time if signatures are printed on coated stock or may cause collating problems.

Figure 11.15 Schedule for estimating perfect binding production.

but we know it will feed well because we have used this kind of cover and varnish before. The BHR for the Muller is $87.25.

Solution

Use Figure 11.15.

Step 1. Determine the production time to perfect bind the job:

$$9.5 \text{ M bks. x } 0.15 \text{ hr./M bk.} = 1.43 \text{ hr.}$$

Step 2. Determine the preparatory time:
Time for pocket (pk.):

$$4 \text{ pks. x } 0.10 \text{ hr./pk.} = 0.40 \text{ hr.}$$

Time for covers (cvs.): 0.20 hr./cv.
Total preparatory time:

$$0.40 \text{ hr.} + 0.20 \text{ hr.} = 0.60 \text{ hr.}$$

Step 3. Determine the total perfect binding production time:

$$1.43 \text{ hr.} + 0.60 \text{ hr.} = 2.03 \text{ hr.}$$

Step 4. Determine the total production cost to per the job:

$$2.03 \text{ hr. x } \$87.25/\text{hr.} = \$177.12$$

Step 5. Summarize the findings:
Total perfect binding time: 2.03 hr
Total perfect binding cost: $177.12

Pamphlet and Book Trimming

Pamphlet and books are trimmed using split-back gauge cutting machines and three-knife trimmers. Example 11.14 is provided to demonstrate the estimating procedure for split-back gauge production, and Example 11.15 demonstrates how to complete estimating for three-knife trimming production.

Split-Back Gauge and Autospacing Cutting Machines. Figure 11.16 is provided for estimating the trimming production time and cost for booklets and pamphlets. Schedule data apply to cutting machines with split-back gauges and cutters with automatic, programmed spacing systems. Production is based on a single operator. The schedule basis is the number of lifts cut per hour of production. Determine the number of booklets in a lift by dividing the number of sheets of paper in one booklet into the approximate number of sheets per load, as indicated in the schedule.

For example, a 32-page booklet contains 16 sheets of paper. If substance 70 wove finish book stock (caliper 0.005 inch) is the substrate, then 800 sheets of paper represent the approximate sheets per load (see Figure 11.16). Dividing 800 sheets per lift by 16 sheets per booklet calculates that each lift will contain 50 booklets. At a trimming rate of 60 lifts per hour (again, see Figure 11.16), approximately 3,000 of these booklets can be trimmed out during 1 hour of production. If the job consists of 5,000 copies, dividing 5,000 total booklets by 3,000 booklets per hour results in a trimming production time of 1.67 hours. (See Appendix B for formulas for pamphlet/book trimming production time and cost.)

Example 11.14. We want to estimate the trimming time for 8,200 copies of a 186-page, self-cover, perfect-bound book printed on basis 70 dull enamel book stock. We will use our Polar 76 auto-spacing cutter with a BHR of $47.25.

Solution

Use Figure 11.16.

Step 1. Determine the number of books per lift:

$$186 \text{ pp.} \div 2 = 93 \text{ pp./bk.}$$

$$1,200 \text{ shts./lift} \div 93 \text{ pp./bk.} \cdot 12.9 \text{ bks./lift.} = 13 \text{ bks./lift}$$

Step 2. Determine the number of books trimmed per hour:

$$13 \text{ bks./lift} \times 60 \text{ lifts/hr.} = 780 \text{ bks./hr.}$$

Caliper and Kind of Paper	Approximate Sheets Per Load	Lifts Cut Per Hour
.0025" 13# Bond, 50# Enamel Book	1,600	60
.0035" 70# Enamel Book	1,200	60
.0040" 20# Bond, 80# Enamel Book, 60# Wove Offset	1,000	60
.0050" 24# Bond, 100# Enamel Book, 70# Wove Offset	800	60
.0060" 80# Wove Offset, 60# Enamel Cover	700	60
.0080" 80# Enamel Cover, 90# Bristol	500	60
.0110" 65# Antique Cover, 140# Bristol	400	60

Setup time 0.20 hr. Schedule basis is number of lifts cut or trimmed per hour.

Figure 11.16 Schedule for estimating pamphlet or booklet trimming production using an auto spacing cutter or split-back gauge. (Reproduced with permission of Printing Industries Association of Southern California from its *1994-95 Blue Book of Production Standards and Costs.*)

Step 3. Determine the trimming time:

8,200 bks. ÷ 780 bks./hr. = 10.51 hr.

Step 4. Determine the total production cost to trim:

10.51 hr. x $47.25/hr. = $496.60

Step 5. Summarize the findings:
Total book trimming time: 10.51 hr.
Total book trimming cost: $496.60

Three-Knife Trimmers. High-production commercial printing companies and most trade binderies typically have three-, four-, and five-knife trimmers that are used to cut apart and trim books, booklets, and pamphlets after binding. Generally, such units are set up to operate in line with the stitching, sewing, or perfect binding units, which expedites production because the final product is fully finished and ready for boxing or wrapping.

Figure 11.17 is provided to estimate book, booklet, and pamphlet production using a three-knife trimmer. Speed is determined by the size of the finished book, with penalties for very thin booklets and pamphlets and for odd-sized publications. Schedule data are presented for example only and should be modified for individual plant production. (See Appendix B for formulas for three-knife trimming production time and cost.)

Booklet Finish Size in Inches	Trimming Time in Hours per M Pieces
Up to and including 6 × 9	0.14
Over 6 × 9 and up to and including 8 ½ × 11	0.17
Over 8 ½ × 11	0.19

Setup time 0.20 hr. Schedule basis number of sets per hour gathered.

Penalities: Add 25% to schedule time for booklets containing less than 16 pages. Add 20% to total time for odd size books, booklets, or pamphlets.

Figure 11.17 Schedule for estimating pamphlet and book trimming using a three-knife trimmer.

Example 11.15. We want to estimate the time and cost to 3-knife trim a 48-page self-cover booklet using plant equipment. The booklet was printed and folded with 3 16-page signatures in an upright format and with a trimmed page size of 11 inches x 8 1/2 inches. The BHR for the 3-knife trimmer is $52.70. Add the trimming times and costs to the estimated times and costs from Example 11.11 for hand gathering and saddle stitching the book, then compare these totals to the times and costs for automatically gathering and saddle stitching this job using the McCain system in Example 11.12.

Solution

Use Figure 11.17.

Step 1. Determine the total production time to use a 3-knife trimmer on the job:
Time to trim:

$$5.2 \text{ M bkts. x } 0.17 \text{ hr./M bkt.} = 0.88 \text{ hr.}$$

Time for preparation: 0.20 hr.
Total production time:

$$0.88 \text{ hr.} + 0.20 \text{ hr.} = 1.08 \text{ hr.}$$

Step 2. Determine the total production cost to trim:

$$1.08 \text{ hr. x } \$52.70/\text{hr.} = \$56.92$$

Step 3. Determine the total production time and cost to stitch and trim the booklets (total of times from Example 11.11 and this example):

Total production time:

$$1.08 \text{ hr.} + 21.40 = 22.48 \text{ hr.}$$

Total production cost:

$$\$702.33 + \$56.92 = \$759.25$$

Step 4. Compare the answers in Step 3 with those of Example 11.12 for fully automated McCain production:

Total production time difference: 22.48 hr. - 2.35 hr. yields 20.13 hr. less using fully automated McCain equipment

Total production cost difference: $759.25 - $169.67 yields $589.58 less using fully automated McCain equipment.

11.5   Estimating Banding, Wrapping, Mailing, and Shipping Operations

The final area of binding and finishing to be estimated involves the concluding operations prior to shipment of the product. These operations include five separate procedures: banding and boxing (Figure 11.18), kraft and corrugated wrapping (Figure 11.19), shrink-wrapping (Figure 11.20), wrapping and inserting, and mailing operations (Figure 11.21).

Banding, Boxing, and Paper Wrapping

Both banding and boxing and kraft and corrugated wrapping operations, which are estimated with Figures 11.18 and 11.19, are frequent procedures prior to delivering the job to the customer. Banding and boxing or wrapping should not be estimated when incorporated as a portion of an earlier bindery procedure, such as the rubber banding and boxing of pamphlets during folding. In instances when banding and boxing or wrapping represents a necessary portion of the order, for example, when the customer specifically requests shrink-wrapping of letterheads, it should be included in the estimate as a separate operation. Plant policy should dictate such packaging procedures.

Shrink-Wrapping Production

Figure 11.20 is provided for estimating shrink-wrapping production using semi-automated equipment. Typically, the sealing of the shrink-wrap film is done manually by the operator, after which the package is placed on a conveyor transport that moves it through the heating unit that causes the film to shrink and seal the package tightly. Different models and speeds of equipment provide different production output. Thus, the figures indicated in Figure 11.20 are for

Type of Banding and Type of Package	Banding Time in Hours per M Packages		
	Under 25 Inches*	26–50 Inches*	Over 50 Inches*
Kraft paper band (firm, solid package wrapped with precut bands)	4.00	5.00	6.50
Kraft paper band (spongy package with precut bands)	6.50	8.00	9.25
Rubber bands: Single	2.20	2.50	2.90
Rubber bands: Double	4.00	4.50	5.00
String-tied packages (completed by hand)	5.00	5.70	6.60
String-tied packages (completed with tying machine)	2.80	3.10	3.50

Package measurements

height

width

length

Girth = 2 widths + 2 heights

Setup time 0.10 hr. Schedule basis is hours per 1,000 packages banded.

* Package girth plus length.

Figure 11.18 Schedule for estimating banding and boxing production

example only. (See Appendix B for formulas for shrink-wrapping production time and cost.)

Example 11.16. We have been asked to shrink-wrap 3,000 120-page books using our semiautomatic equipment. They have been perfect bound and are finished at 8 1/2 inches x 11 inches. The customer wants them shrink-wrapped in groups of 12 per package (pkg). The BHR for our shrink-wrap machine is $31.50. Determine the time and cost to shrink-wrap this job.

Solution

Use Figure 11.20.

Step 1. Determine the total production time to shrink-wrap:
Number of packages:

$$3,000 \text{ bks.} \div 12 \text{ bks./pkg.} = 250 \text{ pkg.}$$

Time to shrink-wrap:

$$250 \text{ pkgs.} \times 0.006 \text{ hr./pkg.} = 1.5 \text{ hr.}$$

Cubic Inch Volume (width × length × height)	Wrapping and Sealing Time in Hours per Package	
	Kraft Paper Roll and Paper Tape	Corrugated Material for Shipment; Kraft Wrap Also Included
Under 120 cubic inches (4 × 6 × 5, 3 × 5 × 6, or less)	0.020	0.033
121–200 cubic inches (4 × 6 × 6, 5½ × 8½ × 4, etc.)	0.022	0.040
201–350 inches (8½ × 11 × 3, 5½ × 8½ × 8, etc.)	0.025	0.050
350–500 cubic inches (8½ × 13 × 4, 8½ × 11 × 5, etc.)	0.029	0.067
501–600 cubic inches (11 × 14 × 3, 12 × 18 × 2, etc.)	0.033	0.100
Over 600 cubic inches (11 × 14 × 5, 19 × 25 × 3, etc.)	0.050	0.125

Setup time is 0.10 hr. Schedule basis is wrapping and sealing time in hours per package.

Penalties: Add 15% if the contents of the materials to be wrapped are spongy or unfirm.

Figure 11.19 Schedule for estimating kraft and corrugated wrapping production.

Time for preparation: 0.10 hr.
Total production time:

$$1.5 \text{ hr.} + 0.1 \text{ hr.} = 1.6 \text{ hr.}$$

Step 2. Determine the total production cost to shrink-wrap:

$$1.6 \text{ hr. x } \$31.50/\text{hr.} = \$50.40$$

Step 3. Summarize the findings:
Total production time: 1.6 hr.
Total production cost: $50.40

Type of Item	Shrink-Wrap Time in Hours per Package
Loose Sheets in Easy-to-Handle Amounts/Lifts	
Up to and including 6 × 9 in. (54 sq in.) finish size	0.003
6 × 9 in. up to and including 10 × 15 in. (150 sq in.) finish size	0.004
Individual Booklets	
Up to 10 × 12 in. (120 sq in.) finish size and 64 or fewer pages	0.003
Up to 10 × 12 in. (120 sq in.) finish size and more than 64 pages	0.004
Packages of Books or Booklets in Easy-to-Handle Amounts	
Up to and including 5 ½ × 8 ½ in. (48 sq in.) finish size	0.005
5 ½ × 8 ½ in. up to and including 10 × 12 in. (120 sq in.) finish size	0.006

Setup time is 0.10 hr. Schedule time is hours per package wrapped using semi-automated shrink-wrapping equipment.

Figure 11.20 Schedule for shrink-wrapping production.

Operation	Average Production Per Hour
Hand Wrap Packages & Label (4″ Depth)	40 Packages
Shrink Wrap Packages (Flat Sheets)	500 Packages
Shrink Wrap Packages (Booklets)	400 Packages
Insert 1 Piece into envelope, flap tucked	500 Pieces
Adjust for each additional piece inserted	95 per Piece
Insert 1 Piece into envelope, seal and hand stamp	300 Pieces
Insert brochure/booklet in catalog envelope	250 Pieces
Seal standard envelopes by hand	1,000 Pieces
Seal standard envelopes by machine	4,000 Pieces
Affix stamps by hand	770 Pieces
Insert one poster into mailing tube	90 Pieces
Affix label to tube	320 Labels

Setup time for each operation used is 0.10 hr.

Figure 11.21 Schedule for estimating mailing/shipping operations. (Reproduced with permission of Printing Industries Association of Southern California from its *1994-95 Blue Book of Production Standards and Costs*.)

Mailing Operations

Figure 11.21 provides estimating data for estimating mailing operations, of which the major production elements include inserting, addressing, and sorting mail to be sent through normal post office channels. Depending upon the setup of the binding and shipping facilities of the plant, mailing may or may not be considered a portion of the bindery area. Nevertheless, mailing operations have been included here as part of the bindery process, along with banding and wrapping, because they are concluding procedures and may utilize, or at least share, binding and shipping floor space.

Figure 11.21 is based on the number of completed packages or pieces per hour. Select the mailing operations to be completed and then determine the number of pieces subject to such mailing procedures.

Chapter 12

Estimating Web Printing Production

12.1 Introduction

12.2 Overview of Web Presses, Papers, and Inks
Web Press Production   Web Inks
Web Paper

12.3 Advantages and Disadvantages of Web Printing

12.4 Changes in Web Printing Products and Web Technology
Increased Press Speeds   Waterless Web Printing
Reduced Makeready Time   Wide-Width Web Technology
Increased Use of Prefolders   Improved Rotary Cutting Technology
Redesigned Postprinting Delivery   Web Products and Services to Meet
    Systems to Expedite Material Flow   Competition with Other Media

635

12.5   Estimating Web Paper

12.6   Estimating Web Production

12.1   Introduction

The primary difference between web and sheetfed printing is that sheetfed printing requires paper stock to be passed through the press as single pieces of paper, while web printing requires paper to be imaged from a continuously unwinding roll. Web's primary popularity comes from the exceptionally high speed at which a web press can operate: A typical full-width web can produce an output equal to that of approximately five sheetfed presses. Such high press speeds are not without limitations, however, such as high paper spoilage, the need for sophisticated registration controls for web equipment, and a pressroom technology that is different from the more commonly understood sheetfed operation. Also, the fixed cutoff of a web press, which is the repeat of the image around the cylinder, presents a significant problem because it limits product size to changes in web width only. Sheetfed presses can produce almost any size of press sheet within the length and width dimensions of the maximum pss, and therefore can produce nearly any finished product size desired by the customer.

This chapter begins with an overview of web presses, web papers, and web inks followed by a detailed discussion of the advantages and disadvantages of web production. Changes occurring in web production are discussed as they pertain to process improvement, enhanced product differentiation, and emerging markets. Estimating web production, which is discussed next, requires a thorough knowledge of web paper, including how to estimate roll footage, the number of cutoffs per roll, weight per 1,000 (M) cutoffs, roll weight, and slabbing waste. The final section of this chapter details the estimating processes for web production, including paper spoilage, ink consumption, and press time and cost.

12.2   Overview of Web Presses, Papers, and Inks

All web presses consist of infeed, printing, and postprinting segments. These three units vary widely in terms of their configurations, technical sophistication, and operating methods.

The infeed system includes roll stands, web tension control devices, roll changing devices, and all other preprinting equipment. Infeed operations include the preparation and mounting of one or more rolls of paper on the number of roll stands needed, after which the paper webs are carefully threaded through devices that carefully control the tension of the paper as it unwinds during printing. Controlling web tension is a key to ensuring precise image registration and minimum web breaks as the web of paper unwinds at high speed. Roll changes are necessary when rolls are depleted and new rolls are started. These roll changes can be completed by stopping the press and manually mounting new rolls on the roll stands or by using automated systems known as flying pasters.

The printing units of web presses image the substrate. Most web presses operate on lithographic, gravure, or flexographic imaging principles, but waterless printing is emerging as a viable web printing process. Xeikon and Agfa are webfed digital presses. Almost all web printing units print both sides of the sheet in one pass, which is commonly referred to as "perfecting" or "duplexing." Web offset presses perfect using blanket-to-blanket technology. Newer web printing units are console driven whereby operators electronically monitor and control all press production from a central location. In contrast, older webs require constant operator contact during production.

Web press printing units are typically configured in one of three ways: (1) in line, (2) stacked, or (3) common impression cylinder. In the in-line arrangement, the printing units are lined up one after another in direct sequence, and the substrate sequentially passes through each unit during printing. In the stacked unit configuration, which is designed to save floor space, the printing units are stacked one on top of another. During printing, the web is fed through the units using roll bars and other directional mechanisms so that many printing combinations are possible. Common impression cylinder webs have the printing units arranged around a large central cylinder, and printing occurs as the web passes by each unit in sequence.

Because many variations are possible with stacked and in-line web presses, and because each web press may be installed with different printing unit configurations, estimating web production requires a working knowledge of webbing procedures for the specific press on which the job is likely to run. An important component of a web estimate is a webbing diagram, which shows how the paper will move through the press to generate the final product.

It is important to note that there are both heatset webs, which are also known as closed webs, and nonheatset, or open, webs. Heatset webs, which are used to produce thousands of printed products on coated and uncoated book stocks, are equipped with both chillers and dryers as postprinting operations. The printed ribbon of paper passes through a chiller unit that solidifies the wet inks, then the heated dryers evaporate the solvents fully and harden the inks for immediate postprinting finishing operations. Nonheatset webs, which are found largely in the newspaper and newspaper preprint industry, allow for ink drying by absorption of the ink vehicle into the substrate. Thus, the ink is somewhat wet immediately after printing and dries slowly over time.

Postprinting production is of great importance because finishing operations affect the quality of the job as much as the quality of the printed image. Postprint finishing involves converting the web of paper into sheets, called cutoffs, and completing other operations so that, upon completion, the product is fully finished or prepared for additional finishing production.

When finishing is done immediately after printing and in one operation, it is termed "in-line finishing," while finishing that is done as a separate operation is known as "off-line finishing." In-line finishing provides a complete product in a single production activity, which tends to be more productive than off-line finishing because the product is handled only once. Off-line finishing is completed when the finishing processes require complex manufacturing steps, when finishing operations would slow press output, or when there is no in-line equipment to properly perform the desired result.

Both in-line and off-line finishing cover many production operations, including folding, die cutting, stitching, sewing, perfect binding, gluing, inserting, ink-jet addressing, and various packaging arrangements. Given this variety of finishing choices, web finishing equipment varies widely from press to press and company to company.

Web Press Production

There are three general classifications of web presses: newspaper web presses, commercial web presses, and specialty web presses. They are discussed in the following.

Newspaper Web Presses. The newspaper web is commonly used for printing on newsprint stocks for newspapers, freestanding inserts, advertising flyers, and other products. The usual substrate with newspaper webs is newsprint, but both book and bond stocks can also be used. Most newspaper webs are coldset or open webs.

As competition with other media has driven newspapers to print multicolor images, the technical sophistication of newspaper web presses has grown significantly in the past ten years. Older newspaper webs are usually characterized by an equal number of roll stands to printing units, which indicates that the presses are primarily for printing all rolls in a 1/1 configuration or black ink on newsprint. Newer newspaper webs have the capacity to provide multicolor printing, but their cutoff sizes, dampening systems, and other equipment aspects are similar to older newspaper webs.

Commercial Web Presses. There are two categories of commercial web presses used extensively in the printing industry: full-width and half-width. This discussion centers around lithographic web presses—the largest category of commercial webs—although gravure (intaglio) and flexographic webs are also used and are discussed as appropriate.

Full-width web lithographic presses, which are also known as 16-page webs, typically deliver a cutoff or cut sheet of approximately 24 inches x 36 inches or 16-page (8 1/2 inch x 11 inch) signatures imposed in an SW page lay with 8 pages per side. A 16-page web prints with the image repeat or cylinder circumference in the 24-inch dimension and the maximum width of the web in 36 inches. The circumferential printing area or image repeat is built into the press and cannot be changed, while the width of the roll of paper can be any dimension up to 36 inches.

Half-width webs, which are also known as 8-page or narrow-width webs, typically accommodate a maximum web width of approximately 24 inches and produce a maximum cutoff of 19 inches x 24 inches. However, there is no fixed definition of maximum web width in half-width webs. Image repeat is fixed at 19 inches, and webs can be any width up to 24 inches.

Full-width commercial webs are popular for the production of book signatures, magazines, catalogs, packaging products, and many higher volume advertising materials, while narrow-width webs are used to produce smaller signatures, a wide variety of commercial and advertising products, and generally shorter run jobs.

Eight-page webs experienced great popularity for about a ten-year period beginning in the mid-1970s, largely due to their fast startup, quick changeover during production, and suitability for shorter runs. Most web printers found that the older full-width web press was too slow and cumbersome to stand up against the faster, more flexible narrow-width press.

During the early 1980s, web press manufacturers began to modify the 16-page web to make it more suitable as a fast-turnaround production unit. The changes incorporated faster plate mounting techniques, improved inking systems, and electronic consoles that greatly quickened makeready procedures. As a result, the production output of such presses increased from a top speed of 1,500 feet per minute (fpm) to 2,500 fpm. Thus, the full-width web became faster not only with respect to its gross speed, but in its capacity to deliver twice the product because of its double maximum web width. Also, the makeready times of the full-width web were significantly reduced compared to its half-width counterpart, making the full-width web the press of choice for newer web installations and for customers whose budgets are critical.

At this writing, both older 16-page webs and newer 16-page webs, as well as a variety of half-width webs, are found throughout the industry. It is clear that older 16-page webs cannot address the same customer needs as their newer, full-width counterparts. It is also clear that the half-width web remains a viable, competitive production press against both the older and the newer 16-page web units. An emerging generation of half-width presses will improve in largely the same ways as their full-width counterparts. However, when considering new purchases, many web printers are opting for full-width webs with the hope of being able to keep the presses busy because their output is so high.

The purchase of a commercial web lithographic press requires that the printing company determine the product lines to be produced with the equipment. Web printing is both a process and a product specialization. Purchasing considerations include the type of roll-changing apparatus, the number of roll stands, and the number and configuration of printing units (stacked or in line), as well as the web-tensioning devices, the plate-dampening units, and the postprinting finishing and binding equipment. If the press is heatset, chillers and driers with the accompanying air quality assurance equipment must be purchased.

Gravure (intaglio) web presses, which are sometimes termed "rotogravure," are popular for high-volume publishing production such as weekly news magazines. Cylinders are carefully etched and expensive to produce, but they provide millions of impressions. Gravure web widths may be 60 inches or greater, and most gravure presses are equipped with complete in-line finishing. Gravure presses are manufactured to meet specific product sizes and imaging requirements, and they frequently cost millions of dollars. Typically their substrates include newsprint, coated and uncoated book stocks, and thinner board stocks for packaging products.

Specialty Web Presses. Specialty webs are narrow-width webs used for the manufacture of specialized products. Their generally defined maximum web width is 14 inches, with image repeat at 10 inches or fewer. Thus, while specialty presses have built-in inflexibility for small cutoffs, they also represent a very profitable segment of the printing industry because of their increased output in producing highly specialized, nontypical products. For example, in the production of business forms, there may be in-line printing, perforating, numbering, scoring, and carbon interleaving procedures.

Specialized web substrates are linked to the type of web press. Label presses handle most types of adhesive stocks and paper, while forms presses handle "no carbon required" (NCR) and other types of papers. Inks are matched to the substrates, and drying methods and equipment are specialized to meet the substrate and ink combinations.

Specialized web printing may be done using lithographic or waterless, intaglio (gravure), flexographic, or digital methods. Flexographic webs are common to packaging, labels, business forms, and similar specialized products. Rotary flexographic printing is completed from raised-image photopolymer rubber plates to many different substrates, including papers, foils, plastics, and transparent packaging materials. This type of printing is a direct impression to the substrate that is easy to control, and its quality has improved greatly since the mid-1980s. Flexographic plates are easy to make and provide high mileage, while their cost is lower than lithographic plates or the very expensive gravure cylinders. Labels are a popular application of flexographic printing. They are frequently produced on Mark Andy narrow-width rotary flexographic web presses.

Web Paper

The three most common types of paper purchased for web lithographic printing are book (coated and uncoated), bond, and newsprint. Coated book paper, which is used largely with the commercial web press, is popular for most glossy (fancy) publications, magazines, and annual reports, especially where process color is desired. Uncoated book paper is used predominantly in the production of textbooks, calendars, and for thousands of other general commercial products. Uncoated book paper is probably the single largest seller of all web papers. Bond stocks are generally used with specialty web operations in business forms, but they are used for many commercial products also. Newsprint has its greatest application with newspaper web presses. It is also used with newspaper and commercial web equipment for preprint, supplement advertisements, inserts, and many other products requiring less expensive substrates.

There are some general facts regarding web paper. Thin caliper stocks seem to run better and offer a large number of linear feet per roll. Heavy papers and those with thick caliper have lower footages (and therefore require more frequent roll changes) and seem to print and convert with more difficulty. In terms of winding, all rolls should be wound as tightly and as uniformly as possible at the mill, regardless of the type of paper. The cores for web paper are made of either metal or fiber (paperboard), but there are also coreless rolls. Metal cores are preferred for wide rolls and coated stocks. Fiber cores are preferred by many plants because they are easy to work with and do not require storage and return to the mill—a necessity with metal cores. Common inside diameters for cores are 3 inches and 4 inches. With either type of core roll, weight is high.

Web paper can be wound at the mill either felt (smooth) side in or felt side out and slit at the specific width desired. Moisture content of most web stocks resembles that of sheeted stock—it is between 4 percent and 6 percent. Flags or roll markings are used to indicate splices and flawed sheet formation areas; many flags mean there is a greater probability of web breaks and production problems. Wrapping the rolls for shipment from the mill may be done using either moisture-proof or nonmoisture-proof material. When ordering paper, felt side in or out, the number of acceptable flags and type of wrapping should be specified. Of course, roll dimension (width), roll weight, and the type of paper should also be indicated, as should any special instructions and delivery information.

Rolls of web paper are frequently specified using a notation system of width in inches by diameter in inches by thickness in inches. For example, a roll of uncoated book paper measuring 34 inches wide, 0.004 inch thick, and 40 inches in diameter is specified as a roll 34 x 40 x 0.004. This notation system is used to specify web paper later in this chapter.

Web Inks

Web lithographic inks vary from manufacturer to manufacturer. Generally, differences in print quality, production performance, and working conditions are noticeable between the more expensive inks and those in the reduced price group.

Web ink consumption is contingent upon constant and variable factors. The constant factors relate to the amount of ink necessary for initially inking the system and the amount of ink lost during washups. Both of these factors, once they are determined for a specific web press, change very little over time. Variable ink consumption is an entirely different matter, however. Two factors relate here: the mileage of the ink on the press and the absorption rate of the substrate. As with sheetfed inks, both press mileage and absorption are difficult to determine precisely because even slight changes in the type of ink or substrate can result in pronounced shifts in either category.

Web inks can be purchased in 5-pound cans, in 10-pound and 25-pound sizes, by the 55-gallon drum, and by the tanker truckload or railroad tank car. Overall, the prices of the more fluid web inks are lower than the costs of the sheetfed paste inks. Many large web offset printers buy and store large volumes of ink so that they are ensured the desired quantities. Ink transportation from storage tank to press fountain is completed using dedicated pipes and pumping equipment.

Web inks are usually estimated on the basis of the number of pounds of ink per 1,000 press cutoffs. For example, a 35-inch web with a 23-inch cutoff that prints a 16-page signature on coated stock might be estimated for ink using a factor of "2.9 pounds of ink per 1,000 cutoffs." This same job, if printed on uncoated paper but with all other factors equal, might have a factor of "3.9 pounds per 1,000 cutoffs." Ink mileage data can vary widely based on the coverage of the printed image, the type of paper, the color of ink, and the web press. It is recommended that each company determine its ink consumption based on its actual web press performance. In this manner, companies can fit their inks to standard paper stocks, printing conditions, and presses. Web ink estimating is demonstrated later in this chapter.

12.3   Advantages and Disadvantages of Web Printing

The discussion that follows provides a perspective on the major advantages and disadvantages of printing using the web process. The following are advantages of web production.

Advantage No. 1: High-Speed Production for High-Volume Output

Web presses, with stock that is fed from rapidly unwinding rolls and is not limited by sheetfed registration and sheet transporting procedures, print at very high speeds. For example, the average speed of a 4-color, 40-inch sheetfed perfecting press printing 2/2 on a 24 inch x 36 inch finished sheet produces about 7,500 iph. A comparable 4-color perfecting web press, when producing roughly the same 24 inch x 36 inch finished sheet (called a cutoff by the web printer), can realistically run at 1,000 fpm, which translates to 30,000 finished cutoffs per hour. These cutoffs would be printed 4/4 because the web press would perfect, or print both sides of the sheet in one pass. Thus, compared to the sheetfed press, the typical web press can produce from three to four times the sheet volume and double the image capacity because it perfects.

Advantage No. 2: In-Line Finishing Reduces Production Time

Most web presses, while feeding from rolls of paper that allow for high production output, are equipped with postprinting converting attachments. These attachments are designed to cut the ribbon of paper into sheets at high speed, then fold these sheets, and finally collect them in sequence to make up a booklet or a collection of pages for a particular job. Thus, web printing production provides a built-in bindery, where a job is not only printed, but it is then partially or completely finished as a single, in-line operation.

In fact, many large magazine publishers and catalog publishers build complete binding lines at the converting ends of their presses. Thus, signatures are printed, sheeted, folded, and then collected at extremely high speeds, and direct in-line final binding equipment (such as perfect binding units) is used to produce the final catalog, telephone book, or magazine. Because binding and finishing share similar labor and capital intensity with the pressroom, having an in-line bindery that is linked to the press can save many hours of production time and thereby reduce manufacturing cost with high-volume usage.

It should be noted that other postprinting operations, such as gluing, slitting, perforating, numbering, and scoring, can also be done with proper web press attachments. Also, some web equipment is designed to print roll to roll. That is, the ribbon of paper is rewound after printing as a roll of paper, with no converting or finishing performed during presswork. Finishing will be completed later on the roll of stock, perhaps during a follow-up imprinting.

Advantage No. 3: High-Quality Products

The consideration of print quality has been a much discussed point between sheetfed and web experts over the years, and generally it is agreed that, all other factors being equal, equally high quality is achievable using either lithographic sheetfed or web printing.

Perhaps the two most important categories of quality measurement of printed products are image registration and color valuation. Recent years have seen many changes in web tension controls and in the electronic devices for precision and consistency of web registration during printing. On-press color density measurement devices, which are linked to plate scanner technology for faster makeready, aid in focusing immediately on accurate ink coverage and color valuation. They also save on makeready time and avoid wasted paper. Advances in ink technology and ink distribution on press have improved both the quality and the speed of drying for both heatset and nonheatset printed products.

Advantage No. 4: Paper Cost Is Less than Sheetfed Paper

A final major advantage of web printing is that the cost of paper stock is generally from 3 percent to 7 percent less in roll form when compared to the same type of paper in sheets. Sheeting and cartoning of paper at the mill require extra time and equipment, thus increasing the cost of sheeted papers. Even though this reduction may not seem significant, because paper represents approximately 50 percent of the average cost of a web printing order, even a slight cost reduction passed on to the customer may win the job for the web printer. Because paper is a direct material cost, the greater the quantity desired by the customer, the greater the savings.

While the advantages of web are significant, the following disadvantages must be considered as well.

Disadvantage No. 1: High Paper Spoilage during Production

As paper costs increase, the issue of high paper spoilage remains critical to web printers everywhere. Paper spoilage during web press makeready and printing is higher with web production than with sheetfed procedures. A number of factors contribute to this high spoilage environment. First are web breaks, which occur when the ribbon of paper that is moving rapidly through the printing units is torn or snapped apart. Web breaks require immediate stopping of the press, rewebbing, and then startup throwaways until desired print quality is achieved. One or two web breaks at maximum production speed can mean the difference between profit and loss on many web jobs. Although the industry practice is to charge the customer for normal job-related paper spoilage, competitive conditions do not permit the printer to charge for unplanned or excess spoilage. Obviously, reducing web breaks is an important factor for improving web production and job profitability.

Second, because most web presses are used to print multicolor jobs, all printing units must image in exact relation to one another. As the press is made ready, the registering of these units to one another requires startup spoilage, and this register must be maintained during the press run itself. If either makeready or running registration becomes problematic, spoilage increases above normal.

For example, we are in the middle of a pressrun of a 4/4 job on our 4-unit, 36-inch web press that has a 22 3/4 inch cutoff and is running 800 fpm. Two printing units begin to print out of register, compromising quality and providing a product the customer would not accept. At this speed, the press prints 25,319 cutoffs per hour (see Figure 12.4). If the problem is not discovered or cannot be stopped for three minutes, spoilage will be 1,266 cutoffs measuring 22 3/4 inches x 36 inches. If the paper is sub 60 book, the estimated poundage of unusable paper is 131 pounds. If the paper prices at $0.80 per pound, the cost of the spoiled paper is $104.80.

The third factor contributing to high spoilage is that web lithographic presses require an intricate balance between ink and water, as well as a large number of other technical setup and running considerations. During production, changes in these preestablished printing conditions can translate into an excessive number of spoiled cutoffs. As with web breaks and registration problems, lack of control of technical printing factors can adversely affect the profitability of the job through increased paper cost. This disadvantage is partially resolved with the use of waterless printing, which is discussed later in this chapter.

Disadvantage No. 2: Fixed Cutoff

A clear limitation of web printing is that web presses are built with an unchangeable cutoff length, which limits their product sizes. Cutoff measurement defines the circumferential distance of the blanket cylinder of the press and usually represents the smaller dimension of the cutoff sheet. For example, if the circumferential cutoff for a full-width 36-inch web press is 22 inches and the web paper is 34 inches wide, then the sheet cutoff measures 22 inches x 34 inches. Normally the maximum printing area is slightly less than the cutoff dimension, so a 22-inch cutoff might provide for the printing of a 21-inch image.

This size inflexibility makes it necessary for web printers to establish and standardize their product lines to this fixed cutoff measurement, understanding that product flexibility can be provided only by varying web width. For example, assume a full-width web press can handle up to a 36-inch wide web and has a 22-inch circumferential cutoff. Most printers would select certain web widths for this 22-inch cutoff and plan products to each sheet cutoff dimension. Assume the printer decided on web widths of 30 inches, 32 1/2 inches, 34 inches, and 36 inches to deliver products his customers desired. These widths would provide sheet cutoffs dimensions of 22 inches x 30 inches, 22 inches x 32 1/2 inches, 22 inches x 34 inches, and 22 inches x 36 inches. As products using these four sheet cutoff sizes were developed and sold, the printer's web paper inventory for this press would consist of roll widths measuring 30 inches, 32 1/2 inches, 34 inches, and 36 inches.

Disadvantage No. 3: High Costs for Heatset Web

As has already been noted, ink setting can utilize either heatset or nonheatset technology. For fancier products on book stock, which represent a major group of products purchased by advertising agencies and other customers, heatset web is the chosen process. This process allows for immediate setting of inks and complete postpress finishing operations, so the entire product is manufactured in one operation.

However, there are serious environmental concerns over air quality with respect to heatset web offset driers, and many states now require expensive afterburners to reduce the volatile organic compound (VOC) emissions from these presses to established levels. Adding such expensive peripheral equipment represents a major fixed cost to the printer, but it adds no significant production output to the press. Increased variable costs are also required because the afterburner requires energy to operate. Both the peripheral equipment and its energy requirements increase the cost of the final product. Generally, however, the owner of the heatset web press accepts these additional costs with little complaint in an effort to cooperate in improving the environment.

Disadvantage No. 4: Highly Skilled Web Press Operators Are Hard to Find

Web printing involves a number of interrelated preprinting, printing, and postprinting operations that utilizing high-speed production. Although sheetfed printing technology can be complex, the process is generally done at a slow, measured pace. Given the range of technology and the speed with which web presses operate, web press operators must posses a high degree of technical skill and be able to respond quickly and correctly.

The problem is that highly skilled web press operators—operators who are knowledgeable about roll preparation, web tension, web breaks, technical printing factors, postpress finishing, product quality, and a myriad of other technical production elements—are frequently hard to find. Because web presses operate at such high speeds and represent significant capital expense, the press operator is a key ingredient to ensure efficient production with minimum paper waste, low downtime, and quality products. It is clear that the technically skilled web press operator is an absolute necessity and management cannot operate under profitable conditions without this skilled, frequently hard-to-find technician.

12.4 Changes in Web Printing Products and Web Technology

Web printing, as are all other parts of the printing industry, is changing. The following itemizes and briefly discusses the emerging technologies.

Increased Press Speeds

Web press production, which is measured in fpm, has been steadily increasing since the mid-1980s. As noted in Figure 12.4 later in this chapter, a web press with a 22-inch cutoff running at 1,000 fpm produces 32,727 cutoffs per hour. If this press can be enhanced to print at 2,000 fpm, the cutoff quantity doubles to 65,455 cutoffs per hour. Every 100 fpm increase is the equivalent of a 10 percent productivity increase.

Web press speeds have been slowed largely by infeeding and postpress equipment limitations. Infeeding problems include tension control and web breaks, which, as discussed earlier, cause significant registration and spoilage problems. Postpress systems that retard press speed include many in-line operations such as folding, perfect binding, and product delivery mechanisms.

Reduced Makeready Time

The more quickly a makeready is completed, the lower the fixed costs the customer must pay to produce usable cutoffs for his job. Reducing makeready time from 1 hour to 20 minutes on a $300 per hour press saves the customer $200.

Reduced makeready time for web production has been achieved using largely the same techniques found in the sheetfed press area. These include fast plate registration, optical plate scanning to set ink densities, console controls that provide instantaneous response, faster webbing systems, and automated washup systems.

Increased Use of Prefolders

A prefolder is an in-line finishing device that can be used to increase the number of folds in the sheet or to provide certain types of folds at high web press speeds. The prefolder is positioned before the web enters the folder. Using angle bars and plow folding methods, the prefolder positions the web to create a variety of fold configurations. For some web printers, prefolders are a way to add product flexibility to their conventional web presses.

Redesigned Postprinting Delivery Systems to Expedite Material Flow

Many web printers have experienced frustration in their inability to handle final products that are delivered at high speeds at the very ends of finishing lines. This has created a bottleneck that is difficult to overcome, even with the addition of employees who can get in each other's way. This has been largely resolved with the development of single- and multiple-stacking equipment, which allows web press crews additional time to jog, band, wrap, or skid load the finished product.

Waterless Web Printing

As waterless printing has begun to make inroads in lithographic sheetfed production, it is emerging as a viable web printing process as well. As discussed in detail in Chapter 10, waterless printing is accomplished using waterless Toray plates, waterless inks, and temperature-controlled inking methods. The advantages of sheetfed and web production are largely the same. Waterless web provides faster makereadies, generally better control during printing, greater color fidelity and resolution because no water is used, and less spoilage during the run. Because the waterless process does not require careful ink-water balance, monitoring web production is less problematic. Although waterless plates are more than double the cost of lithographic plates, and although retrofitting of inking systems is expensive, the advantage of reduced paper spoilage alone can provide a fast payback for web printers adopting waterless technology.

Wide-Width Web Technology

Although full-width, 36-inch webs provide significant production output, double-wide and other wide-width web presses are emerging. These presses typically are offered in widths of over 50 inches for both lithographic and gravure processes. Wide-width webs are purchased and installed to meet very specific production and product requirements and cost millions of dollars each. Their press speeds can be as high as 2,500 fpm and finishing is done in line. Thus, if a 36-inch, full-width web with a 22-inch cutoff ran at 1,500 fpm, it would produce 49,091 cutoffs per hour (see Figure 12.4). Therefore, a double-wide, 72-inch press would produce 98,182 cutoffs per hour (49,091 x 2). However, this output capacity can be justified only by very large, high-volume printing companies for long-run publishing and packaging orders.

Improved Rotary Cutting Technology

Rotary cutters slice the web into sheet form early in the postprinting sequence. The operating speed of these cutters has been one of the key problems in achieving high web press speeds because the cutters have mechanical limitations. This is changing because a number of vendors have developed high-speed rotary cutting devices that are easy to make ready and operate at press speeds of over 1,500 fpm. The cost of blades, which are also called knives, and the time needed to change them have also been reduced.

Web Products and Services to Meet Competition with Other Media

The investment in web press equipment is high, and the competition between web printers and with other media is intense. This means that web printers must reduce cycle times and provide customers with ever-improving products and services. High-volume web printers constantly strive to keep their costly web press equipment and skilled employees working on chargeable activities. A key approach to achieve this is for the printers to aggressively develop and tailor their web products to meet specific customer needs. The following is a discussion of some of the specialized services and products web printers offer their customers. It should be noted that some of these products and services are also discussed in Chapter 11 as postpress operations completed by the sheetfed printer.

Use Lighter Weight Papers. The choice to use lighter weight papers is among the printer's first solutions when evaluating methods to save postal or delivery costs. However, one problem with lighter weight substrates is that they tend to increase the number of web breaks during printing. The number of breaks depends on the specific infeed equipment on many web presses, including the web tensioning and roll changing apparatus. Thus, shifting to a lighter weight paper is a reasonable solution to cutting mailing costs only when paper spoilage during production is not adversely affected.

Reduce Product Sizes. Catalog, magazine, and other customers using the postal service are constantly monitoring mailing costs. One practical solution to reducing mailing costs is to reduce the size of the product so that it weighs less. Changing the size of a web product typically requires a careful analysis of paper factors, including web cutoff size, prefolding and folding, and binding. A small reduction in product size, for example making a catalog one-half inch smaller in one dimension, could easily translate into thousands of dollars in saved paper, as well as reduced mailing costs since the catalog weighs less.

Comailing. Comailing is the mailing of two or more products as a single item to save mailing costs. Comailing generally involves placing all products into a transparent plastic carrier or bag, through which the mailing label can be seen. Comailing provides a cost savings in delivery, but it increases product costs because the products must be collated, addressed, and bagged at the printing plant or another site.

Mailing and Alternative Delivery Services. Because many web products are mailed to customers from the printing plant, providing mailing and product delivery expertise is a critical service for most web printers. Given the complexities of the United States Postal Service in terms of its mail classifications, bulk mailing, delivery effectiveness, bureaucratic snaffles, and other issues and problems, successful web printers are forced into becoming mailing experts. Also, as alternative delivery services have developed and grown in some regional geographic areas, providing this expertise is a VA service that some customers consider essential.

Ink-Jet Addressing and In-Line Address Sorting. This is a popular service that many high-volume catalog and magazine customers consider essential. Computer technology and ink-jet improvements have made this service a requirement for any high-volume web printer wishing to remain competitive.

The "ZIP + four" program, in which the five-digit ZIP code is followed by a four-digit number that provides more accurate sorting of mail, is one way the United States Postal Service provides expedited mailing at bulk rates. During production of jobs, in-line sorting achieves this goal. Ink-jet addressing systems are essential in completing this process because they are computer driven and easily provide sorting and cross-sorting methods.

Selective Binding. Selective binding is the tailoring of a catalog, magazine, or other product to a targeted audience within a larger population. For example, a farm magazine wishes to target certain farming groups for advertising purposes. To do this, the magazine prepares a general-purpose edition, then develops a special section for poultry farm readers, another section for dairy farmers, and still another section for cattle farmers. The magazine is produced by converging the general-purpose edition and each special section for each specific farming group. The magazine is ink-jet addressed at the same time. All of this is done in line and is sorted for expedited mailing. Selective binding, which was originally conceived and perfected by R.R. Donnelley & Sons in the 1970s, is a popular in-line process with many high-volume web printers and is also used by sheetfed printers as an off-line process.

12.5   Estimating Web Paper

For many estimators who understand sheet paper costing and mathematics (see Chapter 6), web estimating holds an aura of mystery. This perception is unfortunate because estimating web paper is not really difficult. The accompanying formulas have been simplified and presented in such a manner that substitution of variable data is all that is required. It is important to note that the calculation of each segment, such as roll footage or the number of cutoffs per roll, should be mastered because such information coordinates with the data required when estimating the complete web problem.

Determining Roll Footage

The following formula allows for the calculation of the number of feet in a roll of paper when the roll diameter, core diameter, and stock caliper of the stock are known:

$$\text{roll footage} = \frac{0.06545\,(D^2 - d^2)}{T}$$

where
  D = roll diameter in inches
  d = core diameter in inches

T = stock caliper in inches

0.06545 = a constant that provides for conversion of inches to feet

Example 12.1. Determine the footage of a roll of substance 55 book, with caliper 0.004 inch and a roll diameter of 40 inches, that is wound on a 3-inch metal core.

Solution

Determine the roll footage:

$$\text{roll footage} = \frac{0.06545\ (40\ \text{in.}^2 - 3\ \text{in.}^{2)}}{0.004}\ \text{in.} = \frac{0.06545\ (1{,}600\ \text{in.} - 9\ \text{in.})}{0.004\ \text{in.}}$$

$$= \frac{0.06545\ (1{,}591\ \text{in.})}{0.004\ \text{in.}} = 26{,}033\ \text{ft. (rounded up)}$$

The roll footage formula works for all types of paper stocks in precisely the substitution procedure indicated. It should be noted that roll width plays no part in the amount of linear feet in a roll of paper. Therefore, the linear feet value is excluded from any portion of these calculations.

Determining the Number of Cutoffs per Roll

Essentially, the number of cutoffs per roll can be translated to mean the number of pieces, sheets, or signatures that the roll of paper will produce during printing. To determine this "quantity per roll" figure, the estimator must know the number of feet per roll and the cutoff size of the press to be used for printing. The following formula is used:

$$\text{number of cutoffs per roll} = \frac{\text{number of feet per roll x 12 inches per foot}}{\text{press cutoff}}$$

where press cutoff is given in inches and 12 inches per foot is a constant.

Example 12.2. A roll of newsprint, which contains 26,033 linear feet of paper, will run on a web press with a cutoff of 23 1/2 inches. How many cutoffs (cts.) are in the roll if the entire roll will be used?

Solution

Determine the number of cutoffs in the entire roll:

$$\text{number of cutoffs} = \frac{26{,}033\ \text{ft. x 12 in./ft.}}{23.5\ \text{in.}} = 13{,}293\ \text{cts.}$$

It is unrealistic to expect that the total roll will be used during printing. There is generally a built-in waste factor to accommodate for what is sometimes termed "core waste."

Determining the Weight per 1,000 (M) Cutoffs

The weight per 1,000 cutoffs is the actual weight of 1,000 printed and finished pieces at the delivery end of the web press. The reason such a calculation is made is twofold:

1. Ink estimating is sometimes based on the "weight/M cutoffs" figure (which is detailed later in this chapter).
2. Such weight information can be used to calculate relative shipping weights of printed materials.

The formula for calculating the weight per 1,000 cutoffs is the same formula used for comparative weight calculations (see Chapter 6). It is:

$$\text{weight per M cutoffs} = \frac{\text{area (sq. in.) of cutoff size}}{\text{area (sq. in.) of basic size}} \times \text{sub weight doubled}$$

Example 12.3. Determine the weight per 1,000 cutoffs for a press with a cutoff of 22 3/4 inches running a roll 36 inches wide of substance 55 book (see Chapter 6, Figure 6.2, for a list of basic sizes and substance numbers). Add 3 percent to compensate for core waste, white waste (trim-off waste during printing), and spoilage.

Solution

Determine the weight per M cutoffs:

$$\text{weight/M cutoffs} = \frac{22.75 \text{ in.} \times 36 \text{ in.}}{25 \text{ in.} \times 38 \text{ in.}} \times 55 \text{ (2)} = 94.83 \text{ lbs}$$

Total weight including spoilage: 94.83 lbs. x 1.03 = 97.67 lbs.

To save time, some estimators prefer to calculate the weight per M cutoffs (or weight per M sheets for sheet papers) using the "constant schedule" provided in Figure 12.1. The constant factor is calculated by doubling the basis weight of the identified shock and dividing that figure by the square inches of the basic size. For example, the constant factor for sub 50 book with a basic size of 25 inches x 38 inches would calculate as sub 50 x 2 = 100 ÷ 950 sq. in. = 0.1053. If a cutoff of sub 50 book measured 24 inches x 36 inches, the weight per M cutoffs would then be 24 in. x 36 in. or 864 sq. in. x 0.1053 (constant factor), which equals 90.98 or approximately 91 M.

NEWSPRINT TAG KRAFT		BONDS, WRITING & LEDGER		BOOK PAPER	
Basis Wt.	1000	Basis Wt.	1000	Basis Wt.	1000
24 × 36/500	Sheet Factor	17 × 22/500	Sheet Factor	25 × 38/500	Sheet Factor
32	.0741	8	.0428	35	.0737
34	.0787	9	.0481	40	.0842
35	.0810	11	.0588	45	.0947
40	.0926	12	.0642	50	.1053
50	.1157	13	.0695	60	.1263
60	.1389	16	.0856	70	.1474
100	.2315	20	.1070	80	.1684
125	.2894	24	.1283	100	.2105
150	.3472	28	.1497	120	.2526
175	.4051	32	.1711		
200	.4630	36	.1925		

BRISTOL		COVER PAPER		INDEX BRISTOL	
Basis Wt.	1000	Basis Wt.	1000	Basis Wt.	1000
22 1/2 × 28 1/2/500	Sheet Factor	20 × 26/500	Sheet Factor	25 1/2 × 30 1/2/500	Sheet Factor
67	.2090	50	.1923	90	.2314
80	.2489	60	.2308	110	.2829
90	.2807	65	.2500	140	.3600
100	.3119	80	.3077		
120	.3743	90	.3462		
140	.4366	100	.3846		
160	.4990	130	.5000		

Figure 12.1 Constant factors used to determine the weight per M cutoffs or weight per M sheets.

Determining the Weight of a Roll of Paper

The total weight of a roll of paper is important for shipping, warehousing, and costing purposes. The total weight of a roll of paper depends on many factors: the type of paper, its thickness, the coatings used, sizing compounds, and wrapping materials, as well as the roll dimensions. The following formula is used to calculate roll weight:

$$\text{roll weight} = \frac{0.00156\,(D^2 - d^2)\ x\ w\ x\ b}{T\ x\ s}$$

where
  D = outside roll diameter in inches
  d = core diameter in inches
  w = roll width in inches
  b = basis weight of the paper
  T = stock thickness (or caliper) in inches
  s = basic size of the paper in inches
  0.06545 = a constant that provides for conversion of inches to feet

Example 12.4. Determine the weight of a roll of newsprint that measures 36 inches wide and 40 inches in diameter. The roll is wound on a 3-inch core. The stock is substance 30 with a caliper of 0.0025 inch. (Note: This roll could be specified as 36 x 40 x 0.0025 as indicated earlier in the Web Paper section of this chapter).

Solution

Determine the roll weight:

$$\text{roll weight} = \frac{0.00157\,(40\ \text{in.}^2 - 3\ \text{in.}^2)\ x\ 36\ \text{in.}\ x\ 30\ \text{lbs.}}{0.0025\ \text{in.}\ x\ (24\text{in.}\ x\ 36\ \text{in.})} = 1{,}249\ \text{lbs.}$$

Determining Slabbing Waste

The slabbing of paper rolls is a process by which the outside of the paper roll is cut away, usually with a knife or power. The paper that is removed from the roll is typically discarded. Because the outside of the roll contains a significant portion of the paper on the roll, cutting off an inch or more may represent a major loss of paper. The roll will produce fewer cutoffs than originally estimated, and perhaps the job will require additional rolls and roll changes to make up for this paper loss. Thus, slabbing is generally undesirable.

The usual reason for slabbing paper from rolls is because the roll was damaged during transit, by the shipping agent, or in the plant. For example, foreign matter may become embedded in the roll and require slabbing to remove it, or a gouge of the outer roll might occur due to careless forklift operation. If the damage occurs during shipping, this fact should be noted on the delivery forms when the roll is delivered to the plant. Typically, the shipper will acknowledge the imperfection and make restitution through insurance or other means once the amount for the damage is determined. Of course, any damage occurring inside the plant that is not shipping related represents lost paper and lost company dollars because the slabbed paper becomes a company expense and cannot be charged to the customer's account. Not only is the slabbed paper thrown away, which represents a dollar loss to the printer, but additional paper will be needed to substitute in its place, which may affect roll inventories for other jobs. The following formula is used for calculating slabbing waste:

$$\text{slabbing waste} = \frac{4\,(DS - S^2)}{D^2} \times ORW$$

where
   D   = original roll diameter
   S   = slab thickness in inches to be cut away
   ORW = original roll weight
   4   = a constant

Example 12.5. A 2-inch slab must be cut from a roll of basis 50 book due to damage by the shipper. The original roll diameter is 36 inches, and the original roll weight is 1,850 pounds. The cost of the paper is $1,350 per ton. Determine the poundage and cost of the slabbed paper.

Solution

Step 1. Determine the weight of the slabbing waste:

$$\text{stabbing waste} = \frac{4[(36\text{ in. x }2\text{ in.}) - 2\text{ in.}^2]}{36\text{ in.}^2} \times 1{,}850\text{ lb.} = \frac{272}{1{,}296} \times 1{,}850 = 388\text{ lb.}$$

Note: The waste is about 21 percent of the total roll.

Step 2. Determine the cost of the paper:

$$388\text{ lbs. x }(\$1{,}350.00 \div 2{,}000\text{ lbs.}) = \$261.90$$

12.6 Estimating Web Production

Web production estimating is divided into three segments:

1. estimating paper requirements including spoilage
2. estimating ink consumption
3. estimating press makeready and running times and costs

Because production on the press must include paper additions, the estimate must be built by first determining total paper requirements. Ink quantity is then estimated to include paper spoilage, and press time and cost are then calculated based on the total estimated paper needs. The previously presented roll formulas are applied.

All categories of web production data must be developed for each web press on an individual basis. As is noted in the accompanying discussion regarding paper spoilage, there are many equipment and production differences, and no two webs are exactly the same. These inconsistencies apply not only to paper consumption, but they also materially affect ink and press operations. For this reason, all web estimating schedule data in this text are presented for example only. While data may appear realistic for one web operating under a certain production-equipment discipline, they may be totally off base for another. The only way to ensure accurate web estimating data is through individual developing and continually maintaining this information.

Three general points regarding the establishment of tailor-made web production standards should be made. First, it is best if only one individual, working in a careful and scientific manner, determines such data. This practice ensures there is a consistent orientation. Of course, the individual must be fully conversant in web procedures and technology and especially aware of requirements for establishing accurate production standards and BHRs (see Chapter 3).

Second, it will probably be necessary for this individual to design web production forms. For example, because ordering web paper is an important factor, the ordering procedure should be carefully detailed so that its many variables are considered and specified accurately. In terms of estimating web production, it is important that the webbing of the press be detailed with each job or when major webbing changes are evident. This procedure requires that a webbing diagram form be completed to aid platemaking and press production. The diagram must precisely represent the printing units and on-press converting operations and should accompany the job through the plant during production. Form design for web requires careful effort to minimize costly production errors and ensure recovery of accurate production times for modification of production standards.

Third, the development and maintenance of web data should be periodically reviewed with the head press operator on the web press for which the data apply. This individual is the most knowledgeable of all plant personnel regarding the press operating conditions, technical printing factors, and spoilage information. Some web estimators consult with the head press operator about complicated jobs or when estimating data do not seem to fit the job under consideration. The competent web operator is a most valuable source of information to the web estimator and should not be ignored.

Estimating Roll Paper Spoilage

Figure 12.2 demonstrates one method of estimating web paper spoilage. Schedule data are based on a 16-page, coldset lithographic web press. The process requires estimating the base spoilage, then adding spoilage for roll changes, stock penalties, in-line operation penalties, and off-line operation penalties. Process adjustments for heatset production, half-width webs, or waterless production are then made to the total spoilage amount.

The basic spoilage percentage includes spoilage for core waste; wrap; normal waste for webbing, prepress setup, and makeready; usual running conditions; and on-press binding operations. Penalties indicated apply as a total percentage to the basic percentage (see Example 12.6 later in this chapter). All data in Figure 12.2 are for example only and must be modified to reflect variations in production, press, and binding for the individual web equipment.

There are a large number of equipment and production variables affecting the data presented in Figure 12.2. They are as follows:

1. There are differences in the types of web presses, the number of roll stands, and the number of printing units.
2. There are differences in technical printing attachments and special controls for improved consistency and greater production.
3. There are differences in the types of products produced and the special operations they require.
4. There are differences in types of paper stock and other substrates. Coated stocks may blister or pick; thick papers may reduce press speeds considerably. Coordinating these stocks with drying units is also important.
5. There are differences in the types of roll feeding and roll change techniques. Web paper can be fed from manually loaded roll stands or from roll stands that contain automatic splicing equipment. Manual roll changes increase spoilage dramatically because the press must be stopped, while automatic pasting devices connect rolls at nominal press speeds.
6. There are important differences to be considered with postprinting production. Some jobs allow for the entire job to be done in line so that infeed, printing, and postprinting operations complete the job. Other jobs may require off-line finishing, in which cases postprinting equipment may not be available in line or when the finishing is too specialized. It is possible that postpress paper spoilage may be as high, or higher than, spoilage from the press run.
7. There are differences in the number of stops and startups for plate changes and other identified production operations.
8. There are differences in job scheduling. Spoilage can increase significantly when complete stock changeover is needed from one job to the next or when webbing conditions are completely different between jobs.
9. There are differences in job quality factors wherein special color matches, intricate register, or other quality requirements cause increased throwaways during printing.

Web press paper spoilage schedule
(schedule data for a 36-inch coldset lithographic web press)

Base spoilage

Number of copies	Base spoilage percentage*
Under 10,000	13 %
10,001 - 25,000	11
25,001 - 50,000	9
50,001 - 100,000	7
100,001 - 250,000	5
Over 250,000	3

* Percentage includes makeready setup for startup rolls (including webbing) and base running spoilage for the quantity indicated for a 36-inch (16-page) coldset web press. Penalities and process adjustments below apply as appropriate.

Penalties (add to base spoilage percentage above)

Roll changes

Manual roll changes during press run, after startup roll: 0.50% per roll change

Automatic (flying) roll changes during press run, after startup roll: 0.10 % per roll change

Stock penalties

Newsprint	0%: Sub 28, 30, 32	
	1.0%: Under sub 28 or over sub 32	
Uncoated book and bond	0%: Sub 45 - sub 75	0%: Sub 16 - sub 24
	1.5%: Under sub 45	1.5%: Under sub 16
	2.5%: Over sub 75	2.5%: Over sub 24
Coated book	0%: Sub 45 - sub 75	
	2%: Under sub 45	
	3%: Over sub 75	

In-line operation penalities

Color (per printing unit)	0.5 %
Gluing	1.0
Rotary die cutting	1.0
Prefolding/folding	1.5
Ink-jet addressing	1.0
Stitching	2.0
Perfect binding	2.5

Off-line operation penalities

Roll-to-roll conversion	0.5%
Folding/collating/binding	1.0

Process or production adjustments (apply if appropriate)

Heatset web: Total spoilage (base plus penalities) then add 10%

Half-width web (8-page web): Total spoilage (base plus penalities) then deduct 20%

Waterless web (experienced crew): Total spoilage (base plus penalities) then deduct 20%

Figure 12.2 Schedule for estimating web press paper spoilage. Schedule data are for example only.

Example 12.6. We have an full-width, coldset lithographic web press feeding one roll stand into one perfecting printing unit. Rolls measure 35 inches wide x 40 inches in diameter and are wound on 3-inch cores. Stock is substance 50 book with a caliper of 0.0035 inch. Press cutoff is 22 1/2 inches, making the final signature size 22 inches x 35 inches; pages measure 8 3/4 inches x 11 1/4 inches. Each signature contains 16 pages. Estimate the amount of paper required to run 60,000 (16-page) signatures, black-and-white only using this one-unit web press. There are manual roll changes. Determine:

- the number of total cutoffs that will be printed, including spoilage
- the poundage and cost of paper, including spoilage
- the number of rolls that will be required, including spoilage

Also, if the cost of this paper is $1,560 per ton, determine the total cost of paper for this job.

Solution

Use the given formulas and Figure 12.2 as necessary.

Step 1. Determine the basic roll paper information:
Number of linear feet per roll:

$$[0.06545 \, (40 \text{ in.}^2 - 3 \text{ in.}^2)] \div 0.0035 \text{ in} = 29{,}752 \text{ ft./roll}$$

Number of cutoffs per roll:

$$(29{,}752 \times 12 \text{ in./ft.}) \div 22.5 \text{ in.} = 15{,}868 \text{ cts.}$$

Step 2. Add the spoilage percentage (see Figure 12.2):
Base percentage at 60,000 copies: 7%
Number of manual roll changes:

$$60{,}000 \text{ copies} \div 15{,}868 \text{ cts.} = 3.78 \text{ rolls} = 4 \text{ rolls on press} -$$
$$1 \text{ roll (with setup)} = 3 \text{ roll changes}$$

Percentage of roll changes:

$$3 \text{ rolls} \times 0.50 = 1.5\%$$

Note: There are no stock penalties or penalties for in-line or off-line production.

Total spoilage required:

$$7.00\% + 1.50\% = 8.50\%$$

Step 3. Determine the total paper required using cutoff data:
Total cutoffs with spoilage:

$$60{,}000 \text{ cps.} \times (100.00\% + 8.5\% \div 100) = 65{,}100 \text{ cts.}$$

Web ink estimating schedule
(schedule data for a 36-inch coldset lithographic web press)

Schedule basis is black ink in pounds per 1,000 cutoffs by coverage % and type of paper

% black coverage for 24 x 36 (approx.) inch (8-page) plate or form	Type of paper		
	Newsprint	Uncoated book and bond	Coated book
10 %	0.27	0.25	0.17
15	0.41	0.37	0.25
20	0.55	0.49	0.33
25	0.68	0.61	0.41
30	0.82	0.74	0.50
35	0.95	0.86	0.58
40	1.09	0.98	0.66
45	1.22	1.10	0.74
50	1.36	1.22	0.83
60	1.63	1.46	0.99
70	1.90	1.71	1.16
80	2.18	1.95	1.32
90	2.45	2.20	1.49
100	2.72	2.44	1.65

Color ink adjustment (black coverage multiplier)

Color of ink	Newsprint	Uncoated book and bond	Coated book
Process blue	1.11	1.07	1.06
Process red	1.23	1.18	1.10
Process yellow	1.16	1.13	1.09
Opaque red (PMS)	1.72	1.68	1.51
Opaque blue (PMS)	1.72	1.68	1.51
Opaque green (PMS)	1.94	1.88	1.69
Opaque yellow (PMS)	1.84	1.80	1.62

Process or production adjustments (apply if appropriate)

Heatset web: Total ink pounds then add 10%

Half-width (8-page) web (4-page form): Total ink pounds then deduct 50%

Waterless web (experienced crew): No adjustment

Figure 12.3 Schedule for estimating web ink consumption. Schedule data are for example only.

Number of pounds per M cutoffs using basic formula:

$$\frac{(22.5 \text{ in. x } 35 \text{ in.}) \, 100 \text{ lbs.}}{(25 \text{ in. x } 39 \text{ in.})} = 82.89 \text{ lbs.}$$

Total stock poundage:

82.89 lbs./M ct x 65.1 M cts. = 5,396 lbs.

Step 4. Determine the total paper required using roll data:
Total rolls required:

3.78 rolls x (100.00% + 8.5% ÷ 100) = 4.101 rolls

Roll weight using basic formula:

$$\frac{0.00157 \, (40 \text{ in.}^2 - 3 \text{ in.}^2) \text{ x } 35 \text{ in. x } 50\text{lbs.}}{0.0035 \text{ in. x } (25 \text{ in. x } 38 \text{ in.})} = 1,315 \text{ lbs.}$$

Total weight of paper:

4.101 rolls x 1,315 lbs./roll = 5,393 lbs.

Step 5. Determine the paper cost:

5,393 lbs. x ($1,560.00 ÷ 2,000 lbs.) = $4,206.54

Step 6. Summarize the findings:
Total cutoffs: 65,100 cts.
Total weight: 5,393 lbs.
Total paper cost: $4,206.54
Total rolls needed: 4.101 rolls

Estimating Web Ink Consumption

Just as with paper spoilage, there are many variables affecting ink consumption during web printing. Perhaps the most prevalent is the difference in ink mileage from one web press to another. This difference can be attributed to variations in ink fountain setup (where the setting might be light or heavy with little visible difference in density during printing), different press operators, different kinds of presses, and variations between different brands of ink and paper.

When estimating web ink, too frequently "rules of thumb" are used instead of more clearly identified data. In addition, sometimes ink is estimated on the number of finished pieces only (or the number of ordered cutoffs), while press spoilage may have a significant bearing on increased ink requirements.

The rules for sheetfed inks presented in Chapter 7 generally hold true for web inks. One difference is that web inks are purchased in larger quantities because it is consumed at a much faster rate. As with sheetfed inks, differences in web ink cost normally translate into differences in quality: The less expensive inks characteristically perform poorly when compared to the more expensive formulations.

The accompanying web ink estimating schedule in Figure 12.3 is based on the number of pounds of ink per 1,000 cutoffs per 24 inch x 36 inch form or plate. Consider the following example:

We have one full-width, closed, perfecting unit web press printing black newsink on newsprint. Cutoff measures 24 inches x 36 inches. Coverage for Form 1 is 35 percent and coverage for Form 2 is 50 percent. Therefore, Form 1 will require 0.95 pound of ink per 1,000 cutoffs, and Form 2 will consume 1.36 pounds of black ink per 1,000 cutoffs printed. Because the ink type and color are the same, these figures may be added. Thus, each set of 1,000 cutoffs measuring approximately 24 inches x 36 inches, printed on both sides with black newsink, will require 2.31 pounds of ink.

Estimating colored inks requires first establishing an initial estimate using black data, then multiplying using the color ink multiplier The previous example required 2.31 pounds of black ink for each 1,000 cutoffs. If opaque red ink were used instead of black, the estimated weight per 1,000 cutoffs would be: 2.31 lbs./M cuts x 1.72 (multiplier) or 3.97 lbs.

As indicated at the bottom of Figure 12.3, process or production adjustments should be made if they apply. If heatset web inks are used (with the appropriate heatset equipment), total poundage is increased by 10 percent. When half-width webs are used with an approximate cutoff of 18 inches x 24 inches, ink poundage would be one-half of the full-width amount. Waterless web production has no adjustment for ink quantity because approximately the same amount of ink is used when the two process are compared relative to ink consumption.

The following formulas are used to calculate web ink poundage:

> total black ink poundage = (black ink poundage per M cutoffs for
> Form 1 + black ink poundage per M cutoffs for Form 2) x
> process/production adjustment factor (if applicable) x
> (total number of cutoffs including spoilage ÷ 1,000)

> total color ink poundage = [(black ink poundage per M cutoffs for
> Form 1 + black ink poundage per M cutoffs for Form 2) x
> color ink adjustment (black coverage multiplier)] x
> process/production adjustment factor (if applicable) x
> (total number of cutoffs including spoilage ÷ 1,000)

Example 12.7. A 4-unit perfecting web is used in the production of process color booklets, 9 inches x 12 inches (untrimmed page) in 16-page signatures. Press cutoff is 24 inches; all rolls are 36 inches wide. We have an order for a process color booklet to be printed on coated book, basis 60. Ink coverage, by unit and color, is:

Unit I: Process yellow: Left form 40 percent, right form 50 percent
Unit II: Process blue: Left form 55 percent, right form 60 percent
Unit III: Process red: Left form 40 percent, right form 70 percent
Unit IV: Process black including typematter: Left form 45 percent, right form 40 percent

Ink costs per pound are $5.20 for process blue, $4.60 for process yellow and red, and $2.90 for black. Determine the ink quantity and cost of ink for a gross press run of 52,300 cutoffs (copies).

Solution

Use Figure 12.3.

Step 1. Determine the ink quantity and cost for process yellow:
Base pounds from black schedule:

$$0.66 \text{ lb./M ct.} + 0.83 \text{ lbs./M ct.} = 1.49 \text{ lbs./M ct.}$$

Adjustment using factor from color schedule:

$$1.49 \text{ lbs./M ct.} \times 1.09 = 1.62 \text{ lbs./M ct.}$$

Total amount of ink:

$$1.62 \text{ lbs./M ct.} \times 52.3 \text{ M ct.} = 84.7 \text{ lbs.}$$

Total cost:

$$84.73 \text{ lbs.} \times \$4.60 \text{ lbs.} = \$389.76$$

Step 2. Determine the ink quantity and cost for process blue. (Note: You must use a chart figure halfway between 50 percent at 0.83 lb. and 60 percent at 0.99 lb.)
Base pounds from black schedule:

$$0.91 \text{ lb./M ct.} + 0.99 \text{ lb./M ct.} = 1.9 \text{ lbs./M ct.}$$

Adjustment using factor from color schedule:

$$1.9 \text{ lbs./M ct.} \times 1.06 = 2.01 \text{ lbs./M ct.}$$

Total amount of ink:

$$2.01 \text{ lbs./M ct.} \times 52.3 \text{ M cts.} = 105.12 \text{ lbs.}$$

Total cost:

$$105.12 \text{ lbs.} \times \$5.20/\text{lb.} = \$546.62$$

Step 3. Determine the ink quantity and cost for process red:
Base pounds from black schedule:

$$0.66 \text{ lb./M ct.} + 1.16 \text{ lbs./M ct.} = 1.82 \text{ lbs./M ct.}$$

Adjustment using factor from color schedule:

$$1.82 \text{ lbs./M ct.} \times 1.10 = 2 \text{ lbs./M ct.}$$

Total amount of ink:

$$2 \text{ lbs./M ct.} \times 52.3 \text{ M ct.} = 104.6 \text{ lbs.}$$

Total cost:

$$104.6 \text{ lbs.} \times \$4.60 \text{ lb.} = \$481.16$$

Step 4. Determine the ink quantity and cost for black:
Base pounds from black schedule:

$$0.74 \text{ lb./M ct.} + 0.66 \text{ lb./M ct.} = 1.4 \text{ lbs./M ct.}$$

Adjustment: None
Total amount of ink:

$$1.4 \text{ lbs./M ct.} \times 52.3 \text{ M ct.} = 73.2 \text{ lbs.}$$

Total cost:

$$73.22 \text{ lbs.} \times \$2.90 \text{ lbs.} = \$212.34$$

Step 5. Summarize the findings:
Process yellow: 84.7 lbs.; cost, $389.76
Process blue: 105.1 lbs.; cost, $546.62
Process red: 104.6 lbs.; cost, $481.16
Black: 73.2 lbs.; cost, $212.34

Estimating Web Lithographic Press Production

Estimating of lithographic web press production is divided into two major operational segments: press preparation and press running. Some plants lump press preparation operations together to include all major preparatory elements: webbing the press, adjusting web controls, mounting rolls on roll stands, hanging plates, setting ink and dampening controls, makeready, setting converting and folding units, and all washups required during the run and afterward. Other plants break out the preparatory operations where they find individual attention must be directed during production. For example, a plant might consider all of the previous items together with the exception of press washups, which would be added to the estimate on an individual basis.

Individual judgment on the part of plant management and the estimator is necessary if estimated press preparation time is to be accurate. In this book, preparatory time is lumped, thus combining all operations into one "per printing unit" hourly figure. For example, "1.3 hours/unit" covers all preparatory time for one perfecting printing unit (two plates). There is no de facto standard for web press makeready in the industry because equipment and production techniques vary widely throughout the industry. Estimating press running time can be done in either cutoffs per hour or fpm. Figure 12.4 is provided to cross-reference these data for cutoffs from 8 1/2 inches to 44 1/2 inches and running speeds from 100 fpm to 2,500 fpm. For cutoffs that are not listed, the formula for calculating the number of cutoffs per hour when running speed in feet per minute and circumferential cutoff in inches is known is shown at the bottom of Figure 12.4.

Generally speaking, estimating web press output is a simple process because all that must be identified is the fpm and the press cutoff in inches. This process is further simplified in that a web press is frequently locked into a certain type of job—it uses papers and inks that are continuously the same, and it is manned with same experienced press crew day after day. Thus, time for makeready and running is reasonably predictable.

Estimating web press makeready and running time can be more difficult when work begins to depart from normal procedures, however. For example, different web widths in the same press run, unusual or less typical paper stocks, webbing changes that produce a unique product, or unpredictable in-line finishing devices all make estimating web press production difficult.

Most web estimators learn from early experience that it is best to check with plant production staff and pressroom personnel when deviations from normal web press running are likely. The head press operator, on whose web press the job will likely run, is an excellent source for such information, as might be the production supervisor or the web pressroom superintendent. Involved discussions and consultation allow the estimator to determine with some accuracy the expected running speeds in fpm, cutoffs per hour, or finished pieces per hour.

Once the press speed and the cutoff length are known, the estimator then consults Figure 12.4 to determine the estimated number of cutoffs, sheets, or signatures that will be produced per hour on the press. This figure is then divided into the total number of copies to be printed (including spoilage) to determine the press time required for the job. Total press cost is then the sum of the makeready time and the running time, which is then multiplied by the BHR for the press. Consumable materials such as paper, ink, and plates are added separately to the estimate.

Example 12.8 is provided to demonstrate how estimating web presswork is completed. Example 12.9 is provided to show how an entire web estimating problem is done. The following formulas may be used when working the examples:

No. linear feet per minute (fpm)	8.5	11	14	17	17.5	22	22.75	23	23.5	23.625	24	25.5	26	35	41.5	44.5
100	8471	6545	5143	4235	4114	3273	3165	3130	3064	3048	3000	2824	2769	2057	1735	1618
200	16941	13091	10286	8471	8229	6545	6330	6261	6128	6095	6000	5647	5538	4114	3470	3236
300	25412	19636	15429	12706	12343	9818	9495	9391	9191	9143	9000	8471	8308	6171	5205	4854
400	33882	26182	20571	16941	16457	13091	12659	12522	12255	12190	12000	11294	11077	8229	6940	6472
500	42353	32727	25714	21176	20571	16364	15824	15652	15319	15238	15000	14118	13846	10286	8675	8090
600	50824	39273	30857	25412	24686	19636	18989	18783	18383	18286	18000	16941	16615	12343	10410	9708
700	59294	45818	36000	29647	28800	22909	22154	21913	21447	21333	21000	19765	19385	14400	12145	11326
800	67765	52364	41143	33882	32914	26182	25319	25043	24511	24381	24000	22588	22154	16457	13880	12944
900	76235	58909	46286	38118	37029	29455	28484	28174	27574	27429	27000	25412	24923	18514	15614	14562
1000	84706	65455	51429	42353	41143	32727	31648	31304	30638	30476	30000	28235	27692	20571	17349	16180
1100	93176	72000	56571	46588	45257	36000	34813	34435	33702	33524	33000	31059	30462	22629	19084	17798
1200	101647	78545	61714	50824	49371	39273	37978	37565	36766	36571	36000	33882	33231	24686	20819	19416
1300	110118	85091	66857	55059	53486	42545	41143	40696	39830	39619	39000	36706	36000	26743	22554	21034
1400	118588	91636	72000	59294	57600	45818	44308	43826	42894	42667	42000	39529	38769	28800	24289	22652
1500	127059	98182	77143	63529	61714	49091	47473	46957	45957	45714	45000	42353	41538	30857	26024	24270
1600	135529	104727	82286	67765	65829	52364	50637	50087	49021	48762	48000	45176	44308	32914	27759	25888
1700	144000	111273	87429	72000	69943	55636	53802	53217	52085	51810	51000	48000	47077	34971	29494	27506
1800	152471	117818	92571	76235	74057	58909	56967	56348	55149	54857	54000	50824	49846	37029	31229	29124
1900	160941	124364	97714	80471	78171	62182	60132	59478	58213	57905	57000	53647	52615	39086	32964	30742
2000	169412	130909	102857	84706	82286	65455	63297	62609	61277	60952	60000	56471	55385	41143	34699	32360
2100	177882	137455	108000	88941	86400	68727	66462	65739	64340	64000	63000	59294	58154	43200	36434	33978
2200	186353	144000	113143	93176	90514	72000	69626	68870	67404	67048	66000	62118	60923	45257	38169	35596
2300	194824	150545	118286	97412	94629	75273	72791	72000	70468	70095	69000	64941	63692	47314	39904	37213
2400	203294	157091	123429	101647	98743	78545	75956	75130	73532	73143	72000	67765	66462	49371	41639	38831
2500	211765	163636	128571	105882	102857	81818	79121	78261	76596	76190	75000	70588	69231	51429	43373	40449

Web press cutoff in inches

Note: To convert press cutoffs not in this schedule, use the following formula: No. ft./min. x 12 in./ft. x 60 min./hr. + press cutoff (in.)

Figure 12.4 Number of press cutoffs at various cylinder circumferences for webs running at speeds from 100 to 2,500 fpm.

total web press production time = (number of units printing x makeready time per unit) + (total number of cutoffs, including spoilage ÷ press running speed in cutoffs per hour)

total web press production cost = total web press production time x web press BHR

Example 12.8. We have a 4-unit web press feeding 2 roll stands into 2 units each to produce a 2-color finished product. Preparation and makeready time per printing unit is 0.75 hour, which includes roll mounting and webbing. The press will run at 670 fpm. The BHR for this web press is $152.50. Determine the time and cost for presswork for this job if the gross press run is 72,600 pieces. Press cutoff is 22 3/4 inches.

Solution

Use Figure 12.4 as necessary.

Step 1. Determine the press preparation time:

$$4 \text{ units x } 0.75 \text{ hr./unit} = 3.0 \text{ hr.}$$

Step 2. Determine the press running time at 22 3/4 inches in cutoff (see Figure 12.4):
Press speed at 670 fpm:

$$3,165 \text{ cts./hr. at } 100 \text{ fpm x } (670 \text{ fpm} \div 100 \text{ fpm}) = 21,206 \text{ cts./hr.}$$

Press time:

$$72,600 \text{ cts.} \div 21,206 \text{ cts/hr.} = 3.42 \text{ hr.}$$

Step 3. Determine the total production time and cost:
Total production time:

$$3.0 \text{ hr.} + 3.42 \text{ hr.} = 6.42 \text{ hr.}$$

Total production cost:

$$6.42 \text{ hr. x } \$152.50/\text{hr.} = \$979.05$$

Example 12.9. A printer has a 3-unit perfecting coldset newspaper web press with 3 roll stands. Each unit can produce 8-page tabloids running from standard size rolls 34 inches (wide) x 45 inches (diameter) x 0.0025 inch caliper newsprint, substance 30. There are manual roll changes. The paper costs $1,460 per ton. All rolls are wound on 3-inch cores. Press cutoff is 22 3/4 inches. The press BHR is $175.00. A customer wants 45,000 copies of a tabloid-sized advertising circular. It will run 8 pages, black only, with another 8 pages black with process blue as a spot color. (Note: This means that 2 roll stands will feed 2 rolls for printing. One roll will feed into one unit and print black only, the second roll will feed into two consecutive units, and the first will print black and the second will print blue on both sides of the sheet.) Ink coverage, by unit and plates, is as follows:

Unit 1: Black: Left form 30 percent, right form 40 percent
Unit 2: Black: Left form 25 percent, right form 35 percent
Unit 3: Process blue: Left form 20 percent, right form 30 percent

Ink costs $2.70 per pound for newsblack and $4.95 per pound for process blue (use the uncoated book schedule data in Figure 12.3 for estimating). The press will print at 700 fpm. The preparatory time is estimated to be 0.8 hour per unit. Determine:

- total number of cutoffs and rolls necessary including spoilage (for inventory purposes)
- the poundage and cost of paper
- the poundage and cost of ink
- the press time and cost

Solution

Use Figures 12.2, 12.3, and 12.4 as necessary.

Step 1. Determine the configuration for running: Feed 2 rolls from 2 roll stands. The first roll prints black only (Unit 1), while the second roll prints black and spot blue (Units 2 and 3). There is a total of 6 plates. All units perfect.

Step 2. Determine the basic roll paper information using basic formulas: Number of linear feet per roll:

$$\frac{0.06545 \ (45 \ \text{in.}^2 - 3 \ \text{in.}^2)}{0.0025 \ \text{in.}} = 52{,}779 \ \text{ft.}$$

Number of cutoffs per roll:

$$\frac{52{,}779 \ \text{ft.} \times 12 \ \text{in./ft.}}{22.75 \ \text{in.}} = 27{,}839 \ \text{cts.}$$

Step 3. Determine the spoilage percentage per roll stand (see Figure 12.2):
Base percentage at 45,000 copies: 9%
Roll changes per stand:

$$45{,}000 \ \text{cps.} \div 27{,}839 \ \text{cts.} = 1.616 \ \text{rolls} = 2 \ \text{rolls on stand} -$$
$$1 \ \text{roll (setup)} = 1 \ \text{roll change/stand}$$

Percentage of roll changes per stand:

$$1 \ \text{roll} \times 0.50 = 0.5\%$$

Total color spoilage: 1% (spot blue)
Total spoilage per roll stand (base percentage + roll change percentage + color percentage = total spoilage percentage):

$$9.00\% + 0.50\% + 1.00\% = 10.5\%$$

Note: Because the rolls feed together, this maximum percentage applies to all stands.

Step 4. Determine the amount of newsprint required using cutoff data:
Cutoffs per roll stand:

$$45,000 \text{ cps. x } (100.00\% + 10.5\% \div 100) = 49,725 \text{ cts.}$$

Weight per M cutoffs per roll stand:

$$\frac{(22.75 \text{ in. x } 34 \text{ in.}) \, 60 \text{ lbs.}}{(24 \text{ in. x } 36 \text{ in.})} = \frac{(773.5 \text{ sq. in. } 60 \text{ lbs.}}{864 \text{ sq. in.}} = 53.72 \text{ lbs./m ct./stand}$$

Weight per M cutoffs for both stands:

$$53.72 \text{ lbs./M ct./stand x 2 stands} = 107.44 \text{ lbs./M cts.}$$

Total stock weight:

$$107.44 \text{ lbs./M ct. x } 49.725 \text{ M cts.} = 5,342 \text{ lbs.}$$

Step 5. Determine the amount of newsprint required using roll data:
Total rolls needed per stand:

$$1.616 \text{ rolls x } (100.00\% + 10.5 \% \div 100) = 1.786 \text{ rolls}$$

Roll weight (basic formula):

$$\frac{0.00157 \text{ x } (45 \text{ in.}^2 - 3 \text{ in.}^2) \text{ x } 34 \text{ in. x } 30 \text{ lb.}}{0.0025 \text{ in. x } (24 \text{ in. x } 36 \text{ in.})} = 1,495 \text{ lbs./roll}$$

Total rolls required (rolls per stand x stands feeding = total rolls):

$$1.786 \text{ rolls/stand x 2 stands} = 3.572 \text{ rolls}$$

Total paper weight:

$$3.572 \text{ rolls x } 1,495 \text{ lbs./roll} = 5,340 \text{ lbs.}$$

Note: The difference of 3 pounds between two methods is not considered significant.

Step 6. Determine the paper cost:

$$5,340 \text{ lbs. x } (\$1,460.00 \div 2,000 \text{ lbs.}) = \$3,898.20$$

Step 7. Determine the ink quantity and cost (see Figure 12.3):
Amount of newsblack for Unit 1 (30%/40%):

$$0.82 \text{ lb./M ct.} + 1.09 \text{ lbs./M ct.} = 1.91 \text{ lbs./M ct.}$$

Amount of newsblack for Unit 2 (25%/35%):

0.68 lb./M ct. + 0.95 lb./M ct. = 1.63 lbs./M ct.

Amount of newsblack for Units 1 and 2:

1.91 lbs./M ct. + 1.63 lbs./M ct. = 3.54 lbs./M ct.

Total amount of newsblack:

3.54 lbs./M ct. x 49.725 M ct. = 176.03 lbs.

Newsblack cost:

176.03 lbs. x $2.70/lbs. = $475.28

Amount of process blue for Unit 3 (20%/30%):

0.55 lb./M ct. + 0.82 lb./M ct. = 1.37 lbs./M ct.

Adjustment:

1.37 lbs./M ct. x 1.11 = 1.52 lbs./M ct.

Total amount of process blue:

1.52 lbs./M ct. x 49.725 M cts. = 75.58 lbs.

Process blue cost:

75.58 lbs. x $4.95/lbs. = $374.12

Total ink weight:

176.03 lbs. (black); 75.58 lbs. (blue)

Total ink cost:

$475.28 + $374.12 = $849.40

Step 8. Determine the press time and cost (see Figure 12.4):
Press preparation time:

3 units x 0.8 hr./unit = 2.40 hr.

Press running time:

49,725 cts. ÷ 22,154 cts./hr. = 2.24 hr.

Total press time:

2.40 hr. + 2.24 hr. = 4.64 hr.

Total press cost:

4.64 hr. x $175.00/hr. = $812.00

Step 9. Summarize the findings:

Total number of cutoffs: 49,725 cts./stand
Total rolls required: 3.572 rolls
Total paper weight: 5,340 lbs.
Total paper cost: $3,898.20
Total ink weight: black = 176.03 lbs., blue = 75.58 lbs.
Total ink cost: $849.40
Total press time: 4.64 hr.
Total press cost: $812.00

Chapter 13

Contemporary Marketing and Management Issues in Printing

⊕   ⊕

13.4 *Printing 2000 Update: Bridging to a Digital Future*

13.5 Marketing Graphic Products and Services in a Digital Environment

Market Niching: Product, Process, and Service Specializations in Printing

Developing a Marketing Plan

Some Suggested Markets for Conventional and Digital Products and Services

Customer Partnerships and World-Class Customer Service

13.6 Dynamic Factors Affecting the Printing Industry into the Twenty-First Century

Great Opportunities for Graphic Imaging Entrepreneurs and Innovators Continue to Be Extensive

Total Quality Management Replaces Hierarchical Management Methods

Partnerships, Strategic Alliances, and ISO 9000

Reducing Cycle Time and Industry Overcapacity

Workforce and Training Issues

Growth of Facilities Management

Global Competition

Company Consolidations, Mergers, and Acquisitions

Environmental Issues for Printers

Governmental Regulation

13.7 Industry Associations and the Services They Provide

Graphic Arts Technical Foundation (GATF)

Graphic Communications Association (GCA)

International Digital Imaging Association (IDIA)

International Prepress Association (IPA)

International Publishing Management Association (IPMA)

National Association of Desktop Publishers (NADTP)

National Association of Printers and Lithographers (NAPL)

National Association of Quick Printers (NAQP)

Printing Industries of America (PIA) and Its Regional Affiliate Offices

Waterless Printing Association (WPA)

13.1   Introduction

The printing industry has entered a new and increasingly complex era. The industry has been forever changed by digital and electronic technology. No longer do some of the old rules apply, and the emerging new rules are written outside the industry. For an industry that has shown exceptional employment and technological stability for the past forty or more years, the dynamics of this change are frightening on the one hand and filled with intriguing possibilities on the other. That such change will continue is one of the few predictable absolutes as the industry moves into the next millennium.

This chapter addresses a range of important issues, including the all-electronic printing company, the general characteristics of the industry, *Printing 2000 Update* findings, an overview of marketing strategies and tactics, TQM, human resources, facilities management, global competition, government issues, mergers and acquisitions, and environmental concerns.

The conclusion of this chapter lists a number of important associations and foundations serving the printing industry. These industry-supported groups provide essential services to printing managers everywhere, including industrial and human relations, credit referrals, costing and production data, individual consultation on business matters, technical assistance, and many other valuable aids. These groups assist printers in making careful, prudent decisions. Associations or foundations include the Graphic Arts Technical Foundation (GATF), the Graphic Communications Association (GCA), the International Digital Imaging Association (IDIA), the International Prepress Association (IPA), the International Publishing Management Association (IPMA), the National Association of Desktop Publishers (NADTP), the National Association of Printers and Lithographers (NAPL), the National Association of Quick Printers (NAQP), the Printing Industries of America (PIA) and its regional affiliate offices, and the Waterless Printing Association (WPA).

13.2   The Electronic Printing Company

Printers are in a transition stage in all segments of the graphic arts—there is rapid movement from conventional, photomechanical methods, and ink-on-paper products to digital methods and electronic products. The transition is well underway and the result will be the "electronic printing company."

Today's graphic arts enterprise can be described as a business that uses an increasing number of electronic platforms and electronic devices to manufacture ink-on-paper products. Conventional production methods are still used, particularly in press and postpress areas, but new equipment in these areas is increasingly driven by digital methods as well.

Increasingly as well, this electronic equipment is tied into an electronic computer management system. As jobs enter production, they are converted from CAEs to electronic job tickets. The customers provide the electronic artwork, and the production is monitored by electronic data collection and DMI tools. Sometimes digital presses are used to print the job, and postpress mailing operations utilize computer-driven ink-jet addressing methods and ink-jet product personalization. To operate the company, management uses various decision-making tools such as electronic spreadsheets and database accounting. In sum, a typical printing plant increasingly functions in a digital environment at most levels of production and management.

The employees working in a typical printing company have become less craft oriented and increasingly computer literate. The move is toward employing highly skilled technologists who receive extensive training on a continuous basis. Hierarchical management methods are less often the norm and are instead being replaced with various forms of TQM. Employee empowerment, continuous improvement, SPC, and outstanding customer service are increasingly understood and accepted concepts. Customers are electronically connected to the company for e-mail communication, fax exchange, data transmission to transfer digital files, and other purposes.

There is no question that, in various forms, the previous description fits a growing number of printing companies as we approach the year 2000. Another, more major component of the graphic arts company is likely to go electronic—the product. Certain ink-on-paper products are in transition to various forms of magnetic media. Computer-based information systems are replicated (printed) on CD-ROM to replace encyclopedias printed on paper. Electronically interactive products such as maps, reference manuals, and catalogs have been reconfigured and "printed" in electronic form, not on paper. Paper products in some forms will remain viable for many years because they are portable, easy to use, flexible, and inexpensive, but as public acceptance increases and cost diminishes, electronic graphic products will become common. The electronic printing company will be a completely integrated electronic enterprise in all areas: product, process, and management.

There is no force on the horizon to challenge the electronic revolution inside the graphic arts or among customers and buyers as they slowly shift from ink-on-paper to electronic products. There will be no return to traditional photomechanical methods. An increasing number of graphic arts companies today have become purveyors of both ink-on-paper and electronic products; they use electronic equipment and computer management systems. These businesses represent the electronic printing companies of the present. As the transition continues, it appears likely that someday, perhaps not too far in the future, the all-electronic printing company will produce electronic graphic products on digital equipment and will manage them with fully integrated computer MISs.

13.3   General Characteristics of the Printing Industry

Printing plants across the United States vary with respect to their types of conventional and electronic equipment, production outputs, management philosophies, skill levels of personnel, labor and factory costs, and in dozens of additional ways. However, seven generally recognized characteristics common to the printing industry as a whole remain true even in these times of extensive digitization and shifting technology. They are classic signs of the pure competition seen in the industry for many years and are as follows.

The Printing Industry Is Dominated by Smaller Businesses

Although figures regarding the size of the printing industry vary, it is generally acknowledged that in the mid-1990s, there were approximately 40,000 independent printing firms engaging in printing manufacturing across the United States. In addition, there were an estimated 25,000 in-plant printing firms serving the graphic needs of parent companies, such as insurance companies or banks, and another 25,000 quick printing firms in convenient locations in thousands of cities throughout the United States. In sum, there were an estimated 90,000 to 100,000 firms engaged in some form of graphic reproduction at that time.

Studies have shown that the majority of these firms—commercial printers, quick printers, and in-plant printers—are classified as small and employ twenty workers or fewer. Over the years, the United States Department of Commerce statistics have indicated that printing leads all manufacturers in terms of the highest number of small business establishments, with an estimated 80 percent of all printing companies (Standard Industrial Classification or SIC 2700) having twenty or fewer employees. Although estimates of company size differ, the average printing company has about fourteen employees, the average quick printer has about six employees, and the average in-plant printer has slightly over eight workers.

These data can be viewed from another perspective: The 1995 *Graphic Arts Monthly* "GAM 101: Official Ranking of the Top 101 Printing Firms in the U.S." shows the largest United States printer, R.R. Donnelley & Sons, with 41,000 employees, while one firm in the top 101 lists 225 employees. Because there are an estimated 90,000 or more firms engaged in printing in the United States, and because one company in the top 101 has 225 employees (a number of the others are in the 250 to 300 range), it is clear that the printing industry is dominated by smaller firms.

The Printing Industry Has Generally Low Entry Barriers when Beginning a Business Enterprise

Although emerging technology has somewhat shifted upward the base amount of capital needed to enter the printing industry, it is still possible to open and successfully operate a printing-related establishment on a modest amount of money. Examples include the woman who buys a used sheetfed press, sells her own jobs, then prints the orders on weekends in her garage or basement. Also consider the entrepreneur who, with a modest amount of operating cash, designs and prints T-shirts by screen printing techniques, or the printing brokers who sell and service client printing needs but own no equipment and outsource all production to printers who are anxious to produce it. There is also the small graphic design studio that uses its DTP equipment to provide service bureau skills in addition to electronic design or its digital output device as a limited-run printing press. Given such low barriers, hundreds of small printing-related businesses open yearly only to replace other such printing firms that were not successful and forced to close. Such business turnover is constant in the printing industry.

Printing Is a Materials-, Labor-, and Capital-Intensive Business

Printing companies operate in a material-intensive, labor-intensive, and capital-intensive environment. Statistics from the 1994 PIA Ratio Studies demonstrate that approximately 36 percent of every sales dollar goes to material and outside purchases, with another 26 percent going to labor and factory costs. Thus, when these figures are summed, approximately 62 percent of each sales dollar goes toward "hard" costs, which do not contribute to profit and represent a "pass through" relationship from customer to printer to supplier or employee.

For example, when the customer pays his $100 printing bill for an average job, about $36 will be paid directly to the paper company or other suppliers, and another $25 will be paid for out-of-pocket costs to the employees who produced the job. Because the payouts are pass throughs, they do not contribute to profit. This concept, which is called value added (VA), demonstrates that printing may not be extremely profitable unless the printer finds ways to improve the value of the product to the customer beyond the high material and buyout costs.

There is no question that the industry has become more capital intensive in the past ten years as well. For example, in the 1970s and 1980s a "major" purchase for the typical printer was a press, and other equipment purchases were considered less significant. The EPP systems and electronic devices for postpress have changed this focus. Today costs of equipment are high in every production area, so any bad purchase can cause problems.

Finally, there is the issue of printing as a labor-intensive industry. While it is true that numerous labor-saving devices, particularly electronic devices, are now commonly available to a printer of any size, these devices have kept the number of people needed to produce a typical printing job largely the same, instead of reducing the number of people needed. The shift has been from manual production with skilled craftspeople to digital production with skilled technologists. Thus, employees are skilled printing technicians dealing with complex, sophisticated equipment.

Printing's Dichotomy: Is It Manufacturing and Service?

Printing production is the manufacturing conversion of raw and semiraw materials to a finished product that is desired by the customer. To support this effort, many printers offer clients a range of services including design, photography, delivery alternatives, revised estimates to assist in budgeting, and advice on product size, graphic impact of the product, and many other services. While manufacturing typically requires extensive use of company equipment and personnel, support services are provided by the printing sales representative, the CSR, the estimator, or another company employee and tend to require less equipment and fewer personnel.

At issue is the dichotomy of whether printing should be strictly a manufacturing enterprise that makes products for customers or an enterprise that provides tailor-made services to meet customer needs, which includes printed products. From a tax perspective, state governments across the United States and the federal government classify printing as a manufacturing enterprise.

This dichotomy may seem unimportant until profitability and company success are used to evaluate the two areas. Based on the *McKinsey Report to PIA* in 1966 and follow-up studies since that time, successfully providing support services in addition to manufacturing a printed product increases the likelihood of company success. As discussed in Chapter 4 and as illustrated in Figure 4.10, the more printing company management views their company as a service business, the more likely they will be to enjoy high profits. Conversely, the more company management views their company as a manufacturing enterprise, the less likely the company will be to enjoy high profits.

There Are Hundreds of Market Categories for Printed Products

All business establishments require printing in some form or another—packages in the supermarket, pharmacy labels in the drugstore, forms for the operation of an insurance agency, textbooks for education, business cards, and so on. The list is extensive and wide. Printed consumer products add to the list and include newspapers, magazines, catalogs, directories, restaurant menus, freestanding advertising inserts, and hundreds of other products. In addition, almost all graphic products are tailored to specifically meet a customer's purposes, needs, and requirements, which further segments and expands the range of potential products.

Hundreds of demand categories creates an environment of potentially great opportunity for success. However, the problem is that too many printers try to produce any product the customer wants. These printers effectively compromise their success because they average their most profitable jobs with numerous loss leaders which they produce at cost or below. This operating method ultimately compromises business growth and may threaten the survival of businesses over the long term.

There Is Intense Competition between Printing Companies with Each Other and with Other Media

Owing to the five previous factors, the competition for customers is unusually intense at two levels: (1) between printing companies and (2) with competing media such as television, radio, and digital products. Consider this: There are thousands of small printing businesses, each attempting to serve many demand categories, but very few with exactly the same equipment array. All of these companies work in a materials-, labor-, and capital-intensive environment. Furthermore, there is constant turnover of new, smaller printing establishments that are willing to cut prices (perhaps below costs, if they know them) simply to survive and larger, high-volume printers that have their presses to fill and require volume needed simply to break even. There is also competition with other media in certain markets where printing may not be the most cost-effective way to reach the largest number of people.

The result of this inter- and intra-industry competition can be brutal. Unless printers target customers, practice excellent customer service, and consciously work with customers in other ways to encourage their continuing business, competition is fierce and profits low.

There Are Defined Price Ceilings on Many Printed Goods

While there is no question that printers serving any targeted group of customers or certain vertical markets can raise their prices if they desire to, such price increases may jeopardize the profit pictures of these businesses. For example, if the management of Plant A decided to raise prices even by a slight amount, the competition at Plant B would use this price umbrella and underbid Plant A. This underbid would result in a loss of volume for Plant A, which translates into a loss in dollar profits. If the volume reduction is greater than the slight increase in price, the future survival of Plant A is not good.

It is clear that artificial price ceilings, particularly in demand categories where competition is intense, keep profits low because price is a major contributor to profitability.

13.4 *Printing 2000 Update: Bridging to a Digital Future*

In September 1990, PIA released *Printing 2000*, which was completed by the Stanford Research Institute. The eighteen-month study was undertaken to provide printers with a working strategy for change in order to prepare them for the year 2000 in terms of customers, technology, and business operation. However, the extremely swift and massive shift to digital technology in the late 1980s and early 1990s had revolutionized the industry at all levels, and in 1992 PIA initiated a follow-up study to the original *Printing 2000*. In January 1994, *Printing 2000 Update: Bridging to a Digital Future* was released. (Further information and a copy of the study can be obtained from PIA by calling 800/742-2666.) The following is a summary of this important study.

Printing 2000 Update: Bridging to a Digital Future confirmed that the printer's role in the digital future of the communication industry is yet to be determined. There is a blurring of technology where publishers of certain products move from ink-on-paper to electronic media of different kinds. This shifting will rearrange the priorities for numerous ink-on-paper products, and it is expected that as much as 50 percent of the sales revenue of printers in the year 2000 will come from products and services they did not produce or provide when the study was completed in 1992 and 1993. This means that the role of printers and the customers and markets they serve will be redefined. While in the long term there may be a significant diminishing or complete loss of certain printed products and services, the short term is likely to focus on small changes in directions that will be manageable and fairly predictable. Most emerging graphic products and services will be driven by electronic or digital methods or systems.

Printing 2000 Update projects that company growth will be linked to skill in digital technology. The study also indicates that large and high-volume printers will become even bigger at the expense of weaker large companies and middle-sized firms, and that smaller printers will remain small but face serious problems if they do not innovate and shift to digital imaging technology that is appropriate to their customers. Printers of all sizes will be forced into targeting and niching markets if they are to survive. It is expected that profit margins will continue to be generally under pressure, with the profit leaders most likely to be those companies that integrate two overlapping concepts: (1) they will successfully buy and implement digital technology at all levels of the company, and (2) they will shift their overall business strategy so that market niching of products and services, with an emphasis on customers needs, and flexibility at all levels of the business are practiced.

Printing 2000 Update: Bridging to a Digital Future lists the following seven critical factors for success:

1. Printers must shift their focus from specializing in printing processes to specific value added products and services. Printing sales representatives must become computer literate and provide their customers with consulting services and not just products.

2. Printers must segment their markets and target customer groups with care and precision.

3. Printers must embrace and exploit nontraditional thinking at all levels of the company.

4. Printers must accept the fact that competition will change and intensify, not only from other printers but from other media as well.

5. Printers must fully understand new and emerging technology and properly assess and implement it with a focus on profitability.

6. Printers must develop and utilize critical management skills in finance, human resources, production, and technology. Printers can no longer practice "seat of the pants" management methods and expect to grow.

7. Printers must acknowledge that investment decisions will become more risky, with the risk-takers "betting the company" to achieve success.

In general, the long-term future of the successful printing company will be linked to products and services that include new or emerging digital media such as CD-ROM, multimedia, and personal digital applications. The all-electronic printing company, which was discussed earlier, will be the result. Products will include ink-on-paper and electronic media, and services will emerge that support these products. Customers will select the technology applications and printers will provide products and services that support their choices.

13.5 Marketing Graphic Products and Services in a Digital Environment

As the printing industry approaches the next millennium, the "Number One Commandment" for overall success remains "Know Thy Market." According to every measurement tool available, and by applying both quantitative or anecdotal evaluation, success in printing begins with a successful marketing program that is supported with proactive selling and outstanding customer service.

Market Niching: Product, Process, and Service Specializations in Printing

The advent of niche marketing, which is also known as "market specialization" or "target marketing," has been successfully used by printers for many years. Essentially it requires the identification of graphic products, services, or processes, or a combination of these, which translates into narrowing the manufacturing and service range the printing company provides. Because of the specialized nature of what the company offers, production tends to be streamlined and per unit costs reduced, which together make the company very price competitive. As noted in Chapter 4, controlling markets results in providing the company with a price lever so that the printer can charge more for the products and services she provides, which in turn increases overall profitability for the company.

The *McKinsey Report 1966* to PIA is considered to be a cornerstone investigation of markets and pricing strategy for commercial printing. In general, the report states that profit variation between printing companies is not always related to cost, volume, or price—even though each of these factors plays a part in the profit picture—but is instead related to market demand, the services provided by the printer, and the factors of competition experienced by companies vying for work in those markets. The study stresses that printing management should consider marketing as well as production manufacturing for enhanced profitability because the industry is market driven. Almost thirty years after the McKinsey report was released, its findings are still considered relevant to commercial printers because there has been little change in the competitive factors at work in the industry.

In terms of products, the McKinsey Report found that the demand for tailor-made printed products was diversified, but that no printer could reasonably expect to provide all products and services for all customers, even though many seemed to try. In terms of procedures used for manufacturing printed products, McKinsey reports that there was extreme diversity in process: Some equipment was automated and high speed, while other equipment was slow and required the individual operator's attention. In fact, the study observed that printing companies were beginning to branch out by adding nonimaging processes. Conventional printing techniques of ink-on-paper still were used during printing when the report was published, but extra equipment, such as special wrapping equipment, was being installed to provide additional services to entice the customer's business.

The McKinsey Report concluded that market diversity and process variation both contributed to the significant and intense competition in the printing industry. Thus, if printers practiced specialization of product or process, or both, the intense competition between them for the same types of work would lessen. If a printing company could enter a specialized market and control it, the company could then control prices in that market. If such prices were under control, profits would be greater because price exerts tremendous leverage on profitability. Specialization is a way out of the intense, price-cutting free-for-all that most printing managers dislike.

Product specialization in printing is the production of an item that is difficult to produce economically by most other printers. Process specialization relates to the application of a unique process to accomplish production output of a printed product. An example of a specialized product is the manufacture of theater tickets. An example of a specialized process is the use of shrink-wrap to seal packages for delivery after printing and finishing are completed.

It is possible to specialize in a product line using nonspecialized printing equipment, as many printing plants do. It is also possible to specialize in a process area, such as web printing, and produce a nonspecialized product. Analysis has shown that a combination of both product and process specialization yields the most profitability; it provides the company with excellent market leverage and high production output.

Advantages of Specialization. The following list outlines some advantages of specialization in printing:

1. Competition, in terms of large numbers of companies doing the same type of work and producing the same kind of product, is significantly reduced.
2. Specialized products, services, and processes allow for definite cost advantages, such as higher volume and reduced preparatory costs, thus providing price leverage over less specialized competition.
3. Production during manufacturing is usually streamlined, which saves both time and money.
4. Production control and quality control, which ensure consistent products and may be vital facets of the product, are simplified.
5. Employees working with specialized products, services, and processes usually have specific and defined job assignments, which translates to fewer job errors.
6. Marketing and selling activities can be focused and highly targeted because the products and services are defined and clarified by everyone in the company.

Disadvantages of Specialization. There are also disadvantages associated with specialization, as the following list indicates:

1. The more specialized the process, product, or service, the greater the inherent inflexibility for manufacturing other products. Specialization means that printers cannot manufacture products to meet every customer's need. Thus, specialization locks the printer into continually depending upon the demand of his particular product or process.
2. Although the overall number of competitors is reduced, those who remain exert significant competitive pressure. If the market for the specialized product or process is not broad enough, there may eventually be too few customers for even a limited number of firms. The inevitability of price cutting then results.
3. Obsolescence can be a problem. One major technological advance can destroy a specialized product or process. In addition, skills craftspeople developed in learning the specialized methods may become useless.
4. In many cases, specialization requires dependence upon a few suppliers

who provide specialized products and services. Although it may be beneficial to deal with a limited number of suppliers in general, specialized suppliers use their specialization as a price lever just as the printer does. In the long run, supplies and materials may be more, and not less, expensive.

5. There is a human tendency to resist change, even if the product or process specialization is no longer profitable. Firms locked into a specialty may have a tendency, because of their initial very profitable years, to continue doing the same things over extended periods of time and may therefore pass up changes in technology and products. Over these time periods, profits and sales may begin to decline as the competition shifts to a more modern or different process or product specialty. Eventually, it could become necessary for the company to file for bankruptcy or to merge because of its resistance to change.

It should be noted that market specialization naturally leads to manufacturing standardization. For example, quick printing is geared to smaller pss, and such reduced product sizes lead to similar paper handling techniques, common sizes of all products, and so on. In sum, specialization and standardization go hand in hand to provide additional impetus for any printer to consider market specialization.

Developing a Marketing Plan

Developing and maintaining a marketing plan for a printing company should be a continuing priority for top management. It deserves a deep commitment, fierce passion, and continuous energy. The marketing plan represents a key strategy position upon which many business decisions pivot. Overall the marketing plan affects the short- and long-term survival of the business, company stability, business growth, and the financial success or failure of the company. The importance of a functional marketing plan cannot be overstated. Given the intense competition and low price ceilings that many printers experience, having a marketing plan allows the printing company the chance to achieve success. Without a marketing plan the company is far more likely to sputter, stumble, and ultimately fail.

There is no cookbook solution to successful marketing in printing. Some companies find success with "rolling" marketing programs whereby they make modest but continuous changes over time, while other companies are successful with plans by which they reinvent their companies every few years. Some companies pattern their marketing efforts to mirror the competition, while others take innovative approaches and formulate their marketing efforts around unique products and services. Some printers are manufacturing driven and focus on process, while others are market driven and direct their company efforts into markets where they see opportunities. Still others are customer driven and focus their marketing on meeting current and new customer demand for products and services.

Regardless of the way a printing company approaches its markets and customers with printed products and ancillary services, three rules must be ever present:

1. The marketing plan must be flexible and always open to change.
2. The marketing plan must be realistic enough so that every company employee can understand and implement it in her own way.
3. The marketing plan must be driven by a passion for customers as people, and not by printing as a commodity.

The marketing plan should be written, but some companies record their marketing plans in audio or video format. Using outsiders as input or sounding boards is a good idea; these outsiders can be past or current customers, business acquaintances, or suppliers. Engaging a marketing consultant can be of great benefit, but only when the consultant is thoroughly familiar with conventional and digital printing technology, business operations, personnel issues, and financial factors typically experienced by the company. Superior marketing consultants are information-based, innovative, and provide exceptional service to their clients.

Some Suggested Markets for Conventional and Digital Products and Services

The shift from ink-on-paper products and conventional photolithographic manufacturing methods to electronically generated products at this time—and to fully digital products in the future—is a reality that all printers must face. Although some experts predict the shift to be swift and to cover many products and services, the transition is likely to be slow and to follow a generally predictable pattern.

The key to survival for printers is to remain flexible and to provide their customers—human beings, not markets—with VA products and services. Because it has become difficult to separate VA products from VA services, success in marketing graphic images requires "bundling" these two functions into one. Thus, printers should consider digital products and services one function of their marketing plan unless the two are clearly distinguishable and separate.

Previous chapters of this text detail numerous VA products and services that successful printers are offering their customers. The following summarizes these products and services and is intended as a starting point when considering potential customers and markets.

- Train sales representatives to take complete job specifications for both conventional and electronic production (Chapter 5).
- Turn estimates/proposals/quotes around within one day or sooner (Chapter 5)
- Train CSRs to be front-line customer champions (Chapter 5).
- Encourage teamwork and cross-training between estimating, customer service, and sales so that the entire process is smooth and fast (Chapter 5).
- Provide an excellent selection of papers so that the customer's products are unique (Chapter 6).
- Provide the type of ink-and-paper products that yield the type of product the customer desires (Chapters 6 and 7).
- Offer prepress film or CTP output (Chapter 8).
- Provide prepress services to correct or repair files (Chapter 8).
- Offer related digital products such as CD-ROM (Chapter 8).
- Provide total digital services, including file archiving, and interface into other digital media, including the Internet and the World Wide Web (Chapter 8).
- Provide photomechanical and analog production when cost and time factors make the process more cost effective or of higher quality (Chapter 9).
- Offer black-and-white POD services using high-speed copiers or the Xerox DocuTech (Chapter 10).
- Offer color POD using the Heidelberg-DI and QM presses, and the Indigo, Xeikon, ChromaPress, Canon, and Spontane (Chapter 10).
- Offer products that are unique in size, such as wide-format products (Chapter 10).
- Offer variable imaging through digital presses and ink-jet production (Chapter 10).
- Enhance product quality through waterless printing (Chapter 10).
- Offer postpress services to support target marketing (Chapter 11).
- Suggest ways to differentiate the customer's products and services (Chapter 11).
- Become the key resource for distributing and delivering the customer's products (Chapter 11).
- Provide specific technical advances, such as lay-flat adhesive binding, selective binding, and ink-jet addressing, which includes postpress product personalization (Chapter 11).
- If web printing is being used, enhance the web products (Chapter 12).
- Provide outstanding customer service to support every printing company product or service (Chapter 13).

Customer Partnerships and World-Class Customer Service

If there is one clearly distinguishable difference between a typical printer and a profit leader in the 1990s, it is the way they treat their customers. Before DPP technology emerged, printers controlled the entire spectrum of printing manufacturing, from photographic methods to postpress production. Many printers did not wish to share production or manufacturing decisions with their customers unless liability or contractual issues were involved. Today this situation has been moderated and customer-driven choices are numerous through extensive digital options in prepress, which carry over to press and postpress manufacturing as well.

This shared responsibility has encouraged the development of alliances between printers and customers. To the surprise of some printers, this partnership association has resulted in satisfied, happy customers who handle their shared status with dignity. However, some printers, particularly those driven by hierarchical or traditional management methods, continue to have great difficulty working with customers on an equal-partnership basis. These printers operate on the assumption that delivering an acceptable graphic product at a reasonable price is good enough, and that their customers will always come back because of this. A further discussion of customer partnerships is provided later in this chapter.

Quantitative studies and anecdotal observation show that providing outstanding customer service is a major factor in customer satisfaction, which in turn encourages continuing customer purchases. The following are key ingredients for printers who wish to provide customer service that is of world-class caliber.

- Every customer is treated with dignity and respect, regardless of the job.
- Promises to customers are always kept.
- All company employees, from the president to the janitor, acknowledge that the customer is "the only thing that matters" and take a personal interest in providing positive customer relations.
- Every aspect that goes into generating positive customer perception is monitored. This includes telephone manners, speed of callbacks, politeness, presentable physical appearance by company employees, "can do" attitudes, careful listening and responding, honesty, fairness, and enthusiasm.
- All customer inquiries are answered within one day.
- Customer relations issues are continuously monitored using quantifiable measurement methods such as SPC and Likert Scale tools.
- Customer suggestions for improvement are encouraged and acted upon as appropriate.
- Telephone help and assistance are available during business hours and additional hours on a customer-needed basis.
- Customers with work-in-process or accepted proposals are encouraged to call for information or visit the plant. In the case of customer-supplied electronic art, customers are oriented to minimum job rework through disk pretesting and job preflighting.

- Customer training, such as in EPP, is available upon request. Customers are not charged for training time as long as the time they require is reasonable and appropriate to the work they are ordering from the company.
- Employees value customer complaints as vital feedback to improve the products and services the company provides. Complaints are handled between the individuals most involved in the issues. Employees diligently work to resolve customer complaints in a manner that both the company and customer are satisfied, even if this requires a nontraditional or unconventional solution.
- All permanent company employees spend at least two weeks annually in some type of customer service capacity, preferably in direct contact with customers.

One interesting fact bears emphasizing regarding customers and world-class customer service: It is estimated that it costs five times more to obtain a new customer than it does to keep an existing customer. Because treating customers with dignity, answering their inquiries within one day, and resolving their complaints quickly have negligible out-of-pocket costs, implementing a program of outstanding customer service is a wise business decision.

13.6 Dynamic Factors Affecting the Printing Industry into the Twenty-First Century

The printing and publishing industry is in a paradigm shift driven by ever-changing technology and shifting customer demands. The industry's stable and steady environment has been challenged at almost every level, from its products to the processes used to manufacture them.

The discussion that follows addresses a group of emerging issues that are important to printers. Because of the expansiveness, viability, and core strength of the industry as a whole, the net effect of some of these issues on a company or employee will occur slowly over time. Because these changes affect printers and the industry overall in a parallel, overlapping fashion, the changes also occur subtly.

Great Opportunities for Graphic Imaging Entrepreneurs and Innovators Continue to Be Extensive

Historically the printing industry has always attracted motivated individuals with great entrepreneurial spirit. These men and women have been challenged by the potential they saw and took risks others refused to take. They innovatively developed new graphic products, grew start-up companies into huge corporations, or introduced unique services. They sometimes failed, only to move into other areas that appeared to hold greater promise. Their attraction to printing was the mix of technology, opportunity, and challenge. As technology was introduced—from foundry type to hot metal, from letterpress to offset lithography, from slow electrostatic copiers to the Xerox DocuTech, from photomechanical prepress to DPP—innovative, intelligent men and women took chances.

Today's shift to digital imaging technology continues to offer the possibility of great success for those who are willing to take the risk. One of the findings of the *Printing 2000 Update* discussed earlier in this chapter states that printers must acknowledge that investment decisions will become more risky, with the risk-takers "betting the company" to achieve success. While risking the company may be considered extreme to some printing company owners, the possibility of great opportunity provides a certain challenge that energizes most entrepreneurs.

As the industry shifts from photomechanical to digital products and services, the opportunities for substantial success are greater than at any other time in the industry. Although it is difficult to accurately predict the next paradigm shift in technology or customer need, two general rules describe many successful entrepreneurs and innovators:

1. They are "information seekers" in that they constantly are looking for and evaluating information and ideas of all kinds, even when the information may not be directly related to their companies' missions or personal areas of expertise. They constantly watch, listen, evaluate, and learn in a continuous, open environment.
2. They look beyond the big picture to the details of an emerging innovation, new technology, or unique idea. They remain mentally flexible. They study the details of an idea or emerging technology and seek possible applications for customer products and services. They do not let the suggested or obvious applications of a new product or service obscure their analyses of the potential, which may lie in the details.

The challenge for the industry innovator or entrepreneur is his willingness to actively seek new products or services, and then take the personal and financial risk to address that need. Digital imaging technology offers great potential for those who are willing to take the chance. Those entrepreneurs who are wise enough to take the time to develop new graphic products, offer unique services, or seek customers with superior approaches stand to win both personally and financially in a big way.

Total Quality Management Replaces Hierarchical Management Methods

Many books have been written in the past ten years on Total Quality Management (TQM). This section summarizes TQM as it relates to the printing industry.

In its most general terms, TQM provides an all-encompassing, panoramic shift in how work is assigned, produced, and evaluated. It relies on employee empowerment and continuous improvement of each employee and replaces the hierarchically driven, top-to-bottom decision making that has been practiced throughout the industry for many years. Printing managers who successfully learn and apply TQM principles manage more people with less effort, have more productive employees, enjoy their jobs more, work with less stress, and, as a consequence of all of these factors, increase the profitability of their companies.

Although it is difficult to generalize, a printing or publishing company practicing TQM is committed to two essential components:

1. an intense focus on producing the highest quality product or service it is possible to produce
2. a deep and sincere personal commitment of continuous improvement of every employee in the printing company.

The following "guiding rules" summarize the critical aspects of TQM.

First, the TQM process is simple in concept but complex in detail. Clearly the guiding principles of TQM—high quality and continuous improvement—are easily communicated to any employee. However, integrating TQM into a printing company requires a different management approach. Empowering employees, pushing decision making to the lowest level, removing layers of middle management, and monitoring and controlling process improvement through SPC methods are a few of the important components of TQM.

Second, if TQM is to be successful in a company, each employee must freely and consciously make a personal, passionate commitment to the principles of high quality and continuous improvement. This is a critical, important, personal choice and is, for most employees, a long-term or lifelong commitment. In addition, this commitment must exist in the corporate culture of "can-do" thinking, with an enthusiasm for work, a positive company environment, and the expectation of success in the program over the long term.

Third, TQM is not a process that can be coerced, threatened, insisted upon, or otherwise forced upon employees. Certainly all employees can be trained in methods and processes to achieve high quality and continuous improvement. However, if TQM is to be successful over the long term—where the gains for both the company and the employee will be most significant—employees must voluntarily and freely accept the program.

Fourth, TQM programs are most successful when the consensus of employee opinion in the company indicates that there is a critical need for changing the process by which the company is managed. In a given company or working environment, most employees are sensitive to management's interests and would cooperate to achieve what management wants if it could be done in a friendly, team-oriented manner. In talking with TQM managers, statements as to why they adopted the program include "Management has been the problem," or "The employees wanted a change so they could do their jobs better." In a hierarchically driven company, management tends to avoid listening to employee input, even though the management team may be addressing such critical areas as work flow improvements, quality of product, or cycle-time factors.

Fifth, TQM requires that company leaders establish an "environment of trust" throughout the organization. The element of trust brings to bear the critical issues of risk and failure as components of the process. For example, when employees are trusted to make their own decisions as to how to best accomplish their jobs, managers effectively relinquish control of numerous decisions they would otherwise make. Thus, when allowing employees to make their own job decisions, management risks failure in some of these decisions.

However, TQM managers, who know the importance of this "environment of trust," take such risks—and cope with failure as needed—and continuously maintain a positive attitude and fully expect employee success. The trust/risk/failure relationship thus moves the employee and manager closer under an umbrella of partnership and teamwork and with an accepted vulnerability to error and failure. Although it is usually difficult for hierarchically oriented managers to provide this "environment of trust," once the "ice is broken" and trust is rewarded with success, both management and employees are strengthened and grow together, almost as a family. As the "environment of trust" continues over time, managers develop a natural trust in their employees. The result of this is that the best decisions are made at the lowest level, which allows managers to focus on the more critical business and strategic issues facing the company.

Sixth, managers must clearly understand that any TQM program shifts and redirects their personal power to lower levels where it can be used more effectively. In any organization, power rests in the hands of the employees who make decisions. In a functioning TQM environment, when management relinquishes decision making to lower-level employees, these managers relinquish a certain amount of power and control over these decisions. For many hierarchically oriented managers, empowering generally less-educated, lower-paid workers with decision making is a difficult transition to make, because they see "giving up" power as the first step to losing control of the company. In fact, TQM companies find that decision-making empowerment actually enhances leadership because managers have the freedom to take on new, important projects and leave the less important, day-to-day decisions where they are best made. A significant benefit of decision-making empowerment is that it allows for faster, more immediate decision responses, which allows the company to respond more quickly and thus deal more effectively with time compression and cycle-time factors.

Seventh, because TQM requires line employees and those at the operating level to be empowered to take more responsibility and to maintain a personal passion for achieving high quality and continuous improvement, an "environment of change" exists as a natural by-product. This makes change much easier to accept on a day-to-day basis. Thus, because change brings shifts and revisions to the very core of how work is done, TQM methods allow for more significant shifts that are done more quickly and in response to customer and workplace needs. In the TQM environment, change is not hierarchically driven by promise, force, or threat, but rather by employees who want the changes because they want to continuously improve. The only true way to successfully cope with change is to establish a continuous improvement program, because it goes to the very core of employee involvement and participation in the company.

It should be clear that TQM printing companies have a defined structure and a chain of command—they are not disorganized nor do they operate chaotically or in disarray. Furthermore, TQM companies have a continuous fix on profitability and financial success, for without these the companies cannot move forward. Typically TQM companies provide their employees with information about production and profits, and they ask their employees to participate in making decisions on long-term company matters such as equipment purchases, plant remodels, and so on. Employees are treated as adults who are capable of weighing various issues and making mature decisions based on the facts with which they are presented.

Partnerships, Strategic Alliances, and ISO 9000

Printers purchase raw and semiraw materials from suppliers and convert them, through manufacturing, to the products desired by customers. However, raw materials from suppliers sometimes vary in consistency or quality, which in turn causes quality problems for the printer. At other times, the printing process during production varies because of printer—controlled problems, which causes some portion of the print run to be of a lesser quality than desired. Thus, print quality in any customer's job is subject to variation from numerous, and sometimes unpredictable, causes. To ensure a specified level of quality in printed products, the three affected groups-the suppliers, the printers, and the customers—are adopting two interrelated concepts: partnerships and ISO 9000. These are both considered important components of a TQM program.

There are two types of partnerships: legal and voluntary. A legal partnership is the cooperative joining of two or more parties whereby each party provides specified goods, services, or compensation to the other parties on an equivalent basis, as subscribed by written agreement. Legal partnerships are common between individuals sharing company ownership. Voluntary partnerships, sometimes termed "alliances," are formed when two or more partners agree to work together in a manner that benefits both, but there is no legal or binding commitment. In a voluntary alliance, if either party wishes to discontinue the relationship, she is free to do so without obligation to the other party.

A growing number of voluntary partnerships can be seen between printers and specific customers or suppliers. These voluntary arrangements allow both parties greater freedom, but they also provide a basis of commitment for a long-term business relationship as long as both parties wish to continue. For example, the customer may ask his printer-partner to provide overnight delivery on a special job when most jobs require five-day turnarounds, and the printer-partner may do this without complaint or excessive overcharges. In another case, the printer may ask her partner-paper supplier for a certain kind or size of paper that is not normally available, and the supplier would provide the paper quickly and without additional charges.

Voluntary alliances are held together by goodwill between the parties, although business transactions that require legally contracted obligations between the two partners are used as they would normally apply (e.g., purchase orders form a legal contract). With a voluntary partnership either party is free to discontinue the partnership at any point as long as there is no outstanding obligation owed by one party to the other, such as an overdue invoice.

The emergence of strategic partnerships or strategic alliances have been frequent in the past few years, driven primarily by opportunities in digital technology. Strategic partnerships are typically formed when two companies recognize the value of combining their talents to produce a needed product or service. For example, the manufacturer of a bar code inventory device may enter into a strategic partnership with a printer whereby the printer site-tests the device. Compensation for the printer's testing and feedback for improvements might be free equipment, while the bar code manufacturer might obtain advertising testimonials from the printer. Strategic partnerships are typically bound by legal agreement.

A critical problem for printers is that there are sometimes variations in the supplier's products, which in turn causes the printer to vary product quality to the customer. Although these variations can be extreme enough to cause product quality shifts that are unacceptable to customers, customers frequently lack the sophistication to quantitatively define quality or to be certain it is maintained throughout their jobs. To ensure quality by each partner in the process—the printer, the supplier, and the customer—a growing number of companies are adopting ISO 9000.

ISO 9000 is a component-based quality assurance system for establishing, measuring, and maintaining quality. Originally developed to ensure a defined, basic quality level between suppliers for the European Common Market, ISO 9000 has emerged into global acceptance, particularly in the United States and Canada. The American version, which is known as Q90, was developed by the American Society for Quality Control (ASQC) and the American National Standards Institute and is compatible with the ISO 9000 system in Europe. In 1993, there were over 100 countries endorsing ISO 9000, with approximately 23,000 registered companies in Europe and approximately 1,000 in the United

States either certified or in the process of obtaining certification. The United States Federal Government is currently evaluating whether it will endorse legislative action in Congress mandating ISO 9000 registration for suppliers of products and services throughout the government system.

Printing industry observers generally agree that by the first decade of the next millennium, ISO 9000 will have had a significant effect on printers engaged in sole-source manufacturing, as well as on suppliers such as trade shops and service bureaus. As ISO 9000 catches on in the United States, and it is already occurring, manufacturers and suppliers who have become "ISO 9000 certified" will do business only with each other and not with any non-ISO 9000 certified company. Although the certification process is slow, costly, and somewhat of an academic approach to quality assurance, it provides a concrete set of guidelines that are otherwise missing in the TQM movement.

Although ISO 9000 is progressing, problems with it still exist. In addition to being a time-consuming, costly, and somewhat rigid process, ISO-certification provides a written method that the company has a working quality assurance system. This ISO 9000 certification, in and of itself, does not assure a consistently high quality product, nor does it link the established product quality used for certification to the printing company's output from job to job and customer to customer.

Although "ISO 9000" is the generic term used for this system, the system is actually divided into five parts: ISO 9000 is the basic system framework and ISO 9001, ISO 9002, ISO 9003 are three sets of quality components (ISO 9001 is the most comprehensive and ISO 9003 provides the least number of quality functions). ISO 9004 is set of guidelines for how the process is implemented and maintained, while ISO 8402 provides a working vocabulary of terms and clarification.

To become ISO 9000-certified, company management must select one of the three levels of quality components: ISO 9001, ISO 9002, or ISO 9003. ISO 9001, which has twenty quality components, covers the complete range necessary for a company providing a full range of products and supporting services, including R&D and network distribution. In general, ISO 9001 is too broad for most printing companies, trade shops, and service bureaus. ISO 9002 consists of eighteen quality functions, and omits "purchasing" for example, and seems to more likely fit printing companies, service bureaus, and trade shops. ISO 9003 consists of twelve quality components and best fits nonmanufacturing companies such as distributors of premanufactured products.

ISO 9000 certification requires full management commitment and a developed plan. Typically an outside consultant is used to initiate the process, but it is possible to become certified without outside assistance. To begin the process, a company should contact the ASQC to request a preliminary visit. An application fee and existing quality materials are required to begin the process, and both are reviewed before the preliminary visit. Throughout the certification procedure, ASQC auditors review, inspect, and assist the company.

Reducing Cycle Time and Industry Overcapacity

Cycle time in printing, which is also known as "lead time," is the time required to produce a printing order. In the mid-1980s, prior to DPP and other timesaving devices and methods, the lead time for a job was about twenty days. By the mid-1990s, however, cycle time had been reduced in most printing manufacturing to ten days or fewer, with continuing pressure from customers for even faster job turnarounds. Lead time is usually a customer-driven job requirement that must be met by the printer. However, customers vary in that some must have a five-day or faster production cycle, while others purchase printing based on long lead times and usually at price advantages. Because lead time is customer driven, it is an important issue for many printers.

The pressure to reduce cycle times in printing manufacturing remains a critical issue from both competitive and production viewpoints. As long as price and quality remain fairly equal, it is not unusual for customers to shift their work from slower lead time printers to printers who provide faster job turnarounds. When this occurs with a number of customers, a common reaction of the slower printer is to purchase faster but more expensive technology. If no other changes are made, this purchase tends to compromise the financial position of the business in the long term and may not solve the problem.

Reducing lead times can be achieved using a number of approaches that overlap and are frequently used in combination. Seven are listed in the following. Some of these require additional equipment or skilled employees, which have an immediate cost impact on the company and must be carefully evaluated. Lead time can be reduced by:

1. combining production processes through electronic technology applications
2. using automation, robotics, and in-line production
3. increasing product output using a "faster or bigger" approach
4. training employees so they work more efficiently
5. accepting customer artwork that has few or no errors and requires no rework
6. scheduling production carefully and accurately to reduce overlaps and bottlenecks
7. shortening the estimating/quoting cycle (because some customers consider estimating and quoting part of the lead time)

One of the problems with reducing cycle times is that it exacerbates the issue of overcapacity. This is because reduced cycle time increases the capacity of a company to generate products. For example, when product turnaround in a given printing company is cut from ten days to five days, the company has effectively doubled its available capacity. When management recognizes this, their common response is to seek additional work to fill the void, thereby intensifying industry competition. Price cutting, which is discussed in Chapter 4, is frequently a sign of overcapacity.

In terms of defining overcapacity, an industry is not considered to have true overcapacity unless: (1) prices on the goods are dropping quickly and uncontrollably, (2) there are massive employee layoffs, (3) bankruptcies are being filed throughout the industry, and (4) the number of new companies entering the industry is low.

The problem of overcapacity in printing manufacturing is likely to be exacerbated further as some customers shift certain products from ink-on-paper to digital format. Although this is likely to occur slowly, the shift will open blocks of press time to the lowest bidder. Complicating the overcapacity problem are global competition, increasing paper prices, a less-skilled workforce, mergers and consolidations, government-mandated constraints, and expensive environmental compliance.

Workforce and Training Issues

The printing industry is growing an average of three percent per year ahead of the gross domestic product (GDP). Although such growth is expected to continue, certain vertical markets will shrink or disappear as they convert to digital formats. The printing industry workforce is projected to grow in proportion to industry growth and become more ethnically diverse, more competitive, and more female. New employees will seek stable employment opportunities, training benefits, health-care benefits, good financial compensation, and a challenging work experience. Unionization is projected to remain unchanged or to decline slightly.

Entry-level employees will need a high school diploma and the ability to successfully handle basic mathematics, writing, and speech communication skills. These basic education areas have been an perplexing problem for printing employers and have led to the development of programs such as NAPL's Carl Didde WorkPLACE®. A knowledge of printing manufacturing will be helpful but not necessary for new entrants. In both production and management areas, employees will be expected to be computer literate or to be able to quickly gain requisite computer skills. New employees must also possess or learn science and technology as it applies to their jobs.

Management employees will rise through the ranks or come from college and university programs with majors in business, technology, and the liberal arts. Success will be linked to performance on the job and not to background or academic pedigree. Women and ethnically diverse individuals will occupy more management positions than ever before.

Training programs will be available for all employees with a focus on continuous personal improvement. A growing number of companies will offer training by volunteer employees and managers during off-hours. On-the-job training will continue to be used extensively at all levels, as will modular training programs that mix various types of training methods and offer training flexibility. The use of seminars and short courses will continue to be popular as well.

The keys to personal success are unchanged from past years: Employees should demonstrate a positive work ethic, motivation, self-reliance, team participation, and the desire to continuously learn and improve. Success will not be tied to seniority or time on the job. Opportunities will range widely from line production and staff positions, such as estimating and customer service, to a variety of management positions.

Growth of Facilities Management

Facilities management is the franchising out of all or part of a client or company's operational services. The services are then handled by an outside service provider. As corporations downsize, one way they reconfigure is to eliminate all but their core segments and to outsource some or all of the support services needed to operate the company. Thousands of corporations have used facilities management for years through service bureau support for computer services, advertising agencies for advertising programs, and similar types outsources.

The use of facilities management is a growing trend for procuring graphic arts products. To do this, the company or corporation engages the facilities management firm as the sole-source provider for all of its printing services and needs. Products and services include prepress, printing manufacturing, postpress, distribution, or any other graphic need.

Facilities management has threatened in-plant printing departments for many years because it frequently replaces these departments entirely. For example, a large insurance corporation finds that its in-plant printing department can produce only certain products, that job turnaround takes ten days on average, and that there has been a recent proposal requesting $15,000 to buy DTP computer and software. The facilities management provider, who is perhaps a printer looking for new customers, approaches company executives with a proposal to provide all graphic products and services needed by the corporation in a reduced cycle time mode. Inherent with this proposal would the opportunity for the insurance company to disband its in-plant printing department completely, which would also eliminate employees and facilities and cut overhead costs. The decision requires that executives weigh the advantages and disadvantages of the facilities management proposal versus keeping the in-plant department operational.

Facilities management clients can be any organization that needs printing or graphic services. For example, facilities management could provide a large law firm with its varying but continuous printing needs. In another example, a corporation may desire to develop a new product line and may engage a facilities management company to provide graphic design and EPP services to parallel the product development cycle and save time when the product is ready for the market.

As the printing industry adjusts to emerging digital technology, and as competition for customers heats up more intensely than ever, facilities management is one of the fastest growing areas of the industry. Even so, in order to deliver graphic products and services in the reduced cycle times customers want, a growing number of facilities management companies are finding that they must become print manufacturers and not simply the purchasing agents of the graphic products and services printed by others. This condition requires an investment of substantial dollars in POD equipment such as the Xerox DocuTech and digital presses such as Xeikon and Indigo.

Global Competition

There is a significant increase in printing activity, with United States printers trading in Mexico and Canada, and increasingly vying for work in European and Asian markets. Although competing for printing orders outside the United States borders offers certain drawbacks, those printing companies that take the risk stand to enjoy significant financial and other gains. The drawbacks include language barriers, currency exchange rates, incompatible prepress methods, and shipping costs and related delivery issues. The gains for United States printers are long-term partnerships with high-volume buyers who desire quality products and are willing to pay for them.

Passage of the North American Free Trade Agreement (NAFTA) in November 1993 has spurred printing exchanges—both export and import—with Canada and Mexico. The general pattern is that printers in northern American states concentrate on Canadian markets, while printers in states that border Mexico pursue those markets. The biggest difficulties for United States printers are startup connections and sales arrangements, but once these are overcome, customers in both Canada and Mexico enjoy doing business with United States printers because of their consistent quality and timely delivery. However, shipping and distribution within Mexico can be problematic.

The size and versatility of Mexico offers a panorama of potential for United States printers. Mexican and Latin American printers have a history of what amounts to monopolies over their customers, which has kept their printing prices high until now. American competition is what has changed this. In

Canada there are numerous huge graphic arts markets that have not always been properly served by Canadian printers and that as a result sought business with United States customers. Except for certain regions, Canada does not have the language barrier evident with Mexico or Latin America, Europe, or Asia.

Customers in Europe and Asia offer United States printers unique problems. To compete in Europe, some printers opt to establish full manufacturing facilities from scratch, while other printers purchase existing European printing facilities and then staff and manage them with the assistance of local employees. Asian business opportunities are even more complex and tend to be more risky, but the markets are huge and the payoffs are great if success is achieved. Entering and competing in either European and Asian printing markets is expensive given the currency exchange rates, the labor laws, the political climate, the availability of skilled employees, cultural issues, government intervention, and shipping and distribution problems once the product is printed.

Company Consolidations, Mergers, and Acquisitions

Consolidation of companies through mergers and acquisitions is expected to continue at a steady pace into the next millennium. Reasons vary, but the following are among them:

1. Foreign companies have recognized that buying American printing or publishing businesses gives them immediate access to huge American markets, which is therefore an advantage.
2. Some printing firms, which are in trouble because of poor cash positions or other financial reasons, are ripe for purchase. Their counterpart cash-rich printing companies carefully buy these companies to provide immediate new markets.
3. More than ever before, printing has been recognized as a way to make money, and it therefore attracts investors from other business areas.
4. There has been an acceleration in leveraged buyouts.

A number of consolidations between some of the industry's largest printing companies occurred in the 1990s. Thus, very large printers continue to grow even bigger. These industry giants are also diversifying into digital products and services beyond their core markets, which consisted primarily of ink-on-paper products only a few years ago. The spin-off digital divisions have fast growth and consume a significant amount of corporate investment. The integration of digital production methods in the ink-on-paper divisions of these large companies is also extensive and is pushing conventional photomechanical printing processes into the background quickly.

Small and medium printers are also affected by mergers and acquisitions. Production is increasingly digital, but these small and medium size companies tend to remain more focused on conventional ink-on-paper products and related services. Some experts predict that medium and small printing companies will either consolidate or go out of business as they work to maintain production equilibrium between ink-on-paper and digital products and services. Thus, there are two important structural changes occurring in parallel as the industry enters the twenty-first century: (1) continuing industry-wide consolidations that will change the competitive landscape of the industry both in the United States and abroad and (2) extremely fast shifts to digital production and digital products.

There is no doubt that the result of consolidation through mergers and acquisitions will have a significant, long-term bearing on the overall printing and publishing industry. They will reshape certain markets and affect the core structure of the industry in ways that are unpredictable at this time.

Environmental Issues for Printers

Printing manufacturing, as well as the paper, ink, and other raw and semiraw materials used in printing, are subject to extensive environmental government regulation. Clearly this is a critical issue given the desire of many Americans for clean air, clean water, and improved long-term health benefits.

During the middle and late 1990s a number of federal environmental laws are slated for review, and careful attention should have been paid them so that the American public is protected from environmental disaster. Some of the laws to be reviewed include the Clean Air Amendment controlling VOC emissions; the Clean Water Act (CWA), which sets effluent and water quality standards; the Compensation and Liability Act (CERCLA), which brings small printing companies into superfund litigation; the Occupational Safety and Health Act (OSHA), which covers health monitoring in the workplace; the Comprehensive Environmental Response, Resource Conservation, and Recovery Act (RCRA); and the Superfund Amendment and Reauthorization Act (SARA Title III).

In general, the ink and paper suppliers shoulder a major environmental burden with the products they produce. As legislation revision is discussed, costs of retrofitting or the development of cleaner paper and ink manufacturing methods will be evaluated. Stricter guidelines to provide cleaner water and air would be a cost burden passed from the paper and ink manufacturer to the printer, who would in turn pass it to the customer.

If there is one area of concern over all of the others, it is the effect of toxic products on human health. Existing federal laws include built-in, mandatory reductions of hazardous and toxic substances that are effective in 1996 or 1997. These are accompanied by worker notification procedures, employee training of how to properly handle toxic materials, and monitoring of air and water emissions to ensure compliance. When any company, including any printing company, is monitored and found to be beyond the limits prescribed by law, penalties, fines, and/or criminal prosecution will follow. It is likely that there will be an increase in monitoring and penalties in the future. In addition, it is likely that disposal fee costs will increase and VOC emission permits will be more stringently enforced.

Becoming a "green" or an environmentally sensitive printer has a positive effect on customers. Every printer is faced with similar costs to be in compliance, which are passed to the customers, so taking the positive approach is best. Suggesting that customers use recycled papers and soya inks is wise. Informing customers about the steps taken by the company to ensure clean air and water and to reduce the effects of toxic substances on company employees and the community at large is good marketing and environmentally desirable as well.

Governmental Regulation

There is an direct link between the laws written to regulate commercial business and the daily operation of the enterprise. It is up to the executives of the company to learn about, and follow, the legal parameters established by ordinance in their towns or municipalities, by state statute, and by federal law.

One problem that arises is learning which laws, statutes, and ordinances affect a given company. Another problem is the frustration of dealing with certain laws, statutes, and ordinances that appear to be useless, unnecessary, or frivolous. Also, as a business grows, and as time passes, laws change and the company is obligated to change with them.

With all of the other pressing issues a busy executive must cope, the regulatory aspect of municipal, state, and federal government can be a major impediment. Two key points need to be made here. First, government regulation is an interactive part of the capitalistic system and will always be integrated into the operation of the business. Whether we agree or not with any law, statute, or ordinance, there are rational reasons the legislation was enacted. The democratic process requires extensive discussion before any law is passed. In general, our laws, statutes, and ordinances have been enacted by well-intentioned people to protect, limit, control, regulate, or monitor the conditions by which a business is run.

The second point is that there is every reason for printing executives and others in the industry to participate in writing or to provide input as any ordinance, statute, or law is being drafted. Although this may involve entering the political arena, which can be distasteful and time consuming, there is no one to better help draft a law, ordinance, or statue than the person who is directly affected by it from regulatory and cost standpoints. In a democracy, unfair, unnecessary, or inappropriate laws, statutes, and ordinances can only be changed by taking a proactive stance to modify the situation.

If there is one area that frustrates printing executives, but one in which they frequently refuse to participate, it is in the writing of laws that affect their companies. Clearly, government regulation will remain a major issue for printing executives and the printing industry as a whole into the next millennium and beyond. The proactive participation of knowledgeable printing industry executives in drafting the laws, statutes, and ordinances that affect their business activities is important.

13.7 Industry Associations and the Services They Provide

The following industry associations and foundations provide extensive resources and information for printers. Listed alphabetically, each is briefly described relative to the services it provides. Addresses, telephone, fax, Internet, and World Wide Web numbers (if available) are provided to expedite contacting them for information.

Graphic Arts Technical Foundation (GATF)

The Graphic Arts Technical Foundation (GATF) is a member-supported, not-for-profit, scientific, technical, and educational organization that serves the international graphic communication industries. GATF's educational programs encompass the graphic processes and related areas, including electronic publishing, environmental control, SPC, TQM, and the development of skill standards for the graphic arts. The Foundation publishes college-level textbooks covering every aspect of the lithographic process, as well as developments in digital color imaging, CTP technology, and other topics that cut across the boundaries of different printing processes. Videotapes, audiovisuals, and learning-module training tools are also available.

Through its technical articles, the bimonthly *GATFWORLD Magazine* helps GATF members stay on top of the latest issues affecting the ever-changing graphic communications field. As administrator of the National Scholarship Trust Fund, GATF disburses scholarships and fellowships established by industry associations, companies, and individual leaders interested in investing in the future of graphic communication.

Established in 1924, the GATF continues to conduct specialized research in areas, such as materials testing, and to develop test images that assist industry professionals in achieving quality print reproductions. GATF is located at 4615 Forbes Avenue, Pittsburgh, PA 15213. Telephone: 412/621-6941. Fax: 412/621-3049.

Graphic Communications Association (GCA)

GCA's strategic mission is to be the leading global membership organization for advancing the processes of information and image management and distribution through the development and application of new technologies, standards, and management methods. In order to address the graphic communication industry as a whole, GCA's efforts are focused in two areas: print media information and information technologies.

Print Media Information. This section is subdivided into three areas of emphasis: management technologies, spectrum, and address/distribution. Management technologies focuses on total quality in the printing, publishing, and paper industries. GCA covers issues such as pressroom automation, statistical analysis of operations, and waste reduction/environmental issues. This area also develops and manages almost all of the industry's electronic data interchange (EDI) standards for the exchange of business, order, and TQM information and manages graphic arts industry bar code programs.

Spectrum is dedicated to color issues—color in DTP, color in prepublishing, color in print, and color in multimedia. From concept through delivery, this area focuses on resolving challenges that affect the process and effectiveness of color production and reproduction.

Addressing/distribution focuses on postal and mail management issues and standardization in order to facilitate the full utilization of current technologies for mail preparation and postal processes. GCA covers improvements in communication between service bureaus, list houses, and printers, as well as improvements to make the business of addressing and producing mail more efficient and cost effective.

Information Technologies. This section of GCA deals with structured electronic information management for technical, reference, and commercial publishing applications. The information technologies (IT) track also fosters the development and implementation of the Standard Generalized Markup Language (SGML) and all of its derivatives, such as HTML, DSSSL, HyTime, and so on. SGML is the backbone of the international electronic information infrastructure and GCA is considered the worldwide leader for publications, training seminars, and conferences on SGML and electronic publishing.

Products and Services. GCA runs a number of conferences and tutorials focusing on all aspects of the graphic communication industry. Annual conferences include Spectrum, Impact, Direct, Electronic Partnership, Addressing/Distribution Conference, and Print Media Executive Conference.

In addition, GCA has developed a broad array of publications and standards for the industry. Specific to the printing estimating process, GCA's committees have worked together to formulate industry standards for paper control in the printing process, such as Sheeted Paper Identifiers Specification EMS: Electronic Mechanical Specifications; EFEX: Electronic Front-End Exchange; Specification EMBARC/X12: Electronic Manifesting of Paper Stock Shipments in ANSI X12

Format; Paper Quality EDI Transaction (PAQET); and North American Roll Identifier. In addition, GCA has focused on developing two newer EDI standards for production orders and invoicing: Production Order Specifications/EDI (PROSE) and Electronic Printer Invoice Transaction (ELPRINT). For a complete list of publications and standards, contact the GCA Publications Department, 100 Daingerfield Road, Alexandria VA 22314. Telephone: (703) 519-8157.

For more information, contact Graphic Communications Association, 100 Daingerfield Road, Alexandria, Virginia 22314. Telephone: (703) 519-8160. Fax: (703) 548-2867

International Digital Imaging Association (IDIA)

The International Digital Imaging Association (IDIA) is a trade association serving the digital imaging industry. Founded in 1990, IDIA dedicates its resources to furthering the interests of digital imaging professionals by supporting their education, sharing information, increasing their purchasing power, and increasing their network opportunities.

IDIA is the combined power of nearly five hundred members worldwide who share a common idea. As rapidly changing as digital imaging is, IDIA members are not only in step with those changes, they help steer them. Its members encompass digital imaging professionals, including imaging service providers, printers, publishers, corporations, advertising agencies, designers, educators, and leading manufacturers of imaging hardware and software.

Through its membership directory, IDIA members have access to a powerful resource for critical decisions, such as equipment acquisition or support. Information on industry trends, marketing strategies, and technical issues and solutions that help grow imaging businesses are founded in %%*Time Out*, IDIA's bimonthly newsletter. In addition, the *Glitch Report* is faxed to IDIA members' desktops monthly to alert them of hardware and software bugs and provide them with the fixes. IDIA members also save thousands of dollars by taking advantage of discounts on products, services, and educational conferences. However, the most important benefit is the interactive exchange of ideas among IDIA members that brings them to the knowledge of a worldwide network.

For more information about the International Digital Imaging Association, contact IDIA, 5601 Roanne Way, Suite 608, Greensboro, NC 27409. Telephone: 800/844-2472. Fax: 910/854-5956. Compuserve: 75300,750

International Prepress Association (IPA)

The International Prepress Association (IPA), which was founded in 1897, represents the fastest changing and most innovative segment of the graphic communication and information industry-professional imaging and prepress.

Widely regarded for its economic, management, and technology reports, the IPA dedicates its resources to programs and studies that provide members the information they need to stay one step ahead in this dynamic industry.

The IPA publishes *The Prepress Bulletin, Tech Focus,* and *Images,* and copublishes the *Prepress Market Watch.* The IPA has also founded the Advanced Color Imaging Forum on America Online. This service permits members to access pertinent technology issues and to network with one another. Over 2,000 downloads have been made since the program was inaugurated. In addition, the IPA aids its members in defining many of the new opportunities presented through multimedia, digital distribution, and digital transmission, as well as through database marketing in electronic prepress.

Reports regularly issued by IPA include:

Annual Economic Study Provides an update of sales and production costs as well as imaging services and markets. It has proven to be a critical tool for management decisions.

In-Depth Economic Report Tracks several firms over a three-year period, thus uncovering key trends taking place.

Sales Compensation Survey Provides input from prepress imaging firms to identify compensation levels within the industry. It also defines the forms of compensation that are in use as well as analyzes their effectiveness.

Customer Service Study Assists companies with the assessment of their CSR's function and the CSR's changing structure and emphasis.

Labor Wage Summary Examines compensation practices for prepress companies under both union and nonunion contracts.

In addition, the IPA commissions specific industry reports covering special marketing and technology aspects. Those of recent issue include:

Prepress . . . Its Changing Role This in-depth analysis of changing prepress dynamics uncovers opportunities available in both existing and emerging markets.

Optimizing Production Communications This comprehensive and sophisticated overview studies the systems needed to achieve optimum job profitability.

Multimedia Opportunities for Prepress This report addresses both the risks and the opportunities of this emerging technology, as well as new methods of structuring and extending customer relationships.

The Association's two major conferences are the most highly acclaimed in the industry. The IPA Management Conference brings together owners and managers from around North America to meet, share concerns, develop relationships, and access information. The IPA Technical Seminar is a multiday, intensive, interactive forum that is designed to focus on practical technology and processes. It is often the first opportunity for attendees to see new technology in action. The IPA also holds several issue and occupational-specific seminars throughout each year.

As a major participant in SWOP, DDAP, OSCA, and several other key industry standards committees, the IPA affords its membership the opportunity for input and update on current standards issues.

For a complete listing of publications and services offered by the IPA, contact the International Prepress Association, 7200 France Avenue South, Edina, MN 55435. Telephone: 612/896-1908. Fax: 612/896-0181

International Publishing Management Association (IPMA)

The International Publishing Management Association (IPMA) is the professional association for in-house corporate publishing (design, prepress, press, distribution) professionals who work for educational institutions, governments, and private industry. These industries comprise some 60,000 departments that produce more than $50 billion in merchandise each year. Nearly 35 percent of in-house corporate publishing departments employ five or fewer individuals; almost 95 percent have fewer than fifty employees.

The IPMA is a thriving organization that was founded in 1964 as the In-Plant Printing Management Association. It exists to provide corporate publishing and distribution professionals the resources to attain greater productivity and cost effectiveness through education, certification, and information exchange while promoting technological advancements. As an association, IPMA promotes the value of in-house corporate publishing and distribution while advocating high ethical standards and environmental and safety awareness.

Members can network with more than 2,200 in-house managers in the United States, Australia, and Canada. Nineteen percent of IPMA's members work for higher education institutions, 12 percent for insurance companies, 11 percent each for manufacturing companies and governments, and 9 percent for health-related organizations. Thirteen other industries are also represented. Associate membership may be held by persons representing equipment manufacturers, ink and toner suppliers, or paper manufacturer or resellers. IPMA facilitates two-way communication between in-house professionals and suppliers to share the latest technologies. Associate members count for 15 percent of the membership. Members may join as members-at-large, or they may join one of the nearly fifty local chapters. The following lists of some of IPMA's services:

- annual international conferences and exhibits with over fifty concurrent seminars on topics such as the Internet, the World Wide Web, high-fi color,

environmental issues, mail management, copy, on-demand printing, and marketing
- yearly regional conferences
- professional certification programs for in-house print and mail managers
- award recognition for superior printing and effective management
- *Perspectives*, a monthly publication offering industry news and management articles
- books, audio tapes, and videotapes (for which members receive substantial discounts)
- industry studies, such as the exclusive in-house salary and compensation survey
- employment leads
- an annual grant for the educational institution that most furthers the in-house graphic arts industry
- scholarships for students from many local chapters
- leadership opportunities and the chance to hone public speaking skills
- public relations offered in support of in-house publishing
- mailing list rental for networking and marketing

For further information, contact the International Publishing Management Association, The IPMA Building, 1205 W. College Street, Liberty, MO 64068. Telephone: 816/781-1111. Fax: 816/781-2790. Internet: 71674.1647@compuserve.com.

National Association of Desktop Publishers (NADTP)

The National Association of Desktop Publishers (NADTP) is the nation's leading professional organization for desktop publishers, graphic designers, and multimedia originators. Founded in 1987, NADTP is designed to serve the information, education, and support needs of its members. Its membership totals more than 40,000 and it continues to grow as computer-based technology dominates production and distribution of documents to paper and alternative media.

The NADTP is a member-driven organization with member services developed from member surveys. Services are invaluable to desktop publishers of all skill levels who utilize either Macintosh or PC-based publishing systems. The NADTP members operate in enriched computing environments that require the latest technology in hardware, software, peripherals, and networking.

The monthly *Desktop Publishers Journal* is the official publication of the association and is a prime resource for professional communicators using desktop technology. Another service of the association is the NADTP Bookstore, which stocks hard-to-find, industry-specific titles offered at members-only prices. Because NADTP is a member-driven organization, the NADTP

Member HelpLine Network provides free technical support from more than 250 DTP experts. Membership in NADTP provides access to a free Member HelpLine Network Directory, which is updated quarterly and organized in a convenient, user-friendly format.

For further information, contact the National Association of Desktop Publishers, 462 Old Boston Street, Topsfield, MA 01983. Telephone: 508/887-7900. Fax: 508/887-6117/9245. e-mail: nadtp1@shore.net; nadtp@aol.com; 74064.2334-@compuserve.com.

National Association of Printers and Lithographers (NAPL)

Chartered in 1933, the National Association of Printers and Lithographers (NAPL) is a dynamic printing association known for innovative, quality products and highly personal service for the printing and allied industries worldwide. NAPL's mission is to prepare the printing community to profit from change through a vast array of management and educational services. NAPL offers a growing list of impressive studies and reports that are too numerous to list.

Cost Studies. One of NAPL's most popular and significant contributions to the printing industry is represented in its cost studies, which detail production center costs for all areas of a printing company—from prepress to bindery—enabling users to develop their own BHRs. A comprehensive study is even available for print operations with up to fifteen employees. Also available is the Computer Modeling Package, a PC-based program that enables purchasers to develop their own hourly rates using NAPL's model.

Economic Reports. NAPL's quarterly *Printing Business Report* is considered one of the industry's most important economic tools due to its accuracy, timeliness, and quality of information. For benchmarking purposes, the report includes sales performance figures, price trends, profitability levels, capacity utilization data, and other information from in-depth surveys of a core group of commercial printing companies of all sizes from across the United States and Canada. The report's forecasts are based on NAPL's exclusive, detailed industry economic model of data from over sixty indicators, which allow NAPL to closely track the industry's performance and accurately predict employment and sales growth figures over a five-year period.

NAPL's Printing Economic Research Center also produces the quarterly *Prepress Market Watch* report and the *NAPL Print Demand Yearbook* for tracking new print markets and segments.

On-Line Benchmarking. The ability to confidentially benchmark and download individual financial performance measures against industry standards is now available on line through *NAPL's Profit Connection*® on the World Wide Web at http;//www.napl.org. Free startup software is available through NAPL for individuals not already on the Web.

All Facets of Printing Management. Beyond economics and cost studies, NAPL produces and distributes hundreds of publications and audio- and videocassettes on topical business issues ranging from administrative to sales and marketing topics, desktop and production matters, environmental concerns, and every other aspect needed for a printing company to profit from change. NAPL also provides on-site consulting services and seminars on virtually every topic and is well-known for its thorough and expedient responses to the numerous and varied member questions that come through the association's toll-free phone line.

Of particular import is the NAPL Management Institute, the industry's *only* executive certification program in Financial Management, Sales and Marketing Management, Production Management, and Strategic Management through intensive, job-specific coursework. NAPL's groundbreaking Carl Didde Work-PLACE® Program is the industry's only comprehensive training program to improve workers' job-related skills in math, reading, writing, critical thinking, and problem-solving, as well as their understanding of the graphic arts processes.

For further information, contact NAPL, 780 Palisade Avenue, Teaneck, NJ 07666. Telephone: 800/642-6275 or 201/342-0700. Fax: 201/692-0286. On line: http://www.napl.org

National Association of Quick Printers (NAQP)

NAQP was founded in 1975 by George Pataky and has about 4,500 member companies representing about 6,000 quick printing and copying shops throughout the United States, Canada, and several foreign countries. The purpose of NAQP is to provide its members with pertinent, up-to-date information on all facets of the quick printing business. The association releases numerous reports and other information, such as:

- Member shop profiles provide data and information on NAQP members with respect to current equipment, services provided, and demographics.
- *The Quick Printing Industry Operating Study* summarizes in detail the financial and other operating characteristics of NAQP respondent firms.
- *Desktop Publishing Studies* tells about the methods and procedures used by NAQP members in providing DTP services to their customers and clients.
- *The Pricing Study/Final Report* provides information to members on profit leaders, owner's compensation, sales per employee, and regional pricing differences.

The focus of NAQP is to help its members in all areas of business operation. A key way this is done is using NAQP Online, which is available through American Online. Access provides connection to NAQP Online Resources, the NAQP Message Board, and NAQP Live! where the first and third Tuesday of each month (8-11 p.m. EST) members have the opportunity to chat with an industry expert or consultant on pertinent business issues. NAQP also offers a range of publications, including *NAQP Bookshelf*, *Mailing Services Group Newsletter*, *Quick Bytes Newsletter*, and *Public Affairs Council Positions*. NAQP has local chapters across the United States and provides members with group discount purchasing.

Contact NAQP at 401 North Michigan Avenue, Chicago, IL 60611. Telephone: 312/644-6610. Fax: 312/321-6869. It can also be reached through America Online using the key word NAQP.

Printing Industries of America (PIA) and Its Regional Affiliate Offices

Printing Industries of America (PIA) is a national trade association dedicated to the promotion of the general welfare of the graphic arts industries. PIA serves as the graphic arts industry's advocate and advances the management of member firms throughout North America. PIA, which is one of the United States's oldest trade associations in continuous operation, was organized in 1887 and is now headquartered in Alexandria, Virginia. PIA is the world's largest trade association, representing nearly 14,000 member firms throughout North America.

Although the majority of PIA's members are general commercial printers, its membership also includes allied graphic arts firms, such as electronic imaging companies, equipment manufacturers, and suppliers. Members join through a network of state and regional printing associations that are affiliated with PIA. PIA also offers a diversified array of publications, audio tapes, videos, and services for the industry that are listed in the *Printer's Resource Catalog*, which is available by contacting PIA or a regional printing industries office.

PIA provides a broad spectrum of important services, including:

- government relations
- economics and research
- human resources and industrial relations
- insurance programs
- buying power programs
- PIA Ratio Studies
- business and financial services
- marketing assistance programs
- environmental and safety programs
- education and training programs
- Premier Print Awards ("The Bennys")

- a national bookstore
- PIA Solutions, an on-site consulting service
- Executive Development Program (EDP)
- seminars, conferences, and workshops

PIA also has several special industry groups and sections to meet members' specific needs, including the Graphic Arts Marketing Information Service (GAMIS), the Graphic Communications Association (GCA), the International Thermographers Association (ITA), the Label Printing Industries of America (LPIA), the Web Offset Association (WOA), and the NonHeatset Web Section (NWS). Special PIA sections include Printing Industry Financial Executives (PIFE), Electronic Prepress Section (EPS), Sales and Marketing Executives (S&ME), and a customer service training alliance.

The mission of PIA is to help its members stay profitable and competitive with a broad list of products and services. For further information, contact Printing Industries of America, 100 Daingerfield Road, Alexandria, VA 22314. Telephone 800/742-2666 or 703/519-8100. Fax: 703/548-3227.

Waterless Printing Association (WPA)

The not-for-profit Waterless Printing Association (WPA) was formed to encourage the use of analog and digital waterless printing technology through educational and informational efforts aimed at both printers and print buyers. The WPA's purposes include:

- educating the print-buying public to drive the demand for the waterless printing process
- educating printers about all phases of waterless printing
- providing a central source of information about pioneering developments occurring with waterless printers and the products they are producing
- offering print buyers and designers knowledge about the high quality of waterless
- encouraging waterless as a method to increase pressroom productivity
- promoting the environmental advantages of waterless printing
- promoting R&D of waterless printing methods

The WPA offers memberships to printers, suppliers, and the print-buying community. Members receive a monthly newsletter and special discounts for events and publications. For further information, contact the Waterless Printing Association, P.O. Box 59800, Chicago, IL 60659. Telephone: 312/743-5677. Fax: 312/743-5756.

Appendix A

List of Abbreviations

Measurement Terms

BU	basic unit of production
cm	centimeter
ctn	carton
CWT	hundred weight (100 pounds)
dp	depth
fpm	feet per minute
ft	foot, feet
gsm	grams per square meter
hp	horsepower
hp-hr	horsepower hours
hr	hour
in	inch
kB	kilobyte = 1024 bytes
k	1000
kg	kilogram
kW	kilowatt
kWh	kilowatt hour
l	liter
lb	pound
M	thousand
m	meter
max	maximum
mB	megabyte = 1 million bytes
mm	millimeter
no	number
pkg	package
sq	square
sub	substance
wk	week
yr	year

Electronic Prepress, Computer, and Data Processing Terms

bits	binary digits
CAD/CAM	computer-aided design/computer-aided manufacturing
CCD scanner	desktop flatbed scanner

CD-ROM	compact disk—read only memory
CPU	central processing unit
d-base	database
DBMS	database management system
DFC	digital file creator
DMI	direct machine interface (for data collection)
DOS	disk operating system developed by Microsoft
dpi	dots per inch
DPP	digital prepress
DTP	desktop publishing
EFDC	electronic factory data collection
EPP	electronic prepress
EPS	encapsulated PostScript (digital file format)
EXCEL	MicroSoft spreadsheet and database program
FAX	facsimile transmission
FAX modem	facsimile transmission using a modem
FDC	factory data collection
FFP	final film provider
FOP	final output provider
FORTRAN	formula translation
I/O	input/output hardware IBM
IBM-compatible	Personal computers (PCs) compatible with International Business Machines computer equipment and related software
IDSN	Integrated Digital Services Network telecommunication
LAN	local area network
Lotus 1-2-3	spreadsheet program
Mac	Macintosh computer
MHR	machine hour rate
MIS	management information system
modem	modulator-demodulator telecommunication device
MS-DOS	Microsoft Disk Operating System
Multiplan	spreadsheet program
PC	Personal Computer
PICT	image format for digital files
PMT scanner	desktop drum scanner
PostScript	code used to communicate with laser printing equipment
RAM	random access memory
RGB-CMYK	converting colors from red, blue, and green to process colors for printing
RIP	raster image processor
ROM	read only memory
SBC	small business computer
SDPPP	successful digital prepress provider

SFDC	shop floor data collection
TIFF	Tagged Image File Format
UNIX	operating language
Windows 95	Microsoft operating system introduced in 1995
WWW	World Wide Web

Estimating, Printing, and Related Terms

$/MBU	dollar cost per 1000 basic units
8-page web	half-width web press
16-page web	full-width web press
AA	Author's Alteration
adj	adjustment
AIC	all-inclusive center
ARCP	account receivable collection period
b	basis weight of paper
BEP	breakeven point
BHR	budgeted hour cost rate
bk	book
bkt	booklet
bt	(income) before taxes
BU	basic unit
c	cutoff in inches
C1S	coated on one side
C2S	coated on two sides
CAA	chargeable Author's Alteration
CAE	computer-assisted estimating
CAP	computer-assisted pricing
CAS	computer-assisted scheduling
ccm	color correction mask
CEPS	color electronic prepress system
CGE	computer-generated estimating
char	characters
CMYK	abbreviation for process colors: cyan, magenta, yellow, black
col	column
COP	change-over point
cp	copies
cps	characters per second
CREF	Computer Ready Electronic Files
CSR	customer service representative
ct	cutoff
CTP	computer-to-plate
cv	cover

D	roll diameter
d	core diameter
dpi	dots per inch
DTP	desktop publishing
E-B (or e-b)	emulsion-to-base
E-E (or e-e)	emulsion-to-emulsion
FC	fixed cost
fm	front matter
fss	finish size sheet
GCBP	Graphic Communications Business Practices
GTO-DI	Heidelberg press with digital direct image capability
HE	house error
imp	impression
imp/hr	impressions per hour
ISO-9000	quality management system developed by the International Standards Organization
ISO-A series	metric paper dimensions for business papers
ISO-B series	metric paper dimensions for posters and large-size goods
ISO-C series	metric paper dimensions for envelopes and post cards
JIT	just-in-time
JSF	job specification form
M weight	1000 sheet weight
MBU	1000 basic units
MF	machine-finished
MHR	machine hour rate
ms	manuscript
msp	manuscript page
NAA	nonchargeable Author's Alteration
NAPS	Enco negative-acting proofing system
OOP	out-of-pocket
p(p)	page(s)
PAF	production adjustment factor
pars	parent size sheet
PC	production center
pc	piece
pi	pica
pk	pocket
PMS	Pantone Matching System
PMT	Kodak photo-mechanical transfer
POD	print-on-demand
prep	preparation
pss	press size sheet
pt(s)	point(s)

PTC	Printing Trade Customs
QM	Heidelberg press with digital direct image capability
RAO	metric paper sizes including normal trim added
RFE	request for estimate
RFP	request for purchase
RFQ	request for quotation
ROI	return on investment
ROS	return on sales
S	slab thickness in inches to be cut away
s	basic sheet size in square inches
S&SC	sized and supercalendered
sep	separations
sht	sheet
sig	signature
SOP	standard operating procedure
SP	selling price
SPC	statistical process control
SRAO	metric paper sizes with extra trim added
sss	stock sheet size
SW	sheetwise (work-and-back)
T	stock thickness (or caliper)
TCF	totally chlorine-free paper
TQM	Total Quality Management
VA	value added
VC	variable cost
VOC	volatile organic compound
w	roll width in inches
W&B	work-and-back (sheetwise)
W&T	work-and-turn
w&t	work-and-tumble
wp	washup

Appendix B

Estimating and Related Formulas
and Calculation Methods

Chapter 1

Cost estimate = (standard production time x budgeted hour
cost rate) + material cost + (buyout cost + markup)
= estimated cost to produce the job

Chapter 3

Production standard conversions
To convert pieces per hour to hours per M pieces:

number of hours per M pieces = 1000 ÷ number of pieces per hour

To convert hours per M pieces to pieces per hour:

number of pieces per hour = 1000 ÷ number of hours per M pieces

BHR spreadsheet formulas
See Figure 3.5 for formulas used when developing BHRs by electronic spreadsheet.

719

Cost of electrical power when completing BHRs

> Lighting cost = [(number of annual hours worked x wattage per square foot) ÷ 1000 watts per kilowatt] x cost per kilowatt hour x number of square feet in center

> Power cost = total horsepower of motors x number of annual hours worked x 0.746 kilowatt per horsepower x cost per kilowatt hour

> Arc lamp cost = (number of rated input watts of source ÷ 1000 watts per kilowatt) x number of annual hours worked x cost per kilowatt hour

> Note: The number of annual hours is sometimes lowered for some types of arc lamp sources because of the intermittent use of the source during production.

Calculating chargeable hours for BHRs

> Chargeable hours = (number of annual hours – hours for vacations and holidays) x percentage utilization

Calculating manufacturing cost for BHRs

> Manufacturing cost per chargeable hour = total factory cost ÷ number of chargeable hours

Calculating budgeted hour cost rates

> BHR cost = total annual center cost ÷ number of chargeable hours

Prorated costing formulas
See Figure 3.13 and 3.14 for formulas used when developing prorated costing using AIC and PC methods.

Chapter 4

Calculating return on investment

> Gross asset return on investment (ROI) = net income ÷ gross assets

> Net asset return on investment (ROI) = net income ÷ (gross assets – depreciation)

Calculating return on sales

> Return on sales (ROS) = net income ÷ annual gross sales

Calculating value added

> Value added = sales dollars – (material costs + buyout costs)

Chapter 5

Estimated cost to produce a job = (estimated production time using standard production data x budgeted hour cost rate) + material cost including markup + buyout cost including markup

Estimating selling price = estimated cost to produce the job + desired profit dollars

Chapter 6

Ply thickness conversion

Ply thickness = (number of plies x 0.003 inch per ply) + 0.006 inch

Comparative or equivalent weight of paper

Comparative weight = (area of desired or parent size ÷ area of basic size) x sub weight of basic size doubled

M sheet kilogram weight

1000 sheet weight in kg = length of sheet (mm) x width of sheet (mm) x grams per square meter (gsm) ÷ 1,000,000

Estimating paper cost

Note: Accuracy requires that paper prices be obtained from a current or up-to-date paper price catalog.

Changing CWT price to M sheet price = (CWT price from catalog ÷ 100) x poundage per M sheets

Changing M sheet price to CWT price = (M sheet price from catalog) ÷ poundage per M sheets) x 100

(Note: In the above two formulas, use double the equivalent weight - for example, the M weight, for sizes other than the basic size; for the basic size, use the sub weight doubled.)

Cost of paper using CWT price = paper poundage expressed in M weight or equivalent weight x price per CWT from catalog

Cost of paper using M sheet price = (number of parent sheets ÷ 1000) x price per M sheets from catalog

Cost of paper using the 100 sheet price = (number of parent sheets ÷ 100) x price per 100 sheets from catalog

Estimating flat sheet cutting

Number-up on a press size sheet = press size sheet ÷ finish size sheet

Number-out of a parent size sheet = parent size sheet ÷ press size sheet

(Note: Cutting or imposition diagrams should be drawn to verify mathematics.)

To determine the maximum number-out when stagger-cutting finish sheets out of press size sheets = area (sq. in.) of press size sheet ÷ area (sq. in.) of finish size sheet

To determine the maximum number-out when stagger-cutting press size sheets out of parent size sheets = area (sq. in.) of parent size sheet ÷ area (sq. in.) of press size sheet

Estimating flat sheet paper quantity

Number of press size sheets needed for a certain quantity of finished sheets = number of finish size sheets ÷ number-up on the press size sheet

Number of parent size sheets needed for a certain quantity of press size sheets = number of press size sheets ÷ number cutting out of the parent size sheet

Number of parent sheets needed for a job including spoilage = number of press sheets + spoilage (Fig. 6.32) ÷ number cutting out of the parent sheet

Carton level to be used from the paper catalog = number of parent sheets ÷ number of sheets per carton

Estimating number of impressions for flat sheet work on a sheetfed press

Calculating maximum number of impressions per press sheet using forms method = number of press size sheets including spoilage x (total number of forms ÷ number of forms press can print in one pass)

Calculating maximum number of impressions per press sheet using pass method = number of press size sheets including spoilage x number of passes per press sheet

Estimating paper waste

Paper waste percentage = 1 − (area of sheet used in sq. in. ÷ total area of sheet in sq. in.) x 100

Estimating sheetfed paper for bookwork impositions

Note: These formulas assume that no duplicate pages will be imposed on a press sheet, such as in the use of step-and-repeat techniques for multiple signature production.

Size of the press sheet, number of pages per press sheet, number of forms

Size of press sheet = untrimmed page size x number-up imposed on one side of the press size sheet

Number of pages per press sheet = maximum press size sheet ÷ untrimmed booklet page size

Number of forms = total number of booklet pages ÷ number of pages per form

Number of signatures

Number of sheetwise signatures for a booklet of known number of pages = total number of booklet pages ÷ (number of pages per form x 2)

Number of work-and-turn signatures for a booklet of known number of pages = total number of booklet pages ÷ number of pages per form

Number of press size sheets

Number of press size sheets using sheetwise imposition = (number of sheetwise signatures per booklet x 1 press size sheet per signature x number of copies) + spoilage

Number of press size sheets using work-and-turn imposition = (number of work-and-turn signatures per booklet x 1/2 press size sheet per signature x number of copies) + spoilage

Number of Impressions

Number of impressions without spoilage = total number of forms x number of copies

number of impressions using a straight percentage spoilage figure = total number of forms x number of copies x percentage spoilage

Chapter 7

Estimating ink quantity and cost

Number of pounds of ink = (total form area in sq. in. x percentage of coverage x total number of copies x anticipated percentage of ink waste) ÷ ink mileage factor where total form area is measured in square inches, number of copies includes press spoilage, and the ink mileage factor is derived from the appropriate ink mileage schedule.

To determine form area in square inches:

Given page measurements in inches = inches width x inches depth

Given page measurements in picas = (pica page width ÷ 6 picas per inch) x (pica page depth ÷ 6 picas per inch)

Chapter 8

Estimating desktop publishing production time and cost

Time for DTP production = time for job setup + time for text processing + [time for first image created + time for additional images created at 70%] + [time for first image processes + time for additional images processed at 70%] + [time for first image manipulated + time for additional images manipulated at 70%]

Time for output production = time for laser output + time for proof output + time for film output

Total cost for DTP production = (total time for job setup + text processing + image creation + image processing + image manipulation) x BHR + (total time for output production x BHR cost) + output consumable costs

Estimating digital prepress job setup time and cost

Time for job setup production = (minutes for job preflight and preliminary review + file setup and management + loading fonts + archiving files ÷ 60 min/hr) + (minutes for remote file transfer ÷ 60 min/hr]). Apply PAF as needed.

Cost for job setup production = (total time for file acquisition and management production x BHR cost)+ (total time for remote transfer x BHR cost) + (media consumable costs)

Estimating drum (PMT) scanning time and cost

Time for drum scanning = time for prescan production + time for scanning production + time for post-scan production + additional time penalties

Cost for drum scanning = (time for drum scanning x BHR) + consumable materials

Estimating flatbed (CCD) scanning time and cost

Time for flatbed scanning = time for prescan production + time for scanning production + time for post-scan production + time for RGB-CMYK conversion and sharpening + additional time penalties

Cost for flatbed scanning = (time for flatbed scanning x BHR) + consumable materials

Estimating digital page layout and illustration production time and cost

Time for page layout and illustration production = [minutes for page layout ÷ 60 min/hr] + [minutes for editing pages ÷ 60 min/hr] + [minutes for illustration creation ÷ 60 min/hr] + [minutes for illustration editing ÷ 60 min/hr]. Apply PAF as needed.

Cost for page layout and illustration production = [total time for page layout production x BHR cost] + [total time for editing pages x BHR] + [total time for illustration production x BHR cost] + [total time for illustration editing x BHR]. Add material costs if required.

Estimating electronic trapping and image manipulation production

Time for electronic trapping and image manipulation production = [minutes for electronic trapping ÷ 60 min/hr] + [minutes for image manipulation operation 1 ÷ 60 min/hr] + [minutes for image manipulation operation 2 ÷ 60 min/hr] + [minutes for image manipulation operation 3 ÷ 60 min/hr] + [minutes for image manipulation operation 4 ÷ 60 min/hr], etc. Apply PAF as needed.

Cost for page layout and illustration production = [total time for electronic trapping x BHR cost] + [total time for image manipulation operation 1 x BHR] + [total time for image manipulation operation 2 x BHR cost] + [total time for image manipulation operation 3 x BHR]. Add material costs if any are incurred.

Estimating electronic imposition time and cost

Time for electronic imposition production (assuming page files are properly prepared and edited in a page layout program) = [minutes to generate PostScript pages/files ÷ 60 min/hr] + [minutes to define imposition and marks ÷ 60 min/hr] + [minutes to import PostScript pages or files ÷ 60 min/hr]. Apply PAF as needed.

Total cost for electronic imposition production = total time for electronic imposition x BHR cost

Estimating digital film output or computer-to-plate output

Time for film output (assuming page files are properly prepared and edited in a page layout program) = [minutes to RIP page ÷ 60 min/hr] + [minutes to image and process film ÷ 60 min/hr]. Apply PAF as needed.

Time for film output = total time for electronic imposition x BHR cost. Add material cost as needed.

Chapter 9

Estimating mechanical and paste-up production time and cost

Total time for mechanical production = (board layout time x number of boards) + (number of pieces to be pasted x production time per piece) + (overlay attachment production time x number of boards) + (number of pieces to be pasted per overlay x production time per piece)

Total production cost for mechanical art = (mechanical production time x artist BHR) + cost of materials used

Estimating hourly mechanical art page production time and cost

Hourly page production time = total production time for preparing similar mechanical art ÷ number of pages of finished mechanical art

Hourly page production cost = total production time for preparing similar mechanical art x employee BHR) + cost of materials used ÷ number of pages of finished mechanical art

Estimating phototypesetting time and cost

Keyboard production time = (number of characters ÷ 1000) x keyboard hours per M characters

Keyboard production cost = keyboard production
time x keyboarding BHR

Phototype unit production time = keyboard production time
x phototype unit multiplier

Phototype unit production cost = phototype unit production
time x phototype BHR

Proofreading production time = (number of characters ÷ 1000)x
proofreading hours per M characters

Proofreading production cost = proofreading production time x
proofreading BHR

Total production time = keyboard production time +
phototype production time + proofreading production time

Estimating process camera production time and cost

Process camera production time = (number of pieces of art to
be photographed ÷ number-up on copyboard) x
production time per piece

Process camera production cost = camera production time
x camera BHR

Material and film cost = number of pieces of material and film x
number of square inches per piece x material and film cost per square inch

Total cost for process camera production = camera production
cost + material cost

Estimating film contacting and duplicating production time and cost

Duplicating/contacting production time = preparation and setup +
duplicating/contacting production time + adjustments (as required)

Duplicating/contacting production cost = duplicating/contacting
production time x duplicating and contacting BHR

Material and film cost = number of pieces of film or paper x
number of square inches per piece x film cost per square inch

Total duplicating/contacting production cost =
duplicating/contacting production cost + film and material cost

Estimating digital scanner production time and cost

Digital scanner production time = image review (per image)

+ image mounting (per image) + scanner setup and
prescan adjustment (per image) + scanning time (per scanned
set) + automatic processing (per scanned set)

Digital scanner production cost = digital scanner production
time x digital scanner BHR

Material and film cost = number of pieces of film or paper x
square inches per piece x film cost per square inch

Total digital scanner production cost = digital scanner
production cost + film and material cost

Estimating table stripping production time and cost

Total table stripping production time = flat preparation time
(key flats + master flats + marks flat) + laying
and cutting time + additions

Laying and cutting time for goldenrod stripping = number of pieces
of film to be laid in and cut x production time per piece

Laying and cutting time for clearbase stripping = number
of separations film images to be laid in x production time
per piece + number of windows to be cut (in common-window flat)
x the production time per window

Cost of flat materials (clearbase or vinyl) = number of pieces
needed x cost per piece

Total table stripping production cost = (total table stripping
production time x table stripping BHR) + material cost

Estimating platemaking and proofing

Platemaking and proofing production time = (number of first exposure
flats x first exposure production time) + (number of
additional exposure flats x additional exposure production time)

Platemaking and proofing production cost = platemaking and proofing
production time x platemaking and proofing BHR

Plate cost = number of plates x cost per plate

Proof cost = number of proofs x size of proof in
square inches x cost per square inch

Total cost for platemaking and proofing = production
cost + platemaking and proofing material cost

Chapter 10

Establishing changeover (or breakeven) points

Changeover point = (fixed costs$_1$ - fixed cost$_2$) ÷ dollars per M basic units$_2$ - dollars per M basic units$_1$)

Dollar per MBU = [(BHR ÷ impressions per hour) ÷ number-up on press sheet] x 1000 units

Estimating sheetfed press production time and cost

Total number of press sheets required = (total number of finished pieces ÷ number-up on the press sheet) x (spoilage percentage + 100%)

Preparation and makeready production time = number of forms per job x hours per form for preparation and makeready

Hours of press time per form = total number of press sheets required + number of impressions per hour per form

Press-running time = hours of press time per form x number of forms per job

Number of washups per form = hours of press time per form ÷ hours of press time per form per washup

Production time for washups = number of washups per form x hours of washup time per form x number of forms per job

Total production time per job = preparation and makeready time + press running time + production time for washups

Total production cost per job = total production time per job x press BHR

Chapter 11

Estimating cutting production time and cost

Total number of press size sheets required = (number of finish size sheets required ÷ number-up on the press size sheet) x (percentage of spoilage + 100%)

Total number of parent size sheets required = number of press size sheets required, including spoilage ÷ number-out of parent size sheet

Total prepress cutting production time = [(total number of parent size sheets required ÷ number of sheets per lift) x cutting time per lift] + cutter setup time

Total postpress cutting production time = [(total number of press size sheets required ÷ number of sheets per lift) x cutting time per lift] + cutter setup time

Total cutting production time = total prepress cutting production time + total postpress cutting production time

Total production cost = total cutting production time x cutter BHR

Estimating parallel folding production time and cost

Total parallel folder production time = [setup time + running time (where running time is calculated by the number of sheets to be folded ÷ folder output in sheets per hour from schedule)] x applicable penalties

Total parallel folding production cost = total folding production time x folder BHR

Estimating signature (right-angle) folding production time and cost

Total signature (right-angle) folder running time = [setup time + running time (where running time is calculated by the total number of signatures to be folded ÷ number of signatures per hour from schedule)] x applicable penalties

Total signature folding production cost = total folding production time x folder BHR

Estimating hand gathering production time and cost

Total gathering production time = [(number of sets to be gathered x number of pieces per set) ÷ number of gathered sets per hour] + penalty additions + setup time

Total gathering production cost = total gathering production time x gathering BHR

Estimating jogging production time and cost

Total jogging production time = [(number of sheets to be jogged ÷ 1000) x jogging time per M sheets] + penalty additions + setup time

Total jogging production cost = total jogging production time x jogging BHR

Estimating counting production time and cost

Total counting production time = [(number of sheets to be counted including spoilage ÷ 1000) x counting time per M sheets] + penalty additions + setup time

Total counting production cost = total counting production
time x counting BHR

Estimating padding production time and cost

Total padding production time = [(number of sets to be padded
x number of sheets per set) ÷ 1000] x padding time per M sheets
+ setup time

Total padding production cost = total padding production
time x padding BHR

Estimating drilling production time and cost

Total drilling production time = [(number of pieces to be
drilled ÷ 1000) x drilling time per M sheets] + setup time
+ penalty additions

Total drilling production cost = total drilling production
time x drilling BHR

Estimating signature gathering production time and cost

Total signature gathering production time = [(number of booklets to be
gathered ÷ 1000) x gathering time per M booklets] + setup time
+ penalty additions

Total signature gathering production cost = total signature gathering
production time x gathering BHR

Estimating saddle-wire stitching production time and cost

Total saddle-wire stitching production time = [(number of booklets to be
stitched ÷ number of booklets stitched per hour)] + preparatory time
+ penalty additions

Total saddle-wire stitching production cost = total saddle-wire stitching
production time x saddle-wire stitching BHR

Estimating signature side-wire stitching production time and cost

Total side-wire stitching production time = [(number of booklets to
be stitched ÷ 1000) x stitching time per M booklets]
+ preparatory time + penalty additions

Total side-wire stitching production cost = total side-wire stitching
production time x side-wire stitching BHR

Estimating fully automatic saddle-wire stitching production time and cost

Total automated saddle-wire stitching production time = [number of books to be automatically saddle-stitched ÷ number of books per hour] + setup time

Total automated saddle-wire stitching production cost = total automated saddle-wire stitching production time x automated saddle-wire stitcher BHR

Estimating perfect binding production time and cost

Total perfect binding production time = [(number of booklets to be perfect bound ÷1000) x binding time per M booklets] + setup time + penalty additions

Total perfect binding production cost = total perfect binding production time x perfect binding BHR

Estimating pamphlet/booklet trimming production time and cost

Total pamphlet/booklet trimming production time = number of books to be trimmed ÷ [number of books per lift x number of lifts trimmed per hour] + setup time

Total pamphlet/booklet trimming production cost = total pamphlet/booklet trimming production time x pamphlet/booklet trimming equipment BHR

Estimating three-knife trimming production time and cost

Total three-knife trimming production time = [(number of booklets to be trimmed ÷ 1000) x trimming time per M booklets] + setup time + penalty additions

Total three-knife trimmer production cost = total trimming production time x trimmer BHR

Estimating shrink-wrapping production time and cost

Total shrink-wrapping production time = [(number of packages to be wrapped ÷ number of pieces per package) x shrink-wrapping time per package] + setup time

Total shrink-wrapping production cost = total shrink-wrapping production time x shrink-wrapping BHR

Chapter 12

Estimating roll paper quantity and cost:
Note: Use formulas that apply and add press spoilage as appropriate.

Estimating roll footage

Number of linear feet = [0.06545, a constant x (outside roll diameter squared – inside roll diameter squared)] – stock caliper in inches

Estimating the number of cutoffs per roll

Number of cutoffs per roll = (number of linear feet per roll x 12 inches per foot) ÷ press cutoff in inches

Estimating the weight per M cutoffs

Weight per M cutoffs = [press cutoff in inches x roll width in inches x (basis weight of paper x 2)] ÷ basic size of paper in square inches

Estimating the weight per M cutoffs using "constant factor"

Weight per M cutoffs = constant factor* x Qs in of cutoff

* constant factor = basis weight x 2 ÷ Qs in of basic size

Estimating the weight of a roll of paper

Roll weight = [0.0157, a constant x (outside roll diameter in square inches – inside roll diameter in square inches) x roll width in inches x basis weight of paper)] ÷ (stock caliper in inches x basic size of paper in square inches)

Estimating slabbing waste

Slabbing waste = [4, a constant x (original roll diameter x slab thickness to be removed) – slab thickness squared ÷ original roll diameter squared] x original roll weight

Estimating web ink poundage and cost

Total black ink poundage = (black ink poundage per M cutoffs for Form 1 + black ink poundage per M cutoffs for Form 2) x process/production adjustment factor (if applicable) x (total number of cutoffs including spoilage ÷ 1,000)

Total color ink poundage = [(black ink poundage per M cutoffs for Form 1 + black ink poundage per M cutoffs for Form 2) x color ink adjustment (black coverage multiplier)] x process/production adjustment factor (if applicable) x (total number of cutoffs including spoilage ÷ 1,000)

Estimating web press production time and cost

Total web press production time = (number of units printing x preparation time per unit) + (total number of cutoffs including spoilage ÷ press-running speed in cutoffs per hour)

Total web press production cost = total web press production time x web press BHR

Appendix C

**Vendors of Printing Industry
Estimating and MIS Systems**

Vendor name and address: Arrowhead Software, 1617 Barclay Dr., Arlington, TX 76018
Telephone and fax numbers: 817/465-5573
Contact person: Bill Russell
Target market: 1,2,3,4
Product: SW

Vendor name and address: Asta Software Corporation, 969 Monroe Avenue, Rochester, NY 14620
Telephone and fax numbers: 716/473-0372, 716/473-9005
Contact person: Harry Puff
Target market: 2,3
Product: TK

Vendor name and address: Avant Computer Associates, 102 Powers Ferry Rd., Marietta, GA 30067
Telephone and fax numbers: 404/977-7255, 404/977-5692
Contact person: Bill Gilmer
Target market: 1,2
Product: SW&TK

Vendor name and address: Avanti Computer Systems, 2788 Bathurst St., Suite, Toronto, CAN M6B3A
Telephone and fax numbers: 416/785-0424, 416/785-0478
Contact person: Harold Rapp
Target market: 2,3,4
Product: SW

Vendor name and address: BASCORP, 116 Courtland Rd., Cherry Hill, NJ 08034
Telephone and fax numbers: 609/429-2573
Contact person: Ernie Jellinek
Target market: 1,2
Product: SW

Vendor name and address: BFE Systems, 625 Dallas Drive, Suite 525, Denton, TX 76205
Telephone and fax numbers: 800/852-5568, 817/382-4610
Contact person: Doug Giles
Target market: 4
Product: SW&TK

Vendor name and address: Accu-Graphic Systems, P.O. Box 3816, Winter Springs, FL 32708
Telephone and fax numbers: 407/359-7000, 407/359-7001
Contact person: Drew Alvarez
Target market: 1,2,3,4
Product: SW&TK

Vendor name and address: AccuData, Inc., P.O. Box 651, Salt Lake City, UT 84115
Telephone and fax numbers: 800/624-6841, 801/485-7417
Contact person: Bert Pugh
Target market: 1,2
Product: Job Cost

Vendor name and address: Advanced Computer Systems, 6746 S. Revere Pkwy., Englewood, CO 80112
Telephone and fax numbers: 303/792-9779, 303/792-9786
Contact person: Vince Lawrence
Target market: 2,3
Product: SW&TK

Vendor name and address: Advantage Computer Systems, 12400 Olive Blvd., Suite, St. Louis, MO 63144
Telephone and fax numbers: 314/275-4165, 314/275-8131
Contact person: Richard Tews
Target market:
Product: SW&TK

Vendor name and address: AHP Systems, 3166 Des Plaines Ave., Des Plaines, IL 60018
Telephone and fax numbers: 708/296-6040, 708/296-0626
Contact person: Udi Ariel/J.Ritchie
Target market: 2,3,4
Product: SW&TK

Vendor name and address: Alphalmage, 2819 Elliot Avenue, Seattle, WA 98121
Telephone and fax numbers: 206/871-2795, 206/871-2926
Contact person: Walt Garfield
Target market: 1
Product: SW&TK

Vendor name and address	Bill Friday's Computer Program 7089 Crystal Blvd. Diamond Springs CA 95619
Telephone and fax numbers	916/620-5580 916/620-6825
Contact person	Bill Friday
Target market	1
Product	SW

Vendor name and address	CompuSoft Services 18 Keith Hill Rd. Grafton MA 01519
Telephone and fax numbers	800/932-7894 508/839-3675
Contact person	Tom Ticknor
Target market	1,2
Product	SW&TK

Vendor name and address	Computer Dynamics P.O. Box 490 Grimesland NC 27837
Telephone and fax numbers	919/758-9948 919/758-8858
Contact person	Dale/Terry Brooks
Target market	1,2,3,4
Product	SW

Vendor name and address	Computer Management 6327 204th St., SW Lynnwood WA 98036
Telephone and fax numbers	206/672-2470 206/774-3956
Contact person	Daniel Kenyon
Target market	1,2,3,4
Product	SW&TK

Vendor name and address	Computer Sys. for Graphic Arts 2005 DeLaCruz Blvd., Santa Clara CA 95050
Telephone and fax numbers	408/980-9037 408/980-9390
Contact person	Ray Gabler
Target market	2
Product	SW&TK

Vendor name and address	Computerized Pricing Systems 13650 Silverton Drive Broomfield CO 80020
Telephone and fax numbers	303/469-0557
Contact person	Mark Yelich
Target market	1,2,3,4
Product	SW

Vendor name and address	Covalent Systems 47436 Fremont Blvd. Fremont CA 94538
Telephone and fax numbers	800/321-0405 510/683-6779
Contact person	Rod Murray
Target market	2,3
Product	SW

Vendor name and address	CRC Information Systems 9700 N. 91st St. Scottsdale AZ 85258
Telephone and fax numbers	602/451-7474 602/451-7075
Contact person	Jim Drisler
Target market	2,3,4
Product	SW&TK

Vendor name and address	Crouser & Associates 235 Dutch Road Charleston WV 25302
Telephone and fax numbers	304/342-5100 304/342-5187
Contact person	Tom Crouser
Target market	1
Product	SW

Vendor name and address	DHA Systems & Software 333 I Street, Niles District Fremont CA 94536
Telephone and fax numbers	510/795-9522 510/795-9586
Contact person	Doug Haylock
Target market	1,2,3,4
Product	SW&TK

Vendor name and address	E-Z Esti P.O. Box 77094 Greensboro NC 27417
Telephone and fax numbers	910/855-0909 910/294-8042
Contact person	Dean White
Target market	1
Product	SW

Vendor name and address	Effective Management Systems 100 Foxborough Blvd., Foxborough MA 02035
Telephone and fax numbers	800/962-1279 508/698-0116
Contact person	Paul Lavallee
Target market	1,2,3,4
Product	SW

Vendor name and address: GAMX, 497 Lighthouse Avenue, Monterey, CA 93940
Telephone and fax numbers: 408/375-9994, 408/649-5656
Contact person: Dave Christensen
Target market: 1,2
Product: SW&TK

Vendor name and address: Globe-Tek Systems, 1065 N. Queen St., Suite, Etobicoke, CAN M9C1A
Telephone and fax numbers: 416/622-0444, 416/622-0574
Contact person: Richard Brack
Target market: 2,3,4
Product: SW&TK

Vendor name and address: Graphic Arts Software, 4098 N. Buffalo Rd., Orchard Park, NY 14127
Telephone and fax numbers: 716/662-6634, 716/662-7677
Contact person: Bucky Larusch
Target market: 2,3
Product: SW&TK

Vendor name and address: Graphic Arts Software Solutions, 1055 Kensington Pk., Altamonde, FL 32714
Telephone and fax numbers: 407/774-8312, 407/774-9481
Contact person: Bob Baillargeon, Prepress
Target market: 1,2
Product: SW

Vendor name and address: Graphic Data Systems, 8066 North Point Blvd., Winston-Salem, NC 27106
Telephone and fax numbers: 910/759-2211, 910/759-2228
Contact person: Mark Idol
Target market: 1,2
Product: SW&TK

Vendor name and address: Graphic Systems Technology, 11 Spiral Drive, Suite 12, Florence, KY 41042
Telephone and fax numbers: 800/232-9750, 606/283-9769
Contact person: Stacy Ward
Target market: 1,2,3,4
Product: SW

Vendor name and address: Electromat Electronics, Inc., 3819 Holland Blvd., Chesapeake, VA 23323
Telephone and fax numbers: 804/487-8849, 804/487-9272
Contact person: Mike Griese
Target market: 2,3
Product: TK

Vendor name and address: Electronet Information Systems, 1605 King Street, Alexandria, VA 22314
Telephone and fax numbers: 703/739-5510, 703/739-9444
Contact person: Henry Freedman
Target market: 1,2,3,4
Product: SW&TK

Vendor name and address: Epic Data International, 7280 River Road, Richmond, BC, CAN V6X1X5
Telephone and fax numbers: 800/663-5386, 604/273-1930
Contact person: Karen Slessor
Target market:
Product: SW&TK

Vendor name and address: EST-PAC (Prof. Auto. Srvcs.), 265 Cinnamon Way, Suite, Boulder, CO 80303
Telephone and fax numbers: 303/494-1861, 303/499-9487
Contact person: Brian Anderson
Target market: 1,2
Product: SW&TK

Vendor name and address: Excalibur Systems, Inc., 27281 Las Ramblas, #155, Mission Viejo, CA 92691
Telephone and fax numbers: 800/932-9320, 619/723-9076
Contact person: Ed Kirchner
Target market: 1,2
Product: SW

Vendor name and address: Franklin Estimating Systems, P.O. Box 16690, Salt Lake City, UT 84116
Telephone and fax numbers: 800/346-7363, 801/322-5822
Contact person: Duaine Scadlock
Target market: 1,2
Product: SW

Vendor name and address	GraphiTech Computer Systems 2161 Palm Beach Lakes W. Palm Beach FL 33409
Telephone and fax numbers	800/634-8324 407/684-8590
Contact person	Scott Thatcher
Target market	1,2,3,4
Product	SW&TK

Vendor name and address	Green Systems Box 15414 Biltmore Station Asheville NC 28813
Telephone and fax numbers	704/274-3518 704/254-0940
Contact person	Lynn Yarbrough
Target market	2,3
Product	SW

Vendor name and address	Hagen Systems, Inc. 6438 City W. Parkway Eden Prairie MN 55344
Telephone and fax numbers	800/284-2436 612/946-8513
Contact person	Steve Peterson
Target market	2,3,4
Product	SW&TK

Vendor name and address	Hi-Tek Computer Products 308 W. Erie St., Suite 500 Chicago IL 60610
Telephone and fax numbers	312/787-2000 312/787-3786
Contact person	Wayne Cohen
Target market	2,3
Product	SW&TK

Vendor name and address	Infonet P.O. Box 370 Warner NH 03278
Telephone and fax numbers	603/456-3581 603/456-2536
Contact person	Ken Davis
Target market	1,2,3,4
Product	SW&TK

Vendor name and address	Innovative Solutions 350 Crenshaw Blvd., Suite Torrance CA 92503
Telephone and fax numbers	310/787-3260 310/782-2723
Contact person	Bill Crispin
Target market	2,3,4
Product	SW&TK

Vendor name and address	J. P. Brown & Associates 780 Gordon Baker Rd. Willowdale, CAN M2H 3B
Telephone and fax numbers	416/494-0472 416/494-0504
Contact person	Peter Greer
Target market	
Product	SW&TK

Vendor name and address	Kelley World 61501 Bremen Highway Mishawaka IN 46544
Telephone and fax numbers	219/255-4926 219/255-5817
Contact person	Karen Kelley
Target market	3
Product	SW&TK

Vendor name and address	Kenex Systems 575 E. 4500, S., Suite Salt Lake City UT 84107
Telephone and fax numbers	801/263-3276 801/261-2529
Contact person	Dennis Johnson
Target market	1,2
Product	SW&TK

Vendor name and address	Logic Associates P.O. Box 765 White River VT 05001
Telephone and fax numbers	802/295-5661 802/295-5512
Contact person	Lydia Bos
Target market	2,3,4
Product	TK

Vendor name and address	MasterFlo Technology 30-B Kent Street West Lindsay, Ontario CAN K9V 2Y1
Telephone and fax numbers	705/324-0603 705/32-0603
Contact person	Debra Wilson
Target market	2,3
Product	TK

Vendor name and address	Micro Ink 1600 Boston Providence Walpole MA 02081
Telephone and fax numbers	800/842-5667 508/291-8900
Contact person	Carol Anderson
Target market	1,2,3,4
Product	SW

Vendor name and address	Microprint Developments 32 Breckenridge Blvd. St. Catharines, CAN L2WIA7
Telephone and fax numbers	800/461-8114 905/688-6132
Contact person	Mark Porter
Target market	2,3,4
Product	SW&TK

Vendor name and address	Modular Graphic Services 611 S. Front Wilmington NC 28401
Telephone and fax numbers	919/763-2012 919/251-0384
Contact person	Dennis Walsak
Target market	1
Product	SW

Vendor name and address	Noguska Industries 741 N. Countyline Road Fostoria OH 44830
Telephone and fax numbers	419/435-0404 419/435-1844
Contact person	Stephanie Spires
Target market	1,2,3,4
Product	SW&TK

Vendor name and address	Pace Systems (Springfield) 4209 Baymeadows Rd., Jacksonville FL 32217
Telephone and fax numbers	800/624-5999 904/367-0601
Contact person	Rick Kaestner
Target market	2,3
Product	SW&TK

Vendor name and address	Parsec Corporation 5624 Yarrow Street Arvada CO 80002
Telephone and fax numbers	303/423-4546 303/423-5579
Contact person	Steve Hallberg
Target market	2,3
Product	SW&TK

Vendor name and address	Performance Group (The) 170 Duffield Drive Markham, Ontario CAN L6G1B5
Telephone and fax numbers	800/667-3289 905/475-7985
Contact person	Dennis Stroud
Target market	2,3,4
Product	BHR SW

Vendor name and address	PICCA 5309 Lincoln Avenue, Suite Skokie IL 60077
Telephone and fax numbers	708/674-4055 708/674-4782
Contact person	Paul Betancourt
Target market	2,3
Product	SW&TK

Vendor name and address	PlanFirst by Soft USE 116 Old Padonia Rd. Hunt Valley MD 21030
Telephone and fax numbers	800/638-7526 410/560-1934
Contact person	Tulin Edev
Target market	1
Product	SW

Vendor name and address	Plantrol Systems, Ltd. 71 E. Main St. Westfield NY 14787
Telephone and fax numbers	716/326-4900 716/326-4944
Contact person	Dan Smith
Target market	3,4
Product	SW&TK

Vendor name and address	Press-Tige Software 501 S. First Avenue Arcadia CA 91006
Telephone and fax numbers	800/223-9861 818/574-7106
Contact person	Don Jones
Target market	2
Product	SW

Vendor name and address	Primac Systems, Inc. 4601 Langland Rd., Suite Dallas TX 75244
Telephone and fax numbers	214/661-9336 214/960-2461
Contact person	Van Price/John Knowlton
Target market	2,3,4
Product	SW&TK

Vendor name and address	Print Systems Corp. 269 S. Jefferson St. Berne IN 46711
Telephone and fax numbers	219/589-3151 219/589-3499
Contact person	Chris Hester
Target market	2,3
Product	SW&TK

Vendor name and address . . . . **printLEADER Software**
1105 S.W. Martin Downs
Palm City   FL   34990
Telephone and fax numbers 800/752-4624
407/220-1882
Contact person . . . . John Fleming
Target market 1,2
Product . . . . SW&TK

Vendor name and address . . . . **PrintPoint (MicroGuide)**
57 Ludlow Lane
Palisades   NY   10964
Telephone and fax numbers 800/774-6853
914/359-3468
Contact person . . . . Morrie Brown
Target market 1,2,3
Product . . . . SW

Vendor name and address . . . . **PrintSmith (M Data, Inc.)**
1702 E. Highland, Suite
Phoenix   AZ   85016
Telephone and fax numbers 800/426-4963
602/234-0309
Contact person . . . . Neil Miller
Target market 1,2,4
Product . . . . SW&TK

Vendor name and address . . . . **Profit Control Systems, Inc.**
90-30 Metropolitan Ave.
Rego Park   NY   11374
Telephone and fax numbers 718/830-7900
718/897-0034
Contact person . . . . Ron Berg
Target market 2,3,4
Product . . . . SW&TK

Vendor name and address . . . . **Programmed Solutions, Inc.**
25 Third Street
Stamford   CT   06905
Telephone and fax numbers 203/358-9955
203/324-2797
Contact person . . . . Mary Rowan
Target market 2,3,4
Product . . . . SW

Vendor name and address . . . . **QCX Corporation**
261 Circle Ct.
Palatine   IL   60067
Telephone and fax numbers 708/884-9292
Contact person . . . . George Manthey
Target market 1
Product . . . . SW

Vendor name and address . . . . **Printer's Management Control**
1007 First Avenue
Salt Lake City   UT   84103
Telephone and fax numbers 801/531-8721
801/537-1944
Contact person . . . . Jim Webster
Target market 1,2,3,4
Product . . . . SW&TK

Vendor name and address . . . . **Printer's Plan by Soft USE**
116 Old Padonia Rd.
Hunt Valley   MD   21030
Telephone and fax numbers 800/638-7526
410/560-1934
Contact person . . . . Tulin Edev
Target market 1,2
Product . . . . SW

Vendor name and address . . . . **Printer's Plus (by Compuware)**
31440 Northwestern
Farmington Hills   MI   48334
Telephone and fax numbers 800/325-6344
313/737-7919
Contact person . . . . Bill Remijan
Target market 1
Product . . . . SW&TK

Vendor name and address . . . . **Printer's Shareware**
5019-5021 W. Lovers Lane
Dallas   TX   75209
Telephone and fax numbers 214/350-5353
214/350-2610
Contact person . . . . George Croft
Target market 1,2,3,4
Product . . . . SW

Vendor name and address . . . . **Printer's Software, Inc.**
3665 Bee Ridge Road
Sarasota   FL   34233
Telephone and fax numbers 813/923-9010
813/925-1007
Contact person . . . . Paul Grieco
Target market 1,2,3,4
Product . . . . SW

Vendor name and address . . . . **Printers Inc./Data Specialists**
715 Florida Avenue, Suite
Minneapolis   MN   55426
Telephone and fax numbers 612/541-0440
612/541-1149
Contact person . . . . James W. Jones
Target market 1,2,4
Product . . . . SW&TK

	Streamline Solutions
Vendor name and address	P.O. Box 1311
	Mill Valley CA 94941
Telephone and fax numbers	800/950-8687 415/331-9336
Contact person	Lawrence Snyder
Target market	2,3,4
Product	SW&TK

	Time Tracks
Vendor name and address	P.O. Box 159
	Crestwood KY 40014
Telephone and fax numbers	502/241-1424
Contact person	Rick Kaestner
Target market	1,2,3,4
Product	SW

	Timothy Hill Enterprises
Vendor name and address	12465 Via Cabezon
	San Diego CA 92129
Telephone and fax numbers	619/484-8250 619/484-8250
Contact person	Ed Turner
Target market	1,2,3,4
Product	SW&TK

	Turquoise Products
Vendor name and address	9709 E. 2nd Street
	Tucson AZ 85748
Telephone and fax numbers	602/885-9671 602/722-0025
Contact person	William Kastner
Target market	1
Product	SW

	Quality Solutions of America
Vendor name and address	1040 Park Creek Circle
	Lawrenceville GA 30244
Telephone and fax numbers	404/931-3742 404/931-3892
Contact person	Terry Potter
Target market	2,3,4
Product	SW/Sched

	RPT Business Systems
Vendor name and address	P.O. Box 4233
	Collingwood, Ont CAN L9Y4T9
Telephone and fax numbers	800/267-4792 705/444-5125
Contact person	Jeff Belanger
Target market	2,3,4
Product	SW&TK

	SDI Systems
Vendor name and address	4889 Sinclair Rd., Suite
	Columbus OH 43229
Telephone and fax numbers	614/785-1127 614/785-1129
Contact person	William Immel
Target market	1
Product	SW&TK

	Softprint
Vendor name and address	1754 Maplelawn
	Troy MI 48084
Telephone and fax numbers	800/522-5443 313/649-9009
Contact person	Harry Neely
Target market	2
Product	SW&TK

	Software Specialists
Vendor name and address	8433 N. Black Canyon Hwy
	Phoenix AZ 85021
Telephone and fax numbers	602/995-7538 602/995-4408
Contact person	Kirk Schramm
Target market	BusForms
Product	SW&TK

	State Printing Company
Vendor name and address	1210 Key Road, Box 1388
	Columbia SC 29202
Telephone and fax numbers	803/799-9550 803/252-2852
Contact person	Cary Czajkowski
Target market	2
Product	SW

Appendix D

Bibliographic reference and sources of information

The following is a list of books and sources of information for the printing estimator, professional printing manager, or person interested in information on traditional printing or digital graphic imaging methods and procedures. A telephone number is provided in parentheses to facilitate contacting the publisher or source listed.

Adams, J. Michael, David Faux, and Lloyd Rieber. *Printing Technology*. Delmar Publishers, 4th ed., 1996. (800/347-7707)

Agfa Digital Color Prepress publications (800/395-7007):
   An Introduction to Digital Color Prepress
   An Introduction to Digital Scanning
   A Guide to Color Separation
   An Introduction to Digital Photo Imaging
   Working with Prepress and Printing Suppliers
   PostScript Process Color Guide

Brenner, Robert C. *Pricing Guide for Desktop Publishing Services*. Brenner Information Group, 4th ed., 1995. (619/538-0093)

Cavuoto, James and Stephen Beale. *Guide to Desktop Publishing*. Graphic Arts Technical Foundation, 2nd ed., 1995. (412/621-6941)

Delmar Publishers. Offers an extensive list of current desktop publishing and digital imaging technology books. Catalog available. (800/347-7707)

Graphic Artists Guild. *Handbook of Pricing and Ethical Guidelines*. Graphic Artists Guild, Inc., 8th ed., 1994. (212/463-7730)

Graphic Arts Technical Foundation. Offers an extensive range of traditional printing and digital imaging books and other products. Catalog available. (412/621-6941)

Graphic Communications Association. Offers books and other services focused primarily on digital imaging technology. Catalog available. (703) 519-8160)

International Digital Imaging Association. Offers books and other services focused primarily on digital imaging technology. (800/844-2472)

International Prepress Association. Offers an extensive range of traditional printing and digital imaging books and other products aimed primarily at prepress. Catalog available. (612/896-1908)

International Publishing Management Association. Offers an extensive range of traditional printing and digital imaging books and other products aimed primarily at in-plant publishing. Catalog available. (816/781-1111)

Levenson, Harvey R. *Complete Dictionary of Graphic Arts and Desktop Publishing Terminology*. Summa Books, 1994. (805/524-3903)

National Association of Desktop Publishers. Offers books and other services focused primarily on digital imaging technology. Catalog available. (508/887-7900)

National Association of Printers and Lithographers. Offers an extensive range of traditional printing and digital imaging books and other products. Catalog available. (800/642-6275). Cost studies published by NAPL include:
1995–96 Cost Study on Lithographic Preparatory Operations
1994–95 Cost Study on Desktop/Electronic Publishing
1992–93 Cost Study on Bindery, Finishing & Mailing Operations
1992–93 Cost Study on Sheetfed Presses
1992–93 Cost Study For Print Operations with Up To 15 Employees
1989–90 Cost Study for Heatset and Non-Heatset Web Press Operations

National Association of Quick Printers. Offers a range of traditional and digital imaging books and other products aimed primarily at quick printers. Catalog available. (312/644-6610). Studies by NAQP include:
1995 NAQP Industry Pricing Study
1994 Industry Operating Ratio Study
1993 NAQP Industry Pricing Study
1992 Membership Services Profile
1991 Quick Printing Industry Equipment Usage Study
1991 Wage and Benefit Survey
1991 Quick Printing Industry Color Study
1990 NAQP Desktop Publishing Study Guide

Parsons, Bill. *Introduction to Electronic Prepress*. Delmar Publishers, 1994. (800/347-7707)

Peachpit Press. Provides an extensive list of current desktop publishing and digital imaging technology books. Catalog available. (800/283-9444)

Printing Industries of America. Offers an extensive range of traditional printing and digital imaging books and other products. Catalog available. (800/742-2666). The *PIA Ratio Studies*, published annually, are available in the following volumes:

Management Guide to the PIA Ratios
    All Printers by Sales Volume and Geographic Area
    All Printers by Product Specialty
    Sheetfed Printers by Sales Volume and Geographic Area
    Web Offset Printers/Heatset
    Web Offset Printers/Non-heatset
    Combination Offset–Sheetfed/Web
    Book Manufacturers Ratios
    Printers with Sales Over $10,000,000
    Prepress Specialists Ratios
    Binders Ratios
    Printers with Sales Under $1,500,000
    Quick Printers
    Business Forms

Printing Industries of Southern California. *PIA-SC Blue Book of Production Standards and Costs, 1994-95*. (213/728-9500)

Romano, Frank J. *Pocket Guide to Digital Prepress*. Delmar Publishers, 1995. (800/347-7707)

Ruggles, Philip K. *Desktop Dividends: Managing Electronic Prepress for Profit*. Printing Management Services, 1993. (805/543-5968)

Ruggles, Philip K. *Computer Dividends: Management Information Systems for the Graphic Arts*. Printing Management Services, 1994. (805/543-5968)

Ruggles, Philip K. *Printing Estimating Workbook*. Printing Management Services, 4th ed., 1996. (805/543-5968) (Companion text to the 4th ed. of *Printing Estimating*)

Ruggles, Philip K. *Printing Estimating Workbook*. Printing Management Services, 3rd ed., 1991. (805/543-5968) (Companion text to the 3rd ed. of *Printing Estimating*)

Silver, Gerald A. *Professional Printing Estimating*. Editorial Enterprises, 3rd ed., 1991.

Stettinius, Wallace. *Running in the Black*. Printing Industries of America, 1985.

Stettinius, Wallace. *Winning in a Changing Environment,* 1995.

Waterless Printing Association. Offers books and other products aimed primarily at waterless printing technology and production. Catalog available. (312/743-5677)

Glossary

account payable: Money owed to a supplier or other vendor by the printer for materials and services.

account receivable collection period (ARCP): The amount of time, in days, from the date of mailing an invoice to the date the invoice is paid.

account receivable: Money owed to a printing firm for printing goods and services.

additive surface plate: A lithographic printing plate that requires the addition of a developing lacquer to improve plate life.

Adobe Illustrator: A popular graphics software program originally developed for the Macintosh, used to draw and develop illustrations on computer.

all-inclusive center (AIC) method: A prorated costing procedure that allows administrative areas to cost data just as if they were used during printing production.

analog-digital color scanner: Older type of color scanner that scans directly to film, with fairly complex manual controls.

analog: Parallel production whereby an image can be generated using more than one process or method.

anodized plate: A lithographic plate manufactured with a passivation barrier of aluminum oxide to prevent chemical reactions with diazo coatings and provide improved press performance during printing.

applications program: Software written to perform a specific task by the computer system, such as estimating, job costing, and inventory.

aqueous plate: Plate coatings that are water-soluble and thus less harmful to the environment.

archival storage: The storing of data and information in such a manner that it will represent a permanent record.

art director: An individual working in an art studio who is in charge of a group of artists; directs artists' efforts for a studio.

art work: Any image prepared for graphic reproduction using either mechanical or electronic methods

Author's Alteration (AA): Change initiated by or approved to be made by the customer or originator of the image.

auto-trapping: Process by which images are slightly overlapped using automated methods built into electronic prepress software.

automatic film processing: Equipment that provides automatic developing and fixing of silver halide film products; both older, conventional "lith" and new rapid-access processing systems are popular.

automatic plate processing: Equipment that provides automatic developing and finishing of lithographic plates.

automatic roll change: Process by which rolls of paper stock are automatically changed during web printing production; devices sometimes termed "flying pasters" or "automatic pasters."

automatic spacing: Mechanical or electronic equipment used with cutting machines to precisely position the position of the back gauge.

back gauge: That mechanical segment of a cutting machine that moves to establish a precise sheet dimension or distance from the cutting blade.

backward compatible: When upgraded software for desktop publishing and electronic prepress can be used without difficulty on files created with previous, older versions of the software.

ballpark estimating: Estimating using approximation methods.

banding: The wrapping of a package with string, rubber bands, or other material to secure the contents as a complete unit.

bar code data collection: Process of collecting shop floor data using a bar code wand and bar code strips.

bar code strip: A printed series of lines used to communicate a message to a computer system through some type of optical reading device.

basic size: Established size of a paper stock upon which the basis weight is calculated; each major class of paper has one basic size.

basic unit (BU): A standard product selected as the basis for comparison of changeover points with presses.

basis weight: The scale weight of 500 sheets of the basic size of a particular class of paper; also termed substance (sub) weight, or pounds.

bastard cut: Procedure by which some small sheets cut from a larger parent sheet will have the grain in the short direction, while other sheets cut from the same parent sheet will have grain going in the long direction; also termed stagger cut or Dutch cut.

baud: Term used to describe the speed of transmission for sending and receiving information and data by telecommunication methods.

benchmarking: Selecting and using a standard item, element or routine to measure output or production when comparing or analyzing a system, or process.

billing: The process of preparing and producing documents to be sent to customers indicating the amount of money owed for printing and other services.

black-and-white laser printer: Desktop output device used to generate high contrast images.

blanket-to-blanket: See perfector.

blotter paper: A paper class, basic size 19 x 24 inches, used when ink blotting is necessary (such as for checkbook backs).

blueline: A photographic proof that has blue images contained on a white background; a Dylux proofing material made by DuPont which uses photo-encapsulated blue dye to produce an image upon exposure.

bond paper: A paper class, basic size 17 x 22 inches, used for many types of business communications; rag and sulfite subgroups.

book paper: A class of printing paper commonly used for book manufacturing with a basic size of 25 x 38 inches; subcategories include coated, uncoated, and text groups.

book: A published work containing more than 64 pages.

booklet: A published work containing 64 or fewer pages..

bookwork: A general term describing the manufacturing procedures required for the production of books and booklets.

break-even point (BEP): A procedure that allows for quick comparison between outputs of similar equipment producing a similar product; also called change-over point.

buckle folder: A piece of bindery equipment with knurled rollers used to fold paper.

budgeted hour cost rate (BHR): A calculated dollar figure based on defined fixed and variable costs for a specific production area (center).

business paper: A class of printing paper commonly used for business purposes, with a basic size of 1 7 x 22 inches; subcategories include bond, ledger, thin, duplicator, and safety paper groups.

buyout: A service purchased by a printer from an outside source; trade services include composition, bindery, and prepress segments.

Byer's Micromodifier: A machine that produces extremely accurate spreads and chokes through the use of a carefully controlled, orbital rotating bed.

c-prints: Color prints.

C1S: A term used to describe paper stock that is coated on one side.

C2S: A term used to describe paper stock that is coated on both sides.

calendering: A buffing process completed during paper manufacturing that polishes the sheet surface, making it less prone to printing production difficulties.

caliper: See paper caliper.

camera-ready art: Mechanical artwork that is ready for photographic reproduction.

canned software: Software that has been developed to be ready for use without further work; also called packaged software.

capital intensive: A term describing the condition of business where large sums of money (capital) are required to enter and work in a specific sector.

cardboard paper: A class of printing paper that is generally thick and bulky; major categories include index bristol, tagboard, blanks, printing bristol, and wedding bristol.

Carl Didde WorkPLACE® program: A program for evaluating and educating printing employees in basic skills; developed by NAPL.

cash flow: The movement of working capital through a business.

CD-ROM: Digital storage method whereby a compact disc contains information or images which can only be read into a computer system.

cell: A specific location on a spreadsheet program matrix referenced by a letter and number.

cellulose fiber: A wood fiber used as the major ingredient in most printing papers.

centimeter: A metric measurement whereby a meter (39.37 inches) is divided into 100 equal parts thus equaling 0.3937 inches; about the thickness of a pencil.

changeover point (COP): See break-even point.

Chargeable Author's Alteration (CAA): An alteration approved by the customer or author which the customer agrees to pay without question.

chargeable hours: Production time spent on a customer's job that can be directly charged to that customer and for which he or she must pay.

chargeback system: A procedure wherein actual times are recorded during printing production and used as a basis to calculate the selling price of a customer's job.

chiller unit: A postprinting process in heatset web production where the web of paper passes through a refrigeration unit following heating of the web to set the ink.

choke: An image slightly reduced in size; produced from a positive film original to raw film using contacting procedures or orbital techniques; also termed a "shrink" or "squeeze."

ChromaPress: A webfed digital press sold by Agfa.

circumferential repeat: Distance around the web press cylinder which defines the length of image.

clear stripping base: Transparent acetate or polyester on which imaged film negatives and positives are stripped; also termed "clearbase."

clearbase stripping: Process of assembling and taping film images to clear stripping base material.

clip-out art: Preprinted art image sold to printers, which can be cut out and used directly in a paste-up.

closed web: A heat-set web press.

CMYK: Abbreviation for process colors; cyan, magenta, yellow, and black.

co-mailing: The mailing of more than one item or product in the same package or container to reduce mailing costs.

coated paper: Paper manufactured with a fine coat of a mineral substance to increase reflectivity or printability of the final product; a category of book papers.

cold web: See non-heatset web.

collating: See gathering.

Color Electronic Prepress System (CEPS): Process by which high resolution electronic systems are used to produce complex color using digital methods; Crosfield, Hell, DS America and Scitex are manufacturers of such equipment.

color separation: A photographic procedure by which a color image is divided into magenta (red-blue), cyan (blue-green), yellow (red-green), and black film images using red, blue, green, and amber filters.

commercial pin registration systems: Pin registration systems that are available to the printer for purchase from commercial sources.

commercial web press: A term used to describe a type of web press used for a wide variety of commercial printing and advertising production.

common-window flat: A flat that contains only windows or cut openings in masking material and used as a knockout flat when proofing and plating process color separations stripped to clearbase.

comparative weight formula: A mathematical formula used to calculate a weight for a standard size of paper; also called equivalent weight formula.

component estimating: An estimating process by which a job is carefully broken into component parts or elements.

composite film: A film contacting process by which a film sheet receives multiple exposures from different film images of all one color or type, thereby collecting the film images together on one film sheet; procedure termed "compositing."

comprehensive: A completed visualization of an image prepared by an artist; final step before preparation of artwork for graphic reproduction.

computer literacy: A general understanding of electronic computing, including an understanding of the general technology and application of computers to solve problems.

computer-assisted estimating (CAE): Estimating procedures that utilize computers to determine job planning and production costs.

computer-assisted pricing (CAP): Pricing using a computer system with appropriate pricing software.

computer-assisted scheduling (CAS): Scheduling using a computer system with appropriate scheduling software.

computer-generated estimating (CGE): Process of estimating where the computer system makes choices and generates an estimate based on those choices.

computer-to-plate (CTP): Digital production whereby graphic imaging is direct from digital file to printing plate, bypassing film output and related prepress operations.

continuous improvement: Condition by which employees choose to improve their job and personal skills as an essential element of improving the products and services of the company.

continuous-tone: Any image that consists of a range of values from light to intermediate to dark with no defined breaks between values.

conventional prepress: Used to describe printing production that does not utilize electronic imaging processes, systems or equipment; also termed photomechanical production.

conversion: The process of changing information from one form to another for computer use.

cookbook solution: Solving similar problems using the same set of ingredients and procedures which may not fit the details of each problem.

copy drum: The segment of a color scanner where the copy to be separated is positioned.

copy preparation: A term generally used to describe the coordination of artwork into a form suitable for graphic reproduction.

copy: To duplicate a file or program to provide a backup; the copy is then used and the original saved. A term also used to indicate manuscript and other materials supplied to the printer by the customer, representing the essential parts of a printing job.

core: A circular tube made of metal or fiberboard on which roll paper is wound.

cost estimating: The process by which a printing job is broken into detailed manufacturing components representative of anticipated production, after which production times and costs are determined, and to which material costs and outside services are added.

cost markup: An additional dollar amount added to material, outside purchase, or labor and overhead costs for handling and servicing requirements.

cost-benefit analysis: A procedure by which costs and benefits are weighed by management when purchasing a computer, piece of equipment, or other potentially expensive item or service.

cover paper: A class of printing paper commonly used for book covers and when thick, durable stocks are required; basic size of cover paper is 20 x 26 inches.

credit association: A firm organized to determine the credit status of companies and individuals doing business with their member firms.

credit referral service: A procedure by which credit information about a customer is given; generally a free service offered through a regional PIA office for member firms.

CREF guidelines: Computer Ready Electronic Files; set of guidelines for preparing electronic files developed by the Scitex Graphic Arts Users Association.

customer service representative (CSR): A person working as a liaison between customer and printing company to streamline production and ensure that the final printed product is manufactured properly and to the customer's satisfaction.

cutoff: The measured distance around the blanket cylinder of a web press that established the length of repeatability of the image; term used to describe the printed product as a sheet or signature in web production.

cutoffs per roll: The number of sheets or signatures that can be cut from a roll of web paper; sometimes abbreviated as "cuts per roll."

cutting machine: A piece of equipment used for the cutting of larger sheets of paper into smaller pieces and for the trimming of finished goods to final size.

cutting: Process of slicing sheets paper into smaller sizes.

CWT: A term used in the paper industry meaning hundred weight or weight per 100 pounds of paper; common paper pricing system used to provide a price per hundred pounds.

cycle time: Time required to complete a cycle or sequence; used in printing to define the time required to complete a printing order from beginning to end; see lead time.

DAT tape: Method of storing electronic information, typically used as a backup system for digital prepress.

data collection: The process by which data are gathered.

data transmission: Method by which data are sent and received, commonly referring to telecommunication or satellite media.

database management system (DBMS): A program that manages a database.

database: A collection of data.

daylight contacting: Process of contacting film products in fairly normal lighting conditions; sometimes also termed "roomlight" or "brightlight" contacting.

debugging: Finding and fixing the errors in a computer program.

decimal hours: Division of a clock hour into hundredths or tenths.

default pricing: Using a standard or pre-established markup method when pricing by computer, thereby pricing jobs automatically.

depreciation: A dollar amount assigned as compensation for the wearout of printing plant equipment and facilities.

desktop drum scanner (or PMT scanner): Tabletop digital imaging system where one or more transmission or reflection images are placed on a drum, after which drum rotation converts the images into electronic impulses captured in computer memory.

desktop publishing (DTP): An integrated application of microcomputer hardware, software, input, and output devices that allows the electronic generation, assembling, and printing of graphic images.

detail estimate: Estimating where each job or production detail is broken out for review and cost analysis.

diazo: A coal-tar by-product popular as a plate coating for presensitized lithographic plates and overlay proofs.

diffusion-transfer: A photographic material used with photographic equipment to produce paste-up art; commonly known as PMT.

digital data: Information or image converted to numeric format.

digital file creator (DFC): Person who originates or creates one or more images or files using a computer platform, software, and related input and output devices.

digital photography: Process of capturing images using a digital camera and associated computer equipment.

digital: Numeric form of an image, color separation or type, which is electronically produced.

digitized image: An electronic file that represents an image of any kind that can be manipulated, retrieved, or massaged, in electronic form.

digitizing platform: An integrated mix of electronic hardware and software developed and used to digitize, retrieve, manipulate, or massage electronic files.

digitizing: Rendering typematter or graphic images into electronic form.

direct contacting: A film contacting procedure wherein the resultant contacted image has the same tonality as the original.

direct digital proofing: Production of a visible hard proof directly from an electronic or digital output device.

direct machine interface (DMI): A form of data collection whereby production equipment is directly connected to a computer system so that gathering data as the equipment operates is automatic.

disk operating system (DOS): The program that instructs the computer's CPU in coordinating data, managing files, and transferring information to and from a disk.

distribution services: Services provided by the printer or others which distribute the customer's products.

documentation: Operator manuals for a computer system; documents that detail a computer system, software usage, operating systems, and other information for user reference.

DocuTech: A stand-alone, high-speed printing device manufactured by Xerox that provides in-line image scanning, printing, and finishing.

dot-for-dot registration: The placement of images in precisely required relation to other images with no variation between printed sheets.

dots per inch (dpi): The number of dots per linear inch of measure; used to describe the fineness of halftones, tinted materials and electronic display terminals; also termed "lines per inch."

double washup: Cleaning a printing unit two times in sequence so that the next ink color will not be tainted by residual ink from the previous job.

double-burned: A term used to describe multiple exposures on a plate of proofing material.

double-faced proofing paper: A proofing paper that contains a photographic coating on both sides (C2S).

dry-tapping: The printing of a new ink film layer over a previously printed and dry film layer.

dryer unit: A postprinting process in heatset web production, where the web of paper passes through a heating unit to set the ink.

dummy: A folded sample representing a book, booklet, or image to be graphically reproduced; used for production planning and estimating purposes.

duplexing: Printing a sheet of paper on both sides.

duplicator paper: A paper class, basic size 17 x 22 inches, used specifically with mimeographic reproduction units.

Dutch cut: Procedure by which some small sheets cut from a larger parent sheet will have the grain in the short direction, while other sheets cut from the same parent sheet will have grain going in the long direction; also termed stagger cut or bastard cut.

dye sublimation printer: Digital output device for color proofing that creates continuous-tone images by heating CMYK dyes until they sublimate (turn to a gas).

Dylux proof: A stable-based photographic proof, also called a blueline proof or blueline.

eight-page web: A lithographic web press capable of producing 8-page sheetwise signatures with a cutoff size of up to 19 x 24 inches; also termed a half-width web.

elastic market demand: A theory that states that as the price of goods increases, the volume sold decreases, and as the price of goods decreases, the volume sold increases.

electronic (or digital) artwork: Graphic artwork for printing prepared exclusively using computer imaging hardware and software.

electronic factory data collection (EFDC): A process by which production data is collected from shop floor employees when production is completed, then stored in a computer system for analysis and review, sometimes termed shop data collection (SFDC).

electronic image manipulation: Changing or modifying images using digital methods.

electronic imaging: The process by which images of any kind are produced electronically, in digitized form.

electronic imposition: Process of placing electronic images in precise arrangement to one another using computer hardware and software.

electronic platform: An assemblage of interrelated electronic hardware and software designed for production of digitized type and graphic images; also termed a platform.

electronic trapping: Process of overlapping images using digital methods; software packages allow for automatic or non-automatic trapping methods.

emulsion-to-base (e-b) contacting: A film contacting procedure where the emulsion of the imaged piece of film is placed in direct contact with the base of an unimaged film sheet.

emulsion-to-emulsion (e-e) contacting: A film contacting procedure where the emulsion of the imaged piece of film is placed in direct contact with the emulsion of an unimaged film sheet.

emulsion: Photosensitive silver salts or other emulsified product, typically coated on a support base.

Encapsulated PostScript(EPS): A digital file format that stores images in PostScript language commands.

entrepreneurial philosophy: Management philosophy whereby the company, shop, or business is operated with little regard to maximizing profit on any given job, with the hopes of making a profit over the long term.

equivalent weight: See comparative weight.

estimate worksheet: A predesigned form used by the estimator to estimate the job either by computer or manually.

facilities management: The franchising out of all or part of a company's operational services to an outside provider.

fake color: Producing a rainbow of different colors through a mix of solids, screen tints and process colors, when printed in superimposed form in a predetermined manner.

fast pass estimating: A process of estimating where the job components are reviewed in general and not specific terms, saving time and speeding up the estimating/quoting process.

FAX modem: A device which provides for the sending of facsimile telecommunication transmissions directly from a computer platform.

FAX: A transmission sent and received by telecommunication using paper for input and output; images are facsimile of the original.

feet per minute (fpm): Unit of measurement of web printing production as paper is unwound.

file compression/decompression: Process by which digital files are compacted or uncompacted so as to reduce memory space.

file size: The measure of a digital file is megabytes.

file-checking software: Software provided to check files for missing fonts, linked graphics, screen previews, colors, PostScript errors, RIP time and other digital components.

file: Data that can stand alone but represent a complete set of information on a topic or subject.

filler work: Printing jobs taken into the plant to smooth out peaks and valleys of the production schedule.

film contacting: The procedure by which an imaged piece of film is placed to touch an unimaged film sheet; after exposure and processing, a copy of the original is produced.

film dupe: Abbreviation for the final product as a result of film duplication.

film duplication: The reproduction of precisely the same film image using film contacting procedures.

film imagesetter: Output device which converts digital files into final film.

final film provider (FFP): Company or person who provides fully imaged film ready to platemaking; see final output provider.

final output provider (FOP): Company or person who provides fully imaged digital output to film, paper, or other substrate.

financial statement: A document representing the financial condition of a business such as a balance sheet, income statement, and ratio information; also called a financial by accountants and management.

finish size sheet (fss): The final trimmed size of paper when a printing job is finished; also called finish size.

finished goods inventory: A listing of all work that has been completed and is held in inventory for future delivery to a customer or customer pickup.

fixed costs: All cost that do not change with changes in production; also termed setup costs in changeover point calculations.

fixed overhead: All costs required to maintain the space and environment of a defined plant area or production center.

flag: A marker in a roll of web paper indicating a weak area or imperfection in the paper at that point.

flat color: A color that is specifically mixed to match a given sample swatch.

flat configuration plan: A plan developed and written for stripping a job, particularly helpful when estimating complex or difficult jobs.

flat file: A group or collection of flats making up one complete printing job.

flat: An assemblage of film and masking base materials produced during the image assembly (stripping) procedure.

flatbed (or CCD) scanner: An image capture device which consists of a flat surface upon which an image to be scanned is placed, with scanning done via a image-sensing charge-coupled device.

folding: A procedure by which printed paper is creased, thereby reducing it in size; a common bindery and finishing procedure.

form: A collection of images on one plate that will be printed in the same color; also termed a printer or plate.

form chart: A planning tool showing arrangement of pages in a book or booklet with which stitching conditions may be determined.

Fourdrinier machine: A long machine with a revolving copper screen upon which a slurry is deposited, which ultimately will become paper.

freelance artist: Self-employed individual who produces graphic art; also called a freelancer.

full-width web: A web press capable of producing 16- page sheetwise signatures with a cutoff size of approximately 24 x 36 inches; also termed a 16-page web.

goldenrod masking material: A common term used to describe yellow or amber materials used to assemble images into flats.

goldenrod stripping: The process of assembling film images into flats using goldenrod materials.

grain direction: The predominant alignment of cellulose fibers in a sheet of paper; see paper grain.

grammage: The metric weight of paper in grams per square meter; similar measurement to paper basis weight in the United States system.

grams per square meter: Same as grammage.

Graphic Communications Business Practices (GCBP): These 23 business practices or conditions of operation were revised from the Printing Trade Customs in 1994; see Printing Trade Customs.

graphical (or gooey) interface: A computer interface characterized by the use of graphical icons or bit-mapped images to represent common computer functions.

grayscale: A measure of the number of gray levels in an image; important when scanning continuous tone images on the desktop.

gross profit: The amount of money made by a business before administration, sales expenses, and taxes have been deducted.

groundwood paper: A paper stock that is made by grinding logs into particle form; typical groundwood product is newsprint.

half-width web: A web press capable of producing 8- page sheetwise signatures with a cutoff size of approximately 19 x 24 inches or less; also termed an eight-page web.

halftone: The reproduction of a continuous-tone photograph or image by a pattern of fine dots of varying sizes and shapes, as related to the light or dark values of the continuous-tone image; contact or glassline screens are used for this procedure.

heatset web: Web presses that have dryers and chillers to set ink immediately after printing, thereby allowing for finishing production to be completed in-line, immediately following the pressrun; also termed closed web.

Heidelberg GTO-DI: A print-on-demand 14 x 20 inch printing press equipped with a spark-discharge computer-to-plate system for making waterless plates on press.

Heidelberg Quickmaster (QM): A print-on-demand, 13 x 18 inch printing press with a common impression cylinder surrounded by four imaging units and equipped with a spark-discharge computer-to-plate system for making waterless plates.

hierarchically-driven company: A company managed in a top-down, controlled manner where employees are given little freedom to make their own work-related decisions.

high contrast: A term used to describe images typically drawn in black ink on white paper; denotes extreme difference in value between two materials.

high-profit printers: A term defined by PIA as those printing firms that earn 8% or more return on sales annually.

House Error (HE): An error made during production that is fully the printer's responsibility to rectify.

hundred sheet price: See price per 100 sheets.

hundred weight: See CWT.

IBM-compatible: A group of computer platforms that are manufactured to comply with IBM standards and perform exactly like IBM platforms.

icon-based: Software that is picture-based.

Illustrator: Popular software package for drawing and illustration developed by Adobe Systems.

image assembly: The procedure by which film images are positioned in a precise order for platemaking; also called stripping.

image capture: Process of securing an image using a camera, scanner, or other device.

image repeat: Circumferential distance around a cylinder that defines the length of an image.

imposition: The exact positions of book pages as they will fall on a press sheet, ultimately folded to produce a signature; positioning of images in a precise order on a form.

impression: Process of transferring an image to a substrate through the printing process.

impressions per hour (imp/hr): A system used to measure the output of printing presses.

in-line: A term used to describe production operations performed in a sequential manner.

income before taxes: See net profit.

index bristol: A paper class, basic size 25 1/2 x 30 1/2 inches, used when moderately thick paper material is required.

Indigo E-1000: Sheetfed digital press.

indirect contacting: A film contacting procedure wherein the resultant contacted image has the opposite tonality of the original.

inelastic market demand: A theory that states that there is no relationship between price and volume of goods sold; prices may rise or fall with no direct reduction or increase in volume.

ink coverage: A percentage factor related to the size of the form to be printed and the kind of form.

ink mileage: The volume of ink required to print a certain coverage and specified number of copies.

ink-jet: Process whereby ink is pushed through fine jets and imaged to a substrate with the image formation controlled by a computer.

Integrated Digital Services Network (IDSN): a dial-up method of telecommunication through public telephone lines for digital data exchange.

integrated standards: Output values reflecting the combination of manual and automated (person-machine) production.

Internet: An integrated, world-wide network of computer users for communication and information exchange.

intuitive estimating: Determining the cost or price of a printed job using guesswork or intuition.

investment community philosophy: Management philosophy whereby the company, shop, or business is operated with careful cost, manufacturing, and management controls so as to maximize profits on each job, with every expectation of making a profit over the long-term.

Iris color proofing: Type of ink-jet proofing which provides high resolution, high quality proofs.

ISO 9000: A component-based quality assurance system for establishing, measuring, and maintaining quality.

ISO: International Standards Organization, a group created to promote the development of worldwide standards; developed metric paper standards and quality standards used throughout much of the world.

job cost summary: A procedure completed after a job has been delivered that compares actual to estimated production times and costs; production data used to revise estimating standards.

job costing: A computer software system wherein actual and estimated times and costs are compared after the fact to note variations in the data and to revise estimating standards.

job loading/scheduling: A process by which printing equipment is organized to complete production.

job specification form (JSF): A form used to record job specifications upon which estimates are based.

job specifications: The specific details of a job to be printed, typically indicated by the sales representative to the estimator on a job specification form; also termed job specs.

job summary: A technique comparing actual production times and costs to estimated times and costs; see also job cost summary.

job ticket: An envelope or other document in paper or digital form that indicates all production details of a job in production and that travels with the job during production; sometimes called a job docket.

just-in-time: A concept whereby a printing company operates on an "immediate need" basis with customers or suppliers. Commonly abbreviated as JIT.

kenaf fibers: Fibers from the kenaf plant used as a substitute for cellulose fibers in papermaking.

key color: The base, or first, color pasted to illustration board when preparing mechanicals to which overlay colors are registered.

keyline art: The base or key mechanical art image to which all other images register.

keypad data collection: System of collecting shop floor data using electronic keypads developed to match company activities, materials, employees, and production processes.

kilobyte (K): 2^{10}, or 1024, bytes of memory capacity in a computer system.

kilowatt hours (kWh): A measurement of power consumption or usage for job-costing procedures.

knife folder: A type of folding equipment that creases the paper and forces it into two knurled rollers that complete the fold.

knockout: Dropping out or removing an image using some type of masking material such as peelcoat, goldenrod, or film.

labor-intensive: Production that requires a high complement of employees.

laser printer: Term used to refer to a generic line of computer printers that print digitized graphic images from a microcomputer.

LaserWriter: A computer printing device introduced by Apple Computer in 1985; first laser printer commercially available in the U.S.

lead time: Time required to produce a printing job; see cycle time.

ledger paper: A paper class, basic size 17 x 22 inches, used for record keeping and accounting work.

letterpress: A printing process wherein type-high relief forms are inked and impressed to transfer the image directly to the paper.

lift value: The approximate number of sheets of paper in a hand-held lift; also called load value.

lift: A hand-held stack or pile of paper to be cut, trimmed, or worked in production.

line copy: Material prepared for reproduction containing only high contrast images, lines or dots.

line film: A category of film generally used for the photographic imaging of line work.

line work: Graphic images in line or solid block form; also termed lineart.

lithography: A printing process whereby image transfer is accomplished through the use of plates with a planographic (flat) surface; plates accept ink in the sensitized (image) areas and accept water, which repels ink, in the nonimage areas.

local area network (LAN): A group of computers in a relatively small area that are interconnected to allow sharing of printers and other devices.

M (sheet) weight: The scale weight, in pounds, of 1000 sheets of paper of a given size; also termed thousand sheet weight.

M sheet price: Paper price expressed as a cost per 1000 sheets of an established size; also termed thousand sheet price.

machine hour rates: A term used interchangeably with BHR.

machine standard: The output value for a piece of equipment that is fully automated and requires no employee operation.

management information system (MIS): A system designed to provide management with the necessary data and information to run a business.

manual roll change: Changing rolls using manual methods during a web press run; requires stopping the press, which generally increases spoilage and waste.

manufacturing cost: The production cost of producing a printing order that does not include administrative and sales costs for the product.

market niche: A specific customer, product, or service targeted by a company for sales efforts.

markup: See cost markup.

master flat: Key flat of a flat file to which other flats are registered.

materials-intensive: Product or service that requires a high or extensive amount of materials

mechanical: Artwork that has been fully prepared for photographic reproduction as

MHR: Machine hour rate; same as budgeted hour rate.

millimeter (mm): A metric measurement whereby a meter (39.37 inches) is divided into 1000 equal parts thus equaling 0.03937 inches; about the thickness of a paper clip wire.

minimum-change reprint: Reprint of a printing order which has minor or very few changes.

MIS: Management Information System.

modem: The abbreviation for modulator-demodulator, an input/output device used to link systems together by telecommunications.

modular computer system: A computer system logically divided into parts, segments, or modules whereby each part can operate independently of all other segments.

moiré: A generally undesirable pattern formed when two or more screen tints or halftones are overlapped incorrectly.

monochromatic proof: A one-color, high contrast proof typically containing a colored image on a white background.

multicolor stripping: Complex image assembly procedure whereby process color and fake color techniques are integrated together; can be completed manually, electronically, or as a mix of both.

multimetal plates: Long-run lithographic plates that are layered using a base metal, copper, and stainless steel or chromium.

narrow-width web: A class of web presses made to run web widths in the range of 16 to twenty inches.

negative-acting: A term used to describe photographic products that reverse tonality with each photographic step.

negative: An image on film or paper where the image is reproduced as clear or white and the surrounding background is dark or black.

net profit: The amount of dollars remaining after all costs have been deducted, but before taxes are paid; also called net profit before taxes or income before taxes (bt).

newspaper web: A web press typically made and used for newspaper production.

newsprint: A paper class, basic size 24 x 36 inches, used as the printing base for newspaper and other less expensive products, see also groundwood paper.

niche marketing: A marketing program whereby customers are evaluated and selected based on specific characteristics or factors; see selective marketing and target marketing.

non-chargeable Author's Alternation (NAA): An alteration to a customer's job that is not charged to them; may be gratis or rework of an alteration that was incorrectly completed initially.

non-chargeable hours: All work that cannot be directly related to a specific job or customer order nor charged to any specific account.

non-heatset web: Web printing that utilizes no chiller/dryer postprinting units to set ink; term commonly applied to newspaper production where ink dries by absorption; also known as cold-set web or open web; also termed open web.

numbering: An operation wherein consecutive numbers are printed on goods.

off-line production: Work completed on a customer's job that is done separate from other production.

offset paper: Same as book paper with a basic size of 25 x 38 inches.

open web: See non-heatset web.

Opti-copy: An accurate projection technique for step-and-repeating images to photographic film.

orbital (micromodifier) technique: One of two methods used to produce spreads and chokes; process required the Byer's Micromodifier, which produces extremely accurate spreads and chokes using a carefully controlled, orbital rotating bed.

order entry: The beginning data necessary to enter a job into a production system or to initiate production on a printing order.

orthochromatic material: Light-sensitive material such as film products that is not sensitive to red light.

out-of-pocket (OOP) cost: A cost incurred by the printer that must be paid immediately or within a short period of time.

out: The number of sheets that will be cut from a larger sheet of paper.

output device: Equipment used in conjunction with a computer platform to produce visible images.

output per time unit: Basis for some production standards; example would be "6000 sheets per hour."

outside service supplier: A vendor or firm that supplies services, such as a trade house, service bureau, or timesharing firm.

over-the-counter sales: Taking orders face-to-face from customers who present themselves at the shop or company.

overcapacity: The concept of having too much available production time or equipment; in a purely competitive economic environment, generally leads to reduced prices.

overlay proof: Proofs that consist of two or more layers of color substrate that are exposed, processed, and mounted in register to one other.

overprint: To print over or on top of another ink color; also termed a surprint.

page editing production: Desktop production where pages are modified or edited.

page layout production: Desktop production where pages are graphically arranged.

PageMaker: First desktop publishing page design software program.

pallet: See skid.

Pantone Matching System (PMS): An ink and color matching system that has become the standard for the printing industry; PMS colors are referenced by number and are formulated using exact quantity measurements so the color value is always consistent.

paper caliper: The thickness of a paper stock measured in thousandths of an inch (or points).

paper catalog: A published price book indicating all paper offered for sale by a paper merchant.

paper grain: The alignment of cellulose fibers (or other type of fibers) in a sheet of paper; when writing dimensions, "grain long" or "grain short" may be indicated with a line above or below the appropriate dimension of paper.

paper micrometer: A device used to determine accurately the thickness of paper stocks.

paper point: The equivalent of one thousandth of an inch; used to indicate paper thickness (caliper).

paper ratio system: An estimating system that uses a ratio of the cost of paper to the total job cost or price of the job.

parallel folding: A procedure by which sequential folds in paper are completed parallel to one another.

parent size sheet (pars): The size of paper to be purchased from the paper merchant; also termed stock size sheet.

pass: Movement of a sheet of paper through a press.

passivation: A procedure used when manufacturing lithographic plates to reduce undesirable chemical reactions between coating materials and aluminum plate bases.

past work basis: An estimating/pricing system, which uses the value of past printing jobs done as a basis for quoting on current work.

paste ink: Ink with thick body.

peelcoat: A red or yellow gelatin material coated on a clear carrier sheet that is manually cut and peeled to produce a graphic image.

penalties: Adjustments for special operations or less typical production procedures.

percentage markup: A method by which profit is added to a job based on a percentage of the estimated cost or some other basis; percentage markup is a top management decision.

perfect binding: Finishing of a book or booklet where signatures are glued to a paper cover.

perfecting: A term used to describe a printing or press that prints an image on both sides of the sheet simultaneously; also called blanket-to-blanket or perfector.

perforated: A term used to describe paper that has small dashed cuts made close to one edge to facilitate tearing the paper out of a book or booklet.

personal computer (PC): Generally, a microcomputer designed for single-person use with primary applications to small businesses and home use.

Photo CD: A process developed by Kodak for scanning and storing images on a compact disk.

photo-composed film: A process by which images are combined or collected on film using photographic techniques; most common reference is to the production of composite film materials.

photomechanical production: Producing a printing order where imaging equipment and materials utilize photographic and mechanical technologies, not digital methods.

photomechanical transfer (PMT): A camera-speed, diffusion- transfer product used to go directly from camera copy to paste- up or film positive.

photopolymer coating: A light-sensitive coating used principally for presensitized lithographic plates.

Photoshop: A popular software program used in conjunction with scanning hardware.

phototypesetting: A procedure by which type is set photographically; requires keyboarding or punching of a paper input tape on a typewriter unit, with sequential typesetting in a photographic unit containing a light source, a font on film or magnetic medium, and photographic paper or film.

pica: A common unit of measurement in copy preparation and typesetting; one pica equals 12 points, and there are approximately 6 picas in 1 inch.

PICT: An image format used by Macintosh graphics programs.

pin registration: The use of metal or plastic pins to align flats, film, or prepared copy during prepress operations.

pixel: the smallest unit of a bit-mapped image on a computer screen; abbreviation for picture element.

plate scanner: An electronic device used to read printing plate densities prior to plate mounting and press makeready; the densities are then input into the press computer console, which automatically adjusts ink coverage relative to the density values.

plate screen: A piece of film used to divide normally solid areas into a design or dot pattern; same as screen tint.

platemaker: A vacuum frame with a light source used principally to expose offset plates to film images and flats.

platemaking and proofing configuration plan: A plan developed and written for plating and proofing a job, particularly helpful when estimating complex or difficult jobs.

platemaking: The procedure of preparing, exposing, and developing lithographic plates.

platform: An assemblage of interrelated electronic hardware and software designed for production of digitized type and graphic images; also termed an electronic platform.

ply: A term used to indicate thickness of cardboard stocks; to convert ply thickness to caliper, multiply the ply value by 3 and then add 6 to that result.

point (paper): The equivalent of one thousandth of an inch; used as a measurement of paper thickness.

point (printer's point): The basis for typesetting, where one point equals 1/72 inch; U.S. Bureau of Standards indicates the equivalent of 1 point is 0.013837 inch.

point-of-purchase system: A microcomputer system used for transacting cash business with customers, which may also include software for estimating or pricing jobs as the customer waits.

positive-acting: A term used to describe photographic products that maintain the same tonality (or polarity) from image to image.

positive: An image on film or paper wherein black copy is reproduced on a light or clear background.

postpress: Production on a job which occurs after the printing is completed.

PostScript code: The most common language for driving laser printers and output devices.

pound: See basis weight.

ppi: pixels per inch; a measure of the resolution of scanned images.

preflight: The review of electronic or mechanical artwork prior to initiating production on the job.

prefolder: In-line web finishing device used to increase the number of folds or provide certain types of folds.

presensitized plates: A lithographic surface plate that is coated during manufacture and shipped to the printer in coated form.

press preparation and makeready: That segment of press operation that sets up the press for the particular job to be run; includes such factors as setting grippers and guides, adjusting ink distribution, and setting feeder and delivery mechanisms.

press proof: A proof that has been manufacturing using conventional printing production including color separation, stripping, plating, and press operations.

press running: The continuous operation of a printing press by which acceptable press sheets are printed.

press size sheet (pss): The size of paper stock that will receive the image during press-running operations.

press spoilage: An additional amount of paper included at the beginning of the production of a job to compensate for throwaways and unusable sheets generated during presswork and finishing operations.

presswork: The mechanical reproduction of copy using a printing press.

price ceiling: Top or highest pricing point that can be charged for a product or service.

price collusion: The illegal establishment of prices for a product, good, or service within a geographic region; price fixing.

price cutting: Reducing or lowering the price on a given printing job; typically found when competition for customers is intense, although considered an unwise practice if costs and prices have been carefully predetermined.

price estimating: Estimating the price of a job from a price list or price matrix.

price list estimating: Estimating a job from a listing of prices which have been developed for product lines standard to a particular company.

price matrix estimating: Estimating a job from a matrix of prices for specific products or services offered by the company.

price per 100 sheets: A paper catalog price expressed as a dollar amount per each 100 sheets; also called hundred sheet price.

price per 1000 sheets: A paper catalog price expressed as a dollar amount per each 1000 sheets; also called price per M sheets.

price proposal: A written offer from the printer to the print buyer or customer proposing a tentative price and job specifications that describe the work to be done.

price quotation: A final, written offer from the printer to the print buyer or customer, locking up price, quantity desired, and all other vital job particulars.

pricing template: A pre-formatted spreadsheet or other worksheet used to develop final prices for a good or service.

pricing: The establishment by the top management of a printing plant of the selling price of a printed good, product, or service.

print buyer: A representative of a business, advertising agency, or corporation who purchases printing on a consistent basis.

print-on-demand (POD): Producing a printing order immediately when requested, in a reduced cycle time environment.

Printing Trade Customs: A compilation of operating and business practices held as legal based on court precedent, typically printed on the back of a quotation or proposal; revised and termed the Graphic Communication Business Practices in 1994.

printing broker: A person who sells printing goods and services to customers and print buyers, then arranges for printing manufacturing through printers willing to produce the job.

printing consultants: A person retained by the customer or print buyer to ensure consistent print quality and coordinate printing projects at different stages of manufacturing.

printing cost estimating: A mathematical procedure used to determine the cost of a printing job prior to production using BHRs and standard production times and adding all additional material costs.

printing estimator: An individual who completes cost estimates in a printing company.

procedural standard: A recognized technique or procedure used to complete a given job or task; also termed a technical standard.

process camera: A piece of equipment used to reduce or enlarge artwork as a major step in prepress operations of printing manufacturing.

process color: A specifically formulated pigment used to print process color separations; cyan (blue-green), magenta (red-blue), yellow (red-green) and black (K) as transparent colors; also called process blue, process red, process yellow, and process black and abbreviated CMYK.

process specialization: Concentrating on a market based on a specific process available from a printing company.

process standardization: Focus on similar production techniques that allow for streamlined manufacturing procedures.

product differentiation: Distinguishing or enhancing one product from all other competing products so that it is different or unique.

product specialization: Concentrating on a market based on a specific product manufactured by a printing company.

product standardization: Focus on similar production techniques that allow for streamlined production of a printed product.

production adjustment factor (PAF): Used to adjust for production variations that are unique to a product, customer, or service.

production center method (PC): A prorated costing procedure that does not include administrative areas, thereby spreading job costs over only those areas that have a defined printing production function.

production center: A defined work area where a certain segment of printing production is completed.

production coordinator: An individual who works with sales representatives, estimators, and production personnel to ensure smooth movement of jobs through plant production.

production planner: An individual who determines the production flow for a specific printing job; also called a job planner.

production scheduling: The assignment of jobs into the sequence of production in a printing plant.

production standard: An hourly value representing the average output of a particular operating area producing under specified conditions.

production standards manual: A book or notebook containing all production standard times and procedures for a printing facility.

profit markup: The addition of an amount of dollars over the cost of a job.

profit: The excess dollars remaining after all costs have been accounted for in a particular job.

proforma estimating: The establishment of a standard method or process by which estimating is completed; also termed template estimating.

proof-to-satisfaction: Process that requires the printer or prepress service provider to supply whatever number of proofs will be necessary to obtain customer approval.

proofing: A visual check of a job in production; may be completed in monochromatic or multicolor form depending upon the job.

proposal: An offer make to a customer for production of printing goods and services that specifically states all job requirements, specifications, and prices for such goods; may be accepted, rejected, or modified by the customer.

prorated costing: A costing process by which fixed and variable costs are identified, divided up using some index reflective of the company, and then distributed back over the company's operating areas.

purchase order control: A computer report providing management with information and data regarding purchases made by company employees for company materials and supplies.

purchasing: The arrangement for buying of materials and services for a job in production; may be assigned to the estimator as a related job duty.

QuarkXPress: A popular page design software program.

quotation: A legal, binding agreement between customer and printer for specified printing goods and services; typically a written form.

rag content paper: A paper manufactured with a specified percentage of cotton fiber.

random access memory (RAM): Short-term memory required by a computer for immediate needs, which is lost when computer power is interrupted.

rapid-access processing: A film processing system whereby exposed film is developed and fixed using predetermined chemical controls, allowing for fast development and consistent final film images.

raster image processor (RIP): A hardware device used to electronically prepare a file for output.

recycled paper: Paper made from previously printed or used stock.

registration mark: A mark or symbol used throughout printing production to align (register) images; typically appears as two perpendicular lines in crossed form centered in a circle or oval.

regular cutting: The procedure by which all small sheets cut from a larger parent sheet will have the same grain direction.

repeat work: Printing jobs that are reordered by a customer with little or no change.

report generator: Software that allows report data to be formatted in various ways to be customized to the database available.

request for estimate (RFE) form: A form used primarily by printing sales representatives to clarify and detail job specifications for a printing order.

request for purchase (RFP): A form used to request prices on an item to be purchased.

return on investment (ROI): The ratio of income (profit) earned as compared to assets (capital) required to earn that income; can be based on either gross or net assets.

return on sales (ROS): Income as a percentage of sales; found by dividing the earned profit (income before taxes) by the total gross sales required to generate that profit.

RGB-CMYK: An abbreviation to indicate the color conversion of digital color images from red, green, and blue to cyan, magenta, yellow, and black

right angle folding: The procedure by which each fold is made at right angles to the preceding fold.

right-reading: A term used to describe images that can be read or deciphered from left to right; typically implies that the negative or positive reads correctly through the base side.

RIP: The process of electronically preparing a digital file for output using a raster image processor; also termed RIPping.

Robinson-Patman Act: Actually a segment of the Clayton Act, this federal law prohibits the seller of a product, good, or service from offering goods or services of like grade and quality to two or more buyers at different prices.

robotics: The process of using automated mechanical-electrical devices to perform numerous sequential production operations.

roll footage: The number of linear feet in a roll of paper.

roll-to-roll: A web production technique where rolls of paper are printed and then rewound in roll form for shipment and future conversion to sheets.

roll: Paper stock that remains as one continuous ribbon; also called a web of paper.

rotary cutter: Web press device used to cut a roll of paper into sheet form.

Rubylith: A popular peelcoat product that is red in color, made by the Ulano Company.

saddle stitching: The placement of wire or string along the binding spine (saddle) of gathered signatures, holding them together as a book or booklet.

safety paper: A paper class, basic size 17 x 22 inches, used when no change of written image is desired, such as for many types of documents requiring financial exchange (checkbooks).

sales per employee: A dollar figure derived by taking the gross sales dollars of the company and dividing by the number of employees required to generate that sales volume; considered an important measurement tool although the average figure varies by industry segment.

sales representative: A person who meets with customers, determines their printing needs, and then arranges for production of products to meet these needs; also termed salesperson or sales rep.

scanner: Drum and flatbed equipment used to digitize images for storage, manipulation, and output.

screen tint: A piece of film used to divide normally solid areas into a design or pattern; two major categories are dot and special effect patterns.

selective binding: Products which are tailored to a certain market through the selection of signatures or printed materials that address the needs of customers in that market.

selective marketing: A marketing program whereby customers are evaluated and selected based on specific characteristics or factors; see target marketing and niche marketing.

selling price (SP): The amount of money a customer pays for particular printing

separation master flat: The first set of separation images assembled to which all other separations will be registered.

service bureau: A company offering computer, typesetting, or electronic imaging services.

shareware: Computer software which is developed and initially shared at no cost with potential buyers, with the understanding that the potential buyer will pay for the software if it serves a useful purpose.

sheetfed: Printing or feeding sheets of paper; used to describe types of presses that are designed around printing paper in sheet form.

sheeting: The conversion of rolls of paper into sheet form with the use of sheeting equipment (called sheeters).

sheetwise (SW) imposition: A press sheet that has one-half of the pages of a signature printed on one side and the other half on the opposite side in direct relation; also called work-and-back imposition.

shop floor data collection (SFDC): A process by which production data are collected from shop floor employees when production is completed, then stored in a computer system for analysis and review; sometimes termed electronic factory data collection (EFDC).

side stitching: The placement of wire or string through the side of gathered signatures, holding them together as a book or booklet.

signature: A collection of printed pages folded in a prearranged sequence to make all or part of a book or booklet.

simplexing: Printing on one side of the sheet.

single washup: Cleaning a printing unit one time because the next ink color is approximately the same darkness or lightness as the ink color from the previous job.

single-faced proofing paper: A paper coated with a photographic material on one side (C1S).

single-sheet proof: A proof upon which all proofing layers or colors are adhered or laminated to a base carrier sheet; DuPont's Cromalin and 3M's Matchprint are popular proofs in this category.

sixteen-page web: A lithographic web press capable of producing 16-page web sheetwise signatures with a cutoff size of approximately 24 x 36 inches; also termed a full-width.

sized and supercalendered (S&SC) paper: A paper stock that has been sized with necessary products and then highly calendered to produce a paper that has excellent surface requirements for printing.

sizing: Chemical products added to paper during manufacture that physically make the paper more suitable for printing production or ultimate product usage.

skid: A wooden or metal base with runners upon which paper is stacked in large quantities and then wrapped for shipment; a pallet is similar to a skid, but is about half the size.

slabbing waste: Unusable paper stock cut (or "slabbed") away from the outside of a roll of paper, required because of damage to the roll.

slurry: A mixture of cellulose fiber, additives, and water that is flowed to the Fourdrinier machine in the papermaking process.

soft proof: An image on a color monitor or screen to ascertain approximate color values of an image, as opposed to a hard proof on paper or other substrate which can be mailed or physically sent to a customer.

soya ink: Vehicle used in ink that is made from soya (soybean) oil which reduces VOC emissions and toxic waste.

specialty web: A web press, typically narrow-width, built and used for production of a specialized product.

specified form: A form used for ordering and detailing papers; a specified information sequence indicating all important ordering data.

splicing equipment: Web equipment that provides for automatic change of rolls during a pressrun; sometimes called flying pasters or automatic pasters.

split back gauge: Component part of a cutting machine that can be precisely separated to allow for accurate trimming of books or signatures on different sides at one time.

split invoice: A technique whereby the customer pays a deposit for out-of-pocket costs before a job begins production; after the job is delivered, the customer is invoiced for the remaining costs.

spoilage: Unusable, throw-away, or spoiled paper from the pressrun portion of the production of the job.

spread: A film image that is slightly larger in size; produced from a negative film original to raw film using film contacting procedures; also termed a fatty or swell.

spreadsheet program: Packaged software for microcomputers wherein a large matrix of rows and columns of numerical data can be built to answer "what if " questions as the data are changed.

stagger cutting: A procedure by which some small sheets cut from a large parent sheet will have grain in the short direction while other sheets cut from the same parent sheet will have grain going in the long direction; also termed dutch or bastard cutting.

standard production data: See production standard.

standard production time: An hourly value representing the average output of a particular operating area producing printing under specified conditions.

standard size paper: A paper in sizes or dimensions other than the basic size that is offered for sale by paper merchants.

standardization: The establishment of a defined production procedure that does not vary from day to day; also refers to products that have established and unchanging requirements.

statistical process control (SPC): A statistical procedure designed to measure and improve the quality of products and services.

step-and-repeat: A procedure by which a single film image or a group of the same image is exposed to a lithographic plate or sheet of film in a defined manner to provide multiple images on the plate or film sheet.

stock size sheet (sss): See parent size sheet.

straight cutting: Paper stock cuts where the resultant cut sheets all have the grain going in the same direction, as opposed to stagger cutting where some of the cut sheets have grain direction one way, and other cut sheets having grain direction the opposite way.

straight reprint: The reprint of an printing order which has no changes.

strategic alliance: The partnership of two (or more) selected companies to produce a product or service that requires the combined talents of both companies; also termed a strategic partnership.

stripper: An individual who mounts film images into flats to complete image assembly in a printing plant.

stripping tab: A small piece of film, with a prepunched hole at one end; pairs of these are attached to the edges of masking sheets to provide a pin registration procedure.

stripping: See image assembly.

substance weight: See basis weight.

subtractive surface plate: A presensitized lithographic plate that requires removal of nonimage (unexposed) areas during processing.

sulfite papers: A large group of paper products made using chemical breakup of cellulose fibers with subsequent cooking, beating, and refining procedures.

summary estimate: An estimate report which shows totals or a summary only, with no details included.

supercalendered: A term used to describe paper stock that has been calendered extensively by manufacturing procedures that produce a paper surface that is very smooth and has excellent printability.

surface plates: A major category of lithographic plates that carry their image on the surface; divided into presensitized and wipe-on subgroups.

surprint: Overprint of one image over another.

SyQuest: A popular magnetic media storage process

table stripping: The process of assembling images manually using a light table, masking materials, and other tools, as opposed to electronic stripping using CEPS or CAD/CAM systems such as the Gerber Autoprep.

tagboard: A paper class, basic size 24 x 36 inches, used generally for the making of tags and other products where inexpensive yet strong papers are needed.

Tagged Image File Format (TIFF): A file format for bit-mapped images.

target marketing: A marketing program whereby customers are evaluated and selected based on specific characteristics or factors; see selective marketing and niche marketing.

telecommunications: Communications via telephone or other signal system.

template estimating: Establishment of a standard method or process by which estimating is completed manually or by computer; also termed proforma estimating.

template spreadsheet estimating: Completing template estimating using a computer spreadsheet format.

template: A pre-designed form to estimate or price a printing job

text paper: A paper class, basic size 25 x 38 inches, used for the production of books and booklets; subgroup of book paper; very colorful stocks typically offered for sale with matching cover papers.

thermal wax printer: A type of digital output device that produces colors by melting dots from RGB or CMYK images onto a substrate.

thousand sheet price: See M sheet price.

thousand sheet weight: See M (sheet) weight.

three-knife trimming: Production operation where books are trimmed on three sides using a three-knife trimmer or split back gauge.

thumbnail: A rough sketch produced by an artist during the initial phase of artwork development for a graphic image.

time and motion study: A procedure by which employees are studied during production, with resultant recommendations for improved efficiency and establishment of production time standards.

time compression: Reducing the time needed to complete a task.

time per output quantity: Conversion of a production standard into a calculated time value related to output; an example would be "0.1667 hours per thousand sheets."

Total Quality Management (TQM): Management technique which requires employee empowerment, statistical process control, continuous improvement, zero defects, and other components to ensure a high quality of product or service on a constant basis.

total cost: With changeover points, the resultant cost when fixed and variable costs are summed together.

totally chlorine-free (TCF) paper: Paper which is produced without chorine as a bleaching agent to conform to Clean Water Act emission requirements.

trade customs: See Printing Trade Customs or Graphic Communication Business Practices.

trade house: A firm or company that produces a segment of a printing order; common trade services are composition, prepress, postpress, and special operations.

trap: An area where color is to be printed, which is surrounded by another printed area; normally requires a spread or choke to provide for a slight overlap or undercutting of the two printed areas.

tri-linear scanner: Flatbed scanners which require three passes to scan a color image into RGB files.

trimming: The removal of edges or segments of paper stock to bring the final printed product to the desired size.

turnkey vendor: A company providing computer systems that have been designed, programmed, checked, and then sold as a package to a customer; the client "turns the key" to begin to operate the system.

ultraviolet: A specific range of light wavelengths that is not visible and to which many photographic films and lithographic plates are sensitive.

uncoated paper: A paper stock, in the book class, that does not receive an additional coating of clay.

unit cost: The cost for an individual item or product.

up: A term used to describe the number of finish size sheets that can be positioned (imposed) on a press size sheet.

utilization: A percentage of time that a production center is used for chargeable work, as compared to total time available.

vacuum back: A vacuum board used to hold film securely during exposure in a process camera or enlarger; essentially the same as the focal plane.

vacuum frame: A unit for film contacting that utilizes a vacuum drawdown to obtain intimate contact between pieces of film; sometimes termed a contact frame.

value added: A concept used by printing management to measure the dollar amount added by the manufacturing process using a "sales minus materials and buyouts" formula.

variable costs: Costs that do change with charges in output.

variable data: Information that changes with each estimate, such as a customer's name.

volatile organic compounds (VOC): Compounds classified by the federal government as volatile with a focus on emission control of such toxic compounds under the Clean Air Act.

washup: The procedure used to remove ink from a press.

waste: A percentage comparison of paper that must be thrown away to the total surface area of the sheet.

waterless lithography: Elimination of water from the lithographic printing process; waterless inks print by adhering to image areas on a plate that are not covered with a silicon rubber coating.

watermark: A design or image pressed into the wet paper sheet by a dandy roll during manufacture.

web break: The accidental tearing apart of web paper during production.

web printing: The production of printed goods from rolls of paper that are passed through the press in one continuous piece.

webbing diagram: A picture that is drawn by a press operator or production planner to show exactly how a web will be run through the press.

weight per 1000 cutoffs. The scale weight of 1000 cutoff sheets or signatures; used for estimating ink consumption and determination of shipping weight factors.

weight per M (1000) sheets: The actual scale weight of 1,000 sheets of paper of a given size and type; can be calculated from the substance weight using a comparative weight formula.

wet-trapping: Printing wet colors of ink over other wet colors of ink; common with both multicolor sheetfed and web production.

wide-width web: Web presses that print webs of greater than 36 inches wide.

window: An area in a masking sheet that has been cut away and through which light will pass.

Windows 95: Icon-based operating system developed by Microsoft for personal computers and introduced in August 1995.

wipe-on plate: A kind of surface lithographic plate that is coated ("wiped-on" with coating) as the first step in platemaking.

work-and-back (W&B) imposition: See sheetwise imposition.

work-and-turn (W&T) imposition: A procedure wherein all pages for a signature are positioned in one form that is then printed on both sides of the sheet; after printing, the sheet is cut apart, producing two signatures exactly alike.

World Wide Web: International computer network of business and other users established for advertising and promotion purposes.

wrapping: The enclosing of a completed product in a package or box for shipment.

wrong-reading: A term used to describe images that read from right to left; typically implies that the film emulsion faces upward toward the viewer.

Xeikon DCP: Webfed digital press.

Index

Page numbers in italic indicate information to be found in table(s) or figure(s).